COMMERCIAL PRACTICE

COMMERCIAL PRACTICE

Inns of Court School of Law

BLACKSTONE
PRESS LIMITED

First edition published in Great Britain 1990 by Blackstone Press Limited, 9–15 Aldine Street, London W12 8AW. Telephone: 0181-740 1173

ISBN: 1 85431 488 2

First edition, 1990
Second edition, 1991
Reprinted, 1991
Third edition, 1992
Fourth edition 1993
Fifth edition, 1994
Sixth edition, 1995
Seventh edition, 1996

British Library Cataloguing in Publication Data
A CIP Catalogue record for this book is available from the British Library

Typeset by Montage Studios Ltd, Tonbridge, Kent
Printed by Ashford Colour Press, Gosport, Hampshire

Foreword

These manuals are published in conjunction with the Vocational Course for the Bar which is run at the Inns of Court School of Law. The course, which was introduced in 1989, was specifically designed to equip students with the procedural and evidential knowledge and the practical skills they will need to start their professional careers. It is gratifying to find that this course has been greeted as a major step forward in legal vocational training, and that it has attracted substantial interest.

These Manuals have been produced specifically to support this course, and they have been written both by teaching staff at the Inns of Court School of Law and by a range of members of the Bar. The Manuals are designed to cover all the areas of skill and knowledge which research showed were important for the new practitioner, and the emphasis throughout is on the practical, professional approach. Although the Manuals are produced for a specific course, their range is such that they should be of interest to all those concerned with legal training.

The Manuals are revised annually, to keep them up-to-date, and to improve content with the benefit of experience and of the many useful comments made by practitioners and by students. The development of legal vocational training can only be an ongoing process for all those concerned in achieving and maintaining high standards, and further comments are always welcome. Such comments may be addressed either to the Dean or the Course Director at the Inns of Court School of Law.

The enthusiasm of the staff of Blackstone Press Ltd and their efficiency in arranging the production and publication of these Manuals is much appreciated.

Lord Justice Phillips
Chairman of The Council of Legal Education
December 1995

Contents

EUROPEAN COMMUNITY
COMPETITION LAW

1 Introduction

1.1 Extracts from the Treaty of Rome

PRINCIPLES

ARTICLE 1

By this Treaty, the High Contracting Parties establish among themselves a EUROPEAN COMMUNITY.

ARTICLE 2

The Community shall have as its task, by establishing a common market and an economic and monetary union and by implementing the common policies or activities referred to in Articles 3 and 3a, to promote throughout the Community a harmonious and balanced development of economic activities, sustainable and non-inflationary growth respecting the environment, a high degree of convergence of economic performance, a high level of employment and of social protection, the raising of the standard of living and quality of life, and economic and social cohesion and solidarity among Member States.

ARTICLE 3

For the purposes set out in Article 2, the activities of the Community shall include, as provided in this Treaty and in accordance with the timetable set out therein:

(a)   the elimination, as between Member States, of customs duties and of quantitative restrictions on the import and export of goods, and of all other measures having equivalent effect;
(b)   a common commercial policy;
(c)   an internal market characterised by the abolition, as between Member States of obstacles to the free movement of goods, persons, services and capital;
(d)   measures concerning the entry and movement of persons in the internal market as provided for in Article 100c; ...
(g)   a system ensuring that competition in the internal market is not distorted;
(h)   the approximation of the laws of the Member States to the extent required for the functioning of the common market; ...
(j)   the strengthening of economic and social cohesion; ...
(l)   the strengthening of the competitiveness of Community industry;
(m)   the promotion of research and technological development; ...
(s)   a contribution to the strengthening of consumer protection; ...

[Treaty text shown as amended by the Maastricht Treaty 1992.]

1.2   Where are the Rules?

The EC has, among its aims, the raising of living standards and a harmonious development of economic activities (Article 2, EC Treaty). It seeks to achieve these aims largely through the mechanism of a common market. To this end, certain specific tasks (or 'activities') are imposed on the Community in Article 3, EC Treaty; primarily (for our purposes) a system ensuring that competition in the internal market is not distorted'. In Part Three of the Treaty, under 'Title One. Common Rules', you find 'Chapter I. Rules on Competition'. This is divided into three sections:

Section 1. Rules applying to undertakings
Section 2. Dumping
Section 3. Aids granted by States

We are mainly concerned here with those Articles which deal with undertakings, that is, Articles 85-90 and, in the space available, we shall concentrate almost exclusively on the 'substantive' competition laws — Articles 85 and 86. The European Court of First Instance has described these Articles as 'independent and complementary provisions designed, in general, to regulate distinct situations by different rules'.

These Articles are interpreted and applied primarily by the European Commission. Article 87, EC Treaty, requires the EC Council to pass legislation to give effect to the principles set out in Articles 85 and 86 — it refers explicitly to the need to 'define the respective functions of the Commission and of the Court of Justice in applying' the legislation. This is taken further in Article 89, EC Treaty, which states that, as soon as the Commission takes up its duties, it shall ensure the application of the principles laid down in Articles 85 and 86. The Commission is to investigate cases of suspected infringement. If proved, the Commission is to propose appropriate measures to bring the infringement to an end.

In addition to the relevant Articles in the Treaty, the competition rules of the European Community are found in regulations issued under the authority of the Treaty by the Council or Commission and in case law, that is, decisions of the Commission made in individual cases and the judgments of the Court of Justice and Court of First Instance. The Commission also issues notices from time to time indicating its policy on certain topics (e.g., the Notice on Agreements of Minor Importance, 3 September 1986).

For ease of reference, Articles 85 and 86 and Council Regulation 17/62 are printed in full in **8.1–8.3**. You will also find a full list of the cases cited in this part of the Manual at **Chapter 9**. Other measures are not printed in full but are set out in the text as appropriate (e.g., Articles from the 'block exemption' regulation 1983/83–**3.6**).

It was said above that we are going to concentrate on Articles 85 and 86 — the 'competition' rules. However, it is also important to be aware of related topics which sometimes interact with or are relevant to the operation of Articles 85 and 86. So **Chapter 7** looks briefly at the rules governing free movement of goods throughout the Community, and includes a short explanation of intellectual property rights.

We should note, in passing, that the Agreement on a European Economic Area ('EEA') came into force on 1 January 1994. This has, among its aims, the regulation of trade within the territory of the EC *and* the countries of EFTA, excluding Switzerland. Articles 53 and 54 of the EEA mirror Articles 85 and 86; in the future, business behaviour will need to be assessed in the light of both EC and EEA competition rules, in addition to any discrete national rules that might apply. For the sake of simplicity, we will not consider further the impact of the EEA in this part of the Manual.

1.3   Regulation 17/62

The first piece of secondary legislation to appear was Council Regulation 17/62 (in force from 13 March 1962). This sets out in detail the powers and duties of the Commission in the field of competition. It will be examined in detail later (see **Chapters 3, 5** and **8**).

The recital to Regulation 17 makes the point that all decisions taken by the Commission under the Regulation are subject to review by the Court of Justice of the European Communities (ECJ), in accordance with the Court's jurisdiction as laid down by the Treaty. This allows the Court to review the procedural or substantive merits of a decision. Increasingly, the *initial* judicial review will be undertaken by the Court of First Instance.

1.4 The Role of the European Commission

Subject to any review by the Court of Justice, the European Commission is the investigator, judge and jury in competition 'trials'. A complaint was made in *Musique Diffusion Française* v *Commission* (1980) (the 'Pioneer' case) that this multiplicity of roles was a breach of due process of law, contrary to Article 6 of the European Convention on Human Rights. The complaint was rejected by the Court of Justice, who indicated that the Commission was not a tribunal within the meaning of Article 6 of the Convention. The same point was raised subsequently before the European Commission on Human Rights in *Société Stenuit* v *France* (1992). The Commission felt that the nature of investigations under Regulation 17 was such that Article 6(1) of the European Convention should apply to them. The Commission on Human Rights said that, regardless of the procedural safeguards that competition proceedings now have, the European Community Commission is both plaintiff/prosecutor and judge, there is no presumption of innocence and the burden of proof on the EC Commission is only to a civil standard. It was felt that none of these elements complied with Article 6(1) of the Convention. There have been suggestions recently that there should be an independent 'Competition Authority', distinct from the Commission. For example, in October 1994 the head of the German Cartel Office recommended that the competition decisions which are currently made by the Commission should instead be made by an independent authority so that political interference might be reduced (see *Financial Times*, 3.10.94). However, this is unlikely to be created in the short- to medium-term. Indeed, the head of DG IV, Dr Claus-Dieter Ehlermann, has expressed the opinion that the Commission, rather than the Council of Ministers, possessed the fundamental power in the matter of competition policy.

The Commission investigates either on its own initiative or following a complaint made to it, using its own officials to elicit information; it then decides whether the law has been infringed. If it has, the conduct is prohibited and the Commission either requires termination of the conduct and/or imposes a fine or (under Article 85 only) grants an exemption.

1.5 Direct Effect of Articles 85 and 86

Both Articles 85 and 86 have been held by the Court of Justice to be directly effective and therefore capable of use in the national courts of Member States: see *BRT* v *SV Sabam* (1973):

> It must ... be examined whether the national courts, before which the prohibitions contained in Articles 85 and 86 are invoked in a dispute governed by private law, must be considered as 'authorities of the Member States'.

> The competence of those courts to apply the provisions of Community law, particularly in the case of such disputes, derives from the direct effect of those provisions.

> As the prohibitions of Articles 85(1) and 86 tend by their very nature to produce direct effects in relations between individuals, these Articles create direct rights in respect of the individuals concerned, which the national courts must safeguard.

> [I]f the Commission initiates a procedure in application of Article 3 of Regulation No. 17 such a court may, if it considers it necessary for reasons of legal certainty, stay the proceedings before it while awaiting the outcome of the Commission's action.

On the other hand, the national court should generally allow proceedings before it to continue when it decides either that the behaviour in dispute is clearly not capable of having any appreciable effect on competition or on trade between Member States, or that there is no doubt of the incompatibility of that behaviour with Article 86 (*BRT* v *SV SABAM*, paras 14-16, 21 and 22).

1.6   National Use

The extent to which national courts make use of Articles 85 and 86 varies from state to state. This was examined by the Commission through a questionnaire sent to the Member States in 1985. Although the response was very patchy (due to an absence of systematic gathering of information) the Commission concluded that:

> ... in principle, there are no fundamental obstacles to the application of Community competition law by national courts.... Until now it is clear that the Community competition rules have generally been pleaded as a basis for obtaining an injunction or other interim relief or as a defence to an action for breach of contract. There does not appear, to the Commission's knowledge, to be any case in which damages have been awarded by a national court for a breach of either Article 85 or Article 86 of the EC Treaty. (16th Report on Competition Policy, 1987.)

In 1993, the Commission issued Guidelines for national courts when applying Articles 85 and 86 in 'domestic' litigation. The use of Articles 85 and 86 in English courts is examined in **Chapter 6**.

It is also now possible in some Member States for their competition authorities to use Articles 85 and 86 (or suitably amended variants) against undertakings whose activities do not attract the attention of the European Commission. This is not presently the case in the United Kingdom, where bodies such as the Monopolies and Mergers Commission and the Office of Fair Trading work under different rules (e.g., Restrictive Trade Practices Act, Competition Act). However, this may change in the future; it is thought that the RTPA may be replaced by legislation closely modelled on Article 85 EC and with the Maastricht treaty currently containing ideas of 'delegation', it is possible that the European Commission could send cases to (e.g.) the OFT for investigation, while retaining jurisdiction over the case itself. Currently, OFT officials assist those of the European Commission when they investigate cases in the UK and in such circumstances (but only then), the OFT can exercise the investigative powers vested in the European Commission by EC Regulation 17. (See **5.5** etc.)

The influence of the EC competition rules can be found in rather unexpected areas in the United Kingdom. Recently, the London Stock Exchange was found (by the Minister for Corporate Affairs) to be in breach of Article 86 by virtue of its rules on the dissemination of news about companies. Under the Financial Services Act, the Minister is empowered to direct the Stock Exchange to take specific action if he considers that its conduct conflicts with the Community obligations of the United Kingdom.

1.7   Preliminary Work

Before reading anything else, turn to **Chapter 8** and read the text of Articles 85 and 86 of the Treaty.

2 Article 85 — Anti-competitive Agreements

2.1 Relevant Types of Conduct

Article 85 prohibits three forms of business conduct as being 'incompatible with the common market':

(a) agreements between undertakings,
(b) decisions by associations of undertakings,
(c) concerted practices,

which prevent, restrict or distort competition.

These are not entirely outlawed — the world of commerce could not operate without agreements between undertakings, for example. Such business conduct will be prohibited if it has the ability to affect trade between the Member States and to prevent, restrict or distort competition within the common market. If this can be proved, the conduct has no legal effect — any agreements or decisions which are prohibited by Article 85(1) shall be automatically void (Article 85(2)).

Article 85 is aimed at businesses which *combine* in some way to distort competition, for example:

(a) deals between manufacturer and wholesaler(s) to give exclusive selling rights in a territory;
(b) contracts between wholesaler and retailer that require a retailer to purchase a whole range of products when maybe only one or two types are wanted;
(c) decisions of trade associations to set common prices for their members' products; and
(d) deals made by executives behind closed doors where nothing ever gets written down.

These may all infringe Article 85, exposing the guilty parties to swingeing fines and the consequences of void contracts. In contrast, Article 86 is concerned mainly with the behaviour of *individual* businesses — those who have a monopoly power which is being misused.

The following sections examine the criteria in Article 85(1) more closely to illustrate when and why conduct might be prohibited.

2.2 Agreements between Undertakings

'Undertakings' is a term that has been referred to several times already. There is no definition of it in the EC Treaty, nor in the secondary legislation, although Regulation 17/62 gives some clues as to the probable scope when it deals (in Article 11) with requests to undertakings for information. Article 11 imposes a duty (to supply information) upon:

(a) the owners of undertakings (or their representatives);
(b) the authorised representatives of legal persons, companies or firms;
(c) the authorised representatives of associations which have no legal personality.

It seems in practice that any form of entity which engages in economic activity will be considered by the Commission (and the Court of Justice) to be an undertaking.

Examples have included:

(a)   individuals (e.g. *AOIP/Beyrard* (1976) — an inventor who gave exclusive rights in his invention to a commercial organisation; even opera singers — *RAI/Unitel* (1978));
(b)   corporations — even of non-EC origin (*Europembellage Corp. and Continental Can Co.* v *Commission* (1972); *Ahlstroem Oy* v *Commission* (1985) — the woodpulp cartel);
(c)   partnerships (*Re William Prym-Werke* (1973));
(d)   non-profit-making organisations which operate to collect artists' royalties commercially (e.g., *GVL* (1983) — a German society which collects copyright royalties); and
(e)   organisations which are part of the 'State', where they carry on economic or commercial activities (an example in the UK might be the Post Office).

To fall within Article 85(1), an agreement must be made *between* undertakings, not *within* a single undertaking. So one needs to know when more than one undertaking is involved. This can become problematic when a parent company and its subsidiaries are parties to an agreement. The Commission and the Court have said that parent companies and their subsidiaries form a single economic unit: *Hydrotherm* v *Andreoli* (1983). Any agreements between them (sometimes known as a 'bathtub conspiracy'!) cannot fall foul of Article 85. Thus in *Centrafarm* v *Sterling* (1974) the ECJ said:

[There is no violation of Article 85 by] agreements or concerted practices between undertakings belonging to the same concern and having the status of parent company and subsidiary, if the undertakings form an economic unit within which the subsidiary has *no real freedom to determine* its course of action on the market, and if the agreements or practices are concerned merely with the internal allocation of tasks as between the undertakings. (Emphasis added.)

(Conversely, this idea of economic unity has been used to fine a parent company for the misdeeds of its subsidiary: see, e.g., *Eurim Pharm GmbH* v *Johnson & Johnson* (1981); see also *Commercial Solvents Corp.* v *Commission* (1973).)

What constitutes an agreement for present purposes? It is clear that legally binding contracts are included but it seems that the meaning is broader than this. 'Gentlemen's agreements' are included — in *Boeringer* v *Commission* (1972) a quinine cartel divided up the world market and fixed prices, but its contract expressly excluded the common market. The members of the cartel then wrote down a gentlemen's agreement, which extended the application of the contract to the common market. This was held to be an agreement for the purposes of Article 85 even after its operation was suspended by the members, as the prices set under its terms continued to be used. If two or more entities pursue a joint plan then it may not matter that it cannot be classified as an 'agreement' — it may be labelled as a 'concerted practice' (see **2.4**) and still be within the net of Article 85.

The polypropylene cartel which was investigated by the Commission in the early 1980s (see OJ 1986 L230) was alleged to be a 'rolling' agreement which lasted some six years. It was asserted that it had a variety of members at any point in time, who sometimes undercut their (covertly) agreed prices and where meetings occurred at different levels of importance ('bosses' meetings and 'experts' meetings). The Commission found that the basic, detailed plan constructing the cartel was an agreement for the purposes of Article 85(1). We should note that, in the present judicial climate, the Commission would be put to strict proof as to who belonged to the cartel and for what period(s) — see the Court of First Instance in its judgments on the polypropylene cartel decision; e.g., *BASF AG* v *Commission* (T-4/89). That the Commission has accepted and discharged that burden of proof may be seen in *Re Cartonboard Cartel* (1994) where the participants in a series of regular 'secret and institutionalised meetings' were divided into four groups by the Commission, according to the period of their participation.

The Court of Justice returned to the definition of an agreement in the *Sandoz* case (C277/87) and concluded that, where a customer raised no protest about detailed stipulations contained in a company's standard invoice, this could amount to 'tacit acquiescence' in the clauses thus stipulated. The dispatch of such invoices was not unilateral conduct on the part of the company but was part of the general commercial relations maintained between the company and its customers. The stipulations therefore were part of an 'agreement' within the ambit of Article 85. For a recent example of an agreement being inferred from behaviour, see *Tipp-Ex* v *Commission* (C279/87).

2.3 Decisions by Associations

This covers matters such as formal decisions which are approved by the members of a trade association. These could be classified as a collection of agreements between the member undertakings (see, e.g., *Groupement des Fabricants de Papiers Peints* v *Commission* (1974)), so it is clear that the different categories of business conduct are not mutually exclusive. Even non-binding recommendations made by a trade association to its members may be caught as a 'decision': see, e.g., *FEDETAB* v *Commission* (1982); *Vereeniging van Cementhandelaren* v *Commission* (1972). If two trade associations reach an agreement, the terms of which will affect their respective members, this may be regarded as decisions of the associations *and* an agreement between the members, rendering everyone liable to fines if the agreement infringes Article 85: see, e.g., *FRUBO* v *Commission* (1974).

2.4 Concerted Practices

This concept has been very broadly interpreted by the Commission and Court of Justice, so that it really encompasses the first two categories and expands further. The Court has defined concerted practice as (*ICI* v *Commission* (1969) — 'Dyestuffs'):

> ... a form of coordination between enterprises that has not yet reached the point where there is a contract in the true sense of the word but which, in practice, *consciously substitutes a practical cooperation for the risks of competition.* (Emphasis added.)

Perhaps the best attempt to describe in practical terms what is a concerted practice can be found in the judgment of the Court of First Instance in *Rhône-Poulenc SA* v *Commission* (1991). This was an appeal by a member of the alleged polypropylene cartel. The Court indicated that each company must work out its policies for itself; although that does not mean that they cannot adapt their policies intelligently to the existing and anticipated conduct of their rivals. What is forbidden is:

(a)   to have contact, whether direct or not, with one's competitors
(b)   if such contact is intended to (or does) either
(c)   influence the conduct of a competitor (actual or potential) or
(d)   discloses to such competitors the intended or possible conduct of one's own company.

In the *Rhône-Poulenc* case itself, the evidence showed that R-P had attended meetings with its competitors; and at such meetings had expressed its general support for a policy of price increases begun by one competitor, while also indicating its own future policy. According to the Court of First Instance, this was evidence of 'concerted action'.

The notion of contact between competitors may be easy to establish where it occurs directly between them. Where it is alleged to be indirect, though, problems of proof may arise. For example, faxing your competitors with advance news of your price increases is clearly contact; but what if you just tell your customers about pending price increases and they then go to a competitor of yours and say, 'X is going to charge us £10 per unit from next month, can you sell to us cheaper?' Your customer is simply being sensible, but your competitor now knows of your price strategy — is this contact or not? The ECJ in the *Woodpulp* case (1993) found that this type of behaviour was not indicative of a concerted practice, but that finding may be specific to the circumstances of the *Woodpulp* case.

2.4.1 PARALLEL CONDUCT

Proving a concerted practice may be a problem where no record exists of an agreement between the undertakings. For example, in the *Rhône-Poulenc* case (polypropylene cartel), the Court of First Instance concluded that the cartel members must have been aware that their actions infringed Article 85 but went on to act 'deliberately and in the greatest secrecy'. One of the allegations against the cartel was price-fixing — the Commission was unable to produce evidence of R-P's price policy to the Court of First Instance but the Court considered that this was because R-P 'did not preserve any evidence of that policy'. The Court allowed the Commission to adduce evidence of other policies adopted by R-P (relating to sales volume) — as these corresponded to the results of cartel meetings, the Court considered that it had sufficient evidence of R-P's actual policy.

This problem of proof can occur quite easily in an oligopoly industry — that is, one with only a few members (usually fewer than 12) in the market, e.g. European airlines, or major petrochemical companies. It may happen that all of the companies engage in similar behaviour — increasing prices at the same time or by the same amount or percentage. This behaviour may be enough to raise the suspicion of a concerted practice. Evidence of meetings between such companies may be conclusive of the matter.

2.4.1.1 Economic theory and the Aniline Dyes cartel

Such behaviour *can* be explained by economic theory as simply the way in which an oligopolistic market operates, but the European Commission may regard this sort of behaviour as evidence of an agreement/concerted practice and start an investigation if it happens too often or appears to be orchestrated. In *ICI* v *Commission* (1969), where 10 major producers who had, between them, 80 per cent of the relevant sales of dyestuffs, all raised their prices by similar amounts on three separate occasions, the Commission stated:

A first element of proof of the concerted nature of these increases can be found in the fact that the rates of the individual price increases were identical in all the countries, as well as in the fact that with very few exceptions the price increases applied to the same dyestuffs. In addition, the concerted nature of these price increases is confirmed by the fact that they were put into effect by the producers concerned, on almost — or even exactly — the same day in the individual countries of the Common Market in which they were applied. It is inconceivable that, without first meticulously working out an arrangement in concert, the major producers supplying the Common Market would have raised the price for the same products produced in large quantities, repeatedly and practically at the same time, and at the same rate, and even in several countries, in which the market conditions for dyestuffs are different.

Further proof of the concerted nature of these price increases is the similarity of the wording of the instructions given by the producers to their subsidiaries or representatives on the various markets. . . . The orders sent by several producers contain very similar wording, even to the extent that some sentences are exactly the same. . . . This cannot be explained otherwise than by a prior agreement between the enterprises concerned, since these instructions were often sent on the same day, sometimes even at the same hour. . . .

The producers exchanged information repeatedly, in particular at meetings held in Basel and London.

The ECJ thought that 'viewed as a whole, the three consecutive increases reveal progressive cooperation between the undertakings concerned' (*ICI* v *Commission* (1969) para. 99).

In *Re Polypropylene Cartel* (1986), the Commission stated that, whilst Article 85 distinguishes between the two concepts of the 'agreement' and the 'concerted practice', nevertheless there can be cases where apparent collusion between companies indicates the presence of both forms of prohibited conduct. The Commission felt that it was not very important to maintain a strict distinction between agreements and concerted practices; what mattered was distinguishing a concerted practice from the simple parallel behaviour of companies who were not colluding.

In *ICI* v *Commission* (1969) the ECJ said that parallel conduct of itself does not constitute a concerted practice but it is 'a decisive indication of it' if it leads to a departure from the normal conditions of a competitive market. They further stated (paras 65-67):

> By its very nature ... a concerted practice does not have all the elements of a contract but may *inter alia* arise out of coordination which becomes apparent from the behaviour of the participants.

> Although parallel behaviour may not by itself be identified with a concerted practice, it may, however, amount to strong evidence of such a practice if it leads to conditions of competition which do not correspond to the normal conditions of the market, having regard to the nature of the products, the size and number of the undertakings, and the volume of the said market.

> This is especially the case if the parallel conduct is such as to enable those concerned to attempt to stabilize prices at a level different from that to which competition would have led, and to consolidate established positions to the detriment of effective freedom of movement of the products in the Common Market and of the freedom of consumers to choose their suppliers.

The view of the ECJ in *ICI* that parallel conduct may be a 'decisive indication' of a concerted practice has been modified by its judgment in the *Woodpulp* case (1993): here, the ECJ stated that

> In determining the probative value of [the behaviour in question], it must be noted that parallel conduct cannot be regarded as furnishing proof of concentration unless concentration constitutes the only plausible explanation for such [behaviour].

2.4.2 BURDEN OF PROOF IN CASES OF PARALLEL CONDUCT

Tactically, it would make sense for both the Commission and the 'defendant' undertakings to try to adduce sufficient evidence to establish (or rebut) the proposition that there has been a concerted practice. It might be thought that, once the Commission has proved the existence of parallel conduct, the burden of proof should shift to the 'defendants' to explain how their behaviour might have occurred *without* concertation. In fact, the burden of proof remains with the Commission; it must prove that there is no credible explanation for the conduct *except* concertation between the undertakings. See, e.g., the Opinion of A-G Darmon in *Re Woodpulp Cartel: Ahlstroem Osakeyhtiö and others* v *Commission* (1993) at para. 195. It may be easier for the Commission to discharge this burden when the market is not oligopolistic. See further Van Gerven and Verona, [1994] CMLR 31, at p. 601.

2.4.2.1 The *CRAM* case

The defendants successfully discharged this burden of proof in *CRAM and Rheinzink* v *Commission* (1983). The Commission had determined that four facts in the history of the three companies concerned could be explained only on the basis of a concerted practice.

CRAM and its fellow defendant, RZ, were zinc suppliers. CRAM and RZ were alleged by the Commission to have colluded to stop cheap, unauthorised imports of zinc coming into Germany. They had a common customer, Schiltz. Schiltz was sold zinc on condition that he sold it outside the EC, e.g. in Egypt. The four facts found by the Commission were:

(a) On 21 October 1976 CRAM suspended deliveries to Schiltz and RZ accused Schiltz of breaking an agreement to resell its zinc only to Egypt.

(b) On 26 October 1976 RZ told CRAM that it was going to reduce its prices in Germany by about 3 per cent.

(c) On 29 October 1976 RZ ceased its deliveries to Schiltz.

(d) CRAM delayed pressing Schiltz for payment of sums owed until 8 November 1976.

This finding was overturned by the Court as it held that the defendants had established good reasons for these four actions. CRAM's cessation of deliveries came at the end of a particular contract to supply Schiltz and it had a history of problems getting payment from Schiltz. The communication of price policy by RZ appeared to have had no effect on CRAM's prices and thus, by itself, could not prove a concerted practice.

2.5 'Effect on Trade between Member States'

2.5.1 WHY DO YOU NEED TO CONSIDER THIS?

This phrase introduces the intra-Community element into Article 85, an idea similar to that which can be seen in some of the cases on free movement of workers (e.g. *Morson & Jahnjan* v *Netherlands* (35 and 36/82) [1982] ECR 3723). The idea is that there should be a single common market with goods circulating freely within it. If one's behaviour cannot affect trade *between* Member States, then it is outside the scope of the EC Treaty.

This phrase may be taken, then, as indicating the boundary between the jurisdiction of the EC rules on competition and the competition laws of the Member States. This was certainly the position adopted by the Court in *Hugin/Liptons* v *Commission* (1978). However, it is quite limited because the Court usually gives a generous interpretation of those matters which may affect trade between Member States — for example, it will acknowledge the jurisdiction of the Community rules even where behaviour has only an indirect or even potential effect on trade between Member States: see, e.g., Advocate-General Trabucchi in *Groupement des Fabricants de Papiers Peints* v *Commission* (1974), who suggested that, in time, the idea of 'an effect on trade between Member States' would simply mean that the effect of the behaviour must be '... such as to be significant at Community level', regardless of frontiers or geographic areas.

It has been suggested (by Dr Ehlermann of DG IV) that the inclusion of a requirement of an 'effect on inter-state trade' in Article 85 was an early forerunner of the subsidiarity principle (introduced by the Maastricht Treaty to indicate that matters of purely local/national importance should fall outside the scope of the European Community).

Agreements have been found to have an effect on trade between Member States even though they are restricted expressly to cover a single country. Examples are:

(a) *Vereeniging van Cementhandelaren* v *Commission* (1972) — price fixing between Dutch cement producers, limited to sales in the Netherlands but which, the Court said, made the Dutch market more difficult for foreign cement producers to operate in or penetrate.

(b) *Papiers Peints (supra)* — loyalty discounts to customers who bought in bulk from Groupement members, but only within Belgium. The Court acknowledged that, in theory, the alleged behaviour could have an effect on trade between Member States, but quashed the decision of the Commission because it was not sufficiently reasoned (and thus fell foul of Article 190, EC Treaty).

A typical example of a clause which had a direct effect on inter-state trade is the case of *Consten and Grundig* v *Commission* (1964). Specific terms of contracts prohibited exports of Grundig machines from Germany into France other than by the authorised French dealer, Consten. Grundig transferred its French trademark, 'Gint', to Consten. When an unauthorised exporter shipped (cheaper) German Grundig machines into France and undercut Consten's prices, Consten started litigation in France alleging, *inter alia,* breach of its trademark rights. The matter was then brought to the attention of the Commission and subsequently to the European Court on appeal. The insulation of the French market from imports clearly affected trade between Member States.

2.5.2 AGREEMENTS OF MINOR IMPORTANCE

Returning to the remark of Advocate-General Trabucchi that the effect of the behaviour must be 'significant at Community level', it is important to note that not all effects on inter-state trade will fulfil this criterion of Article 85. The Commission has issued notices defining what constitutes economically significant activity for the purposes of Article 85. These 'Notices on Agreements of Minor Importance' try to remove small and medium-sized companies from the purview of Article 85(1). The philosophy of the Commission is that such companies must be encouraged, especially if they are to grow and provide a challenge to the bigger enterprises (i.e. greater long-term competition). One way to encourage them is to allow them to work together in situations where their cooperation does not really have any meaningful effect on trade between Member States.

The Commission's latest Notice (1986) excuses from Article 85(1) those agreements whose effect on inter-state trade or on competition are 'negligible' or which have no 'appreciable effect' on inter-state trade. The Notice defines what is meant by 'not appreciable' (see below) but also states that even behaviour that produces an 'appreciable' effect may nevertheless fall outside Article 85(1) if its effect is negligible (which is not defined).

The Commission acknowledges the possibility that an agreement may be of minor importance yet fall foul of Article 85(1) 'in exceptional circumstances'. If this proves to be the case, the Commission will not impose fines for the breach of Article 85. Such 'exceptional' incidents are unlikely to be uncovered because the Commission has said (in the Notice) that, as a general rule, in cases covered by the Notice it will not open a Regulation 17 investigation.

'Appreciable effect' is defined by paras 7-9 of the Notice in terms of market share and turnover:

(a) *Market share* — the contract goods or services must have no more than a 5 per cent share of their market. (To the market share of the contract goods/services must be added the market share of any equivalent products made by the participating undertakings.)

(b) *Turnover* — the annual aggregate turnover of the participating undertakings must not exceed 300 million ECU (European Currency Units). This figure was last increased in 1994: OJ 1994 C 368/20. (Calculations should include turnover in all goods and services, net of tax, in the last financial year. Disregard deals between participating undertakings.)

Both market share and turnover may be exceeded by up to 10 per cent in any two successive financial years.

'Participating undertakings' (see (a) and (b) above) is defined widely. As well as the parties to the agreement, the following must be included:

(a) undertakings in which a party to the agreement, directly or indirectly,
   (i) owns more than half the capital or business assets, or
   (ii) has the power to exercise more than half the voting rights, or
   (iii) has the power to appoint more than half the members of the supervisory board, board of management or bodies legally representing the undertakings, or
   (iv) has the right to manage the affairs;
(b) undertakings which directly or indirectly have in or over a party to the agreement the rights or powers listed in (a);
(c) undertakings in or over which an undertaking referred to in (b) directly or indirectly has the rights or powers listed in (a);
(d) undertakings in which several undertakings as referred to above jointly have, directly or indirectly, the rights or powers set out in (a).

Decisions of associations and concerted practices may also have the benefit of the Notice.

2.5.3   A REASONED TEST?

The determination of an effect on inter-State trade may now be subject to a 'rule of reason' test, in similar fashion to the rest of Article 85(1). We can draw this conclusion from the decision of the ECJ in the *Delimitis* case (1989). The court considered an 'access' clause in the beer supply agreement between the litigants, which purported to allow the customer to purchase beer from other suppliers, including those in other Member States. If it was a genuine clause, and foreign suppliers could have access to the customer, then the effect on inter-State trade of an exclusive purchase agreement could be minimised so that Article 85(1) need not apply. See further **2.9.6** on *Delimitis*.

Against this introduction of a 'rule of reason' must be balanced the interesting opinion of both the CFI and ECJ that a contractual clause which has *never* been implemented may nevertheless have an effect on trade between Member States because its existence may create a 'visual and psychological' effect which contributes to a partitioning of the market. See e.g., the CFI in *Parker Pen Ltd* v *Commission* (1994).

When considering whether there is an 'effect on trade between Member States,' remember that 'trade' has been broadly construed to cover trade in services as well as goods.

2.6   Object of Prevention, Restriction or Distortion of Competition within the Common Market

The European Court treats 'object' as separate from 'effect'. If you are concerned with the object of an agreement, you need not analyse the market to see the effects of the agreement — purpose (or intention) alone is enough: see, e.g., *Re Polypropylene Cartel* (1986), where the Commission was satisfied that the producers' cartel had an anti-competitive object; it was unnecessary to demonstrate that competition had been affected. You should remember, though, that even if a company is found 'guilty' of having an unlawful objective, the degree of any consequential effect may be examined in order to determine the amount of any financial penalty to be imposed on the company.

Subject to problems of proof, the ability to prohibit conduct intended to have anti-competitive effects may be used to prevent business plans from coming into effect or stop them at an early stage. This criterion has been interpreted quite liberally — see, e.g., *Consten and Grundig* v *Commission* (1964): '... it is not necessary to take into consideration the actual effects of an agreement where its purpose is to prevent, restrict or distort competition'. The agreements were *designed* to isolate the French market and artificially maintain separate national markets within the Community for products of a widely distributed brand. This meant that there was a distortion of competition within the common market.

These matters were considered recently by the Court of Justice in the *Sandoz* case (C277/87) where Sandoz raised three objections to the allegation that its conduct had the object or effect of preventing, restricting or distorting competition. Sandoz said:

   (a)   the conduct (inclusion of the words 'not to be exported' on an invoice) was void under national (Italian) law;

   (b)   there had been no allegation that its conduct had an adverse effect on trade between Member States;

   (c)   it had done nothing to enforce observance of the clause by its customers.

All three points were rejected by the Court: it was unnecessary that the agreement be valid in national law — Article 85 was concerned only with the parties' intention; if it appeared that an agreement had the objective of preventing (etc.) competition within the common market, it was unnecessary to have regard to the specific effects of the agreement; the absence of enforcement was not sufficient to excuse the clause from the prohibition in Article 85(1). One can see that the Court of Justice is still determined to take a tough line on 'offenders' by its adherence to a teleological interpretation of the phrase 'object or effect' in Article 85(1). That the Court of First Instance adopts the same attitude can be seen in, e.g., *Solvay* v *Commission* (1992).

2.7   Effect of Preventing, Restricting or Distorting Competition within the Common Market

The effect must be established by means of a market analysis. In *Volk* v *Vervaecke* (1969) the Court demanded that there must be an 'appreciable' or not insignificant effect on the market. This means that agreements between small businesses may fall outside the scope of Article 85. The idea has been given formal detail by the Commission in its *Notice on Agreements of Minor Importance* (first issued in 1970), which is intended to facilitate cooperation between enterprises in the small to medium size range.

The Court considered the concept of behaviour which has the effect of restricting competition within the common market in *Ahlstroem Oy* v *Commission* (1985) (the woodpulp cartel). The defendant undertakings were non-EC-based companies who sold woodpulp to paper manufacturers based in the EC and who had been found guilty (by the Commission) of fixing the prices of these sales by means of agreements and other concerted practices. On appeal, the defendants alleged that they were outside the jurisdiction of the EC competition rules. The Court held that if woodpulp producers established in non-EC countries sold directly to purchasers established in the Community and engaged in price competition in order to win orders from those customers, that would constitute competition within the common market. Where, as here, those woodpulp producers jointly fixed the prices at which they would sell to EC customers and then sold at such prices: '... they are taking part in concertation which has the object and effect of restricting competition within the common market'. This is a very simplistic analysis but is perhaps best explained by the fact that the Court was only concerned with the jurisdiction of the Commission to investigate and fine the non-EC enterprises, rather than the merits of the Commission's decision.

Whilst one should not demean the significance of this element in Article 85(1), the usual finding of the Commission is that competition has been restricted in some way without too rigorous an analysis. This is because an agreement which infringes Article 85(1) is automatically void (Article 85(2)) unless it is granted an exemption under Article 85(3). According to Regulation 17/62, only the Commission has the power to grant an exemption and it can impose conditions on an undertaking in order to qualify for an exemption. Thus, by finding that an undertaking has infringed Article 85(1), the Commission concentrates a lot of power in its hands.

2.8   Rule of Reason

Examples of behaviour which has been found to have the effect of preventing, restricting or distorting competition and which may be prohibited by Article 85(1) include:

(a) non-competition clauses;
(b) restrictions on use of know-how, patents;
(c) non-challenge clauses;
(d) restrictions on conditions of resale;
(e) price-fixing (other than within a specific contract);
(f) export bans;
(g) tying the sale of one product to that of another;
(h) exclusive purchase clauses;
(i) exclusive sale clauses.

The Court of Justice indicated in *Pronuptia de Paris* v *Schillgalis* (1984) that it was prepared to consider the necessity of such clauses or, in other words, how reasonable it is that commercial agreements contain such clauses. Prior to this case, such matters had been considered but only when the Commission was deciding whether to grant an exemption to an otherwise void agreement. In *Pronuptia* the Court considered whether such clauses were justified in order to determine whether the agreement was prohibited by Article 85(1) at all. In this case the Court determined that franchising was a business method which promoted competition and that, without certain types of protection, the franchisor would not grant a franchise that obliged him to supply know-how and training and generally to support a franchisee. Certain clauses which were prima facie restrictive of competition were fundamental to the franchisor's willingness to grant a franchise, e.g. clauses which prohibited the franchisee from competing with the franchise network or disclosing confidential information to people outside the network. (See further **3.3** below.)

The ECJ seemed to have significantly altered the way we should analyse agreements under Article 85(1). This received confirmation in the subsequent case of *Delimitis* v *Henninger Brau AG* (1989), considered below at **2.9.6** and was further reinforced by the reliance of the ECJ on economic experts' reports in the *Ahlstroem Oy* case (1993).

2.9 Some Examples

It is useful to look at several types of behaviour mentioned in Article 85(1), to see how and why such behaviour might fall foul of Article 85(1). The examples chosen are: price fixing, limiting production, controlling markets, sharing markets, ties and exclusive purchasing.

2.9.1 PRICE FIXING

Price fixing is a real 'no-no', particularly when the parties operate in cartel form, i.e. in a *horizontal* arrangement. The reason for this emphasis on horizontal cooperation is that it removes price competition from an entire level of the market place (e.g. all manufacturers of this product) and is thus seen as against the interest of consumers. See, for example, the judgment of the ECJ in *ICI* v *Commission* (1969), at paras 12 and 17.

Horizontal price fixing is traditionally not allowed — it is never acknowledged as 'necessary' or as setting a 'reasonable price'. A good illustration of horizontal price fixing is the case of *Vereeniging van Cementhandelaren* v *Commission* (1972), which involved the Dutch Cement Dealers' Association.

> CDA alleged that its system of 'target prices' was rarely adhered to in practice, and did not constitute a restraint on members (see para. 16 of judgment). ECJ said (para. 21) that price fixing, even of a target, has an effect on competition as it enables all participants to 'predict with a reasonable degree of certainty' what their competitors' pricing policy is going to be.

A similar attitude can be seen in the recent Commission Decision (in OJ 1992 L246/37) *Re Scottish Salmon Board*:

> there was a price-fixing agreement on farmed salmon, between the Scottish Salmon Growers' Association and the Norwegian Fish Farmers' Sales Organisation. This agreement infringed Article 85 but there was no fine even though neither party had notified the Commission of the agreement, perhaps as this was the first infringement of Article 85 in the economic sector of fish farming. The Commission observed that any concern about low Norwegian prices could be attacked through the anti-dumping procedure in the EC Treaty, not via an illegal arrangement.

The ban on horizontal price fixing includes indirectly fixing prices, for example, through exchange of information about prices (e.g. discussions on proposed increases; press conferences; exchange of new price lists), or through concertation on discounts (i.e. how much or even deciding not to give them).

The same prohibitory attitude does not exist for *vertical* agreements. This division of approach between horizontal and vertical agreements is quite general, and does not apply just in the area of price fixing. The distinction can be seen in the block exemptions which exclude the application of Article 85(1) — they are usually couched in the form of vertical arrangements, with agreements between competitors often specifically excluded. See, e.g., Recital 10 and Article 3(a) of Regulation 1983/83; Article 3(a) of Regulation 1984/83.

2.9.2 LIMITING PRODUCTION

This might involve, for example, establishing quotas for existing companies. It is likely to be linked to price increases with a corresponding fall in production. The idea is to preserve everyone's market share. The victim is the consumer — he has to pay more money to buy the product, there are fewer satisfactory goods available and he is driven to consume inferior substitutes. It should be noted that if there are *acceptable* substitutes, such a system breaks down: see the *Rhône-Poulenc* case (1989).

Limiting technical development is a related prohibition for reasons which are partly economic, partly social. The ban is economic in the sense of preventing wasted resources — money could be better spent in other ways; it is social in the sense of Article 2 EC — seeking to guarantee an acceleration in the increase in living standards.

2.9.3   CONTROLLING MARKETS

This might be done through the use of guarantees, e.g. if they are valid only in the country of manufacture, not the country of purchase or use. This would act as a disincentive to buy 'foreign' goods. Typical instances can be seen in the consumer journals for SLR cameras or computer games and equipment, which often warn consumers against the otherwise tempting offers in the 'grey' unofficial import market.

In another field, see the recent proceedings involving *Honda* (Commission press release, August 1992). The Commission looked at, *inter alia,* Honda's spare parts distribution system in Europe. This had allowed Honda importers in single Member States to set up exclusive distribution networks designed to protect their distributors against parallel imports. In the light of the Commission's interest, Honda agreed to introduce a single standard form distribution and servicing agreement for the whole Community. This gave distributors an exclusive right to provide in their territory the guarantee services offered by Honda to purchasers of its motorbikes. In exchange, distributors had to service all users who had a guarantee certificate from Honda, which must accompany the motorbike until it reaches the end user.

Also consider the Commission's response to a question asked in the European Parliament by Commissioner Van Miert (OJ 1992 C66/40). He stated that the Commission was concerned about major manufacturers who operate over a Community-wide market, offering guarantees which claim to be 'European'. They are actually valid in all Member States but their content and scope vary considerably from one Member State to another. This was seen by the Commission as very unsatisfactory and the Commission had still to investigate the explanations given.

2.9.4   SHARING MARKETS

This might involve quotas as the means of restricting competition. It prevents price competition, e.g. through export bans or absolute territorial exclusion, a ban on either an active or passive 'foreign' sales policy. Isolation lessens competition (either inter- or intra-brand) because everyone has their own exclusive territory.

The Commission has often been strongly against such territorial protection but may justify it in certain circumstances, e.g. a new product or market or process. If the risks involved are such that no one would venture into the market without 'protection', it may be in the long-term interests of consumers to permit such protection for at least a short period. It is more likely to be allowed in vertical, rather than horizontal, arrangements. See, e.g., *Nungesser* (1978); *Pronuptia* (1984).

Absolute territorial protection is probably the one major example of a *vertical prohibition,* In this context, we could usefully consider the recent proceedings involving *Fyffes/Chiquita Europe* (1992). C was the largest importer of bananas into the EC, selling principally under the Chiquita trade mark in continental Europe. Prior to 1986, its UK sales were made through Fyffes Group Ltd (FGL), a wholly-owned subsidiary. C also sold bananas under the Fyffes trade mark through Europe, as a secondary brand after introducing its Chiquita brand.

In 1986, C sold off FGL. In an agreement on trade marks, FGL granted C exclusive rights to use the Fyffes trade mark outside the UK and Ireland for three years and a non-use clause, stopping FGL using the Fyffes trade mark for any fresh fruit outside the UK and Ireland until 2006 (or such earlier date as C might decide). After 1989, C stopped using the Fyffes trade mark but would not allow FGL to use it in continental Europe. Following FGL's complaint, the Commission felt the non-use clause restricted competition because of loss of competitive advantage in selling under a strong trade mark. The clause could not be regarded as legitimate protection of C's continental goodwill following sale of the UK company. After agreement on the worldwide use of the trade mark between the parties, the Commission agreed to close its file.

On a similar note, see *Viho/Parker Pen* (1992). V, a Dutch company, tried to buy Parker pens in Germany and Italy for resale in The Netherlands. P's distributors in both countries refused to sell to V, alleging that a clause in their contracts with P, making them distributors for their national market, forbad them to sell outside their territory. V complained to the Commission. On investigation, P submitted that the express export ban was inserted into the distribution agreements on a marketing director's personal initiative, acting without P's authority. P immediately revoked the restrictions. The infringement lasted over two years. P was fined ECU 700,000 (reduced to ECU 400,000 on appeal to CFI), the German distributor Herlitz was fined ECU 40,000. The Commission observed that export bans are always restrictions of competition. The director's lack of authority was irrelevant — the company was still liable, either because it had allowed him to act in that fashion or because it had failed to supervise him properly.

2.9.5   TIES

This is the name given to an arrangement where you can buy the thing you want but only if you buy something else which you do not want (either at all or at that price). The more natural home for the prohibition of ties is Article 86, where market power would allow an undertaking to compel the acceptance of unwanted terms or products. However, it is also an example given in Article 85. Maybe the example is intended to regulate contractual relations with third parties?

Examples of ties can be found in *Vaessen/Moris*. There was a patented machine to make saucissons de Boulogne; the machines were sold under a requirement to buy all sausage casings from the manufacturer too. See also *Hilti* (although this involved Article 86), a Commission decision recently confirmed by the Court.

These ties can be justified — for example, if the price for the machine is paid via *use* of the machine; this can be policed through the number of casings sold (you would need to check thoroughly by stamping your mark on the casings).

Another recent example of tying might be the freezer exclusivity arrangements concluded by Langnese and Schöller, regarding retail ice cream sales in Germany. See, e.g., 1993 ECLR at R-41 and below at **2.9.6**. These have also been the subject of recent litigation in Ireland, involving the Mars Corporation.

2.9.6   EXCLUSIVE PURCHASING

The Commission has issued block exemptions dealing with exclusive distribution and exclusive purchasing (1983/83 and 84/83). The exclusive purchasing regulation was considered in *Delimitis* v *Henninger Brau AG* in 1991. In this case, the ECJ looked at beer supply agreements in Germany. It considered the advantages offered to both supplier and reseller by such an agreement, e.g. the supplier gets guaranteed outlets, a motivated reseller and the ability to plan production and distribution more effectively; the reseller gets access to the beer resale market under favourable conditions (favourable loans, technical installations), guaranteed supply, and help in securing product quality.

The ECJ concluded that such agreements *may not* have the *object* of restricting competition, but it is still necessary to examine their *effect*. The ECJ said that one must look at the totality of such beer supply agreements to get the full picture; in the present case it was 'necessary to analyse the effects of a beer supply agreement, taken together with other contracts of the same type, on the opportunities of national competitors or those from other Member States, to gain access to the market for beer consumption or to increase their market share and, accordingly, the effects on the range of products offered to consumers'.

First, you must define the market in terms of product and territory. Here, distribution of beer through premises for the sale and consumption of drinks (*not* retail outlets) in Germany. Secondly, see if the existence of several beer supply agreements impedes *access* to that market. You need to examine the effect of all of them, not just the one you are presently concerned with. Relevant factors are the proportion of tied outlets compared to 'free' houses, duration of agreements, quantities of beer involved and how that compares to quantities sold by free houses.

Even if there is 'a considerable effect' on chances to gain access, that is insufficient in itself to allow a finding that the market is inaccessible. It is simply one factor among several, economic and legal. For example, you also consider opportunities for access — a competitor might take over an existing national brewery with its tied sales outlets, or build new pubs. You need to examine any laws relating to such actions and (an economic factor) find the minimum number of outlets needed to operate a distribution system economically. Then see how the market itself works, competitively, to see how easy access is. Find the number and size of producers on the market, the degree of saturation of the market and customers' brand loyalty. A saturated market with high brand loyalty to a few large producers is more difficult to break into 'than a market in full expansion in which a large number of small producers are operating without any strong brand names'.

Lastly, if this examination of the totality of such contracts shows that they do *not* have the cumulative effect of denying access to new national or foreign competitors, the individual agreements cannot restrict competition within Article 85(1) and so are not prohibited.

If access is found to be hard to attain, it is still necessary to assess the extent to which the 'suspect' brewery's contracts contribute to the cumulative effect of all such agreements. Breweries whose beer supply agreements make an *insignificant* contribution to the cumulative effect are not prohibited by Article 85(1).

Whether the contribution is significant or not is determined by:

(a)   the brewery's market share (and that of any group it belongs to);
(b)   the number of outlets tied to it (or its group) compared to the total number of such outlets in the relevant market;
(c)   the duration of the agreement compared to the average for that market, e.g. a brewery with a relatively small market share but which ties up sales outlets for many years may make as significant a contribution to sealing-off the market as a brewery with a relatively strong market position which regularly releases outlets at shorter intervals.

Applying those principles to the case, the ECJ considered the economic and legal effect of an *access clause* in the beer supply agreement (this was the referring court's fourth question, shown as A(4) in the Report). Such a clause allows the reseller to buy beer from other Member States. In theory, this should reduce the scope of the prohibition on competition in a beer supply agreement. If, in practice, the effect of the access clause is hypothetical or economically insignificant, one can ignore the clause. This may be the situation where the clause only authorises the reseller directly to buy beers from other Member States, rather than allowing him to buy beers imported by other companies into his Member State. Similarly, if the agreement has a clause requiring minimum quantities to be purchased by the reseller from the brewery (especially if backed by financial penalties for failure), those minimum amounts may be high in comparison to sales normally achieved by the pub in question; any 'freeing-up' of access here would be illusory.

If the access clause allows a national/foreign supplier '*a real possibility*' of supplying the pub in question, the agreement is not in principle capable of affecting trade between Member States. It therefore falls outside the prohibition in Article 85(1).

The *Delimitis* case has many other facets to it, but is of great importance here because it shows the ECJ going to considerable lengths to conduct more than a knee-jerk analysis under Article 85(1). A great deal of economic and legal analysis is going on and the Commission would clearly be expected to follow this lead in future investigations. Already, the Commission has responded by putting out a Notice on 'beer supply agreements of minor importance', putting into practice some of the ECJ's thoughts on economic significance. See the OJ 1992, C121/2, amending 1983/83 and 84/83.

The Commission had to consider exclusive purchase in the context of 'impulse' ice cream sales in Germany in *Langnese-Iglo, Schöller-Lebensmittel* (1993). It said that, in *normal* market conditions, exclusivity agreements are beneficial to competition because they strengthen the position of the undertaking which concluded the agreement. But, if access to the market by other suppliers is impeded *as a result of the market structure* and other significant barriers to entry, then exclusivity is unacceptable. That appears to have been the case here. Two companies had a duopoly over wholesale ice cream sales in Germany and access to that market was difficult because of the 'freezer exclusivity' arrangements they had with retailers. Generally, there is room for one ice cream freezer in a shop selling other goods (newspapers, etc.). If that freezer is supplied to the shopkeeper by the wholesaler on condition that it is used to stock only a specific manufacturer's goods, then no other manufacturer can get access to that retail outlet. In its final Decisions in these two cases, the Commission distinguished between 'outlet exclusivity' and 'freezer exclusivity'. The former was anti-competitive because it foreclosed that outlet for other suppliers, while the latter was permissible as a *quid pro quo* for making the ice creams available.

For a cogent criticism of the Commission's Decisions in the 'ice cream' cases, based on its failure to follow or distinguish *Delimitis*, see Korah [1994] 3 ECLR 171.

3 Escape from Nullity under Article 85

Having seen that an agreement will be void if it falls within Article 85(1), we must consider the possibility of its resurrection! Under Article 85(3), the Commission may exempt an agreement from the application of Article 85(1) and (2) if it falls within certain criteria.

A person or organisation seeking exemption must apply to the Commission. This is done by *notifying* the Commission of the agreement. Alternatively, if a company is unsure whether one of its agreements falls within Article 85(1) at all, it can seek the opinion of the Commission on this point. If the Commission decides in the company's favour, it gives the agreement *negative clearance*.

Whether a company is applying for negative clearance or giving notification of an agreement to be exempted, the same form is used. Form A/B must be filled in and 15 copies sent to the Commission. Form A/B was originally published in Commission Regulation 27/62; an example is reproduced in **3.5**. There must be full disclosure of information in Form A/B and its Annexe. Any failure to do so, whether intentional or simply negligent, may result in the Commission imposing a fine (see Article 15(1)(a), Regulation 17). This fine can range between 100 and 5,000 units of account. If a company appeals against the fine to the Court of First Instance, the Court has power to cancel, reduce or increase it.

3.1 Notification

Regulation 17/62 introduced the idea of notification — essentially, taking a pre-emptive step to forestall accusations of anti-competitive behaviour. There is no need to notify the Commission of agreements, etc., which you are sure will not infringe Article 85, EC Treaty, but otherwise notification is probably a good idea. It does carry potential disadvantages, e.g. it alerts the Commission to your existence — who knows what else they may find in the filing cabinet?

The main purpose of notification is to get your agreement exempted by the Commission — there can be no exemption of an agreement which has not been notified. Ancillary benefits are an immunity from fines under Article 15(5) of Regulation 17/62 (see further **5.13–5.15**) and the possibility that the undertaking will acquire a reputation for being 'Community-spirited' — something which may stand it in good stead should it ever need some goodwill in its dealings with the Commission.

Under Regulation 17/62, both new and old agreements should be notified, that is, agreements created after 13 March 1962 (or the date of accession for newer Member States) and those which existed prior to 13 March 1962. The latter are known as old agreements and have provisional validity (see the **Glossary, Chapter 10** for further details).

3.2 Negative Clearance

The purpose of the negative clearance procedure is to allow businesses to ascertain whether or not the Commission considers that any of their arrangements or behaviour are prohibited under Articles

85(1) or 86 of the Treaty. (It is governed by Article 2 of Regulation No. 17.) Clearance takes the form of a decision by the Commission certifying that, on the basis of the facts in its possession, there are no grounds under Article 85(1) or 86 of the Treaty for action on its part.

(Complementary Note to Commission Regulation 27/62.)

Negative clearance is not an exemption, but is a simple statement of the Commission's opinion. It is, therefore, binding on neither the Court of Justice nor the national courts. The clearance may be withdrawn if the circumstances change or if new information is revealed.

Insofar as negative clearance represents the end of a full investigation, it is quite rare for an undertaking to achieve this result. The Commission completes only a few individual cases each year. This is one reason why it introduced block exemptions. An application for negative clearance could end up by being the subject of a comfort letter (see **3.4.3**). The number of decisions resolved by negative clearance is likely to increase relative to exemptions as the Commission (encouraged by the ECJ in *Pronuptia* and subsequently in *Delimitis*) adopts a rule of reason approach to its analysis under Article 85(1), i.e. it should test the arguments pro- and anti-competition before deciding whether there is an infringement.

3.3   Exemption

3.3.1   UNCERTAINTY

An agreement is notified formally for the purpose of getting an exemption for it from the Commission. It is possible that the Commission may find that it does not infringe Article 85(1) in the first place and therefore does not need exemption (i.e. it will grant negative clearance). This used to be unlikely but seems to be more frequent since the Court's judgment in *Pronuptia de Paris* v *Schillgalis* (1984) encouraged the Commission to take a more reasonable look at the competitive pros and cons of an agreement before condemning it as anti-competitive, rather than leaving this analysis until the time for consideration of the grant of an exemption.

The consequence now seems to be (at the least) prima facie inconsistent conclusions being reached by the Commission on the application of Article 85(1). Two recent illustrations may help to make the point.

In *Halifax Building Society/Bank of Scotland* (1991), the two parties had a cooperation agreement for the issue of a new credit card. A clause in the agreement required the Halifax BS not to promote any competing credit cards in its branches. The Commission found this to be anti-competitive insofar as it continued beyond a reasonable start-up period. The parties limited the requirement to the first five years of the agreement and the Commission gave a negative clearance.

In *IATA Passenger Agency Programme* (1991), the Commission took the view that a cooperation agreement between the member airlines of IATA restricted competition between themselves (they all agreed to use an identical distribution system for their tickets). But, as the agreement offered various pro-consumer advantages, an exemption was granted.

It is suggested that the *IATA* case represents the traditional mode of thought for Commission decisions, whereas *Halifax* seems to apply a *Pronuptia*-like test. As the two decisions were taken about a month apart, a logical distinction is hard to divine. It has been suggested to the writer that there was in fact more similarity between these two cases than the published versions might indicate. That may well be the case but, as most of us have to rely on published information and reasoning rather than first-hand knowledge of (perhaps) confidential information, we may have problems when advising clients.

3.3.2   QUALIFYING FOR EXEMPTION

Only the Commission can grant an exemption; the burden rests on the company seeking exemption to show it is merited. Under Article 85(3) (the substantive provision on exemptions), agreements etc., will be exempted if they help to improve the production or distribution of goods (i.e. make available a larger amount of a product) or promote technical or economic progress (acceleration in raising of living standards). They must also:

(a)   give consumers a fair share of the resulting benefit;
(b)   only restrict competition to the extent and in ways which are totally necessary to achieve these procompetitive ends; and
(c)   not allow the companies concerned to wipe out competition to any great degree.

In this respect, see, e.g., *Pronuptia de Paris* itself, where some clauses did not infringe Article 85(1) at all, whilst those that did qualified for exemption under Article 85(3).

Exemption is granted from a specific date which, generally, cannot be earlier than the date of notification. It will be granted for a limited, renewable period. It may be withdrawn; it may be granted subject to conditions (usually requiring alteration of some of the terms of the agreement).

3.3.3   FOUR CONDITIONS

We must remember a caveat from Barry Hawk when looking at individual exemption decisions — to a large extent they are 'fact-specific', i.e. *ad hoc,* and give few, if any, general principles to use. As he says, 'This makes hazardous the extrapolation of general rules beyond the four express statutory conditions in Article 85(3) itself.'

The four conditions are as follows:

(a)   *The agreement must contribute to either an improvement in production/distribution of goods or the promotion of technical/economic progress.* This harks back to Article 2 EC. This condition is the most important of the four. It is used to overcome the original anti-competitive diagnosis under Article 85(1). The question to ask is, 'Does the agreement as presently constituted give *benefits* which would not be available in the absence of such agreement?'. Or, as asked by the Commission, do the restrictions 'bring about an improvement over the situation which would have existed in their absence?' (*GERO-fabrik* (1977), Commission Decision). Such benefits might be, for example, a reduced cost per unit because of longer production runs; the facilitation of entry into new markets (either product or geographical); an improvement in distribution through continuity of supplies, or the availability of a wider range of products. If this condition is met, we can consider the second one.

(b)   *Consumers must receive a fair share of the resulting benefits* (e.g., better standard of living; wider choice of products). Remember that 'consumer' here has a broad definition — not just the ultimate user but everyone down the manufacturing-marketing chain who makes use of the goods or services affected by the agreement. Korah notes the case of *ACEC/Berliet* (1968), where the 'consumers' of a bus were held to be the bus companies and tour operators, not the likely passengers; 'consumer' is a translation of the French *utilisateur* — the ultimate buyer, whether for private or business use. The 'benefit' may be given to consumers in price or other terms, e.g. the provision of qualified staff or service, a repair facility or the availability of a guarantee of quality. This condition is one of the less demanding to satisfy. Once it is met, we can turn to the third condition.

(c)   *The restrictions on competition which the agreement makes must be* indispensable *to attaining the identifiable benefits.* This is a recurring EC theme — an exception to a fundamental principle (e.g. free movement of workers, or normal competition) may be permitted but will be very strictly construed. The exception must do no more than is absolutely necessary to achieve the legitimate goal. The major question must be, 'Are less restrictive alternatives available which achieve the same benefits?' For example, could we get the same advantages over a shorter timespan, or with a smaller territory? There is an obvious link with the first condition here.

A good recent example of exactly how strictly this requirement can be construed is the judgment of the CFI in *UK Publishers Association* v *Commission* (1992) — general restrictions covering all Member States will not be allowed if the only benefit occurs within a single Member State. The case concerned the Net Book Agreement (NBA) between publishers in the UK. A Decision by the Commission that it was contrary to Article 85(1) and did not merit exemption under Article 85(3) was challenged. The CFI was not persuaded that the restrictions on competition did not go beyond what was strictly necessary to attain the objectives permitted by Article 85(3) so the Commission's decision was upheld.

The CFI felt that, even if one accepted that the NBA produced beneficial effects within the UK, if that occurred at the cost of trade between Member States then the benefit was irrelevant:

> ... a price maintenance system that restricts competition within the *common market* cannot qualify for exemption on the ground that it must continue to operate in order to produce beneficial effects inside a *national market*.

However, this judgment only affects the trade between Member States, i.e. books imported into the UK, *not* domestic publications (a result similar in many respects to an earlier case on the Dutch and Flemish book industries, *VBVB/VBBB* (1984)). The Commission originally felt that the publishers could achieve their desired effect without recourse to the NBA (i.e. the restriction went beyond that which was necessary to attain an identifiable benefit). Christopher Bright of Linklaters and Paines, at 1992 ECLR 269, presumes that this means the imposition of resale price maintenance as a standard condition of sale. It is debatable whether or not this could be a legitimate tactic to adopt.

In a rather bizarre series of events, in January 1995, the ECJ overturned the judgment of the CFI. In the spring, it was announced that the OFT had applied to the Restrictive Practices Court for leave to apply to end the NBA. At the time of writing (September 1995), the NBA appears to have collapsed following the resignation from it of several large publishers.

It should be noted that this third condition probably ranks second in importance behind the first one. If it is met, we can turn finally to the fourth and least important condition.

(d)   *The parties to the agreement must not have been given the chance to* eradicate *competition regarding a substantial part of the products in question.* It is sufficient to say that, if an agreement satisfies the other three conditions, it is most unlikely to lose out under this head.

3.3.4   INDIVIDUAL VERSUS BLOCK EXEMPTIONS

We have considered the four conditions in Article 85(3) so far in the context of a notification for individual exemption. The Commission has also established rules governing exemption of agreements by type — these are known as block exemptions and are considered further at **3.4.1**. For now, you should note that all four conditions in Article 85(3) are applied by the Commission in the block exemption Regulations.

See, for example, the case of the *Scandinavian Ferry Operators* (1992). Three companies each provided a ferry service between a Danish port and a Swedish port (Helsingor-Helsinborg). They decided to operate a joint ferry service and notified the agreement under block exemption 4056/86 on maritime transport, utilising the opposition procedure (see **3.4.2**). There was no opposition by the Commission. Its view was that, although the agreement would impose substantial restrictions *if not total elimination* of competition on *this route* (author's emphasis), the agreement would improve services on the route and promote technical and economic progress, while consumers would get a fair share of the benefits — more frequent sailings, larger new vessels and better ability to match capacity to demand so producing lower costs and prices. Also, there was still sufficient competition on the market, e.g., through direct ferry services between Sweden and Germany.

If you look at the block exemption Regulations themselves, you can see how the Commission has tried to demonstrate compliance with the four conditions. See, for example, Regulation 1983/83 recitals (5) to (12) in **3.6** below.

3.4 Alternatives to Individual Exemption: Block Exemptions, Comfort Letters and Undertakings

After Regulation 17/62 was introduced, the Commission quickly became snowed under with notifications seeking exemption for existing agreements. The Commission is able to grant very few individual exemptions each year so there was soon a huge backlog of unprocessed notifications. To deal with this, the Commission introduced two new procedures — the block exemption and the comfort letter.

3.4.1 BLOCK EXEMPTIONS

First, it enacted secondary legislation creating block exemptions — these deal with specific, common types of agreement (e.g. exclusive distribution agreements) — where commonly-encountered clauses are set out in 'black lists' or 'white lists'. Both lists contain clauses which are usually seen as being anti-competitive. In the white list are clauses which, in the circumstances described in the block exemption, are deemed to be acceptable (i.e. exemptable); while the black list contains those clauses which cannot be permitted on an unseen basis.

If the subject-matter of an agreement appears to fall within a block exemption but the agreement contains black-listed clauses, the parties have three options. First, they can keep quiet and hope the Commission never finds out about it (thus running the risk of substantial fines); second, they can delete the offending clauses; or, third, they can notify the agreement to the Commission and seek individual exemption (Article 85(3)) based on the particular circumstances of their case. If an agreement contains anti-competitive clauses which are white-listed, the block exemption applies and there is no need to notify the Commission of the agreement. Be warned that some block exemptions also contain a 'grey list' (e.g. Regulation 2349/84, Article 2; see **3.8**)!

Block exemptions have been enacted (in the form of Commission regulations) in various fields to date. These include:

(a) Regulation 1983/83 on exclusive distribution agreements;
(b) Regulation 1984/83 on exclusive purchasing agreements; and
(c) Regulation 2349/84 on patent licensing agreements.

Two more recent block exemptions are those on franchising and know-how licences (Regulations 4087/88 and 556/89 respectively). These regulations (and others) are printed in the Official Journal and most of them are in a Commission publication, *Competition Law, in the EEC and the ECSC* (available from HMSO). Extracts from some block exemptions are set out later in this chapter.

On a slightly different topic, the Council of Ministers adopted a regulation (4064/89) in December 1989 establishing a policy for corporate mergers within the EC. This came into force on 21 September 1990, and the Directorate responsible for competition policy at the Commission (DG IV) now contains a merger task force. See also **4.1** below.

3.4.2 THE OPPOSITION PROCEDURE

Some of the block exemption regulations contain a provision known as the 'opposition procedure', notably the patent licensing regulation, 2349/84 (Article 4 — see **3.8**). Some patent licence agreements contain clauses which restrict competition but which appear in neither the white list nor the black list. The opposition procedure indicates that such an agreement should be notified to the Commission, with an indication that the opposition procedure could be used. The result is that the Commission has six months to indicate its opposition to the block exemption being applied to the agreement. If it does not oppose within six months, the agreement automatically falls within the block exemption.

A problem associated with the current opposition procedure is that there is no requirement for the Commission to publicise those agreements which are notified under the opposition procedure. This makes it very difficult for those who might wish to object to an exemption — they are unlikely to be able to make representations or present evidence to the Commission simply through their ignorance of what is happening.

3.4.3   COMFORT LETTERS

The second step was the introduction of comfort letters. These give neither an exemption nor a negative clearance, but were created for reasons of administrative convenience. Rather than take a formal decision in a case, the Commission will send a letter, announcing that it has closed its file, i.e., terminating proceedings against the undertaking or conduct under investigation.

The issue of a comfort letter may be preceded by negotiations between the undertakings and the Commission, intended to bring about modifications in the notified agreement. An example is *ICL/Fujitsu* (1986). ICL entered into several agreements providing for the transfer of knowhow and industrial property rights relating to computer components. Another agreement covered sales of Fujitsu mainframe computers to ICL, to be resold under the ICL brand. The agreements were notified to the Commission. The Commission decided that the sales agreement was outside the scope of the block exemption for exclusive distribution agreements and probably did not qualify for individual exemption either. This agreement was cancelled. The remaining agreements were seen as enabling an important transfer of technology to take place; the anti-competitive restrictions in them were indispensable and thus the agreements merited individual exemption under Article 85(3). A comfort letter was issued to this effect.

A comfort letter may be sent on various grounds:

(a)   On the facts, the agreement does not seem to infringe Article 85(1).
(b)   The agreement falls within a block exemption.
(c)   The agreement merits exemption.

3.4.4   PROBLEMS WITH THE *ROVIN* COMFORT LETTER

This type of comfort letter (see (c) above) is a recent innovation. Its first reported use was in the *Rovin* case (1983) (and see *ICL/Fujitsu (supra)*). It probably causes more problems than it solves because, by saying that the agreement merits exemption, it suggests that the agreement infringes Article 85(1).

If the parties to an agreement fall out, their dispute often comes before the courts of a member state. The party who wishes to escape from the agreement may allege it is void, being within Article 85(1), EC Treaty. If the other party tries to rebut this allegation by producing a comfort letter from the Commission, a *Rovin* letter may provoke the following argument from the 'escapee':

(a)   The letter implies the agreement is within Article 85(1).
(b)   It is therefore void unless exempted.
(c)   The comfort letter is not an exemption.
(d)   National courts cannot grant an exemption.
(e)   It follows that the agreement is unenforceable.

Rather than stop any litigation on this 'technical' point, it might be better to adjourn the national case and seek a final ruling on the original investigation from the Commission.

A comfort letter may be taken into account by a national court in litigation concerning an agreement but it is not binding on that court: see *Guerlain* (1978); *Lancôme v Etos* (1979). This permissive language is echoed in the Commission's Notice on Cooperation between National Courts and the Commission (1993) and leaves the legal effect of any comfort letter as the subject of speculation.

3.4.5 UNDERTAKINGS

The Commission is sometimes prepared to accept undertakings from a company that it will modify its suspect behaviour. This may be for the duration of the investigation — this will count as a mitigating factor if the company is eventually fined (see, e.g., *Hilti* (1985)). Alternatively, the Commission may agree to suspend its investigation indefinitely in return for the company giving appropriate undertakings as to its future conduct. Perhaps the best example of this is the *IBM* case (1984). The Commission issued a Notice, saying that its investigation of IBM under Article 86 would be suspended in return for certain promises. The Notice made it clear that IBM's future conduct would be monitored carefully to ensure compliance.

Undertakings are effectively binding on the Commission, once accepted by someone with the authority to do so (see, e.g., *FRUBO* (1974)). This is the result of applying the general principle of legitimate expectations; it would cease to apply if new facts were discovered, or there was a change in circumstances. See generally Bourgeois, in Slot and McDonnell (eds) (1993).

3.4.6 NEGOTIATED SETTLEMENTS

These are closely connected with undertakings given by 'suspect' companies. An investigation under Regulation 17/62 can stop at an early stage if the company being investigated agrees maybe on a non-admission basis) to modify its behaviour. A good recent example is the Italian Coca-Cola case — *San Pellegrino SpA* v *Coca-Cola Export Corp.-Filiale Italiana* (1989). San Pellegrino complained to the Commission that Filiale Italiana had a dominant position in the Italian cola market and was excluding competitors by offering discounts to distributors who agreed to sell no one else's cola. After a preliminary investigation, the Commission told Filiale Italiana that it agreed with the complaint. Filiale Italiana amended its contracts to remove the offending clauses and the Commission simply closed its file on the investigation.

3.5 Extracts from Regulation 3385/94 — Form A/B

Commission Regulation 3385/94

[Regulation No. 3385 of the Commission of 21 December 1994]
(form, content and other details of applications and notifications provided for in Council Regulation No. 17)

THE COMMISSION OF THE EUROPEAN COMMUNITIES,

Having regard to the Treaty establishing the European Community,

Having regard to the Agreement on the European Economic Area,

Having regard to Council Regulation No. 17 of 6 February 1962, First Regulation implementing Articles 85 and 86 of the Treaty, as last amended by the Act of Accession of Spain and Portugal, and in particular Article 24 thereof,

Whereas Commission Regulation No. 27 of 3 May 1962, First Regulation implementing Council Regulation No. 17, as last amended by Regulation (EC) 3666/93, no longer meets the requirements of efficient administrative procedure; whereas it should therefore be replaced by a new Regulation;

Whereas, on the one hand, applications for negative clearance under Article 2 and notifications under Articles 4, 5 and 25 of Regulation No. 17 have important legal consequences, which are favourable to the parties to an agreement, a decision or a practice, while, on the other hand, incorrect or misleading information in such applications or notifications may lead to the imposition of fines and may also entail civil law disadvantages for the parties; whereas it is therefore necessary in the interests of legal certainty to define precisely the persons entitled to submit applications and notifications, the subject matter and content of the information which such applications and notifications must contain, and the time when they become effective;

Whereas each of the parties should have the right to submit the application or the notification to the Commission; whereas, furthermore, a party exercising the right should inform the other parties in order to enable them to protect their interests; whereas applications and notifications relating to agreements, decisions or practices of associations of undertakings should be submitted only by such association;

Whereas it is for the applicants and the notifying parties to make full and honest disclosure to the Commission of the facts and circumstances which are relevant for coming to a decision on the agreements, decisions or practices concerned;

Whereas, in order to simplify and expedite their examination, it is desirable to prescribe that a form be used for applications for negative clearance relating to Article 85(1) and for notification relating to Article 85(3); whereas the use of this form should also be possible in the case of applications for negative clearance relating to Article 86;

Whereas the Commission, in appropriate cases, will give the parties, if they so request, an opportunity before the application or the notification to discuss the intended agreement, decision or practice informally and in strict confidence; whereas, in addition, it will, after the application or notification, maintain close contact with the parties to the extent necessary to discuss with them any practical or legal problems which it discovers on a first examination of the case and if possible to remove such problems by mutual agreement;

Whereas the provisions of this Regulation must also cover cases in which applications for negative clearance relating to Article 53(1) or Article 54 of the EEA Agreement, or notifications, relating to Article 53(3) of the EEA Agreement are submitted to the Commission,

HAS ADOPTED THIS REGULATION:

Article 1

Persons entitled to submit applications and notifications

1.   The following may submit an application under Article 2 of Regulation No. 17 relating to Article 85(1) of the Treaty or a notification under Articles 4, 5 and 25 of Regulation No. 17;

   (a)   any undertaking and any association of undertakings being a party to agreements or to concerted practices; and

   (b)   any association of undertakings adopting decisions or engaging in practices;

which may fall within the scope of Article 85(1).

Where the application or notification is submitted by some, but not all, of the parties, referred to in point (a) of the first subparagraph, they shall give notice to the other parties.

2.   Any undertaking which may hold, alone or with other undertakings, a dominant position within the common market or in a substantial part of it, may submit an application under Article 2 of Regulation No. 17 relating to Article 86 of the Treaty.

3.   Where the application or notification is signed by representatives of persons, undertakings or associations of undertakings, such representatives shall produce written proof that they are authorised to act.

4.   Where a joint application or notification is made, a joint representative should be appointed who is authorised to transmit and receive documents on behalf of all the applicants or notifying parties.

Article 2

Submission of applications and notifications

1. Applications under Article 2 of Regulation No. 17 relating to Article 85(1) of the Treaty and notifications under Articles 4, 5 and 25 of Regulation No. 17 shall be submitted in the manner prescribed by Form A/B as shown in the Annex to this Regulation. Form A/B may also be used for applications under Article 2 of Regulation No. 17 relating to Article 86 of the Treaty. Joint applications and joint notifications shall be submitted on a single form.

2. Seventeen copies of each application and notification and three copies of the Annexes thereto shall be submitted to the Commission at the address indicated in Form A/B.

3. The documents annexed to the application or notification shall be either originals or copies of the originals; in the latter case the applicant or notifying party shall confirm that they are true copies of the originals and complete.

4. Applications and notifications shall be in one of the official languages of the Community. This language shall also be the language of the proceeding for the applicant or notifying party. Documents shall be submitted in their original language. Where the original language is not one of the official languages, a translation into the language of the proceeding shall be attached.

5. Where applications for negative clearance relating to Article 53(1) or Article 54 of the EEA Agreement or notifications relating to Article 53(3) of the EEA Agreement are submitted, they may also be in one of the official languages of the EFTA States or the working language of the EFTA Surveillance Authority. If the language chosen for the application or notification is not an official language of the Community, the applicant or notifying party shall supplement all documentation with a translation into an official language of the Community. The language which is chosen for the translation shall be the language of the proceeding for the applicant or notifying party.

Article 3

Content of applications and notifications

1. Applications and notifications shall contain the information, including documents, required by Form A/B. The information must be correct and complete.

2. Applications under Article 2 of Regulation No. 17 relating to Article 86 of the Treaty shall contain a full statement of the facts, specifying, in particular, the practice concerned and the position of the undertaking or undertakings within the common market or a substantial part thereof in regard to the products or services to which the practice relates.

3. The Commission may dispense with the obligation to provide any particular information, including documents, required by Form A/B where the Commission considers that such information is not necessary for the examination of the case.

4. The Commission shall, without delay, acknowledge in writing to the applicant or notifying party receipt of the application or notification, and of any reply to a letter sent by the Commission pursuant to Article 4(2).

Article 4

Effective date of submission of applications and notifications

1. Without prejudice to paragraphs 2 to 5, applications and notifications shall become effective on the date on which they are received by the Commission. Where, however, the application or notification is

sent by registered post, it shall become effective on the date shown on the postmark of the place of posting.

2. Where the Commission finds that the information, including documents, contained in the application or notification is incomplete in a material respect, it shall, without delay, inform the applicant or notifying party in writing of this fact and shall fix an appropriate time limit for the completion of the information. In such cases, the application or notification shall become effective on the date on which the complete information is received by the Commission.

3. Material changes in the facts contained in the application or notification which the applicant or notifying party knows or ought to know must be communicated to the Commission voluntarily and without delay.

4. Incorrect or misleading information shall be considered to be incomplete information.

5. Where, at the expiry of a period of one month following the date on which the application or notification has been received, the Commission has not provided the applicant or notifying party with the information referred to in paragraph 2, the application or notification shall be deemed to have become effective on the date of its receipt by the Commission.

Article 5

Repeal

Regulation No. 27 is repealed.

Article 6

Entry into force

This Regulation shall enter into force on 1 March 1995.

This Regulation shall be binding in its entirety and directly applicable in all Member States.

Done at Brussels, 21 December 1994.

FORM A/B

INTRODUCTION

Form A/B, as its Annex, is an integral part of the Commission Regulation (EC) 3385/94 of 21 December 1994 on the form, content and other details of applications and notifications provided for in Council Regulation No. 17 (hereinafter referred to as 'the Regulation'). It allows undertakings and associations of undertakings to apply to the Commission for negative clearance agreements or practices which may fall within the prohibitions of Article 85(1) and Article 86 of the EC Treaty, or within Articles 53(1) and 54 of the EEA Agreement or to notify such agreement and apply to have it exempted from the prohibition set out in Article 85(1) by virtue of the provisions of Articles 85(3) of the EC Treaty or from the prohibition of Article 53(1) by virtue of the provisions of Article 53(3) of the EEA Agreement.

To facilitate the use of the Form A/B the following pages set out:

— in which situations it is necessary to make an application or a notification (Point A),
— to which authority (the Commission or the EFTA Surveillance Authority) the application or notification should be made (Point B),
— for which purposes the application or notification can be used (Point C),
— what information must be given in the application or notification (Points D, E and F),

— who can make an application or notification (Point G),
— how to make an application or notification (Point H),
— how the business secrets of the undertakings can be protected (Point I),
— how certain technical terms used in the operational part of the Form A/B should be interpreted (Point J), and
— the subsequent procedure after the application or notification has been made (Point K).

A IN WHICH SITUATIONS IS IT NECESSARY TO MAKE AN APPLICATION OR A NOTIFICATION?

I. PURPOSE OF THE COMPETITION RULES OF THE EC TREATY AND THE EEA AGREEMENT

1. Purpose of the EC competition rules

The purpose of the competition rules is to prevent the distortion of competition in the common market by restrictive practices or the abuse of dominant positions. They apply to any enterprise trading directly or indirectly in the common market, wherever established.

Article 85(1) of the EC Treaty (the text of Articles 85 and 86 is reproduced in Annex I to this form) prohibits restrictive agreements, decisions or concerted practices (arrangements) which may affect trade between Member States, and Article 85(2) declares agreements and decisions containing such restrictions void (although the Court of Justice had held that if restrictive terms of agreements are severable, only those terms are void); Article 85(3), however, provides for exemption of arrangements with beneficial effects, if its conditions are met. Article 86 prohibits the abuse of a dominant position which may affect trade between Member States. The original procedures for implementing these Articles, which provide for 'negative clearance' and exemption pursuant to Article 85(3), were laid down in Regulation No. 17.

2. Purpose of the EEA competition rules

The competition rules of the Agreement on the European Economic Area (concluded between the Community, the Member States and the EFTA States) are based on the same principles as those contained in the Community competition rules and have the same purpose, i.e., to prevent the distortion of competition in the EEA territory by cartels or the abuse of dominant position. They apply to any enterprise trading directly or indirectly in the EEA territory, wherever established.

Article 53(1) of the EEA Agreement (the text of Articles 53, 54 and 56 of the EEA Agreement is reproduced in Annex I) prohibits restrictive agreements, decisions or concerted practices (arrangements) which may affect trade between the Community and one or more EFTA States (or between EFTA States), and Article 53(2) declares agreements or decisions containing such restrictions void; Article 53(3), however, provides for exemption of arrangements with beneficial effects, if its conditions are met. Article 54 prohibits the abuse of a dominant position which may affect trade between the Community and one or more EFTA States (or between EFTA States). The procedures for implementing these Articles, which provide for 'negative clearance' and exemption pursuant to Article 53(3), are laid down in Regulation No. 17, supplemented for EEA purposes, by Protocols 21, 22 and 23 to the EEA Agreement.

II. THE SCOPE OF THE COMPETITION RULES OF THE EC TREATY AND THE EEA AGREEMENT

The applicability of Articles 85 and 86 of the EC Treaty and Articles 53 and 54 of the EEA Agreement depends on the circumstances of each individual case. It presupposes that the arrangement or behaviour satisfies all the conditions set out in the relevant provisions. This question must consequently be examined before any application for negative clearance or any notification is made.

1. Negative clearance

The negative clearance procedure allows undertakings to ascertain whether the Commission considers that their arrangement or their behaviour is or is not prohibited by Article 85(1), or Article 86 of the EC Treaty or by Article 53(1) or Article 54 of the EEA Agreement. This procedure is governed by Article 2 of Regulation No. 17. The negative clearance takes the form of a decision by which the Commission certifies that, on the basis of the facts in its possession, there are no grounds pursuant to Article 85(1) or Article 86 of the EC Treaty or under Article 53(1) or Article 54 of the EEA Agreement for action on its part in respect of the arrangement or behaviour.

There is, however, no point in making an application when the arrangements or the behaviour are manifestly not prohibited by the abovementioned provisions. Nor is the Commission obliged to give negative clearance. Article 2 of Regulation No. 17 states that '... the Commission may certify ...'. The Commission issues negative clearance decisions only where an important problem of interpretation has to be solved. In the other cases it reacts to the application by sending a comfort letter.

The Commission has published several notices relating the interpretation of Article 85(1) of the EC Treaty. They define certain categories of agreements which, by their nature or because of their minor importance, are not caught by the prohibition.

2. Exemption

The procedure for exemption pursuant to Article 85(3) of the EC Treaty and Article 53(3) of the EEA Agreement allows companies to enter into arrangements which, in fact, offer economic advantages but which, without exemption, would be prohibited by Article 85(1) of the EC Treaty or by Article 53(1) of the EEA Agreement. This procedure is governed by Articles 4, 6 and 8 and, for the new Member States, also by Articles 5, 7 and 25 of Regulation No. 17. The exemption takes the form of a decision by the Commission declaring Article 85(1) of the EC Treaty or Article 53(1) of the EEA Agreement to be inapplicable to the arrangements described in the decision. Article 8 requires the Commission to specify the period of validity of any such decision, allows the Commission to attach conditions and obligations and provides for decisions to be amended or revoked or specified acts by the parties to be prohibited in certain circumstances, notably if the decisions were based on incorrect information or if there is any material change in the facts.

The Commission has adopted a number of regulations granting exemptions to categories of agreements. Some of these regulations provide that some agreements may benefit from exemption only if they are notified to the Commission pursuant to Article 4 or 5 of Regulation No. 17 with a view to obtaining exemption, and the benefit of the opposition procedure is claimed in the notification.

A decision granting exemption may have retroactive effect, but, with certain exceptions, cannot be made effective earlier than the date of notification (Article 6 of Regulation No. 17). Should the Commission find that notified arrangements are indeed prohibited and cannot be exempted and, therefore, take a decision condemning them, the participants are nevertheless protected, between the date of the notification and the date of the decision, against fines for any infringement described in the notification (Article 3 and Article 15(5) and (6) of Regulation No. 17).

Normally the Commission issues exemption decisions only in cases of particular legal, economic or political importance. In the other cases it terminates the procedure by sending a comfort letter.

B   TO WHICH AUTHORITY SHOULD APPLICATION OR NOTIFICATION BE MADE?

The applications and notifications must be made to the authority which has competence for the matter. The Commission is responsible for the application of the competition rules of the EC Treaty. However there is shared competence in relation to the application of the competition rules of the EEA agreement.

The competence of the Commission and of the EFTA Surveillance Authority to apply the EEA competition rules follows from Article 56 of the EEA Agreement. Applications and notifications relating to agreements, decisions or concerted practices liable to affect trade between Member States should be addressed to the Commission unless their effects on trade between Member States or on competition within the Community are not appreciable within the meaning of the Commission notice of 1986 on agreements of minor importance. Furthermore, all restrictive agreements, decisions or concerted practices affecting trade between one Member State and one or more EFTA States fall within the competence of the Commission, provided that the undertakings concerned achieve more than 67% of their combined EEA-wide turnover within the Community. However, if the effects of such agreements, decisions or concerted practices on trade between Member States or on competition within the Community are not appreciable, the notification should, where necessary, be addressed to the EFTA Surveillance Authority. All other agreements, decisions and concerted practices falling under Article 53 of the EEA Agreement should be notified to the EFTA Surveillance Authority (the address of which is given in Annex III).

Applications for negative clearance regarding Article 54 of the EEA Agreements should be lodged with the Commission if the dominant position exists only in the Community, or with the EFTA Surveillance Authority, if the dominant position exists only in the whole of the territory of the EFTA States, or a substantial part of it. Only where the dominant position exists within both territories should the rules outlined above with respect to Article 53 be applied.

The Commission will apply, as a basis for appraisal, the competition rules of the EC Treaty. Where the case falls under the EEA Agreement and is attributed to the Commission pursuant to Article 56 of that Agreement, it will simultaneously apply the EEA rules.

C THE PURPOSE OF THIS FORM

Form A/B lists the questions that must be answered and the information and documents that must be provided when applying for the following:

—a negative clearance with regard to Article 85(1) of the EC Treaty and/or Article 53(1) of EEA Agreement, pursuant to Article 2 of Regulation No. 17, with respect to agreements between undertakings, decisions by associations of undertakings and concerted practices,
—an exemption pursuant to Article 85(3) of the EC Treaty and/or Article 53(3) of the EEA Agreement with respect to agreements between undertakings, decisions by associations of undertakings and concerted practices,
—the benefit of the opposition procedure contained in certain Commission regulations granting exemption by category.

This form allows undertakings applying for negative clearance to notify, at the same time, in order to obtain an exemption in the event that the Commission reaches the conclusion that no negative clearance can be granted.

Applications for negative clearance and notifications relating to Article 85 of the EC Treaty shall be submitted in the manner prescribed by form A/B (see Article 2(1), first sentence of the Regulation).

This form can also be used by undertakings that wish to apply for a negative clearance from Article 86 of the EC Treaty or Article 53 of the EEA Agreement, pursuant to Article 2 of Regulation No. 17. Applicants requesting negative clearance from Article 86 are not required to use form A/B. They are nonetheless strongly recommended to give all the information requested below to ensure that their application gives a full statement of the facts (see Article 2(1), second sentence of the Regulation).

The applications or notifications made on the form A/B issued by the EFTA side are equally valid. However, if the agreements, decisions or practices concerned fall solely within Articles 85 or 86 of the EC Treaty, i.e., have no EEA relevance whatsoever, it is advisable to use the present form established by the Commission.

D WHICH CHAPTERS OF THE FORM SHOULD BE COMPLETED?

The operational part of this form is sub-divided into four chapters. Undertakings wishing to make an application for a negative clearance or a notification must complete Chapters I, II and IV. An exception to this rule is provided for in the case where the application or notification concerns an agreement concerning the creation of a cooperative joint venture of a structural character if the parties wish to benefit from an accelerated procedure. In this situation Chapters I, III and IV should be completed.

In 1992, the Commission announced that it had adopted new internal administrative rules that provided that certain applications and notifications — those of cooperative joint ventures which are structural in nature — would be dealt with within fixed deadlines. In such cases the services of the Commission will, within two months of receipt of the complete notification of the agreement, inform the parties in writing of the results of the initial analysis of the case and, as appropriate, the nature and probable length of the administrative procedure they intend to engage.

The contents of this letter may vary according to the characteristics of the case under investigation:

— in cases not posing any problems, the Commission will send a comfort letter confirming the compatibility of the agreement with Article 85(1) or (3),
— if a comfort letter cannot be sent because of the need to settle the case by formal decision, the Commission will inform the undertakings concerned of its intention to adopt a decision either granting or rejecting exemption,
— if the Commission has serious doubts as to the compatibility of the agreement with the competition rules, it will send a letter to the parties giving notice of an in-depth examination which may, depending on the case, result in a decision either prohibiting, exempting subject to conditions and obligations, or simply exempting the agreement in question.

This new accelerated procedure, applicable since 1 January 1993, is based entirely on the principle of self-discipline. The deadline of two months from the complete notification — intended for the initial examination of the case — does not constitute a statutory term and is therefore in no way legally binding. However, the Commission will do its best to abide by it. The Commission reserves the right, moreover, to extend this accelerated procedure to other forms of cooperation between undertakings.

A cooperative joint venture of a structural nature is one that involves an important change in the structure and organisation of the business assets of the parties to the agreement. This may occur because the joint venture takes over or extends existing activities of the parent companies or because it undertakes new activities on their behalf. Such operations are characterised by the commitment of significant financial, material and/or non-tangible assets such as intellectual property rights and know how. Structural joint ventures are therefore normally intended to operate on a medium- or long-term basis.

This concept includes certain 'partial function' joint ventures which take over one or several specific functions within the parents' business activity without access to the market, in particular research and development and/or production. It also covers those 'full function' joint ventures which give rise to coordination of the competitive behaviour of independent undertakings, in particular between the parties to the joint venture or between them and the joint venture.

In order to respect the internal deadline, it is important that the Commission has available on notification all the relevant information reasonably available to the notifying parties that is necessary for it to assess the impact of the operation in question on competition. Form A/B therefore contains a special section (Chapter III) that must be completed only by persons notifying cooperative joint ventures of a structural character that wish to benefit from the accelerated procedure.

Persons notifying joint ventures of a structural character that wish to claim the benefit of the aforementioned accelerated procedure should therefore complete Chapters I, III and IV of this form. Chapter III contains a series of detailed questions necessary for the Commission to assess the relevant market(s) and the position of the parties to the joint venture on that (those) market(s).

Where the parties do not wish to claim the benefit of an accelerated procedure for their joint ventures of a structural character they should complete Chapters I, II and IV of this form. Chapter II contains a far more limited range of questions on the relevant market(s) and the position of the parties to the operation in question on that (those) market(s), but sufficient to enable the Commission to commence its examination and investigation.

E THE NEED FOR COMPLETE INFORMATION

The receipt of a valid notification by the Commission has two main consequences. First, it affords immunity from fines from the date that the valid notification is received by the Commission with respect to applications made in order to obtain exemption (see Article 15(5) of Regulation No. 17). Second, until a valid notification is received, the Commission cannot grant an exemption pursuant to Article 85(3) of the EC Treaty and/or Article 53(3) of the EEA Agreement, and any exemption that is granted can be effective only from the date of receipt of a valid notification. Thus, whilst there is no legal obligation to notify as such, unless and until an arrangement that falls within the scope of Article 85(1) and/or Article 53(1) has not been notified and is, therefore, not capable of being exempted, it may be declared void by a national court pursuant to Article 85(2) and/or Article 53(2).

Where an undertaking is claiming the benefit of a group exemption by recourse to an opposition procedure, the period within which the Commission must oppose the exemption by category only applies from the date that a valid notification is received. This is also true of the two months' period imposed on the Commission services for an initial analysis of applications for negative clearance and notifications relating to cooperative joint ventures of a structural character which benefit from the accelerated procedure.

A valid application or notification for this purpose means one that is not incomplete (see Article 3(1) of the Regulation). This is subject to two qualifications. First, if the information or documents required by this form are not reasonably available to you in part or in whole, the Commission will accept that a notification is complete and thus valid notwithstanding the failure to provide such information, providing that you give reasons for the unavailability of the information, and provide your best estimates for missing data together with the sources for the estimates. Indications as to where any of the requested information or documents that are unavailable to you could be obtained by the Commission must also be provided. Second, the Commission only requires the submission of information relevant and necessary to its inquiry into the notified operation. In some cases not all the information required by this form will be necessary for this purpose. The Commission may therefore dispense with the obligation to provide certain information required by this form (see Article 3(3) of the Regulation). This provision enables, where appropriate, each application or notification to be tailored to each case so that only the information strictly necessary for the Commission's examination is provided. This avoids unnecessary administrative burdens being imposed on undertakings, in particular on small and medium-sized ones. Where the information or documents required by this form are not provided for this reason, the application or notification should indicate the reasons why the information is considered to be unnecessary to the Commission's investigation.

Where the Commission finds that the information contained in the application or notification is incomplete in a material respect, it will, within one month from receipt, inform the applicant or the notifying party in writing of this fact and the nature of the missing information. In such cases, the application or notification shall become effective on the date on which the complete information is received by the Commission. If the Commission has not informed the applicant or the notifying party within the one month period that the application or notification is incomplete in a material respect, the application or notification will be deemed to be complete and valid (see Article 4 of the Regulation).

It is also important that undertakings inform the Commission of important changes in the factual situation including those of which they become aware after the application or notification has been submitted. The Commission must, therefore, be informed immediately of any changes to an agreement, decision or practice which is the subject of an application or notification (see Article 4(3) of the Regulation). Failure to inform the Commission of such relevant changes could result in any negative clearance decision being without effect or in the withdrawal of any exemption decision adopted by the Commission on the basis of the notification.

F THE NEED FOR ACCURATE INFORMATION

In addition to the requirement that the application or notification be complete, it is important that you ensure that the information provided is accurate (see Article 3(1) of the Regulation). Article 15(1)(a) of Regulation No. 17 states that the Commission may, by decision, impose on undertakings or associations of undertakings fines of up to ECU 5,000 where, intentionally or negligently, they supply incorrect or misleading information in an application for negative clearance or notification. Such information is, moreover, considered to be incomplete (see Article 4(4) of the Regulation), so that the parties cannot benefit from the advantages of the opposition procedure or accelerated procedure (see above, Point E).

G WHO CAN LODGE AN APPLICATION OR A NOTIFICATION?

Any of the undertakings party to an agreement, decision or practice of the kind described in Articles 85 or 86 of the EC Treaty and Articles 53 or 54 of the EEA Agreement may submit an application for negative clearance, in relation to Article 85 and Article 53, or a notification requesting an exemption. An association of undertakings may submit an application or a notification in relation to decisions taken or practices pursued into in the operation of the association.

In relation to agreements and concerted practices between undertakings it is common practice for all the parties involved to submit a joint application or notification. Although the Commission strongly recommends this approach, because it is helpful to have the views of all the parties directly concerned at the same time, it is not obligatory. Any of the parties to an agreement may submit an application or notification in their individual capacities, but in such circumstances the notifying party should inform all the other parties to the agreement, decision or practice of that fact (see Article 1(3) of the Regulation). They may also provide them with a copy of the completed form, where relevant, once confidential information and business secrets have been deleted (see below, operational part, question 1.2).

Where a joint application or notification is submitted, it has also become common practice to appoint a joint representative to act on behalf of all the undertakings involved, both in making the application or notification, and in dealing with any subsequent contacts with the Commission (see Article 1(4) of the Regulation). Again, whilst this is helpful, it is not obligatory, and all the undertakings jointly submitting an application or a notification may sign it in their individual capacities.

H HOW TO SUBMIT AN APPLICATION OR NOTIFICATION

Applications and notifications may be submitted in any of the official languages of the European Community or of an EFTA State (see Article 2(4) and (5) of the Regulation). In order to ensure rapid proceedings, it is, however, recommended to use, in case of an application or notification to the EFTA Surveillance Authority one of the official languages of an EFTA State or the working language of the EFTA Surveillance Authority, which is English, or, in the case of an application or notification to the Commission, one of the official languages of the Community or the working language of the EFTA Surveillance Authority. This language will thereafter be the language of the proceeding for the applicant or notifying party.

Form A/B is not a form to be filled in. Undertakings should simply provide the information requested by this form, using its sections and paragraph numbers, signing a declaration as stated in Section 19 below, and annexing the required supporting documentation.

Supporting documents shall be submitted in their original language; where this is not an official language of the Community they must be translated into the language of the proceeding. The supporting documents may be originals or copies of the originals (see Article 2(4) of the Regulation).

All information requested in this form shall, unless otherwise stated, relate to the calendar year preceding that of the application or notification. Where information is not reasonably available on this basis (for example if accounting periods are used that are not based on the calendar year, or the previous year's figures are not yet available) the most recently available information should be provided and reasons given why figures on the basis of the calendar year preceding that of the application or notification cannot be provided.

Financial data may be provided in the currency in which the official audited accounts of the undertaking(s) concerned are prepared or in Ecus. In the latter case the exchange rate used for the conversion must be stated.

Seventeen copies of each application or notification, but only three copies of all supporting documents must be provided (see Article 2(2) of the Regulation).

The application or notification is to be sent to:

Commission of the European Communities,
Directorate-General for Competition (DG IV),
The Registrar,
200 Rue de la Loi,
B-1049 Brussels

or be delivered by hand during Commission working days and official working hours at the following address:

Commission of the European Communities,
Directorate-General for Competition (DG IV),
The Registrar,
158 Avenue de Cortenberg,
B-1040 Brussels.

I CONFIDENTIALITY

Article 214 of the EC Treaty, Article 20 of Regulation No. 17, Article 9 of Protocol 23 to the EEA Agreement, Article 122 of the EEA Agreement and Articles 20 and 21 of Chapter II of Protocol 4 to the Agreement between the EFTA States on the establishment of a Surveillance Authority and of a Court of Justice require the Commission, the Member States, the EEA Surveillance Authority and EFTA States not to disclose information of the kind covered by the obligation of professional secrecy. On the other hand, Regulation No. 17 requires the Commission to publish a summary of the application or notification, should it intend to take a favourable decision. In this publication, the Commission '. . . shall have regard to the legitimate interest of undertakings in the protection of their business secrets' (Article 19(3) of Regulation No. 17; see also Article 21(2) in relation to the publication of decisions). In this connection, if an undertaking believes that its interests would be harmed if any of the information it is asked to supply were to be published or otherwise divulged to other undertakings, it should put all such information in a separate annex with each page clearly marked 'Business Secrets'. It should also give reasons why any information identified as confidential or secret should not be divulged or published. (See below, Section 5 of the operational part that requests a non-confidential summary of the notification.)

J SUBSEQUENT PROCEDURE

The application or notification is registered in the Registry of the Directorate-General for Competition (DG IV). The date of receipt by the Commission (or the date of posting if sent by registered post) is the effective date of the submission (see Article 4(1) of the Regulation). However, special rules apply to incomplete applications and notifications (see above under Point E).

The Commission will acknowledge receipt of all applications and notifications in writing, indicating the case number attributed to the file. This number must be used in all future correspondence regarding the notification. The receipt of acknowledgement does not prejudge the question whether the application or notification is valid.

Further information may be sought from the parties or from third parties (Articles 11 to 14 of Regulation No. 17) and suggestions might be made as to amendments to the arrangements that might make them acceptable. Equally, a short preliminary notice may be published in the C series of the *Official Journal of the European Communities*, stating the names of the interested undertakings, the groups to which they belong, the economic sectors involved and the nature of the arrangements, and inviting third party comments (see below, operational part, Section 5).

Where a notification is made together for the purpose of the application of the opposition procedure, the Commission may oppose the grant of the benefit of the group exemption with respect to the notified agreement. If the Commission opposes the claim, and unless it subsequently withdraws its opposition, that notification will then be treated as an application for an individual exemption.

If, after examination, the Commission intends to grant the application for negative clearance or exemption, it is obliged (by Article 19(3) of Regulation No. 17) to publish a summary and invite comments from third parties. Subsequently, a preliminary draft decision has to be submitted to and discussed with the Advisory Committee on Restrictive Practices and Dominant Positions composed of officials of the competent authorities of the Member States in the matter of restrictive practices and monopolies (Article 10 of Regulation No. 17) and attended, where the case falls within the EEA Agreement, by representatives of the EFTA Surveillance Authority and the EFTA States which will already have received a copy of the application or notification. Only then, and providing nothing has happened to change the Commission's intention, can it adopt the envisaged decision.

Files are often closed without any formal decision being taken, for example, because it is found that the arrangements are already covered by a block exemption, or because they do not call for any action by the Commission, at least in circumstances at that time. In such cases comfort letters are sent. Although not a Commission decision, a comfort letter indicates how the Commission's departments view the case on the facts currently in their possession which means that the Commission could where necessary — for example, if it were to be asserted that a contract was void under Article 85(2) of the EC Treaty and/or Article 53(2) of the EEA Agreement — take an appropriate decision to clarify the legal situation.

K   DEFINITIONS USED IN THE OPERATIONAL PART OF THIS FORM

Agreement: The word 'agreement' is used to refer to all categories of arrangements, i.e., agreements between undertakings, decisions by associations of undertakings and concerted practices.

Year: All references to the word 'year' in this form shall be read as meaning calendar year, unless otherwise stated.

Group: A group relationship exists for the purpose of this form where one undertaking:

— owns more than half the capital or business assets of another undertaking, or
— has the power to exercise more than half the voting rights in another undertaking, or
— has the power to appoint more than half the members of the supervisory board, board of directors or bodies legally representing the undertaking, or
— has the right to manage the affairs of another undertaking.

An undertaking which is jointly controlled by several other undertakings (joint venture) forms part of the group of each of these undertakings.

Relevant product market: questions 6.1 and 11.1 of this form require the undertaking or individual submitting the notification to define the relevant product and/or service market(s) that are likely to be affected by the agreement in question. That definition(s) is then used as the basis for a number of other questions contained in this form. The definition(s) thus submitted by the notifying parties are referred to in this form as the relevant product market(s). These words can refer to a market made up either of products or of services.

Relevant geographic market: questions 6.2 and 11.2 of this form require the undertaking or individual submitting the notification to define the relevant geographic market(s) that are likely to be affected by the agreement in question. That definition(s) is then used as the basis for a number of other questions contained in this form. The definition(s) thus submitted by the notifying parties are referred to in this form as the relevant geographic market(s).

Relevant product and geographic market: by virtue of the combination of their replies to questions 6 and 11 the parties provide their definition of the relevant market(s) affected by the notified agreement(s). That (those) definition(s) is (are) then used as the basis for a number of other questions contained in this form. The definition(s) thus submitted by the notifying parties is referred to in this form as the relevant geographic and product market(s).

Notification: this form can be used to make an application for negative clearance and/or a notification requesting an exemption. The word 'notification' is used to refer to either an application or a notification.

Parties and notifying party: the word 'party' is used to refer to all the undertakings which are party to the agreement being notified. As a notification may be submitted by only one of the undertakings which are party to an agreement, 'notifying party' is used to refer only to the undertaking or undertakings actually submitting the notification.

OPERATIONAL PART

PLEASE MAKE SURE THAT THE FIRST PAGE OF YOUR APPLICATION OR NOTIFICATION CONTAINS THE WORDS 'APPLICATION FOR NEGATIVE CLEARANCE/NOTIFICATION IN ACCORDANCE WITH FORM A/B'

CHAPTER I   SECTIONS CONCERNING THE PARTIES, THEIR GROUPS AND THE AGREEMENT (TO BE COMPLETED FOR ALL NOTIFICATIONS)

Section 1   Identity of the undertakings or persons submitting the notification

1.1   Please list the undertakings on behalf of which the notification is being submitted and indicate their legal denomination or commercial name, shortened or commonly used as appropriate (if it differs from the legal denomination).

1.2   If the notification is being submitted on behalf of only one or some of the undertakings party to the agreement being notified, please confirm that the remaining undertakings have been informed of that fact and indicate whether they have received a copy of the notification, with relevant confidential information and business secrets deleted.[1] (In such circumstances a copy of the edited copy of the notification which has been provided to such other undertakings should be annexed to this notification.)

1.3   If a joint notification is being submitted, has a joint representative[2] been appointed?[3]

If yes, please give the details requested in 1.3.1 to 1.3.3 below.

If no, please give details of any representatives who have been authorised to act for each or either of the parties to the agreement indicating who they represent.

1.3.1   Name of representative.

1.3.2   Address of representative.

1.3.3   Telephone and fax number of representative.

1.4   In cases where one or more representatives have been appointed, an authority to act on behalf of the undertaking(s) submitting the notification must accompany the notification.

Notes
1.   The Commission is aware that in exceptional cases it may not be practicable to inform non-notifying parties to the notified agreement of the fact that it has been notified, or to provide them a copy of the notification. This may be the case, for example, where a standard agreement is being notified that is concluded with a large number of undertakings. Where this is the case you should state the reason why it has not been practicable to follow the standard procedure set out in this question.
2.   For the purposes of this question a representative means an individual or undertaking formally appointed to make the notification or application on behalf of the party or parties submitting the notification. This should be distinguished from the situation where the notification is signed by an officer of the company or companies in question. In the latter situation no representative is appointed.
3.   It is not mandatory to appoint representatives for the purpose of completing and/or submitting this notification. This question only requires the identification of representatives where the notifying parties have chosen to appoint them.

Section 2   Information on the parties to the agreement and the groups to which they belong

2.1   State the name and address of the parties to the agreement being notified, and the country of their incorporation.

2.2   State the nature of the business of each of the parties to the agreement being notified.

2.3   For each of the parties to the agreement, give the name of a person that can be contacted, together with his or her name, address, telephone number, fax number and position held in the undertaking.

2.4   Identify the corporate groups to which the parties to the agreement being notified belong. State the sectors in which these groups are active, and the world-wide turnover of each group.

Section 3   Procedural matters

3.1   Please state whether you have made any formal submission to any other competition authorities in relation to the agreement in question. If yes, state which authorities, the individual or department in question, and the nature of the contact. In addition to this, mention any earlier proceedings or informal contacts, of which you are aware, with the Commission and/or the EFTA Surveillance Authority and any earlier proceedings with any national authorities or courts in the Community or in EFTA concerning these or any related agreements.

3.2   Please summarise any reasons for any claim that the case involves an issue of exceptional urgency.

3.3   The Commission has stated that where notifications do not have particular political, economic or legal significance for the Community they will normally be dealt with by means of comfort letter. Would you be satisfied with a comfort letter? If you consider that it would be inappropriate to deal with the notified agreement in this manner, please explain the reasons for this view.

3.4   State whether you intend to produce further supporting facts or arguments not yet available and, if so, on which points.

Section 4   Full details of the arrangements

4.1   Please summarise the nature, content and objectives pursued by the agreement being notified.

4.2   Detail any provisions contained in the agreements which may restrict the parties in their freedom to take independent commercial decisions, for example regarding:

— buying or selling prices, discounts or other trading conditions,
— the quantities of goods to be manufactured or distributed or services to be offered,
— technical development or investment,
— the choice of markets or sources of supply,
— purchases from or sales to third parties,
— whether to apply similar terms for the supply of equivalent goods or services,
— whether to offer different services separately or together.

If you are claiming the benefit of the opposition procedure, identify in this list the restrictions that exceed those automatically exempted by the relevant regulation.

4.3   State between which Member States of the Community and/or EFTA States trade may be affected by the arrangements. Please give reasons for your reply to this question, giving data on trade flows where relevant. Furthermore please state whether trade between the Community or the EEA territory and any third countries is affected, again giving reasons for your reply.

Section 5   Non-confidential summary

Shortly following receipt of a notification, the Commission may publish a short notice inviting third party comments on the agreement in question. As the objective pursued by the Commission in publishing an informal preliminary notice is to receive third party comments as soon as possible after the notification has been received, such a notice is usually published without first providing it to the notifying parties for their comments. This section requests the information to be used in an informal preliminary notice in the event that the Commission decides to issue one. It is important, therefore, that your replies to these questions do not contain any business secrets or other confidential information.

1.   State the names of the parties to the agreement notified and the groups of undertakings to which they belong.
2.   Give a short summary of the nature and objectives of the agreement. As a guideline this summary should not exceed 100 words.
3.   Identify the product sectors affected by the agreement in question.

CHAPTER II   SECTION CONCERNING THE RELEVANT MARKET (TO BE COMPLETED FOR ALL NOTIFICATIONS EXCEPT THOSE RELATING TO STRUCTURAL JOINT VENTURES FOR WHICH ACCELERATED TREATMENT IS CLAIMED)

Section 6   The relevant market

A relevant product market comprises all those products and/or services which are regarded as interchangeable or substitutable by the consumer, by reason of the products' characteristics, their prices and their intended use.

The following factors are normally considered to be relevant to the determination of the relevant product market and should be taken into account in this analysis:[1]

— the degree of physical similarity between the products/services in question,
— any differences in the end use to which the goods are put,
— differences in price between two products,
— the cost of switching between two potentially competing products,
— established or entrenched consumer preferences for one type or category of product over another,
— industry-wide product classifications (e.g., classifications maintained by trade associations).

The relevant geographic market comprises the area in which the undertakings concerned are involved in the supply of products or services, in which the conditions of competition are sufficiently homogeneous and which can be distinguished from neighbouring areas because, in particular, conditions of competition are appreciably different in those areas.

Factors relevant to the assessment of the relevant geographic market include[1] the nature and characteristics of the products or services concerned, the existence of entry barriers or consumer preferences, appreciable differences of the undertakings' market share or substantial price differences between neighbouring areas, and transport costs.

6.1   In the light of the above please explain the definition of the relevant product market or markets that in your opinion should form the basis of the Commission's analysis of the notification.

In your answer, please give reasons for assumptions or findings, and explain how the factors outlined above have been taken into account. In particular, please state the specific products or services directly or indirectly affected by the agreement being notified and identify the categories of goods viewed as substitutable in your market definition.

In the questions figuring below, this (or these) definition(s) will be referred to as 'the relevant product market(s)'.

6.2   Please explain the definition of the relevant geographic market or markets that in your opinion should form the basis of the Commission's analysis of the notification. In your answer, please give reasons for assumptions or findings, and explain how the factors outlined above have been taken into account. In particular, please identify the countries in which the parties are active in the relevant product market(s), and in the event that you consider the relevant geographic market to be wider than the individual Member States of the Community or EFTA on which the parties to the agreement are active, give the reasons for this.

In the questions below, this (or these) definition(s) will be referred to as 'the relevant geographic market(s)'.

Note
1.   This list is not, however, exhaustive, and notifying parties may refer to other factors.

Section 7   Group members operating on the same markets as the parties

7.1   For each of the parties to the agreement being notified, provide a list of all undertakings belonging to the same group which are:

7.1.1   active in the relevant product market(s);

7.1.2   active in markets neighbouring the *relevant product market(s)* (i.e., active in products and/or services that represent imperfect and partial substitutes for those included in your definition of the relevant product market(s)).

Such undertakings must be identified even if they sell the product or service in question in other geographic areas than those in which the parties to the notified agreement operate. Please list the name, place of incorporation, exact product manufactured and the geographic scope of operation of each group member.

Section 8   The position of the parties on the affected relevant product markets

Information requested in this section must be provided for the groups of the parties as a whole. It is not sufficient to provide such information only in relation to the individual undertakings directly concerned by the agreement.

8.1 In relation to each relevant product market(s) identified in your reply to question 6.1 please provide the following information:

8.1.1 the market shares of the parties on the *relevant geographic market* during the previous three years;

8.1.2 where different, the market shares of the parties in (a) the EEA territory as a whole, (b) the Community, (c) the territory of the EFTA States and (d) each EC Member State and EFTA State during the previous three years.[1] For this section, where market shares are less than 20%, please state simply which of the following bands are relevant: 0 to 5%, 5 to 10%, 10 to 15%, 15 to 20%.

For the purpose of answering these questions, market share may be calculated either on the basis of value or volume. Justification for the figures provided must be given. Thus, for each answer, total market value/volume must be stated, together with the sales/turnover of each of the parties in question. The source or sources of the information should also be given (e.g., official statistics, estimates, etc.), and where possible, copies should be provided of documents from which information has been taken.

Note
1. I.e. Where the relevant geographic market has been defined as world wide, these figures must be given regarding the EEA, the Community, the territory of the EFTA States, and each EC Member States. Where the relevant geographic market has been defined as the Community, these figures must be given for the EEA, the territory of the EFTA States, and each EC Member State. Where the market has been defined as national, these figures must be given for the EEA, the Community and the territory of the EFTA States.

Section 9   The position of competitors and customers on the relevant product market(s)

Information requested in this section must be provided for the group of the parties as a whole and not in relation to the individual companies directly concerned by the agreement notified.

For the (all) relevant product and geographic market(s) in which the parties have a combined market share exceeding 15%, the following questions must be answered.

9.1 Please identify the five main competitors of the parties. Please identify the company and give your best estimate as to their market share in the relevant geographic market(s). Please also provide address, telephone and fax number, and, where possible, the name of a contact person at each company identified.

9.2 Please identify the five main customers of each of the parties. State company name, address, telephone and fax numbers, together with the name of a contact person.

Section 10   Market entry and potential competition in product and geographic terms

For the (all) relevant product and geographic market(s) in which the parties have a combined market share exceeding 15%, the following questions must be answered.

10.1 Describe the various factors influencing entry in product terms into the *relevant product market(s)* that exist in the present case (i.e., what barriers exist to prevent undertakings that do not presently manufacture goods within the relevant product market(s) entering this market(s)). In so doing take account of the following where appropriate:

— to what extent is entry to the markets influenced by the requirement of government authorisation or standard setting in any form? Are there any legal or regulatory controls on entry to these markets?
— to what extent is entry to the markets influenced by the availability of raw materials?
— to what extent is entry to the markets influenced by the length of contracts between an undertaking and its suppliers and/or customers?
— describe the importance of research and development and in particular the importance of licensing patents, know-how and other rights in these markets.

10.2   Describe the various factors influencing entry in geographic terms into the relevant geographic market(s) that exist in the present case (i.e., what barriers exist to prevent undertakings already producing and/or marketing products within the relevant product market(s) but in areas outside the relevant geographic market(s) extending the scope of their sales into the relevant geographic market(s)?).

Please give reasons for your answer, explaining, where relevant, the importance of the following factors:

— trade barriers imposed by law, such as tariffs, quotas etc.,
— local specification or technical requirements,
— procurement policies,
— the existence of adequate and available local distribution and retailing facilities,
— transport costs,
— entrenched consumer preferences for local brands or products,
— language.

10.3   Have any new undertakings entered the relevant product market(s) in geographic areas where the parties sell during the last three years? Please provide this information with respect to both new entrants in product terms and new entrants in geographic terms. If such entry has occurred, please identify the undertaking(s) concerned (name, address, telephone and fax numbers, and, where possible, contact person), and provide your best estimate of their market share in the relevant product and geographic market(s).

CHAPTER III   SECTION CONCERNING THE RELEVANT MARKET ONLY FOR STRUCTURAL JOINT VENTURES FOR WHICH ACCELERATED TREATMENT IS CLAIMED

[Not reproduced here.]

CHAPTER IV   FINAL SECTIONS (TO BE COMPLETED FOR ALL NOTIFICATIONS)

Section 16   Reasons for the application for negative clearance

If you are applying for negative clearance state:

16.1   why, i.e. state which provision or effects of the agreement or behaviour might, in your view, raise questions of compatibility with the Community's and/or the EEA rules of competition. The object of this subheading is to give the Commission the clearest possible idea of the doubts you have about your agreement or behaviour that you wish to have resolved by a negative clearance.

Then, under the following three references, give a statement of the relevant facts and reasons as to why you consider Article 85(1) or 86 of the EC Treaty and/or Article 53(1) or 54 of the EEA Agreement to be inapplicable, i.e.:

16.2   why the agreements or behaviour do not have the object or effect of preventing, restricting or distorting competition within the common market or within the territory of the EFTA States to any appreciable extent, or why your undertaking does not have or its behaviour does not abuse a dominant position; and/or

16.3   why the agreements or behaviour do not have the object or effect of preventing, restricting or distorting competition within the EEA territory to any appreciable extent, or why your undertaking does not have or its behaviour does not abuse a dominant position; and/or

16.4   why the agreements or behaviour are not such as may affect trade between Member States or between the Community and one or more EFTA States, or between EFTA States to any appreciable extent.

Section 17 Reasons for the application for exemption

If you are notifying the agreement, even if only as a precaution, in order to obtain an exemption under Article 85(3) of the EC Treaty and/or Article 53(3) of the EEA Agreement, explain how:

17.1 the agreement contributes to improving production or distribution, and/or promoting technical or economic progress. In particular, please explain the reasons why these benefits are expected to result from the collaboration; for example, do the parties to the agreement possess complementary technologies or distribution systems that will produce important synergies? (if so, please state which). Also please state whether any documents or studies were drawn up by the notifying parties when assessing the feasibility of the operation and the benefits likely to result therefrom, and whether any such documents or studies provided estimates of the savings or efficiencies likely to result. Please provide copies of any such documents or studies;

17.2 a proper share of the benefits arising from such improvement or progress accrues to consumers;

17.3 all restrictive provisions of the agreement are indispensable to the attainment of the aims set out under 17.1 (if you are claiming the benefit of the opposition procedure, it is particularly important that you should identify and justify restrictions that exceed those automatically exempted by the relevant Regulations). In this respect please explain how the benefits resulting from the agreement identified in your reply to question 17.1 could not be achieved, or could not be achieved so quickly or efficiently or only at higher cost or with less certainty of success (i) without the conclusion of the agreement as a whole and (ii) without those particular clauses and provisions of the agreement identified in your reply to question 4.2;

17.4 the agreement does not eliminate competition in respect of a substantial part of the goods or services concerned.

Section 18 Supporting documentation

The completed notification must be drawn up and submitted in one original. It shall contain the last versions of all agreements which are the subject of the notification and be accompanied by the following:

(a) sixteen copies of the notification itself;
(b) three copies of the annual reports and accounts of all the parties to the notified agreement, decision or practice for the last three years;
(c) three copies of the most recent in-house or external long-term market studies or planning documents (for the purpose of assessing or analysing the affected markets) with respect to competitive conditions, competitors (actual and potential), and market conditions. Each document should indicate the name and position of the author;
(d) three copies of reports and analyses which have been prepared by or for any officer(s) or director(s) for the purposes of evaluating or analysing the notified agreement.

Section 19 Declaration

The notification must conclude with the following declaration which is to be signed by or on behalf of all the applicants or notifying parties.[1]

The undersigned declare that the information given in this notification is correct to the best of their knowledge and belief, that complete copies of all documents requested by form A/B have been supplied to the extent that they are in the possession of the group of undertakings to which the applicant(s) or notifying party(ies) belong(s) and are accessible to the latter, that all estimates are identified as such and are their best estimates of the underlying facts and that all the opinions expressed are sincere.

They are aware of the provisions of Article 15(1)(a) of Regulation No. 17.

Place and date:

Signatures:

Please add the name(s) of the person(s) signing the application or notification and their function(s).

Note
1. Applications and notifications which have not been signed are invalid.

3.6 Extracts from Regulation 1983/83 — the Block Exemption for Exclusive Distribution Agreements

COMMISSION REGULATION (EEC) No. 1983/83 OF 22 JUNE 1983

on the application of Article 85(3) of the Treaty to categories of exclusive distribution agreements

THE COMMISSION OF THE EUROPEAN COMMUNITIES,

Having regard to the Treaty establishing the European Economic Community,

Having regard to Council Regulation No. 19/65/EEC of 2 March 1965 on the application of Article 85(3) of the Treaty to certain categories of agreements and concerted practices as last amended by the Act of Accession of Greece, and in particular Article 1 thereof,

Having published a draft of this Regulation,

Having consulted the Advisory Committee on Restrictive Practices and Dominant Positions,

(1) Whereas Regulation No. 19/65/EEC empowers the Commission to apply Article 85(3) of the Treaty by regulation to certain categories of bilateral exclusive distribution agreements and analogous concerted practices falling within Article 85(1);

(2) Whereas experience to date makes it possible to define a category of agreements and concerted practices which can be regarded as normally satisfying the conditions laid down in Article 85(3);

(3) Whereas exclusive distribution agreements of the category defined in Article 1 of this Regulation may fall within the prohibition contained in Article 85(1) of the Treaty; whereas this will apply only in exceptional cases to exclusive agreements of this kind to which only undertakings from one Member State are party and which concern the resale of goods within that Member State; whereas, however, to the extent that such agreements may affect trade between Member States and also satisfy all the requirements set out in this Regulation there is no reason to withhold from them the benefit of the exemption by category;

(4) Whereas it is not necessary expressly to exclude from the defined category those agreements which do not fulfil the conditions of Article 85(1) of the Treaty;

(5) Whereas exclusive distribution agreements lead in general to an improvement in distribution because the undertaking is able to concentrate its sales activities, does not need to maintain numerous business relations with a larger number of dealers and is able, by dealing with only one dealer, to overcome more easily distribution difficulties in international trade resulting from linguistic, legal and other differences;

(6)   Whereas exclusive distribution agreements facilitate the promotion of sales of a product and lead to intensive marketing and to continuity of supplies while at the same time rationalizing distribution; whereas they stimulate competition between the products of different manufacturers; whereas the appointment of an exclusive distributor who will take over sales promotion, customer services and carrying of stocks is often the most effective way, and sometimes indeed the only way, for the manufacturer to enter a market and compete with other manufacturers already present; whereas this is particularly so in the case of small and medium-sized undertakings; whereas it must be left to the contracting parties to decide whether and to what extent they consider it desirable to incorporate in the agreements terms providing for the promotion of sales;

(7)   Whereas, as a rule, such exclusive distribution agreements also allow consumers a fair share of the resulting benefit as they gain directly from the improvement in distribution, and their economic and supply position is improved as they can obtain products manufactured in particular in other countries more quickly and more easily;

(8)   Whereas this Regulation must define the obligations restricting competition which may be included in exclusive distribution agreements; whereas the other restrictions on competition allowed under this Regulation in addition to the exclusive supply obligation produce a clear division of functions between the parties and compel the exclusive distributor to concentrate his sales efforts on the contract goods and the contract territory; whereas they are, where they are agreed only for the duration of the agreement, generally necessary in order to attain the improvement in the distribution of goods sought through exclusive distribution; whereas it may be left to the contracting parties to decide which of these obligations they include in their agreements; whereas further restrictive obligations and in particular those which limit the exclusive distributor's choice of customers or his freedom to determine his prices and conditions of sale cannot be exempted under this Regulation;

(9)   Whereas the exemption by category should be reserved for agreements for which it can be assumed with sufficient certainty that they satisfy the conditions of Article 85(3) of the Treaty;

(10)   Whereas it is not possible, in the absence of a case-by-case examination, to consider that adequate improvements in distribution occur where a manufacturer entrusts the distribution of his goods to another manufacturer with whom he is in competition; whereas such agreements should, therefore, be excluded from the exemption by category; whereas certain derogations from this rule in favour of small and medium-sized undertakings can be allowed;

(11)   Whereas consumers will be assured of a fair share of the benefits resulting from exclusive distribution only if parallel imports remain possible; whereas agreements relating to goods which the user can obtain only from the exclusive distributor should therefore be excluded from the exemption by category; whereas the parties cannot be allowed to abuse industrial property rights or other rights in order to create absolute territorial protection; whereas this does not prejudice the relationship between competition law and industrial property rights, since the sole object here is to determine the conditions for exemption by category;

(12)   Whereas, since competition at the distribution stage is ensured by the possibility of parallel imports, the exclusive distribution agreements covered by this Regulation will not normally afford any possibility of eliminating competition in respect of a substantial part of the products in question; whereas this is also true of agreements that allot to the exclusive distributor a contract territory covering the whole of the common market;

(13)   Whereas, in particular cases in which agreements or concerted practices satisfying the requirements of this Regulation nevertheless have effects incompatible with Article 85(3) of the Treaty, the Commission may withdraw the benefit of the exemption by category from the undertakings party to them;

(14)   Whereas agreements and concerted practices which satisfy the conditions set out in this Regulation need not be notified; whereas an undertaking may none the less in a particular case where

real doubt exists, request the Commission to declare whether its agreements comply with this Regulation;

(15)   Whereas this Regulation does not affect the applicability of Commission Regulation (EEC) No. 3604/82 of 23 December 1982 on the application of Article 85(3) of the Treaty to categories of specialization agreements; whereas it does not exclude the application of Article 86 of the Treaty,

HAS ADOPTED THIS REGULATION:

Article 1

Pursuant to Article 85(3) of the Treaty and subject to the provisions of this Regulation, it is hereby declared that Article 85(1) of the Treaty shall not apply to agreements to which only two undertakings are party and whereby one party agrees with the other to supply certain goods for resale within the whole or a defined area of the common market only to that other.

Article 2

1.   Apart from the obligation referred to in Article 1 no restriction on competition shall be imposed on the supplier other than the obligation not to supply the contract goods to users in the contract territory.

2.   No restriction on competition shall be imposed on the exclusive distributor other than:

(a)   the obligation not to manufacture or distribute goods which compete with the contract goods;

(b)   the obligation to obtain the contract goods for resale only from the other party;

(c)   the obligation to refrain, outside the contract territory and in relation to the contract goods,

from seeking customers, from establishing any branch and from maintaining any distribution depot.

3.   Article 1 shall apply notwithstanding that the exclusive distributor undertakes all or any of the following obligations:

(a)   to purchase complete ranges of goods or minimum quantities;

(b)   to sell the contract goods under trademarks, or packed and presented as specified by the other party;

(c)   to take measures for promotion of sales in particular:

— to advertise,

— to maintain a sales network or stock of goods,

— to provide customer and guarantee services,

— to employ staff having specialized or technical training.

Article 3

Article 1 shall not apply where:

(a)   manufacturers of identical goods or of goods which are considered by users as equivalent in view of their characteristics, price and intended use enter into reciprocal exclusive distribution agreements between themselves in respect of such goods;

(b)   manufacturers of identical goods or of goods which are considered by users as equivalent in view of their characteristics, price and intended use enter into a non-reciprocal exclusive distribution agreement between themselves in respect of such goods; unless at least one of them has a total annual turnover of no more than 100 million ECU;

(c)   users can obtain the contract goods in the contract territory only from the exclusive distributor and have no alternative source of supply outside the contract territory;

(d)   one or both of the parties makes it difficult for intermediaries or users to obtain the contract goods from other dealers inside the common market or, in so far as no alternative source of supply is available there, from outside the common market, in particular where one or both of them:

(1)   exercises industrial property rights so as to prevent dealers or users from obtaining outside, or from selling in, the contract territory properly marked or otherwise properly marketed contract goods;

(2)   exercises other rights or takes other measures so as to prevent dealers or users from obtaining outside, or from selling in, the contract territory contract goods.

Article 6

The Commission may withdraw the benefit of this Regulation, pursuant to Article 7 of Regulation No. 19/65/EEC, when it finds in a particular case that an agreement which is exempted by this Regulation nevertheless has certain effects which are incompatible with the conditions set out in Article 85(3) of the Treaty, and in particular where:

(a)   the contract goods are not subject, in the contract territory, to effective competition from identical goods or goods considered by users as equivalent in view of their characteristics, price and intended use;

(b)   access by other suppliers to the different stages of distribution within the contract territory is made difficult to a significant extent;

(c)   for reasons other than those referred to in Article 3(c) and (d) it is not possible for intermediaries or users to obtain supplies of the contract goods from dealers outside the contract territory on the terms there customary;

(d)   the exclusive distributor:

(1)   without any objectively justified reason refuses to supply in the contract territory categories of purchasers who cannot obtain contract goods elsewhere on suitable terms or applies to them differing prices or conditions of sale;

(2)   sells the contract goods at excessively high prices.

3.7   Extracts from Regulation 1984/83 — the Block Exemption for Exclusive Purchasing Agreements

COMMISSION REGULATION (EEC) No. 1984/83 OF 22 JUNE 1983

on the application of Article 85(3) of the Treaty to categories of exclusive purchasing agreements

[Recitals omitted]

THE COMMISSION OF THE EUROPEAN COMMUNITIES,

HAS ADOPTED THIS REGULATION:

TITLE 1

General provisions

Article 1

Pursuant to Article 85(3) of the Treaty, and subject to the conditions set out in Articles 2 to 5 of this Regulation, it is hereby declared that Article 85(1) of the Treaty shall not apply to agreements to which only two undertakings are party and whereby one party, the reseller, agrees with the other, the supplier, to purchase certain goods specified in the agreement for resale only from the supplier or from a connected undertaking or from another undertaking which the supplier has entrusted with the sale of his goods.

Article 2

1.   No other restriction of competition shall be imposed on the supplier than the obligation not to distribute the contract goods or goods which compete with the contract goods in the reseller's principal sales area and at the reseller's level of distribution.

2.   Apart from the obligation described in Article 1, no other restriction of competition shall be imposed on the reseller than the obligation not to manufacture or distribute goods which compete with the contract goods.

3.   Article 1 shall apply notwithstanding that the reseller undertakes any or all of the following obligations;

   (a)   to purchase complete ranges of goods;

   (b)   to purchase minimum quantities of goods which are subject to the exclusive purchasing obligation;

   (c)   to sell the contract goods under trademarks, or packed and presented as specified by the supplier;

   (d)   to take measures for the promotion of sales, in particular:

— to advertise,

— to maintain a sales network or stock of goods,

— to provide customer and guarantee services,

— to employ staff having specialized or technical training.

Article 3

Article 1 shall not apply where:

   (a)   manufacturers of identical goods or of goods which are considered by users as equivalent in view of their characteristics, price and intended use enter into reciprocal exclusive purchasing agreements between themselves in respect of such goods;

   (b)   manufacturers of identical goods or of goods which are considered by users as equivalent in view of their characteristics, price and intended use enter into a non-reciprocal exclusive purchasing agreement between themselves in respect of such goods, unless at least one of them has a total annual turnover of no more than 100 million ECU;

50

(c)   the exclusive purchasing obligation is agreed for more than one type of goods where these are neither by their nature nor according to commercial usage connected to each other;

(d)   the agreement is concluded for an indefinite duration or for a period of more than five years.

Miscellaneous provisions

Article 14

The Commission may withdraw the benefit of this Regulation, pursuant to Article 7 of Regulation No. 19/65/EEC, when it finds in a particular case that an agreement which is exempted by this Regulation nevertheless has certain effects which are incompatible with the conditions set out in Article 85(3) of the Treaty, and in particular where:

(a)   the contract goods are not subject, in a substantial part of the common market, to effective competition from identical goods or goods considered by users as equivalent in view of their characteristics, price and intended use;

(b)   access by other suppliers to the different stages of distribution in a substantial part of the common market is made difficult to a significant extent;

(c)   the supplier without any objectively justified reason:

(1)   refuses to supply categories of resellers who cannot obtain the contract goods elsewhere on suitable terms or applies to them differing prices or conditions of sale;

(2)   applies less favourable prices or conditions of sale to resellers bound by an exclusive purchasing obligation as compared with other resellers at the same level of distribution.

3.8   Extracts from Regulation 2349/84 — the Block Exemption for Patent Licensing Agreements

COMMISSION REGULATION (EEC) NO. 2349/84 OF 23 JULY 1984

on the application of Article 85(3) of the Treaty to certain categories of patent licensing agreements

Whereas:

(1)   Regulation No 19/65/EEC empowers the Commission to apply Article 85(3) of the Treaty by Regulation to certain categories of agreements and concerted practices falling within the scope of Article 85(1) to which only two undertakings are party and which include restrictions imposed in relation to the acquisition or use of industrial property rights, in particular patents, utility models, designs or trade marks, or to the rights arising out of contracts for assignment of, or the right to use, a method of manufacture or knowledge relating to the use or application of industrial processes.

(2)   Patent licensing agreements are agreements whereby one undertaking, the holder of a patent (the licensor), permits another undertaking (the licensee) to exploit the patented invention by one or more of the means of exploitation afforded by patent law, in particular manufacture, use or putting on the market.

(3)   In the light of experience acquired so far, it is possible to define a category of patent licensing agreements which are capable of falling within the scope of Article 85(1), but which can normally be regarded as satisfying the conditions laid down in Article 85(3). To the extent that patent licensing

agreements to which undertakings in only one Member State are party and which concern only one or more patents for that Member State are capable of affecting trade between Member States, it is appropriate to include them in the exempted category.

(4)   The present Regulation applies to licences issued in respect of national patents of the Member States, Community patents, or European patents granted for Member States, licences in respect of utility models or 'certified d'utilité' issued in the Member States, and licences in respect of inventions for which a patent application is made within one year. Where such patent licensing agreements contain obligations relating not only to territories within the common market but also obligations relating to non-member countries, the presence of the latter does not prevent the present Regulation from applying to the obligations relating to territories within the common market.

(5)   However, where licensing agreements for non-member countries or for territories which extend beyond the frontiers of the Community have effects within the common market which may fall within the scope of Article 85(1), such agreements should be covered by the Regulation to the same extent as would agreements for territories within the common market.

(6)   The Regulation should also apply to agreements concerning the assignment and acquisition of the rights referred to in point 4 above where the risk associated with exploitation remains with the assignor, patent licensing agreements in which the licensor is not the patentee but is authorised by the patentee to grant the licence (as in the case of sub-licences) and patent licensing agreements in which the parties' rights or obligations are assumed by connected undertakings.

(7)   The Regulation does not apply to agreements concerning sales alone, which are governed by the provisions of Commission Regulation (EEC) No 1983/83 of 22 June 1983 concerning the application of Article 85(3) of the Treaty to categories of exclusive distribution agreements.

(8)   Since the experience so far acquired is inadequate, it is not appropriate to include within the scope of the Regulation patent pools, licensing agreements entered into in connection with joint ventures, reciprocal licensing, or licensing agreements in respect of plant breeder's rights. Reciprocal agreements which do not involve any territorial restrictions within the common market should, however, be so included.

(9)   On the other hand, it is appropriate to extend the scope of the Regulation to patent licensing agreements which also contain provisions assigning, or granting the rights to use, non-patented technical knowledge, since such mixed agreements are commonly concluded in order to allow the transfer of a complex technology containing both patented and non-patented elements. Such agreements can only be regarded as fulfilling the conditions of Article 85(3) for the purposes of this Regulation where the communicated technical knowledge is secret and permits a better exploitation of the licensed patents (know-how). Provisions concerning know-how are covered by the Regulation only in so far as the licensed patents are necessary for achieving the objects of the licensed technology and as long as at least one of the licensed patents remains in force.

(10)   It is also appropriate to extend the scope of the Regulation to patent licensing agreements containing ancillary provisions relating to trade marks, subject to ensuring that the trade mark licence is not used to extend the effects of the patent licence beyond the life of the patents. For this purpose it is necessary to allow the licensee to identify himself within the 'licensed territory', i.e., the territory covering all or part of the common market where the licensor holds patents which the licensee is authorised to exploit, as the manufacturer of the 'licensed product', i.e., the product which is the subject matter of the licensed patent or which has been obtained directly from the process which is the subject matter of the licensed patent, to avoid his having to enter into a new trade mark agreement with the licensor when the licensed patents expire in order not to lose the goodwill attaching to the licensed product.

(11)   Exclusive licensing agreements, i.e., agreements in which the licensor undertakes not to exploit the 'licensed invention', i.e., the licensed patented invention and any know-how communicated to the

licensee, in the licensed territory himself and not to grant further licences there, are not in themselves incompatible with Article 85(1) where they are concerned with the introduction and protection of a new technology in the licensed territory, by reason of the scale of the research which has been undertaken and of the risk that is involved in manufacturing and marketing a product which is unfamiliar to users in the licensed territory at the time the agreement is made. This may also be the case where the agreements are concerned with the introduction and protection of a new process for manufacturing a product which is already known. In so far as in other cases agreements of this kind may fall within the scope of Article 85(1), it is useful for the purposes of legal certainty to include them in Article 1, in order that they may also benefit from the exemption. However, the exemption of exclusive licensing agreements and certain export bans imposed on the licensor and his licensees is without prejudice to subsequent developments in the case law of the Court of Justice regarding the status of such agreements under Article 85(1).

(12)   The obligations listed in Article 1 generally contribute to improving the production of goods and to promoting technical progress; they make patentees more willing to grant licences and licensees more inclined to undertake the investment required to manufacture, use and put on the market a new product or to use a new process, so that undertakings other than the patentee acquire the possibility of manufacturing their products with the aid of the latest techniques and of developing those techniques further. The result is that the number of production facilities and the quantity and quality of goods produced in the common market are increased. This is true, in particular, of obligations on the licensor and on the licensee not to exploit the licensed invention in, and in particular not to export the licensed product into, the licensed territory in the case of the licensor and the 'territories reserved for the licensor', that is to say, territories within the common market in which the licensor has patent protection and has not granted any licences, in the case of the licensee. This is also true both of the obligation of the licensee not to conduct an active policy of putting the product on the market (i.e., a prohibition of active competition as defined in Article 1(1)(5)) in the territories of other licensees for a period which may equal the duration of the licence and also the obligation of the licensee not to put the licensed product on the market in the territories of other licensees for a limited period of a few years (i.e., a prohibition not only of active competition but also of 'passive competition' whereby the licensee of a territory simply responds to requests which he has not solicited from users or resellers established in the territories of other licensees — Article 1(1)(6)). However, such obligations may be permitted under the Regulation only in respect of territories in which the licensed product is protected by 'parallel patents', that is to say, patents covering the same invention, within the meaning of the case law of the Court of Justice, and as long as the patents remain in force.

(13)   Consumers will as a rule be allowed a fair share of the benefit resulting from this improvement in the supply of goods on the market. To safeguard this effect, however, it is right to exclude from the application of Article 1 cases where the parties agree to refuse to meet demand from users or resellers within their respective territories who would resell for export, or to take other steps to impede parallel imports, or where the licensee is obliged to refuse to meet unsolicited demand from the territory of other licensees (passive sales). The same applies where such action is the result of a concerted practice between the licensor and the licensee.

(14)   The obligations referred to above thus do not impose restrictions which are not indispensable to the attainment of the abovementioned objectives.

(15)   Competition at the distribution stage is safeguarded by the possibility of parallel imports and passive sales. The exclusivity obligations covered by the Regulation thus do not normally entail the possibility of eliminating competition in respect of a substantial part of the products in question. This is so even in the case of agreements which grant exclusive licences for a territory covering the whole of the common market.

(16)   To the extent that in their agreements the parties undertake obligations of the type referred to in Articles 1 and 2 but which are of more limited scope and thus less restrictive of competition than is permitted by those Articles, it is appropriate that these obligations should also benefit under the exemptions provided for in the Regulation.

(17)   If in a particular case an agreement covered by this Regulation is found to have effects which are incompatible with the provisions of Article 85(3) of the Treaty, the Commission may withdraw the benefit of the block exemption from the undertakings concerned, in accordance with Article 7 of Regulation No 19/65/EEC.

(18)   It is not necessary expressly to exclude from the category defined in the Regulation agreements which do not fulfil the conditions of Article 85(1). Nevertheless it is advisable, in the interests of legal certainty for the undertakings concerned, to list in Article 2 a number of obligations which are not normally restrictive of competition, so that these also may benefit from the exemption in the event that, because of particular economic or legal circumstances, they should exceptionally fall within the scope of Article 85(1). The list of such obligations given in Article 2 is not exhaustive.

(19)   The Regulation must also specify what restrictions or provisions may not be included in patent licensing agreements if these are to benefit from the block exemption. The restrictions listed in Article 3 may fall under the prohibition of Article 85(1); in these cases there can be no general presumption that they will lead to the positive effects required by Article 85(3), as would be necessary for the granting of a block exemption.

(20)   Such restrictions include those which deny the licensee the right enjoyed by any third party to challenge the validity of the patent or which automatically prolong the agreement by the life of any new patent granted during the life of the licensed patents which are in existence at the time the agreement is entered into. Nevertheless, the parties are free to extend their contractual relationship by entering into new agreements concerning such new patents, or to agree the payment of royalties for as long as the licensee continues to use know-how communicated by the licensor which has not entered into the public domain, regardless of the duration of the original patents and of any new patents that are licensed.

(21)   They also include restrictions on the freedom of one party to compete with the other and in particular to involve himself in techniques other than those licensed, since such restrictions impede technical and economic progress. The prohibition of such restrictions should however be reconciled with the legitimate interest of the licensor in having his patented invention exploited to the full and to this end to require the licensee to use his best endeavours to manufacture and market the licensed product.

(22)   Such restrictions include, further, an obligation on the licensee to continue to pay royalties after all the licensed patents ceased to be in force and the communicated know-how has entered into the public domain, since such an obligation would place the licensee at a disadvantage by comparison with his competitors, unless it is established that this obligation results from arrangements for spreading payments in respect of previous use of the licensed invention.

(23)   They also include restrictions imposed on the parties regarding prices, customers or marketing of the licensed products or regarding the quantities to be manufactured or sold, especially since restrictions of the latter type may have the same effect as export bans.

(24)   Finally, they include restrictions to which the licensee submits at the time the agreement is made because he wishes to obtain the licence, but which give the licensor an unjustified competitive advantage, such as an obligation to assign to the licensor any improvements the licensee may make to the invention, or to accept other licences or goods and services that the licensee does not want from the licensor.

(25)   It is appropriate to offer to parties to patent licensing agreements containing obligations which do not come within the terms of Articles 1 and 2 and yet do not entail any of the effects restrictive of competition referred to in Article 3 a simplified means of benefiting, upon notification, from the legal certainty provided by the block exemption (Article 4). This procedure should at the same time allow the Commission to ensure effective supervision as well as simplifying the administrative control of agreements.

(26)   The Regulation should apply with retroactive effect to patent licensing agreements in existence when the Regulation comes into force where such agreements already fulfil the conditions for application of the Regulation or are modified to do so (Articles 6 to 8). Under Article 4(3) of Regulation No 19/65/EEC, the benefit of these provisions may not be claimed in actions pending at the date of entry into force of this Regulation, nor may it be relied on as grounds for claims for damages against third parties.

(27)   Agreements which come within the terms of Articles 1 and 2 and which have neither the object nor the effect of restricting competition in any other way need no longer be notified. Nevertheless, undertakings will still have the right to apply in individual cases for negative clearance under Article 2 of Council Regulation No 17 or for exemption under Article 85(3),

HAS ADOPTED THIS REGULATION:

Article 1

1.   Pursuant to Article 85(3) of the Treaty and subject to the provisions of this Regulation, it is hereby declared that Article 85(1) of the Treaty shall not apply to patent licensing agreements, and agreements combining the licensing of patents and the communication of know-how, to which only two undertakings are party and which include one or more of the following obligations:

(1)   an obligation on the licensor not to license other undertakings to exploit the licensed invention in the licensed territory, covering all or part of the common market, in so far and as long as one of the licensed patents remains in force;

(2)   an obligation on the licensor not to exploit the licensed invention in the licensed territory himself in so far and as long as one of the licensed patents remains in force;

(3)   an obligation on the licensee not to exploit the licensed invention in territories within the common market which are reserved for the licensor, in so far and as long as the patented product is protected in those territories by parallel patents;

(4)   an obligation on the licensee not to manufacture or use the licensed product, or use the patented process or the communicated know-how, in territories within the common market which are licensed to other licensees, in so far and as long as the licensed product is protected in those territories by parallel patents;

(5)   an obligation on the licensee not to pursue an active policy of putting the licensed product on the market in the territories within the common market which are licensed to other licensees, and in particular not to engage in advertising specifically aimed at those territories or to establish any branch or maintain any distribution depot there, in so far and as long as the licensed product is protected in those territories by parallel patents;

(6)   an obligation on the licensee not to put the licensed product on the market in the territories licensed to other licensees within the common market for a period not exceeding five years from the date when the product is first put on the market within the common market by the licensor or one of his licensees, in so far as and for as long as the product is protected in these territories by parallel patents;

(7)   an obligation on the licensee to use only the licensor's trade mark or the get-up determined by the licensor to distinguish the licensed product, provided that the licensee is not prevented from identifying himself as the manufacturer of the licensed product.

2.   The exemption of restrictions on putting the licensed product on the market resulting from the obligations referred to in paragraph 1(2), (3), (5) and (6) shall apply only if the licensee manufactures the licensed product himself or has it manufactured by a connected undertaking or by a subcontractor.

3.   The exemption provided for in paragraph 1 shall also apply where in a particular agreement the parties undertake obligations of the types referred to in that paragraph but with a more limited scope than is permitted by the paragraph.

Article 2

1.   Article 1 shall apply notwithstanding the presence in particular of any of the following obligations, which are generally not restrictive of competition:

(1)   an obligation on the licensee to procure goods or services from the licensor or from an undertaking designated by the licensor, in so far as such products or services are necessary for a technically satisfactory exploitation of the licensed invention;

(2)   an obligation on the licensee to pay a minimum royalty or to produce a minimum quantity of the licensed product or to carry out a minimum number of operations exploiting the licensed invention;

(3)   an obligation on the licensee to restrict his exploitation of the licensed invention to one or more technical fields of application covered by the licensed patent;

(4)   an obligation on the licensee not to exploit the patent after termination of the agreement in so far as the patent is still in force;

(5)   an obligation on the licensee not to grant sub-licences or assign the licence;

(6)   an obligation on the licensee to mark the licensed product with an indication of the patentee's name, the licensed patent or the patent licensing agreement;

(7)   an obligation on the licensee not to divulge know-how communicated by the licensor; the licensee may be held to this obligation even after the agreement has expired;

(8)   obligations:

(a)   to inform the licensor of infringements of the patent,

(b)   to take legal action against an infringer,

(c)   to assist the licensor in any legal action against an infringer,

provided that these obligations are without prejudice to the licensee's right to challenge the validity of the licensed patent;

(9)   an obligation on the licensee to observe specifications concerning the minimum quality of the licensed product, provided that such specifications are necessary for a technically satisfactory exploitation of the licensed invention, and to allow the licensor to carry out related checks;

(10)   an obligation on the parties to communicate to one another any experience gained in exploiting the licensed invention and to grant one another a licence in respect of inventions relating to improvements and new applications, provided that such communication or licence is non-exclusive;

(11)   an obligation on the licensor to grant the licensee any more favourable terms that the licensor may grant to another undertaking after the agreement is entered into.

2.   In the event that, because of particular circumstances, the obligations referred to in paragraph 1 fall within the scope of Article 85(1), they shall also be exempted even if they are not accompanied by any of the obligations exempted by Article 1.

The exemption provided for in this paragraph shall also apply where in an agreement the parties undertake obligations of the types referred to in paragraph 1 but with a more limited scope than is permitted by that paragraph.

Article 3

Articles 1 and 2(2) shall not apply where:

(1)   the licensee is prohibited from challenging the validity of licensed patents or other industrial or commercial property rights within the common market belonging to the licensor or undertakings connected with him, without prejudice to the right of the licensor to terminate the licensing agreement in the event of such a challenge;

(2)   the duration of the licensing agreement is automatically prolonged beyond the expiry of the licensed patents existing at the time the agreement was entered into by the inclusion in it of any new patent obtained by the licensor, unless the agreement provides each party with the right to terminate the agreement at least annually after the expiry of the licensed patents existing at the time the agreement was entered into, without prejudice to the right of the licensor to charge royalties for the full period during which the licensee continues to use know-how communicated by the licensor which has not entered into the public domain, even if that period exceeds the life of the patents;

(3)   one party is restricted from competing with the other party, with undertakings connected with the other party or with other undertakings within the common market in respect of research and development, manufacture, use or sales, save as provided in Article 1 and without prejudice to an obligation on the licensee to use his best endeavours to exploit the licensed invention;

(4)   the licensee is charged royalties on products which are not entirely or partially patented or manufactured by means of a patented process, or for the use of know-how which has entered into the public domain otherwise than by the fault of the licensee or an undertaking connected with him, without prejudice to arrangements whereby, in order to facilitate payment, the royalty payments for the use of a licensed invention are spread over a period extending beyond the life of the licensed patents or the entry of the know-how into the public domain;

(5)   the quantity of licensed products one party may manufacture or sell or the number of operations exploiting the licensed invention he may carry out are subject to limitations;

(6)   one party is restricted in the determination of prices, components of prices or discounts for the licensed products;

(7)   one party is restricted as to the customers he may serve, in particular by being prohibited from supplying certain classes of user, employing certain forms of distribution or, with the aim of sharing customers, using certain types of packaging for the products, save as provided in Article 1(1)(7) and Article 2(1)(3);

(8)   the licensee is obliged to assign wholly or in part to the licensor rights in or to patents for improvements or for new applications of the licensed patents;

(9)   the licensee is induced at the time the agreement is entered into to accept further licences which he does not want or to agree to use patents, goods or services which he does not want, unless such patents, products or services are necessary for a technically satisfactory exploitation of the licensed invention;

(10)   without prejudice to Article 1(1)(5), the licensee is required, for a period exceeding that permitted under Article 1(1)(6), not to put the licensed product on the market in territories licensed to other licensees within the common market or does not do so as a result of a concerted practice between the parties;

(11)   one or both of the parties are required:

(a)   to refuse without any objectively justified reason to meet demand from users or resellers in their respective territories who would market products in other territories within the common market;

(b)   to make it difficult for users or resellers to obtain the products from other resellers within the common market, and in particular to exercise industrial or commercial property rights or take measures so as to prevent users or resellers from obtaining outside, or from putting on the market in, the licensed territory products which have been lawfully put on the market within the common market by the patentee or with his consent;

or do so as result of a concerted practice between them.

Article 4

1.   The exemption provided for in Articles 1 and 2 shall also apply to agreements containing obligations restrictive of competition which are not covered by those Articles and do not fall within the Scope of Article 3, on condition that the agreements in question are notified to the Commission in accordance with the provisions of Commission Regulation No. 27[1], as last amended by Regulation (EEC) No. 1699/75[2], and that the Commission does not oppose such exemption within a period of six months.

2.   The period of six months shall run from the date on which the notification is received by the Commission. Where, however, the notification is made by registered post, the period shall run from the date shown on the postmark of the place of posting.

3.   Paragraph 1 shall apply only if:

(a)   express reference is made to this Article in the notification or in a communication accompanying it; and

(b)   the information furnished with the notification is complete and in accordance with the facts.

4.   The benefit of paragraph 1 may be claimed for agreements notified before the entry into force of this Regulation by submitting a communication to the Commission referring expressly to this Article and to the notification. Paragraphs 2 and 3(b) shall apply *mutatis mutandis*.

5.   The Commission may oppose the exemption. It shall oppose exemption if it receives a request to do so from a Member State within three months of the transmission to the Member State of the notification referred to in paragraph 1 or of the communication referred to in paragraph 4. This request must be justified on the basis of considerations relating to the competition rules of the Treaty.

6.   The Commission may withdraw the opposition to the exemption at any time. However, where the opposition was raised at the request of a Member State and this request is maintained, it may be withdrawn only after consultation of the Advisory Committee on Restrictive Practices and Dominant Positions.

7.   If the opposition is withdrawn because the undertakings concerned have shown that the conditions of Article 85(3) are fulfilled, the exemption shall apply from the date of notification.

8.   If the opposition is withdrawn because the undertakings concerned have amended the agreement so that the conditions of Article 85(3) are fulfilled, the exemption shall apply from the date on which the amendments take effect.

[1] OJ 35, 10.5. 1962, p. 118/62.
[2] OJ L172, 3.7. 1975, p. 11.

9. If the Commission opposes exemption and the opposition is not withdrawn, the effects of the notification shall be governed by the provisions of Regulation No. 17.

Article 5

1. This Regulation shall not apply:

(1) to agreements between members of a patent pool which relate to the pooled patents;

(2) to patent licensing agreements between competitors who hold interests in a joint venture or between one of them and the joint venture, if the licensing agreements relate to the activities of the joint venture;

(3) to agreements under which one party grants to the other party a patent licence and that other party, albeit in separate agreements or through connected undertakings, grants to the first party a licence under patents or trade marks or reciprocal sales rights for unprotected products or communicates to him know-how, where the parties are competitors in relation to the products covered by those agreements;

(4) to licensing agreements in respect of plant breeder's rights.

2. However, this Regulation shall apply to reciprocal licences of the types referred to in paragraph 1(3) where the parties are not subject to any territorial restriction within the common market on the manufacture, use or putting on the market of the products covered by these agreements or on the use of the licensed processes.

Article 6

1. As regards agreements existing on 13 March 1962 and notified before 1 February 1963 and agreements, whether notified or not, to which Article 4(2)(2)(b) of Regulation No 17 applies, the declaration of inapplicability of Article 85(1) of the Treaty contained in this Regulation shall have retroactive effect from the time at which the conditions for application of this Regulation were fulfilled.

2. As regards all other agreements notified before this Regulation entered into force, the declaration of inapplicability of Article 85(1) of the Treaty contained in this Regulation shall have retroactive effect from the time at which the conditions for application of this Regulation were fulfilled, or from the date of notification, whichever is the later.

Article 7

If agreements existing on 13 March 1962 and notified before 1 February 1963 or agreements to which Article 4(2)(2)(b) of Regulation No 17 applies and notified before 1 January 1967 are amended before 1 April 1985 so as to fulfil the conditions for application of this Regulation, and if the amendment is communicated to the Commission before 1 July 1985 the prohibition in Article 85(1) of the Treaty shall not apply in respect of the period prior to the amendment. The communication shall take effect from the time of its receipt by the Commission. Where the communication is sent by registered post, it shall take effect from the date shown on the postmark of the place of posting.

Article 8

1. As regards agreements to which Article 85 of the Treaty applies as a result of the accession of the United Kingdom, Ireland and Denmark, Articles 6 and 7 shall apply except that the relevant dates shall be 1 January 1973 instead of 13 March 1962 and 1 July 1973 instead of 1 February 1963 and 1 January 1967.

2. As regards agreements to which Article 85 of the Treaty applies as a result of the accession of Greece, Articles 6 and 7 shall apply except that the relevant dates shall be 1 January 1981 instead of 13 March 1962 and 1 July 1981 instead of 1 February 1963 and 1 January 1967.

Article 9

The Commission may withdraw the benefit of this Regulation, pursuant to Article 7 of Regulation No 19/65/EEC, where it finds in a particular case that an agreement exempted by this Regulation nevertheless has certain effects which are incompatible with the conditions laid down in Article 85(3) of the Treaty, and in particular where:

(1)   such effects arise from an arbitration award;

(2)   the licensed products or the services provided using a licensed process are not exposed to effective competition in the licensed territory from identical products or services or products or services considered by users as equivalent in view of their characteristics, price and intended use;

(3)   the licensor does not have the right to terminate the exclusivity granted to the licensee at the latest five years from the date the agreement was entered into and at least annually thereafter if, without legitimate reason, the licensee fails to exploit the patent or to do so adequately;

(4)   without prejudice to Article 1(1)(6), the licensee refuses, without objectively valid reason, to meet unsolicited demand from users or resellers in the territory of other licensees;

(5)   one or both of the parties:

(a)   without any objectively justified reason, refuse to meet demand from users or resellers in their respective territories who would market the products in other territories within the common market; or

(b)   make it difficult for users or resellers to obtain the products from other resellers within the common market, and in particular where they exercise industrial or commercial property rights or take measures so as to prevent resellers or users from obtaining outside, or from putting on the market in, the licensed territory products which have been lawfully put on the market within the common market by the patentee or with his consent.

Article 10

1.   This Regulation shall apply to:

(a)   patent applications;

(b)   utility models;

(c)   applications for registration of utility models;

(d)   'certificats d'utilité' and 'certificats d'addition' under French law; and

(e)   applications for 'certificats d'utilité' and 'certificats d'addition' under French law;

equally as it applies to patents.

2.   This Regulation shall also apply to agreements relating to the exploitation of an invention if an application within the meaning of paragraph 1 is made in respect of the invention for the licensed territory within one year from the date when the agreement was entered into.

Article 11

This Regulation shall also apply to:

(1)   patent licensing agreements where the licensor is not the patentee but is authorised by the patentee to grant a licence or a sub-licence;

(2)   assignments of a patent or of a right to a patent where the sum payable in consideration of the assignment is dependent upon the turnover attained by the assignee in respect of the patented products, the quantity of such products manufactured or the number of operations carried out employing the patented invention;

(3)   patent licensing agreements in which rights or obligations of the licensor or the licensee are assumed by undertakings connected with them.

Article 12

1.   'Connected undertakings' for the purposes of this Regulation means:

(a)   undertakings in which a party to the agreement directly or indirectly:

— owns more than half the capital or business assets, or

— has the power to exercise more than half the voting rights, or

— has the power to appoint more than half the members of the supervisory board, board of directors or bodies legally representing the undertaking, or

— has the right to manage the affairs of the undertaking;

(b)   undertakings which directly or indirectly have in or over a party to the agreement the rights or powers listed in (a);

(c)   undertakings in which an undertaking referred to in (b) directly or indirectly has the rights or powers listed in (a).

2.   Undertakings in which the parties to the agreement or undertakings connected with them jointly have directly or indirectly the rights or powers set out in paragraph 1(a) shall be considered to be connected with each of the parties to the agreement.

Article 13

1.   Information acquired pursuant to Article 4 shall be used only for the purposes of this Regulation.

2.   The Commission and the authorities of the Member States, their officials and other servants shall not disclose information acquired by them pursuant to this Regulation of the kind covered by the obligation of professional secrecy.

3.   The provisions of paragraphs 1 and 2 shall not prevent publication of general information or surveys which do not contain information relating to particular undertakings or associations of undertakings.

Article 14

This Regulation shall enter into force on 1 January 1985.

It shall apply until 31 December 1994.

[Subsequently extended to 30 June 1995.]

4 Article 86 — Abuse of a Dominant Position

Generally speaking, the competition rules are not concerned with the acquisition of monopoly power by an individual enterprise but rather with the way in which such power is used — or abused (see **4.9**). Only those businesses which are dominant within the common market or a substantial part of it are at risk of infringing Article 86, EC Treaty — the Community is not concerned with big fishes in insignificant pools. Article 86 may be broken up into several elements:

(a) relevant product market (plus)
(b) relevant geographical market (leads to)
(c) dominant position
(d) in a substantial part of the Common Market;
(e) abusive behaviour;
(f) effect on trade between Member States.

We shall examine each of these in this chapter.

4.1 Article 86 and Merger Control

Article 86 has been used to control the acquisition of monopoly power — in *Europembellage Corp. and Continental Can Co.* v *Commission* (1972) — but this was really a 'one-off', used to resolve the lack of jurisdiction to deal with mergers under Article 85. Since the *Continental Can Co.* case, Article 86 has not been used in this way. In *BAT and Reynolds* v *Commission* (1984), the ECJ indicated that the mere acquisition of a minority shareholding in a rival company may be an abuse of a dominant position if it 'results in effective control of the [rival] or at least in some influence on its commercial policy'.

The Commission tried to finalise secondary legislation to control mergers for several years — for example, a draft regulation was laid before the Council of Ministers in 1973. The Commission's 1988 version was approved by the Council in 1989 and took effect in September 1990 (Council Regulation 4064/89-OJ 1989 L395/1[1]). The test adopted for rejection of a proposed merger is essentially that set out in the *Continental Can Co.* case, i.e. mergers which establish or strengthen a dominant position, although minor mergers will fall through the net and be caught only (if at all) by national controls.

Over the summer of 1990, various pieces of ancillary legislation were passed — on joint ventures; creation of a standard form to use (like form A/B); and dealing with ancillary restraints. The first implementing regulation was 2367/90 (OJ 1990 L219/5) and there were Commission Notices on joint ventures and ancillary restraints (both in OJ 1990 C203).

---

[1] Although the Regulation was published in the OJ as stated, the published version had many errors. A corrected text was subsequently published in the OJ and must be regarded as the authentic text of the Regulation: see OJ 1990 L257/13. It has since been amended by the EEA Agreement, Annex XIV.

It should be noted that the Commissioner then responsible for competition matters, Sir Leon Brittan, has expressed the opinion that Articles 85 and 86 no longer provide any means of control over mergers. It is clear that the procedures established in Regulation 17/62 do not apply to mergers. (See further 1988 ECLR, at pp. 29 et seq.; 'The Law and Policy of Merger Control in the EEC', Sir Leon Brittan, 1990 ELR, at p. 351.)

4.2 One or More Undertakings

This element of Article 86 does not require a great deal of elaboration. The Article clearly envisages a situation where two or more undertakings abuse a dominant position. This seems to be aimed at corporate groups which act as a single unit, e.g. parent and subsidiary, as in *Commercial Solvents Corp. v Commission* (1973).

An alternative meaning is that one can take a number of separate undertakings, add together their market shares, and see if they have a dominant position between them. The ECJ seems to have accepted this in situations where several companies have agreed to act in concert but, as this behaviour will usually fall within Article 85(1), the additional infringement of Article 86 adds little. The ECJ seems to avoid suggesting that independent companies, against whom there is no evidence of collusion, should be examined to see if they have joint dominance even though no individual has a dominant position. The ECJ concept of dominance relies on a *unilateral* exercise of power: see the decision of the Court in *Zuchner v Bayerische Vereinsbank* (1981) and the opinion of (then) Advocate-General Slynn who said:

> [O]ne of the hallmarks of a dominant position covered by Article 86 is its unilateral nature. As a result... it is right to point out that only [Article 85] applies if the facts establish the existence of a concerted practice.

The concept of 'one or more undertakings' has been the subject of recent attention from the Court of First Instance. In the 'Italian Flat Glass' case (*Società Italiana Vetro SpA et al v Commission* (1992) three companies each made flat glass in Italy. They allegedly operated a cartel. The Commission alleged that this cartel (clearly a breach of Article 85) also contravened Article 86 as, taken together, the three companies held a dominant position on the Italian market for flat glass. The Court rejected the suggestion that the same factors which showed a breach of Article 85 could also be used to demonstrate a breach of Article 86. However, the Court accepted the argument that circumstances could arise where several undertakings together abuse a dominant position, although that was only likely to be the case where they were united by 'economic links' of some form. It remains to be seen whether this represents any real advance beyond the position noted above in *Commercial Solvents*.

4.3 Dominant Position

4.3.1 FOUR QUESTIONS TO ASK

It has been said (Korah, *Introduction to EEC Competition Law & Practice*, p. 58) that, in order to determine whether there is a dominant position, you must ask four questions:

(a) Which firm is accused?
(b) Which products sold by it are involved in the complaint?
(c) Who buys them?
(d) What else could be used by those customers with minimal adaptation to their business? (i.e. what substitutes are there?)

Identification of the products and the location of customers is very important because these factors will be crucial in determining the relevant market share of the suspect undertaking.

The analysis is usually described as defining the relevant product market and the relevant geographical market. The ECJ has consistently said that an undertaking can have a dominant position only if it dominates in a relevant product and geographical market. It may seem to be stating the obvious but you cannot ascertain market share (or power) unless you first ascertain what the appropriate market is.

4.4   Relevant Product Market

The issue here is essentially what product(s) are we interested in? To assist in defining the product market, we could try to answer Korah's four questions (at **4.3.1**):

(a)   Identify your suspect undertaking. It may be a corporate group or a parent and subsidiary.
(b)   Identify which of its products are the subject of the investigation.
(c)   Who buys them? This is important for three reasons. First, because, having identified the customers, you can start to see what alternative products would satisfy them. Then, having decided who are the customers, you can see *where* they are. It is useful to know what territory should be considered. Why do you need to know this?

(i)   To define the geographical market for the product. This will be the next step in defining the market — an undertaking's share of sales will vary according to both what is sold and over what territory. A good example is *Michelin* (see **4.6.2**). A company's market share of saloon car tyres will probably differ from its market share for all types of motor vehicle tyres. Again, market share will vary according to whether we look at (say) just The Netherlands or the whole common market.
(ii)   Jurisdiction. If you have a dominant position in an insubstantial part of the common market, a *de minimis* argument will apply. No matter how abusive your behaviour, if you are a big fish in a little pond the European Commission is not likely to be interested. See, e.g., *Cutsforth, Hugin* and, by analogy, the Commission's Notices on Agreements of Minor Importance.

(d)   What acceptable substitutes there are (on both the supply side and demand side)? We need to know because we are concerned with the undertaking's ability to act independently of others.

4.5   Substitution

The way(s) in which the Commission and ECJ define 'market' has (have) been criticised by economists. They complain that the notion of a single, compartmentalised market is usually unattainable because there will often be substitutes. Further, as Barry Hawk, has observed, 'market definition more often than not reflects a legal conclusion, not an economic fact'.

As a general rule, the broader the definition of the relevant product market (and the same applies for the geographical market), the less likely you are to find a dominant position. Why? Because of *substitutes,* basically,

For the product market, let us return to the example of *Michelin*. If we define the relevant product as 'tyres', the company faces competition from all other sources of tyre; every other tyre is a potential substitute and so the company's market share is likely to be low. We may wish to define the product more narrowly — not simply 'tyres', but 'new tyres'. At least we now remove second-hand tyres from our analysis. We could go further and define the product ever more narrowly — new tyres; new tyres for vehicles other than saloon cars; new tyres for commercial goods vehicles; new tyres for heavy goods vehicles; new replacement tyres for HGVS. As we continue down this road, the number of potential substitutes drops and thus our company's market share rises. If we then look at the geographical market we could find that over different areas tastes may change; transport costs may inhibit long-range shipment of goods so that market share drops — so, the larger the territory, the smaller the market share is likely to be. It may be concluded that if the product is defined very narrowly and the chosen geographical market is small, substitution becomes less likely and market share will rise.

Reference was made above to substitutes being either supply-side (who else could step into your shoes?) or demand-side (what else could customers use to replace your product?) An example of a case where the Commission looked at *supply-side* substitutes is *Continental Can*. The product was found to be light metal containers for meat and fish, and lids for jars. The Commission cast around for other manufacturers who could step into the shoes of Continental Can but seemed unable to conclude that companies who make light metal containers for fruit and vegetables (for example) might be able to supply Continental Can's customers. However, the Commission was criticised for its confused thinking by the ECJ (see paras 33–36 of ECJ judgment). This may explain why the Commission does not undertake this supply-side analysis very often.

A case where the Commission looked at *demand-side* substitutes is *United Brands*. The Commission found the product market was limited to fresh bananas (as opposed to fresh fruit generally, or non-citrus fruits). The Commission's decision was upheld by the ECJ, rather surprisingly given the apparent fluctuations in the price of bananas during the year coinciding with the availability of other fruits (see, e.g., paras 15 and 16 of the judgment). Apparently, the banana has particular qualities of softness and seedlessness and is good for the young, the old and the sick (described by Barry Hawk as a Clint Eastwood classification). The ECJ described the banana as a 'privileged fruit' (see paras 23-5 of the judgment).

A recent consideration of product definition and substitutability came outside the European Community, in the Full Federal Court of Australia (see *Singapore Airlines Ltd* v *Taprobane Tours WA Pty Ltd*) (1992). T was a wholesale travel agent. One of its products was package tours to the Maldives from Australia, with the flights provided by Singapore Airlines (SA). After three years, SA reduced the number of flights between Australia and the Maldives, limited them to departures from one state in Australia and raised the prices it charged to T but not to other wholesalers. T sued, alleging an abuse of market power (analogous to Article 86 EC). The full Federal Court held that the relevant product market was 'airline services to destinations outside mainland Australia' and package tours to such places, *not* return air flights to the Maldives. SA was dominant in such flights but there were many other holiday destinations and many other package tours to them, i.e. plenty of substitutes, so the court held that SA had insufficient market power for the case to succeed.

Time is also important when considering the possibility of substitution. When the Commission looks at supply-side substitutes, it usually does so in the short-term (who could step in and meet demand now?), while a longer-term view might result in more substitutes being able to come forward (e.g. other companies could re-tool their plant, retrain staff, end existing contracts). A good illustration of the Commission's use of this short time-span is found in the 'Vitamins' case, see **4.7.4**.

4.6   Relevant Geographical Market

As mentioned earlier, we need to consider this for three reasons:

(a)   it helps to define the market (and, indirectly, dominance);

(b)   it determines whether a substantial part of the common market is involved;

(c)   it helps to see if there is any effect on trade between Member States.

4.6.1   HOW MIGHT WE DEFINE THE GEOGRAPHICAL MARKET?

The geographical market may be delimited by, for example, consumer tastes and transport costs — those matters which establish a separate market. In fact, we also need to see where goods sold in the market come from. If 'local' prices are high, this may encourage some suppliers, who are geographically remote, to transport their product from there to here. This may suggest that the geographical market is to include here and there too.

Barry Hawk has stated that in most decisions of the Commission, there is little or no analysis of the relevant geographical market. He says that this may be because it was obvious in the particular case

— he gives the example of *Commercial Solvents* (the company was found to possess a worldwide monopoly and thus a dominant position in the common market).

Often an abstract formulation is offered by either Court or Commission but this is of little practical assistance in forecasting the way a decision will go (or advising one's clients).

The ECJ has insisted that different territories must present homogenous conditions for trade to form a comparable basis for analysis of market power. The ECJ and Commission seem very keen to use single Member States as the geographical market — where they go beyond this, similarity of trading conditions is important.

4.6.2 THREE EXAMPLES OF DEFINING THE GEOGRAPHICAL MARKET

(a) A simple example is *Alsatel* (1988). A was found by the Regional Court, Strasbourg, to have a major share of the regional market in the relevant product (telephone installations) but the ECJ held, on a preliminary reference, that 'the relevant context within which the conditions of competition are sufficiently uniform to enable the economic strength of the undertaking in question to be assessed is the market in telephone installations for *the whole of France*'. Since A was dominant only in the Alsace-Lorraine area and had no dominant position in the relevant product market for the whole of France, the ECJ found that Article 86 did not apply.

(b) *United Brands* (see paras 36-53 of the judgment). The Commission was right to consider Germany, Denmark, Ireland, The Netherlands and Belgium/Luxembourg as the geographical market because all six had free competition in bananas (whilst not necessarily being the same in trading conditions, e.g. transport costs), while in the other three Member States (i.e. France, Italy, the United Kingdom) there was State interference in the market (see, e.g., paras 36, 38, 44, 46, 51-3 of the judgment).

(c) *Michelin*. The Commission took The Netherlands as the relevant geographical market for heavy truck tyres. Michelin NV (which was the undertaking under investigation) complained to the ECJ that this was too narrow (see para 23 of the judgment). Michelin NV relied on the fact that the Commission had considered factors pertaining to the whole Michelin group when looking at market power, e.g. its technological lead over rivals and group financial strength. Michelin said that this suggested 'a much wider market' or even the world market. Its main competitors are worldwide. The Commission's response was that tyre makers have chosen to sell tyres through national subsidiaries in the national markets; thus, Michelin NV faces competition on The Netherlands market. The ECJ upheld the Commission's decision — tyre dealers who are established in The Netherlands in practice obtain their supplies only from suppliers operating in The Netherlands. So, Michelin NV's competition is 'mainly' on The Netherlands market and it is at that level that the objective conditions of competition are the same for traders.

4.6.3 CONCLUSION

It may be concluded that both the Commission and the ECJ are often prepared to limit the relevant geographical market to the territory of a single Member State. They may be unlikely to consider a larger territory even where there is (apparently) clear evidence of competition from outside the Member State or cross-elasticity of supply.

Remember, we must also determine the geographical market in order to establish whether the area under consideration is at least a '*substantial part of the common market*' (the fourth element of Article 86). This is related to the jurisdictional point referred to earlier (i.e. whether there is any effect on inter-State trade). See **4.15.**

4.7 Market Power — the Ability to Act Independently

Once you have defined the market, you can then try to assess the undertaking's market power, Barry Hawk says that 'Neither the definition nor the determination of dominant position under Article 86 bears much resemblance to the economic analysis of market power'.

We must remember that we are looking at the ways in which people who are basically lawyers have interpreted and applied Article 86. Bearing that in mind, what are the symbols of such power in a market that we can say the undertaking has a dominant position? According to decided cases, they are:

    (a) the power to prevent effective competition; and/or

    (b) the power to behave independently of competitors, suppliers and customers, to an appreciable extent.

We can see this test in the following extract from the Court's judgment in *Hoffmann-La Roche* v *Commission* (1976) (the 'Vitamins' case):

[D]ominant position relates to a position of economic strength enjoyed by an undertaking which enables it to prevent effective competition being maintained on the relevant market by affording it the power to behave to an appreciable extent independently of its competitors, its customers and ultimately of the consumers.

In *Michelin* v *Commission* (1981) the Court stated:

[I]t is not a precondition for finding that a dominant position exists in the case of a given product that there should be a complete absence of competition from other partially interchangeable products so long as such competition does not affect the undertaking's ability to influence appreciably the conditions in which that competition may be exerted or at any rate to conduct itself to a large extent without having to take account of that competition and without suffering any adverse effects as a result of its attitude.

It should be noted that although most of the reported cases on 'dominant position' refer to an independence of action over one's competitors, this 'horizontal' form of dominance is not the only way to achieve a dominant position. One may be 'vertically' dominant — that is, a company may dominate its supplier (or its customers). An example of customer-dominance may be seen in the *Volvo* v *Veng* case (see **4.8, 6.2.1**), while supplier-dominance could be illustrated by the purchasing power of the National Health Service in the United Kingdom (or British Telecom or the Ministry of Defence) regarding appropriate products.

4.7.1   ABSOLUTE DOMINATION IS UNNECESSARY

Although the ECJ said in *Hoffmann-La Roche* v *Commission* (1976) that the possession of a very large share of the market was a highly important element in establishing a dominant position, it is clear that absolute domination of the market is not needed. This is best illustrated by *United Brands* v *Commission* (1976), where the 'dominant' enterprise was engaged in losing a price war with its main competitor (Chiquita against Dole bananas). What you do have to do is analyse the market share of the suspect undertaking.

4.7.2   DIAGNOSING MARKET POWER

We have seen the criteria set out by the Court for a dominant position, but how are we to determine whether those criteria have been satisfied in any particular case? It seems that the existence of a dominant position may derive from several factors which, taken separately, are not necessarily determinative; but among these factors a highly important one is the existence of very large market shares. See *Hoffmann-La Roche* v *Commission* (1976).

An economist might assert that market power can be directly measured by examining (for example):

    (a) whether the company's customers can buy the product from someone else;

    (b) whether the company is charging an excessively high price compared to its marginal cost;

    (c) whether the company is making monopoly profits;

    (d) whether the company is engaging in price discrimination.

4.7.3   MARKET SHARE

In practice, all of these four measurements are difficult to determine with certainty. The most simple symptom to spot (and therefore the one most relied on) is *market share*. This gives a 'rough and ready' diagnosis and may affirm the presence of a dominant position where a more sophisticated analysis would reject it; but often such sophisticated analysis is very difficult to do. Barry Hawk describes the use of market share as a benchmark as 'a necessary evil'.

So, how has this worked in practice? We can use *Hoffmann-La Roche* to illustrate the situation. In this case the Commission relied on Hoffmann-La Roche's market share in seven vitamins to demonstrate its dominance, especially when compared to the market shares of its competitors (see p. 504 of the judgment).

The ECJ reiterated its 'test' of whether an undertaking can prevent effective competition and act, to an appreciable extent, independently. It then went on (para. 41):

> ... the view may legitimately be taken that very large shares are *in themselves,* and save in exceptional circumstances, evidence of the existence of a dominant position.

We can see the same analysis in the later case of *AKZO Chemie* (C-62/86), where market share of over 50 per cent appears to show a dominant position in the absence of exceptional circumstances and the onus of proof shifts to the suspect undertaking to disprove its dominance (see further **4.7.5**).

The same approach has been used by the Court of First Instance, in *Hilti* (1991) where market shares between 70 and 80 per cent was in itself a clear indication of a dominant position. Rather oddly, Hilti disputed these figures before the CFI, saying they were unreliable, Hilti's credibility was rather stretched by the fact that it had supplied the figures in response to a request from the Commission (pursuant to Article 11, Regulation 17).

The Court of First Instance also observed that the several patents which Hilti possessed went towards strengthening its position on the market. This leads on to a consideration of the secondary symptoms which may support the initial diagnosis.

4.7.4   ANCILLARY FACTORS

In *Hoffmann-La Roche*, the significant factors for the Commission were (see para. 42 of judgment):

   (a)   the size of Hoffmann's market share;
   (b)   the size of the disparity between its market share and that of its rivals;
   *(c)   the fact that it produces a much wider range of vitamins than its competitors;
   *(d)   the fact that Hoffmann is the largest manufacturer of vitamins in the world with a turnover exceeding that of all the other producers;
   (e)   its technological advantages over the others, originally given by patent but now achieved by its 'leading role' in the field;
   (f)   its very extensive and highly specialised sales network;
   (g)   the absence of potential competition.

In addition to market share, heads (b), (e), (f) and (g) were all relevant factors according to the ECJ. Head (b) enables an undertaking's competitive strength to be assessed; (e) and (f) represent technical and commercial advantages; (g) is the result of having obstacles which prevent entry to the market by potential competitors.

*Conversely, head (c) was rejected by the ECJ as immaterial — there are separate markets for each vitamin. Head (d) was also rejected by the ECJ — other companies who make vitamins play on the world market with other products and enjoy the freedom to set off one market against another.

The ECJ then applied each of these factors to the seven different product markets under consideration.

Looking at the *Michelin* case, we can see the Court attaching significance to the relative economic strengths of Michelin and its Dutch competitors. Michelin is part of a group of undertakings operating throughout Europe and the world. This gives it an advantage in investment and research. It also has an unusually large product range — for certain types of tyre, Michelin is the only supplier in The Netherlands. Michelin has a larger network of sales representatives than its competitors, offering an excellent service. (The French Government intervened, alleging that Michelin was being penalised for providing a good product and service — the argument was rejected by the ECJ.)

A similar analysis can be clearly seen in the *United Brands* case (1976). The Commission found United Brands' market share to be 45 per cent. United Brands pointed out that in 1975 this dropped to 41 per cent. The ECJ observed that a trader can only be in a dominant position with a product if it has 'succeeded in winning a large part' of the market. The Court said the evidence showed that United Brands' market share was always more than 40 per cent and nearly 45 per cent. 'This percentage does NOT permit the conclusion that the company automatically controls the market.' So the Court had to look at other factors — for example, it must take into consideration the strength and number of United Brands' competitors. United Brands' market share was several times greater than its nearest competitor, with the rest far behind. This situation can indicate its preponderant strength in the market.

4.7.5 DISPROVING DOMINANCE

As noted above, in the *Akzo Chemie* case (1986), the ECJ held that mere possession of a market share in excess of 50 per cent would, in the absence of exceptional circumstances, shift the onus of proof onto the company to disprove dominance. How might a company discharge that onus?

In *Hoffmann-La Roche*, the company argued that it faced 'lively competition'. The ECJ said that this does not preclude a dominant position. A dominant position means that such competition goes on without the dominant undertaking having to modify its behaviour or suffering any detrimental effects from not modifying its behaviour. But if a competitor's price reductions compelled an undertaking to cut its own prices, this behaviour would be incompatible with the independence which marks out a dominant position. (See paras 69-71 of the judgment.)

Again, turning to *Michelin*, the company argued that over recent years it had made a loss. The ECJ observed that — 'temporary unprofitability or even losses are not inconsistent with the existence of a dominant position'. (See para. 59 of the judgment.)

Similar arguments had been tried and found wanting in *United Brands*. The company complained that it had suffered 'fierce competition'. The ECJ said that it is unnecessary to have eliminated all competition in order to be in a dominant position — United Brands always held out successfully against the attacks of its competitors. Also, United Brands pointed out that it had made losses for five years while its competitors made profits; if a dominant position gave a company the power to fix prices, then making a loss did not show a dominant position. The ECJ rejected this — over the five years customers continued to buy more bananas from United Brands even though it was the dearest vendor: this was a more significant factor. It is a particular feature of a dominant position and was determinative in this particular case.

4.7.6 THE TIME FACTOR

The timescale which is used when measuring the possibility of other companies entering the market is an important consideration in determining if there are potential supply-side substitutes for the relevant product. The Commission and ECJ have both relied on a very short-term look at the possible competitors. In *Hoffmann-La Roche*, the test was, if Hoffmann-La Roche pushed prices up (or decreased production), would those companies with smaller market shares 'be able to meet *rapidly* the demand from those who would like to break away from the undertaking which has the largest market share?'. This short timespan for potential competitors to become actual competition can be criticised.

Again, in *Commercial Solvents* (1973), the ECJ said that if there was a raw material on the market which could be substituted without difficulty for nitropropane or aminobutanol when making ethambutol, this could mean that Commercial Solvents did not have a dominant position, but no such raw material then existed.

In *Michelin*, you might be forgiven for thinking that as the relevant product was a specific type of tyre, it would be quite easy for other tyre manufacturers to switch production over to that type and so provide a substitute for Michelin's product. The ECJ took a different view (at para. 41):

> ... there is no elasticity of supply between tyres for heavy vehicles and car tyres owing to significant differences in production techniques and in the plant and tools needed for their manufacture. The fact that time and considerable investment are required in order to modify production plant for the manufacture of light-vehicle tyres instead of heavy-vehicle tyres or vice versa means that there is no discernible relationship between the two categories of tyre, enabling production to be adapted to demand on the market.

4.8   Legal Monopolies and Dominant Positions

It might seem that to hold a legal monopoly in a product — e.g. through a patent, copyright or registered design — might lead to the relevant company having a dominant position with regard to that product. Of course, whether this was the situation in fact should depend on the availability of substitute products to satisfy customer demand. The Court of Justice has not said that mere possession of a legal monopoly over a product is enough to create a dominant position: e.g. *Deutsche Grammophon* v *Metro-SB Grossmarkte* (1970).

In *Volvo AB* v *Erik Veng (UK) Ltd* (1987) the ECJ was specifically asked by the High Court, on a preliminary reference, whether the possession of exclusive rights to manufacture and import certain car body panels gave Volvo a dominant position. (Volvo had the exclusive rights because they held the UK registered designs for those parts.) The ECJ was also asked a second question — whether a refusal to license others to import the panels constituted an abuse under Article 86. The ECJ answered the second question, saying that there was no proof of abuse, and therefore it found it unnecessary to answer the first question.

The topic was raised again in 1988 in an Italian case involving Renault car parts (*Consorzio Italiano della Componentistica di Ricambio per Autoveicoli and SpA Maxicar* v *Regie Nationale des Usines Renault* (1988)). One question posed by the Italian court was whether the obtaining of protective rights in respect of ornamental models for car bodywork components and the exercise of the resultant exclusive rights constitute an abuse of a dominant position within Article 86? With respect to the drafter of the preliminary reference, this seems to roll up two questions into one, and the ECJ gave a straightforward answer: 'the mere fact of obtaining protective rights in respect of ornamental designs for car bodywork components does not constitute an abuse of a dominant position within the meaning of Article 86 of the Treaty.' It does appear, though, from the subsequent text of the judgment that the ECJ still thought that the mere possession of an exclusive right did not constitute a dominant position. (See, in particular, para. 18 of the judgment.)

This straightforward view may be in the process of changing, though. In the recent case of *Radio Telefis Eireann et al* v *Commission* (1989), the Commission initially found that various broadcasting organisations had a factual monopoly over television listings. This meant that any third parties who were interested in publishing a weekly guide to such listings were in a position of economic dependence on those organisations. (Such dependence is often owed to those who are in a dominant position.) The Commission found that this factual monopoly was strengthened into a legal monopoly by the use of copyright. The Commission found that the organisations did not permit third-party competition and inferred that they each held a dominant position.

The decision was challenged in the Court of First Instance. The Court decided that the relevant product was 'weekly television guides with comprehensive listings for the week'. Because of their copyright, the organisations had a monopoly over publication of such listings and a dominant position on the market for the listings. They also had a dominant position in the secondary market for magazines in which such listings are published. This has subsequently been upheld by the ECJ (1995).

We can see that the nub of the judgment may be the decision to extend the copyright monopoly over listings into a different market — that of printed weekly television guides. We can apply this argument to the *Volvo* situation and see that Volvo are likely to have a dominant position in the market for new spare parts for Volvo vehicles. This could be regarded as a secondary market (the primary one being the market for new, factory-fresh Volvos) and we would then have the answer to the question that the ECJ dodged answering in *Volvo* itself. However, the ECJ stated explicitly in the *RTE* appeal (1995) that the mere ownership of an intellectual property right does *not* confer a dominant position.

Before leaving this topic, we should note also the assertion by Claus-Dieter Ehlermann, in 1993 14 ECLR 61, that it is the 'well-established case-law of the [ECJ] that an undertaking which holds *an exclusive right* in a substantial part of the Common Market can be considered to be in a dominant position within Article 86'. He cites *CBEM/CLT* (1985) as authority for this (the 'Telemarketing' case). However, these exclusive rights appear to be basically those permitting public utilities to have a form of monopoly (e.g. BT, British Gas, etc.). The position there may be much clearer than it is in the 'pure' private sector. Lastly, on a national note, we should be aware of a recent judgment in the English Patents Court — *Chiron Corporation and others* v *Organon Teknika Ltd and others* (1992).

4.9 Within the Common Market or a Substantial Part of It

The relevant territory was considered as an element within 'dominant position' because we need to establish the relevant geographical market before we can begin to ascertain the market share of a company. The phrase 'within the Common Market or a substantial part of it' appears in Article 86 to shift attention to jurisdiction. If the dominant position is not held over the whole of the Community or an economically significant part of it, there is no 'Community interest' in how the dominant company behaves. That is not to say that national authorities will be similarly uninterested in the behaviour; it just means that the Commission, as Community watchdog, will not need to get involved.

Examples of geographical areas which have fulfilled this requirement are:

(a)   the entire common market: *Hoffmann-La Roche* v *Commission* (1976) ('Vitamins');
(b)   the United Kingdom: *Hugin/Liptons* v *Commission* (1978);
(c)   the Netherlands: *Michelin* v *Commission* (1981); *BP* v *Commission* (1977) (oil traders);
(d)   south-western Germany: *Suiker Unie* v *Commission* (1973) (the sugar cartel);
(e)   Italian ports: *Merci Convenzionali Porto di Genova* v *Siderurgica Gabrielli* (1990).

It remains open to question whether the smallest Member States (in terms of numbers of consumers) — Denmark, Ireland and Luxembourg — are substantial parts of the common market. In *BAT and Reynolds* v *Commission* (1984) the Commission found Rothmans International was dominant in Belgium *and* Luxembourg with 47.8 per cent of that market. This territory was a substantial part of the EEC. It is likely that political expediency, if nothing else, will dictate that the smaller states are all found to be substantial parts of the Common Market.

We can see an example of such expediency, perhaps, in the *Radio Telefis Eireann* case (1989). RTE alleged that the geographical area under consideration (Eire and Northern Ireland) did not constitute a substantial part of the common market. This allegation was based on the number of households in the territory (i.e. 1 million; or less than 1 per cent of the Community total). This type of test had been used before by the ECJ — see, for example, the *Sulker Unie* case — but the Court of First Instance held that the island of Ireland was 'undeniably a substantial part of the common market'.

The notion of 'a substantial part' has also entered the domestic law of the United Kingdom. The Monopolies and Mergers Commission is required to have a 'reference area' when it conducts a merger investigation under the Fair Trading Act. This area should be 'a substantial part of the United Kingdom'. A recommendation of the MMC, relating to activities of South Yorkshire Transport Limited (a bus company) was quashed by the High Court as the reference area was not a substantial part of the UK. This judgment was upheld by the Court of Appeal — see *The Times Law Reports*, 9.12.91.

4.10   Abuse

In the French language version of the EC Treaty this is rendered as 'abusive exploitation', which may make its scope clearer. Unlike Article 85, which caught behaviour that was *intended* to restrict competition or had that effect, Article 86 is concerned with *conduct*. Article 86 gives several examples of behaviour that will constitute an abuse. You should note that there is no possibility of getting an exemption from prohibition if the abuse in question in fact has some beneficial effects for consumers (unlike Article 85(3)).

The Court of Justice considered the meaning of 'abuse' in *Europembellage Corp. and Continental Can Co.* v *Commission* (1972) — it said that Article 86 aimed at stopping not just behaviour which was directly detrimental to consumers (e.g. selling at unfair prices or deliberately cutting back on production in order to obtain a higher price for the product), but also behaviour which could harm consumers indirectly, usually by terminating effective competition in the market (i.e. wiping out the existing competition or making it more difficult for others to enter the market and compete).

In *Hoffmann-La Roche* v *Commission* (1976) the Court returned to the notion of 'abuse' and this time noted that an abuse was abnormal behaviour (that which would not occur in conditions of normal competition) which had the effect of either causing existing competition to wither or remain (stagnant) at present levels.

'Abuse' requires a company to engage in an activity; merely possessing a dominant position is not an abuse in itself. This was made clear by the ECJ in *Michelin* (1981):

A finding that an undertaking has a dominant position is not in itself a recrimination but simply means that, irrespective of the reasons for which it has such a dominant position, the undertaking concerned has a *special responsibility* not to allow its conduct to impair genuine undistorted competition on the common market.

None of this really helps us to determine what specific types of behaviour might be found to be an abuse. Article 86 itself offers some assistance in heads (a)–(d). These are not intended to be exhaustive; see *Continental Can* (1972) at para. 26: 'The list merely gives examples, not an exhaustive enumeration....'

Article 86, heads (a) and (b) are indicative of attempts to regulate performance directly — unfair prices (price increases) or restrictions on output have a direct effect on the customer/consumer (although price *cuts* may benefit consumers; but not perhaps in the long term?), By looking at Article 86 (c) and (d), one sees that the provision aims not only at 'practices which may cause damage to consumers directly, but also at those which are detrimental to them [i.e. consumers] through their impact on an effective competition structure' (*Continental Can*, para. 26).

Examples (c) and (d) show that unfair or discriminatory conduct is covered by Article 86 (e.g. price discrimination and tie-ins). We should remember that *Continental Can* was a merger case (in a time before the Merger Regulation). This may explain the bold statement in the judgment that simply strengthening a dominant position may be an abuse within Article 86, *regardless of the means and procedure by which it is achieved*, if it has the effect of substantially fettering the competition.

Is it useful to try to *classify* the types of abuse that fall within Article 86? Arguably, this is what the Article itself does with the four examples. However, the Commission and Court often fail to refer to heads (a)–(d) specifically; or else they refer to more than one of them; or, if they do use just one, they fail to state how it is that the example is demonstrated by the facts in the particular case. We may need to create a classification for ourselves,

4.11   Three Classes of Abuse?

It has been suggested (by John Temple Lang) that there are three basic classes of abuse:

(a)   exploitative abuses, e.g. excessive prices;
(b)   anti-competitive abuses, e.g. tie-ins, mergers and discriminatory pricing;
(c)   reprisal abuses, e.g. refusals to deal, predatory pricing.

It should be noted that these provide a basic framework but are not necessarily mutually exclusive: e.g. tie-ins are anti-competitive but also allow exploitation; predatory pricing is anti-competitive but may be used as a reprisal weapon. The United Kingdom Government's Green Paper on 'Abuse of Market Power' (November 1992) uses 'anti-competitive' and 'exploitative' abuses as a system to underpin several practical examples of abusive behaviour (see p. 19 of the Green Paper).

Examples of abuse were found in the following cases:

(a)   *Commercial Solvents Corp.* v *Commission* (1973): refusal to supply a competitor (see extract quoted in **4.11**).
(b)   *United Brands* v *Commission* (1976): discriminatory pricing — different prices applied to sales of bananas brought by ship from the Caribbean (see Korah at p. 135 and the judgment of the Court in **4.12**). Also refusal to deal — termination of dealer in Denmark after it became an exclusive for another brand of bananas.
(c)   *AKZO* (1991): threats to enter the victim's market, coupled with a predatory pricing policy.

An alternative to classification is to look at *particular types of conduct* and see what is indicated by precedent. We can examine three types:

(a)   discounts (**4.12**);
(b)   refusals to deal (**4.13**);
(c)   unfair pricing (**4.14**).

4.12   Discounts

This activity had been tried by *Hoffmann-La Roche* (1976). The company had a variety of exclusive or preferential supply contracts with several bulk vitamin 'users'. The customers were required either to buy *only* from Hoffmann-La Roche, or to buy most of their requirements from the company. In return, they got a *fidelity rebate*, i.e. a discount based on past purchases. The customers had to get past a threshold percentage of their previous requirements. The principle behind the rebate was said to be, the more you buy the cheaper it gets. The rebate also applied to more than one vitamin, so if a customer bought more of any Hoffmann-La Roche vitamin, this increased their discount on purchases of any other Hoffmann-La Roche vitamin.

These fidelity rebates were rejected by the ECJ as abusive, even if they were entered into willingly by the customer. They were not based on an economic transaction which justified this burden but were designed to *deprive or restrict* the customer's *choice* in sources of supply. This rebate system also hindered other vitamin producers from getting *access* to the market. The rebates were wrong because they were based on loyalty (i.e. Hoffmann tied up an outlet against its competitors) rather than simple *quantity of purchase*. One *can* discount on quantity usually because of economies of scale — these can be passed on to the customer. Here, customers qualified on a percentage of their *need*, whether great or small.

Incidentally, Hoffmann-La Roche also had so-called 'English' clauses in their rebate agreements. These allowed the customer to buy the product elsewhere if they had a better offer but they were obliged to tell Hoffmann about the better offer. The ECJ held that 'English' clauses were unacceptable — although superficially they *prevented foreclosure*, the fact of an obligation to inform Hoffmann-La Roche of its competitors' moves helped it to identify competitors and deal with them.

Discounts were also considered in *Michelin* (1981): the ECJ observed that discounts *per se* are not abusive (para. 71 of its judgment) but loyalty rebates are. The problem is that discounts, especially for quantity, can be offered on a one-off basis but loyalty rebates operate on a rolling basis and require continuity of purchase. This results in competitors being denied access to one's customers. Discounts must be justified by some economic service. Here, discount periods were measured over a one-year qualifying period. Customers came under heavy pressure to buy Michelin tyres over the whole period. Also, Michelin kept changing the qualifying rules and not telling customers, so uncertainty prevailed and customers were less likely to switch to another supplier. This stopped free selection by customers and was not competitively-justified behaviour.

4.13   Refusal to Deal

A useful article has been written by Romano Subiotto, 'The right to deal with whom one pleases under EC competition law: a small contribution to a necessary debate' 1992 ECLR 234.

Refusals to deal occur in various ways, e.g. as a response to shortages; as a threat of punishment for misconduct; as a result of forward vertical integration. Refusals can be competitively justified — for example, in *United Brands* (1976), the company argued that its ban on resale was to protect both its brand name and consumers by guaranteeing the quality of the product. The ECJ said it was permissible if it did not raise obstacles, the effect of which went beyond the (legitimate) objective to be achieved.

Examples of legitimate refusal might be:

(a)   in a selective distribution system where a distributor fails to meet (proper) requirements;

(b)   genuine shortages, if properly dealt with (cf the Dutch Oil case, *AGB/BP* (1977);

(c)   a customer which transfers its central activity to promoting a rival brand. The supplier could review its relationship with the customer and legitimately terminate that relationship, giving adequate notice (taken from the Subiotto article, citing the Commission decision in *BBI/Boosey & Hawkes* (1987). But this must be compared with *United Brands* (1976): United Brands terminated supplies to a long-standing customer (Olesen) after Olesen gave priority to a competing brand of bananas. This was held to be a 'penalty' used to discourage others from following Olesen's example of independent action. It was designed to have a serious adverse effect on competition. (see paras. 169-178, 182-96 of the judgment).

If a company engages in forward vertical integration, the desire of the Commission to protect its *competitors* seems overwhelming. See, for example, *Commercial Solvents* (1973), where the refusal to supply is condemned even though one can see it as the simple replacement of one company by another. The case is often seen thus by its critics, *but* we should note that *potential* competition was eliminated — the situation changed from one actual supplier plus one potential supplier to just one actual supplier. A very strict test was applied in *Commercial Solvents* — intention seemed to be irrelevant — the Court noted that the company's objective had been to reserve the raw materials it produced for its own in-house fabrication of the finished product.

This approach finds an echo in a recent decision of the French *Conseil de la Concurrence* (or Competition Board): *Re Supply of Metallic Calcium* (1992). Here, a dominant supplier of standard industrial calcium supplied the product to a smaller company producing high-grade calcium granules.

The dominant company was slow in making deliveries and failed to provide necessary technical information about the product. So the customer went to other, more expensive, sources and had to raise its own prices. According to the *Conseil*, the requests for supply were normal and it found that the delays were due to the supplier's wish to develop its own in-house production of the high-grade product.

Urgency of supply seems to be irrelevant, as may be seen from para. 26 of the judgment in *Commercial Solvents*.

The Subiotto article (above) refers to the American 'doctrine of *essential facilities*'. This idea, that an undertaking which possesses such a facility is under some obligation to its competitors in a 'downstream' market, seems to be assuming significance in Europe. A good example is *B & I/Sealink Harbours and Stena Sealink* (1992).

Sealink is both a British ferry operator and the port authority at Holyhead, Wales. Both Sealink and B & I use berths at Holyhead. The B & I berth is at the harbour mouth and, when Sealink's ferries pass, the water level rises so that B & I have to interrupt loading or unloading of their ferry. Only one such incident occurred per B & I ferry until October 1991 when Sealink announced new sailing times which would involve two ships passing each docked B & I ferry. B & I sought interim measures which the Commission granted.

The Commission said that a dominant undertaking which owns or controls an essential facility and which uses that facility will be guilty of an abuse within Article 86 if it either:

(a) refuses access to competitors; or
(b) grants access on terms less favourable than those which it gives to its own services.

An essential facility is one to which competitors must have access in order to provide a service to customers. One might easily draw parallels between such a (typically physical) situation and that where access to information protected by an intellectual property right in one market is necessary to enable a separate market to be developed (cp. *Volvo v Veng* (1987) and *RTE* (1995). The ECJ said that a refusal to grant a licence for an intellectual property right would only constitute abusive behaviour in 'exceptional circumstances'.

4.14 Unfair Pricing

A basic problem in proving unfair or predatory pricing lies in the assessment of the cost structure of the suspect. Various theories exist on how costs are to be assessed but there is no real consensus. The task is easiest where a bald threat exists but this really seeks to punish behaviour (intent) with little consideration of effect. A good example of this is the *ECS/AKZO* litigation, where there was a 'smoking gun' letter and the issue of intent seems to have been accorded great significance.

The fact that behaviour, rather than effect, is caught by the notion of predatory pricing can be shown by the words of the ECJ in *Sirena v Eda*:

... as regards the abuse of a dominant position, although the price level of the product may not of itself necessarily suffice to disclose such an abuse, it may, however, if unjustified by any objective criteria, and if it is particularly high, be a determining factor.

So, price increases may be caught, as well as price reductions!

In *United Brands* (1976), the ECJ said that 'charging a price which is excessive because it has no reasonable relation to the economic value of the product supplied is ... an abuse' (see p. 252 of the judgment). When calculating the economic value of a product, we must take into consideration the production costs.

The formula set out by the ECJ for establishing whether predatory pricing has occurred looks like this:

First, find £ x (i.e. price actually charged for a unit of product)
then deduct £ y (i.e. costs actually incurred on making it)
Result? £ z

We should then determine whether £ z is excessive or not. Assuming that someone (usually the Commission) can answer 'Yes' to the question 'Is £ z excessive?', we should next see if £ x is unfair, either in itself or in comparison with competing products. If this can be answered affirmatively, we have a case of unfair or predatory pricing.

The formula is useless to apply in practice for two reasons. First, no one can agree on the method of costs analysis which should be used. Secondly, the notion that '£ z is excessive' implies a comparison with something else but it is not clear what we should use for the comparison. The ECJ has appreciated the difficulties involved in an analysis of production costs but has suggested (correctly) that some tests exist for determining excessive prices and that the Commission should use them when alleging excessive pricing. A problem remains, in that there is a plurality of such tests.

Let us take the *AKZO* case as an illustration. The Court said that prices which are lower than the average variable cost (AVC) and which are used as a tool to lever out a rival *must* be regarded as an abuse; a dominant undertaking has no interest in such action except to eliminate rivals in order to then raise prices. The reason it has no interest other than this is that every one of its sales represents a *loss*, i.e. all the fixed costs plus at least part of the variable costs for each unit sold.

Where an undertaking charges prices above AVC but below average total cost (i.e. the sum of its fixed costs plus variable costs — ATC), these prices must be an abuse where they form part of an elimination plan. The dominant undertaking is able to remove undertakings who are as effective as the dominant undertaking but who cannot resist the competition due to their inferior financial capacity.

The ECJ defines variable costs as only those which vary according to the level of output. The Court says that labour costs fail to do this and so they are fixed costs. On the facts, AKZO's prices were below AVC only once. Other pricing abuses fell in the range between AVC and ATC. These were still abusive as they could not be explained away as reactions to offers made by AKZO's competitors and they continued over a long period. No abuse was proved by the Commission regarding the alleged selectivity of offers to AKZO's customers. The variation in availability of offers properly reflected the differences in the types of customer. For a cogent argument showing the limitations of the *AKZO* formula for predatory pricing, see Soames and Ryan [1994] 3 ECLR 157. National courts seem quite willing to detect predatory pricing. See, e.g., the French 'Competition Council' in *Béton de France* (1994), and the Italian Antitrust Authority in *Tekal/Italcementi* (1995).

4.15 Effect on Trade between Member States

The same element occurs in Article 85, and there is little else to say beyond that which was said earlier (see **2.5**) except for two points. First, occasionally the Court has interpreted this requirement quite strictly. In *Hugin/Liptons* v *Commission* (1978) a Swedish parent company with a UK subsidiary terminated supplies of spare parts for its cash tills to the 'victim', Liptons. Liptons was a small company which operated in the Greater London area, providing a cash till repair service. The ECJ said that Liptons would normally have bought the spares from Hugin's subsidiary in the UK; the volume of trade was so small as to be insignificant and not attractive enough for other companies to want to import spares and satisfy Liptons' demand; finally there was no evidence that Liptons was likely to expand its business into another member state. Thus there was no effect on trade between Member States and therefore no breach of Article 86.

Secondly, under Article 86 the Court and the Commission are more likely to consider the harm done to one's competitors as affecting inter-state trade, even where this does no immediate harm to the ultimate consumer. The most typical example is the actual or threatened elimination of a rival (e.g. *AKZO* (Commission Decision); *Commercial Solvents Corp.* v *Commission* (1973)) or someone in a rival 'camp' (e.g. *United Brands* v *Commission* (1976) — trade buyer deciding to promote a rival brand). This is a rather broader test than that used for Article 85, so conduct which distorts the structure of the market may be regarded as affecting the inter-state trade.

4.16   Notification

Can you notify the Commission of your own abuse of a dominant position? Naturally, an undertaking is unlikely to want to volunteer information about its abusive conduct to the Commission, but companies may want to notify the Commission of certain agreements or practices so that it can put the company's mind at rest. It can do this by giving the agreement etc., negative clearance, i.e. stating that, on the facts then known to the Commission, the agreement etc., does not infringe Article 86. (See Article 2, Regulation 17/62.) What a company cannot do is notify its agreements or practices and hope to have those which infringe Article 86 exempted from prohibition. Exemption is only possible for breaches of Article 85.

4.17   The Relationship between Article 86 and Exemption under Article 85(3)

In the recent *Tetra Pak* case (T-51/89) the Court of First Instance considered the relationship between Article 86 and exemption under Article 85, when the same behaviour is under examination.

The Court concluded that if behaviour is illegal under Article 86, then that is conclusive of the matter. The fact of exemption under Article 85(3) (in this case via the patent licensing block exemption) is irrelevant. If conduct was exempt under Article 85(3), the usual consequences would follow but undertakings in a dominant position still had a separate obligation to comply with Article 86. Tetra Pak's complaint about being left in a position of legal uncertainty was dismissed. Tetra Pak has recently been fined a record sum by the European Commission for these activities — see **5.14**.

For further reading on Article 86, see chapter 4 in Korah; chapter 12 in Hawk; or chapter 14 in Steiner — all works cited in the bibliography. See also the European Economic Area Agreement, Article 54, which replicates Article 86 *mutatis mutandis*. (Text in 1993 14 ECLR supplement.)

5 Investigations and their Consequences

As mentioned previously, Regulation 17/62 is the main item of secondary legislation in the competition regime. It lays down quite explicit rules about how the law on competition is to be applied.

5.1 Starting an Investigation

Under Article 89, EC Treaty, the Commission is to investigate cases of suspected infringement either on its own initiative or on application by a member state. One example of an investigation on its own initiative in the proceeding against a cartel of PVC producers (see OJ 1994 L239/14). Regulation 17/62 has expanded this to include investigation following complaints from '... natural or legal persons who claim a legitimate interest'. A special form — Form C — exists for complainants to use. Its use is not mandatory but complainants should always ensure that their reasons for alleging a breach of Article 85 and/or 86 are clearly set out in writing for the Commission.

5.2 Who might Complain?

Such people are likely to be:

(a) competitors of the suspect enterprise who perhaps are being excluded from a market;
(b) those who have contracts with the suspect enterprise and are suffering from bad contract terms imposed because of a lack of bargaining power;
(c) those who have contracts with an enterprise but for whom, because of a change in the conditions of the market, it is now advantageous to try to get out of the contract, i.e. such a complaint can be used as a *tactical* weapon in an essentially commercial struggle. This can also occur in domestic litigation, e.g. X sues Y for breach of contract in a national court; Y's defence is that the contract contains terms which infringe Article 85, and therefore it is void and unenforceable.

An unusual complainant can be seen in the *Official Journal* (1992) C2/32, In the course of questions asked in the European Parliament by Scottish MEPs, it became clear that the Commission had received a formal complaint in 1990 from a 'pressure group', the Scottish Steel Campaign Trust, about the alleged anti-competitive behaviour of British Steel in shutting down the Ravenscraig hot strip mill. Sir Leon Brittan, for the Commission, stated that the complaint had been investigated and a decision had been taken by the Commission.

Bear in mind that a complaint may not stir the Commission into action. Although it seems clear that the Commission is under an obligation to investigate when it is 'notified' of a matter, the Court of First Instance has declared that the Commission is under no such obligation regarding complaints (see the judgment in *Automec* (1992)). The Commission has a margin of discretion to refer certain complaints to the appropriate national authorities, in order that it may give priority to matters of significance at the Community level. This seems to be in accordance with the current (Maastricht) idea of subsidiarity and also eases some of the work-load on the Commission. It has been suggested by Dr Claus-Dieter Ehlerman, that if the Court of First Instance had not decided *Automec* in the way that it did, the Commission might have had to seek amendment of Regulation 17 in order to achieve a similar result as the number of complaints received by the Commission was too great. According to Bo Vesterdorf, a judge at the Court of First Instance, the Commission gets about 100 complaints annually, although for some reason 'exact figures are hard to come by and tend to be contradictory' (CMLR 31:77). If the Commission does reject a complaint without investigation, it will inform the complainant by letter. That letter must explain clearly the reasons for rejection and it may be challenged by judicial review in the CFI, pursuant to Article 173, EC Treaty. See, e.g., *BEUC* v *Commission* (1994).

5.3 Rights of a Complainant

If an investigation starts after a complaint has been made by a natural or legal person, what rights does that complainant have? It has been suggested (by Korah, *An Introductory Guide to EEC Competition Law and Practice,* p. 90) that if the complainant plays an active part in the investigation (by making representations or submitting evidence), the proceedings become 'almost adversarial'. This suggestion received a blow in *BAT and Reynolds* v *Commission* (1984).

BAT complained to the Commission about a joint venture company established by two of its rivals in the European cigarette industry. The Commission began an investigation but the two suspect companies, Philip Morris and Rembrandt, then modified their agreement in such a way that the Commission decided that there were no longer any grounds for investigating. The Commission told BAT that it was closing its file on the matter.

BAT sought to challenge this in the European Court of Justice, using Article 173, EC Treaty. The Court, following its judgment in *Metro SB-Grossmarkte* v *Commission* (1976), held that BAT had the *locus standi* to use Article 173. BAT was the addressee of a letter from the Commission — all it had to do was show that the letter was a reviewable act, i.e. produced legal effects. This it had done by suggesting that the 'approved' change in the market structure meant that it was likely to suffer financial losses in the future. (See also the **Remedies and Practical Background Manual, 11.3.**)

BAT's ground of complaint was that it had been denied a fair hearing. Article 19 of Regulation 17/62 permits the Commission to hear natural or legal persons during an investigation, if necessary. If those people show 'a sufficient interest', they must be heard. All that the Court was prepared to acknowledge, though, was that complainants must have an opportunity to defend their legitimate interests. This means that the Commission must consider all legal and factual material which the complainant draws to its attention. The complainant's rights are not coextensive with those of the suspect company, the investigation is *not* adversarial in nature. Complainants' rights expire when they start to conflict with the right of the suspect to a fair hearing.

5.4 Access to the Commission's File

A complainant may be given access to the Commission's case-file in order for the Commission to obtain the opinion of the complainant on documents therein, if to do so is necessary for the proper conduct of the investigation. This will include access to documents containing confidential information but not those which contain business secrets: see *BAT and Reynolds* v *Commission* (1984) and *AKZO Chemie* v *Commission* (1985).

The decision whether a document contains business secrets is one for the Commission to take. In the *AKZO* case, the ECJ set out the procedure that the Commission should follow, prior to disclosure:

(a)   Before it makes any disclosure of the document to a complainant, the Commission must allow the company whose secrets they are, the chance to make representations about disclosure.

(b)   Then the Commission must adopt a decision (either to disclose or not), which should state the reasons on which it is based.

(c)   This decision must be notified to the relevant company.

(d)   If the Commission decides in favour of disclosure, it must delay making disclosure in order to allow the company to seek judicial review of the decision under Article 173 of the Treaty.

The Court of First Instance has also had to consider the degree of access to a file that the Commission must allow a '*defendant*' company — see *SA Hercules Chemicals NV* (1991). The Court observed that the right to a fair hearing meant that a 'defendant' must be allowed to express its views on the Commission's statement of objections and the supporting evidence, annexed to the statement (see **5.12**). The right to a fair hearing did not require that the 'defendant' had to be able to comment on everything in the Commission's file. Thus full access was not required as ancillary to that right. However, in its Twelfth Report on Competition Policy, the Commission laid down rules on disclosure going beyond what the Court itself required. The Commission could not go back on its own self-imposed rules and was, therefore, under an obligation to give a 'defendant' access to *all* of the documents that it had acquired during the investigation (other than those containing other companies' business secrets, the Commission's internal documents and other confidential information).

This degree of access must now be contrasted with the judgment of the Court of First Instance in *Cimenteries CBR SA and others* v *Commission* (1992). Various companies were being investigated pursuant to Regulation 17; they sought access to files relating to the investigation and were allowed access only to selected documents by the Commission. They challenged this via an action under Article 173 EC. The action was held to be inadmissible by the Court — access to files may underpin the right to be heard but there was no legal effect on the companies until such time as the Commission found that the competition rules had been violated and, perhaps, had imposed a fine. In other words, the action was premature, With respect to the Court, this wait-and-see approach is unlikely to leave many observers feeling that justice has been seen to be done, regardless of the fact that many companies involved in an investigation may be content with the eventual decision of the Commission on the merits of their case. The topics of confidentiality and disclosure are the subject of a recent article by Julian M. Joshua [1994] 2 ECLR 68.

5.5   Conducting the Investigation

Article 11 of Regulation 17/62 empowers the Commission to get information from governments, state authorities and undertakings. The Commission sends a request for information, setting out:

(a) the purpose of the request;
(b) its legal basis;
(c) a time-limit for compliance; and
(d) the possibility of fines for the supply of incorrect information. (Article 15 of Regulation 17/62 allows a fine to be imposed where incorrect information is supplied, whether *intentionally or negligently*; see **5.13**.)

The owners of the undertakings or the officers of the company (if a separate legal personality) *must* supply the information requested.

If either no information is forthcoming or it is incomplete, the Commission can take a formal decision which:

(a) requires the information to be supplied;
(b) specifies what information is wanted;
(c) gives a new time-limit for compliance; and
(d) contains a reminder about possible fines (either one-off or day-by-day) if information is incorrect or not supplied (see Article 11(5)).

The CFI has stated that Article 11 sets up a two-stage process and the Commission cannot proceed to the second stage (taking a formal decision) unless it has requested information first and this has proved unsuccessful. The CFI has said that an undertaking which receives a request is under a duty to 'cooperate actively' — a passive reaction to a request may now be enough to lead to a formal decision, without the need to show any manifest obstruction by the undertaking (see *Scottish FA* v *Commission* (1994)).

The Commission is empowered to undertake all necessary investigations: Article 14 of Regulation 17/62. Its authorised officials can examine all the records of a business, take copies of them, ask for 'oral explanations on the spot' and go anywhere on the property of an undertaking.

There are two types of 'visit' — one is where the officials arrive and simply ask to come in: Article 14(2). It seems that there is no obligation to allow entry here (although any goodwill generated now may stand the company in good stead if a fine has to be imposed later). The second is the 'dawn raid' — see **5.6**.

It seems that the powers vested in the Commission by Articles 11 and 14 are quite separate. In the *Orkem* case (374/87), the Commission had used Article 14 to try to obtain documents from the company. Later, the Commission purported to use its powers under Article 11 to ask questions *and* seek documents. Orkem alleged this to be an abuse of Article 11. The suggestion was rejected by the Court of Justice, which said that the two procedures were wholly independent of each other. The previous (unsuccessful) use of Article 14 was not an obstacle to the use of Article 11, even where the same information was still being sought.

5.6   'Dawn Raids'

The second type of visit occurs when the Commission takes a formal decision to order an investigation (under Article 14(3)). Undertakings are under a duty to submit to this investigation. This type often occurs without prior warning to the suspect and is commonly known as the dawn raid.

The legality of such unannounced raids was challenged by one investigated company in *National Panasonic v Commission* (1979). It made two allegations. First, that the Commission could only take a formal decision to investigate after an unsuccessful attempt to investigate by simply sending authorised officials. Secondly, that to take such a decision without allowing the company either a chance to offer its views about an investigation or apply for a stay of execution was a violation of its fundamental rights (on analogy with Article 8, European Convention on Human Rights). Both arguments were rejected by the ECJ (paras 11, 19 and 20):

> [Article 14(3)] does not ... prevent the Commission from carrying out an investigation solely pursuant to a written authorisation given to its officials without adopting a decision, but in other respects it contains nothing to indicate that it may only adopt a decision within the meaning of Article 14(3) if it has previously attempted to carry out an investigation by mere authorisation. Whereas Article 11(5) expressly makes the adoption of a Commission decision subject to the condition that the latter has previously asked for the necessary information by means of a request addressed to those concerned and specifies in Article 11(3) the essentials which such a request must contain, Article 14 makes the investigating procedure by means of a decision subject to no preliminary of this kind.

> [I]t is necessary to point out that Article 8(2) of the European Convention, in so far as it applies to legal persons, whilst stating the principle that public authorities should not interfere with the exercise of the rights referred to in Article 8(1), acknowledges that such interference is permissible to the extent to which it 'is in accordance with the law and is necessary in a democratic society....'

> ...[T]he aim of the powers given to the Commission by Article 14 [of Regulation 17/62] is to enable it to carry out its duty under the EEC Treaty of ensuring that the rules on competition are applied in the common market... [I]t does not ... appear that Regulation No. 17, by giving the Commission the powers to carry out investigations without previous notification, infringes the rights invoked by the applicant.

5.7   Searches

In *Hoechst v Commission* (1987) and (1988) the ECJ stated that, as part of its investigative powers under Article 14, the Commission officials are entitled to enter all of the 'suspect's' premises and seek out information which is not already known about or fully identified, i.e. they can search for useful information, they need not know of its existence. (See the Bulletin of the Court No. 18/89.)

5.8 Penalty for Non-cooperation

Failure to cooperate with an investigation (once it has been ordered by Commission decision) can lead to lump sum fines or daily penalty payments (Articles 15 and 16 of Regulation 17/62). If a company is recalcitrant about permitting entry, Member States are required to afford any assistance necessary to enable the Commission officials to do their job. (In the UK this might mean getting an injunction, similar to an *Anton Piller* order, from the Commercial Court.) See further *Hoechst* v *Commission* (*supra*).

5.9 Legal Professional Privilege; Self-incrimination

Not all documents have to be shown to the officials. The European Court of Justice has recognised the right of a suspect company to withhold documents which are protected by legal professional privilege: *AM & S Europe* v *Commission* (1979). The privilege attaches to written advice from independent (i.e. not in-house) lawyers who are registered and practising in the EC. Protection extends to all written communications exchanged between lawyer and client after the start of the administrative procedure under Regulation 17/62 and it will cover earlier written communications which relate to the subject-matter of that procedure.

Until recently, neither the Commission nor the ECJ had recognised the existence of a privilege against self-incrimination. In the *Orkem* case (374/87), the applicant company sought to invoke such a privilege in a novel manner. Orkem alleged that the Commission had asked questions (in an Article 11, Regulation 17 request for information) which, if answered would compel the company to incriminate itself and others. Orkem asserted that by so doing, the Commission had infringed Orkem's right to a fair hearing. The Court of Justice considered that several of the questions asked did compel Orkem to confess its infringement and ruled that they were void. It remains to be seen how this ruling will work in practice, in particular whether it will simply encourage the Commission to ask more general questions and go on to the sort of vague fishing expeditions that the Hoechst and Dow companies recently complained about (see, the *Dow* case (85/87)). Indeed, a vague, catch-all trawl through the filing cabinets may be almost all that is available to the Commission in the future, *if* the judgment of the European Court of Human Rights in *Funke/France* (1993) is applied to competition investigations. In *Funke*, the Court of Human Rights acknowledged the right (under Article 6 of the ECHR) to remain silent and not incriminate oneself. Whilst the Commission could simply look for documentary material on company premises, once its officials wanted to ask questions they would presumably have to administer some sort of caution, analogous to that in a criminal investigation.

One response to *Funke* at a national level has occurred in Norway. In *Norway* v *Rieber & Son AS*, the Norwegian Supreme Court held that the reasoning in *Funke* was too brief to be relied upon for the purpose of overturning 'long-established procedures under Norwegian competition law concerning the duty to render information to investigating officers': see [1995] 2 ECLR R-51. Also van Overbeek [1994] 3 ECLR 127.

5.10 Interim Relief during an Investigation

Sometimes a company may complain, for instance, that it is being driven out of business by a dominant rival (see, e.g., *ECS/AKZO* (Commission Decision) or *Brass Band Instruments/Boosey & Hawkes* (1987)). If the 'victim' merely awaits the outcome of a Commission investigation then, even if there is a finding in its favour, it may come too late for the victim. Its business or financial position may have been irredeemably damaged during the lifetime of the investigation. Rather than allow this to happen, the victim should take immediate steps to have the illegal behaviour stopped while the investigation is being carried out.

The ECJ has express powers to grant temporary relief, under Articles 185 and 186, EC Treaty. These powers are limited to situations where an action is proceeding at the ECJ. During the investigative stages, a victim may seek relief only from the Commission.

In *Camera Care* v *Commission* (1979) the Court held that the Commission has implied powers to grant interim relief during an investigation. This power exists in order to prevent any decisions taken by the Commission at the conclusion of an investigation 'becoming ineffectual or even illusory'. The power can only be exercised if certain criteria are satisfied:

(a)   The applicant must prove that the measures are needed urgently in order to avoid
(b)   a situation likely to cause serious and irreparable damage to the applicant or
(c)   which is intolerable for the public interest.
(d)   The measures must be temporary and
(e)   conservatory and
(f)   restricted to what is required in the given situation (i.e. proportionality).

In *Ford* v *Commission* (1982) the Court affirmed the basic principle in *Camera Care* — that the Commission has implied power to take interim measures. But it went on to state that, because the purpose of the implied powers is to allow the final decision to have a meaningful effect, any interim measures which are taken must fall within the scope of the final decision which may be taken by the Commission. In other words, the Commission cannot do something on an interim application that goes beyond what it could do in its final decision. See also *Brass Band Instruments/Boosey & Hawkes* (1987).

The Court of First Instance has stated (*La Cinq* (1992)) that the applicant need only show a prima facie case that the competition rules had been broken; proof of a clear and flagrant breach was *not* needed. Further, the Commission should not impose too high a standard of proof regarding 'serious and irreparable damage'.

5.11   Hearings

Article 19 of Regulation 17/62 requires the Commission to hear the views of the suspect undertaking before taking a decision in several instances, e.g.:

(a)   before granting negative clearance;
(b)   before requiring an infringement to be terminated;
(c)   before deciding whether or not to exempt behaviour; and
(d)   before imposing financial penalties.

In 1963 the Commission enacted Regulation 99/63 specifically to regulate those hearings which are required by Article 19 of Regulation 17/62.

5.12   Procedure for Hearings

Essentially, the Commission must give a suspect undertaking written notice of what is alleged against it (this is called a statement of objections). The Commission should give the suspect company access to its case-file, upon application (as with a complainant). Documents which reveal other companies' business secrets may not be disclosed, although a summary of the other information in such a document could be supplied. See also **5.4**.

The Commission must then give the undertaking the opportunity to respond in writing before it takes a decision. A time-limit for receipt of views will be imposed. This written stage may be followed by an oral hearing, if requested by the suspect company. Complainants will also have the chance to submit written views and request an oral hearing, particularly if the Commission has published (in the *Official Journal* its intention either to give negative clearance or grant an exemption.

A Hearing Officer (employed by the Commission's Competition Department) will be appointed by the Commission to chair the oral hearing. The Hearing Officer is intended to be independent of the investigation — this is said to be demonstrated by their right to present an opinion on the case directly to the Commissioner for Competition Affairs. This opinion will not usually be disclosed to anyone outside the Commission but an application (by complainant or defendant companies) might succeed in certain, narrow circumstances: see the Court of First Instance in, e.g., *BASF AG* v *Commission* (1991). A useful article by CS Kerse on oral hearings is to be found in [1994] ECLR 40. (Details of the terms of reference for Hearing Officers can be found in Commission Decision 94/810 — see OJ 1994 L330/67.

When the Commission takes its decision it should rely only on the objectionable conduct of which the suspect undertaking has been notified and on which it has been able to offer its views. The Court of Justice has offered its opinion that Regulation 17/62 '... applies the general rule that a person whose interests are perceptibly affected by a decision taken by a public authority must be given the opportunity to make his point of view known'. See, e.g., *Musique Diffusion Française* v *Commission* (1980) (the 'Pioneer' case).

The company must be told in good time of the Commission's objections/proposals (e.g. conditions for granting an exemption or the amount of a fine) and it must have the opportunity to submit its observations to the Commission.

5.13   Fines and other Penalties

The power to impose a fine or periodic penalty is provided by Article 15 (fines) and Article 16 (periodic penalty payments) of Regulation 17/62. An organisation may be fined whether its shortcoming is intentional or negligent — it pays to be careful. The fine can be for not being helpful during the investigation or in order to 'compel' helpfulness. A company can be fined very large sums if found guilty of infringing Articles 85 and 86, EC Treaty.

Recently, the Tipp-Ex firm was fined by the Commission for infringing Article 85. On appeal to the Court of Justice, it challenged the fine on the basis that its infringement was not intentional or negligent. Tipp-Ex pleaded guilty only to ignorance and the receipt of wrong legal advice. The Court held that the Commission had the power to impose a fine — knowledge that the company was in breach of Article 85 was unnecessary. It is enough if it could not have failed to be aware that the purpose of its conduct was to restrict competition. (See case C-279/87). In such circumstances, its infringement is likely to be considered intentional — see the CFI in *Parker Pen Ltd* v *Commission* (1994).

5.14   Fines for Breaches of Articles 85 and 86

For breaches of Articles 85 or 86, Regulation 17/62, Article 15 allows fines of up to 1 million ECU or 10 per cent of the turnover of the undertaking for the previous year, whichever is the greater figure. Turnover here refers to global turnover of the undertaking, across all of its products. Article 15 does not prescribe a threshold for fines but the Commission has said that it will regard any 'ill-gotten gains' that can be identified as the starting-point of its calculation (see the XXIst Report on Competition Policy). Before imposing a fine, the Commission must allow the undertaking a chance to express its views, both written and oral. In fixing the fine, the Commission must take into account the gravity and duration of the infringement and any mitigating factors. In practice, DG IV will advise the Commissioner for Competition on the amount of any fine; the Commissioner will then make a recommendation to the College of Commissioners who make the final decision. Recently, there have been calls for the Commission's methodology when quantifying fines to be made more transparent and that its wide discretion should be curtailed. See, e.g., 'Fining à la carte: the lottery of EU Competition law', *Ivo van Bael* [1995] 4 ECLR 237.

Examples of recent fines imposed by the Commission are:

(a) *Re Konica UK Ltd* (1988) — 75,000 ECU;

(b) *Re Quaker Oats UK Ltd* (1988) — 300,000 ECU;

(c) *Hilti* (1988) — 6 million ECU for a very serious breach of Article 86, even taking into account mitigating factors like:

(i) Hilti's cooperation;

(ii) its voluntary offer of a remedial undertaking prior to the outcome of the investigation;

and

(iii) its introduction of a compliance programme governing its future conduct.

The Hilti fine was upheld by the Court of First Instance — see Case T-30/89, judgment of 12.12.91. Hilti's subsequent appeal to the ECJ was unsuccessful (1994).

(d) *Re Polypropylene Cartel* (1986) — a cartel amongst the major polypropylene producers in the EC which infringed Article 85 led to fines being imposed on some 15 firms, e.g. Hoechst (9 million ECU), ICI (10 million ECU), and Shell (9 million ECU). The producers appealed to the ECJ. Their cases were transferred to the Court of First Instance. Several were unsuccessful (e.g. Hoechst), while others managed to get their fines reduced, usually on the basis that the Commission could not prove that they had been a party to the cartel for as long as originally alleged in the Decision.

(e) *AKZO Chemie BV* (1991) — the ECJ reduced the fine imposed by the Commission by 25 per cent. Two reasons for the reduction were:

(i) that the Community policy on predatory pricing was largely unknown when AKZO embarked on its conduct; and

(ii) that the market shares of AKZO and its rival, ECS, had not been significantly affected by the conduct.

The fine was reduced to 7.5 million ECU.

(f) *Tetra Pak II* (1991) — for an abuse of dominant position (Article 86), Tetra Pak (a Swiss company, owned by Swedes) was fined some 75 million ECU. It was found guilty of carrying out a 'deliberate policy aiming to eliminate actual or potential competitors'. The fine was a record and the subject of an unsuccessful appeal to the CFI (1994). The CFI observed that the amount of the fine represented some 2.2% of the appellant's total turnover for 1990.

(g) *Re Cartonboard Cartel* (1994) — a cartel of producers of cardboard was fined in excess of 130 million ECU, with several individual members fined in excess of 15 million ECU.

5.15 Immunity from Fines

The parties to an agreement usually notify the Commission about it because they want a negative clearance or exemption from the Commission. Once the agreement is notified, the parties benefit from an immunity from fines for the period between notification and the Commission's final decision on the merits (see Article 15(5), Regulation 17). This immunity may be removed by the Commission if it makes *a preliminary finding* that Article 85(1) has been breached and exemption is not justified (see Article 15(6), Regulation 17). In respect of lost immunity the question of whether such a preliminary finding was a reviewable act within Article 173, EC Treaty, was examined in *Re Noordwijk's Cement Accord* (1966). Note also the five-year limitation period on fines — see Regulation 2988/74, referred to, e.g., in *PVC Cartel* (1994).

6   National Impact

As mentioned earlier, the requirement that the conduct which is the subject-matter of the complaint has an effect on trade between Member States is often seen as marking the boundary between the behaviour that the EC rules regulate and that which is left to the national authorities of the Member States to deal with. You may have to consider two sets of competition rules when advising whether a company's behaviour is illegal or not.

Whilst it is true to say that certain behaviour will fall outside the coverage of EC law because it has no, or only an insignificant, effect on Community trade, nevertheless there are situations where the two codes overlap. In *Wilhelm* v *Bundeskartellamt* (1968), the Court of Justice considered the situation where a firm's conduct appeared to have broken both EC and national (German) competition laws. The ECJ thought that, in principle, since the two codes have different aims in mind, both should be applied to the suspect undertaking. There are certain points to take into account, though.

6.1   Contradictions between EC and National Competition Rules

First, EC law prevails over national law (see, e.g., *Costa* v *ENEL* (1964)). This means that if conduct is legal in national law but illegal under EC rules, both national courts and the ECJ must treat it as illegal — both Article 85 and Article 86 refer to the conduct being prohibited. (This also helps to ensure that similar conduct is treated similarly throughout the Community.) However, if conduct is legal under EC rules, it may still be illegal under national rules. The ECJ seems to think that national courts cannot contradict a decision by the Commission to exempt an agreement under Article 85(3): *Anne Marty SA* v *Esteé Lauder SA* (1979). However, the Director General of the Office of Fair Trading, Sir Bryan Carsberg, has stated his opinion that there is 'no clear indication' whether UK rules may prohibit an agreement which has been exempted by the Commission.

Secondly, if the Commission and national authorities both proceed to use their separate powers, a company should not be punished twice for the same behaviour. It should not be fined twice, there should be a sort of set-off. (Note that this idea does not apply to fines imposed outside the EC, at least where the fine is imposed for conduct having an effect outside the Common Market: *Boehringer Mannheim* v *Commission* (1969).)

6.2   Use of Articles 85 and 86 Offensively and Defensively in National Courts

There is a role for EC rules in the national courts of the Community. Both Articles 85 and 86 have been held by the Court of Justice to be directly effective: *BRT* v *SV SABAM* (1973); see **1.5**. This has given rise to the EC competition laws being prayed in aid by parties to domestic litigation — either as a sword or a shield.

6.2.1 DEFENSIVELY

As a shield, one finds the rules used in cases like *British Leyland* v *Armstrong* (1985), *Volvo AB* v *Erik Veng (UK)* (1987), and *R* v *Henn and Darby* (1979). Where people are sued in national courts for infringement of intellectual property rights (patents, copyright, trademarks, etc.), they may allege that the litigation is an abuse of a dominant position or that the grant of the property right is the fruit of an anti-competitive agreement between undertakings.

One should note in passing that ancillary arguments, made by way of 'Euro-defences', can include reliance on the rules providing for free movement of goods within the Community (see **Chapter 7**). This has occurred both in the field of infringement of intellectual property rights and in criminal prosecution for importation of obscene material where the offending subject-matter had come, quite lawfully, from another member state. (See, e.g., *R* v *Henn and Darby* (1979), and cases on free movement of goods such as *Hoffman-La Roche* v *Commission* (1976) and *Centrafarm* v *Sterling* (1974).)

6.2.2 OFFENSIVELY

As a sword, certainly within the United Kingdom, attempts to rely on the EC competition rules have met with a varied reaction. Several years ago Lord Denning suggested that Articles 85 and 86 represented 'new economic torts' — see, e.g., his speech in *Application des Gaz SA* v *Falks Veritas* (1974) — and could be used as causes of action in order to sue someone. This idea was not enthusiastically received by his judicial brethren.

The way forward seems to be indicated by cases like *Cutsforth* v *Mansfield Inns Ltd* (1986), *Argyll* v *Distillers and Guinness* (1986), and, particularly, *Garden Cottage Foods* v *Milk Marketing Board* (1984). The plaintiffs in these cases have not sought to put forward the EC rules as creating some new cause(s) of action, but instead have sought (or strained) to fit them into existing categories. The most acceptable, in judicial terms, seems to be the tort of breach of statutory duty, with its attendant remedies — namely, damages and interlocutory relief.

In *Cutsforth* the plaintiffs owned coin-operated machines such as juke boxes and game machines which were placed in public houses. As a result of a take-over of Northern Breweries by Mansfield Brewery plc, the brewery told the plaintiffs to take their machines out of some 160 tenanted pubs under brewery control. The tenants were told that they could have such machines in the pubs but that they must come from a nominated supplier. Mansfield Brewery refused to put the plaintiffs on their list of approved suppliers.

The plaintiffs issued a writ, then applied for an *ex parte* injunction. The application was successful and was followed subsequently by an *inter partes* hearing. The High Court judge (Sir Neil Lawson) accepted that, if the plaintiffs could raise a serious question as to whether or not the defendants were guilty of infringing either Article 85 or Article 86, EC Treaty, they should get their injunction. He said (at p. 563) that such conduct would be unlawful; the plaintiffs would be entitled to seek its prohibition in the High Court:

> ... as it is clear on the authorities that breaches of the relevant provisions of the EEC Treaty give rise to a cause of action in the domestic courts by a plaintiff who contends that he is the victim of such breaches.

The judge also considered whether the brewery's modified agreement with its tenants fell within the block exemption for exclusive purchase agreements (Regulation 1984/83), but decided it did not. He concluded that there was a serious question to be tried in relation to Article 85 and that damages would not be an adequate remedy for the plaintiffs, whereas they would for the defendant.

Conversely, the plaintiffs lost their argument under Article 86. Sir Neil Lawson held that:

(a) there was no evidence that the brewery held a dominant position;

(b) the area in which the brewery operated was not a 'substantial part of the common market' (although there is nothing in the judgment to indicate their area of operations, as distinct from that of the plaintiffs whose territory was 'Humberside and the surrounding district'); and

(c) no effect on inter-state trade had been shown.

The take-over battle for Distillers plc was the subject of (at least) two court cases between Argyll Group plc and Guinness plc — one in England and one in Scotland. In Scotland, when a revised bid by Guinness was not referred to the Monopolies and Mergers Commission, Argyll applied to the Court of Session for an interim interdict, to prevent the merger on the basis that it would contravene Article 86, EC Treaty.

The court accepted the proposition (from *Garden Cottage Foods* v *Milk Marketing Board* (1984), apparently, rather than *BRT* v *SV SABAM* (1973)) that Article 86 is directly effective. It said that it was entitled to consider breaches of Article 86 on an application for interim relief and noted that, taking *Europembellage and Continental Can Co.* v *Commission* (1972) into account, it is possible for a merger to infringe Article 86.

All three parties argued about the effect of *Continental Can Co.* on the merits of the case (all with contradictory opinions), but the judge concluded that, on the available evidence, there was no prima facie case that a dominant position existed (or would exist); nor that the proposed merger would be an abuse. (The judge considered the relevant market in terms of geography and product.)

In *Garden Cottage Foods* the House of Lords considered the uses of Article 86 in English courts. The defendants had cut off supplies of butter which the plaintiffs needed to carry on their business. They sought an interlocutory injunction, restraining the defendants from withdrawing supplies.

The House (Lord Wilberforce dissenting) held that it was clearly arguable that a breach of Article 86 would give rise to a cause of action in English law at the behest of an individual who has suffered pecuniary loss by reason of the infringement; and that the remedy of damages would be available to compensate for such loss. Lord Diplock noted that Article 86 has been held to be directly effective, citing *BRT* v *SV SABAM*, and that this was binding on English courts. A breach of Article 86:

... can thus be categorised in English law as a breach of statutory duty that is imposed ... for the benefit of private individuals to whom loss or damage is caused by a breach of that duty.

According to Lord Diplock, whilst it was barely arguable that a breach of Article 86 was not actionable as a breach of statutory duty in English courts, it could not be disputed that, if the cause of action existed, a remedy in damages must be available. In a dissenting speech, Lord Wilberforce thought that an open mind should be kept on whether or not a breach of Article 86 simply gave rise to the remedy of an injunction; furthermore, it was still debatable what the nature of the cause of action was — it need not be defined as a tort or a 'breach of statutory duty'. The remaining three Law Lords agreed with Lord Diplock.

By way of completeness, we must also take note of *Bourgoin* v *Ministry of Agriculture, Fisheries and Food* (1986). The case involved decisions of MAFF to keep French turkeys out of the UK. These decisions were subsequently declared to be illegal by the ECJ (under Article 30, EC Treaty — free movement of goods). The plaintiffs were French turkey producers and distributors. They claimed damages from MAFF, alleging substantial loss. The causes of action were stated to be:

(a) breach of statutory duty under Article 30, EC Treaty;
(b) the commission of an 'innominate tort' by so breaching Article 30; and
(c) misfeasance in a public office (i.e. deliberate abuse of power).

The Court of Appeal held (by a two to one majority) that, although Article 30 gave rights to individuals and imposed obligations on Member States, it said nothing about procedures or remedies. National courts had to offer the same remedies as are available for breach of a similar right in national law. A breach of Article 30 was akin to an ultra vires act under an English statute. It would give rise to judicial review, a declaration on the invalidity of the measure containing the illegality, and possibly an order of mandamus, but *not* a claim for damages.

The majority in the Court of Appeal held that a prima facie cause of action existed for misfeasance in public office, but there was no cause of action under the 'innominate tort' or breach of statutory duty (cp. Oliver LJ). The distinction between this case and *Garden Cottage Foods (supra)* was that the latter dealt with 'private law rights'. The present case involved breach of negative obligations by a member state and 'public law rights', which were only susceptible to judicial review. Even Lord Justice Oliver (who dissented in the result) pointed to the decisions of the Court of Justice in cases like *Bayerische HNL Vermehrungsbetriebe GmbH & Co. KG* v *Council and Commission of the EC* (1978) (the skimmed milk powder case), which limit the rights of individuals to claim damages for the legislative acts of the Community under Article 215(2), EC Treaty.

For another examination of the impact of EC Article 30 on our national law (this time by the Court of Justice, although note in the law reports the acceptance of it by the House of Lords), see the judgment in the *Allen & Hanburys* case (1989).

6.3   Equal and Effective Protection

In *Bourgoin* Lord Justice Oliver stated that the English courts are under a twofold obligation. First, to protect the rights of any individual infringed by a breach of a directly effective Article of the Treaty, in a manner not inferior to the protection given for similar rights in domestic law (equal protection). Secondly, to do so effectively (effective protection). To withhold a remedy of damages from a claim against the Crown would deny equal and effective protection to the individual. It would not be equal and effective because the infringement should be classified as the tort of breach of statutory duty and attract the same remedies. Although this was a dissenting judgment, it was by far the longest in the case and very well argued. The Court gave leave to appeal to the House of Lords but the case was subsequently settled. The EC points raised in this case have not subsequently been aired in an appellate court in England and remain, at least temporarily, unresolved. (See also *R* v *Pharmaceutical Society of Great Britain* — a preliminary reference to the ECJ by the Queen's Bench Divisional Court.)

English courts may now be required to accord better than equal protection to claimants who rely on Community law — see the *ex parte Factortame* case (C-213/89). The Court of Justice ruled (on a preliminary reference from the House of Lords) that interim relief could be granted to a litigant in a case concerning Community law if the 'sole obstacle' to such relief was a rule of national law. The relief in that case was the temporary suspension of an Act of Parliament in respect of the applicants. See now also the substantive judgment of the ECJ in *Factortame*, July 1991.

The judgment of the ECJ in *Francovich and others* v *Italian Republic* (1991) may prove to be a landmark in the development of national remedies for breaches of EC laws. In essence, the ECJ held that a Member State may become liable in damages for failure to implement an EC directive. There are clear limits on how far one may infer from this judgment some broader right to damages, in particular between private individuals (as distinct from 'vertically' where an individual sues the State) but the case offers a way forward. It is, of course, binding on English courts.

6.4   Conclusion

The upshot in reality is a state of confusion. The distinction between public and private law seemed settled (having been dealt with in several cases), although the judgment of the Court of Justice in *ex parte Factortame* may have upset that delicate balance.

What can be said is that no new causes of action have been acknowledged by English courts; it seems to be easier to rely on Community law in a defensive sense. When a litigant seeks to rely on Community law, it is necessary to find a domestic cause of action and struggle to fit the facts to the law. Pleadings give rise to a similar difficulty — examination of the standard practitioner encyclopaedias giving little assistance in Community matters, with the exception of precedents for preliminary references to the Court of Justice. It seems that there is still some way to go until a proper comprehension of the practical impact of Community law on our legal system is achieved.

Unfortunately, this incomprehension has now been overtaken by an EC imperative. The doctrine of subsidiarity having been taken out of its box at Maastricht, we now find that national courts are to play a much more significant role in the application of Articles 85 and 86. The ECJ and Court of First Instance made moves to push work away from the Commission and towards national courts in *Delimitis* (1991) and *Automec* (1992) respectively. The Commission issued a Notice in 1993 on cooperation between the courts of the Member States and itself on the application of Articles 85 and 86; this includes the notion that English judges will adjourn court proceedings in order to obtain some expert assistance from the Commission on the merits of the case at hand.

Certainly our judges may be more familiar with the EC competition rules now, but those rules will necessarily have to be moulded to fit existing English court rules and procedures. This process still has a considerable way to go. (Compare a call for the Member States to develop *common* procedural rules when pleading claims for damages based upon Community law: [1995] 1 ECLR 49.) Interestingly, the UK Government is proposing to introduce legislation to regulate domestic competition along lines very similar to Articles 85 and 86. This will be part of a shake-up of the current restrictive trade practices regime. Such legislation will no doubt become the familiar province of a tiny percentage of the judiciary. One is left to speculate on the likelihood of such judges being available to hear cases founded on the EC rules.

7 Free Movement of Goods and Intellectual Property

7.1 The Rules on Free Movement

The Treaty rules on the free movement of goods are often understood to be those contained in Articles 30-37 of the Treaty. However, these Articles are simply 'Chapter 2' of a larger body of Articles which begin with Article 9. Article 9 appears under the heading 'Title I Free Movement of Goods'; the Articles with which we are concerned appear under the rather daunting heading of 'Elimination of Quantitative Restrictions between Member States'.

The basic principle relates to the concept of a 'common market', and in Article 3(a) of the Treaty, the Community is set the task of ensuring the elimination (as between Member States) of quantitative restrictions on the import and export of goods, and of all other measures having equivalent effect (see **1.1** above). In essence, this elimination is carried into effect by Article 30 of the Treaty. Although some of the terminology may seem prolix, we are really concerned with one of the two main ways in which countries seek to protect their domestic economy. One way is to impose tariffs on imports from other countries — the removal of such tariffs (or customs duties) is the aim of Articles 9-17 of the Treaty. Articles 30-37 deal with the other basic way to stop imports — the use of quotas.

7.2 Article 30 — No Quantitative Restrictions

It seems that Article 30 has been used by litigants in national courts with much greater frequency than the EC competition rules. Partly this is no doubt due to expediency — there is no enforcement mechanism equivalent to Regulation 17/62 in this field; so if firms want to have the benefit of the principle of free movement, they must invoke it for themselves in the courts of the Member States. This is possible since, from the end of the transitional period (1 January 1962), Article 30 has been directly effective in the national legal systems of the Member States.

Use of Article 30 by individuals in national courts tends to be defensive — often the owner of, say, a patent will start an action alleging infringement of the patent by a rival who is importing the offending product into the country from another member state. The defendant may rely on Article 30 to try and overcome the (national) right to exclusivity held by the patentee. See, for example, *Allen & Hanburys Ltd v Generics (UK) Ltd* (1988). In such a situation, the litigation is a purely private matter. An alternative, still using Article 30 defensively, is where an individual or firm faces prosecution by either central or local government for commission of a regulatory offence.

Examples of such use occurring in the United Kingdom include *R v Henn and Darby* (1979). This case turned on the conflict between the basic EC freedom to import into a Member State goods which have been legally put onto the market in another Member State and the UK rules on the importation of obscene material. A more recent and highly-publicised use of Article 30 came in the spate of prosecutions of shops for trading on Sundays, in contravention of the Shops Act 1950. The basic defence in most of these cases was Article 30 — the suggestion being that the inability to trade on Sundays meant fewer sales and therefore fewer imports (i.e. an indirect quota). See *Torfaen Borough*

Council v *B & Q plc* (1990); *WH Smith Do-It-All Ltd* v *Peterborough City Council* (1990); *Stoke-on-Trent City Council* v *B & Q plc* (1991).

As may be seen above, the use of Article 30 has grown over the years, and sometimes in rather unexpected ways. This has been the result of imaginative use of a typically broad interpretation of Article 30 by the ECJ several years ago — *Cassis de Dijon* (1979). A recent judgment of the ECJ marked a watering-down of the impact of Article 30 on the circulation of goods around the Community: see *Keck and Mithouard* (1993). This case, which turned on French legislation prohibiting the use of 'loss leaders' in retailing, found the ECJ in retreat from *Cassis*. In *Keck*, the ECJ held that rules governing selling arrangements and which applied to all traders alike in the territory were not caught by Article 30.

Useful article: Anthony Arnull, 'What shall we do on Sunday?', (1991) ELR 112.

7.3 Free Movement and Intellectual Property Rights

As stated above, Article 30 aims to stop quotas — that is, the ability of a member state to limit the volume of imports into the country. The same effect as a quota can be achieved in a much more absolute fashion by reliance on intellectual property rights. These are held (usually) in the hands of natural or legal persons rather than the state, and are much more specific than state-imposed quotas. For example, AB plc may hold a UK patent for a baby buggy. They can then stop imports into the UK of buggies which infringe their patent, but not of other buggies. The state may (in theory) impose a quota limit on imports of *all* baby buggies if it chooses; or, to alter the illustration, the state may impose a blanket ban on the import of French baby buggies only — no individual intellectual property right holder could (or would) do this.

The main difference which usually exists between state action and that taken by individuals using intellectual property rights, is that the state will impose a quota (e.g. no more than 100,000 Korean-built cars will be imported into the UK in 1992), whereas the holder of an intellectual property right wants an absolute ban on all infringing goods. This total prohibition can in principle be attained, because intellectual property rights commonly give their owner a monopoly over the item protected by the right.

7.4 Intellectual Property Rights

When referring above to intellectual property rights, a universal approach was intended, covering all such rights. It is useful to explain, very briefly, what was meant by such an all-embracing term.

7.4.1 PATENTS

The relevant statute is the Patents Act 1977. A patent is the grant of a monopoly right to (usually) the inventor of a product or process for a definite length of time (currently, in the United Kingdom, 20 years). The invention must be clearly defined in the application for a patent and, to quote from WR Cornish (in *Patents, Copyright, Trademarks and Allied Rights*, Sweet and Maxwell), the invention must be 'patentable, i.e. (i) it must be novel, (ii) it must involve an inventive step, (iii) it must be capable of industrial application, and (iv) it must not belong to one of the categories of excluded subject-matter' (see Patents Act 1977, s. 1(1)).

Perhaps the most important consideration is the protection given by a patent to its owner. According to s. 60 of the Patents Act 1977, the patent in a product is infringed if (without the patentee's consent) someone 'makes it; disposes of it; offers to dispose of it; uses it; imports it; or keeps it whether for disposal or otherwise'.

The duration of a United Kingdom patent is from the date of publication of its grant (in the Patent Comptroller's journal) until 20 years after the patent was applied for (s. 25).

7.4.2   COPYRIGHT

The relevant statute is the Copyright, Designs and Patents Act 1988. Basically, copyright is an exclusive right to do certain specific acts in relation to specified types of work. For example, one may have the copyright in 'original literary, dramatic, musical or artistic works' (Copyright, Designs and Patents Act 1988, s. 1(1)(a)). The copyright owner then has the exclusive right to do the following acts in the United Kingdom:

(a)   to copy the work;
(b)   to issue copies of the work to the public;
(c)   to perform, show or play the work in public;
(d)   to broadcast the work or include it in a cable programme service;
(e)   to make an adaptation of the work or do any of the above in relation to an adaptation (s. 16(1)).

For anyone else to do these acts without the licence of the copyright owner is an infringement of copyright, which may give rise to a claim for damages, an injunction and an account (see s. 16(2) and s. 96).

Copyright in a literary, dramatic, musical or artistic work expires at the end of 50 years after the death of the author (s. 12).

7.4.3   TRADEMARK

'Trademark' has a statutory definition in the Trademarks Act 1938. This can be summarised as:

a mark ... used ... in relation to goods for the purpose of indicating a connection in the course of trade between the goods and some person having the right either as proprietor or as registered user to use the mark, whether with or without any identification of the identity of that person.

A mark includes 'a device, brand, heading, label, ticket, name, signature, word, letter, numeral, or any combination thereof'.

Marks applied to services are also protected (see Trade Marks (Amendment) Act 1984, s. 1; Patents, Designs and Marks Act 1986, s. 2).

7.4.4   REGISTERED DESIGNS

The relevant statutes are the Registered Designs Act 1949 and the Copyright, Designs and Patents Act 1988. Often used to protect engineering drawings and the plans used when making a product (e.g. the 'blueprint' for an exhaust pipe on a particular model of car). A 'design right' (the 1988 Act, s. 213) lasts for a maximum of 15 years from the first recording of the design or its first use, whichever was earlier (s. 216). A 'registered design' lasts for five years from the date of registration (1949 Act, s. 8). The problem with both types of design is that they may be used to make the product without permission. An alternative problem is 'reverse engineering' — a 'pirate' manufacturer obtains the product, determines its precise dimensions and composition, etc. and then makes it. The design owner could argue that this infringes the right in the design — see, for example, *British Leyland Motor Corporation v Armstrong Patents Co. Ltd* (1986).

7.4.5   FOREIGN INTELLECTUAL PROPERTY LAW

Finally, it should be noted that the above explanation is concerned with the position in English law. Definitions and the extent of protection given may vary from one country to another. It may be necessary in an individual case to have a knowledge of the particular intellectual property law of the country most closely connected with the proceedings (usually the country which granted the right under consideration). See, for example, the judgment of the ECJ in *Keurkoop v Nancy Kean Gifts* (1982) on the protection of designs and models in the Member States:

in the present state of Community law and in the absence of Community standardization or harmonization of laws the determination of the conditions and procedures under which such protection is granted is a matter for national rules. It is for the national legislature to determine which products qualify for protection, even if they form part of a unit already protected as such.

7.5 Infringement of Intellectual Property Rights

It is important to note that, in order to make their grant effective, intellectual property rights give their holder the ability to stop others from abusing the monopoly. This abuse could occur in a variety of ways — making a patented product or using a patented process, presenting someone else's copyright work as your own, placing someone else's trade mark on your goods, or using another's registered design to make a product. All of these acts can occur without infringing an intellectual property right if the holder of the right has given permission for the act, usually on payment of a royalty. Problems occur when such acts take place without proper permission. The nature of intellectual property law is that the right holder can stop any infringing activity — e.g. making, distributing or selling the offending articles — usually by getting a court injunction. This will forbid repetition, order the destruction of any remaining articles and require the infringer to account to the intellectual property right holder for the profits of the infringement.

7.6 Territorial Scope of Intellectual Property Rights

These rights are granted by the state and are usually good for the whole territory of that country. This results in the possibility that different firms or individuals will hold the same or very similar rights in different countries. There is also the possibility that, in a particular country, no one owns the intellectual property rights, or that no such right can be granted under the law of that country. Two examples may clarify the point.

(a)   In the early years of the EC, Italy did not grant patent protection to pharmaceutical products. So, anyone could make a drug in Italy and sell it there without breaking Italian patent law. If company A imported the pharmaceutical product from Italy into the United Kingdom, where it was protected by a patent granted to company B, could B use its patent to stop the import?

(b)   In Spain, it was not possible to obtain a patent for a new process, as distinct from a new product. If a Spanish firm used such a process to make product x, could the UK holder of a patent covering that process stop imports into the UK of the product from Spain?

The theory of a common market is that once goods are put into circulation legitimately in one Member State, they should be allowed to circulate through all other Member States. But to do so in these two examples would deprive the intellectual property right holder of the legitimate profits of his right. See, for example, the observation of the ECJ in the Italian *Renault* case (1988):

> It should be noted ... that the authority of a proprietor of a protective right in respect of [a design] to oppose the manufacture by third parties, for the purposes of sale on the internal market or export, of products incorporating the design or to prevent the import of such products manufactured without its consent in other Member States constitutes the substance of his exclusive right. To prevent the application of the national legislation in such circumstances would therefore be tantamount to challenging the very existence of that right.

The history of Article 30 and its interpretation by the ECJ has largely revolved around the attempt to resolve the conflict between 'national' intellectual property rights and the 'supranational' Article 30. Those involved with intellectual property rights have tried to solve the problem by creating new intellectual property rights which have a Community-wide scope — e.g., the single Community patent and the Community trademark. These steps should achieve greater harmonisation in the protection of intellectual property rights.

7.7   Abuse of an Intellectual Property Right

As well as 'gaps' in the protection of intellectual property, as indicated in **7.6**, there is also the possibility of intellectual property right holders abusing the protection the law gives them. Abuse is used subjectively here, to cover what might be seen as unjustifiable extensions of the exclusivity given by an intellectual property right. Examples of such behaviour can include the refusal without good reason to supply spare parts (where the design of the part is protected by an intellectual property right); charging an unfairly high price; or the deliberate splitting up of intellectual property rights held by the same firm in different countries in order to prevent parallel imports. A typical example of such market partitioning involved the German firm, Grundig.

Grundig had registered the trademark 'Gint' in several countries, including France. When it appointed an exclusive distributor of its products in France — Consten — it assigned its French trademark 'Gint' to Consten. In theory, this enabled Consten to stop any 'Gint'-marked goods being imported into France without its permission. If 'Gint' products were cheaper in Germany than in France, say, it might be profitable for someone outside the Grundig-Consten system to bulk buy the goods in Germany, then transport them into France and resell them there. This might result in Consten's prices being undercut *but* if Consten could bring a trademark infringement action to stop the unauthorised (parallel) imports, all would be well again for Consten. This was precisely what Consten attempted to do, with the result that the European Commission investigated and found that the two firms, Consten and Grundig, had infringed Article 85 by having an agreement to stop parallel imports.

The ECJ has drawn a firm line between what it calls the existence and the exhaustion of intellectual property rights. Essentially, once a product has been put on the market in a member state with the consent of (or by) the intellectual property right owner, the right is exhausted. That item is now in free circulation throughout the common market. The intellectual property right owner cannot use nationally-defined monopolies to stop parallel imports of the item. *But* whenever the product is marketed *without* the intellectual property owner's consent (e.g. pirate copies), the right has not been exhausted — any infringement may be stopped, using the appropriate national laws and remedies. As well as the *Consten and Grundig* case (1966) mentioned above, see also the 'Cassis de Dijon' case — *Rewe-Zentral AG* v *Bundesmonopolverwaltung fur Branntwein* (1979).

8   The Major Competition Rules

8.1   Article 85

POLICY OF THE COMMUNITY

TITLE 1 — COMMON RULES

CHAPTER 1 — RULES ON COMPETITION

SECTION 1

RULES APPLYING TO UNDERTAKINGS

ARTICLE 85

1. The following shall be prohibited as incompatible with the common market: all agreements between undertakings, decisions by associations of undertakings and concerted practices which may affect trade between Member States and which have as their object or effect the prevention, restriction or distortion of competition within the common market, and in particular those which:

(a)   directly or indirectly fix purchase or selling prices or any other trading conditions;
(b)   limit or control production, markets, technical development, or investment;
(c)   share markets or sources of supply;
(d)   apply dissimilar conditions to equivalent transactions with other trading parties, thereby placing them at a competitive disadvantage;
(e)   make the conclusion of contracts subject to acceptance by the other parties of supplementary obligations which, by their nature or according to commercial usage, have no connection with the subject of such contracts.

2. Any agreements or decisions prohibited pursuant to this Article shall be automatically void.

3. The provisions of paragraph 1 may, however, be declared inapplicable in the case of:

— any agreement or category of agreements between undertakings;
— any decision or category of decisions by associations of undertakings;
— any concerted practice or category of concerted practices;

which contributes to improving the production or distribution of goods or to promoting technical or economic progress, while allowing consumers a fair share of the resulting benefit, and which does not:

(a) impose on the undertakings concerned restrictions which are not indispensable to the attainment of these objectives;

(b) afford such undertakings the possibility of eliminating competition in respect of a substantial part of the products in question.

8.2 Article 86

Any abuse by one or more undertakings of a dominant position within the common market or in a substantial part of it shall be prohibited as incompatible with the common market in so far as it may affect trade between Member States. Such abuse may, in particular, consist in:

(a) directly or indirectly imposing unfair purchase or selling prices or other unfair trading conditions;

(b) limiting production, markets or technical development to the prejudice of consumers;

(c) applying dissimilar conditions to equivalent transactions with other trading parties, thereby placing them at a competitive disadvantage;

(d) making the conclusion of contracts subject to acceptance by the other parties of supplementary obligations which, by their nature or according to commercial usage, have no connection with the subject of such contracts.

8.3 Regulation 17/62

Regulation No. 17 of the Council of 6 February 1962
First Regulation Implementing Articles 85 and 86 of the Treaty amended by
Regulation No. 59, by Regulation No. 118/63 EEC and by Regulation No. 2822/71/EEC

THE COUNCIL OF THE EUROPEAN ECONOMIC COMMUNITY,

Having regard to the Treaty establishing the European Economic Community, and in particular Article 87 thereof,

Having regard to the proposal from the Commission,

Having regard to the Opinion of the Economic and Social Committee,

Having regard to the Opinion of the European Parliament,

Whereas, in order to establish a system ensuring that competition shall not be distorted in the common market, it is necessary to provide for balanced application of Articles 85 and 86 in a uniform manner in the Member States;

Whereas in establishing the rules for applying Article 85(3) account must be taken of the need to ensure effective supervision and to simplify administration to the greatest possible extent;

Whereas it is accordingly necessary to make it obligatory, as a general principle, for undertakings which seek application of Article 85(3) to notify to the Commission their agreements, decisions and concerted practices;

Whereas, on the one hand, such agreements, decisions and concerted practices are probably very numerous and cannot therefore all be examined at the same time and, on the other hand, some of them have special features which may make them less prejudicial to the development of the common market;

Whereas there is consequently a need to make more flexible arrangements for the time being in respect of certain categories of agreement, decisions and concerted practices without prejudging their validity under Article 85;

Whereas it may be in the interest of undertakings to know whether any agreements, decisions or practices to which they are party, or propose to become party, may lead to action on the part of the Commission pursuant to Article 85(1) or Article 86;

Whereas, in order to secure uniform application of Articles 85 and 86 in the common market, rules must be made under which the Commission, acting in close and constant liaison with the competent authorities of the Member States, may take the requisite measures for applying those Articles;

Whereas for this purpose the Commission must have the cooperation of the competent authorities of the Member States and be empowered, throughout the common market, to require such information to be supplied and to undertake such investigations as are necessary to bring to light any agreement, decision or concerted practice prohibited by Article 85(1) or any abuse of a dominant position prohibited by Article 86;

Whereas in order to carry out its duty of ensuring that the provisions of the Treaty are applied the Commission must be empowered to address to undertakings or associations of undertakings recommendations and decisions for the purpose of bringing to an end infringements of Articles 85 and 86;

Whereas compliance with Articles 85 and 86 and the fulfilment of obligations imposed on undertakings and associations of undertakings under this Regulation must be enforceable by means of fines and periodic penalty payments;

Whereas undertakings concerned must be accorded the right to be heard by the Commission, third parties whose interests may be affected by a decision must be given the opportunity of submitting their comments beforehand, and it must be ensured that wide publicity is given to decisions taken;

Whereas all decisions taken by the Commission under this Regulation are subject to review by the Court of Justice under the conditions specified in the Treaty; whereas it is moreover desirable to confer upon the Court of Justice, pursuant to Article 172, unlimited jurisdiction in respect of decisions under which the Commission imposes fines or periodic penalty payments;

Whereas this Regulation may enter into force without prejudice to any other provisions that may hereafter be adopted pursuant to Article 87,

HAS ADOPTED THIS REGULATION:

Article 1

Basic provision

Without prejudice to Articles 6, 7 and 23 of this Regulation, agreements, decisions and concerted practices of the kind described in Article 85(1) of the Treaty and the abuse of a dominant position in the market, within the meaning of Article 86 of the Treaty, shall be prohibited, no prior decision to that effect being required.

Article 2

Negative clearance

Upon application by the undertakings or associations of undertakings concerned, the Commission may certify that, on the basis of the facts in its possession, there are no grounds under Article 85(1) or Article 86 of the Treaty for action on its part in respect of an agreement, decision or practice.

Article 3

Termination of infringements

1. Where the Commission, upon application or upon its own initiative, finds that there is infringement of Article 85 or Article 86 of the Treaty, it may by decision require the undertakings or associations of undertakings concerned to bring such infringement to an end.

2. Those entitled to make application are:

 (a) Member States;
 (b) natural or legal persons who claim a legitimate interest.

3. Without prejudice to the other provisions of this Regulation, the Commission may, before taking a decision under paragraph 1, address to the undertakings or associations of undertakings concerned recommendations for termination of the infringement.

Article 4

Notification of new agreements, decisions and practices

1. Agreements, decisions and concerted practices of the kind described in Article 85(1) of the Treaty which come into existence after the entry into force of this Regulation and in respect of which the parties seek application of Article 85(3) must be notified to the Commission. Until they have been notified, no decision in application of Article 85(3) may be taken.

2. Paragraph 1 shall not apply to agreements, decisions and concerted practices where:

 (1) the only parties thereto are undertakings from one Member State and the agreements, decisions or practices do not relate either to imports or to exports between Member States;
 (2) not more than two undertakings are party thereto, and the agreements only:

 (a) restrict the freedom of one party to the contract in determining the prices or conditions of business upon which the goods which he has obtained from the other party to the contract may be resold; or
 (b) impose restrictions on the exercise of the rights of the assignee or user of industrial property rights — in particular patents, utility models, designs or trade marks — or of the person entitled under a contract to the assignment, or grant, of the right to use a method of manufacture or knowledge relating to the use and to the application of industrial processes;

 (3) they have as their sole object:

 (a) the development or uniform application of standards or types; or
 (b) joint research and development;

(c)   specialization in the manufacture of products, including agreements necessary for achieving this,

— where the products which are the subject of specialization do not, in a substantial part of the common market, represent more than 15% of the volume of business done in identical products or those considered by consumers to be similar by reason of their characteristics, price and use, and
— where the total annual turnover of the participating undertakings does not exceed 200 million units of account.

These agreements, decisions and practices may be notified to the Commission.

Article 5

Notification of existing agreements, decisions and practices

1.   Agreements, decisions and concerted practices of the kind described in Article 85(1) of the Treaty which are in existence at the date of entry into force of this Regulation and in respect of which the parties seek application of Article 85(3) shall be notified to the Commission before 1 November 1962. However notwithstanding the foregoing provisions any agreements, decisions and concerted practice to which not more than two undertakings are party shall be notified before 1 February 1963.

2.   Paragraph 1 shall not apply to agreements, decisions or concerted practices falling within Article 4(2); these may be notified to the Commission.

Article 6

Decisions pursuant to Article 85(3)

1.   Whenever the Commission takes a decision pursuant to Article 85(3) of the Treaty, it shall specify therein the date from which the decision shall take effect. Such date shall not be earlier than the date of notification.

2.   The second sentence of paragraph 1 shall not apply to agreements, decisions or concerted practices falling within Article 4(2) and Article 5(2), nor to those falling within Article 5(1) which have been notified within the time limit specified in Article 5(1).

Article 7

Special provisions for existing agreements, decisions and practices

1.   Where agreements, decisions and concerted practices in existence at the date of entry into force of this Regulation and notified within the time limits specified in Article 5(1) do not satisfy the requirements of Article 85(3) of the Treaty and the undertakings or associations of undertakings concerned cease to give effect to them or modify them in such a manner that they no longer fall within the prohibition contained in Article 85(1) or that they satisfy the requirements of Article 85(3), the prohibition contained in Article 85(1) shall apply only for a period fixed by the Commission. A decision by the Commission pursuant to the foregoing sentence shall not apply as against undertakings and associations of undertakings which did not expressly consent to the notification.

2.   Paragraph 1 shall apply to agreements, decisions and concerted practices falling within Article 4(2) which are in existence at the date of entry into force of this Regulation if they are notified before 1 January 1967.

Article 8

Duration and revocation of decisions under Article 85(3)

1.   A decision in application of Article 85(3) of the Treaty shall be issued for a specified period and conditions and obligations may be attached thereto.

2.   A decision may on application be renewed if the requirements of Article 85(3) of the Treaty continue to be satisfied.

3.   The Commission may revoke or amend its decision or prohibit specified acts by the parties:

(a)   where there has been a change in any of the facts which were basic to the making of the decision;

(b)   where the parties commit a breach of any obligation attached to the decision;

(c)   where the decision is based on incorrect information or was induced by deceit;

(d)   where the parties abuse the exemption from the provisions of Article 85(1) of the Treaty granted to them by the decision.

In cases to which subparagraphs (b), (c) or (d) apply, the decision may be revoked with retroactive effect.

Article 9

Powers

1.   Subject to review of its decision by the Court of Justice, the Commission shall have sole power to declare Article 85(1) inapplicable pursuant to Article 85(3) of the Treaty.

2.   The Commission shall have power to apply Article 85(1) and Article 86 of the Treaty; this power may be exercised notwithstanding that the time limits specified in Article 5(1) and in Article 7(2) relating to notification have not expired.

3.   As long as the Commission has not initiated any procedure under Articles 2, 3, or 6, the authorities of the Member States shall remain competent to apply Article 85(1) and Article 86 in accordance with Article 88 of the Treaty; they shall remain competent in this respect notwithstanding that the time limits specified in Article 5(1) and in Article 7(2) relating to notification have not expired.

Article 10

Liaison with the authorities of the Member States

1.   The Commission shall forthwith transmit to the competent authorities of the Member States a copy of the applications and notifications together with copies of the most important documents lodged with the Commission for the purpose of establishing the existence of infringements of Articles 85 or 86 of the Treaty or of obtaining negative clearance or a decision in application of Article 85(3).

2.   The Commission shall carry out the procedure set out in paragraph 1 in close and constant liaison with the competent authorities of the Member States; such authorities shall have the right to express their views upon that procedure.

3.   An Advisory Committee on Restrictive Practices and Monopolies shall be consulted prior to the taking of any decision following upon a procedure under paragraph 1, and of any decision concerning the renewal, amendment or revocation of a decision pursuant to Article 85(3) of the Treaty.

4.   The Advisory Committee shall be composed of officials competent in the matter of restrictive practices and monopolies. Each Member State shall appoint an official to represent it who, if prevented from attending, may be replaced by another official.

5.   The consultation shall take place at a joint meeting convened by the Commission; such meeting shall be held not earlier than fourteen days after dispatch of the notice convening it. The notice shall, in respect of each case to be examined, be accompanied by a summary of the case together with an indication of the most important documents, and a preliminary draft decision.

6.   The Advisory Committee may deliver an opinion notwithstanding that some of its members or their alternates are not present. A report of the outcome of the consultative proceedings shall be annexed to the draft decision. It shall not be made public.

Article 11

Requests for information

1.   In carrying out the duties assigned to it by Article 89 and by provisions adopted under Article 87 of the Treaty, the Commission may obtain all necessary information from the Governments and competent authorities of the Member States and from undertakings and associations of undertakings.

2.   When sending a request for information to an undertaking or association of undertakings, the Commission shall at the same time forward a copy of the request to the competent authority of the Member State in whose territory the seat of the undertaking or association of undertakings is situated.

3.   In its request the Commission shall state the legal basis and the purpose of the request and also the penalties provided for in Article 15(1)(b) for supplying incorrect information.

4.   The owners of the undertakings or their representatives and, in the case of legal persons, companies or firms, or of associations having no legal personality, the persons authorized to represent them by law or by their constitution, shall supply the information requested.

5.   Where an undertaking or association of undertakings does not supply the information requested within the time limit fixed by the Commission, or supplies incomplete information, the Commission shall by decision require the information to be supplied. The decision shall specify what information is required, fix an appropriate time limit within which it is to be supplied and indicate the penalties provided for in Article 15(1)(b) and Article 16(1)(c) and the right to have the decision reviewed by the Court of Justice.

6.   The Commission shall at the same time forward a copy of its decision to the competent authority of the Member State in whose territory the seat of the undertaking or association of undertakings is situated.

Article 12

Inquiry into sectors of the economy

1.   If in any sector of the economy the trend of trade between Member States, price movements, inflexibility of prices or other circumstances suggest that in the economic sector concerned competition is being restricted or distorted within the common market, the Commission may decide to conduct a general inquiry into that economic sector and in the course thereof may request undertakings in the sector concerned to supply the information necessary for giving effect to the principles formulated in Articles 85 and 86 of the Treaty and for carrying out the duties entrusted to the Commission.

2.   The Commission may in particular request every undertaking or association of undertakings in the economic sector concerned to communicate to it all agreements, decisions and concerted practices which are exempt from notification by virtue of Article 4(2) and Article 5(2).

3.   When making inquiries pursuant to paragraph 2, the Commission shall also request undertakings or groups of undertakings whose size suggests that they occupy a dominant position within the common market or a substantial part thereof to supply to the Commission such particulars of the structure of the undertakings and of their behaviour as are requisite to an appraisal of their position in the light of Article 86 of the Treaty.

4.   Article 10(3) to (6) and Articles 11, 13 and 14 shall apply correspondingly.

Article 13

Investigations by the authorities of the Member States

1.   At the request of the Commission, the competent authorities of the Member States shall undertake the investigations which the Commission considers to be necessary under Article 14(1), or which it has ordered by decision pursuant to Article 14(3). The officials of the competent authorities of the Member States responsible for conducting these investigations shall exercise their powers upon production of an authorization in writing issued by the competent authority of the Member State in whose territory the investigation is to be made. Such authorization shall specify the subject matter and purpose of the investigation.

2.   If so requested by the Commission or by the competent authority of the Member State in whose territory the investigation is to be made, the officials of the Commission may assist the officials of such authority in carrying out their duties.

Article 14

Investigating powers of the Commission

1.   In carrying out the duties assigned to it by Article 89 and by provisions adopted under Article 87 of the Treaty, the Commission may undertake all necessary investigations into undertakings and associations of undertakings. To this end the officials authorized by the Commission are empowered:

(a)   to examine the books and other business records;
(b)   to take copies of or extracts from the books and business records;
(c)   to ask for oral explanations on the spot;
(d)   to enter any premises, land and means of transport of undertakings.

2.   The officials of the Commission authorized for the purpose of these investigations shall exercise their powers upon production of an authorization in writing specifying the subject matter and purpose of the investigation and the penalties provided for in Article 15(1)(c) in cases where production of the required books or other business records is incomplete. In good time before the investigation, the Commission shall inform the competent authority of the Member State in whose territory the same is to be made of the investigation and of the identity of the authorized officials.

3.   Undertakings and associations of undertakings shall submit to investigations ordered by decision of the Commission. The decision shall specify the subject matter and purpose of the investigation, appoint the date on which it is to begin and indicate the penalties provided for in Article 15(1)(c) and Article 16(1)(d) and the right to have the decision reviewed by the Court of Justice.

4.   The Commission shall take decisions referred to in paragraph 3 after consultation with the competent authority of the Member State in whose territory the investigation is to be made.

5. Officials of the competent authority of the Member State in whose territory the investigation is to be made may, at the request of such authority or of the Commission, assist the officials of the Commission in carrying out their duties.

6. Where an undertaking opposes an investigation ordered pursuant to this Article, the Member State concerned shall afford the necessary assistance to the officials authorized by the Commission to enable them to make their investigation. Member States shall, after consultation with the Commission, take the necessary measures to this end before 1 October 1962.

Article 15

Fines

1. The Commission may by decision impose on undertakings or associations of undertakings fines of from 100 to 5,000 units of account where, intentionally or negligently:

(a) they supply incorrect or misleading information in an application pursuant to Article 2 or in a notification pursuant to Article 4 or 5; or

(b) they supply incorrect information in response to a request made pursuant to Article 11(3) or (5) or to Article 12, or do not supply information within the time limit fixed by a decision taken under Article 11(5); or

(c) they produce the required books or other business records in incomplete form during investigations under Article 13 or 14, or refuse to submit to an investigation ordered by decision issued in implementation of Article 14(3).

2. The Commission may by decision impose on undertakings or associations of undertakings fines of from 1,000 to 1,000,000 units of account, or a sum in excess thereof but not exceeding 10% of the turnover in the preceding business year of each of the undertakings participating in the infringement where, either intentionally or negligently:

(a) they infringe Article 85(1) or Article 86 of the Treaty; or

(b) they commit a breach of any obligation imposed pursuant to Article 8(1).

In fixing the amount of the fine, regard shall be had both to the gravity and to the duration of the infringement.

3. Article 10(3) to (6) shall apply.

4. Decisions taken pursuant to paragraphs 1 and 2 shall not be of a criminal law nature.

5. The fines provided for in paragraph 2 (a) shall not be imposed in respect of acts taking place:

(a) after notification to the Commission and before its decision in application of Article 85(3) of the Treaty, provided they fall within the limits of the activity described in the notification;

(b) before notification and in the course of agreements, decisions or concerted practices in existence at the date of entry into force of this Regulation, provided that notification was effected within the time limits specified in Article 5(1) and Article 7(2).

6. Paragraph 5 shall not have effect where the Commission has informed the undertakings concerned that after preliminary examination it is of the opinion that Article 85(1) of the Treaty applies and that application of Article 85(3) is not justified.

Article 16

Periodic penalty payments

1.   The Commission may by decision impose on undertakings or associations of undertakings periodic penalty payments of from 50 to 1,000 units of account *per* day, calculated from the date appointed by the decision, in order to compel them:

(a)   to put an end to an infringement of Article 85 or 86 of the Treaty, in accordance with a decision taken pursuant to Article 3 of this Regulation;

(b)   to refrain from any act prohibited under Article 8(3);

(c)   to supply complete and correct information which it has requested by decision taken pursuant to Article 11(5);

(d)   to submit to an investigation which it has ordered by decision taken pursuant to Article 14(3).

2.   Where the undertakings or associations of undertakings have satisfied the obligation which it was the purpose of the periodic penalty payment to enforce, the Commission may fix the total amount of the periodic penalty payment at a lower figure than that which would arise under the original decision.

3.   Article 10(3) to (6) shall apply.

Article 17

Review by the Court of Justice

The Court of Justice shall have unlimited jurisdiction within the meaning of Article 17 of the Treaty to review decisions whereby the Commission has fixed a fine or periodic penalty payment; it may cancel, reduce or increase the fine or periodic penalty payment imposed.

Article 18

Unit of account

For the purposes of applying Articles 15 to 17 the unit of account shall be that adopted in drawing up the budget of the Community in accordance with Articles 207 and 209 of the Treaty.

Article 19

Hearing of the parties and of third persons

1.   Before taking decisions as provided for in Articles 2, 3, 6, 7, 8, 15 and 16, the Commission shall give the undertakings or associations of undertakings concerned the opportunity of being heard on the matters to which the Commission has taken objection.

2.   If the Commission or the competent authorities of the Member States consider it necessary, they may also hear other natural or legal persons. Applications to be heard on the part of such persons shall, where they show a sufficient interest, be granted.

3.   Where the Commission intends to give negative clearance pursuant to Article 2 or take a decision in application of Article 85(3) of the Treaty, it shall publish a summary of the relevant application or notification and invite all interested third parties to submit their observations within a time limit which it shall fix being not less than one month. Publication shall have regard to the legitimate interest of undertakings in the protection of their business secrets.

Article 20

Professional secrecy

1. Information acquired as a result of the application of Articles 11, 12, 13 and 14 shall be used only for the purpose of the relevant request or investigation.

2. Without prejudice to the provisions of Articles 19 and 21, the Commission and the competent authorities of the Member States, their officials and other servants shall not disclose information acquired by them as a result of the application of this Regulation and of the kind covered by the obligation of professional secrecy.

3. The provisions of paragraphs 1 and 2 shall not prevent publication of general information or surveys which do not contain information relating to particular undertakings or associations of undertakings.

Article 21

Publication of decisions

1. The Commission shall publish the decisions which it takes pursuant to Articles 2, 3, 6, 7 and 8.

2. The publication shall state the names of the parties and the main content of the decision; it shall have regard to the legitimate interest of undertakings in the protection of their business secrets.

Article 22

Special provisions

1. The Commission shall submit to the Council proposals for making certain categories of agreement, decision and concerted practice falling within Article 4(2) or Article 5(2) compulsorily notifiable under Article 4 or 5.

2. Within one year from the date of entry into force of this Regulation, the Council shall examine, on a proposal from the Commission, what special provisions might be made for exempting from the provisions of this Regulation agreements, decisions and concerted practices falling within Article 4(2) or Article 5(2).

Article 23

Transitional provisions applicable to decisions of authorities of the Member States

1. Agreements, decisions and concerted practices of the kind described in Article 85(1) of the Treaty to which, before the entry into force of this Regulation, the competent authority of a Member State has declared Article 85(1) to be inapplicable pursuant to Article 85(3) shall not be subject to compulsory notification under Article 5. The decision of the competent authority of the Member State shall be deemed to be a decision within the meaning of Article 6; it shall cease to be valid upon expiration of the period fixed by such authority but in any event not more than three years after the entry into force of this Regulation. Article 8(3) shall apply.

2. Applications for renewal of decisions of the kind described in paragraph 1 shall be decided upon by the Commission in accordance with Article 8(2).

Article 24

Implementing provisions

The Commission shall have power to adopt implementing provisions concerning the form, content and other details of applications pursuant to Articles 2 and 3, and of notifications pursuant to Articles 4 and 5, and concerning hearings pursuant to Article 19(1) and (2).

This Regulation shall be binding in its entirety and directly applicable in all Member States.[1,2]

---

[1] **Documents concerning the Accession**
Article 25
1.   As regards agreements, decisions and concerted practices to which Article 85 of the Treaty applies by virtue of accession, the date of accession shall be substituted for the date of entry into force of this Regulation in every place where reference is made in this Regulation to this latter date.
2.   Agreements, decisions and concerted practices existing at the date of accession to which Article 85 of the Treaty applies by virtue of accession shall be notified pursuant to Article 5(1) or Article 7(1) and (2) within six months from the date of accession.
3.   Fines under Article 15(2)(a) shall not be imposed in respect of any act prior to notification of the agreements, decisions and practices to which paragraph 2 applies and which have been notified within the period therein specified.
4.   New Member States shall take the measures referred to in Article 14(6) within six months from the date of accession after consulting the Commission.
(OJ L 173, 27.3.1972, p. 92).
[2] **Documents concerning the accession of the Hellenic Republic, the Kingdom of Spain and the Portuguese Republic**
The following paragraph is added to Article 25:
'5.   The provisions of paragraphs 1-4 above still apply in the same way in the case of the accession of the Hellenic Republic, the Kingdom of Spain and of the Portuguese Republic.'
(OJ L 302, 15.11.1985, p. 165).

9 List of Cases

ACEC/Berliet [1968] CMLR D35

AEG Telefunken v Commission (107/82) [1983] ECR 3151

Ahlstroem Oy v Commission (89/85 *et al.*) [1988] 4 CMLR 901

Ahlstroem, A., Oy and others v Commission (re Woodpulp Cartel), (C-89/85 etc.) [1993] ECR I-1307

AKZO Chemie BV, Commission Decision, OJ December 1985 L374/1

AKZO Chemie BV v Commission (53/85) [1987] 1 CMLR 231

AKZO Chemie BV v Commission (62/86) [1991] ECR I-3359

Allen & Hanburys Ltd v Generics (UK) Ltd (434/85) [1988] ECR 1245, [1989] 1 WLR 414

Alsatel Société Alsacienne et Lorraine de Télécommunications et d'Eléctronique v Novasam SA (247/86) [1988] ECR 5987

AM & S Europe v Commission (155/79) [1982] ECR 1575

Anne Marty SA v Estée Lauder SA (37/79) [1981] ECR 2481

AOIP/Beyrard [1976] 1 CMLR D14

Application des Gaz SA v Falks Veritas [1974] 3 All ER 51

Argyll Group plc v The Distillers Company plc and Guinness plc [1986] 1 CMLR 764, 1987 SLT 514

Automec Srl v Commission (T-64/89) [1990] ECR II-0367

Automec v Commission (No. 2) (T-24/90), [1992] ECR II-2223

BAT and Reynolds v Commission (142 & 156/84) [1987] ECR 4487

Bayer AG v Sullhofer (65/86) [1988] ECR 5249

Bayerische HNL Vermehrungsbetriebe GmbH & Co. KG v Council and Commission of the EC (83 and 94/76, 4, 15 and 40/77) [1978] ECR 1209

B & I/Sealink, Commission decision, Press Release IP(92) 478; [1992] 5 CMLR 255

BASF v Commission [1992] ECR II-315, [1992] 4 CMLR 357

Béton de France [1995] 2 ECLR R-45

Boehringer Mannheim GmbH v Commission (45/69) [1970] ECR 769

Boeringer v Commission (7/72) [1972] ECR 1281

Bourgoin v Ministry of Agriculture, Fisheries and Food [1986] QB 716

Boussois/Interpane, Commission Decision, OJ February 1987

BP v Commission (77/77) [1978] ECR 1511

Brass Band Instruments/Boosey & Hawkes, Commission Decision (87/500), OJ 1987 L 286/36

Brasserie de Haecht v Wilkin (23/67) [1967] ECR 407

Brasserie de Haecht v Wilkin (No. 2) (48/72) [1973] ECR 77

British Leyland v Armstrong [1986] AC 577

BRT v SV SABAM (127/73) [1974] ECR 51

Bureau European des Unions de Consommateurs and NCC v Commission (T-37/92) [1994] ECR II-0285

Camera Care v Commission (792/79R) [1980] 1 ECR 119

Cartonboard Cartel 1994 OJ L243/1

CBEM/CLT (311/84) [1985] ECR 3261

Centrafarm v Sterling (15/74) [1974] ECR 1147

Chiron Corporation and others v Organon Teknika Ltd and others [1992] 3 CMLR 813

10   Glossary

Absolute territorial protection

A clause in a distribution agreement whereby a supplier agrees not to supply to others who will sell in the same territory as the first buyer. This is usually accompanied by another clause in the agreement, defining the territory within which the first buyer will operate. This type of protection may involve a ban on passive as well as active sales.

Chiselling

When an individual covertly undercuts the prices agreed by an unlawful cartel of producers/ sellers. It is sometimes suggested that the likelihood of chiselling is so great that cartels do not pose a long-term threat to competition. Since, the theory goes, the cartel members are necessarily prepared to act in an underhand fashion and rip off their customers (in the form of agreed higher prices), they will feel little hesitation in ripping off their fellow cartel members (e.g. by offering secret discounts to customers) and thereby increasing their market share.

Competition

A perfectly competitive market is unattainable in practice. It is a situation towards which one can aim without ever getting there. In a competitive market, no single producer can influence the price of the product — there are enough competitors or competing products to ensure that the quantity sold by a producer does not affect the price. The lack of influence which an individual firm has in a competitive market is best illustrated by the demand curve for a firm in a competitive industry (see **Figure 10A** below). This shows that for this firm there is effectively a set price for the product. As long as it does not try to sell above this price, it can sell as much of the product as it can produce. Once it puts its price above the level indicated, it will sell nothing as there are plenty of available and acceptable substitutes around. Note that for a competitive *industry*, the demand curve will be like that in **Figure 10B** (see demand curve over). See also **Marginal costs and revenue, Figure 10C.**

Figure 10A — Output of a firm in a competitive industry

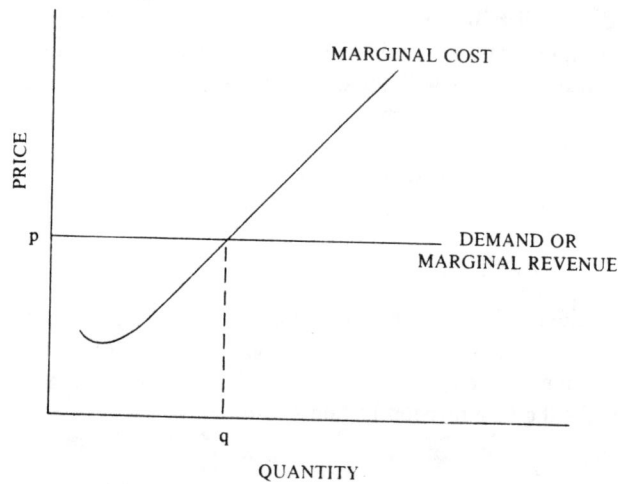

115

Demand curve

Economists are often concerned about the 'demand' for a product. When determining levels of demand, a demand curve is usually constructed. This is simply a graph illustrating the relationship between the number of items that a consumer will buy and the price charged for the item. The demand curve is usually on a negative slope (see **Figure 10B**) because the more you get, the less you want. For example, as the price of coats drops, so the number of coats sold increases, but if you bought, say, two coats at £100 each, you are unlikely to buy yourself another coat unless the price drops. Thus, in order to sell more coats, the seller has to reduce the price. If he charges £150, you'll buy one; if he drops the price to £100, you'll buy two; but you'll only buy three if he drops the price to £70.

Figure 10B — The demand curve

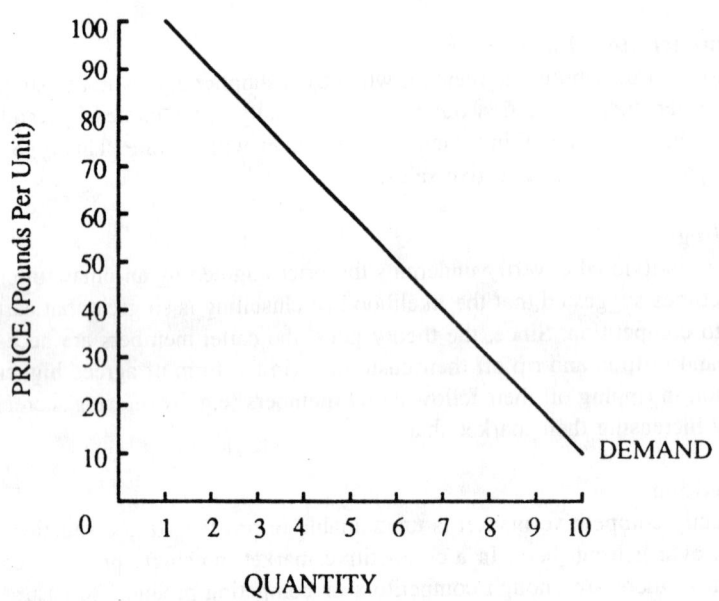

DG IV

The department of the Commission which deals with competition matters, especially investigations.

Exclusionary rebates and discounts

Fidelity rebates (i.e. keep buying from me and you get a rebate); rebates based on improving your volume of purchases from a particular supplier above last year's levels. Basically, financial incentives to stay with a particular supplier and even buy more of his product. These tactics tie up distributors and make it difficult for other suppliers to find an outlet for their products.

Exclusive dealer/distributor

This is an independent distributor who agrees to stock the goods of a particular supplier in return for a promise that the supplier will not supply those goods to another distributor within a defined territory. The distributor is restricted to that territory for his sales. The distributor may also agree to stock the full range of the supplier's goods and not to stock any competing products. Such agreements are regarded by the European Commission as having competitive advantages in certain circumstances — this has lead the Commission to issue block exemptions in this field, notably Regulation 1983/83.

Exclusive purchase

Originally exclusive distribution and exclusive purchasing were treated by the Commission as a single form of business conduct — exclusive dealing (see Regulation 67/67). Since 1983, two block exemptions have existed in this field, with Regulation 1984/83 covering exclusive purchasing agreements. As the Commission has observed,

Regulations ... 1983/83 and ... 1984/83 are both concerned with exclusive agreements between two undertakings for the purpose of the resale of goods.

In an exclusive purchase agreement, the purchaser (or reseller) agrees to buy the relevant goods only from that supplier. Unlike exclusive distribution, the purchaser has no exclusive territory and this has two effects. First, the supplier can supply the same goods to others operating in the vicinity of the exclusive purchaser; secondly, the purchaser is not restricted to a particular area for his sales efforts.

Two particular types of exclusive purchase agreement which are especially dealt with in Regulation 1984/83 are those for the supply of beer in pubs etc. and for petrol in service stations.

Export bans
A contract clause forbidding the purchaser from reselling outside his territory (which may be anything from a 100-metre radius around his shop to the territory of a member state). Such bans may be on active sales only or passive sales, or both. A ban on active sales outside one's territory would prevent the opening of additional shops, for example. A ban on passive sales would prevent one from selling to a customer who came in from outside the allotted territory.

Horizontal agreement
Simply an agreement between companies operating at the same level of the market, e.g. manufacturers (as in *ICI* v *Commission* (1969)). Compare **Vertical agreement.**

Marginal costs and revenue
These terms refer to the additional costs incurred or revenue raised by producing and selling each additional item. Profits are maximised if one sells the quantity at the price indicated by the place where marginal costs and revenue are equal. See **Figure 10C**.

Figure 10C — Profit maximisation by a firm

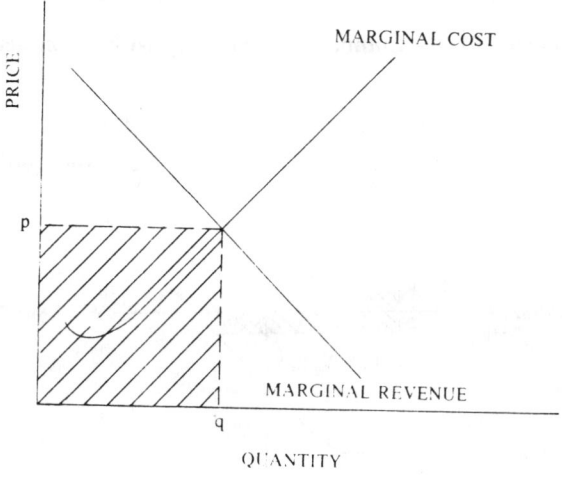

Market share analysis
When determining, for example, whether a company has a dominant position in a market (for use in proceedings under Article 86, EC Treaty), it is necessary to decide on the nature of both the product market and the geographical market. In *United Brands* v *Commission* (1976) the relevant product was bananas, not all soft fruits and certainly not all fruits; in *Michelin* v *Commission* (1981) the relevant product was tyres for heavy trucks, not all truck tyres and not all motor vehicle tyres. The geographical market in *Michelin* was the Netherlands, rather than, say, the Benelux countries; in *United Brands* sales of bananas in France, the UK and Italy were excluded from consideration because of different trading conditions from the other six Member States.

Once the relevant product and geographical markets have been determined, one can gather evidence on the percentage share (either in terms of finance or volume) of that market held by the suspect firm. This is commonly used by the Commission as an indicator of the presence (or absence) of a dominant position. In *United Brands,* the company was found to possess a significant market share and hold a dominant position, even though for at least some of the time it had been incurring losses.

Monopoly

In very simple terms, a monopolist has freedom to charge a price he chooses for his product and (usually) sell less of it, regardless of his competitors' actions and the demands of consumers — he is independent of the other 'players' in that market. One evil of such domination, according to economic theory, is that resources will be misused — higher prices will be charged by the monopolist and some potential customers will either go unsatisfied or will buy inappropriate substitutes. Either way, there is an inefficient allocation of resources ('welfare loss'). Also, the lack of any competition means that the monopolist has less incentive to improve his product or be innovative — this is a disadvantage to consumers.

Some economists argue that monopolies are not necessarily all bad. For example, the greater profits generated may lead both directly and indirectly to more investment in research and development, either by the monopolist or by potential competitors who would like to enter the market.

Figure 10D represents the situation in a perfect monopoly. Note that price and quantity are determined by the spot where marginal costs equal marginal revenue (because this is where profits are maximised). In a competitive industry, marginal revenue and the demand curve are the same so that demand is satisfied. In a monopoly the marginal revenue is always lower than the demand so that when the monopolist maximises profits there is an unsatisfied demand.

The EC prohibits abuse, but not the mere attainment, of a dominant position. Dominant position is not necessarily the same as a monopoly — if a company has a monopoly, then almost certainly it will have a dominant position; but there have been cases in the EC where a company does not seem to have a monopoly but has nevertheless been held to be dominant (see *United Brands* v *Commission* (1976)).

Figure 10D — Comparing monopoly with a competitive industry

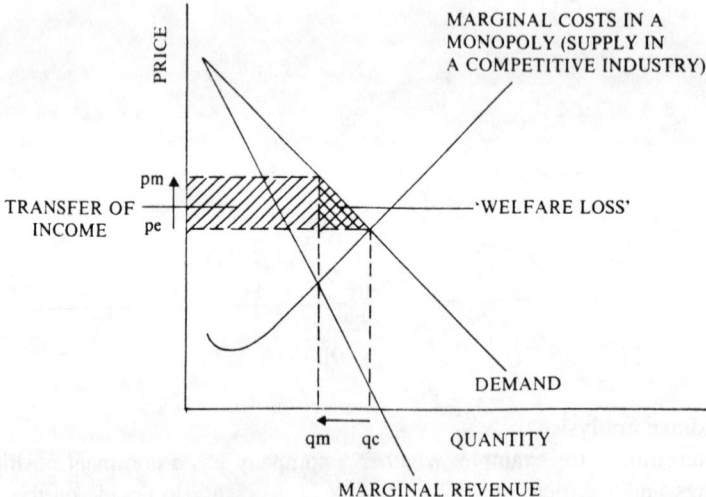

New agreement

One made since March 1962, when the competition rules took effect. Alternatively, one made after the date of accession of a Member State if one of the parties operates in the new Member State and the agreement took effect there. They are specifically dealt with in Article 4, Regulation 17/62, and should be compared with **'old' agreements.**

Non-challenge clause

Basically, this concerns the licensing of intellectual property rights (e.g. patents). (See, e.g., *Bayer* v *Sullhofer* (1986).) The licensor permits the licensee to have access to his patent and manufacture the patented goods, subject to the requirement not to challenge the grant of the patent to the licensor. A licensee might want to do this because, if he could show the patent was invalid, he could make the goods without having to pay a royalty to the licensor. This type of clause is often seen as anti-competitive, although it may not be where the patent licence was granted compulsorily rather than voluntarily.

Non-competition clause

A contract clause requiring one party not to compete with the other or sometimes with third parties. An example is a standard franchise agreement. It may last for the duration of the agreement or extend beyond the lifetime of the agreement. Essentially, the longer it lasts, the more it is likely to be regarded as anti-competitive. Such clauses were considered by the Court of Justice in the *Kai Ottung* case (1989) in the context of a licence for a patented invention. The Court observed that if the licensee was prohibited from manufacture and marketing after termination of the licence, he would be at a disadvantage because, once the patent had expired, others would be free to make and market the product. In such circumstances, the clause would be anti-competitive. It might be saved, though, if the clause were limited in time to the duration of the patent. See also Regulation 2349/84, the block exemption on patent licences.

Old agreement

One which was made between undertakings prior to March 1962 and therefore predated the operation of the EC competition rules. See Article 5 of Regulation 17/62.

Predatory pricing

This is the name given to a theory that a company will reduce the price of its product to below its marginal costs (i.e. deliberately make a loss on each sale) in order to attract many customers to it. In order for its competitors to survive, they too will have to slash prices and face losses. Sooner or later, one of the companies will either go out of business or get out of that product. Either way, that leaves the market free of competition for the survivor who can then charge a monopoly price for the product. After a while, the survivor will recoup his losses and start to make monopoly profits.

This theory has been the subject of some debate. Some economists consider that the theory is unrealistic — once monopoly prices were charged, other companies would be attracted to enter the market. The consequences would then be a drop in price towards that originally charged and the survivor would be unable to recoup the losses in full or make monopoly profits. These views seem to be accepted in the USA (see e.g, *Matsushita Electrical Industries Co.* v *Zenith Radio Corp.* (1986)). In the European Community, predatory behaviour (including pricing policy) is acknowledged as a fact. See, e.g., the investigation of AKZO Chemie by the European Commission (1986), and the 1989 report on predatory pricing by the OECD.

Price fixing

Price fixing has traditionally been condemned by both the Commission and the ECJ. They are often concerned with agreements between competitors (i.e. horizontal agreements or cartels) to sell their products at the same prices — this may occur with homogenous products (like chemical dyes) or similar products (like personal stereos). Such agreements usually cover the whole range of the parties' relevant products. The theory is that such agreements are anti-competitive because the consumer cannot benefit from competition on prices — he cannot purchase the goods cheaper in the store down the road. If the Commission finds competitors even exchanging information about their respective future prices, it may suspect (at the least) a concerted practice which infringes Article 85.

Such horizontal agreements may occur at the level of manufacturers (see, e.g., *ICI* v *Commission* (1969); *Ahlstrom Oy* v *Commission* (1985)); or distributors; or retailers. The economic impact of a similar (but vertical) agreement between, say, a manufacturer and one of its distributors to fix the resale prices for the distributor is likely to be less than if all distributors of competing products agree on prices

— that single distributor will face price competition from other distributors. One can distinguish vertical agreements from horizontal ones and argue that price fixing is less significant in vertical arrangements.

However, one manufacturer may fix the resale prices for all of its distributors — this entirely removes competition on prices for that product, although it may still face such competition from distributors of substitute products. This control over resale prices is still forbidden by the Commission and the ECJ, and they will be alert to find even indirect control being exercised over prices. See, for example, *Pronuptia de Paris* (1986), where the ECJ stated that for a franchisor to *merely* recommend prices to its franchisee was acceptable; what would infringe Article 85 would be where a concerted practice existed between franchisor and franchisee (vertical) or between franchisees (horizontal) to apply the 'recommended' prices as actual prices. A concerted practice of this sort between franchisor and franchisee might be found to exist where the franchisor maintained control over the franchisee's publicity and promotional material (including statements about prices). See also **Chiselling**.

Product market
See **Market share analysis**.

Provisional validity
A term applied to 'old' agreements, referring to a form of prima facie legality which they have. See Regulation 17/62.

Royalties
Often used in patent licences. Considered by the Court of Justice in *Kai Ottung* (1989) where it was held that generally a royalty clause which required payments to continue after expiry of the patent would infringe Article 85(1). However, if the licensee could freely terminate the licence agreement on reasonable notice, an obligation to continue paying for the duration of the licence (i.e. for an indeterminate period) was not prohibited by Article 85(1).

Ties
The notion that a seller with market power can force an unwilling buyer to buy more products than are actually wanted. So if seller S has a monopoly in, say, nail guns (maybe a patent for them) and requires every purchaser of nail guns to buy their supply of nails from him too, even though they could get the nails from another supplier, this represents a tie-in. This type of requirement is often seen as anti-competitive.

Vertical agreement
An agreement made between undertakings operating at different levels of the market, e.g. a manufacturer makes an agreement with a distributor to distribute his products.

11 Bibliography

11.1 Periodical Reports and Journals (English Language)

Common Market Law Reports (much more up-to-date than the European Court Reports), published by European Law Centre Ltd monthly. Has a special series devoted to competition matters. Reports cases in the Court of Justice and cases in national courts which have a EC significance.

Common Market Law Review, covers the whole spectrum of Community affairs; often very good articles on competition matters.

European Competition Law Review, good articles on competition and free movement of goods; good case digests.

European Court Reports (official law reports of the Court of Justice), English-language version is always about two years behind; off-prints of individual cases are usually available from the Court (usually in French) after date of judgment until publication in the ECR.

European Intellectual Property Review, a specialist journal which deals with Community competition matters via case summaries, reports of Community press releases, articles. Also deals with issues concerning free movement of goods.

Official Journal (often abbreviated to OJ, or JO in French texts), this is the organ through which official announcements are made. These may be formal notices in a competition investigation, a declaration of a decision to exempt a company from Article 85(1), or other, legislative, matters. Series L covers the legislation of the Community, divided into those measures which must be published and those which need not be but are published; Series C covers everything else.

11.2 Books

There are both specialist and general books which deal with EC competition law. In the following selection, (G) indicates a book containing a section on competition law, (S) indicates a book devoted to competition law.

Bellamy and Child, *Common Market Law of Competition* 4th edn, 1993, Sweet & Maxwell. (S)
Goyder, J., *EEC Competition Law*, 1988, Oxford University Press. (S)
Green, N., *Commercial Agreements and Competition Law*, 1986, Graham & Trotman. (S)
Hawk, B., *United States, Common Market and International Antitrust — a Comparative Guide* (especially vol. II), Law & Business Inc./Harcourt Brace Jovanovich. (S)
Kapteyn and Verloren van Themaat, *Introduction to the Law of the European Communities: after the coming into force of the Single European Act*, 1989, Kluwer Publishers. (G)
Korah, V., *An Introductory Guide to EEC Competition Law and Practice* 4th edn, 1990, ESC Publishers. (S)

Slot, P.-J., and McDonnell, A. (eds), *Procedure and Enforcement in EC and US Competition Law*, 1993, Sweet & Maxwell. (S)

Steiner, J., *Textbook on EC Law,* 3rd edn, 1992, Blackstone Press. (G)

Van Bael, I. and Bellis, J.-F., *Competition Law of the EEC,* 2nd edn, 1990, CCH Illinois. (S)

Vaughan, D. (ed.), *Law of the European Communities,* 2 vols, 1986, Butterworths. (G)

Weatherill, S. and Beaumont, P., *EC Law*, 1993, Penguin. (G)

Whish, R., *Competition Law,* 3rd edn, 1993, Butterworths. (S)

Wyatt and Dashwood, *The Substantive Law of the EEC* 3rd edn, 1987, Sweet & Maxwell. (G)

11.3   Journal Articles

Easterbrook, Frank H., On identifying exclusionary conduct, [1986] Notre Dame LR 972: an article by a judge on the 7th Circuit Court of Appeals; a radical look at the abuse of a dominant position in US terms.

Farr, Sebastian, Abuse of a Dominant Position — the *Hilti* case [1992] 4 ECLR 174.

Fox, Eleanor M., Monopolization and dominance in the United States and the European Community: efficiency, opportunity and fairness, [1986] Notre Dame 981: a good comparative study, of use when looking at Article 86, EC Treaty.

Furse, Mark, Fines and the Commission's discretion [1995] ECLR 110.

Green, Nicholas, Article 85 in perspective: stretching jurisdiction, narrowing the concept of a restriction and plugging a few gaps, [1988] ECLR 190: looks at actual and potential developments in the application of Article 85.

Hawk, Barry, The American (anti-trust) revolution: lessons for the EEC? [1988] ECLR 53: deals with the changes in competition law enforcement in the USA caused by new economic ideas, and their potential impact for the European Community.

Maitland-Walker, Julian, A Step Closer to a Definitive Ruling on a Right in Damages for Breach of the EC Competition Rules (1992) 1 ECLR 3.

Oliver, Peter, Enforcing Community rights in the English Courts, (1987) 50 MLR 881: looks at some aspects of the use of EC rights in English courts. One case dealt with in some detail is *Bourgoin* v *MAFF* (1986).

Robertson, Aiden and Williams, Mark, An Ice-Cream War: The Law and Economics of Freezer Exclusivity [1995] 1 ECLR 7.

Smith, Helen, The *Francovich* Case: State Liability and the Individual's Right to Damages [1992] 3 ECLR 129.

Steiner, Josephine, How to make the action suit the case — domestic remedies for breach of EEC Law, (1987) 12 *European Law Review* 102: examination of the remedies available in English courts when an alleged breach of EC law is used as a cause of action.

Van Bael, IVO, Fining à la carte: the lottery of EU competition law [1995] 4 ECLR 237.

Whish, Richard, The enforcement of EC competition law in the domestic courts of Member States, (1994) 2 ECLR 60.

11.4   Other Sources

Areeda & Turner, *Antitrust Law: an analysis of antitrust principles and their application:* regarded as an authority on the economic thinking behind the laws on competition; an American work.

Bork, R., *The Antitrust Paradox:* further reading on American challenges to traditional economic thinking; a representative of the 'Chicago' school of economic theory.

Celex: a computer database, available on subscription from the EC itself.

European Commission, *Competition Law in the EEC and in the ECSC:* a collection of the secondary legislation in competition law.

European Communities Legislation Current Status, Butterworth, updated work.

Foster, Nigel, *Blackstone's EC Legislation* 5th edn, 1994, Blackstone Press: an abundance of primary and secondary legislation in the main 'European' areas, including competition and industrial/ intellectual property.

Gellhorn, Ernest, *Antitrust Law and Economics* (in the US 'Nutshell' series): concentrates on competition law and economic theory in the USA but with good, concise sections on basic economic concepts. Available in London through Sweet & Maxwell.

Lexis: another database, supplied by Butterworth Telepublishing and available through their dedicated terminals. Try your Inn library.

Rudden & Wyatt, *Basic Community Laws* 5th edn, 1994, OUP: a materials book containing significant secondary legislation.

12 Flowcharts

The following flowcharts are provided as a quick and simple aid to analysis, when using the competition rules. You may find it useful to see if you can improve them or devise new ones.

12.1 Is the Behaviour Prohibited by Article 85(1)?

START

| Is this an agreement between undertakings? | →NO→ | Is this a decision by associations of undertakings? | →NO→ | Is it a concerted practice? | →NO→ | The activity is outside the scope of Article 85(1) |

YES ↓   YES ↓   YES ↓

May it affect trade between Member States?   NO →

YES ↓

| Is its object the prevention, restriction or distortion of competition within the common market? | →NO→ | Is its effect the prevention, restriction or distortion of competition within the common market? | NO → |

YES ↓   YES ↓

Prima facie, the agreement is prohibited by Article 85(1)

12.2   Is the Behaviour Rendered Void by Article 85(2)?

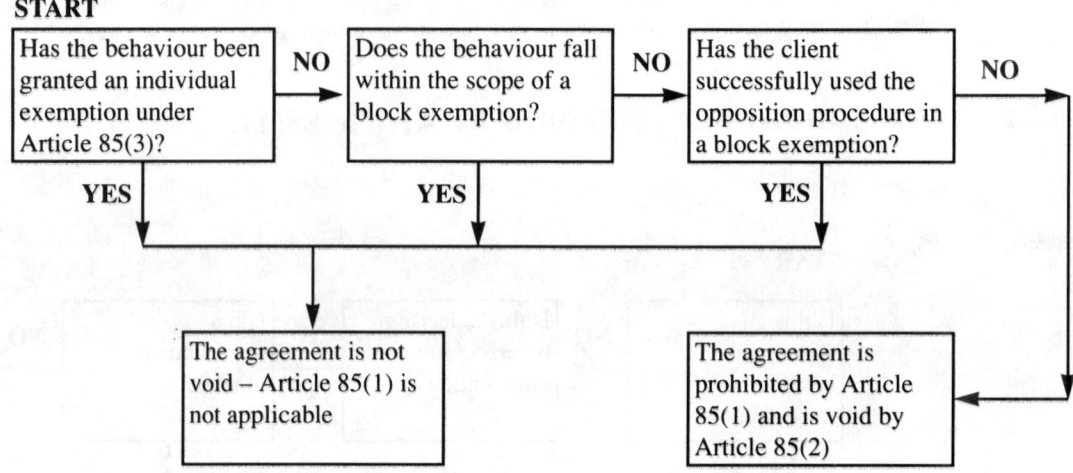

12.3   Individual Exemption: Article 85(3)

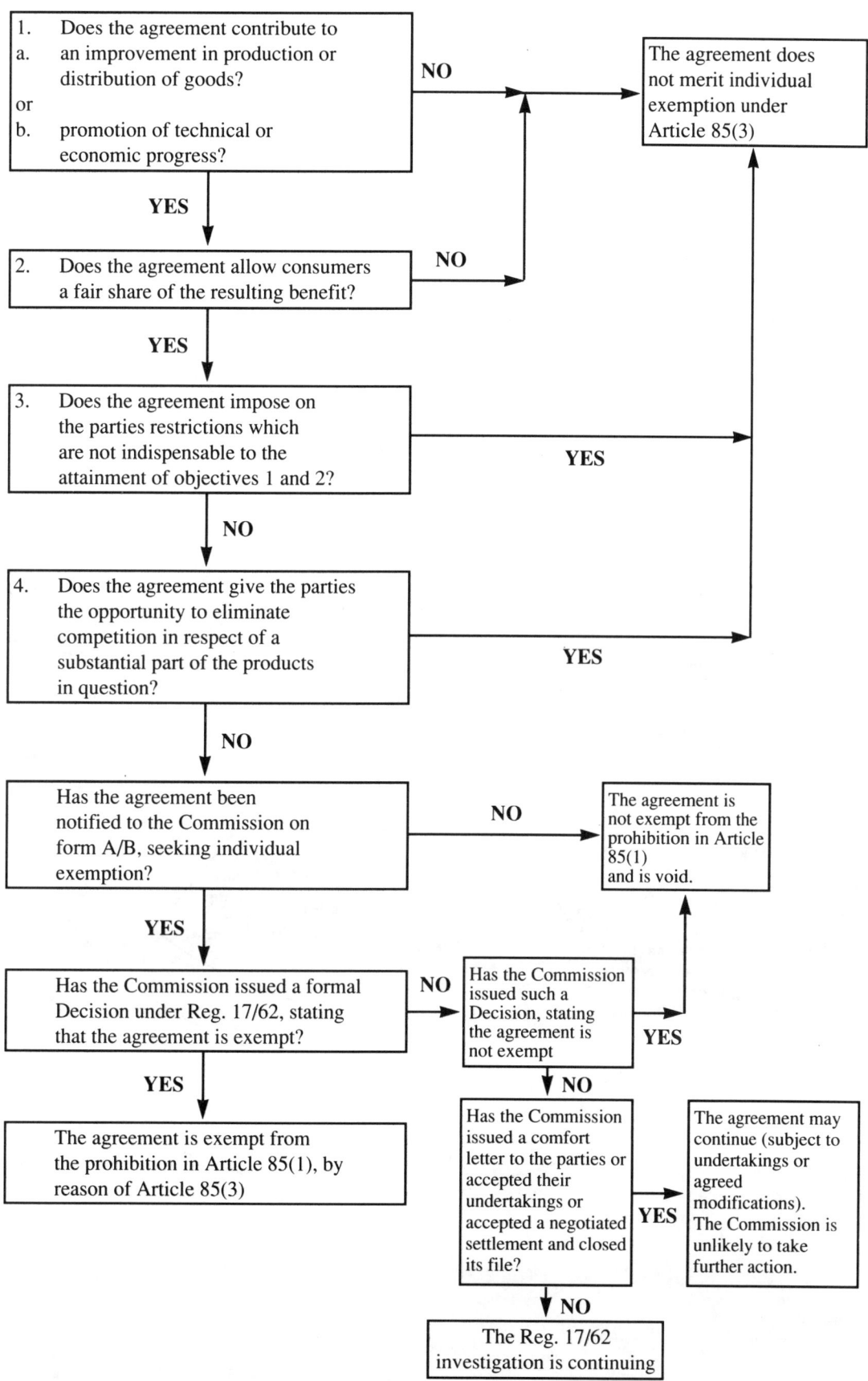

START

1. Does the agreement contribute to
a. an improvement in production or distribution of goods?
or
b. promotion of technical or economic progress?

— **NO** →

The agreement does not merit individual exemption under Article 85(3)

YES ↓

2. Does the agreement allow consumers a fair share of the resulting benefit?

— **NO** →

YES ↓

3. Does the agreement impose on the parties restrictions which are not indispensable to the attainment of objectives 1 and 2?

— **YES** →

NO ↓

4. Does the agreement give the parties the opportunity to eliminate competition in respect of a substantial part of the products in question?

— **YES** →

NO ↓

Has the agreement been notified to the Commission on form A/B, seeking individual exemption?

— **NO** →

The agreement is not exempt from the prohibition in Article 85(1) and is void.

YES ↓

Has the Commission issued a formal Decision under Reg. 17/62, stating that the agreement is exempt?

— **NO** →

Has the Commission issued such a Decision, stating the agreement is not exempt

— **YES** →

YES ↓

The agreement is exempt from the prohibition in Article 85(1), by reason of Article 85(3)

NO ↓

Has the Commission issued a comfort letter to the parties or accepted their undertakings or accepted a negotiated settlement and closed its file?

— **YES** →

The agreement may continue (subject to undertakings or agreed modifications). The Commission is unlikely to take further action.

NO ↓

The Reg. 17/62 investigation is continuing

12.4   Effect on Trade between Member States: Article 85(1)

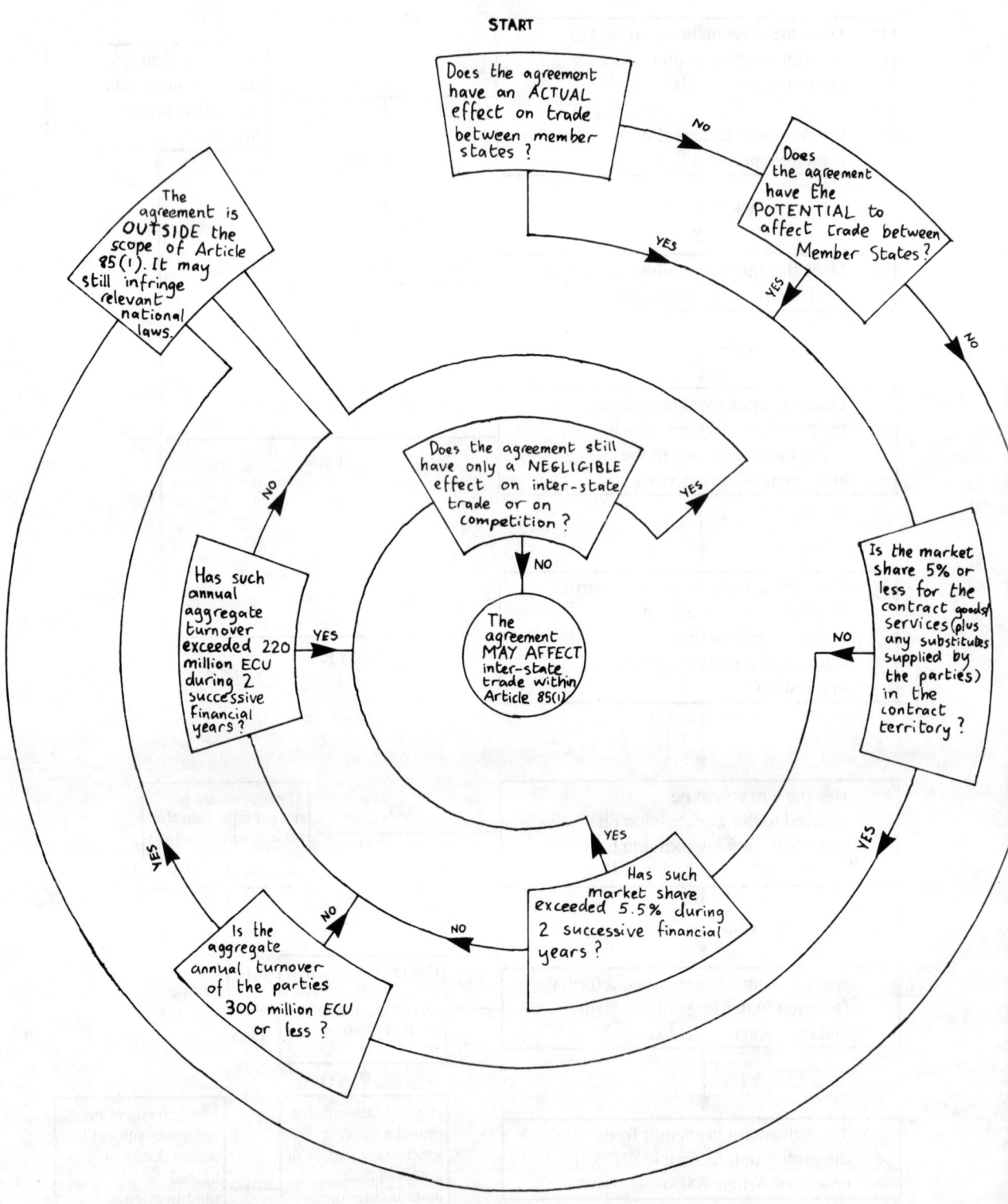

13 Overview of European Community Law

The information which follows is designed only as an introduction to European Community law. It merely outlines the basic concepts, structure and operation of the Community legal order and gives extracts from some source material. An outline of the procedures used to obtain remedies under European Community law can be found in the **Remedies and Practical Background Manual**.

13.1 Why is European Community Law Important to the United Kingdom Practitioner?

European Community law became enforceable law in the United Kingdom by virtue of the European Communities Act 1972 (ECA 1972). Every year, thousands of decisions based on the Community treaties are made by Community institutions which affect the Member States and the lives of their citizens. An individual citizen of a Member State is not only subject to national law but is also affected by European Community law. Practitioners should be well-informed about the Community legal order as well as the national law which affect their clients. For example, in a recent case involving the Tipp-Ex Company, the company was fined for a breach of Community law notwithstanding its illegal action had been approved (wrongly) by their lawyer!

A barrister will be expected to advise on a point of European Community law when it arises in a case, to decide if the client or his opponent can rely on it in their claim or defence and how to deal with the point in the national court or before the European Court of Justice.

A Community law point may arise in a variety of topics with which the ordinary legal practitioner has to deal and is not limited to the commercial sphere only. The practitioner is expected to recognise that a European Community matter has arisen, know where to go to obtain further information about it, how to handle it himself or when to seek specialist advice in relation to it.

13.2 Why and When was the European Community Created and who are its Members?

The European Community grew out of the movement towards international cooperation after World War II. The Council of Europe grew from the same impetus.

The foundations were laid by Robert Schuman, the French Foreign Minister at the time, in his declaration made on 9 May 1950. He set out a plan he and Jean Monnet had devised to combine the European coal and steel industries in a European Community for Coal and Steel. The European Coal and Steel Community (ECSC) was established a year later by the signing of the Treaty of Paris on 18 April 1951 and came into force in 1952.

The European Economic Community and the European Atomic Energy Community (Euratom) were formed by the same original six states (France, Germany, Italy, Belgium, Netherlands, Luxembourg) signing the Treaties of Rome (EEC Treaty and Euratom Treaty) on 25 March 1957.

The United Kingdom, Ireland and Denmark joined on 1 January 1973 and Greece entered in 1981. Spain and Portugal followed in 1986, and most recently Finland, Sweden and Austria, so that total membership is now 15 States.

There is not just one European Community (although from 1 July 1993, the EEC has been known as the European Community. Three separate Communities have existed since the entry into force of the Treaties of Rome, each based on its own foundation treaty. No formal merger of the three Communities has ever taken place although the three share a single Council and a single Commission. Regardless of their differences, the three Communities are regarded as one unit. They share the same basic objectives expressed by the same Member States and share the same legal structure and institutions. All three Communities are by common usage referred to as the European Community. Under the ECSC Treaty the Community has the task of administering the coal and steel industries. The European Atomic Energy Community concerns the utilisation of atomic energy within the Community and research connected with it. Sweden, Finland and Austria are due to become Member States in the near future.

From 1 January 1993, the 12 Member States of the European Community evolved into the 'European Union' (EU) as the result of the Treaty on European Union signed at Maastricht on 7 February 1992. The original EC Treaty of Rome continues in force, though, as amended over the years since 1957, so we need not put aside the idea of the European Community and its laws just yet. (We should also note that the other two 'European' treaties — those establishing the ECSC and Euratom — continue to exist as well.) The Maastricht Treaty made some changes to the EC Treaty but the institutions created in 1957 carry on into the European Union and often continue to derive their functions from the EC Treaty. In particular, Articles B and C of the Maastricht Treaty state that the EU will 'maintain in full', 'respect' and 'build on' the *acquis communautaire* (or the acts of the EC as interpreted and applied since the beginning). The Maastricht Treaty does go further than the Treaty of Rome in one salient respect, though — in Article F the EU states that it will 'respect fundamental rights, as guaranteed by the European Convention for the Protection of Human Rights and Fundamental Freedoms [1950] . . . and as they result from the constitutional traditions common to the Member States, as general principles of Community law'.

Without wishing to confuse the reader too much, we should also remember that on 1 January 1994, the Agreement on a European Economic Area (EEA) came into effect. This brings together, as a single territory, the Member States of the European Community with those countries belonging to the European Free Trade Association (except Switzerland) in many important economic areas, for example free movement of goods and rules governing business competition. Extra institutions have been created for the EEA, together with new rules, but any examination of them in this Manual would make it unduly long and complicated; it should also be remembered that three members of the EFTA subsequently joined the EU (see above).

13.3   What were the Underlying Goals for Creating the European Community?

The underlying goals for creating the European Community are set out in the preamble of the EC Treaty. They are mainly economic but also include social goals, and even political ideals such as laying 'the foundations of an ever closer union among the peoples of Europe' and 'pooling their resources to preserve and strengthen peace and liberty'. These ideals are continued and expanded in the preamble to the Treaty on European Union.

13.4   What is the Task of the European Community and its Sphere of Competence?

The European [Economic] Community was formed to create a single European market uniting the national markets of the Member States and in which goods and services could be offered and sold under common conditions, usually in a free, competitive market.

In order to evolve the common economic market, the national economic policies of the Member States were to be gradually harmonised insofar as they fell within the EC's jurisdiction.

Article 2 of the EC Treaty (as amended) outlines the Community's tasks:

The Community shall have as its task, by establishing a common market and an economic and monetary union and by implementing the common policies or activities referred to in Articles 3 and 3a, to promote throughout the Community a harmonious and balanced development of economic activities, sustainable and non-inflationary growth respecting the environment, a high degree of convergence of economic performance, a high level of employment and of social protection, the raising of the standard of living and quality of life, and economic and social cohesion and solidarity among Member States.

To facilitate the establishment of the market, the Community is to engage in the following activities under Article 3 (as amended):

For the purposes set out in Article 2, the activities of the Community shall include, as provided in this Treaty and in accordance with the timetable set out therein:

(a) the elimination, as between Member States, of customs duties and of quantitative restrictions on the import and export of goods, and of all other measures having equivalent effect;

(b) a common commercial policy;

(c) an internal market characterised by the abolition, as between Member States of obstacles to the free movement of goods, persons, services and capital;

(d) measures concerning the entry and movement of persons in the internal market as provided for in Article 100c;

(e) a common policy in the sphere of agriculture and fisheries;

(f) a common policy in the sphere of transport;

(g) a system ensuring that competition in the internal market is not distorted;

(h) the approximation of the laws of Member States to the extent required for the functioning of the common market;

(i) a policy in the social sphere comprising a European Social Fund;

(j) the strengthening of economic and social cohesion;

(k) a policy in the sphere of the environment;

(l) the strengthening of the competitiveness of Community industry;

(m) the promotion of research and technological development;

(n) encouragement for the establishment and development of trans-European networks;

(o) a contribution to the attainment of a high level of health protection;

(p) a contribution to education and training of quality and to the flowering of the cultures of the Member States;

(q) a policy in the sphere of development cooperation;

(r) the association of the overseas countries and territories in order to increase trade and to promote jointly economic and social development;

(s) a contribution to the strengthening of consumer protection;

(t) measures in the spheres of energy, civil protection and tourism.

These activities are developed in more detail in later provisions of the EC Treaty.

The EC Treaty extends to social matters including inter alia:

(a)   cooperation between Member States on employment, labour law and working conditions, vocational training and social security;

(b)   prevention of occupational accidents and diseases and improvements in occupational hygiene;

(c)   the right of association and collective bargaining between workers and employers (Article 118); and

(d)   equal pay for men and women (Article 119).

The Community has by the EC Treaty assumed competence in all of these areas. However, the founding treaties have not given the Community power to deal with all aspects of national sovereignty so that matters like defence, diplomacy, education and culture remain outside the Community's jurisdiction. Even so, the Community has partial competence in some of these areas (e.g. diplomacy and education).

The Single European Act 1986 (SEA) (Cmnd. 9756, Bull EC suppl. 2/86) amended the EC Treaty. It provided additional objectives and thus enlarged the scope of Community competence. The SEA was signed by all 12 Member States. Incorporation into UK law was brought about by the European Communities (Amendment) Act 1986.

The SEA provided for a formal framework for political cooperation between Member States which had not been covered by the EC Treaty (see below). It set out new goals for economic and monetary cooperation, health and safety of workers, regional policy, research and technological development and environmental protection. It made procedural changes which accelerated progress towards a single internal market by 1992 and moved Member States nearer to European integration. The scope of the Treaty as amended by the SEA was very broad and has been expanded much further by the Treaty on European Union, as can be seen in the amended Article 3 above. The Community has been given competence to deal with important areas of economic and social activity which had hitherto been within the sole competence of Member States.

A Community law point may arise in cases involving any of these areas.

13.5   How are the Tasks Entrusted to the Community Carried Out?

The three Communities share common institutions which carry out their tasks. The major ones are: the European Parliament, the Commission of the European Community, the Council (formerly called the Council of Ministers), the European Court of Justice (ECJ) and the Court of First Instance.

13.5.1   THE FUNCTION AND POWERS OF THE COMMISSION

The Commission, sometimes called the 'guardian of the Treaties', consists of 17 members (Commissioners) who are appointed by the governments of their own Member States and agreed to by all the Member States. They do not represent their own countries as they are supposed to be above national loyalties and their independence should be beyond doubt. In performance of their duties they must 'neither seek nor take instructions from any government or any body'. A breach of this principle by a Commissioner would mean his compulsory retirement which the ECJ would request him to take. The larger Member States (e.g. UK) have two Commissioners, smaller states have one each. See generally Article 157 EC, as inserted by the Treaty on European Union.

The function of the Commission is threefold:

(a)   It is to formulate proposals on any matter provided for under the Treaty (EC Treaty, Articles 152 and 235).

(b)   It acts as the Community watchdog. Article 5 of the EC Treaty states:

Member States shall take all appropriate measures, whether general or particular, to ensure fulfilment of the obligations arising out of this Treaty or resulting from action taken by the institutions of the Community. They shall facilitate the achievement of the Community's tasks.

They shall abstain from any measure which could jeopardise the attainment of the objectives of this Treaty.

The Commission investigates (and takes to the ECJ) any Member State which infringes the EC Treaty, under Article 169 (see Article 169 in the **Remedies and Practical Background Manual, 11.7**). It also has the task of administering and enforcing EC competition policy. It can impose fines and penalties on individuals and companies who are in breach of this policy.

(c) The Commission also acts as the executive branch of the Community. If the Council makes a policy decision, it falls to the Commission to carry it out. This usually means adopting further, detailed, legislation to implement the policy.

13.5.2 THE POWERS AND FUNCTIONS OF THE COUNCIL

The Council ensures the coordination of the general economic policy of the Member States and has the final power to make decisions in the decision-making process of the Community. Its final say is subject usually to consultation with the Parliament. Any legislation it adopts must first, however, be proposed by the Commission.

Each Member State has one member on the Council but the identity of the actual delegate fluctuates and will depend on the topic being decided. The actual member will be the Head of Government for important issues or the appropriate government minister on specialist issues.

As the Council is not a permanent body and meets for only a few days each month, the day-to-day work is done by the Committee of Permanent Representatives, COREPER, and a system of Management Committees.

13.5.3 THE EUROPEAN PARLIAMENT

The European Parliament was originally called the Assembly in the EC Treaty. It has 518 members, including 81 from the UK. It represents the political and other views of all the peoples of the Member States. It does not have the same legislative role as the UK Parliament. Its functions are mainly advisory and supervisory. However, the democratic nature of the Parliament has been strengthened somewhat by the direct election of members to the European Parliament since 1979 and by the SEA (which made procedural amendments such as the cooperation procedure).

The Parliament's powers have been expanded considerably by the Treaty on European Union. For example, Article 189b EC (inserted by the EU Treaty) not only involves the Parliament fully in the procedure for the adoption of an act, but allows Parliament to veto such adoption (i.e. it can prevent proposed legislation from becoming law). Article 189c (an alternative procedure for the adoption of acts) contains no such veto. Under Article 138b (again inserted by the EU Treaty), the Parliament may initiate the legislative process by requesting the Commission to submit proposals on topics that Parliament considers require legislation.

13.6 Why is the Community a Supranational Legal Order?

The Community is often described as a supranational legal order. This is because it is an association of states endowed with autonomous legal authority. Although it was created like a traditional international organisation by international treaties, it is more developed. The same founding documents which established the Community bestowed on it its own sovereign rights and competence. The Community legal system is independent of and superior to those of the Member States. In exchange for membership to the Community, Member States have relinquished some of their own legislative powers and transferred them to the Community institutions which are empowered to enact an autonomous body of Community law. Member States and their citizens are subject to Community law in matters over which the Community has competence. The objectives of the Community are pursued by means of Community legislation and case law and enforced by both the ECJ, the Court of First Instance and the national courts (*Van Gend en Loos* 26/62 [1963] CMLR 105).

13.7 What Powers do the Community Institutions have to Legislate?

The EC Treaty sets out the Community's aims. The Community institutions are left to fill in the details by enacting legislation. As the EC Treaty covers a wide variety of matters, an almost unlimited potential exists for Community legislation (subject to the requirement that the Community institutions may only act within the areas and power laid down by the EC Treaty).

Some Treaty provisions are precise enough not to need further implementation (e.g. the anti-competition rules, Articles 85 and 86). Others specifically call for, or simply require, further measures to be passed. The Council, acting in conjunction with the Commission and the Parliament, has an implicit power to legislate if action by the Community should prove necessary to attain one of the objectives of the Community and the Treaty has not provided the necessary powers (EC Treaty, Article 235).

To facilitate the Community in carrying out its policies towards third countries, the EC Treaty bestows legal personality on the Community (Article 210), enables the Commission to negotiate on its behalf and the Council, after consulting with the Parliament where so required by the Treaty, to conclude Treaties between the Community and third countries or international organisations (Article 228).

By reason of the broad power of the Community institutions to legislate in many areas covered by the EC Treaty, the practitioner has to be constantly alert to keep up to date with the legislation being passed. The best way to do so is through the Official Journal (OJ), published by the Community. Ignorance of EC law is no defence — *Tipp-Ex* case (C-279/87) [1990] ECR 261).

Member States must be vigilant that they are not breaking Community legislation so that an infringement action is not brought against them (see Article 169 in the **Remedies and Practical Background Manual, 11.7**). The practitioner may need to advise on such a matter also.

13.8 How is Legislation Made in the Community?

The legislative process in the Community is based on a division of power between the Commission and the Council. There are only a few cases in which the Commission alone may exercise legislative power. In most cases the Commission proposes and the Council disposes. Before the Council can take a final decision, depending on the subject-matter of the measure, it has to consult the Parliament and sometimes the Economic and Social Committee.

Although the Council is in the strongest position in the decision-making process, the Commission has some tactical advantages. No decision can be taken by the Council without the Commission taking the initiative by proposing the draft Community measure in question. The Commission can amend its proposal up to the time the final decision is made; the Council can only do so by unanimous vote.

13.9 What Kind of Legislative Measures can the Community Institutions Make?

The legislative measures or acts which the Community institutions have power to enact are regulations, directives, decisions, recommendations and opinions. Only the first three are legally binding. All five are described in EC Treaty, Article 189:

In order to carry out their task and in accordance with the provisions of the Treaty, the European Parliament acting jointly with the Council and the Commission shall make regulations and issue directives, take decisions, make recommendations or deliver opinions.

A regulation shall have general application. It shall be binding in its entirety and directly applicable in all Member States.

A directive shall be binding, as to the result to be achieved, upon each Member State to which it is addressed, but shall leave to the national authorities the choice of form and methods. A decision shall be binding in its entirety upon those to whom it is addressed.

Recommendations and opinions shall have no binding force.

A Regulation is best described as a normative measure, laying down general rules which apply to anyone who falls within their scope (like a public Act of Parliament in the UK). They do not need additional implementation to take effect.

A directive may be addressed to all Member States, or an individual Member State. It requires implementation by the Member State(s) before it has the force of law, unless it meets the criteria for direct effect. See **Chapter 15**. The method of implementation is left to the Member State but the result to be achieved is binding.

A decision is an individual act addressed to a specific person or to a Member State. It has the force of law without further enactment. Its nature is essentially administrative, usually affecting just the addressees. It can have judicial undertones, too — see Article 173 in the **Remedies and Practical Background Manual, 11.3**.

The EC Treaty lays down safeguards in the adoption of these measures. The measures must state the reasons on which they are based and refer to any proposals or opinions which were required to be obtained by the Treaty (Article 190). Any act which fails to follow this procedural requirement is at risk of annulment (see Article 173 in the **Remedies and Practical Background Manual, 11.3**). Another safeguard is publication: see Article 191 for details.

Despite Article 189, the ECJ has held that the true nature of an act is determined by its substance and object, and not its form and label (*Confédération Nationale des Producteurs de Fruits et Legumes* v *Council,* Cases 16 and 17/62 [1963] CMLR 160); *International Fruit Co. NV v Commission (No. 1),* Cases 41-4/70 [1975] 2 CMLR 515). The ECJ will re-classify specific measures according to their nature, as distinct from the description applied by the Commission or Council. The ECJ has also developed a category of EC acts which are *sui generis* and not in Article 189 at all. (See the ERTA case.)

13.10   What are the Sources of Community Law?

The sources of law, in the sense of the legal rules that form the Community legal order and bind the Community, its institutions, the Member States and (in some instances) individuals, are the following: the founding treaties; the legal acts of the Community; international agreements entered into by the Community institutions on behalf of the Community; the judgments of the ECJ (and the Court of First Instance) and general principles of law. Member States are obliged by Article 5 (see **13.5.1** above) to 'take all appropriate measures, whether general or particular, to ensure fulfilment' of the obligations which these sources of law impose.

13.10.1   THE FOUNDING TREATIES

The founding treaties are a primary source of Community law. They were created directly by the Member States themselves. They are the EC Treaty and Protocols as amended by subsequent Treaties: the Merger Treaty 1965; Acts of Accession 1972 (UK, Ireland, Denmark), 1979 (Greece), 1985 (Spain, Portugal); Budgetary Treaties 1970, 1975; Single European Act 1986 and the (Maastricht) Treaty on European Union 1992. They form a constitutional skeleton for the Community by setting out the objectives of the Community, its mechanisms, the timetable within which the objectives are to be achieved, and setting up its institutions and conferring on them legislative and administrative powers.

13.10.2 COMMUNITY ACTS: THE SECONDARY LEGISLATION OF THE COMMUNITY

The acts of Community institutions form an important source of Community law (see **13.9**). Note that:

(a) Regulations are directly applicable in national legal systems and apply throughout the Community in all the Member States. Many have direct effect, conferring rights and duties on individuals who can rely on them in the same way as domestic law in their national courts. Unlike national law, however, they have not been passed by the national legislature.

(b) Directives are often used for coordinating the laws of Member States (EC Treaty, Article 100). Member States are obliged to introduce new legislation or redraft or amend existing national legislation and administrative rules to conform to the objectives of a directive. They may have direct effect in certain circumstances.

(c) Decisions are administrative measures. Sometimes the Community institutions themselves are responsible for implementing the treaties or regulations. They can make decisions binding on individuals, firms or Member States. A directive usually requires the addressee to perform some action or refrain therefrom. It also may confer rights or impose obligations on those to whom it is addressed.

13.10.3 INTERNATIONAL AGREEMENTS BETWEEN THE EC AND NON-MEMBER STATES ETC.

The international agreements that the Community enters into with non-Member States and other international organisations on behalf of the Community are a third source of Community law. Such agreements may be new, such as the Rome Convention 1979, or existing agreements for which the Community takes responsibility from Member States on their accession to the Community, such as the General Agreement on Tariffs and Trade (GATT). This agreement was established before the Community existed, but all the Member States were parties to it and it concerned matters over which the Community has competence. 'In so far as the Community has assumed the powers previously exercised by Member States in the area governed by the General Agreement, the provisions of that agreement have the effect of binding the Community' (*Third International Fruit Company* case (Cases 21-4/72 [1972] ECR 1439, para. 18).

13.10.4 INTERNATIONAL AGREEMENTS BETWEEN MEMBER STATES

International agreements between Member States may be concluded on any topic, within or without the scope of the Community law only if their subject-matter is within the jurisdiction of the Community, as defined by the Treaty of Rome and subsequent legislation.

Member States may be under an obligation to reach agreement on a topic as part of a programme determined by the Treaty of Rome. In certain cases these additional conventions are intended to supplement its provisions. For example, EC Treaty, Article 220 enables the Member States to enter into treaties and conventions on specific matters listed in the Article. Two conventions have been concluded: one on the Mutual Recognition of Companies and Legal Persons and a second, on Jurisdiction and the Enforcement of Judgments in Civil and Commercial Matters (both 1968). These agreements will be regarded as Community law.

Alternatively, the States may achieve a binding consensus on a topic entirely of their own choosing. If this has no connection with the work of the Community, then it should not be regarded as a source of Community law. As the Community institutions draw on the fundamental aims and objectives set out in the Treaty of Rome (e.g. in the Single European Act), the topics where Member States have a 'free hand' will be restricted.

In some areas, the Member States seem to have accepted the desirability of broadening the application of European Community law. For example, the Member States have set out to create new intellectual property rights, the Community patent and the Community trademark, which are closely connected to the concept of a single community.

The Treaty of Rome imposes no obligation on Member States to create these new property rights and it might be thought that they are, therefore, no part of Community law. However, the relationship with the Community is clear.

The geographical limit of these intellectual property rights is defined as that of the Community's Member States; the right is described in the agreement as a Community patent (for example). The countries which are involved are all of the existing Member States (and no one else); the European Commission was brought in to advise on the proposed agreement; the European Court of Justice is given jurisdiction over the agreement; and there is a clear connection between the aims of the Community on free movement of goods and services around the common market (and fair competition) and the establishment of a single Community-wide patent together with the single application needed to obtain it. This type of international agreement should clearly be seen as a source of Community law, although subordinate to the Treaty of Rome and its subsequent secondary legislation.

13.11   Judicial Legislation

The entire jurisprudence of the ECJ, including the general principles of law it has recognised and the doctrines it has developed, forms an important source of Community law. This has recently been enlarged by the developing case law of the Court of First Instance.

13.11.1   GENERAL PRINCIPLES OF LAW

The notion of general principles of law has been developed by the ECJ in its judgments; they are often regarded as a separate source of Community law and are based on concepts of law and justice found in most legal systems.

The EC Treaty makes indirect reference to general principles of law in several of its articles. For example:

(a)   Article 164 states that the 'Court of Justice shall ensure that in the interpretation and application of this Treaty the law is observed'. 'Law' here suggests a law which transcends the text of the EC Treaty itself. The practical application of this abstract notion is shown in (b) and (c).

(b)   Article 173 permits the Court of Justice to declare Community acts illegal if, e.g., an act infringes a rule of law relating to the application of the Treaty. This has meant that private or legal persons (if they have locus standi) may challenge a Commission decision on the ground that it infringes a general principle of law, such as equality or legitimate expectations.

(c)   Article 215(2) provides that the non-contractual liability of the Community shall be based on 'the general principles common to the law of the Member States'. For example, the Community is only liable for unlawful acts of a legislative nature (i.e. regulations) if the Court of Justice decides that the act infringed a 'superior rule of law' which was intended to protect the individual, since this is a common basis for state liability for such acts in national courts of the Member States (*Aktien-Zuckerfabrik Schöppenstedt* v *Council*, 5/71 [1971] ECR 975).

(For further information on these articles and on the use of general principles, see the **Remedies and Practical Background Manual, Chapter 11.**)

The particular principles are inspired by those common to the legal systems of Member States and are recognised or developed by the ECJ when required in cases before it. Although the categories of general principles which the ECJ will use are not closed, those which have been considered by the ECJ in its case law, and thus recognised as sources of Community law, have arisen in an *ad hoc* fashion.

(a)   the restrictive nature of the Community's non-contractual liability for legislative acts of its institutions (see *Schöppenstedt*);

(b)   legality in administration (i.e. the institutions comply with the set procedures and act reasonably);

(c)   proportionality: action must be proportionate to the end it seeks to achieve. See *Internationale Handelsgesellschaft*, 11/70 [1970] ECR 1125, and *Bela-Muhle Josef Bergman v Grows-Farm*, 114/76 [1977] ECR 1211;

(d)   legal certainty. See *Germany v Commission*, 44/81 [1982] ECR 1855; *Simmethal*, 92/78 [1979] ECR 77;

(e)   protection of legitimate expectations. See *Amylum v Council*, 108/81 [1982] ECR 2107, para. 4-17 and *CNTA v Commission* 74/74 [1975] ECR 533;

(f)   non-discrimination and equality of treatment. See *Sabbatini v European Parliament*, 20/71 [1972] ECR 345, *Prais v Council* 130/75 [1976] ECR 1589, *Bela-Muhle Josef Bergman v Grows-Farm* 114/76 [1977] ECR 1211;

(g)   entitlement to a hearing. See *Transocean Marine Paint*, 17/74 [1974] ECR 1063;

(h)   professional legal privilege in anti-competition investigations by the Commission. See *AM & S* 155/79 [1982] ECR 1575;

(i)   the right to be assisted by counsel. See *Demont*, 15/80 [1981] ECR 3147;

(j)   the fundamental human rights upon which the constitutional law of Member States is based. See *Stauder v City of Ulm*, 29/69 [1969] ECR 419; *Internationale Handelsgesellschaft*, 11/70 [1970] ECR 1125; *Nold v Commission*, 4/73 [1974] ECR 491.

It is not possible to explain all of these principles here. An explanation of two will illustrate their use.

13.11.1.1   Equality
The principle of equality or non-discrimination means that the Community institutions must treat everyone alike and not make arbitrary distinctions between different groups within the Community. It has been used to challenge decisions of the institutions and staff regulations.

Mrs Sabbatini challenged the Community staff regulation which provided that only 'a head of family' was entitled to an expatriation allowance. The regulation defined this phrase in such a way that only men could receive the allowance. Her claim, based on the general principle of equality, succeeded. Ms Prais challenged the Council's decision to hold a competitive examination on the date of a Jewish festival as religious discrimination. The ECJ held that religious freedom was a general principle of law but on the facts discrimination had not been made out in Ms Prais' case. In *Bela-Muhle Josef Bergman v Grows-Farm* (otherwise known as the *Skimmed Milk Powder* case) the Council passed a measure to force animal feed producers to use skimmed milk in their feed rather than soya. The result of this was to increase the price of animal feed thus harming livestock farmers. The only farmers who benefited from this were dairy farmers as their product was being used in the feedstuffs. The claim that the policy was discriminatory between the two categories of farmers succeeded.

Specific non-discrimination is mentioned in two important EC Treaty Articles. Article 7 prohibits discrimination on the ground of nationality in the application of the Treaty. (This has especially been relied on in relation to the free movement of workers (Article 48) and services (Article 59).) Article 119 provides for equal pay for men and women who do equal work. (Directives also specifically deal with equal treatment between men and women in social security matters, occupational pension schemes and in self-employment.)

13.11.1.2   Human rights
There is no written list of fundamental rights and freedoms in Community law. Some basic rights however are mentioned in the EC Treaty: freedom of movement of workers (Article 48); the right of establishment (Article 52); the freedom to provide services (Article 59); the freedom of movement of goods (Article 9); the right of association (Article 118(1)); the protection of business and professional secrets (Article 214); and numerous prohibitions on discrimination (Articles 7, 48, 52, 60, 85 and 119).

However, the ECJ is still developing the Community's unwritten fundamental rights in its case law.

Stauder was the first case in which it declared that a respect for human rights was a fundamental general principle of Community law that the ECJ would safeguard. In *Internationale Handelsgesellschaft* the ECJ made clear that Community measures would not be judged by the human rights concepts of the national constitutions of Member States, but would be judged by its own concept of human rights. However, Community concepts which the ECJ will protect are those which are common to the constitutions of Member States. These act as inspiration to the development of the Community's concepts (*Nold*). International conventions concerning the protection of human rights to which Member States are parties or have acceded also serve as guidelines for the Community concepts *(Nold)*. In *Rutili* (36/75 [1975] ECR 1219) specific reference in this respect was made to the European Convention on Human Rights.

Examples of human rights concepts that the ECJ has recognised, in addition to the ones which overlap with some of the general principles already listed and discussed above, are the right of ownership, the general right of privacy, freedom to engage in business and to choose and practise a profession, freedom of association, privacy and correspondence.

The ECJ's process of evolving 'European fundamental rights' is a continuing and piecemeal process. The ECJ has been unable to develop rights for all areas in which this might be necessary or desirable because its judgments are confined to the particular cases which are brought before it. In this context, one should see now also Article F of the Treaty on European Union.

14   The Court of Justice of the European Communities

The Treaties, the Statutes of the Court annexed as Protocols to the Treaties, and the Rules of Procedure of the Court provide the framework in which the ECJ operates.

14.1   What is the Jurisdiction of the ECJ?

The supranational aspect of the Community constitution is safeguarded by the ECJ. For the purposes of this chapter, the two courts of the Community — the Court of Justice and the Court of First Instance — have not usually been differentiated. The ECJ ensures that Community law is interpreted and applied uniformly throughout the Member States of the Community. It has sole jurisdiction to decide on the validity of Community legislation. It acts as referee in disputes between the institutions *inter se,* between the Community and Member States, and protects the rights of the individual against the Community bureaucracies, an important role as the democratic element is still quite weak within the Community.

The EC Treaty gives the ECJ a general duty to ensure that, in the interpretation and application of the EC Treaty, Community law is observed (Article 164). This does not mean that the ECJ has a general power to determine any case submitted to it. It has jurisdiction only in the specific topics and procedures which the Treaty has indicated. The kinds of proceedings that may be dealt with by the ECJ are:

(a)   Infringement actions brought against Member States for failing to fulfil their obligations under the EC Treaty or the law derived therefrom (Articles 169-170).

(b)   Annulment actions (Article 173). The ECJ can review the legality of the acts of the institutions on the grounds mentioned in Article 173. If the act is found to be illegal, the ECJ can declare it void (Article 174). The institution concerned is required to take the necessary measures to comply with the ECJ's judgment (Article 176).

(c)   An action for failure of an institution to act (Articles 175 and 176).

(d)   An action for damages for the non-contractual liability of the Community (Articles 178 and 215(2)).

(e)   A reference by a national court or tribunal for a preliminary ruling on the interpretation and validity of Community provisions (Article 177).

(f)   The adjustment of penalties provided for in Council regulations. For example, regulation 17/62 (on competition), allows the ECJ to adjust fines or periodic penalties imposed by the Commission for infringements of the competition rules.

(g)   Staff cases. The ECJ has jurisdiction to resolve disputes between the Community institutions and its servants (Article 179).

(h)   Contractual liability of the Community (Articles 181 and 215). A contract concluded by the Community may give the ECJ jurisdiction to hear disputes arising in relation to the contract.

(i)   Opinions pursuant to Article 228(1) (e.g. the ECJ may give an opinion as to whether a proposed agreement to be concluded by the Community with a third country or international organisation is compatible with EC law).

The more important of these proceedings are dealt with more fully in the **Remedies and Practical Background Manual, Chapter 11.**

The SEA 1986 provided for a Court of First Instance to determine certain classes of action or proceedings brought by national or legal persons. The Court first sat in September 1989. The actions it hears are staff cases, competition and coal and steel cases brought by individuals under Article 173 or 175. Actions started by Member States or the Community institutions and preliminary rulings are expressly excluded from the jurisdiction of the Court of First Instance.

Early indications are that the Court of First Instance will look at the facts in each case in greater detail than often happened in the ECJ. An illustration can be found in the *BASF AG* v *Commission* case (Case T-79/89 etc.) where the annulment of a Commission decision was sought before the Court. The application was dismissed as inadmissible because the decision was so flawed in content and creation as to be legally non-existent thus rendering any annulment unnecessary, The case is now on appeal to the ECJ. The Court of First Instance is perhaps intended to be less 'judicially creative' than the ECJ, although the Decision of the Council which established the Court recited that

in respect of actions requiring close examination of complex facts, the establishment of a second court [Court of First Instance] will improve the judicial protection of individual interests.

14.2   What is the Composition and Organisation of the ECJ?

The ECJ has 13 Judges and six Advocates-General. The qualifications for appointment are similar for both. They must be

persons whose independence is beyond doubt and who possess the qualifications required for appointment to the highest judicial offices in their respective countries or who are jurisconsults of recognised competence. (Article 167.)

Jurisconsults can include academic lawyers. Appointment is 'by common accord of the Governments of the Member States' for a period of six years and is renewable. In practice one Judge is appointed from each Member State and the 13th post is rotated between the different Member States. Every three years there is a partial replacement of six or seven Judges and three Advocates-General. A President of the Court is elected by the Judges themselves.

An Advocate-General is not a Judge but he has equal status. After parties' written and oral submissions have been given in a case and before the Judges deliberate, the Advocates-General appointed to the case gives an Opinion in open court. His Opinion on the case is fully reasoned, impartial and independent and recommends to the Judges the decision to take. It need not be followed by the Judges but it often is. It is published together with the judgment in the law reports and may be cited by counsel and Advocates-General in future cases.

A Judge Rapporteur is chosen by the President of the Court for each case. The Judge Rapporteur has the responsibility of seeing the case through the various stages of the proceedings and preparing reports on the case at different stages. After the Advocate-General's Opinion, the Judge Rapporteur drafts a judgment on which the other Judges deliberate before a final, collective, judgment is reached by them.

The Registrar of the ECJ is responsible for the administration of the court and the reception, transmission and custody of documents relating to the cases.

Cases are decided either in plenary session (i.e. a quorum of seven Judges) or in Chambers of three or five Judges.

The Court of First Instance consists of 12 members, but has no permanent Advocates-General. Instead, any member of the Court may be called upon to perform the task of an Advocate-General in each case (he may not then participate in judging that case). The Court sits in chambers of three or five judges and their decisions may be the subject of an appeal to the ECJ. The First and Second Chambers consist of five judges each, while the Third, Fourth and Fifth Chambers sit with three judges each. The first UK appointment to the Court of First Instance was David Edward QC, a Scots advocate. Following the appointment of Sir Gordon Slynn as a Law Lord, David Edward was appointed as a judge of the ECJ and Christopher Bellamy QC replaced him in the Court of First Instance. The Court seems not to use Advocates-General now.

14.3 What is the Practice and Procedure of the ECJ?

The rules of procedure of the ECJ in relation to its jurisdiction under the EC Treaty can be found in the Protocol on the Statute of the Court of Justice, which is annexed to the EC Treaty, and in the Rules of Procedure of the Court.

The ECJ has jurisdiction over two types of action: direct and indirect. These are explained in more detail in the **Remedies and Practical Background Manual, Chapter 11**. Direct actions commence and end in the ECJ, subject to the work of the Court of First Instance. References for preliminary rulings are indirect actions, which begin and end in the national court. The preliminary ruling of the ECJ is only a step in the proceedings before the national court.

In both types of action greater emphasis is placed on written procedure than oral hearings and the approach at the relatively short oral stage is inquisitorial, not adversarial.

14.3.1 DIRECT ACTIONS

14.3.1.1 Written procedure
Direct actions are initiated by a written application addressed to the President and Members of the ECJ, which is sent to the Registrar of the ECJ. The content of the application is governed by Article 38 of the Rules. Its main function is to define the issues between the parties, set out the grounds on which the application is based, the form of order sought and the nature of evidence relied upon. The Registrar effects service of the documents. The defendant must lodge a defence within a month of the application being served. A default judgment can be obtained. The defendant can contest the admissibility of an action as a preliminary objection by making a separate application to the ECJ. Further optional pleadings can be made, e.g. a reply by the applicant and a rejoinder by the defendant.

14.3.1.2 Fact finding
The ECJ may decide that a preparatory inquiry is necessary to clarify issues of fact. Article 45 of the Rules provides for various 'measures of inquiry', in practice the most usual being written questions devised by the Court and sent to the parties concerned. The parties reply in writing.

14.3.1.3 The oral hearing
A public hearing is held at which oral submissions are made by representatives of the parties. These are relatively short as the Court has already studied the more lengthy written submissions. Members of the Bench sometimes interrupt counsel's speeches to ask questions. Usually their questions are put after all the submissions have been made.

14.3.1.4 The opinion of the Advocate-General
The Advocate-General then delivers his Opinion which can be either *ex tempore* or delivered in open court at a later date.

14.3.1.5 Deliberation and judgment
The Court deliberates in secrecy. Its decision may be taken by majority vote although it is always presented as a collective judgment with all the Judges signing it. No individual judgments, e.g. dissenting judgments, are given. As compromises have to be made this may explain why a judgment (or parts of it) sometimes lacks clarity and cohesion.

A judgment has three parts: the first contains a statement of the facts and a summary of the arguments of the parties; the second contains the reasons for the judgment in numbered paragraphs; and the third is the actual decision. The form of the judgment is terse, formal and abstract like a French court judgment. The short operative third part of the judgment is delivered in open court.

14.3.1.6 Interlocutory relief

The ECJ can provide interlocutory relief (Articles 185 and 186). In practice it is sought most often when a company challenges a Commission decision that the company has infringed the Community rules on competition (*United States* v *Commission*, 27/76 [1976] ECR 425). The rules governing interim measures are found in the Rules of Court (especially Articles 83 and 85) and in ECJ case law (e.g. *Camera Care* v *Commission*, 792/79 [1980] ECR 119, *Ford of Europe Inc and Forde Werke AG* v *Commission*, 228/82 [1982] ECR 3091, *Finsider SPA* v *Commission*, 392/85 [1986] 2 CMLR 290, *Brass Band Instrumets Ltd* v *Boosey and Hawkes Plc* [1988] 4 CMLR 67).

14.3.1.7 Intervention

Member States and institutions of the Community have a right to intervene in proceedings between other parties. Private parties may intervene in an action brought by another private party for annulment, failure to act or for damages, if the private intervener has an interest in the outcome of the case itself (Article 37 of the Statute).

14.3.2 REFERENCES FOR PRELIMINARY RULINGS

Article 20 of the Statute and Article 103 of the Rules govern the procedure before the ECJ.

14.3.2.1 Making the reference

The parties to the national proceedings cannot initiate proceedings for preliminary rulings. The national court can alone make an order for reference. It will ask questions on the interpretation or validity of Community law. In the English High Court see RSC ord. 114.

14.3.2.2 Written procedure

There are no formal pleadings as the proceedings are not contentious. The ECJ is not asked to decide the merits of the dispute between the parties. Its function is simply to assist the national court on the questions asked. It makes no inquiry as to the facts. A statement of agreed or decided facts should be found in the reference for the order or the national court's file on the case.

The Registrar will transmit copies of the preliminary reference to the parties in the national proceedings, to the Member State, the Commission (and to the Council, if the reference concerns an act of the Council). Those notified may submit written observations to the ECJ but there is no obligation on them to do so.

14.3.2.3 Oral procedure

Those notified may also attend the oral hearing and make submissions. The procedure is similar to that for direct actions. After the Advocate-General's Opinion the oral proceedings are closed.

14.3.2.4 Deliberations and judgment

The procedure is the same as for direct actions.

When the preliminary ruling is sent back to the national court, the case before the national court is resumed (proceedings having usually been suspended, pending the outcome of the preliminary reference).

14.3.3 THE LANGUAGE OF THE CASE

The language of the case (i.e. that in which the proceedings should be drafted) may be any one of the nine official Community languages and Irish. In a direct action the applicant can choose the language of the case. However, where the action is brought against a Member State, it is the official language of that State. In references for preliminary rulings the language of the case is the language of the referring court (Rules, Article 29).

The working language of the ECJ is French, although the Advocates-General draft and deliver their Opinions in their own languages. The judgments are drafted and deliberated in French but the authentic version of the judgment will be in the language of the case. If that is not French, it will be a translation into that language from French.

14.3.4 REPRESENTATION BEFORE THE ECJ

Member States and Community institutions are represented by an agent who is often assisted by an advisor or lawyer entitled to practise before a Court in a Member State (e.g. an agent from the Treasury Solicitor's Department, assisted by a barrister). Other parties in direct actions are represented by a lawyer entitled to practise in the courts of a Member State (Article 17 of the Statute). In preliminary rulings the ECJ is to take account of the rules of procedure of the national court making the reference (Rules, Article 194(2)).

14.3.5 COSTS

In direct actions the unsuccessful party shall be ordered to pay costs, if these have been asked for in the pleadings. A successful party may however be ordered to pay costs which the ECJ considers to have been unreasonably or vexatiously caused to the opponent (Rules, Article 69).

In references for preliminary rulings the question of costs is to be determined by the national court or tribunal in question (Rules, Article 104(3)). However, costs incurred by Community institutions or Member States which intervene in such proceedings are not recoverable, i.e. they must be borne by the intervener.

14.3.6 LEGAL AID

In direct actions the ECJ may grant legal aid to a party 'who is wholly or in part unable to meet the cost of the proceedings' (Rules, Article 76).

In references for a preliminary ruling, parties to the national proceedings may be eligible under national law for legal aid in respect of proceedings before the ECJ. In *R v Marlborough Street Stipendiary Magistrates, ex parte Bouchereau* [1977] ECR 1999 an existing legal aid certificate for the case before the national court was held to cover proceedings for a preliminary reference. In exceptional cases the ECJ may also grant legal aid.

14.4 How does the ECJ Interpret the Treaties and Community Legislation?

The ECJ in some ways takes the same approach as an English court: it looks at the words used. It also considers their meaning in the context of the instrument as a whole (contextual interpretation). However, where the contextual interpretation is not helpful it uses the teleological method of interpretation. This means that the ECJ interprets the provision so that it fits into the general aims of the Community legal order, what the Court thinks the Community should be trying to achieve and the needs of the Community. The ECJ differs from the English courts in the extent to which it readily departs from the literal meaning and resorts to the teleological approach and the use of policy in arriving at its decisions.

14.5 How does Policy Feature in the Decision-Making of the ECJ?

One of the distinguishing features of the ECJ is the extent to which the ECJ relies on policy considerations in its decisions. Its policy is the promotion of European integration by:

(a) strengthening the Community and its supranational elements;
(b) developing the scope and effectiveness of Community law;
(c) increasing the powers of the Community institutions.

For example, in *Parti Ecologiste 'Les Verts' v European Parliament*, 294/83 [1987] 2 CMLR 343, the ECJ extended its power of judicial review to cover the legality of acts of the European Parliament as well as those of the Commission and the Council, the only institutions actually mentioned in Article 173, EC. It did this because it thought that such acts ought to be reviewable.

The principle of effectiveness, (i.e. a provision is to be interpreted in the way that enables it to achieve its objective as effectively as possible), has been used by the ECJ to develop the doctrine of direct effect for directives.

Sometimes the Advocates-General make a comparative study of national provisions in order to find a solution which best fits the purposes of Community law (e.g. *AM & S Europe Ltd v Commission* 155/779 [1982] ECR 1575).

The ECJ introduces new doctrines gradually, initially as a general principle subject to qualifications. In later cases it re-affirms the principle and slowly decreases the qualifications. This was its approach to the treaty-making power of the Community and the doctrine of direct effect (e.g. *Defrenne v Sabena* 43/75 [1976] ECR 455).

14.6   Does the Doctrine of Precedent Apply in the ECJ?

There is no formal doctrine of *stare decisis* but the ECJ tends to follow its previous decisions in most cases. Its case law is instrumental in developing Community law. Only rarely does it refer to previous cases in its judgment, although sometimes it may repeat parts of a previous judgment without quotation marks or without mentioning the name of the case. On rare occasions it may not follow precedent, e.g. where the circumstances have changed or the views of the Judges have altered. In such situations the ECJ does not overrule or distinguish the previous case. It merely ignores it. The Opinions of Advocates-General are often cited by lawyers appearing before the ECJ.

15 European Law and National Law

15.1 How does European Community Law Work in our National Legal System?

15.1.1 INTERNATIONAL LAW AND OUR LEGAL SYSTEM

Under English law, international laws (specifically treaties) may be binding on the state and subject to enforcement by legal process. An example is the European Convention on Human Rights and Fundamental Freedoms (ECHR). But international law is unlikely to create rights for individuals which can be enforced through our own courts or tribunals. Again, using the example of the ECHR, a complainant must use the procedures and institutions established by the ECHR in order to complain about a violation of the Convention.

An English court might take note of the principles of the ECHR, especially when interpreting an Act of Parliament as our Parliament is not to be understood as passing legislation which is contrary to the international obligations of the UK unless the Act expresses this intention. But if the victim of an act which was contrary to the ECHR seeks relief from the English courts, the cause of action must be one known to English law (e.g. assault; false imprisonment; a claim for judicial review based on a denial of natural justice) — a writ which simply alleges an infringement of the Convention will be struck out as disclosing no cause of action.

So, international laws generally have no effect on individuals in the UK — they give no rights, impose no obligations, which can be relied on in our courts. These laws bind only the state and are enforceable against the state through procedures totally distinct from our legal system. European Community law is different — it can give rights to individuals or impose obligations on individuals and the state which are enforceable through our courts. It does this by virtue of the European Communities Act 1972 (ECA).

15.1.2 THE EUROPEAN COMMUNITIES ACT 1972

The laws of the European Community became a part of our domestic legal system as a result of this statute. So, the articles of the EC Treaty and the secondary legislation of the Community institutions is as much a part of our legal system as is an Act of Parliament, an Order in Council or a decision of the House of Lords.

Under s. 2(1) of the ECA:

> *all such rights, powers, obligations and restrictions from time to time created or arising* [from the EC Treaty, amongst others], *and all ... remedies and procedures* [provided for by the Treaty] *as in accordance with* [the Treaty] *are without further enactment to be given legal effect or used in the United Kingdom shall be recognised and available in law, and be enforced ... and followed accordingly ...*

The important element here is that some Community laws may give rights and obligations without further enactment, that is they become a part of our laws without any statute or Order in Council to implement them thus.

By s. 2(2) of the ECA, the Government is empowered to pass secondary legislation, when appropriate, to implement any Community obligation of the UK. By s. 2(4) any such legislation (and Acts of Parliament) passed or to be passed 'shall be construed and have effect subject to the foregoing provisions of this section'. This subsection is often relied on as implicitly establishing the supremacy of Community law over English law by 'entrenching' its position.

[NB 'Communities' appears in the short title of the Act as a reference to the three Communities of Europe — the Atomic Energy Community; the Coal and Steel Community; and the Economic Community. This Manual is concerned primarily with what was the European Economic Community.]

15.1.3   THE EUROPEAN COMMUNITIES ACT AND ENGLISH COURTS

Whenever a question arises in legal proceedings as to the interpretation or effect of the EC Treaty (or as to the validity, effect or interpretation of EC secondary legislation), this shall be treated as a question of law, not of fact. The question should either be referred to the European Court of Justice (ECJ) for its opinion or determined by the English judge 'in accordance with the principles laid down by and any relevant decision of the European Court' (s. 3(1) of the ECA). This seems to establish the primacy of the ECJ and its case law in relation to our own courts.

In a similar vein, s. 3(2) requires an English judge to take judicial notice of (i.e. be bound by):

    (a)   the Community Treaties;
    (b)   the Official Journal of the Communities; and
    (c)   'any decision of, or expression of opinion by, the European Court' on the questions of law referred to in s. 3(1).

The two most important 'decisions' by the ECJ, which English judges are bound by are: (a) that Community law takes precedence over national law where the two are in conflict; and (b) that some Community laws give rights or obligations to individuals which can be enforced in our courts without the need for implementing legislation. These two decisions are examined below.

15.2   The Direct Effect of Community Law

Under Article 189 of the EC Treaty, regulations are directly applicable in the Member States. No other type of Community law is thus described. But the ECJ has evolved a concept of 'direct effect' — by this it means that Community laws which meet certain criteria may be used by individuals in national courts. Sometimes such laws may only be used against the state (i.e. they impose no obligation on individuals) — perhaps to claim damages or *certiorari*; other laws proscribe certain conduct — they may be used by one individual to sue another or as a defence to litigation. Some examples may help.

15.2.1   SOME EXAMPLES

15.2.1.1   Example 1
A UK Government minister bans imports of French turkeys. His action is designed to support UK turkey breeders at the expense of French producers. Article 30 of the EC Treaty establishes the principle of free circulation of goods between the Member States of the Community. The ECJ has held this article to be directly effective. The French turkey producers sue the minister in the English High Court for damages, relying on his alleged infringement of Article 30. They establish the right to a declaration that the ban is illegal but the remedy of damages is denied by the court. The case is subsequently settled out of court.

See *Bourgoin* v *Ministry of Agriculture, Fisheries and Food* [1986] QB 716.

15.2.1.2   Example 2

A woman works for a local health authority. When she reaches the age of 62, she is dismissed from her job. There is no reason for this, other than her age. The policy of the health authority is to dismiss female staff when they reach 60, male staff at age 65. She makes a claim in the Industrial Tribunal, alleging that her dismissal contravenes a Community Directive, No. 76/207. This provides that male and female employees shall receive equal treatment in their conditions of work, including dismissal. The question of whether the directive is directly effective is referred to the ECJ. The ECJ decides that it is enforceable against the state (in this case represented by the health authority). The Industrial Tribunal then upholds her claim and awards her several thousand pounds compensation.

See *Marshall v Southampton and SW Hants A.H.A.* [1986] QB 401.

15.2.1.3   Example 3

A French national gets a place at an English university to read for a degree in electrical engineering. His application to the relevant UK Government department for payment of his tuition fees and maintenance grant is refused because he does not meet the requirements for foreign students' grants. He sues the responsible Government minister, claiming that the requirements discriminate against him on the ground of his nationality, contrary to Articles 7 and 48 of the EC Treaty. Both Articles are directly effective, according to the case law of the ECJ. During the proceedings, the Government changes the rules regarding payment of tuition fees for EC nationals; a reference to the ECJ establishes the right of EC workers to move to another Member State and get a maintenance grant from their 'host' country.

See *Brown v Secretary of State for Scotland* [1988] ECR 3237.

15.2.1.4   Example 4

An English company makes dairy products, using milk supplied by the Milk Marketing Board (MMB). The MMB announces it will no longer sell directly to the company; the company must now buy from a middle man with higher prices. The company sues the MMB in the High Court for damages, alleging breach of Article 86 of the Treaty (anti-competitive conduct). The ECJ has held previously that Article 86 is directly effective. The English courts hold that a breach of Article 86 is actionable (as a breach of statutory duty) and can be used to claim damages.

See *Garden Cottage Foods v Milk Marketing Board* [1984] AC 130.

15.2.1.5   Example 5

An English company owns the patent in a pharmaceutical substance 'S'. Another company applies for a licence to import 'S' into the UK from another Member State (Italy). Before the licence is granted (or refused), the applicant starts importing 'S'. The patentee sues in the High Court, alleging infringement of its patent. It claims an injunction to stop the imports. The importer's defence states that its imports have been bought quite lawfully in Italy, although 'S' is not patented there, and it relies on Article 30 of the Treaty (free circulation of goods). A reference to the ECJ makes it clear that the injunction would contradict Article 30 so the English court refuses to grant the injunction.

See *Allen & Hanbury Ltd v Generics (UK) Ltd* [1989] 1 WLR 414.

15.2.1.6   Example 6

Two men are prosecuted for breaking the laws on importation of obscene material. They have imported pornographic literature from another Member State where it is lawfully on sale. Their defence is that they bought the literature legitimately and, under Article 30 of the Treaty, are allowed to export it to any other Member State. This would have succeeded, as Article 30 is directly effective, save that there is an exception to the basic right of free circulation, contained in Article 36. This allows States to derogate from the right on the ground of public morality.

See *R v Henn and Darby* [1981] AC 850.

15.2.2   WHAT COMMUNITY LAWS ARE DIRECTLY EFFECTIVE?

A list of all the Treaty Articles and secondary legislation that has been held to be directly effective would be too long for insertion here. The ECJ has held that several articles of the Treaty are directly effective; also certain regulations, directives and decisions. However, each article, regulation, etc. will be examined individually by the ECJ to see whether it meets the criteria for direct effect. Thus, the contents of a list of directly effective laws is governed by which measures have been referred by national courts to the ECJ for its opinion on the matter. The criteria are examined in **15.2.3.** onwards.

15.2.3   DIRECTLY EFFECTIVE ARTICLES OF THE TREATY

The following Articles have been held to be of direct effect:

(a)   Article 7 (non-discrimination between EC nationals on grounds of nationality); *Gravier* v *City of Liege* [1985] ECR 593. (This is Article 6 as from 1 January 1993.)

(b)   Article 12 (ban on introduction of new customs duties on imports from one Member State to another); *Van Gend En Loos* [1963] ECR 1.

(c)   Article 30 (elimination of quantitative restrictions on the free movement of goods between Member States); *Ianelli & Volpi Spa* v *Ditta Paola Meroni* [1977] ECR 557.

(d)   Article 48 (freedom of workers who are EC nationals to move to another Member State to work there); *Van Duyn* v *Home Office* [1974] ECR 1337.

(e)   Article 52 (freedom of EC nationals who are self-employed or members of a profession, or EC companies, to set themselves up in another Member State); *Reyners* v *Belgian State* [1974] ECR 631.

(f)   Article 59 (freedom of EC nationals to move temporarily to another Member State in order to provide (or receive) a service there); *Van Binsbergen* [1974] ECR 1299.

(g)   Articles 85 and 86 (prohibition on conduct which restricts or distorts competition in the common market); *BRT* v *Sabam* [1974] ECR 313.

(h)   Article 119 (equal pay for male and female staff who do equal work); *Defrenne* v *Sabena* [1976] ECR 455.

Criteria for Articles to be directly effective were first established by the ECJ in the *Van Gend En Loos* case (26/62) and have since been modified. The wording of the Article must be:

(a)   clear and unambiguous;

(b)   unconditional (on the exercise of a power or discretion by, for example, a Member State or the European Commission);

(c)   not dependent on further action.

Clarity and lack of ambiguity are not features of Community law that the man in the street might subscribe to. These features can by supplied by the ECJ, though, often when an EC measure is referred to it for interpretation under Article 177 of the Treaty. The ECJ has also occasionally interpreted an Article in such a way that it has direct effect in certain circumstances but not others. A typical example of this is the litigation between Ms Defrenne and the Belgian national airline, Sabena (43/75). The ECJ was concerned to interpret Article 119 regarding the principle of equal pay for equal work. The ECJ held that it was directly effective so far as 'direct' discrimination was concerned but not for 'indirect' discrimination. The distinction was based on the premise that in some situations discrimination could be determined simply on a legal analysis (direct discrimination) while in others a more complex determination would be required which a court might be ill-equipped to perform (indirect discrimination). So, if Miss A works alongside Mr B doing the same job, they should both receive the same wage, subject to proper reasons for distinction like seniority. On the other hand, if Miss A is a canteen assistant in a shipyard, while Mr B is a welder there, a job evaluation scheme is required to see if their jobs are of equal value; or Miss A may do a job which only women have done for that employer but seeks to argue that, if a man had the job, he would be paid more. Both of the latter examples are indirect discrimination according to the ECJ and Article 119 will not help.

If an Article requires further action, for example by a Member State, then usually it has no direct effect. However, in this situation the Member State would not be allowed to reap the benefit of its own inaction. If a time limit was expressed in the Article (or could be implied) for the further action to be taken but none was, the ECJ is likely to hold that (subject to the first two criteria being satisfied) the Article is now directly effective insofar as it may be enforced against the defaulting Member State.

15.2.4   DIRECTLY EFFECTIVE REGULATIONS

Similar provisions have been held by the ECJ to exist for regulations as have been considered in **15.2.3** for Articles of the Treaty. The regulation must be clear and unambiguous, it must be unconditional and not require further action to be taken.

15.2.5   DIRECTLY EFFECTIVE DIRECTIVES AND DECISIONS

The ECJ has held that directives can have direct effect, a good example being the *Marshall* case, referred to above. Unlike regulations, which are not meant to require any action on the part of Member States to implement them into national law, directives usually specify an aim or general principles and leave choices to the Member States. A good recent example is the Commission's Directive on Product Liability which allowed Member States to take several different options as to liability. The UK enacted the Consumer Protection Act 1987 to implement it.

This might be thought to indicate that a directive should not have direct effect but the ECJ has said that to deprive directives of direct effect would lead to their avoidance by Member States, again through inactivity. This has led the ECJ to declare that once the time limit for implementation of a directive has passed without any (or any proper) implementation, an individual may rely on the directive against the Member State, providing it is clear and precise. The idea is that the Member State cannot rely on its own failure to deprive the individual of a right or remedy. However, the same policy argument cannot be used against another individual it is not Mr Brown's fault if the UK Parliament has not enacted Directive 90/123, for example. This has led the ECJ to declare that directives have vertical direct effect (i.e. impose obligations on the state, give rights to individuals) but not horizontal direct effect (i.e. do not impose obligations on individuals). This view was recently reaffirmed by the ECJ in *Paola Faccini Dori* v *Recreb Srl* (1994).

One result has been several cases in the UK where individual litigants have tried to rely on EC directives against a defendant arguing that the defendant is an 'emanation of the State' and thus subject to vertical direct effect. Two notable cases involved a (then) nationalised corporation, British Gas, and a company wholly-owned by the British Government, Rolls-Royce. They were sued by their employees, who relied on EC directives about equal pay or treatment. Both employees lost since the courts decided that neither organisation represented the state (unlike an area health authority in the *Marshall* case).

Finally, decisions may have direct effect. The criteria are the same as for directives. See, for example, the case of *Grad* (9/70).

For further reading, see *Coming to Terms with EEC Directives*, Josephine Steiner (1990) vol. 106 LQR 144.

15.3   Supremacy of Community Law

There are two points of view to be considered here. First, that of the European Community, second, that of the Member States, The European Community has always taken the view that its law takes precedence over any conflicting national law (see, e.g., the second *Simmenthal* case (106/77)), whether the national law is precedent in time or not. The ECJ is firmly of the opinion that national courts should not apply national law where a Community measure exists.

The doctrine developed by the ECJ is that Community law has primacy over national law. The doctrine of Community primacy was first clarified by the ECJ in a preliminary ruling on a reference from a Milan Justice of the Peace in *Costa* v *ENEL* 6/64 [1964] ECR 585.

When Italy nationalised the production and supply of electricity and transferred the management of it to ENEL, Mr Costa, a shareholder in the Edison Volta company felt that his interests had been adversely affected. He refused to pay his electricity bill which was only a few hundred lire. His defence before the Milan justice was inter alia that the nationalisation of the electricity industry infringed several articles of the EC Treaty. When asked to interpret these Articles in a preliminary reference by the justice, the ECJ used the opportunity to stress that:

> The integration into the Laws of each Member State of provisions which derive from the Community, and more generally the terms and spirit of the Treaty, make it impossible for the States, as a corollary, to accord precedence to a unilateral and subsequent measure over a legal system accepted by them on a basis of reciprocity. The executive force of Community law cannot vary from one State to another in deference to subsequent domestic laws, without jeopardising the attainment of the objectives of the Treaty set out in Article 5(2) and giving rise to discrimination prohibited by Article 7.

Another important ECJ case on this concept is *Internationale Handelsgesellschaft* 11/70 [1970] ECR 1125.

The doctrine of supremacy of EC law has found expression in the Member States in different ways according to their different constitutions (Trevor Hartley's book, *Foundations of European Community Law* has a good chapter reviewing the Member States' constitutions). In the UK s. 2(4) of the ECA seems to establish the supremacy of Community law. Sometimes this concept has been accepted with apparent enthusiasm by English courts (see, e.g., *Pickstone* v *Freemans plc* [1988] 3 WLR 265), but on other occasions a rather narrower view has prevailed (e.g. *Duke* v *GEC Reliance Systems Ltd* [1988] 2 WLR 359). One way to encourage acceptance is through preliminary references by national courts to the ECJ under Article 177 of the EC Treaty. A problem exists with this, though. Such references are usually made at the discretion of the court then dealing with the case; they cannot be insisted upon by the parties to litigation. The more xenophobic a State's judges are, the less likely is any reference to the ECJ where a ruling on supremacy (or at least on an interpretation inconsistent with national law) might emerge. In the long term, the European community can really only rely on the States and all their institutions (including the courts) being *'communautaire'* and embracing the philosophy of the supranational single common market, with all the consequent loss of national sovereignty that that implies.

16   Sources and Further Reading

16.1   Treaties, Statutes, Protocols, Rules

Treaties establishing the European Communities: e.g. The European Economic Community Treaty 1957.
The Single European Act 1986.
Protocol of the Statute of the Court of Justice of the European Economic Community.
Rules of Procedure of the Court.
The European Communities Act 1972.
Rules of the Supreme Court, ord. 114 (in *The White Book*).
Treaty on European Union, Maastricht 1992.

16.2   Practitioners' Works

Halsbury's Laws, Vols 51 and 52.
Vaughan, *The Law of the European Communities* (1986) 2 vol. (reprint of Halsbury's Laws), Butterworth & Co.
Lasok, *The European Court of Justice: Practice and Procedure*, 2nd edn (1994), Butterworth & Co.
Usher, *European Court Practice* (1983), Sweet & Maxwell Ltd.
Kapteyn and Verloran Van Themaat, *Introduction to the law of the European Communities,* 2nd edn, Kluwer.
D'Sa, *European Community Law and Civil Remedies in England and Wales* (1994), Sweet and Maxwell Ltd.

16.3   Digests and Law Reports

Digest of Case Law relating to the European Communities: Series A; Series D, published by the Community.
European Court Reports (Official reports of the Court, English language version often delayed by translation).
Common Market Law Reports (judgments of ECJ, CFI and national courts, quite up-to-date).

16.4   Student Textbooks

Hartley, *The Foundation of European Community Law,* 3rd edn (1994), Oxford University Press.
Steiner, *Textbook on EC Law,* 4th edn (1994), Blackstone Press Ltd.
Weatherill and Beaumont, *EC Law* (1993), Penguin.
Wyatt and Dashwood, *The Substantive Law of the EEC,* (1993), Sweet & Maxwell Ltd.

16.5   Periodicals

The Official Journal of the European Communities.
Common Market Law Review.
European Law Review.

LAW OF INTERNATIONAL TRADE

17 Introduction

In this part of the Manual we shall undertake an analysis of some of the legal problems that arise in an international trade transaction involving sea transport. The issues mostly arise in a contractual context. We shall be examining the following:

(a) contracts of sale;
(b) contracts arising from the use of a bill of exchange;
(c) contracts arising under a documentary credit;
(d) contracts of carriage by sea; and
(e) contracts of marine insurance.

It will be assumed throughout that English law is the proper law of these contracts, unless the contrary is stated. The question of jurisdiction is of central importance in any problem arising in this field and must always be borne in mind. For the sake of clarity, jurisdiction will be dealt with as a separate topic but it is not an issue to be considered in isolation. It will be an integral part of the problem you have before you.

Reference should also be made to the **General Practice Manual, Sale of Goods** when reading **Chapter 18** on International Sales.

Please note:

(a) The Carriage of Goods by Sea Act 1992 (COGSA 1992) applies to bills of lading, seaway bills and ship's delivery orders issued after 15 September 1992.

(b) All references to the Sale of Goods Act 1979 are references to that Act as amended by the Sale and Supply of Goods Act 1994 and the Sale of Goods (Amendment) Act 1995. The amendments introduced by the Sale and Supply of Goods Act 1994 apply to contracts of sale made after 3 January 1995. The amendments introduced by the Sale of Goods (Amendment) Act 1995 apply to contracts of sale made after 18 September 1995.

18   International Sales

18.1   Introduction

An international sale for our purposes will be one where a purchaser in one country, buys from a seller in another country, goods which are to be transported from the seller's premises to the buyer's premises or other agreed place overseas.

The sale contract will define, whether by its express or implied terms, the nature, quantity and quality of the goods that are being bought. It may make specific provisions for the passing of property and/or risk in the goods and on other matters related to the sale proper. It will also stipulate the price.

However, it will be necessary that arrangements be made for:

(a)   The transfer of payment from the buyer in his/her country to the seller in his/her country: the seller may require that provisions be included in the sale agreement which will ensure that he/she does not part with property and/or possession of the goods without at the same time obtaining an entitlement to payment of the purchase price, and which will guarantee that payment. Where payment is made by a bill of exchange or documentary credit, other contracts will be brought into existence.

(b)   The carriage of the goods from the seller's premises to a port in the buyer's country or other agreed place: this may involve transport from the seller's warehouse to the port of loading, carriage by sea to the port of destination and carriage from the port of destination. The goods will have to be loaded and discharged, and may be stored at either port. Thus, a number of different parties will be employed in the transport. It is necessary, therefore, for the parties to the sale contract to agree who is to arrange and who is to pay for these services.

As the provisions of the carriage contract will determine who is responsible for loading and discharge during the carriage operation and the carrier's rights, duties and liabilities generally, the sale agreement may provide that certain terms be included in the contract of carriage.

In addition, the sale contract may determine who is to effect insurance cover for the goods, and who will pay for that cover. It may also lay down certain terms to be included in the contract of insurance. In particular, if the seller is under a duty to conclude the contract of insurance but the risk in the goods is to pass to the buyer at an early stage in the transportation, the buyer may wish to stipulate certain terms over and above, or in substitution for, those which the contract of insurance might normally contain.

Thus, the sale contract will indicate who is to enter into certain ancillary contracts, and, in some circumstances at least, the terms of those contracts. It may also make clear who is to pay under the ancillary contracts. The distribution of the various payments and the incidence of the various risks in the venture determine the contract price. There will be various factors influencing the choice of terms in the sale contract — among them the nature and scope of the seller's and the buyer's respective business operations, and the nature of the goods, as well as geographical and political considerations.

18.2   Types of Contract

Some of the more widely used types of contract will now be explained and considered. In particular, reference will be made to the time at which the payment obligation arises.

Please note that all statutory references in this chapter will be to the Sale of Goods Act 1979 (SOGA 1979) as amended by the Sale and Supply of Goods Act 1994 and the Sale of Goods (Amendment) Act 1995, unless otherwise stated.

Unless there is a contrary agreement, payment is due on delivery: s. 28. Delivery is the voluntary transfer of either actual or constructive possession from one person to another (s. 61(1)) and represents the completion of the seller's performance in relation to the goods. Whether payment is due on actual or constructive delivery will depend on the terms of the contract.

18.2.1   EX-WORKS/EX-WAREHOUSE

The sale contract which involves the minimum of inconvenience and risk to the seller is a sale ex-works or ex-warehouse. If the sale contract is on such terms, the parties agree that the seller will have completed performance by setting the goods aside and making them available for collection by the buyer or his/her agent at the seller's warehouse in the seller's country. The seller is not required to provide an export licence or to enter into ancillary contracts of carriage and insurance. Indeed, although this sale contract may well be between parties carrying on business in different countries, the transport of the goods from one country to another plays no part in the performance of the contract of sale.

Unless there is an agreement to the contrary, payment is due when the goods are set aside and made available for collection. If, however, by the time delivery falls due, the seller has:

(a)   failed to comply with the terms as to quality, description etc. implied into the contract by virtue of SOGA 1979; or

(b)   failed to perform the contract, in such a way that the commercial purpose of the contract is frustrated; or

(c)   manifested an intention not to perform his/her obligation under the contract,

the buyer can refuse payment and reject the goods tendered to him. In (b) and (c) the seller will be in repudiatory breach. In (a) the seller will be in repudiatory breach if it is no longer possible contractually to deliver conforming goods.

Where loss or damage to the goods occurs at a time when the buyer delays *taking* delivery, see s. 20(2). Where the seller incurs loss due to the buyer's failure to *take* delivery on time, see s. 37.

18.2.2   SHIPMENT TO DESTINATION

At almost the other end of the spectrum is a sale on terms shipment to destination. If the contract of sale is a shipment to destination variant, e.g., an ex-ship contract, the form of delivery contemplated is discharge overside the ship at the usual discharge place at the contractual port of delivery. The seller is usually obliged to obtain an export licence. The seller is obliged to discharge any lien arising out of the carriage of the goods, and put the buyer in a position to be able to demand the goods from the ship, e.g., tender to the buyer a bill of lading to the latter's order.

Where the ship has been designated in the contract, e.g., '1,000 tons wheat ex SS Enterprise', the nominated ship forms part of the description of the goods. Failure to deliver from that ship will amount to a failure to comply with a term of the contract (*Yangtsze Insurance* v *Lukmanjee* [1918] AC 585), and may enable the buyer to reject what is tendered and refuse to pay.

It is only on delivery to the buyer overside the ship that payment can be demanded in the absence of contractual provisions to the contrary. If on delivery overside the ship, the goods are found to be damaged, the buyer can refuse to pay. The risk of loss or damage to the goods remains with the seller until delivery.

18.2.3 C.I.F. AND F.O.B. CONTRACTS

In most cases, however, the seller participates in the transport of the goods to a greater extent than in the ex-works or ex-warehouse contract, and at the same time the buyer participates to a greater extent than in the ex-ship contract. There are two intermediate types of sale contract which are particularly used, c.i.f. and f.o.b. contracts. Each has its own complexities.

18.3 Contracts on C.I.F. Terms

The letters c.i.f. stand for 'cost', 'insurance' and 'freight'. They will usually be followed by a named port/place of *destination*. The acronym c.i.f. indicates the initial contract of sale and the two ancillary contracts, of insurance and of carriage, into which the seller agrees to enter. Entry into these contracts enables the seller to obtain the bill of lading representing the contract of carriage and the marine insurance policy evidencing the contract of insurance. The bill of lading and the marine insurance document, together with an invoice, are the usual documents which the seller is required to tender in order to demand payment.

18.3.1 ESSENTIAL ELEMENTS OF C.I.F. CONTRACT

The essence of the c.i.f. contract is as follows:

(a) The seller is entitled to demand payment (in the absence of agreement to the contrary) when he/she tenders to the buyer conforming shipping documents. *The right to payment is not conditional on the arrival of the ship.*

Under the c.i.f. contract *the documents take the place of the goods* when the right to demand payment and the obligation to pay for the goods is considered. In *Gill & Duffus SA v Berger* [1984] 2 WLR 95, Lord Diplock stated:

> It is in my view, a legal characteristic of a c.i.f. contract, so well established in English law as to be beyond the realms of controversy, that the refusal by the buyer under such a contract to pay to the seller, or to a banker nominated in the contract, if the contract so provides, the purchase price on presentation at the place stipulated in the contract, of shipping documents which on their face conform to those called for by the contract, constitutes a fundamental breach of contract, which the seller is entitled to elect to treat as rescinding the contract and relieving him of any obligation to continue to perform any of his own primary obligations under it.

(b) Unlike the ex-ship contract, the *risk* of loss or damage to the goods passes to the buyer before the ship arrives at the port of destination. Risk quite commonly passes on shipment but very rarely before shipment.

18.3.1.1 Risk: what does it mean?

When you have determined that a buyer bears the risk of loss of or damage to goods at the time that loss or damage occurs, it means that the buyer has taken the risk of something happening to those goods and therefore must still pay for them — the loss or damage does not provide an excuse for non-payment.

Where, however, the goods remain at the seller's risk at the time the loss or damage occurs, the seller cannot demand the price for those goods from the buyer. In the c.i.f. contract, the seller might initially be able to demand payment against conforming documents since the obligation to pay arises against tender of documents not goods. However, he may not be legally entitled to *retain* the payments if he bore the risk when loss or damage occurred to the goods (see (a) below). In these circumstances, where the loss or damage amounts to a breach of contract by the seller, he will also be liable in damages subject to the frustration rules.

(For more on risk and frustration — refer to **General Practice Manual, Sale of Goods**.)

Let us very briefly at this stage consider the practical effect of these two essential elements of the c.i.f. contract — that the buyer must pay against conforming documents, and that risk of loss or damage to the goods passes before physical delivery at destination to the buyer:

(a) The buyer must pay against *conforming* documents even though the seller 'ships' (e.g. puts over the ship's rail) non-conforming goods or the goods become damaged whilst still at the seller's risk. However, the buyer may subsequently reject the goods and recover back what he/she has paid and, if the seller is in breach, sue for damages for non-delivery; or the buyer may keep the goods and claim damages for breach of warranty of quality.

(b) Where goods initially conforming at the time of shipment, are lost or damaged whilst at the buyer's risk, i.e. during the sea voyage, the buyer cannot argue a breach of contract by the seller and thus cannot refuse to pay or claim reimbursement.

It is clear, therefore, that a buyer who does not want to pay against documents can argue either that the contract is not on c.i.f. terms but required shipment to destination (see **18.5**), or that there has been a non-conforming tender of documents. In relation to the latter, Lord Diplock in *Gill & Duffus* v *Berger* *(supra)* referred to the obligation of a c.i.f. buyer to pay against documents conforming *on their face*. Yet documents can have an underlying non-conformity and still conform on their face. Before we deal with this problem and try and reconcile it with what Lord Diplock said in the above case, we need to consider what amounts to a conforming tender. Note that if the tender does not legally compel acceptance, the buyer can reject it. He/she will then be rejecting the goods that the documents represent and will not be obliged to pay. Whether the buyer can treat the seller as in breach will depend on the ability of the seller to retender in time.

18.3.2 DOCUMENTARY REQUIREMENTS UNDER C.I.F. CONTRACT

The documents traditionally required to be tendered in order to obtain payment are:

(a) a bill of lading, representing the *freight* element in the c.i.f. contract;
(b) an insurance policy or insurance certificate, representing the *insurance* element in the c.i.f. contract;
(c) an invoice, representing the *cost* element in the c.i.f. contract.

The contract of sale may, however, also require the tender of other documents, such as any export or import licence which the c.i.f. seller is contractually bound to obtain, certificates as to the origin of the goods, and pre-shipment certificates of inspection and quality.

18.3.3 BILL OF LADING

In the absence of any express or implied intention to the contrary, or of a custom in the trade allowing tender of a different shipping document, the c.i.f. purchaser is entitled to a document which:

(a) acts as a receipt for the goods from the sea carrier;
(b) can perform a contractual function if necessary;
(c) gives the purchaser constructive possession of the goods;
(d) allows the purchaser to demand the goods from the carrier on tender of the document.

A shipped bill of lading in transferable form performs the functions set out above. However, please note the following:

(i)   Whilst the cargo on the ship remains in bulk, transfer of a shipped bill of lading in transferable form will not transfer a possessory (or proprietory) interest in the goods. See *Re London Wine Co. (Shippers) Ltd* [1986] PCC 121; *Re Goldcorp Exchange Ltd (in receivership)* [1994] 2 All ER 806. But note now, by virtue of the new s. 20A introduced by the Sale of Goods (Amendment) Act 1995, it is possible, in relation to contracts of sale made after 18 September 1995, for property in an undivided share in the bulk to be transferred to the buyer, if he/she has paid the price or part of it.

(ii)   The shipped bill of lading in transferable form *can* transfer rights to sue in contract even though the goods remain in bulk. See COGSA 1992.

(iii)   By virtue of the operation of COGSA 1992, a 'received for shipment' bill of lading *can* transfer contractual rights to sue.

18.3.3.1   Constructive possession

A few comments need to be made about (c) in **18.3.3**. A buyer will have constructive possession of goods if he/she receives the right to control them. Under the Factors Act 1889, s. 1(2), 'a person is deemed to be in possession of goods where they are held ... by another subject to his control, or for him or on his behalf'.

It is clear that possession by a buyer of a bill of lading in transferable form and appropriately transferred to him/her gives him/her sufficient control over the destiny of goods to amount to constructive possession, first because such a bill of lading requires tender of it to the ship to obtain the goods, and secondly, as the bill is 'to order' (see **18.3.3.2**), the holder of it can direct to whom delivery should be made by transferring on the bill of lading in the appropriate manner. Each new and proper transferee of the bill of lading in transferable form, receives the necessary control over the goods to amount to constructive possession of the goods. Embodied in the transferable bill of lading is an undertaking, called an attornment, by the party in actual possession of the goods (the carrier), that he/she holds the goods for the benefit of the present and proper holder of the bill of lading and subject to the latter's directions, i.e., to the holder's 'order'.

It would appear that by virtue of SOGA 1979, s. 20A (an amendment introduced by the Sale of Goods (Amendment) Act 1995), in those circumstances where property does pass in part of a bulk cargo, thus creating the buyer an owner in common of the bulk, there is now a sufficient degree of control accorded to the buyer to amount to constructive possession. Under s. 20B(2) 'delivery' includes 'such appropriation of goods to the contract as results in property in the goods being transferred to the buyer'.

The bill of lading in transferable form relating to a shipped, identified and separated cargo was recognised as a document of title at common law in *Lickbarrow* v *Mason* (1793) 2 H Bl 211. A document of title at common law is a document relating to goods, the appropriate transfer of which will operate as a transfer of constructive possession of the goods and *may* operate as a transfer of the property in the goods if this is what the parties intended.

A 'received for shipment' bill of lading was not recognised as a document of title at common law in *Lickbarrow* v *Mason* (*supra*). However, the increased use of such documents by merchants and carriers, especially in container transport operations; the acceptability of such a document under the Uniform Customs and Practice for Documentary Credits (1993 Revision) and the inclusion of such a document within the ambit of the COGSA 1992 (see s. 1(2)(b)), provide reason enough for the recognition of a 'received for shipment' bill of lading, like its counterpart, the 'shipped' bill, as a document of title at common law.

18.3.3.2   Transferable form of bill of lading

Unlike a bill of exchange, a bill of lading will only be transferable if designated as such. This can be done by stating that the goods are deliverable:

(a)   to a named consignee <u>OR ORDER</u> (see example 1 at **21.18**); or simply

(b)   <u>TO ORDER</u> (i.e. no named consignee, the goods are to be delivered to the order of the shipper) (see examples 2 and 3 at **21.18**).

When the goods are sold on, the named consignee or the shipper as appropriate can perform his/her contracts of sale by indorsing (i.e., putting his/her own signature) on the bill (usually the back of it) and delivering the bill of lading to the new purchaser. In signing the bill of lading, the consignee/shipper becomes the first *indorser* of the bill of lading. The new purchaser to whom the bill of lading has been transferred becomes the first *indorsee* of the bill of lading and is the proper holder of it. In order to achieve indorsee status it is not necessary for the transferee to have been identified on the bill, when the indorser added his signature. However, the naming of the new indorsee on the back of the bill of lading is relevant when considering the appropriate method of transfer to be adopted *by the indorsee*:

(a)   Where the first indorser, in addition to his/her signature, has added the name of the proposed first indorsee (a 'special' endorsement), that indorsee in transferring on the bill of lading must add his/her signature and deliver the bill of lading, with or without naming the new indorsee. Thus, the first indorsee becomes a second indorser.

(b)   Where the first indorser has not named the new indorsee (a 'blank' endorsement), that indorsee in transferring the bill of lading need only deliver the bill of lading. There is no need for the indorsee's signature. The indorsee does not become an indorser. The bill of lading has become one in which delivery is to be made to *bearer*.

18.3.3.3   Rights against the carrier

Where the bill of lading is in transferable and either 'received for shipment' or 'shipped' form, and issued after 15 September 1992, COGSA 1992 will apply to enable the purchaser to establish rights of suit against the carrier.

Notwithstanding that the contract of sale may require the c.i.f. seller to tender a bill of lading which operates as a document of title at common law and which gives the c.i.f. buyer rights against the carrier, further requirements are placed on the seller in relation to the bill of lading. These can best be discussed in conjunction with a consideration of the obligations generally of a seller under a c.i.f. contract.

18.3.3.4   Straight-consigned bill of lading

A bill of lading issued to a named party with no 'OR ORDER' attached, is not transferable. It is known as a straight-consigned bill of lading. It has not been recognised as a document of title at common law and the bill of lading provisions under COGSA 1992 will not apply to it. However the provisions in COGSA 1992 relating to seaway bills will apply to the straight-consigned bill of lading.

Unless there is an express or implied intention or custom in the trade to the contrary, tender of it amounts to tender of a document non-conforming with the requirements of the c.i.f. contract.

18.3.3.5   Bill of lading — reasonable and usual in the trade

The c.i.f. seller must tender a bill of lading reasonable and usual in the trade and which does not conflict with the terms of the contract of sale: *Burstall* v *Grimsdale* (1906) 11 Com Cas *280; Shipton Anderson & Co.* v *Weston & Co.* (1922) 10 Ll LR 762; *Berger Co. USA* v *Vegoil* [1984] 1 Lloyd's Rep 440, [1982] 2 Lloyd's Rep 762.

Failure on the part of the seller to enter into a contract of carriage reasonable or usual in the trade etc., will usually prevent tender of a bill of lading conforming with the above requirement.

18.3.3.6   Bill of lading to provide for carriage to contractual destination

The seller must enter into a contract of carriage under which the goods will be carried to the destination designated in the contract of sale *and* the bill of lading must provide for the carriage of the goods to that destination: *Colin and Shields* v *Weddel* [1952] 2 All ER 337; *SIAT di del Ferro* v *Tradax Overseas SA* [1980] 1 Lloyd's Rep 53.

Nevertheless, if the bill of lading provides for carriage to the contractual destination and yet entitles the carrier to discharge at other convenient ports in certain events, the seller will still have fulfilled his duty, which is to provide a bill of lading evidencing a contract of carriage customary in the trade. All bills of lading now contain liberty to deviate clauses. The real question will be whether they are drafted in unusually wide terms (see *Shipton Anderson & Co.* v *Weston & Co., supra)* or are in conflict with the express terms of the contract of sale.

The buyer will be able to reject a bill of lading which incorporates a wide and unusual deviation clause whether or not the ship actually deviates. Where the bill of lading tendered does represent a contract of carriage, reasonable and usual in the trade, and a detour from the contractual route (i.e. a deviation) does take place, the buyer's remedy lies against the carrier, *not* against the seller.

18.3.3.7 Bill of lading to give continuous documentary cover

Unless the terms of the contract of sale, or a custom of the trade, require otherwise, the seller must tender a bill of lading which gives continuous documentary cover, that is to say, which will give the buyer rights against the carrier in respect of loss or damage to the goods throughout the time that the goods are at the buyer's risk: *Hansson* v *Hamel and Horley Limited* [1922] 2 AC 36. Thus the presence of a liberty to tranship clause in the bill of lading will make the tender bad unless either the first or subsequent carrier undertakes responsibility for the entire carriage, or the terms of the contract of sale or custom in the trade negate the requirement of continuous documentary cover.

18.3.3.8 Bill of lading must embody a subsisting contract of carriage

The seller must tender a bill of lading which embodies, at that time, a subsisting contract of carriage: *Arnhold Karberg* v *Blythe* [1916] 1 KB 495. The buyer takes the risk of loss or damage to the goods, but he/she does not take the risk of the ancillary contracts becoming unenforceable.

18.3.3.9 Bill of lading must indicate shipment within contractual period

The contract of sale will designate a particular time or, more commonly, a period of time during which the goods must be shipped. Where a period of time is designated, the c.i.f. seller can choose the time to ship within that period.

The c.i.f. seller, in the absence of a term in the contract of sale to the contrary, can perform his/her contract of sale in any of the following ways:

(a) by appropriating (allocating) to the contract with the buyer, goods he/she has previously shipped within the contract dates;

(b) by allowing the supplier to perform the contract of sale by shipping the goods for the seller within the contract dates;

(c) by purchasing afloat and appropriating to the contract with the buyer goods which have been shipped by his/her predecessors in title within the contractual dates and from the contractual port of loading.

In the absence of a term in the contract of sale or of a custom in the trade to the contrary, a c.i.f. purchaser is entitled to receive a 'shipped' bill of lading. By this is meant a bill of lading which, at the time of tender, shows the date on which the goods were delivered over the ship's rail. Where the seller is transporting a bulk cargo such as oil to a c.i.f. purchaser, the 'shipment' point intended by the parties will usually be at an earlier stage, e.g. at the point at which the goods enter the ship's hose connection from the storage tank ashore.

A bill of lading may well have been issued by the carrier to the shipper at the time the goods were received into the custody of the carrier but before shipment. Such a bill of lading is a 'received for shipment' bill of lading and can be converted into a 'shipped' bill of lading by the addition of the words 'and since shipped' followed by the date.

Where a 'received for shipment' bill of lading has been tendered to the buyer and no term of the contract of sale or custom in the trade allows such a tender, the buyer can treat this as a bad tender and reject the documents and thus the goods. This is so even if the goods had in fact been shipped in time. (See also **18.3.3.12.**)

18.3.3.10   Time of issue of bill of lading

The seller must procure the issue, i.e. signing of the bill of lading by or on behalf of the carrier, 'on shipment'. Lord Summer in *Hansson* v *Hamel and Horley* [1922] 2 AC 36 stated:

> 'On shipment' is an expression of some latitude. Bills of lading are constantly signed after loading is complete and in some cases after the ship has sailed. I do not think that they thereby necessarily cease to be procured 'on shipment'.

Where a bulk cargo is being loaded, it is not necessary for the seller to obtain bills of lading issued hold by hold, as long as the bill of lading or bills of lading is/are issued within a reasonable time after completion of loading: *Golodetz (M.) & Co. Inc.* v *Czarnikow-Rionda Co. Inc., The Galatia* [1980] 1 All ER 501.

But note that in relation to a 'shipped' bill of lading the date of issuance must be the date of shipment even though it is in fact issued by the carrier only after the ship leaves port. Where the bill of lading used is 'received for shipment' the date of issuance must be the date when the goods are received into the charge of the carrier.

18.3.3.11   Time of tender of bill of lading

The seller must *send forward* the documents with all reasonable despatch after shipment, in the absence of a stipulation as to time in the contract. As long as the seller does this, there will be a good tender, even if the ship has already arrived: *Sanders Bros* v *Maclean & Co.* (1883) 11 QBD 327. There is no condition implied into the contract of sale that the seller must tender the bill of lading in sufficient time to meet the ship unless a term to that effect exists in the contract of sale.

Where the contract of sale contains an express stipulation as to the time of tender, failure to comply will enable the buyer to reject for breach of condition: *Toepfer* v *Lenersan-Poortman NV* [1980] 1 Lloyd's Rep 143.

Where no time is stated in the contract of sale and tender was not made within a reasonable time of shipment, it is debatable whether such a breach can be treated as a breach of condition giving a right to reject. See Benjamin, *Sale of Goods,* 4th edn, 1992, Sweet and Maxwell, paras 19-059–19–060.

18.3.3.12   Bill of lading must be genuine and accurate

Where the seller tenders a shipped bill of lading showing shipment within the contractual period, when in fact the goods were shipped *outside* that period, the document, although conforming on its face, contains an underlying non-conformity and is not a genuine document: *Kwei Tek Chao* v *British Traders Shippers Limited* [1954] 2 QB 459; *James Finlay* v *Kwik Hoo Tong* [1929] 1 KB 400.

Whether the buyer can reject the tender in these circumstances and refuse to pay, depends on the interpretation of the decision in *Gill & Duffus SA* v *Berger* [1984] 2 WLR 95, where the House of Lords held that the buyer *must* pay against documents conforming *on their face* with the documentary requirements of the contract. Lord Diplock excluded the operation of the principle where the seller is guilty of fraud. He also appeared to exclude the operation of the principle where the seller has shipped or allocated to the contract a shipment of goods fundamentally different from those agreed to be purchased:

> Your Lordships in the instant case are thus not dealing with the converse of Lord Blackburn's well-known aphorism in *Bowes* v *Shand* [(1877) 2 App Cas 455] 'if you contract to sell peas, you cannot oblige a party to take beans!'

In *Gill & Duffus* v *Berger (supra)* the House of Lords did not have to consider the rights of the buyer where the bill of lading contained a latent defect but was good on its face; on the facts the bill of lading did not contain latent defects. However, the court in *Kwei Tek Chao* v *British Traders & Shippers* [1954] 2 QB 459 was concerned with a bill of lading containing a latent defect — the bill of lading had been falsely dated. Devlin J in that case stated:

A c.i.f. contract puts a number of obligations upon the seller, some of which are in relation to the goods and some of which are in relation to the documents. So far as the goods are concerned, he must put on board at the port of shipment goods in conformity with contract description, but he must also send forward documents and those documents must comply with the contract. If he commits a breach, the breaches may in one sense overlap, in that they flow from the same act. If there is a late shipment, as there was in this case, the date of shipment being part of the description of the goods, the seller has not put on board goods which conform to the contract description, and therefore he has broken that obligation. *He has also made it impossible to send forward a bill of lading which at once conforms with the contract and states accurately the date of shipment.* Thus, the same act can cause breaches of two independent obligations. However that may be, they are distinct obligations and *the right to reject the documents arises* when the documents are tendered, and the right to reject the goods arises when they are landed and when after examination they are found not to be in conformity with the contract.

Devlin J emphatically recognised the existence of a right to reject documents where the bill of lading contains a false date of shipment. He recognised the existence of two rights to reject flowing from the one breach. Nowhere in Lord Diplock's speech were the views of Devlin J on this disputed.

In *Proctor & Gamble* v *Becher* [1988] 2 Lloyd's Rep 21, although a case dealing with damages for sending forward a wrongly dated bill of lading, the Court of Appeal accepted that the buyer could have rejected. Lord Justice Nicholls said:

Although the sole question on this appeal concerns damages, it is necessary to note at once, because this is at the heart of the arguments advanced on behalf of the buyers, that a right to damages is not the only remedy which a buyer has in respect of a misdated bill of lading. Before us it was common ground that the buyers in the present case were entitled to reject the bill of lading when it was tendered.

The prevailing view is that nothing in the decision in *Gill & Duffus* v *Berger* has removed the right of the buyer to reject and refuse to pay against documents including a falsely dated bill of lading. (See G. H. Treitel 1984 LMCLQ 565.)

Where the seller tenders a shipped bill of lading showing shipment in time but not the true date of shipment and the goods have been shipped *in time* but on a different date, the buyer can still reject. The document, although conforming on its face, is not a genuine and accurate document. In *Proctor & Gamble* v *Becher* the Court of Appeal accepted the ability of the buyer to reject in this situation. Note that the real difference between a bill of lading showing shipment in time when goods were shipped *out of time* and a bill of lading showing shipment in time when goods were shipped *in time but on a different date* arises when the buyer has accepted the bill of lading, has paid against it and is suing for damages (see **18.9**).

18.3.3.13 Bill of lading must be without reservation as to apparent good order

The seller, in performance of the c.i.f. contract, must ship goods that conform to contract description, that are of satisfactory quality and fit for their purpose and, where appropriate, that conform to sample. (For more information on the statutory implied terms of description, quality and sample, see the **General Practice Manual, Sale of Goods**.) The goods must also, at the time of shipment, conform to any express requirements of the contract.

The seller must, in the absence of a contrary contractual requirement or custom in the trade, tender a bill of lading which is 'clean', i.e. one that does not contain any reservation as to the *apparent* good order or condition of the goods or their packing: *British Imex Industries Ltd* v *Midland Bank Ltd* [1958] 1 QB 542. The time at which one considers whether a shipped bill of lading is clean is usually the time of shipment. If there is any notation on the bill of lading referring to a defective condition or loss of the goods which occurs after shipment (after the seller has completed his performance obligation in relation to the goods), the bill of lading will remain clean unless there is a custom in the trade that such a post-shipment notation or 'clausing' renders the document unmerchantable: *The Galatia* [1980] 1 All ER 501.

A consequence of the above is that a statement in the bill of lading referring to the defective condition of the goods on shipment will enable the buyer to reject the document and refuse to pay even though the defect is not such as would enable the buyer to reject the goods: *Cehave NV v Bremer Handelsgesellschaft mbH, The Hansa Nord* [1976] QB 44.

18.3.3.14 Bill of lading — contract quantity/separation from bulk

The seller must tender a bill of lading which represents only the contractual quantity: *Keighley, Maxstead & Co.* v *Bryant* (1894) 70 LT 155. In addition the bill of lading must, unless there is an express or implied term in the contract of sale to the contrary, represent goods which have been separated from the bulk: *Re Reinhold & Co. and Hansloh* (1896) 12 TLR 422; *Dewar & Webb* v *Joseph Rank* (1923) 14 L1 LR 393. This is necessary because without separation from bulk at the time of tender, the following apply:

(a) There will be no transfer of constructive possession. See *Re Wait* [1927] 1 Ch 606; *Re London Wine (Shippers) Ltd* [1986] PCC 121. The bill of lading cannot therefore operate as a document of title at common law.

(b) The purchaser will have no right to sue the carrier in tort where the purchaser does not have property or possession at the time of the loss or damage. See *The Aliakmon* [1986] 2 All ER 145; *The Filiatra Legacy* [1991] 2 Lloyd's Rep 337 (CA); and **21.4**.

Where the contract is for the sale of goods commonly shipped in bulk and the amount sold to the purchaser does not constitute a full cargo, a term may well be implied into the contract of sale, that the seller can tender a bill of lading for the contractual quantity but representing goods still part of a bulk at the time of tender.

Note that by virtue of the new s. 20A of the SOGA 1979, introduced by the Sale of Goods (Amendment) Act 1995, which applies to contracts of sale made after 18 September 1995, it is now possible for property to pass in part of a bulk cargo if the conditions in s. 20A(1)(a) and (b) are satisfied. In addition, s. 20B(2) allows interest to pass in part of a possessory bulk cargo. The reasons set out in (a) and (b) above for the unacceptability of a bill of lading relating to a bulk cargo no longer apply. Such a bill of lading issued under a contract of sale made after 18 September 1995 in circumstances where s. 20A(1) and (2) are satisfied should therefore be acceptable in the absence of an express provision in the contract of sale to the contrary.

Note, that the transfer of rights and liabilities to a 'holder' of a bill of lading is not affected by the cargo remaining in bulk during transit. See COGSA 1992, s. 5(4)(b).

18.3.3.15 No representation as to quality, weight etc. in bill of lading

The bill of lading tendered by the seller must be usual and customary in the trade. It will not be unusual for the seller to tender a bill of lading which, when issued by the carrier, contains no representation by the carrier as to quantity or weight (e.g. 'shippers load and count') or which makes no representation as to the condition of the goods (e.g. 'weight, quantity, condition, contents and value is unknown'). When goods are packaged or containerised, the statement in the bill of lading as to the contents (inserted into the bill of lading by the shipper or his agent) is qualified by the insertion of words such as 'said to contain'. This is so because the carrier is not bound to make any representation as to quantity, description, condition or contents unless he/she is in a position to ascertain the facts for himself/herself through his/her servants or agents.

18.3.3.16 Incorporation of charterparty terms in bill of lading

Where a bill of lading has been issued, purporting to incorporate some terms of a charterparty, an invalid tender will have been made. However, where it is usual in the trade for the bill of lading to refer to a charterparty, the charterparty must be tendered along with the bill of lading in order for the purchaser to ascertain that there has been a conforming tender of documents: *SIAT di del Ferro* v *Tradax Overseas SA* [1980] 1 Lloyd's Rep 53. However, this is not necessary where, by a previous course of dealing between the parties, the terms of the charterparty are well known to the purchaser: *Finska Cellulosa Forenigen* v *Westfield Paper Co. Ltd* [1940] 4 All ER 473.

18.3.3.17   Right to reject when non-conforming documents tendered

When dealing with the seller's duties in relation to shipment of the goods under the c.i.f. contract, we can see that in most instances failure to comply with those duties will make it impossible for the seller to tender a bill of lading which is genuine, accurate, usual and customary in the trade. Tender of non-conforming documents enables the buyer to reject. However, failing to tender documents *in time* may not enable the buyer to reject. See **18.3.3.11**.

18.3.3.18   Conforming tender of documents — seller in breach

Nevertheless, there are circumstances in which a conforming tender of documents can be made even though the seller is already in breach in relation to the goods. For example, if the seller has shipped non-conforming goods but the defect in the goods is not noted on the bill of lading, the document conforms on its face. The statement 'shipped in apparent good order and condition' is unqualified. If the defect is something that a carrier could not be expected to detect and did not detect on a reasonable external examination of the goods, it is not a defect which *should* have been noted on the bill of lading. It is therefore a genuine bill of lading; it is accurate in what it does say and it is reasonable and usual in the trade. Now the effect of the decision in *Gill & Duffus* v *Berger (supra)* is clear. In the absence of fraud by the seller and if the goods shipped are not fundamentally different from those that form the subject of the contract of sale, the buyer cannot reject what is in *all* respects a conforming tender of documents. The buyer must pay even if he/she knows that the seller has shipped defective goods. The buyer cannot set up his/ her rejection and refusal to pay as his/her termination of the contract because of the repudiatory breach of the seller in relation to the goods.

18.3.3.19   Letters of indemnity

In many instances the c.i.f. contract allows the seller to claim payment against documents which include a letter of indemnity, instead of a bill of lading. The contract of sale will usually make provision for this where the seller contemplates that the buyer will not receive the bill of lading in time. This is likely to happen where the ship is on a short sea trip and/or the bill of lading has to go through the banking system under a letter or letters of credit before it is released.

The letter of indemnity tendered to the purchaser contains an undertaking to indemnify against all losses, costs and liabilities arising from the fact that payment is to be made in the absence of the bill of lading.

It would be most unusual for a court to be persuaded, in the absence of clear wording in the contract of sale to the contrary, that property in the goods was still to remain with the seller once payment had been made against the letter of indemnity. There is usually no reason to maintain a security interest in the goods.

The carrier, in turn, will have agreed to deliver the goods in the absence of the bill of lading, against an undertaking to indemnify in respect of any liability, loss or damage which may be sustained by the carrier, his/her servants or agents by reason of delivery of the goods in the absence of the bill of lading. Depending on the circumstances, this letter of indemnity will be provided to the carrier, either by the seller or the buyer.

18.3.4   INVOICE

As stated earlier, the letters c.i.f. stand for cost, insurance and freight, and indicate how the c.i.f. price is computed. The seller will fix a price which covers the cost of the goods, profit, the premium and the freight charges he/she has agreed to pay on his/her own account. It is the c.i.f. seller who takes the risk of increases in freight and premium charges. Once the c.i.f. price has been concluded, the seller cannot go back for more unless there is an agreement to this effect: *D. I. Henry* v *Wilhelm Clasen* [1973] 1 Lloyd's Rep 159.

Where the freight charges, or a portion of them, are payable to the carrier on delivery of the goods at the port of destination, the c.i.f. seller, in performance of *his/her contract of sale*, must tender an invoice in which there is deducted from the c.i.f. price the freight which is payable by the buyer to the carrier at the port of destination. Normally the contract of sale will make express provision as to the contents of the invoice. However, where the contract of sale is silent, it would appear that there will still be a good tender even though the invoice fails to describe the goods as they were described in the contract of sale, as long as there are sufficient particulars to enable the buyer to identify that which is described in the invoice as the goods he/she has purchased, and as long as the description which is given is not in conflict with the description in the contract of sale.

Where the seller is to receive payment through a bank under a documentary credit, the Uniform Customs and Practice for Documentary Credits demands that the commercial invoice contain a description of the goods which corresponds with the description in the credit: UCP 1993 Revision, Article 37.

18.3.5   INSURANCE DOCUMENT

Where the contract is on c.i.f. terms, the seller's duty is to procure insurance cover at his/ her own cost, which is on 'usual terms' and which satisfies any express requirements on insurance in the contract of sale. It is unclear at what time what is 'usual' is to be considered. The view of the editors of Benjamin on *Sale of Goods* is that this question should be considered at the time the insurance is effected. See Benjamin, *Sale of Goods,* 4th edn, 1992, Sweet and Maxwell, para. 19-042.

Bearing in mind what is usual in the trade and any express requirements of the contract of sale, the seller's duty is:

(a)   To effect insurance with reputable insurers.

(b)   To effect an effective and valid policy of insurance — a policy voidable for non-disclosure or misrepresentation, for example, is not an effective policy unless it has been affirmed by the underwriters.

(c)   To effect a policy which is assignable under Marine Insurance Act 1906, s. 50(3).

(d)   To effect a policy which covers the goods for the period of time or for the voyage as specified in the contract of sale.

(e)   To effect a policy which gives continuous documentary cover, i.e. one which is available for the protection of the purchaser throughout the period of time or the voyage specified in the policy.

(f)   To effect a policy which covers the risks designated in the contract of sale. Note that here the seller does not promise in the contract of sale that the purchaser will be able to recover under the contract of insurance for losses suffered. As long as the seller effected a contract of insurance which covered the risks required to be covered under the contract of sale or which were usual in the trade, the seller, on tendering conforming documents plus the relevant insurance document, can demand payment.

(g)   To insure the goods for the amount stated in the contract of sale. In the absence of contractual provisions, the seller is only obliged to insure the goods for an amount representing their value at the time of shipment, freight payments in advance and insurance premium.

(h)   To tender the required insurance document. The contract of sale will commonly specify whether the seller is required to tender an insurance policy or an insurance certificate. Sometimes the contract of sale gives the seller the choice of one of these two. Older cases denied the right of the seller to tender an insurance certificate in substitution for a policy unless the contract expressly allowed him to do so. See *Diamond Alkali Export Corp.* v *Fl. Bourgeois* [1921] 3 KB 443; *Donald H. Scott Ltd* v *Barclays Bank Ltd* [1923] 2 KB 1; *Malmberg* v *H. & J. Evans* (1924) 30 Com Cas 107. With the changes in export practices, the increased use by sellers of floating policies and open covers, the selling on of portions of a bulk cargo insured under one policy, it may be that there will be greater readiness on the part of the courts to recognise an implied agreement between the parties or custom in the trade to accept an insurance certificate in those circumstances where the insurance certificate gives the right to demand the issue of a policy and which sets out the terms of the insurance. Note, however, that even where tender of a certificate is permitted, where there is a discrepancy between the certificate tendered and the policy, there may be a bad tender: *De Monchy* v *Phoenix Insurance Co. of Hartford* (1928) 33 Com Cas 197.

If the contract of sale is on c. and f. terms, the seller is not obliged to take out insurance at all, unless the seller is to insure at the buyer's request. In this case, although (as in the c.i.f. contract) the seller is required to tender an insurance document, the premium is to be paid by the buyer. It will not be part of the c. and f. price.

18.3.6   CONSISTENCY OF DOCUMENTS REQUIRED FOR CONFORMING TENDER

When the c.i.f. buyer is considering whether there has been a conforming tender, he/she looks not only at each document individually, but also considers them collectively. If there is an inconsistency when all the documents are considered together, the buyer can reject. For example, if a certificate of inspection or quality certifies a defective condition of the goods, this will not render the *certificate* defective, but, looking at the documents as a whole, the stated defective condition in the certificate enables the buyer to reject the tender on the basis that there is a defect in the goods apparent on the face of the document.

18.4   Contracts on F.O.B. Terms

In the f.o.b. contract the time at which the seller can expect payment will depend on the *type* of f.o.b. contract used by the parties. This will be deduced from the terms of the contract.

The letters stand for 'free on board' and are followed by a nominated port of *departure*. Unlike the term c.i.f., these words do not denote a series of contracts. In the absence of provisions in the contract to the contrary, the seller is not obliged to enter into ancillary contracts of carriage and insurance. However, the words indicate how the price is computed and the stage at which the seller will have completed his/her performance obligation in relation to the goods. As in the c.i.f. contract, the seller completes his/her performance obligation in relation to the goods *before* the goods are physically delivered at the port of destination. Whether the seller is also required to tender shipping documents before payment is due, and if so which documents, will depend on the type of f.o.b. contract. There are three basic types according to Devlin J in *Pyrene Co. Ltd* v *Scindia Navigation Co. Ltd* [1954] 2 QB 402 (see also *The El Amria and El Minia* [1982] 2 Lloyd's Rep 28). These are considered in **18.4.1** to **18.4.3**. In all three cases, however, the f.o.b. seller must ship goods from the contractual port of shipment. The nominated port is a condition of the contract viewed as part of the description of the goods. See *Petrograde Inc.* v *Stinnes Handel GmbH,* [1995] Lloyd's Rep 142. The goods shipped must be otherwise of contract description, of satisfactory quality, fit for their purpose and must conform both to sample and to any other express condition of the contract.

18.4.1   BUYER NOMINATES SHIP AND PROCURES SHIPPING SPACE

The type of f.o.b. contract in which the buyer both nominates the ship and procures the shipping space on it, is common when the contract of sale is not a f.o.b. *export* contract but rather a f.o.b. domestic *supply* contract, where a local exporter wishes the goods to be delivered on board ship. In addition, a buyer/importer will be required to use this type of f.o.b. contract where his/her government has restricted foreign currency allocation to the f.o.b. value of the goods thus promoting procurement of carriage and insurance in the local market using domestic currency. This type of f.o.b. contract is also common where the carrier is requiring freight to be paid in advance. The parties in these circumstances will normally intend that payment should be made against a mate's receipt.

18.4.1.1   Mate's receipt
A mate's receipt is a non-negotiable document, acknowledging *receipt* by the carrier of the goods therein described. The mate's receipt can also acknowledge the *shipment* of the goods. It is not a document of title at common law, unless there is a custom in the trade to that effect. See *Kum* v *Wah Tat Bank Ltd* [1971] 1 Lloyd's Rep 439.

The f.o.b. seller, having received the mate's receipt, on delivery of the goods over the ship's rail, will exchange this against payment by the f.o.b. buyer. The f.o.b. buyer, in his/her turn will relinquish it to the carrier in exchange for the issue of a bill of lading, naming him/her as shipper.

Although the f.o.b. seller actually ships the goods, the contractual shipper is the f.o.b. buyer. Nevertheless, the seller may have a contractual right of suit against the carrier. See **21.2**.

In f.o.b. contracts of the type mentioned in **18.4.1** it is the buyer, in the absence of a contrary contractual provision, who has the choice as to the time of shipment within the shipping period designated in the contract. Once the buyer has given effective shipping instructions the f.o.b. seller must begin loading within a reasonable time or load at the contractual rate. See *Nordisk Oversoisk Handelsselskab v Eriksen* (1920) 5 Ll LR 71. For the consequences of failing to load at contractual rate see *Tradax Export v Italgrani* [1986] 1 Lloyd's Rep 112. Risk of loss or damage passes on shipment into designated ship.

As in the c.i.f. contract, the duty to pay will be treated as an independent covenant and therefore in the absence of fraud by the seller or the shipment of goods fundamentally different from those ordered by the purchaser the buyer will not be able to refuse payment against a conforming mate's receipt, even though the buyer is aware that the seller is in breach.

18.4.2   WITH ADDITIONAL SERVICES

It may not be convenient for a f.o.b. buyer to contract directly with the carrier. The buyer may instead ask the f.o.b. seller to choose the vessel and arrange the shipping space. This is called a f.o.b. contract with 'additional services' or an 'extended' f.o.b. contract. By arranging it, the seller is an original party to the contract of carriage. The contract of sale usually calls for payment against a bill of lading, since the f.o.b. seller, as the legal shipper of the goods, is in a position to demand the issue and release to him/her of a bill of lading. Any freight which the f.o.b. seller has had to pay in advance to obtain the issue of the bill of lading, *will be for the buyer's account*. The f.o.b. price does not include any freight element.

As to contractual rights of suit available to the f.o.b. buyer against the carrier see **21.3**.

In the absence of any express provisions in the contract or custom in the trade, what has been said about the requirements of the bill of lading in relation to c.i.f. contracts applies, where relevant, to this type of f.o.b. contract. See *Concordia Trading BV v Richco International* [1991] 1 Lloyd's Rep 475.

The f.o.b. seller will normally (in the absence of a contractual provision to the contrary) take the bill of lading to his/her own order. The effect of this (as in the c.i.f. contract) is prima facie to preserve the seller's right of disposal until payment: s. 19(2). The seller may also agree to take out insurance. Any premium which the seller pays will be for the buyer's account. In tendering the required documents to obtain payment, the seller will tender two invoices, one for the f.o.b. price, the other for freight and insurance premiums which the seller may have been obliged to pay since, unlike the c.i.f. contract, the price does not include any freight charges or insurance premium paid by the seller. This type of f.o.b. contract is almost akin to a c.i.f. contract.

The seller under the f.o.b. contract here is commonly given the option as to the time of shipment during the shipping period. Risk of loss or damage to the goods in transit will pass once a contractual allocation of the goods has taken place. (See also, on risk, **18.8**.) As in the c.i.f. contract, the duty to pay will be treated as an independent covenant.

18.4.3   BUYER NOMINATES SHIP, SELLER PROCURES SHIPPING SPACE

The remaining type of f.o.b. contract to which Devlin J referred in the *Pyrene* case, is unlikely to be much encountered today because of modern shipping practices. It occurs where the buyer nominates the ship to be used but the seller procures the shipping space. The seller is directly a party to the contract of carriage and will obtain the bill of lading, usually to his/her own order. The contract of sale will, in most cases, call for payment against documents including a bill of lading.

The buyer will have the option as to the time of shipment within the shipment period. The danger to the buyer, if this type of contract is used, is that the ship he/she nominates may not have space to take the goods at the required time. The buyer may, in consequence, have made an ineffective nomination.

Risk of loss or damage to the goods in transit will pass on shipment in the designated ship. As in the c.i.f. contract, there is an independent obligation on the buyer to pay against conforming documents irrespective of the conditions of the goods.

As to the ability of a f.o.b. buyer to nominate a substitute vessel refer to *Cargill UK Ltd* v *Continental UK Ltd* [1989] 2 Lloyd's Rep 290.

18.5   C.I.F., F.O.B. or Ex-Ship

In determining whether the buyer must pay if the documents tendered are in order, you need to consider whether the parties agreed that the performance of the contract was to be on c.i.f., f.o.b. or ex-ship terms. A number of points arise here. First, the parties may have used the c.i.f. or f.o.b. terminology merely to indicate the elements in the price to be paid by the purchaser. Secondly, even if the terminology is purporting to define the performance obligations of the parties, mere use of the term will not be decisive: *The Julia* [1949] AC 293. All the terms of the contract must be considered. Where the effect of the terms of the contract of sale, purporting to be on e.g., c.i.f. terms, is to give the purchaser, on payment against documents, no rights against the carrier and no rights against the insurers, the contract is in truth an ex-ship contract: *The Julia* (an example of a contract which could operate c.i.f. or ex-ship depending on which documents the seller chose to tender).

Where the contract is on ex-ship terms, loss/damage to the goods during the voyage will enable the buyer to refuse to pay, or enable him/her to claim back advance payment made. However, it is worth noting the new s. 15A of the SOGA 1979, inserted by the Sale and Supply of Goods Act 1994, which will deprive the non-consumer buyer of his right to reject if 'the breach is so slight that it would be unreasonable for him to reject', the burden in relation to this being on the seller. Section 15A will not apply where a contrary intention is expressed or can be implied in the contract.

The following points should be noted.

18.5.1   TIME OF PAYMENT/OBLIGATION TO PAY

A contract purporting to be on c.i.f. terms will not be treated as in reality on ex-ship terms simply because the *time* of payment only arises on the arrival of the goods. The contract remains on c.i.f. terms where as a matter of construction the *obligation* to pay arises on tender of documents: *Fragano* v *Long* (1825) 4 B & C 219. In these circumstances and as long as on a construction of the contract as a whole there are no other reasons to cease to treat the contract as on c.i.f. terms, if the goods do not arrive, payment must still be made, time being fixed as at the date when the goods would have arrived.

18.5.2   NON-ARRIVAL OF GOODS DUE TO LOSS OF VESSEL OR OTHER UNAVOIDABLE CAUSE

The contract may contain a term 'should the goods not arrive from loss of vessel or other unavoidable cause, then contract is to be void'. This phrase has been interpreted in *Karinjee Jivanjee & Co.* v *William F. Malcolm & Co.* (1926) 25 L1 LR 28 as follows. If loss takes place before the buyer accepts the tender of documents, the seller ceases to be obliged to tender the documents and the buyer to take up and pay for them. There ceases to be an obligation to pay against documents. The seller therefore bears the risk of loss. However, unlike an ex-ship contract the seller will not be liable in damages for non-delivery and will be able to claim the insurance monies himself/herself. (The valuation in the insurance policy may be more than the actual value of the goods lost.) However, where the goods have suffered damage or have deteriorated, or have been lost *after* the buyer has accepted the tender of documents, the contract operates as a normal c.i.f. contract.

18.6   Effects of Documents other than Bills of Lading

We will now consider what sort of benefits the c.i.f./fo.b. purchaser obtains where the seller has the right to, and does, tender a shipping document other than the traditional bill of lading.

18.6.1   DELIVERY ORDER

Although the parties to the contract of sale are able to agree to the tender of a delivery order whatever the type of cargo shipped, the delivery order is more likely to be used where a bulk cargo has been shipped and at that stage purchasers for parts of the bulk have not been found. On shipment, therefore, one bill of lading will have been issued, acting as the receipt for the goods. It will obviously not be possible to use this one document in performance of the several purchases of portions of the bulk. The manufacturer/seller of the bulk might instead provide in the individual contracts of sale that a delivery order can be tendered instead of a bill of lading. The delivery order 'orders' the carrier to deliver the goods to the party named in the order. It does not act as a receipt for the goods. In the absence of a contractual provision or a custom in the trade or a previous course of dealing between the parties permitting tender of a delivery order, the c.i.f./f.o.b. buyer can reject and refuse to pay against a delivery order of whatever type.

If a c.i.f. contract permits the tender of a delivery order, without specifying which type, the c.i.f. buyer is only obliged to accept and pay against a delivery order which places him/her as near as possible in the same position as he/she would have been on receipt of a bill of lading: *The Julia* [1949] AC 293; *Khron* v *Thegra* [1975] 1 Lloyd's Rep 146.

So what benefits does a c.i.f. purchaser receive on receipt of a bill of lading? On receipt of a shipped transferable bill of lading, the buyer obtains, over and above the promise of the seller in the contract of sale that there will be proper performance, the following:

(a)   Transfer to the buyer of constructive possession of the goods, by transfer to the buyer of the bill of lading. The buyer will be able to deal with the goods by means of the documents. The buyer can transfer on constructive possession in the goods by means of transfer of possession of the bill of lading.

(b)   Transfer of property on payment against tender of the appropriate bill of lading.

(c)   The right to sue the carrier in tort for negligence if there has been transfer of constructive possession or property prior to or at the same time as the loss or damage occurred.

(d)   The right to demand the goods from the ship on production of the bill of lading.

(e)   The right to sue the carrier in contract for loss or damage to the goods by virtue of the operation of the COGSA 1992, where the bill of lading was issued after 15 September 1992.

It can be seen that transfer of the bill of lading has proprietary/possessory and contractual consequences. Note that a cargo remaining in bulk during sea-transit can affect the proprietary/possessory position if s. 20A SOGA 1979 is inapplicable.

In **18.6.1.1** to **18.6.1.4** below we will see how far the use of a delivery order produces the same consequences.

18.6.1.1   Delivery orders — proprietary and possessory effect
Constructive possession of goods will vest in the buyer if the following conditions apply:

(a)   the order is addressed *to* the party in possession or control of the goods whilst they are in transit ordering him/her to deliver the goods to the party named in the order; and

(b)   the party in possession or control of the goods in transit promises to hold the goods for the benefit of the person named in the order. This promise is called an 'attornment'; and

(c)   the attornment is given *to* the buyer; and

(d)   at the time of the attornment or thereafter, but whilst the goods remain in possession or control of party who attorns, the goods of the buyer are separated from a bulk. (But note, (d) might be unnecessary in relation to contracts of sale made after 18 September 1995, by virtue of SOGA 1979, s. 20A which allows property to pass in part of a bulk in certain circumstances.)

OR, if on the seller's instructions, the party in possession of the goods in transit issues his/her own 'warrant' undertaking to hold the goods for the benefit of the person named in the warrant. Condition (a) above is unnecessary, condition (b) is automatically satisfied, but conditions (c) and (d) are still relevant.

The promise or 'attornment' given to the buyer by the party in possession or control of the goods in transit, gives the latter the control over the goods necessary to transfer to him/her constructive possession of the goods

Section 29(4) provides:

> *where the goods are at the time of sale in the possession of a third person, there is no delivery by seller to buyer unless and until the third person acknowledges to the buyer that he holds the goods on his behalf ...*

Note that the act of attornment does not make the document negotiable. In other words, a transfer of the attorned delivery order by the buyer would not operate as a transfer of constructive possession of the goods to a sub-purchaser. There would have to be a fresh attornment to the sub-purchaser by the party in possession or control. It is only a bill of lading or other document recognised as a document of title at common law which gives an automatic attornment to each fresh holder of the document. This is so even though COGSA 1992, s. 1(4) and s. 5(3) allow the party identified in the ship's delivery order to be identified as 'order' and thus contemplate the transfer on of the delivery order. COGSA 1992 merely affects contractual consequences of use of a delivery order, although the provisions of the Act as they relate to delivery orders may create a fresh impetus for the recognition of certain types of delivery order as documents of title at common law.

The receipt of the delivery order by the party in possession or control of the goods in transit will not suffice to effect an attornment. A positive act is required, recording that the person in possession holds for the benefit of a party identified in the delivery order: *Laurie & Morewood* v *Dudin & Sons* [1926] 1 KB 223.

Property in the goods will pass when the parties intend it to pass, which may be before or after attornment. Usually, however, the parties will not intend property in the goods to pass until payment is made; and payment, in the absence of intention to the contrary, is due on delivery (s. 28). Thus, the act of attornment will trigger the obligation to pay, and effect the passing of property. Note, however, that property in the goods cannot pass until the goods become ascertained (s. 16), unless SOGA 1979, s. 20A, applies to allow property to pass in part of a bulk. Section 20A applies to contracts of sale made after 18 September 1995.

In order to be able to pursue a claim in negligence against the party in possession of and carrying the goods, it will be necessary to show a proprietary and/or possessory interest in the goods at the time the loss or damage occurs: *The Aliakmon* [1986] 2 All ER 145.

Note in conclusion that the transfer of constructive possession requires the giving of an undertaking *by* the party in possession or control of the goods in transit *to* the *buyer*. Thus, an undertaking given by a party not yet in possession, e.g., sellers warehouseman ... at the port of destination will not suffice. Equally, any undertaking given *to* a party other than the buyer will not transfer constructive possession to the buyer.

18.6.1.2 Delivery orders — contractual consequences
COGSA 1992, which has replaced the Bill of Lading Act 1855 with regard to documents issued after 15 September 1992, has created contractual rights to sue in a party identified in the delivery order.

In order for the buyer to obtain a contractual right of action, COGSA 1992, s. 1(4) provides that the document must identify the buyer and must contain an undertaking which:

(a) *is given under or for the purposes of a contract for the carriage by sea of the goods to which the document relates, or of goods which include those goods; and*
(b) *is an undertaking by the carrier to a person identified in the document to deliver the goods to which the document relates to that person.*

COGSA 1992 describes such a document satisfying (a) and (b) above and which is not a seaway bill or a bill of lading, as a ship's delivery order.

A person to whom delivery is to be made of the goods to which the ship's delivery order relates in accordance with the undertaking contained in the order, shall have transferred to him/her the contract under or for the purposes of which the undertaking contained in the order was given: see COGSA 1992, s. 2(1)(c) and s. 5(1).

A person identified in a ship's delivery order who obtains contractual rights to sue by virtue of COGSA 1992 also obtains the right to demand the goods from the ship. There is no need for tender of the ship's delivery order to obtain release of the goods. Acquiring contractual rights is not dependent on a buyer showing he is a 'holder' of the delivery order. He/she must demonstrate that he/she is identified as the person to whom delivery should be made under the order.

18.6.1.3 Delivery orders — bulk cargoes — proprietary-possessory effect
Any undertaking given by the party in possession or control of a bulk cargo to deliver a quantity of goods to the buyer, will not transfer to the purchaser a legal interest in the goods. Property cannot pass whilst the goods remain unascertained: SOGA 1979, s. 16. Constructive possession will not be transferred: *Re London Wine Co. (Shippers) Ltd* [1986] PCC 121; *Re Goldcorp Exchange Ltd (in receivership)* [1994] 2 All ER 806. But note reversal of this proprietary and possessory position where SOGA 1979, s. 20A applies. Section 20A applies to contracts of sale made after 18 September 1995.

Note, however, that the c.i.f. or f.o.b. purchaser can still bear the risk of loss or damage even though the goods remain in bulk: *Sterns Ltd* v *Vickers Ltd* [1923] 1 KB 78. The House of Lords in *The Aliakmon* [1986] 2 All ER 145, has held that even though goods might be at buyer's risk, a claim in negligence is only available to a person who has 'either the legal ownership of or a possessory title to the property concerned at the time the loss or damage occurred'.

18.6.1.4 Delivery orders — bulk cargoes — contractual effect
COGSA 1992 allows the person 'identified in the ship's delivery order to pursue a contractual remedy even though the goods remained in bulk in transit'. See s. 2(3)(b) and s. 5(4)(b).

18.6.1.5 Type of delivery order acceptable under the c.i.f. contract
If the c.i.f. contract permits tender of a delivery order without expressly or impliedly specifying which type, the c.i.f. buyer is probably only required to accept a document which satisfies the definition of a ship's delivery order under COGSA 1992 *and* which transfers to him/her constructive possession of the goods, i.e., there must be:

(a) an attornment given by the carrier in possession or control of the cargo in transit, *to* the buyer; and
(b) if the cargo, to which the delivery order relates, was shipped in bulk, the attornment must relate to an ascertained cargo unless the provisions of SOGA 1979, s. 20A apply; and
(c) the undertaking is given by the carrier to the buyer identified in the document to deliver the goods to which the document relates; and

(d)   the undertaking to deliver is given under or for the purposes of a contract for carriage by sea of the goods to which the document relates.

18.6.2   SEAWAY BILL

The seaway bill is a straight-consigned bill of lading in printed form. It contains no words indicating transferability but merely indicates a named consignee. See **21.18**, examples 4 and 5. Such a document acts as a receipt for the goods but is not a document of title at common law. It is not a symbol representing the goods. Possession of it does not represent constructive possession of the goods. This is so because it is not necessary to tender such a document to obtain delivery of the goods from the carrier. The carrier does not undertake to deliver to the holder of the seaway bill; he/she undertakes to deliver to the consignee *identified* in the seaway bill or (usually) any other party as directed by the shipper. In consequence, the consignee must identify himself as the party to whom delivery should be made.

However, although the seaway bill has no possessory effect, COGSA 1992 provides a contractual remedy to the person 'to whom delivery of the goods to which the seaway bill relates is to be made by the carrier in accordance with the contract of carriage': s. 2(1)(b). In other words, like the transferable bill of lading, it can have a contractual function if necessary.

18.6.3   DOCUMENTS FOR MULTIMODAL TRANSPORT

Where the seller is transporting goods by container, he/she may use the services of a freight forwarder. Where containers are used to transport goods, there may be several modes of transport and several carriers used in performance of the contract of sale. The freight forwarder may be employed merely to arrange carriage/on carriage as agent for the seller and receive the carriage documents on the seller's behalf (see **Figure 18.1** below). Similarly, while still acting as agent, he may arrange the carriage/on carriage but issue a 'house' bill of lading to the seller (see **Figure 18.2** below). On the other hand, the freight forwarder may undertake the carriage operation as a principal, in which case a contract of carriage is concluded between the freight forwarder and the seller, who receives from the freight forwarder a combined transport document (see **Figure 18.3** below).

18.6.3.1   'House' bill of lading

Where the freight forwarder is 'stuffing' a container with goods in various ownership (this is called a mixed container load) he/she will usually take a bill of lading to his/her own order. It will obviously not be possible to tender this 'groupage' bill of lading, as it is called, to individual owners of cargo in the container. The position is as follows.

Where the freight forwarder is not acting as a principal, but is merely acting in the traditional role of agent for the cargo owners in arranging the transport of the goods, he/she will tender what is known as a 'house' bill of lading to the client. This document enables the holder of it to demand the release of the goods from the freight forwarder's agent at the container depot at the place of destination. It is not a true bill of lading, as in the context described the freight forwarder is not a sea carrier. Indeed the freight forwarder may not undertake any carriage duties at all. The extent of the freight forwarder's responsibilities depends on the contract with the client, but normally the freight forwarder will confine himself/herself to the careful selection of carriers. He/she does not take responsibility for the acts or omissions of the carrier(s) involved in the execution of the transport. Even though the seller can sue the carrier on the contract of carriage as undisclosed principal (see Figure 18.2) there will still be difficulties in determining when the loss or damage occurred and thus which carrier is potentially liable and what conventions apply to govern and limit liability. (Different conventions may apply to the various modes of carriage, i.e. carriage by air governed by the Warsaw Convention; carriage by road by the Convention on the Contract for the International Carriage of Goods by Road (CMR); and carriage by rail by the International Convention concerning the Carriage of Goods by Rail (CIM).)

The 'house' bill of lading is not a true bill of lading. The Carriage of Goods by Sea Act 1992 will not apply to it. In these circumstances, where the seller wishes to sell on, he/she will not be able to transfer to the purchaser the rights to sue on a contract contained in the house bill of lading. Nor will the seller be able to transfer rights to sue on the groupage bill of lading (which is a true bill of lading), as this document is not transferred to the seller by the freight forwarder. No implied contract between the carrier and the holder of the house bill of lading will arise, as that document does not contain an undertaking by the sea carrier to deliver to the purchaser — it is the freight forwarder's agent who has undertaken to deliver to the purchaser. The house bill of lading is not a document of title at common law; possession of it does not represent constructive possession of the goods.

18.6.3.2   Multimodal transport document

Instead of acting merely as agent, the freight forwarder can enter into a contract of services with the client in which he/she agrees to undertake responsibility for the overall carriage of the goods, whether or not he/she actually undertakes any of the carriage operations. The freight forwarder is very likely to enter into such a contract with a client when he/she will be shipping a mixed container load. We call the freight forwarder who undertakes the above responsibilities, a Multimodal Transport Operator (MTO). The MTO will, on receipt of the goods, issue a combined transport document which is usually expressed to be in transferable form. This document will indicate that the MTO undertakes liability as carrier for the whole transport operation. If loss or damage occurs to the goods en route, the client will have a contractual remedy against one party (the MTO), no matter at what stage and in whose custody the goods were when the loss or damage occurred. There will still be the problem of considering the stage at which the loss occurred and thus what convention governs the MTO's liability. It is common for the combined transport document to incorporate the Uniform Rules for a Combined Transport Document.

If it can be said that the MTO is a sea carrier by virtue of his legal responsibility for the sea leg of the journey, the MT document will operate either as a traditional 'received for shipment' bill of lading (if transferable in form), or as a seaway bill, to both of which COGSA 1992 is potentially applicable.

In **Figure 18.1**

(a)   Freight forwarder undertakes with seller/shipper to enter into the various contracts of carriage in order to complete transport of the goods, on behalf of the seller/shipper. The freight forwarder in this scenario does not act as carrier or undertake the responsibilities of a carrier.

(b)   Whether the seller retains the transport documents or transfers them to the purchaser, it may be necessary to establish at what stage in the voyage loss or damage took place and thus which convention applies to govern liability. In addition, circumstances may require the purchaser to establish privity of contract with the carrier.

Figure 18.1

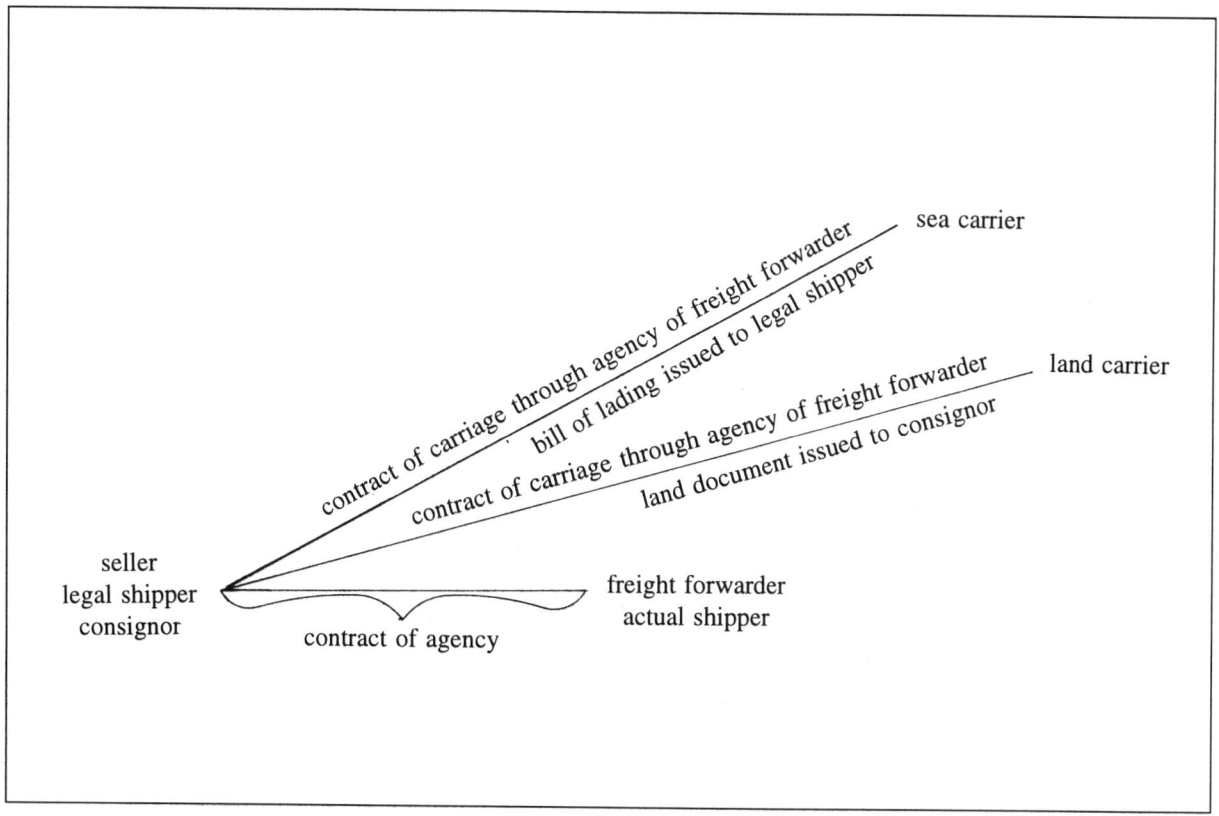

Figure 18.2

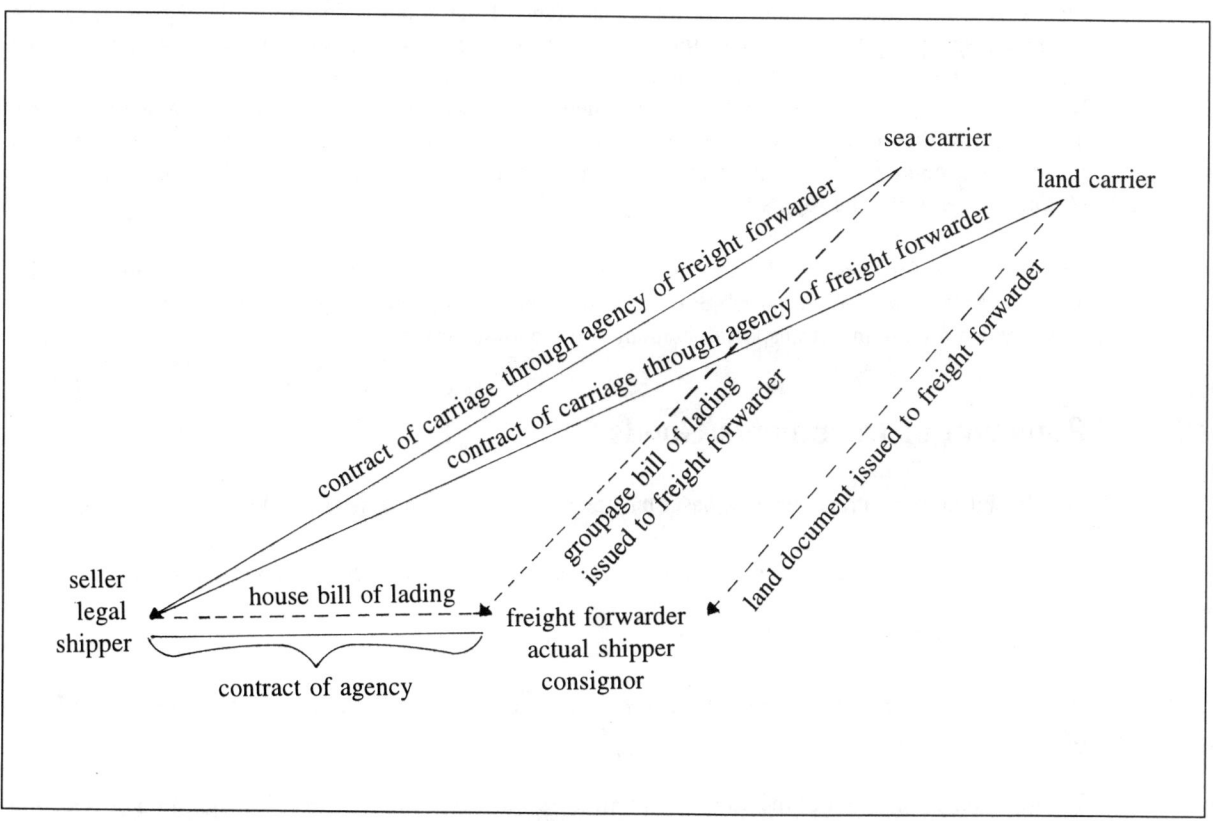

Figure 18.3

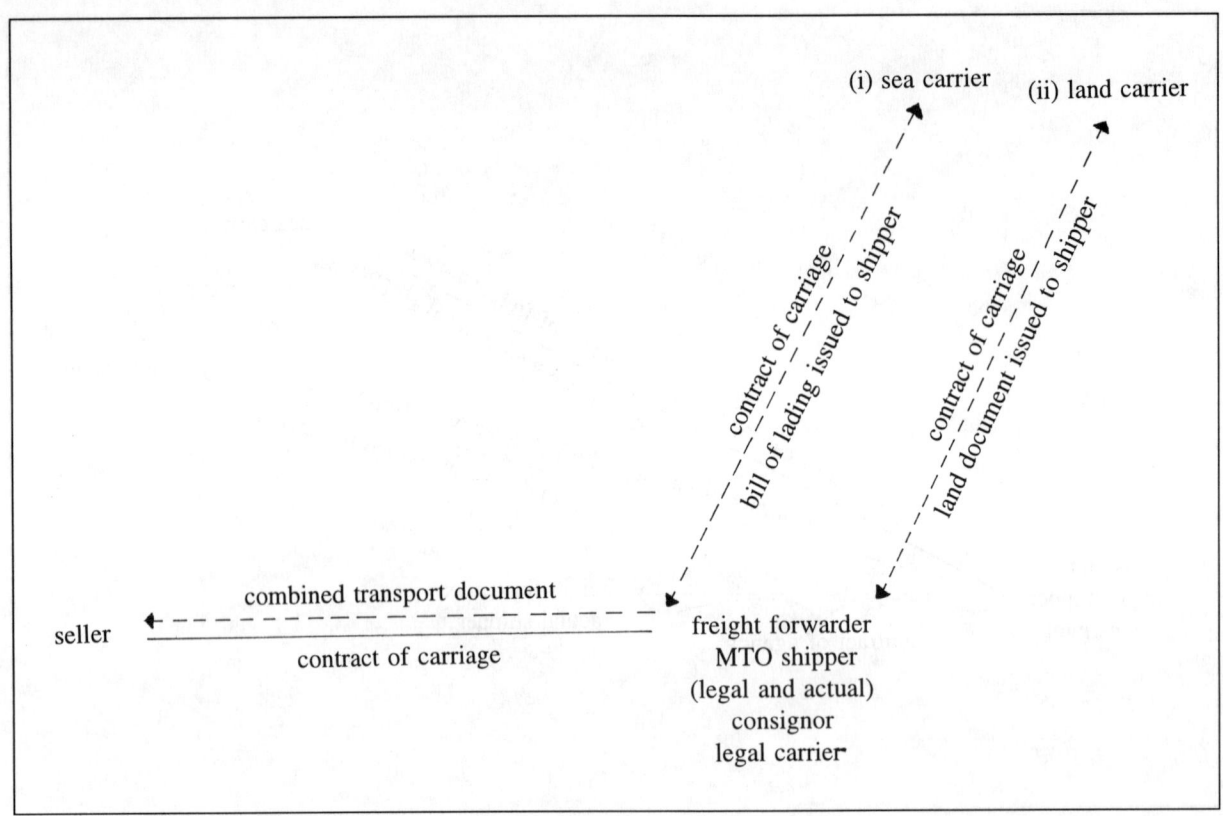

The difference between **Figure 18.3** and **Figures 18.1** and **18.2** is that the freight forwarder (MTO) in **Figure 18.3** undertakes responsibility for the carriage of the goods — he/she is the legal carrier. The combined transport (MT) document that he/she issues to the seller makes this clear. Whether or not he/she is actually carrying, he/she undertakes overall responsibility for the carriage of the goods. Nevertheless, an action in bailment can be pursued by the owner against carriers sub-contracted to carry the goods by the bailee MTO. Sub-contractor carriers might also be able to rely on the terms of sub-bailment contracts in an action pursued against them by the owner of the goods. Refer to *The K. H. Enterprise* [1994] 1 Lloyd's Rep 593.

Since 'received for shipment' bills of lading in transferable form and seaway bills fall within the ambit of COGSA 1992, it may be possible to argue transfer of contractual rights to sue to the purchaser of goods, when a combined transport document is issued/transferred.

18.7 Rejection of Documents/Goods

In c.i.f. and f.o.b. contracts the purchaser has the right to reject in respect of a breach of the obligation:

(a) to ship in time conforming goods or allocate to the contract conforming goods that have been shipped in time; and

(b) to tender conforming documents:

Kwei Tek Chao v *British Traders and Shippers Ltd* [1954] 2 QB 459; *Yelo* v *SM Machado* [1952] 1 Lloyd's Rep 183.

The question of rejection of the *documents* will arise *when they are tendered*. The question of rejection of the goods will not become exercisable:

... until the seller has unconditionally appropriated the goods to the contract. Under a c.i.f. contract this does not happen until his reservation of the right of disposal of the goods by his withholding from the buyer the shipping documents which represent them, is terminated by his transferring the shipping documents to the buyers.

(Per Lord Diplock in *Gill & Duffus SA* v *Berger* [1984] 1 All ER 438.)

18.7.1 REJECTION OF DOCUMENTS

Rejection of documents must therefore be considered first. We have already examined the reasons upon which the buyer can rely to reject the documents (see **18.3.3.5** *et seq.*).

If the documents are rejected, so are the goods, even if the breach, in relation to the goods, would not have given the buyer the right to reject them. If the rejection is lawful the buyer can refuse payment, *and*, if it can also be determined that the seller is then in breach, the buyer can treat the contract as terminated and sue for damages for non-delivery. If the documents are accepted or deemed to be accepted, the buyer, unless he/she has waived the breach altogether, can recover damages for breach of warranty — normally nominal. The right to reject the document is lost on acceptance or deemed acceptance of the documents.

18.7.2 LOSS OF RIGHT TO REJECT GOODS

18.7.2.1 Acceptance of documents

If the documents are accepted or deemed to have been accepted (see **18.7.2.2**), the right to reject them is lost: s. 11(4). However, this will not in every case affect the buyer's right to reject the goods. (See **Sale of Goods** in the **General Practice Manual** for circumstances in which there exists a right to reject goods.) The two rights to reject are independent; essentially, loss of one will not affect the other: Devlin J in *Kwei Tek Chao* v *British Traders and Shippers Ltd* [1954] 2 QB 459. Nevertheless, acceptance of documents will deprive the buyer of the ability to reject the goods in the following circumstances:

(a)   Where there is no non-conformity in relation to the goods or the non-conformity is not such as to allow the remedy of rejection. The failure to reject the documents has, practically speaking, prevented the buyer from placing the goods back in the seller's hands.

(b)   Even if there is a non-conformity in relation to the goods which allows rejection, a buyer who accepts documents, *aware* of defects on the face of the documents, will have waived his right to reject the goods *for the reasons manifested* in the documents. Devlin J said in *Kwei Tek Chao* v *British Traders and Shippers Ltd (supra)*:

It may be that if the actual date of shipment is not in conformity with the contract and the error appears from the documents, the buyer by accepting the documents, not only loses his right to reject the documents but also his right to reject the goods, but that would be because he had waived in advance reliance on the date of shipment.

(c)   The buyer can also be estopped by his/her conduct from rejecting the goods in those circumstances where the accepted documents contain a defect(s) which should have been seen on a reasonable examination. The buyer will be estopped by his/her conduct from rejecting the goods for that/those reasons: *Panchaud Frères* v *Etablissements General Grain Co.* [1970] 1 Lloyd's Rep 53.

18.7.2.2 Deemed acceptance

Apart from the above, an independent right to reject the goods can be lost by a deemed acceptance of the *goods* under s. 35. The deemed acceptance provisions cover three situations:

(a)   Intimation of acceptance.

A buyer will be deemed to have accepted by virtue of an indication of acceptance by words or conduct, but only where he has previously examined them or has had a reasonable opportunity of examining them to determine if they conform with the contract: see s. 35(1) and (2).

(b) Delivery of goods to the buyer c.i.f./f.o.b., followed by an act in relation to them inconsistent with the ownership of the seller after a reasonable opportunity for examination has occurred. See s. 35(1) and (2). Several points need to be considered:

(i) In a c.i.f. contract a reasonable opportunity for examination of the goods will prima facie arise at the time of physical delivery to the purchaser: Molling & Co. v Dean & Son (1901) 18 TLR 217. In a f.o.b. contract, even though there is no presumption as to the time when a reasonable opportunity of examination takes place, the courts usually decide that the time of examination is, as in the c.i.f. contract, when the goods arrive at their destination. This will be so because the f.o.b. seller knows that the goods are to be shipped and is aware that the nature of the packing will usually make inspection at the time and place of shipment impractical. The burden of proving that the buyer had a reasonable opportunity of examination of the goods at the time of shipment lies on the seller: J. W. Schofield v Rownson, Drew and Clydesdale (1922) 10 L1 LR 480. However, in either the c.i.f. or the f.o.b. contract, the place and time of examination can be postponed to the time of delivery to a sub-purchaser if the seller knew or ought to have known that the goods were to be delivered to a sub-purchaser and that examination at the time of delivery to the purchaser would be impractical by reason of the unsuitability of the place of delivery or the nature of the packing: Van den Hurk v Martens [1920] 1 KB 850; Molling v Dean (1901) 18 TLR 217.

(ii) Where property in the goods has passed to the purchaser, the phrase 'act inconsistent with the ownership of the seller' refers to the possible reversionary interest of the seller if the goods are rejected: Kwei Tek Chao v British Traders and Shippers Ltd [1954] 2 QB 459.

(iii) SOGA 1979 does not define what is an act inconsistent with the ownership of a seller but does indicate at s. 35(6) that it will not include a sub-sale or other disposition, or any delivery thereunder.

(c) Lapse of reasonable time.

The right to reject can be lost under s. 35(4) where, after the lapse of a reasonable time, the purchaser retains the goods without intimating to the seller that he/she has rejected them. What is a reasonable time is difficult to determine. The court has to balance the interests of the seller and the buyer; it has to consider the value of the goods (e.g., whether they are perishable), whether there is a volatile market etc. However, s. 35(5) requires there also to be a consideration of whether the buyer has had a reasonable opportunity of examining the goods to determine their conformity.

Once a buyer has proved what on the face of it amounts to a clear and unequivocal rejection of the goods, it is for the seller to prove that the right to reject has been lost by other conduct having a different and inconsistent effect. It is not for the buyer to establish the negative case that he/she did nothing to disentitle himself/herself from rejecting: Tradax Export v European Grain & Shipping [1983] 2 Lloyd's Rep 100.

18.7.2.3 Inability to make restitution

The right to reject the goods can also be lost at common law if the purchaser is unable to make restitution. However, the c.i.f. purchaser will not be prevented from rejecting non-conforming goods, even though they are lost or have received further *damage* whilst at his/her risk, as long as he/she is not at fault. Where the goods cannot be returned in the same condition because of the fault of the buyer, it is arguable that the buyer has lost the right to reject for the initial non-conformity because he/she has done an act 'inconsistent with the ownership of the seller'.

18.7.3 REMEDY ON REJECTION OF GOODS

Where there is a non-conformity of a type allowing the purchaser to reject and the purchaser exercises that right in time, then, *if* the seller is in breach the buyer will be able to sue for the return of all payments made on the grounds of a total failure of consideration, and sue for damages for non-delivery (see **18.9.1**).

Under s. 36 the buyer is not bound to return the goods to the seller when he/she rejects them. It is sufficient that the buyer intimates to the seller that the goods are at the seller's disposal. The goods must be made available to the seller at the place of examination: *Heilbutt* v *Hickson* (1872) LR 7 CP 456/457.

The buyer does not have a lien on the goods he/she has rejected for the return of the price: *J. L. Lyons* v *May & Baker* [1923] 1 KB 685. The prospect of being an unsecured creditor may well persuade the purchaser not to reject the goods (as to the possible measures of damages, see **18.9**).

18.7.4 REMEDY ON ACCEPTANCE OF NON-CONFORMING GOODS

Where the right to reject is lost, the payment obligation remains. The breach about which the buyer is complaining is now relegated to a breach of warranty (s. 11(4)), for which the buyer can still claim damages (see **18.9**).

18.8 Allocation of Risk between Buyer and Seller in C.I.F./F.O.B. Contracts

C.i.f. and f.o.b. sellers have a duty to tender conforming goods, i.e. goods that comply with:

(a) express provisions of the contract; and
(b) the statutory implied terms as to description, quality, fitness for purpose and sample.

SOGA 1979 categorises the statutory implied terms as to description, quality, fitness for purpose and sample as conditions. Failure to comply with a condition gives the buyer the right to reject. However, note s. 15A in which a non-consumer buyer will be deprived of his right to reject the goods, i.e. 'the breach will not be treated as a breach of condition but may be treated as a breach of warranty' where 'the breach is so slight that it would be unreasonable for him to reject them'.

SOGA 1979, s. 30 allows rejection where there is a contractual shortfall or excess in the quantity delivered. But note s. 30(2A) which prevents a non-consumer buyer rejecting a shortfall cargo or the whole consignment where there has been an excess delivery, where 'the shortfall or, as the case may be, the excess is so slight that it would be unreasonable for him to do so'.

With regard to other express provisions, in the absence of an expressed intention as to the status of the term, or previous authority, the courts may construe it as an innominate term, in which case the right of the buyer to reject will depend on the gravity of the breach: *The Hansa Nord* [1976] QB 44.

Instances arise where goods conform at the beginning of their journey from the seller's warehouse to the buyer's warehouse, but at some stage during the transport of the goods they cease to be such as to conform as a result of some external incident. In order to determine whether the seller has made a non-conforming tender and then to discuss the nature of the buyer's rights and remedies, we need to determine who bore the risk of loss or damage at the time the goods ceased to conform.

18.8.1 TIME OF PROVISIONAL DELIVERY

The passing of risk is a matter of intention. However, risk cannot pass until a particular stage in the performance of the contract has been reached — the provisional delivery stage. In both the c.i.f. and f.o.b. contract, once this stage is reached the parties intend that the seller's responsibilities in relation to the goods cease — although the seller may still be obliged to tender documents, and will still be obliged not to prevent physical delivery of the goods to the buyer at the place of destination.

It is said that in traditional c.i.f. and f.o.b. contracts, this provisional delivery stage is reached at the time of shipment, and in consequence risk of loss or damage to the goods is intended to pass on shipment; or *as from* shipment in the case of a c.i.f. contract where the seller chooses to perform his/her contract with the buyer by allocating to the contract goods which have been previously shipped, either by the seller himself/herself or his/her predecessor in title: *The Julia* [1949] AC 293; *C. Groom Ltd* v *Barber* [1915] 1 KB 316; *Manbre Saccharine & Co.* v *Corn Products Co.* [1919] 1 KB 198.

The provisional delivery stage is reached on shipment and thus risk can pass *if at that time*, that shipment has become irrevocably attached to the contract. This attachment of a source to a contract is called a contractual appropriation. This irrevocable act will occur at the time of shipment *if* at that stage the seller can no longer change his/her mind and use another shipment of goods to perform his/her contract with the buyer — if it is known at that stage which source *only* can be used to perform the contract. In other words, the goods are identifiable as a source. The goods are now 'contract goods'.

The mere act of shipment does not always irrevocably attach that shipment or a part of it to the contract. For example, the buyer's contract may be one for the purchase of purely generic, unascertained goods, with the seller choosing and arranging carriage. That seller may have similar contracts with other purchasers. In such a case the mere act of shipment cannot in itself act as an allocation to any one of the seller's contracts. The seller can in these circumstances insist on using any shipment to perform his/her contract with any one of the purchasers. Any one buyer cannot sue in conversion for non-delivery of *one particular shipment.* Something else is required. Unfortunately, in *Groom* v *Barber* and in *Manbre Saccharine* v *Corn Products,* the court did not consider whether the goods were contractual at the time of the loss. The prevailing view is that risk cannot pass before the goods are identified as from a particular source. This means that any deterioration, damage or loss occurring before this time is at the risk of the seller. The buyer can reject the goods tendered. Whether the buyer can sue for damages for non-delivery, depends on whether the seller is able to retender. For passing of risk in contractual/noncontractual goods, see Goode, *Commercial Law,* 1985, Pelican, and Benjamin, *Sale of Goods,* 4th edn, 1992, Sweet and Maxwell, para. 19-096. But see Benjamin, para. 19-095, for a contrary view where the goods are merely damaged.

18.8.2 ALLOCATION OF GOODS TO THE CONTRACT

As it is only when goods become 'the contract goods' that a provisional delivery takes place, it is necessary to consider in more detail when this stage is reached.

18.8.2.1 Specific shipment
Where the contract on c.i.f. or f.o.b. terms is for the sale of a specific shipment, risk of loss or damage can pass at the time the contract is made (and not 'as from' the shipment, which took place before the contract was concluded), since the parties know from the moment of contract which goods *must* be used in performance of the contract of sale.

18.8.2.2 Specific goods
Where the contract on c.i.f or f.o.b. terms is for the sale of specific goods to be shipped, risk may pass before shipment, since it is known at the time the contract is made what are the contract goods. Under s. 20(1) property and risk prima facie pass together. In the absence of contrary intention, therefore, the placement of the property interest between the parties governs the allocation of risk. Property may well pass before shipment if payment has already been made. Indeed, applying s. 18 (r. 1) property (and therefore prima facie risk) could pass at the time the contract is made. If risk were to pass before shipment, the buyer is protected by procuring, or obtaining from the seller, insurance including 'warehouse to warehouse' cover.

18.8.2.3 Unascertained goods
Where the contract is for the sale of unascertained goods, it becomes more difficult to determine which goods become the 'contract goods' and when. In the c.i.f. contract and those f.o.b. contracts in which the seller is given the right to choose the ship, the contract of sale normally provides that the seller should send a notice of appropriation or 'declaration of shipment' to the purchaser, indicating which shipment is to be used to perform the seller's contract with the purchaser. In order to amount to a contractual act of allocation of a shipment to the contract, the notice must comply with all contractual terms relating to it. It must refer to goods of the contractual description and contain all the required particulars, i.e. date of shipment, name of the ship. The notice must be given in time. Goff LJ in *The Post-Chaser* [1981] 2 Lloyd's Rep 695 said:

The requirement of 'declaration of ship' in the present form of contract constitutes an essential step in the seller's performance of his contractual obligations. It is, moreover, an important step, because, once such a declaration is made, the buyer can then appropriate goods from the ship so declared in performance of his obligations to a particular sub-buyer to whom he has already agreed to sell goods of the same contractual description ...

Once the notice complies with the contract *in form,* it amounts to a valid notice and cannot be withdrawn. It is effective, i.e. makes goods contractual, on receipt of the notice: *Continentale Importation* v *Handelsvetretung* (1928) 138 LT 663. If, therefore, the goods have already been damaged by the time the notice is received, the risk of that loss remains with the seller. It will not assist the seller to argue that the goods to which the notice relates conformed at the time of shipment.

In the rare cases where the contracts do not make provision for the service of a notice of appropriation, it will be much more difficult to determine when goods become contractual. However, as the seller must eventually irrevocably bind himself to deliver a shipment or a part of a shipment, a consideration of all the circumstances of the case will point to a particular time when this has occurred. In some instances it may be only when a bill of lading is tendered to the c.i.f. or f.o.b. purchaser.

It must be observed here that, just because the seller has made goods contractual, he will not necessarily be bound to deliver *all* those goods. The phrase 'making the goods contractual' or 'appropriating the goods to the contract' can be understood in this sense — that the seller has bound himself/herself to deliver a portion of those goods on that ship. In other words, the seller has contractually and irrevocably identified his/her source. The goods to be used to perform the seller's contract with the buyer must now come from *that* source. Risk *can* pass in part of a bulk (as long as the source has become contractual): *Sterns Ltd* v *Vickers Ltd* [1923] 1 KB 78. Thus where, after the source has become contractual (e.g. on receipt of a notice of appropriation), the goods or some of them suffer loss or damage, the risk of that loss or damage will be with the c.i.f., or, where appropriate, the f.o.b. purchaser.

18.8.2.4   'Shipment' point

These days many goods are transported in containers. Containerised goods are released into the custody of a combined transport operator, who will organise the shipment and carriage of the goods. The c.i.f./f.o.b. seller may have no further control over the goods, as to when they are shipped and in what condition, once the goods are released to the combined transport operator. Thus it may be that the traditional shipment point, i.e. the goods crossing the ship's rail, is not intended by the parties to the contract of sale as the delivery point. In these circumstances it may be that, subject to what has been said above about the goods being contractual, risk of loss or damage will pass at the time the goods are delivered into the custody of the combined transport operator. The parties themselves may expressly or impliedly put back the shipment point because of the nature of the goods being shipped. Parties in these circumstances may agree that, e.g., the risk of loss or damage should pass on the goods entering the ship's hose connection from a storage tank ashore: *The Sevonia Team* [1983] 2 Lloyd's Rep 640.

18.9   Damages Recoverable where C.I.F./F.O.B. Seller in Breach

Where it is determined that the c.i.f./f.o.b. seller has made a non-conforming tender of documents and/or goods and in consequence the buyer rejects, the buyer will not be able to argue that the seller is in repudiatory breach unless he/she can show that it is no longer possible for the seller to re-tender. See the **General Practice Manual, Sale of Goods, 12.1.**

18.9.1   DAMAGES FOR NON-DELIVERY, DEFECTIVE/LATE DELIVERY

On lawful rejection of documents and/or goods where the seller is in breach, the buyer, if he/she has paid, will be able to sue for the return of payments made as on a total failure of consideration, and claim damages for non-delivery. See the **General Practice Manual, Sale of Goods, 12.5** for damages for non-delivery and Benjamin, *Sale of Goods,* 4th edn, 1992, paras 17–001–17–035.

Where the documents/goods are accepted, the purchaser can sue only for damages for breach of warranty (s. 11(4)). Refer to the **General Practice Manual, Sale of Goods** for damages for defective delivery and damages for delay in delivery.

A buyer who has accepted or is deemed to have accepted goods, may find that although they are non-conforming, there is no difference between the respective values of the conforming and non-conforming goods, e.g., the non-conformity does not prevent them from fetching the same market price: *Taylor & Sons Ltd* v *Bank of Athens* (1922) 10 L1 LR 88. As it is that difference in values which constitutes the purchaser's loss for breach of warranty, the purchaser will recover only nominal damages in such a situation. If, however, the market price has fallen below the contract price (in which case the buyer would have been better off if he/she had rejected the goods and bought substitutes at the lower price), damages representing the difference between the contract price and the lower market price are recoverable where:

(a)   the seller is in breach of his/her obligation to tender a genuine document, i.e. one that is true in all material respects; and

(b)   it can be said that that breach has deprived the buyer of a *right* to reject the goods.

Damages in tendering an inaccurate/non-genuine document are recoverable where there was an independent right to reject the goods *and* the buyer is effectively deprived of the right to reject the goods through the operation of legal, commercial and practical considerations. If, for example, the seller tenders an inaccurately dated bill of lading which, if accurately dated, would have shown shipment outside the shipping period, the buyer would have had an independent right to reject the goods. (But *quaere* whether this would be so under the new SOGA 1979, s. 15A.) He may have been effectively deprived of exercising that right because, after taking up the documents, unaware of the inaccuracy, he sold the goods on and cannot now make restitution, or because having paid against the documents, if he were now to reject the goods, he would be an unsecured creditor for the return of the price. The damages in sending forward an inaccurate/non-genuine document must put the buyer in the same position, as far as money can achieve this, as if there had been no inaccuracy. With no inaccuracy in the bill of lading the buyer would have noted that the goods were shipped out of time and would have been able to reject the documents/goods and thus throw back on the seller the drop in the market. The market price to be used for the assessment of damages is probably that obtaining at the time the buyer becomes aware or ought to have become aware of the inaccuracy.

However, such damages are not recoverable where there remains an inaccuracy in the document alone. Since the first question to be asked in awarding damages for breach of contract is what would be the buyer's position if there had been no inaccuracy in the document, the answer would be that the buyer would have no right to reject the goods. If, for example, a falsely dated bill of lading has been rectified to show the true date and that date is within the shipping period, the buyer has no right to reject the goods. Thus in suing for damages in sending forward a falsely dated bill of lading he cannot argue that he has lost the right to reject the goods through the seller's breach — he never had a right to reject the goods in the first place. See *Kwik Hoo Tong* v *James Finley* (1928) 31 L1 LR 220; *Kwei Tek Chao* v *British Traders & Shippers Ltd* [1954] 1 Lloyd's Rep 16; *Kleinjan & Holst* v *Bremer Handelsgesellschaft GmbH* [1972] 2 Lloyd's Rep 11; *Vargas Pena Apezteguia y Cia* v *Peter Cremer GmbH* [1987] 1 Lloyd's Rep 394; *Proctor & Gamble* v *Becher* [1988] 2 Lloyd's Rep 21.

Nevertheless, the Court of Appeal in *Proctor & Gamble* v *Becher* did contemplate situations where something more than nominal damages might be recovered, even where there was no independent breach in relation to the goods emanating from the inaccuracy in the document. In this case Nicholls LJ said:

I do not doubt that there may be cases where a buyer suffers loss by payment of the price against a bill of lading which was unmerchantable because it misstated the date of shipment even though the actual date of shipment was within the contract period. Such a buyer might by reason of the unmerchantability of the bill, be unable to sell the goods, or complete a prior sale of the goods, whilst the goods were still afloat. In such a case the buyer's prima facie measure of damages would be the difference between the market value of the goods when he ought to have been able to deal with them (viz. when the bill of lading was tendered and accepted) and the market value of the goods when he became able to deal with them.

Besides the possibility of damages where the bill of lading, because of its falsity, has become unmerchantable, the buyer might be able to pursue a claim for fraudulent misrepresentation against the seller at common law, or in certain circumstances under the Misrepresentation Act 1967.

We saw in **18.3.1** that the buyer must, in the absence of fraud, pay against conforming documents. Failure to do so will amount to a repudiatory breach which the seller can treat as terminating the contract. Yet the seller himself may be in breach in shipping non-conforming goods. In an action for damages for non-acceptance the buyer can set off damages for breach of the seller's obligation to ship conforming goods. The buyer will not be able to argue that he/she would have rejected the goods and is therefore under no liability at all to the seller. Lord Diplock in *Gill & Duffus SA* v *Berger* [1984] 1 All ER 438 stated that the right to reject is not exercisable 'until the seller has unconditionally appropriated the goods to the contract'. According to Lord Diplock this occurs on transfer of the shipping documents to the buyer.

18.10   Further Reading

Goode, R. M., *Commercial Law,* rev. ed. 1985, Pelican.
Benjamin/Guest, *Sale of Goods,* 4th ed. 1992, Sweet & Maxwell.
Sassoon, D., *C.I.F. & F.O.B. Contracts,* 3rd ed. 1984, Sweet & Maxwell.
Schmitthoff, C., *Export Trade: Law and Practice of International Trade,* 9th ed. 1990, Sweet & Maxwell.

19 Financing the Contract of Sale

19.1 Introduction

Where the obligation of the buyer is to pay cash, a failure to comply with that obligation within the required time will enable the seller to sue the buyer on the contract of sale for damages or to pursue an action for the price. There are no restrictions on the type of defence, set-off or counterclaim which can be raised thereto by the buyer against the seller.

When a seller deals with a foreign purchaser, however, he/she may not be in a position to obtain a full picture of the purchaser's financial situation. Moreover, the seller may not wish to be put to the inconvenience of pursuing remedies in the courts of the purchaser's country. Certain methods of financing contracts have therefore evolved, in which the seller is protected from the possibility that the purchaser may not be creditworthy or may not, for some other reason, honour his/her obligations. These methods modify, reduce or deny rights to defend or to set off other sums due, and enable the seller to obtain his/her money from a third party or parties usually within the jurisdiction. Two particular methods of financing international sales are the bill of exchange and the documentary credit.

19.2 Bill of Exchange

The bill of exchange as a payment mechanism offers advantages to the seller. By using it not only can the seller obtain a promise to pay from a third party (possibly a more creditworthy institution and within the jurisdiction), but he/she can transfer the legal right to the debt expressed in the bill by merely transferring, or indorsing and transferring, the instrument. There is no need to give notice to the debtor. In addition, the assignee obtains a guarantee of payment from the assignor plus the possibility of obtaining a better title to the debt than that of the assignor.

The seller's and the assignee's right to the debt expressed in the bill of exchange is, in differing degrees, isolated from any underlying transaction and thus enables the creditor to use speedier methods of enforcement.

19.2.1 DEFINITION

The term 'bill of exchange' is defined in the Bills of Exchange Act 1882, s. 3. There must be:

(a) an unconditional order,
(b) in writing (s. 2 includes printing),
(c) addressed by one person (the 'drawer') to another (the 'drawee'),
(d) signed by the drawer — the party giving the order,
(e) requiring the person to whom the order is addressed (the 'drawee') to pay:

    (i) on demand,
    (ii) at a fixed or determinable future time,

(f) a sum of money which is ascertainable,

(g) to:

    (i) the order of a specified person, or

    (ii) to bearer,

in both cases called the 'payee'.

Throughout **Chapter 19** any references to sections of Acts should be taken to be those of the Bills of Exchange Act 1882 unless otherwise stated.

19.2.2 PARTIES

In the context of a sales transaction, the party who draws up the order to pay — the *drawer*— will be the seller. The party to whom the order is addressed — the *drawee* — will either be the buyer himself or some creditworthy institution, e.g. a bank. Commonly the party on whom the order is drawn is the issuing bank or correspondent/confirming bank under a documentary credit, The contract of sale will indicate on whom the bill of exchange is to be drawn. The drawee may be called on to accept the bill of exchange. If he/she complies with the request he/she then becomes known as an *acceptor*.

The party to be paid by the drawee/acceptor, i.e. the payee, is usually, in the context of a sale, the seller. This means that the drawer and the payee are the same party. However, that is not always the case. The seller, as drawer, can draw up a bill of exchange ordering the drawee/acceptor to pay to a party to whom the seller is indebted.

The payee in possession of the bill of exchange is the first *holder* of the bill of exchange: s. 2. It is only the holder of a bill of exchange who can sue on it in his own *name* (s. 38(1)) and it is only a holder who can obtain the right to sue with restrictions on the defences that can be raised against him.

In a c.i.f. or f.o.b. contract the parties may have agreed on an acceptance of the bill of exchange against conforming documents (the D/A system). The seller as drawer/payee will in these circumstances be extending a period of credit to the purchaser, by allowing payment under the bill of exchange to be made subsequent to the constructive delivery of the goods (which occurs on tender of the bill of lading). Even if it is the buyer's bank operating as the drawee, it may not demand to be put in funds until the time for payment falls due and thus the same effect is achieved. To give an example, the bill of exchange may be made payable '90 days after sight' or '90 days after date'. Such bills of exchange are called 'usance' bills.

However, the seller, although recognising the need to extend credit to get his/her goods sold, may not wish to delay receipt of payment for the period of time indicated in the bill of exchange. From the nature of the bill of exchange as a negotiable instrument, the payee can sell the bill or borrow against it. The payee does this by negotiating (see **19.3**) the bill of exchange, usually by indorsing the back of the bill with a signature and delivering it to the party buying the bill of exchange or lending against it. The payee is then known as an *indorser*.

The party, e.g. a bank, to whom the bill of exchange has been *indorsed* and delivered is an *indorsee* of the bill of exchange. The *indorsee in possession* is a holder: s. 2. The *bearer*, i.e. the possessor of a bearer bill of exchange is also a holder: s. 2.

19.3 Negotiation

A bill is negotiated when it is transferred from one person to another in such a manner as to constitute the transferee the holder of the bill: s. 31(1). Two issues arise here:

(a) Which bills are negotiable, i.e. which bills are capable of being so transferred.

(b) If a bill is negotiable, what is the correct manner of its transfer.

In order to consider these two points, we need to be clear about the different types of bills of exchange.

19.3.1 ORDER BILL OF EXCHANGE

This is a bill of exchange which states *on the face* of the bill that it is payable to the order of a named person, or to the named person or to his/her order, or to the named person.

19.3.2 BEARER BILL OF EXCHANGE

There are two ways in which the bearer bill comes into operation:

(a)   where the bill of exchange states *on the face* of the bill that it is payable to bearer, or a named person or bearer;

(b)   where the bill of exchange, *on its face*, is an order bill of exchange but in which the last indorsement is in blank.

An indorsement in blank occurs where the signature of the transferor is placed on the back of the bill of exchange but the transferor does not indicate on the back of the bill of exchange to whom he/she is transferring it (s. 34(1)), i.e. the new indorsee is not specified. For example, where the original payee is Miss Smith (i.e. on its face the bill is payable to her order) and she, in transferring the bill to Mr Doe, merely places her own signature on the back of the bill without indicating Mr Doe as the new payee, the bill of exchange in Mr Doe's hands will thereafter be payable to bearer.

19.3.3 WHICH BILLS ARE NEGOTIABLE?

A bearer bill of exchange is negotiable. An order bill of exchange is negotiable as long as it does not contain words prohibiting transfer or indicating an intention that it should not be transferable. An example of where such a contrary intention is expressed is where the bill of exchange is made payable to 'X only'. A bill made payable thus is, or is no longer, transferable. It will, however, still be valid between the parties to the bill of exchange prior to its losing its character as negotiable: s. 8(1).

19.3.4 VALID TRANSFER OF BILLS

With one exception, it is only when the transfer has been correctly made that the transferee in possession of the bill of exchange becomes capable of calling himself/herself a holder of it: s. 31(1). It is only as a holder that the possessor of the bill can sue in his/her own name and perhaps take the full benefits of negotiability. When correctly negotiated, a bill of exchange is capable of transferring a better title to the bill than that possessed by the transferor.

19.3.4.1 Delivery

A bill payable to bearer, whether the bill was such originally or has become so subsequently, is negotiated by mere delivery: s. 31(2). No indorsement is necessary to pass title to the bill of exchange, i.e. to make the possessor of it a holder. Each possessor in turn will qualify as holder. There are risks, however, attached to a bill in bearer form. Where on the maturity of the bill the acceptor pays out to the holder of the bearer bill, he/she ceases to become liable to the true owner as long as he/she acted in good faith and without notice that the holder's title to the bill was defective: s. 59(1).

Any holder can reconvert a bill which has *become* payable to bearer, back into an order bill by placing above the last indorsement in blank a direction to pay to the order of himself/herself or his/her intended transferee: s. 34(4).

19.3.4.2 Indorsement and delivery

Where the holder wishes to transfer a bill which in his/her hands is an order bill, the holder is required to indorse it and deliver it: s. 31(3). The indorsee in possession will be the new holder of the bill of exchange. If this new holder wishes to negotiate the bill of exchange, the manner in which he/she must negotiate will depend on the status of the bill of exchange in *his/her* hands. This is determined by discovering whether it is an order bill or a bearer bill, which in turn will depend on the type of indorsement the holder received from his/her transferor. If the holder received the bill of exchange specially indorsed, i.e. the transferor not only signed it but indicated the indorsee as the new payee (s. 34(2) and (3)), then the bill in the holder's hands has remained an order bill.

19.3.4.3 Quasi-indorsement: transferor by delivery

More often than not, a bill will start out as an order bill and will remain so throughout its life. This is so because not only will a thief not qualify as a holder, and thus the acceptor cannot rely on s. 59(1) to argue that he/she has paid in due course, but also the indorsement itself attracts liability. On dishonour by non-acceptance or non-payment, there is an immediate right of recourse against the drawer *and indorsers* prior to the holder. The drawer and indorsers undertake liability as guarantors: s. 55(1) and (2). An indorsement adds currency to a bill. If the bill is or has become payable to bearer, no indorsement is necessary to create holder status. And yet, understandably, an intended transferee may be unwilling to buy or lend against a bill without the indorsement of his/her transferor. Section 56 contemplates circumstances in which the bill will be signed, even though it is not essential to create holder status. This indorsement is called a quasi-indorsement. The transferee may be able to insist on this indorsement to impose the liability of a guarantor on his/her transferor. However, this liability arguably only operates in favour of a holder in due course. (See the wording of s. 57, and for an explanation of the term 'holder in due course' see **19.4.2**.)

The transferor of a bearer bill is called, under the 1882 Act, a transferor by delivery: s. 58(1). Even in the absence of an indorsement however, his/her transferee is not totally without a remedy against him/her, although s. 58(2) provides that the transferor by delivery is not liable *on the bill of exchange*. Under s. 58(3) the transferor warrants, but *only* to his/her immediate transferee for value:

(a) that the bill is not a forgery;
(b) that he/she is not aware of any fact which renders it *valueless;*
(c) that he/she has the right to transfer it.

Breach of the warranty entitles the transferee for value to recover damages or recover back money paid as on a total failure of consideration (note that this will not necessarily be the same as the amount of the bill). Nevertheless, the liability of the transferor by delivery is not as attractive to the transferee/holder as an indorsement. The transferee knows that under a transfer by delivery liability extends only to himself/herself and not to any of his/her own transferees. Thus the transferee may have greater difficulty in dealing with the bill. Once an indorsement is given, the obligations as guarantor extend beyond the immediate transferee/indorsee to all subsequent indorsers and holders: s. 55(1) and (2).

19.4   Types of Holder

There are different categories of holder and the rights of a holder will depend on the category into which he/she falls.

19.4.1   HOLDER FOR VALUE

In the transaction between a holder and his/her transferor, the holder will have given value if there is any consideration sufficient to support a simple contract: s. 27(1)(a). It need not be money but can include goods delivered. Therefore the seller who, in performance of his contract of sale, delivers goods (e.g. represented by documents) against the acceptance of a bill of exchange payable to his order or to bearer will be a holder by virtue of s. 2 and will be a holder *for value* by virtue of s. 27(1). He/she may be the holder of a bearer or an order bill of exchange.

A holder will have given value if he/she takes the bill in satisfaction of an antecedent debt or liability owed to the holder by his/her transferor: s. 27(1); *Mackenzie Mills* v *Buono, The Times,* 31 July 1986.

A holder will be deemed to be a holder for value as regards the acceptor and all parties to the bill who became parties *prior to the time that value was given* (s. 27(2)), i.e. the holder need not have given value himself/herself to his/her transferor. Nor need his/her proposed defendant have 'received' value, as long as in the chain of transactions between the plaintiff and defendant value has, at some stage, been given.

Section 27(3) states that if the holder has a lien on the bill, by contract or implication of law, then he/she is deemed to have given value to the extent of the lien. A pertinent example here would be the lien which, by implication of law, the collecting bank has on all securities of its customers which it possesses, as long as the customer has not given instructions as to the use of the bill of exchange which would be inconsistent with the lien (see **19.8.3**).

Note that under s. 30(1) every party whose signature appears on the bill is prima facie *presumed* to have given value. The burden, therefore, is on the defendant to show that no value has been given.

19.4.2   HOLDER IN DUE COURSE

This category of holder is defined in s. 29(1). He/she may be the holder of a bearer or an order bill of exchange. The following conditions are required to be satisfied:

(a)   The bill must have been negotiated to the possessor of it. In *R. E. Jones Ltd* v *Waring & Gillow Ltd* [1926] AC 670 the House of Lords held that the original payee, although a holder by virtue of s. 2, can never be a holder in due course (HDC), as the bill is not negotiated, but rather issued, to him/her. This is defined in s. 2 as the 'first delivery' of the bill. The original payee, in the context of a sales transaction, will be a holder for value.

(b)   The holder must have been taken a bill which was complete and regular on its face. By 'face' is meant both sides of the bill: *Arab Bank Ltd* v *Ross* [1952] 2 QB 216. A bill which is not complete is an inchoate instrument. The bill is incomplete if it is wanting in any material particular, e.g. where the date is omitted from a bill payable a specified number of days after date: *Arab Bank Ltd* v *Ross (supra); Whistler* v *Forster* (1863) 14 CB (NS) 248. The incompleteness of a bill does not make it invalid: s. 3(4). If a bill of exchange transferred to a holder is incomplete, he/she cannot be a HDC, but has, under s.20, prima facie authority to complete the instrument in any way which he/she thinks fit. A bill of exchange is irregular if any thing on it gives rise to doubts or is out of the ordinary: *Arab Bank Lid* v *Ross (supra)*. In that case, the plaintiffs sued as HDCs of two promissory orders made out by the defendants in favour of an Arab company. The indorsement on the back of the note omitted the word 'Co.', which was included on the front of the bill. It was held that there had been an irregular indorsement which prevented the holders from being HDCS. They were holders for value. Note that the absence of an acceptance on a bill does not make it incomplete or irregular: *National Park Bank* v *Berggren* (1914) 110 LT 907. Nor will a restrictive indorsement, e.g. 'for collection', make the bill incomplete or irregular: *Yeoman Credit Ltd* v *Gregory* [1963] 1 All ER 245.

(c)   The holder must have taken the bill before it is overdue, i.e. before the time for payment arises. See *Clifford Chance (a firm)* v *Silver, The Times,* 11 September 1992.

(d)   The holder must have taken the bill without notice that it has been previously dishonoured. Note that a bill can be dishonoured before it is overdue, i.e. on a refusal to accept a bill payable, e.g., 90 days after sight or 90 days after date.

(e)   The holder must have given value *himself/herself.* The holder cannot rely on s. 27(2) to bring himself/herself within s. 29(1). But the holder of a cheque who has a lien on it and who is by virtue of s. 27(3) deemed to have given value, has in fact given value for the purpose of s. 29(1): *Yeoman Credit Ltd* v *Gregory* [1963] 1 All ER 245; *Barclays Bank Ltd* v *Astley Industrial Trust Lid* [1970] 2 QB 527. See also *Lipkin Gorman* v *Karpnale Ltd* [1992] 4 All ER 512.

(f)   The holder must have taken the bill in good faith. Under s. 90 a thing is deemed to be done in good faith within the meaning of the Act where it is in fact done honestly, whether it is done negligently or not.

(g)   At the time of the negotiation, i.e. the indorsement and delivery or delivery depending on the type of bill being transferred to the holder, the holder must not have had *notice* of any *defect in the title* of the person who negotiated the bill, i.e. his/her transferor: see *Clifford Chance (a firm)* v *Silver (supra)*. As regards notice, carelessness will not amount to notice of defects in title although it may be evidence of it: *Jones* v *Gordon* (1877) 2 App Cas 616. However, where the holder turns a 'blind eye', i.e. deliberately or fraudulently omits to discover the true situation when he/she has been put on inquiry, he/she will have actual notice: *Jones* v *Gordon (supra).* It is sufficient that the holder has general notice of some fraud or illegality. The holder need not know the exact details for the purpose of having notice: *Jones* v *Gordon (supra).*

Section 29(2) gives some instances of circumstances where the transferor's title is defective:

(a)   Where the transferor himself/herself *obtained* the bill of exchange, or *obtained its acceptance,* through fraud, force or fear or other unlawful means, or for an illegal consideration.

(b)   Where the transferor *negotiated* the bill of exchange to the present holder in breach of faith or in circumstances amounting to fraud.

Section 29(2) is not exhaustive. The transferor's title can be defective where a party prior to the holder's negotiator falls within category (a) or (b) above.

19.4.3   HOLDER IN DUE COURSE BY DERIVATION

The HDC of a bill which is affected by fraud or illegality etc. as explained above, may have difficulty dealing with that bill if the defects become widely known. To counter this problem s. 29(3) enables a holder:

(a)   who derives his/her title through one who was a HDC; and
(b)   who is not himself/herself a party to any fraud or illegality affecting the bill,

to take all the rights of a HDC as regards the acceptor and all parties to the bill prior to that holder. It is important to note here that:

(a)   To take advantage of s. 29(3) there is no need for value to have been given.
(b)   It does not matter that the holder has notice of fraud or illegality as long as he/she is not a party to it.

Section 29(3) has been used not only in the situation where a bill of exchange has been negotiated on to a new holder but has also been used where a bill of exchange has gone back up the chain of transactions on the exercise of a right of recourse. This right of recourse arises when the bill of exchange has been dishonoured by non-acceptance or non-payment. As to rights of recourse, see **19.6.**

A comparison between a holder for value and a HDC or HDC by derivation (see **19.8.1** and **19.8.2**), shows that a holder claiming HDC status is in a far more secure position when it comes to obtaining the amount of the bill. Thus, where a seller draws a bill to his/her own order, and retains it, he/she can only achieve holder for value status. Once negotiated however, if it were to be returned to him/her on a right of recourse, he/she would be able to claim holder in due course status under s. 29(3).

19.5   Acceptor

If a drawee refuses to accept the bill or pay the bill on the due date, he/she incurs no liability *on the bill:* s. 53(1). The drawee will, however, be liable on any underlying contract in which he/she promised to accept the bill or pay against it. For example, the purchaser/drawee will have promised in the contract of sale, to honour the bill of exchange. Nevertheless, even though this right to sue on the underlying contract is available to the seller, the procedural advantages of an action on the bill are not there. Once accepted, however, the acceptor undertakes a primary liability on the bill. He/she promises 'that he will pay it according to the tenor of his acceptance': s. 54(1). Some bills *must* be presented for acceptance. For further discussion on this, see **19.7.**

19.6   Rights of Recourse

Apart from the acceptor who undertakes primary liability, and apart from one who signs 'sans recour', i.e. undertakes no liability on the bill, each party signing the bill of exchange undertakes the liability of a guarantor towards the holder and towards any indorser in the chain of transaction between himself/herself and the holder who has been compelled to pay the amount of the bill: ss.55(1) and (2), 57. This liability as a guarantor is activated by the exercise of a 'right of recourse' by the party entitled to demand payment, Sometimes however the right of recourse is lost, see **19.7**.

It is no mean advantage to be able, on dishonour, to demand the amount of the bill not only against the acceptor, but also against the guarantors. The holder does not need to depend on the financial stability of just one party. If necessary, the holder can, as a matter of procedure, sue all these prior parties at the same time and obtain judgment against each of them. In relation to judgments obtained, the holder can choose against which one he/she will enforce judgment. Where judgment has been obtained and executed against an indorser, or where the indorser, on dishonour pays the amount of the bill plus interest without action being pursued against him/her, that indorser, too, has the right to demand the same amount from those guarantors prior to himself/herself on the bill of exchange, and the acceptor. Procedurally, he/she can sue all his/her own prior indorsers and the acceptor before he/she has paid out.

Similarly where the drawer has paid out either voluntarily or on execution of a judgment, he/she is entitled to be reimbursed by the acceptor. The drawer can pursue his/her claim to judgment against the acceptor before payment out.

Thus in an action brought by the holder against all prior indorsers and the acceptor, each defendant can bring his/her own third party proceedings, the defendants of which will be the predecessors on the bill of the plaintiff to those third party proceedings. If payment is made by the acceptor, all intervening parties will be discharged. (**See Example I.**)

EXAMPLE I

```
        Acceptor                    Payee (I₁)----------------------I₂

                    Drawer                                          |
                                                                    I₃
                                                                    |
                                                                    I₄
                                                                    |
                                                                    H
```

H = holder: I = indorser

1   On dishonour (in our example by non-payment), H, if unable to receive the amount of the bill, on the exercise of a right of recourse against his prior indorsers, and the drawer, can choose to sue any or all of the prior signatories to the bill.

2   If H decides to sue all, I_4, as one of the defendants to the action, can start third-party proceedings against **his/her** own prior signatories to the bill, i.e. I_3, I_2, I_1, (drawer — if different from I_1) and acceptor.

3   Similarly, I_3, as another defendant, can start third-party proceedings against I_2, I_1, (drawer) and acceptor.

4   In the same way the drawer, a defendant to the action brought by H, can only start third-party proceedings against the acceptor.

5   If H decides to sue I_4 only, the latter's third parties, i.e. I_3, I_2, I_1, (drawer) and acceptor can commence fourth-party proceedings against those signatories to the bill prior to themselves. For example, I_2 as a third party to the proceedings between H and I_4 can fourth party I_1, (drawer) and acceptor.

It is when this right of recourse is exercised that the rights given by s. 29(3) to a HDC by derivation are of particular importance, as is illustrated by *Jade International Steel Stahl und Eisen GmbH & Co. KG* v *Robert Nicholas (Steels) Ltd* [1978] 3 WLR 38, where a bill of exchange was drawn by the plaintiff sellers on the defendant purchaser for a consignment of steel. The sellers were both the drawers/payees of the bill. The bill was negotiated by the plaintiffs to their bank in Germany and was ultimately transferred to the Midland Bank. The Midland Bank presented for and obtained an acceptance to the bill by the drawee defendants. The bill was subsequently dishonoured for non-payment by the acceptor/defendants, who were disputing the quality of the steel. The bill passed back under the right of recourse until it reached the sellers. The question arose, could the purchaser, the acceptor of the bill, set up a defence to the sellers' action on the bill? It was held by the Court of Appeal that the sellers, under s. 29(3), had all the rights of a HDC and therefore no defences could be set up against them. As the original payees, the sellers could not be HDCs: *Jones* v *Waring & Gillow* [1926] AC 670. However, the Court of Appeal stated that they lost their capacity as original payees when they negotiated to their bank in Germany. When the bill was returned to them, on the exercise of the right of recourse, they took as new holders. Although the sellers still could not be HDCs *in fact*, as they had retaken the bill with notice of dishonour (the right of recourse is only exercisable on dishonour), nevertheless they were in the same position as if they were HDCs since they derived their title from one who was a HDC, i.e. they were HDCs by derivation. Lane LJ said:

It seems to me that once the drawers/payees [the plaintiffs in the case] have discounted the bill [to the German bank] they lose the capacity which they had as immediate parties to the bill as drawers. Then when in the effluxion of time they once again become holders of the bill in the way that I have described it is that new fresh capacity of holders via the [German bank] and the other banks that their situation must be judged.

19.7 Loss of Rights of Recourse

The holder and each indorser should be aware that the rights of recourse maintainable against their own prior indorsers can be lost in the following ways.

19.7.1 BILL NOT PRESENTED FOR ACCEPTANCE IN TIME

Where the bill is required to be presented for acceptance under the 1882 Act and was not presented at all or in time, rights of recourse will be lost: ss. 39(3) and 40(2). A bill is required to be presented for acceptance where:

(a)   The bill expressly so stipulates: s. 39(2).
(b)   It is drawn payable elsewhere than at the residence or place of business of the drawee: s. 39(2).
(c)   It is necessary in order to fix the maturity of the bill, i.e. where the bill is payable after sight: s. 39(1). Time can only begin to run after presentment for acceptance.

For the rules as to presentment for acceptance, and excuses for non-presentment. see s. 41. Note that bills are still presented for acceptance even if they are not required to be presented for the purposes of preserving rights of recourse under the Act. This is so because, not only does the acceptance add currency to the bill, but if there is dishonour by non-acceptance, there is an immediate right of recourse against prior indorsees and the drawer. The holder therefore need not wait until the bill matures to receive payment: s. 43(2).

19.7.2 PRESENTMENT FOR PAYMENT NOT ON DUE DATE

Where the bill was required to be presented for *payment,* and it was not presented on the due date, rights of recourse will be lost: s. 45. However, where the bill has already been dishonoured by non-acceptance, there is no requirement on the holder to present for payment: s. 43(2). Note that s. 45 only discharges the liability of the *drawer* and *prior indorsers* if presentment for payment is not made on the due date. The acceptor remains liable. Indeed, there is no need to present for payment at all to the acceptor in order to render him/her liable: s. 52(1).

19.7.2.1 Rules for presentment for payment
Section 45 sets out rules for presentment for payment. It provides as follows:

(a)   Presentment for payment must be made on the due date. Section 14 determines the computation of time. Section 3(2) of the Banking and Financial Dealings Act 1971 has replaced s. 14(1) and provides that the bill is due and payable in all cases on the last day of the time for payment as fixed by the bill, or if that is a non-business day, on the succeeding business day. Under s. 14(2), where a bill of exchange is payable at a fixed period after sight or date or the happening of a specified event, the time for payment is determined by excluding the day from which time is to begin to run and by including the day of payment. In a bill payable after sight, time begins to run from the date of acceptance if the bill is accepted, or from the dating of noting or protesting if the bill is noted or protested for non-acceptance: s.14(3). If the drawee, after initially dishonouring a bill payable after sight, subsequently accepts, s. 18(3) entitles the holder to insist on the acceptance being antedated to the date of first presentation for acceptance.

(b)   There must be a presentment at the 'proper place'. The proper place is defined in s. 45(4). In particular, where the place of payment is expressed on the bill, it is called a domiciled bill. It must be presented there (s. 45(4)(a)), even though the acceptor informs the holder that there are no funds for meeting the bill at that place: *Yeoman Credit Ltd* v *Gregory* [1963] 1 All ER 245. Section 46 sets out the permitted excuses for delay in presentment, or non-presentment, for payment.

19.7.3 NOTICE OF DISHONOUR NOT GIVEN IN TIME

Where the bill was dishonoured by non-acceptance or non-payment and notice of dishonour was not given in time, rights of recourse will be lost: s. 48. The bill is dishonoured by non-acceptance where it is duly presented (as to this, refer to s. 41) for acceptance and acceptance is refused, or cannot be obtained within the customary time (i.e. 24 hours), or where presentment for acceptance is excused and the bill is not accepted: ss. 41 to 43. The bill is dishonoured by non-payment when it is duly presented for payment and payment is refused or cannot be obtained, or when presentment is excused and the bill is overdue and unpaid: ss. 46 and 47.

In order to preserve the liability of the indorsers and the drawer, they must now be given a notice of dishonour: s. 48. This can occur in the following ways.

19.7.3.1 Notice to some or all prior indorsers

The holder can give notice to some or all prior indorsers. In this situation, the notice given by *this* holder can be relied on both by subsequent holders and all indorsers prior to this holder who have a right of recourse against the party to whom it was given: s. 49(3). (**See Example II.**)

EXAMPLE II

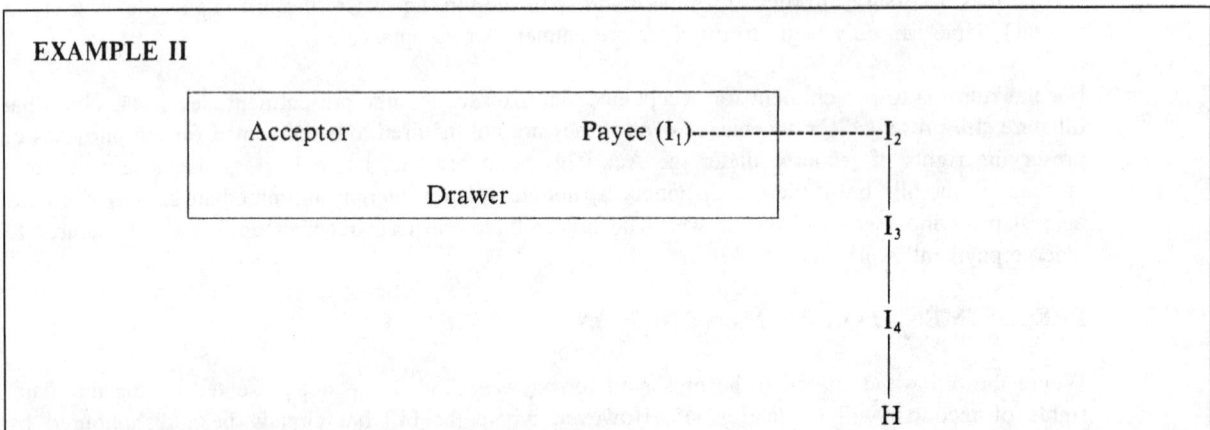

If H, the holder, having given a notice to drawer, and I_1 to I_4 (there is no need to serve a notice on the acceptor—the acceptor remains primarily liable on the bill), exercises his/her right of recourse against I_4 i.e. recovers the amount of the bill from I_4, the latter, although he/she may not have given a notice of dishonour himself/herself, can rely on the notices given by H to the drawer and I_1 to I_3. In consequence, I_4 can still exercise **his/her** own rights of recourse against drawer and I_1 to I_3.

19.7.3.2 Notice to only one prior indorser

In Example II, H may decide to give notice to only one prior indorsee, e.g. I_4. I_4 in his turn, to preserve his/her rights of recourse against his/her own prior indorsers, must give notice of dishonour. I_4 may if he/she wishes, decide to give notice to all prior indorsers or only one, e.g. I_3. In this latter situation, first the notice given by I_4 to I_3 enures for the benefit of H, who can proceed to exercise his/her rights of recourse against I_3 (s. 49(4)). Second, if that notice given by I_4 to I_3 is out of time, then not only is I_3 discharged from liability (s. 49(12)), but so also is every remaining indorsee on the bill, e.g. I_2 and I_1 and the drawer. This is because it will not be possible for I_3 to give a valid notice as s. 49(1) states: 'The notice must be given ... by or on behalf of an indorser who, at the time of giving it, is himself *liable on the bill*'.

19.7.3.3 Form of notice/time of notice

The notice can be either in writing or by personal communication and in any terms as long as it sufficiently identifies the bill and intimates that it has been dishonoured by non-acceptance or non-payment: s. 49(5). The return of the dishonoured bill is in point of form deemed a sufficient notice of dishonour: s. 49(6). The notice must be given within a reasonable time of dishonour. In the absence of special circumstances:

(a) Where the parties 'reside in the same place' notice will be deemed to have been given within a reasonable time only if it is given or sent off in time to reach the person who is to receive the notice on the day after dishonour: s. 49(12)(a). As long as it was duly addressed and posted in time, it will be deemed to have been given in time even if it is subsequently lost in the post: s. 49(15).

(b) Where the parties reside in different places, the notice will be deemed to have been given within a reasonable time if sent off, at the latest, on the day after dishonour of the bill if there is a post on that day and, if not, by the next convenient post: s. 49(12)(b).

The question to be asked in considering whether or not the parties reside in the same place is whether or not it would be reasonable to send the notice by hand rather than by relying on the general post: *Hamilton Finance* v *Coverley* [1969] 1 Lloyd's Rep 53. If an indorser wishes to send off a notice of dishonour, time begins to run under s. 49(12) not from dishonour, but from his/her receipt of a notice of dishonour: s. 49(14).

19.8   Action on the Bill of Exchange

An action on the bill may ensue where the bill has been dishonoured and the drawee/acceptor and indorsers are refusing to make payment. Where the bill has been dishonoured by non-acceptance, action on the bill can proceed against the drawer and/or any one or more indorsers prior to the holder suing (assuming rights of recourse are available or have been preserved). Where the bill has been dishonoured by non-payment, action on the bill can proceed against the drawer and/or indorser (as above) and/or against the acceptor if the bill of exchange has been accepted.

The benefits of pursuing an action on the bill, as opposed to suing on the underlying transaction, are that action on the bill:

(a) enables the plaintiff to sue those with whom there is no *underlying* contractual relationship — e.g. the bank which has negotiated the seller's bill of exchange can sue the buyer, on his acceptance; and
(b) restricts the defences that can be raised against the plaintiff and thus increases the possibility of summary judgment being obtained by the plaintiff, RSC ord. 14.

19.8.1   ACTION BY A HOLDER IN DUE COURSE

Where the party suing is a HDC or HDC by derivation, s. 38(2) provides that he/she takes the bill:

(a) free from defects of title of prior parties; and
(b) free from personal defences available to prior parties between themselves.

The provision also enables the holder to enforce payment against all prior parties liable on it.

Thus a bank to which the seller may have negotiated his/her bill, can, as a HDC, enforce payment from the buyer/acceptor (see **Figure 19.1**) and it will not be possible for the buyer as acceptor to argue that the goods delivered to him/her under the contract of sale were defective and thus rejected and that in consequence he/she is not obliged to pay the amount of the bill. The engagement of the acceptor to pay the bill (see s. 54(1)) is, in these circumstances, completely isolated from the underlying transaction.

The defendant can argue that the holder has not achieved HDC status and that his defence is one that can be raised against a holder for value but the burden of proof will be on the defendant, because the plaintiff is prima facie deemed to be a HDC: s. 38(2). Once, however, the defendant has proved, or it is admitted that the issue, acceptance or negotiation of the bill is affected with fraud, duress, force, fear or illegality, then the burden of proof shifts to the plaintiff holder, to establish that subsequent to the fraud etc, value has in good faith been given for the bill: s. 38(2).

In *Bank für Gemeinwirtschaft A G* v *City of London Garages Ltd* [1971] 1 WLR 149 Cairns LJ formulated the respective positions of the parties on an application by the plaintiff for summary judgment as follows:

> It is clear that if fraud is proved the holders have the onus of proving that they, or the previous holders who endorsed to them, took the bills in good faith and for value. Since in RSC ord. 14, proceedings the defendant cannot be required to establish his defence (it being sufficient for him to show that he has some grounds which would constitute a defence if what he alleges were proved at the trial) it must follow that in an action on a bill of exchange he is entitled to leave to defend if he 'sets up' a case of fraud affecting the bill, unless the plaintiff in his turn can establish that the bill was taken in good faith for value and without notice.... The real question seems to me to be, whether the account given (in the plaintiff's affidavit) standing as it does uncontradicted, and supported by contemporaneous documents, can be said to establish good faith and the giving of value with such a degree of probability that if the case went for trial the defendant's defence of fraud would have no real chance of success.

If the plaintiff's affidavit does so establish good faith and the giving of value, summary judgment will be obtained. If the state of the evidence is such that there is still a real issue as to whether the bills were taken in good faith and for value, leave to defend will be given.

If the bank, instead of proceeding against the acceptor, had exercised a right of recourse against the seller as indorser (see **Figure 19.3**), the seller would have achieved HDC by derivation status. Now even if fraud is 'set up' by the defendants, as long as the seller can establish with the required degree of probability that he/she was not a party to the fraud and that the bank took the bills in good faith and for value, summary judgment will be obtained.

The defendant will also get leave to defend if, in his/her affidavit, he/she raises a triable issue that:

(i)   The plaintiff does not hold a valid bill.

(ii)   The plaintiff is not a *holder,* i.e. there is *no* title to the bill — as opposed to a defective title — because of forgery of an indorsement essential to the passing of title. However, the defendant/acceptor is estopped, as against one who would *otherwise* be a HDC, from denying the genuineness of the drawer's signature: s. 54(2)(a). The defendant/indorser is estopped from denying, as against one who would otherwise be a HDC, the genuineness of *prior* indorsements but he/she is not estopped from disputing the genuineness of a *subsequent* indorsement: s. 55(2)(b)(c). No estoppels operate against a drawer.

(iii)   The plaintiff has lost his/her rights of recourse against the defendant. (This is only applicable where the relevant defendant is a prior indorser or the drawer of the bill — see **Figure 19.2**.) (See s. 55(2)(b) and (c).)

Figure 19.1

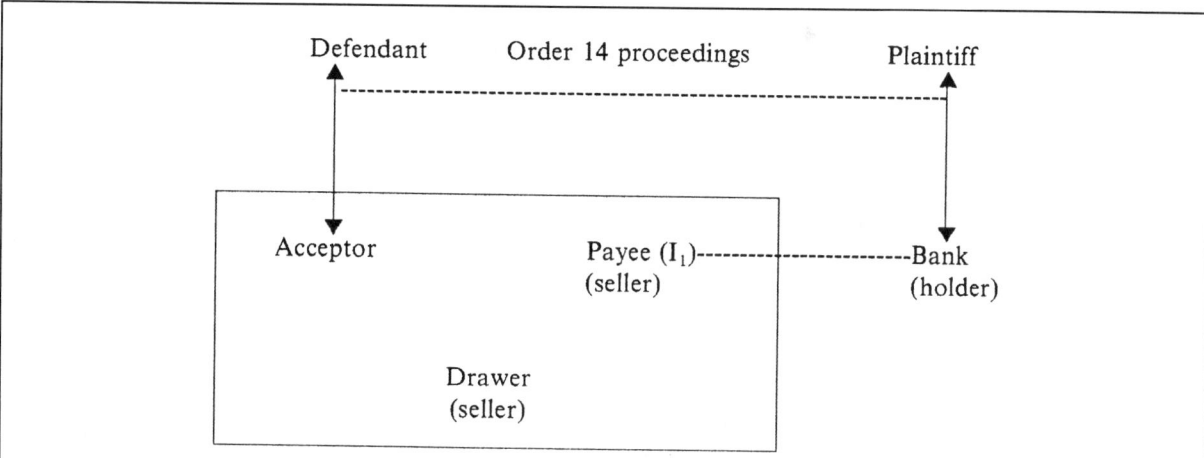

Defences to the ord. 14 proceedings:
(a) Bank does not comply with requirements of s. 29(1) and defences can be raised against bank as holder for value.
(b) Instrument is not a valid bill.
(c) Bank is not a holder.

Figure 19.2

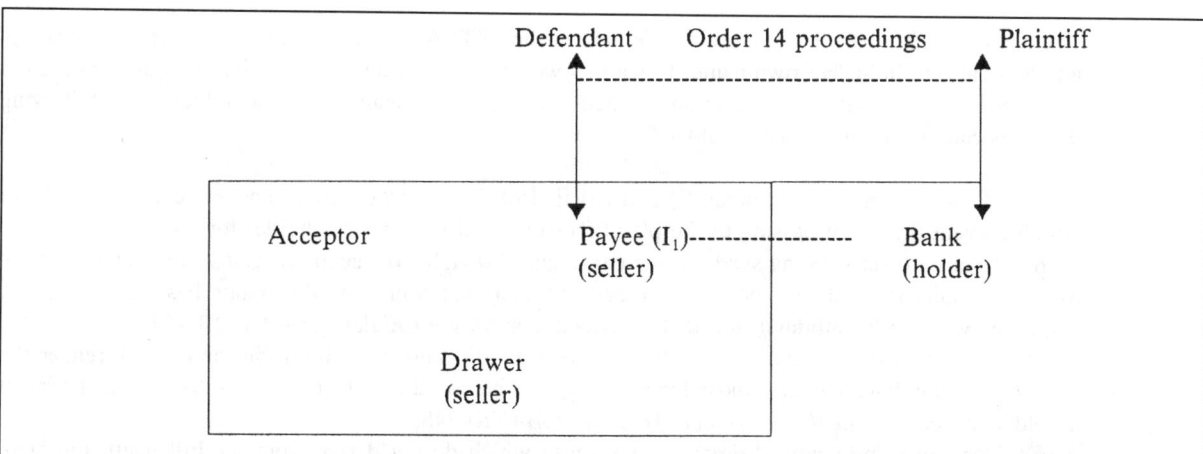

Defences to the ord. 14 proceedings:
(a) Bank does not comply with requirements of s. 29(1) and defences can be raised against bank as holder for value.
(b) Instrument is not a valid bill.
(c) Bank is not a holder.
(d) Right of recourse not available or has been lost.

Figure 19.3

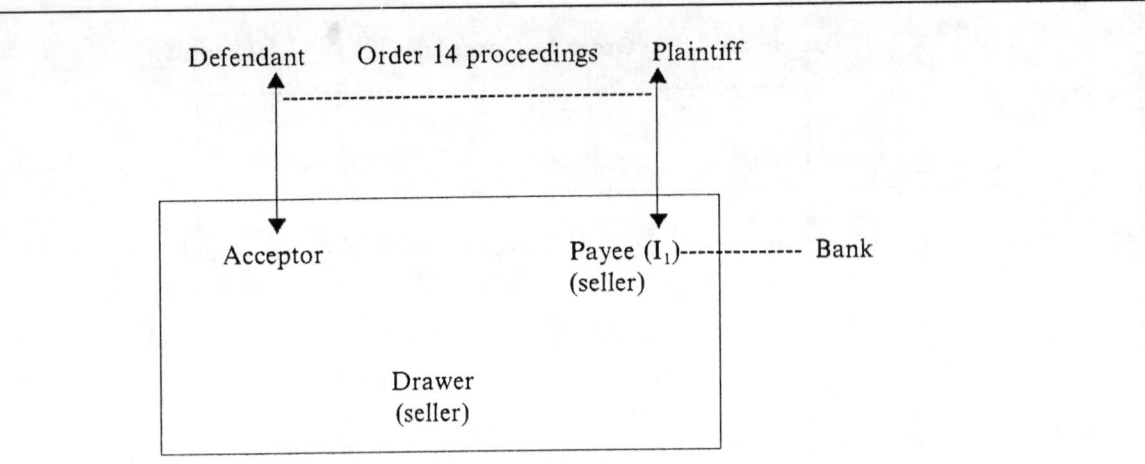

Defences to the ord. 14 proceedings:
(a)   Payee does not satisfy the requirements of s. 29(1) and (3) and the defences can be raised against holder for value.
(b)   Instrument is not a valid bill.
(c)   Payee is not a holder.

19.8.2   ACTION BY A HOLDER FOR VALUE

The rights of a holder for value are not defined in the 1882 Act, apart from s. 38(1), which states that a holder can sue in his/her own name. It is a less well-protected category than that of HDC, with fewer restrictions on the number of defences which can be raised against such a holder. The following defences can be raised against a holder for value:

(a)   'Real' defences (as in paras (i) and (ii) in **19.8.1**, i.e. those which render the bill a nullity or which prevent title from passing to the plaintiff) can be raised against a holder for value.
(b)   If an indorser is being sued, he/she can argue that rights of recourse against him/her have been lost. The plaintiff need not, however, allege the fact that notice of dishonour has been given or dispensed with, in his affidavit in ord. 14 proceedings: *May* v *Chidley* (1894) 1 QB 451.
(c)   The defences of fraud, duress, force or fear, or illegality affecting a bill and which render the transferor's title defective (as opposed to a nullity) can be raised to defeat the claim for payment against a holder for value: *Whistler* v *Forster* (1863) 14 CB (NS) 248.
(d)   The following personal defences, i.e. those which do not derive from the bill itself, but arise from external circumstances existing between plaintiff and defendant or even between the defendant and another party:

(i)   Total failure of consideration for the bill: *Fielding Platt Ltd* v *Selini Najjar* [1969] 2 All ER 150. Where, for example, a buyer rejects a consignment of foods delivered, he/she can argue that there has been a total failure of consideration. In ord. 14 proceedings, if he/she shows the right to reject as a triable issue, leave will be given to defend.

(ii)   Partial failure of consideration for the bill. Where, for example, a buyer rejects that part of the consignment delivered to him/her which is of a different description to that contracted for (SOGA 1979, s. 30(4)), or rejects an instalment delivered under a severable contract, or accepts a short delivery, there will be partial failure of consideration. If this is shown to be a triable issue in ord. 14 proceedings, judgment will be given for the amount not in dispute, with leave to defend as to the remainder: *Brown Shipley & Co. Ltd* v *Alicia Hosiery* [1966] 1 Lloyd's Rep 668.

A claim for unliquidated damages cannot be raised in an action on a bill of exchange. A claim for damages for breach of warranty under SOGA 1979, s. 53(3) (a claim pursued where defective goods are retained by the purchaser), is neither a claim for partial failure of consideration nor a claim for a liquidated sum. See *Nova (Jersey) Knit Ltd* v *Kammgarn Spinnerei GmbH* [1977] 1 WLR 713; *Montebianco Industrie Tessili* v *Carlyle Mills (London) Ltd* [1981] 1 Lloyd's Rep 509; *Thoni GmbH & Co. KG* v *RTP Equipment Ltd* [19791 2 Lloyd's Rep 282; *Cebora SNC* v *SIP (Industrial Products) Ltd* [1976] 1 Lloyd's Rep 271; *James Lamont & Co. Ltd* v *Hyland Ltd (No. 2)* [1950] 1 KB 585.

(iii) Misrepresentation, e.g. where the buyer is induced to accept a bill of exchange on the basis of a non-fraudulent misrepresentation as to the quality of the goods delivered against acceptance. See *Clovertogs* v *Jean Scenes* [1982] Com LR 88.

(iv) Any other mutual debt set-off. No other defences can be raised to the action on the bill against a holder for value. The courts treat the bill of lading as akin to cash and, where no defence can be set up, it will not be possible for the defendant to counterclaim and apply for a stay of execution: *Brown Shipley & Co. Ltd* v *Alicia Hosiery Ltd* [1966] 1 Lloyd's Rep 668; *Montebianco Industrie Tessili* v *Carlyle Mills (London) Ltd* [1981] 1 Lloyd's Rep 509.

Nevertheless, it may be possible for the defendant to safeguard his/her position by applying for a *Mareva* injunction to prevent dissipation of those moneys in the hands of the plaintiff. It does not interfere with the autonomy of the bill of exchange; it merely seeks to prevent a dealing with the sums paid out. However, the right to claim a *Mareva* injunction only arises if there is an underlying cause of action under which the right to claim a *Mareva* arises.

It has been argued that although 'real' defences and defences of defects in title can be raised against parties whether they are immediate or remote, personal defences can only be raised between immediate parties. The position is unclear. See Goode, *Commercial Law,* 1985, Pelican, p. 467. The following parties are immediate: acceptor/drawer; drawer/payee; payee (I$_1$)/indorser (2); indorser (2)/indorser (3); etc.

19.8.3   POSITION OF BANK

Since a seller who has drawn up a time bill rarely retains it, the holder at the time payment falls due will usually be a bank which has either bought the bill or lent against it, or which has merely been instructed to present it for payment and collect the proceeds, i.e. the bank acts as a collecting bank.

Where the bank has bought the bill it will either be a holder for value or a HDC depending on whether the conditions in s. 29(1) have been complied with. No matter the price paid, the bank will be a holder for the full amount of the bill.

Where the bank has agreed to lend money against the bill, it is still capable of achieving HDC status as there will have been a negotiation of it, e.g. an indorsement and a delivery. However, if the bank has only lent a percentage, e.g. 73 per cent, of the value of the bill, it will be a trustee of the seller with regard to the remaining amount, e.g. 27 per cent: *Barclays Bank* v *Aschaffenburger Zellstoffwerke* [1967] 1 Lloyd's Rep 387. The court will therefore order a stay of execution of the amount held on trust by the bank until a decision is reached in an action brought on the contract of sale by the defendant buyer (the acceptor of the bill) against the sellers for delivery of defective goods.

Where the bill is transferred to the bank for collection only, but the customer's account is overdrawn, the bank will obtain a lien over all securities of the customer which it possesses, including the bill of exchange. Under s. 27(3) the bank is deemed to have given value to the extent of the lien and is thus capable of becoming a HDC and being at the same time an agent for collection: *Barclays Bank Ltd* v *Astley Industrial Trust Ltd* [1970] 2 QB 527.

19.8.4   AMOUNTS RECOVERABLE

In the action on the bill, the plaintiff can recover from either the acceptor or the drawer and or a prior indorser:

(a) the amount of the bill as a debt including interest payable on the face of the bill up until its maturity; or

(b) liquidated damages as set out in s. 57, the measure of which is as follows:

(i) the amount of the bill;

(ii) interest on the bill from the time of presentment for payment if the bill was payable on demand, and from the maturity of the bill in any other case;

(iii) the expenses of noting or protesting the bill.

19.9 Further Reading

Goode, R. M., *Commercial Law,* rev., ed. 1985, Pelican.

Benjamin/Guest, *Sale of Goods,* 4th ed. 1992, Sweet & Maxwell.

Byles, J., *Bills of Exchange,* 26th ed. 1988, Sweet & Maxwell.

Richardson, D., *Guide to Negotiable Instruments,* 8th ed. 1991, Butterworths.

Schmitthoff, C., *Export Trade: Law and Practice of International Trade,* 9th ed. 1990, Sweet & Maxwell.

Example 1

In this and the following examples, sections referred to are those within the Bills of Exchange Act 1882, unless otherwise indicated.

---

[1]

£14,365

London 4th January 1995 [7]

AT SIGHT[2] OF THIS SOLA OF EXCHANGE[3]
PAY TO OUR ORDER[4] THE SUM OF sterling pounds

Fourteen thousand, three hundred and sixty five only for value received.

TO:[6]   Bank of Liberia
169 Fishergate
London

FOR AND ON BEHALF OF[5]
Milkemdry & Co. Ltd

. . . .

Director

Notes

1   This is the 'face' of the bill of exchange.

2   It is payable 'at sight' meaning it is payable on demand, or on presentation (see s. 10(1)).

3   'Sola of Exchange' indicates that the bill has not been drawn in a set (see below).

4   'Our order' indicates two things:

(a) the payee is the drawer of the bill[5]

(b) the bill is not on its face a bearer bill.

Therefore if Milkemdry & Co. Ltd, the drawer/payee wishes to negotiate the bill of exchange so as to pass title to the bill, they must put their signature on the back of the bill (see below). However, as a bill payable on demand it is unlikely to be negotiated.

⁵ The document must be signed by the person giving the order so that it can operate as a valid bill (see s. 3).

If it has been signed on behalf of the drawer without authority, or if the drawer's signature has been forged, it is not a valid bill (see ss. 24 and 3).

⁶ This indicates the drawee, the party upon whom the order to pay has been drawn and the place of payment. Note it has not been drawn on the buyer. As a bill payable on demand, it is unlikely to be presented for acceptance.

In addition, since the place for payment is within the British Isles (see s. 45(4)) and the bill has been drawn within the British Isles[7] the bill is an inland bill (see s. 4). See also s. 72 if the bill is negotiated. On the proper law, refer to *G & H Montage GmbH* v *Irvani* [1990] 1 Lloyd's Rep 14.

⁷ This indicates where the bill of exchange has been drawn and also indicates the date of its issue. Its importance in this 'sight' bill can be seen in s. 45(2). In order to prevent the drawer from being discharged from its liability as guarantor (only relevant if the bill is negotiated or the drawer and payee are different parties), presentment for payment must be made within a reasonable time after the bill's issue in order to render the drawer liable.

Example 2

---

[1]

US$14,365.40

London 4th January 1995 [7]

AT 90 DAYS AFTER DATE[2]OF THIS FIRST OF EXCHANGE[3] (SECOND OF THE SAME TENOR AND DATE BEING UNPAID)
PAY TO OUR ORDER[4] THE SUM OF US dollars[8]

Fourteen thousand, three hundred and sixty five and cents forty only for value received.

TO:[6]   Bank of Liberia
         New York

FOR AND ON BEHALF OF[5]
Milkemdry & Co. Ltd

. . . .

Director

Notes

¹ This is the 'face' of the bill of exchange.

² This indicates that the bill is not payable on sight. This phrase sets out 'the tenor' of the bill, i.e. time at which bill must be paid. These bills are sometimes referred to as 'usance' bills.

³ It is quite common in international trade for a bill to be drawn in a set, each part being sent by different mail, so that there are no setbacks if one of the parts is lost in the post. A usance bill of exchange such as this will be presented for acceptance to add currency to the bill. It is important that the drawee accepts only one part of the set. If the drawee were to accept more than one part, he/she would incur a liabilty to pay more than once if the parts were (wrongfully) negotiated to separate holders. In addition, the acceptor must make quite sure that he/she only pays against the accepted bill of exchange (see s. 71).

⁴ See note 4, Example 1. However, as a usance bill of exchange it is likely to be negotiated. Milkemdry & Co. Ltd as payee must indorse the back of the bill of exchange and deliver it to the new payee/indorsee, The indorsement could be 'special' that is to say the new payee is specified, or in blank, i.e. Milkemdry & Co. Ltd will still sign the back of the bill but no new payee will be specified. The back of the above bill of exchange could be set out as follows:

Pay <u>Easy Terms Credit</u> Co. Ltd
per pro Milkemdry & Co. Ltd   *John Smith*[a]

Pay Bank of Novia Scotia
per pro Easy Terms Credit Co. Ltd.   *Jack Dash*[b]

(a) Milkemdry & Co. Ltd will be an indorser ($I_{(1)}$) and liable as such as a guarantor of the bill in the event of dishonour by non-acceptance or non-payment. By indicating a new payee (s. 34(3)), the bill must not only be delivered to Easy Terms Credit Co. Ltd in order to complete the negotiation, and thus pass title to the bill (s. 31), but it will remain an order bill in Easy Terms Credit Co.'s hands. If Easy Terms Credit Co. wishes validly to negotiate the bill, they must indorse it.

(b) You can see Easy Terms Credit Co.'s indorsement here. Suppose they have in fact indorsed in blank and delivered the bill to the Bank of Monrovia — a perfectly valid negotiation to pass title of the bill to the latter (s. 31(3)) — in the hands of the Bank of Monrovia the bill is now a bearer bill (s. 34(4)) and the Bank of Monrovia can negotiate the bill by mere delivery. No indorsement is necessary *to pass title to the bill.*

The blank indorsement can be converted back into a special indorsement and thus back into an order bill by a holder writing above the Easy Terms Credit Co. Ltd signature a direction to pay the bill to the order of himself/herself or some other person (s. 34(4)). In this example, the Bank of Monrovia has placed above Easy Terms Credit Co.'s signature a direction to pay to their proposed new holder — the Bank of Nova Scotia. In the latter's hands the bill is now to order and not to bearer.

These bills have been issued as part of a set. Milkemdry & Co. Ltd as the payee should negotiate them as a whole. However, where they indorse the two parts to different persons, they are liable on each part (s. 71).

5   See note 5, Example 1.

6   This indicates the drawee and the place of payment. Note the following:

(a) Although it is not essential to present this bill for acceptance in order to preserve the liability of indorsers and the drawer on dishonour (s. 39 is not applicable), it is usually done to add currency to the bill.

(b) This is a foreign bill as it is neither drawn *and* payable within the British Isles nor drawn within the British Isles upon some person resident therein (see s. 4).

For consequences of this see ss. 51 and 72 and *G. & H. Montage GmbH* v *Irvani* [1990] 1 Lloyd's Rep 14.

7   This indicates where the bill of exchange has been drawn and also indicates the date of its issue. Its importance in this 'usance' bill is as follows:

(a) The date upon which the bill is to be presented for payment is determined by looking at the date of issue and applying the provisions of s. 14. See s. 14 as amended by the Banking and Financial Dealings Act 1971.

(b) Where the bill is accepted or indorsed, after it has become payable, it is deemed to be payable on demand (s. 10).

(c) Where the bill is expressed to be payable *after date* but no date had been expressed on the face of the bill, the bill is not invalid (s. 3(4)). For consequences of the omission, however, see s. 12.

[8] The amount recoverable is set out in s. 57(1). (Section 57(2) has been repealed by Administration of Justice Act 1977, s. 4(2).) As to judgment expressed in a foreign currency see *Miliangos* v *George Frank (Textiles) Ltd* [1975] 3 All ER 801.

Example 3

---

per pro Bank of Liberia, Jaques Delors [°]

[1]
£14,365.40

London 4th January 1995 [7]

AT 90 DAYS AFTER SIGHT[2] of this first of exchange (second and third of the same tenor and date being unpaid)[3]
PAY TO OUR ORDER[4] THE SUM OF US dollars[8]

Fourteen thousand, three hundred and sixty five and cents forty only for value received.

TO:[6]   Bank of Liberia
         New York

FOR AND ON BEHALF OF[5]
Milkemdry & Co. Ltd

. . . .
Director

Notes

[1] See note 1, Example 1.

[2] This bill is payable *after* sight, i.e. 90 days after its presentment for acceptance to the drawee.

[3] As in Example 2, except here the bill has been drawn in a set of three.

[4] See notes 4, Examples 1 and 2. However, be aware that Milkemdry & Co. Ltd, the payee, need not present for acceptance before they negotiate the bill. An unaccepted bill is not irregular — a holder of it can still achieve holder in due course status. Nevertheless, each subsequent holder of the bill must present it for acceptance *or* negotiate it within a reasonable time (s. 40(1) and (3)). A failure to comply with s. 40(1) discharges the drawer and all indorsers prior to that holder.

[5] See note 5, Example 1.

[6] This indicates the drawee. Note the following:

(a) This bill *must be presented for acceptance in order to fix the maturity date (s. 39(1)). As to when* the bill must be presented for acceptance, see s. 40(1) and note 4 above. As to consequences of failure to present at all, or in time, see s. 40.
If the bill is presented for acceptance too late, *and* acceptance is refused, there can be no action *on the bill* at all — the indorsers and drawer will be discharged and there is no acceptor. A drawee is not liable on the bill until he/she has accepted it.

(b) See note 6(b), Example 2.

[7] This indicates where the bill of exchange has been drawn and also indicates the date of its issue. This date is not of such obvious importance in an 'after sight bill'. It cannot be used to fix the maturity date of the bill.

[8] See note 8, Example 2.

[9] This is the acceptance of the bill of exchange. Where the signature has been forged or placed thereon without the authority of the drawee, the bill remains unaccepted. However, it is still a valid bill and title to it can still pass to subsequent holders. Section 14, as amended by the Banking and Financial Dealings Act 1971, indicates that time for payment begins to run from the date of acceptance *if the bill is accepted.*

If no date accompanies the acceptance, any holder may insert the true date of acceptance (s.12). Even if the wrong date has been inserted, in the hands of a holder in due course, the date is treated as correct (s. 12).

Where the bill is not accepted and the holder notes or protests for non-acceptance, time for payment begins to run from the date of noting or protesting the bill.

Where the bill has initially been refused acceptance, a subsequent acceptance by the drawee entitles the holder, in the absence of any different agreement, to operate the acceptance from the date of first presentation (s. 18(3)).

20   Documentary Letters of Credit

The seller may not wish to depend solely on the creditworthiness of his/her buyer when it comes to payment under the contract of sale. The seller may wish to be assured that the buyer will not obtain possession of the document of title to the goods, e.g. the bill of lading, until after payment has been made. He/she may wish to have an undertaking to pay given in this country which will enable him/her to sue and enter/enforce a judgment within the jurisdiction if problems ensue. The seller may wish to finance a supply contract. He/she may wish to have a right of action immune from attack similar to the rights of a holder in due course of a bill of exchange. All these desires can be accommodated in a payment mechanism called a documentary credit.

In a documentary credit, a bank(s) gives an independent undertaking to credit a named party's account. This party is called the beneficiary and is normally the seller. This undertaking(s) is conditional on the tender, in time, of conforming documents. The mechanism is triggered on the instructions of the buyer.

The requirements vis-à-vis the documentary credit, if this is the method of payment agreed between seller and buyer, are set out in the contract of sale, and include:

    (a)   the documents required to be tendered to the banks in order to obtain payment;
    (b)   an indication whether the buyer can choose the banks to implement the documentary credit or whether the seller has nominated one or more of the banks to be used;
    (c)   the *type* of credit which the seller wants opened;
    (d)   currency of payment.

Compliance with these documentary credit requirements is usually a condition precedent to the obligation of the seller to perform the contract of sale: *Garcia* v *Page & Co. Ltd* (1936) 55 L1 LR 391.

There has been no codification of the law relating to documentary credits into statutory form. However, the International Chamber of Commerce, because of the comparative uniformity of the rules as to letters of credit in different jurisdictions, have codified their understanding of these rules. The latest revision of these rules, called the Uniform Customs and Practice for Documentary Credits (UCP), was in July 1993. The rules do not have statutory force. Nevertheless, all British banks since 1962 have incorporated the UCP into their standard forms used for issuing documentary credits. Note, however, the UCP do *not* dominate over express contractual terms, *(see Royal Bank of Scotland* v *Cassa Di Risparmio Delle Provincie Lombard, Financial Times,* 21 January 1992 (CA)) and remain subject to the application of a country's national law. See Article 1.

20.1   Legal Structure of Documentary Credit

There are three main types of documentary credit:

    (a)   irrevocable/confirmed documentary credit;
    (b)   irrevocable/unconfirmed documentary credit;
    (c)   revocable/unconfirmed documentary credit.

The terms used in (a), (b) and (c) refer to the type of undertaking to be received/received by the beneficiary. Whatever the type of undertaking given to the beneficiary, there will be agency contracts between: the buyer and the issuing bank and the issuing bank and the advising bank or confirming bank. See **20.2.1** and **20.2.2**.

20.2 Contracts of Agency

20.2.1 BUYER AND ISSUING BANK

In each case the buyer will approach a bank, usually in his/her own country and usually one of his/her choice, to request the opening of a documentary credit in favour of the seller, on the terms set out in the contract of sale. If the bank agrees, a contractual relationship comes into existence between the buyer and the bank, known as the issuing bank (IB), in which the IB, as agent of the buyer, agrees to issue the type of credit requested, in the time requested and to arrange payment against conforming documents. The buyer agrees to pay commission and agrees to put the bank in funds before payment out by the bank, or agrees to reimburse the bank when payment is made.

20.2.2 ISSUING BANK AND ADVISING BANK

The IB will now enter into one or maybe two or more contracts. In implementing its instructions in its agency contract with the buyer, the IB will approach another bank, usually in the seller's country, and sometimes already designated in its contract of agency with the buyer. This bank is known as an advising bank (AB). (It is also referred to as a correspondent bank, but the term advising bank will be used here.) AB will be asked by the IB to inform the seller/beneficiary that a credit has been opened by the IB in his/her favour. It may also be asked to take up the documents and make payment. In these circumstances it will be an advising/nominated bank. Note here that not in every case will an advising bank act also as the nominated bank and vice versa. In some cases the issuing bank will approach one of its branches in the beneficiary's country to arrange for it to take up the documents and make payment. Such a branch is a 'nominated bank' for the purposes of the UCP as Article 2 states: 'the branches of a bank in a different country are considered another bank'.

The advising bank (AB) or the advising/nominated bank (AB/NB) may be asked to add its own 'confirmation' (CB) (see **20.2.4**). If the advising or advising/nominated bank accepts the proposals, a contract of agency arises between the IB and the chosen bank, and as appropriate the IB undertakes to pay commission and put the advising/nominated bank in funds before the date for payment, or reimburse.

20.2.3 IRREVOCABLE UNDERTAKING: ISSUING BANK AND BENEFICIARY

Where the IB on the instructions of its principal (the buyer) issues an irrevocable undertaking to pay to the beneficiary, it gives an independent undertaking, i.e. as a principal to the beneficiary. This undertaking becomes binding as soon as the letter of credit — sent by the AB, in performance of its obligation as agent of the IB to inform the beneficiary of the opening of the credit — reaches the hands of the beneficiary: *Hamzeh Malas v British Imex Industries Ltd* [1958] 2 QB 127. There is at this point a binding contract between the IB and the seller/beneficiary, in which the IB undertakes to pay against conforming documents (for more on what amounts to a good tender, see **20.5**). It may be difficult, if not impossible, to find the required consideration for a contract coming into existence at this time. In *Hamzeh Malas v British Imex Industries* Jenkins LJ stated that it must be regarded as established by mercantile custom recognised all over the world that a binding contract comes into existence at the time the documentary credit reaches the hands of the beneficiary. No bank has sought to dispute the existence of a contractual relationship with the beneficiary existing at that time. The credit which has been issued here is called an irrevocable credit. On non-payment against a conforming tender, the seller/beneficiary will have a right of action in contract against the IB.

20.2.4   CONFIRMATION: CONFIRMING BANK AND BENEFICIARY

The AB or AB/NB, in agreeing to advise the seller/beneficiary of the opening of the credit, may have been asked to give its own independent undertaking to pay against conforming documents. Whether it has been asked will depend on what the seller wanted and thus what went into the documentary credit clause in the contract of sale. This in turn would have become part of the buyer's instructions to the IB.

The undertaking given by the AB or AB/NB is called a confirmation, and the AB or AB/ NB becomes a confirming bank (CB). Where the letter of credit issued by the IB is irrevocable and the letter of credit informing the seller/beneficiary of its existence has added to it the confirmation of the CB, the payment mechanism is called an 'irrevocable/confirmed letter of credit'. Again, following *Hamzeh Malas* v *British Imex Industries (supra),* the confirmation becomes binding as soon as the letter of credit is received by the beneficiary. If the CB, the party directly responsible for payment, refuses to make /permit payment against a conforming tender, the seller/beneficiary will have a contractual remedy against it.

20.2.5   IRREVOCABLE/CONFIRMED LETTER OF CREDIT

The irrevocable/confirmed letter of credit is really the best the seller can obtain if a documentary credit is used. On a wrongful refusal to pay, the seller has a contractual remedy against (a) the CB, (b) the IB, *and,* if the letter of credit is a form of conditional payment only, (c) the buyer *on the contract of sale.* The seller/beneficiary will usually pursue his/her remedies against the CB, since this bank is situated in the seller's own country and the disadvantages of foreign litigation and enforcement abroad are thus avoided,

Figure 20.1

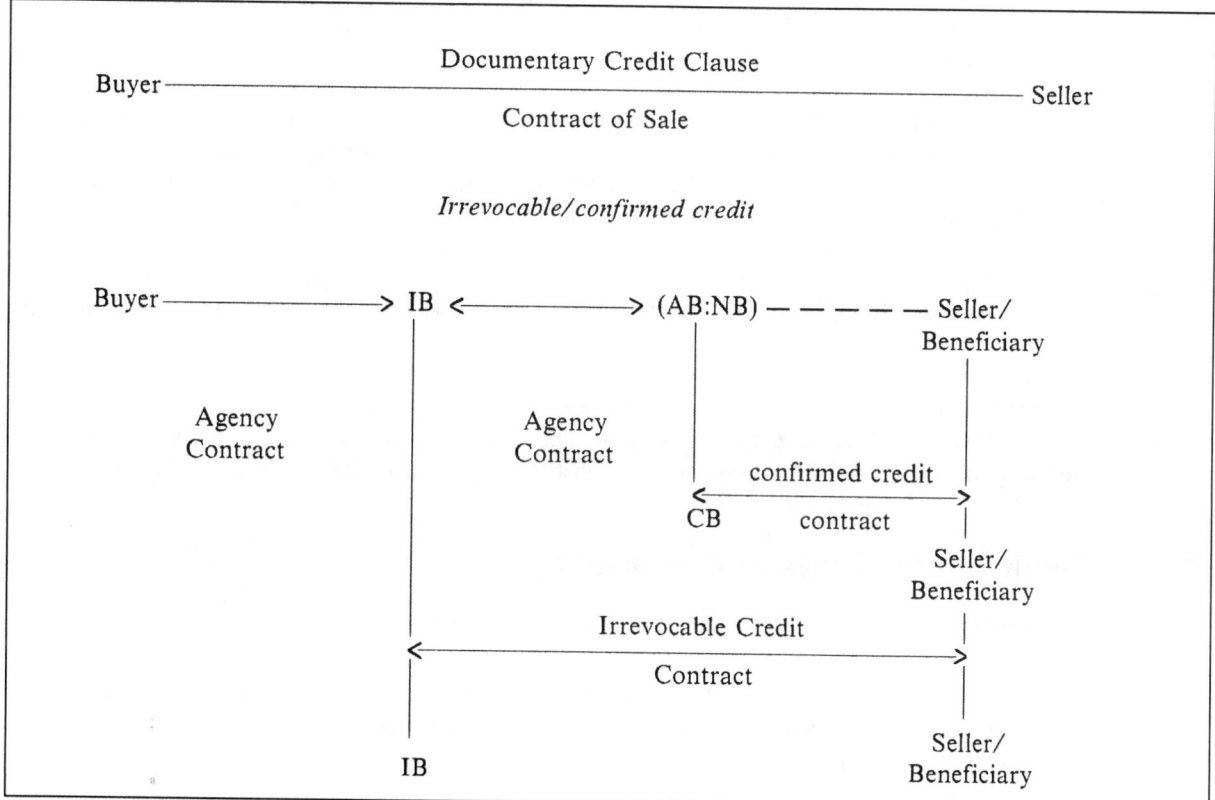

20.2.6   IRREVOCABLE/UNCONFIRMED LETTER OF CREDIT

Where the seller in the contract of sale did not feel it necessary to have, or could not obtain the agreement on the part of the buyer to add the confirmation of an advising or advising/ nominated bank, the credit will be irrevocable/unconfirmed. What has been said above about the position of the buyer and the IB in relation to the seller still applies. However, the advising or advising/nominated bank, by not adding its confirmation cannot be sued on a refusal to pay. There will be no contractual relationship between the beneficiary and the advising or advising/nominated bank. The beneficiary can still pursue a contractual remedy against the IB and perhaps also the buyer, but not the AB.

20.2.7 REVOCABLE/UNCONFIRMED LETTER OF CREDIT

It may be that the parties in the contract of sale agree on the use of a documentary credit in order to enable the seller to obtain payment but they do not feel it necessary from the nature of their relationship, e.g. the parties are associate companies, to open an irrevocable credit. Or it may be that the seller cannot demand the opening of an irrevocable credit because of his/her weak bargaining position. In these circumstances the credit which the seller will receive is a revocable credit. Such a credit will not be confirmed. The credit is thus a revocable/unconfirmed credit. Here the documentary credit, as far as the beneficiary is concerned, merely acts as a conduit pipe for the passage of funds from buyer to seller. Note here that the latest revision of the UCP has revoked the unpopular provision that credits were deemed *revocable* in the absence of a clear indication that they were irrevocable. Article 6 of the 1993 Revision states:

(b)   The credit, therefore, should clearly indicate whether it is revocable or irrevocable.
(c)   In the absence of such indication the credit shall be deemed to be irrevocable.

The onus is now on the applicant and the issuer of the credit to indicate clearly in both the instructions for the credit and the credit itself that the credit is revocable, if that is their intent.

Where the undertaking of the IB is revocable it may be amended or cancelled by the IB at any moment and without prior notice to the beneficiary (UCP, Article 8a), subject to the limitation however that the IB must, by virtue of Article 86

(i)   reimburse another bank with which a revocable credit has been made available for sight payment, acceptance or negotiation for any payment, acceptance or negotiation made by such bank — prior to receipt by it of notice of amendment or cancellation, against documents which appear on their face to be in compliance with the terms and conditions of the Credit.
(ii)   reimburse another bank with which a revocable credit has been made available for deferred payment, if such a bank has, prior to receipt by it of notice of amendment or cancellation, taken up documents which appear on their face to be in compliance with the terms and conditions of the Credit.

Under the revocable/unconfirmed credit, the seller/beneficiary does not receive an undertaking from the IB or AB/NB, but he/she is enabled to tender his/her documents at a bank in his/ her own country. On a refusal to pay, the seller's action will be against the buyer for breach of the contract of sale.

20.3 Bank Undertakings to Beneficiary

20.3.1 IRREVOCABLE CREDIT: UNDERTAKING OF THE ISSUING BANK

UCP, Article 9 provides that where the stipulated documents are presented to the nominated bank or to the issuing bank and all other terms and conditions of the credit are complied with, the IB undertakes to do one of the following:

(a)   to pay at sight if the credit provides for sight payment; or
(b)   where the credit provides for deferred payment, to pay on the appropriate date.

Where a bill of exchange is to be tendered by the beneficiary, the situation is as follows. The IB undertakes either:

(c) to accept the bill of exchange drawn on the IB by the beneficiary *and* pay at the maturity date;or

(d) where the bill of exchange is required to be and is drawn on another bank which fails to accept, to accept a bill of exchange drawn on the IB *and* pay at the maturity date; or

(e) to pay where the bill of exchange is drawn on and accepted by another drawer bank which fails to make payment on the due date.

If the credit provides for negotiation, the situation is as follows. The IB undertakes to:

(f) pay without recourse to drawers and/or bona fide holders, draft(s) drawn by the beneficiary and/or documents presented under the credit.

The latest revision of the UCP requires that a credit should not be issued available by drafts drawn on the applicant for the credit. Nevertheless, if the credit does call for a credit in which the applicant is to be the drawee of the bill of exchange, such a bill of exchange is merely to be considered as an additional document.

Under (f) above, if the bill is negotiated by the IB, the IB excludes its right of recourse against prior indorsers which would otherwise be available on dishonour by non-acceptance or non-payment. To allow the IB to exercise a right of recourse would destroy the efficacy of the irrevocable credit.

20.3.2 CONFIRMED CREDIT: UNDERTAKING OF CONFIRMING BANK

Provided that the stipulated documents are presented to the CB or to any other nominated bank and that the terms and conditions of the credit are complied with, the undertaking of the CB is identical to that of the IB: Article 9(b). Refer to **20.3.1**(a)–(f), substituting CB for IB.

20.4 Obligation of the Buyer under the Documentary Credit

The opening of the credit is usually treated as a condition precedent to the obligation of the seller to perform the contract of sale by delivering the goods.

The credit will be opened when its existence is communicated to the beneficiary (*Bunge Corp.* v *Vegetable Vitamin* (1984) 134 NLJ 125). The obligation to open the correct credit in time is strict — see, for example, *Etablissement Chainbaux* v *Harbourmaster* [1955] 1 Lloyd's Rep 303.

For the time by which the credit must be opened in relation to f.o.b. and c.i.f. contracts refer to *Sinason-Teicher Inter-American Grain Corp.* v *Oil Cakes and Oil Seeds* [1954] 1 WLR 1394; *Ian Stach* v *Baker Bosley* [1958] 2 QB 130.

Failure to open the correct credit in time enables the seller to treat the contract of sale as repudiated and sue for damages. (See *Trans-Trust* v *Danubian Trading* [1952] 2 QB 297; *Transpetrol Ltd* v *Transol* [1989] 1 Lloyd's Rep 309.) Refer also to *State Trading Corporation of India Ltd* v *Golodetz Ltd* [1989] 2 Lloyd's Rep 277.

20.5 Obligations of Beneficiary in order to Obtain Payment, Acceptance or Negotiation

Assuming that the correct credit has been opened in time, we need to examine what the seller/beneficiary must do in order to obtain payment, or, where appropriate, the acceptance or negotiation of a bill of exchange.

20.5.1   DOCUMENTS MUST BE TENDERED IN TIME

In this context there are two time elements to be considered. First, banks will refuse documents presented to them later than a specified period of time after the date of shipment. If no time is specified the documents must be presented not later than 21 days after the date of shipment: Document UCP 43(a). Note the extension of expiry date provision Article 44 (see below).

Where the transport document indicates that shipment has been made on the same means of conveyance and for the same journey and indicates the same destination, the existence of different shipment dates and/or different ports of loading, places of taking in charge or dispatch allows the bank to treat the date of shipment as the last shipment date on any of the transport documents presented: Article 43(b). What is the 'date of shipment'? In relation to a multimodal transport document the expression refers to the 'taking in charge' of the goods. In relation to other transport documents the expression refers to the 'loading on board', 'dispatch', 'acceptance for carriage' and 'the like of the goods'. (See Article 46.)

Secondly, and subject to the time limit set out above, all credits must stipulate an expiry date for presentation of documents (Article 42). All documents required to be tendered under the credit must be so tendered before the expiry date unless it is possible to rely on the extension provision in Article 44(a), which states:

> If the expiry date of the credit and/or the last day of the period of time for presentation of documents stipulated by the credit or applicable by virtue of Article 43 falls on a day on which the bank to which presentation has to be made is closed for reasons other than those referred to in Article 17 '[force majeure]' the stipulated expiry date and/or the last day of the period of time after the date of shipment for presentation of documents, as the case may be, shall be extended to the first following day on which such bank is open.

Note that an extension of the expiry date and/or an extension of the time for tender of documents after 'shipment' does *not* extend the shipping period (Article 44(b)). If the credit fails to indicate a latest date for shipment, documents will not be accepted which indicate a date of shipment beyond the expiry date of the credit (Article 44(b)).

In considering the expiry of a relevant time limit, note that Article 42(a) requires the credit to stipulate a place for presentation of documents unless it is a freely negotiable credit.

Note a further time limitation in relation to credits which allow drawings and/or shipments by instalments. Article 41 indicates that a failure to make an instalment drawing and/or shipment within the given period allowed for that instalment will cause the credit to cease to be available for that or any subsequent instalment, unless otherwise stipulated in the credit.

Note too that Article 22 allows banks, unless otherwise directed, to accept a document bearing *a date of issuance* prior to that of the credit, provided the document is presented within the time limit set out in the credit or in the UCP.

20.5.2   DOCUMENTS MUST CONFORM ON THEIR FACE TO THE REQUIREMENTS OF THE CREDIT

There are several points to note about this requirement. The documentary credit transaction is autonomous and isolated from the underlying sales transaction. The position of the banks is made clear in UCP, Article 4:

> In credit operations all parties concerned deal in documents and not with goods, services and/or other performances to which the documents may relate.

Article 3 provides:

(a)   Credits, by their nature, are separate transactions from the sales or other contract(s) on which they may be based and banks are in no way concerned with or bound by such contract(s), even if any reference whatsoever to such contract(s) is included in the credit. Consequently, the undertaking of a bank to pay, accept and pay Draft(s) or negotiate and/or to fulfil any other obligation under the credit, is not subject to claims or defences by the applicant resulting from his relationships with the issuing bank or the beneficiary.

This means, first, that the banks involved in the credit arrangement cannot rely on, say, the defective nature of the goods shipped as a reason for refusing payment unless the defect appears *on the face* of the document. See below, on the bank's position where there is fraud by the beneficiary or illegality at the place for honouring the credit.

In addition, Article 3(a) makes it clear that the applicant is also prevented from interfering with the bank's obligation to honour the credit by, say, arguing that the beneficiary has breached his contractual obligation with the applicant.

Article 3(b) places the beneficiary in the same position as the applicant. The beneficiary cannot argue that the credit should be issued because of the bank's agreement with the applicant to issue the credit.

(b)   A beneficiary can in no case avail himself of the contractual relationships existing between the banks or between the applicant for the credit and the issuing bank.

The bank is entitled, and indeed obliged, to examine all documents stipulated in the credit to ascertain that they appear 'on their face' to conform: Article 13(a). 'On their face' according to ICC commentary and Article 13, does not mean 'face' as opposed to 'reverse' of a document, but the examination by a banker, with reasonable care and according to international standard banking practice, of the whole document. In addition, documents stipulated in the credit will not conform on their face, and thus not be in compliance with the terms and conditions of the credit, if they are inconsistent with one another.

To reinforce the principle of the autonomy of the credit and to clarify even further the duties of a bank authorised to take up the documents, Article 14 states:

Upon receipt of the documents, the issuing bank and/or confirming bank, if any, or a nominated bank acting on their behalf, must determine on the basis of the documents alone whether or not they appear on their face to be in compliance with the terms and conditions of the credit. If the documents appear on their face not to be in compliance with the terms and conditions of the credit, such banks may refuse to take up the documents.

However, even though the defect is *not* present on the face of the document the banks can refuse payment in the following cases:

(a)   Where there is a fraud *by the beneficiary*, i.e., a fraudulent misrepresentation in the documents tendered under the credit: *United City Merchants* v *Royal Bank of Canada* [1982] 2 All ER 720. Fraud by a supplier or by some other party who is not the agent of the seller, of which fraud the seller is ignorant, will not justify the bank in refusing to pay. Nor can the principal refuse to reimburse the bank which does pay out. Compare with the position of a seller who tenders inaccurate documents for payment directly to a buyer: *Kwei Tek Chao* v *British Traders & Shippers Ltd* [1954] 2 QB 459.
(b)   Where the honouring of the credit would be illegal according to the law of the place where the bank's performance is due. The letter of credit will determine by which bank payment is to be made to the beneficiary. If confirmed it will be the CB. If unconfirmed it is still usually the AB: *United City Merchants* v *Royal Bank of Canada (supra)*; see also *Toprak Mahsulleri Ofisi* v *Finagrain* [1979] 2 Lloyd's Rep 98.
(c)   Where the bank is owed a liquidated sum due from a beneficiary under another transaction; set off could be total or partial, see *Hong Kong & Shanghai Banking Corp.* v *Kloeckner* [1989] 3 All ER 513.

Note that the defences of fraud of the beneficiary or illegality at the place of performance cannot be raised by the IB or CB/AB and/or NB as acceptor or negotiator against a holder in due course (HDC) of a bill of exchange. The bank's liability on the bill of exchange is isolated from both the sale transaction and the letter of credit. Remember that the seller/beneficiary, who is also the drawer/payee of the bill of exchange drawn under the credit, cannot be a HDC whilst the bill remains in his/her hands. He/she will be a holder for value, and the defences of fraud or illegality can be raised against him/her.

The doctrine of strict compliance applies to the tender of documents under a credit: *Equitable Trust Co. of New York* v *Dawson Partners Ltd* (1927) 27 L1 LR 49. This allows the banks to reject a tender which is technically defective, e.g. a difference in terminology. See *J. H. Rayner & Co. Ltd* v *Hambro's Bank Ltd* [1943] 1 KB 37, where the credit described the goods to be shipped and for which documents were to be presented as 'coromandel groundnuts'. The bill of lading tendered referred to 'machine-shelled' groundnuts. The bank was held justified in rejecting documents tendered even though the two descriptions were synonomous. The UCP alleviates the effect of the strict-compliance rule by introducing tolerances in quantity and amount and unit price. Article 39(a) provides:

The words 'about', 'circa' or similar expressions used in connection with the amount of the credit or the quantity or the unit price stated in the credit are to be construed as allowing a difference not to exceed 10% more or 10% less than the amount or the quantity or the unit price to which they refer.

Article 39(b) provides:

Unless a credit stipulates that the quantity of the goods specified must not be exceeded or reduced, a tolerance of 5% more or 5% less will be permissible, always provided that the amount of the drawings does not exceed the amount of the credit. This tolerance does not apply when the credit stipulates the quantity in terms of a stated number of packing units or individual items.

Article 39(c) provides:

Unless a credit which prohibits partial shipment stipulates otherwise, or unless sub-article (b) above is applicable, a tolerance of 5% less in the amounts of the drawing bill will be permissible, provided that if the credit stipulates the quantity of the goods, such quantity of goods is shipped in full, and if the credit stipulates a unit price, such price is not reduced. This provision does not apply when expressions referred to in sub-article (a) above are used in the credit.

Bearing the above general points in mind, a few words need to be said about individual documents. These may be conveniently considered under the headings of transport documents (documents indicating loading on board or dispatch or taking in charge), the commercial invoice, and insurance documents.

20.5.3 MARINE/OCEAN BILL OF LADING: SEAWAY BILL: MULTIMODAL TRANSPORT DOCUMENT

Where the credit stipulates that there should be tender of a bill of lading or seaway bill covering port to port shipment, banks under the credit will accept, unless otherwise stipulated in the credit, a document, *however named*, which indicates that the goods have been loaded on board, or shipped on a named vessel. There is no room here for a 'received for shipment' bill of lading/ seaway bill: (Article 23(a); Article 24(a)).

If the bill of lading or seaway bill is printed as a 'shipped' document, the above condition is satisfied and the date of shipment will be deemed to be the date of issuance of the document.

If the bill of lading/seaway bill is of the 'received for shipment' variety, there must be an on board notation indicating the vessel and the date. This date will be deemed to be the date of shipment.

Whenever the bill of lading or seaway bill refers to an 'intended vessel' or similar qualification in relation to the vessel, loading on board a named vessel must be evidenced by an on board notation on the document indicating the name of the vessel.

The bill of lading or seaway bill must indicate the port of loading and discharge stipulated in the credit. In relation to a 'received for shipment' document, the on board notation must include the port of loading stipulated in the credit.

Where the credit calls for a transport document covering *at least two different modes of transport*, banks will, unless otherwise stipulated in the credit, accept a document *however named*, which indicates that the goods have been dispatched, taken in charge or loaded on board:

> Dispatch, taking in charge or loading on board may be indicated by wording to that effect on the multimodal transport document and the date of issuance will be deemed to be the date of dispatch, taking in charge or loading on board and the date of shipment. However, if the document indicates by stamp or otherwise, a date of dispatch, taking in charge or loading on board, such date will be deemed to be the date of shipment. [Article 26(a)].

The multimodal document will be acceptable to the bank, unless otherwise stipulated in the credit, where it refers to an 'intended vessel' and/or intended port of loading and/or intended port of discharge. The document, must, however, refer to the place of taking in charge and place of destination stipulated in the credit.

Where the credit stipulates tender of a bill of lading or seaway bill covering port to port shipment the banks will, unless otherwise stipulated in the credit, accept a document however named which:

> appears on its face to indicate the name of the carrier and to have been signed or otherwise authenticated by:
> The carrier or a name agent for or on behalf of the carrier, or
> The master or a named agent for or on behalf of the master.

Any signature or authentication of the carrier or master must be identified as that of the carrier or master, as the case may be. An agent signing or authenticating for the carrier or master must also indicate the name and the capacity of the party, i.e. carrier or master, on whose behalf that agent is acting (Article 23; Article 24).

Where the credit calls for a transport document covering at least two different modes of transport banks will, unless otherwise stipulated in the credit, accept a document however named which:

> appears on its face to indicate the name of the carrier or multimodal operation and to have been signed or otherwise authenticated by the carrier or multimodal transport operator or a named agent for or on behalf of the carrier or multimodal operator, or the master or a named agent for or on behalf of the master.

Any signature or authentication of the carrier, multimodal transport operator or master must be identified as that of the carrier, multimodal transport operator or master, as the case may be. An agent signing or authenticating for the carrier, multimodal transport operator or master must also indicate the name and the capacity of the party, i.e. carrier, multimodal transport operator or master, on whose behalf that agent is signing (Article 26).

Note Article 25, which indicates that if the credit calls for or permits a charter party bill of lading, banks will, unless otherwise stipulated in the credit, accept a document however named which:

> appears on its face to have been signed or otherwise authenticated by:
> The master or a named agent for or on behalf of the master, or
> The owner or a named agent for or on behalf of the owner.

Any signature or authentication of the master or owner must be identified as that of the master or owner, as the case may be. An agent signing or authenticating for the master or owner must also indicate the name and the capacity of the party, i.e. master or owner, on whose behalf that agent is acting.

It is not necessary for the document to indicate the name of the carrier.

Note, too, Article 30 which imposes restrictions on the acceptability of transport documents issued by freight forwarders:

unless otherwise authorised in the credit, banks will only accept a transport document issued by a freight forwarder if it appears on its face to indicate:

(i)   the name of the freight forwarder as a carrier or multimodal transport operator and to have been signed or otherwise authenticated by the freight forwarder as carrier or multimodal transport operator, or

(ii)   the name of the carrier or multimodal transport operator and to have been signed or otherwise authenticated by the freight forwarder as a named agent for or on behalf of the carrier or multimodal transport operator.

The transport document generally must (unless the credit stipulates to the contrary):

(a)   be tendered on a full set of originals (Article 23iv; Article 24iv; Article 25iv; Article 26iv);

(b)   appear to contain all of the terms and conditions of carriage, or of some such terms and conditions by reference to a source or document other than the bill of lading/seaway bill or multimodal transport document (Article 23v; Article 24v; Article 26v);

(c)   contain no indication that it is subject to a charterparty (Articles 23vi; 24vi; 26vi).

Where the credit calls for or permits a charterparty bill of lading, a document containing an indication that it is subject to a charterparty is acceptable unless the credit stipulates to the contrary.

20.5.4   TRANSHIPMENT/DECK CARGO

For the purposes of Article 23 (port to port bills of lading) and Article 24 (non-negotiable seaway bills), transhipment is defined as meaning the 'unloading and reloading from one vessel to another vessel during the course of ocean carriage from the port of loading to the port of discharge'.

Where transhipment is not prohibited, banks will accept a port to port bill of lading or seaway bill which indicates that the goods *will* be transhipped but only if the transport document covers the entire ocean carriage.

Where transhipment *is* prohibited by the terms of the credit, a transport document indicating that goods will be transhipped *will* be unacceptable unless the relevant cargo is shipped in containers, trawler(s) and/or 'lash' barges and evidenced by the bill of lading or seaway bill and the transport document covers the entire ocean carriage.

Where transhipment is prohibited by the terms of the credit, banks will accept a port to port bill of lading or seaway bill which indicates the goods may be transhipped.

Where the credit calls for a transport document covering at least two different modes of transport, banks will disregard conditions in the credit prohibiting transhipment and accept': a transport document which indicates that the goods *will* or *may* be transhipped 'provided that the entire carriage is covered by one and the same multimodal transport document': Article 26(b).

Where the mode of transport is, or includes, carriage by sea, banks will reject a transport document which indicates that the goods *are* or *will* be loaded on deck (Article 31(i)) — unless specifically authorised in the credit. However, banks will not reject a transport document which merely indicates that the goods *may* be carried on deck: Article 31(i). The reason for this is that the Hague-Visby Rules, given statutory force in this country under the Carriage of Goods by Sea Act 1971 and which restrict the freedom of the carrier to exclude his liability, will cease to apply, unless expressly incorporated into the carriage contract, if the bill of lading indicates that the goods are being or will be carried on deck. The presence of a liberty clause in the bill of lading permitting carriage on deck without a further indication that the goods are or will be carried on deck does not oust the operation of the Hague-Visby Rules: *Svenska Traktor* v *Maritime Agencies (Southampton) Ltd* [1953] 2 QB 295.

20.5.5   NOTATIONS ON TRANSPORT DOCUMENT

The transport document tendered must be 'clean', i.e. bear no clauses or notation expressly declaring a defective condition of the goods and/or the packaging: Article 32(a). The banks will reject such a tender unless the credit expressly stipulates the clauses or notations which are acceptable: Article 32(b).

The transport document is acceptable in the absence of instructions to the contrary, even if it bears a clause on its face stating, e.g. 'shipper's load and count' or 'said by shipper to contain' or any other phrase indicating that the carrier is making no representation as to the quantity or contents of the goods shipped: Article 31.

20.5.6   COMMERCIAL INVOICE

Unless otherwise stipulated in the credit, banks will accept a commercial invoice which is not signed. However, it must appear on its face to be issued by the beneficiary named in the credit or by the second beneficiary in a transferred credit; it must be made out in the name of the applicant for the credit or the name of the first beneficiary in a transferred credit, and the description of the goods in the commercial invoice must correspond with the description in the credit: Article 37.

20.5.7   INSURANCE DOCUMENTS

UCP, Article 34 indicates that, unless instructed to the contrary, banks will not accept cover notes issued by brokers but will accept insurance certificates or declarations issued under an open cover pre-signed by insurance companies or underwriters or their agents. If the credit specifically calls for an insurance certificate or a declaration under an open cover, an insurance policy is acceptable to the bank in lieu thereof.

An insurance document tendered must appear on its face to be issued and signed by insurance companies, or underwriters or agents.

Unless otherwise stipulated in the credit, the insurance document must, at minimum, cover the goods up to their C.I.F. value (cost, insurance, freight) or C.I.P. (carriage and insurance paid to named place of destination) value of the goods plus 10 per cent. However, where the bank cannot determine the C.I.F. or C.I.P. value from the face of the documents tendered it will accept as such minimum amount 110 per cent of the amount for which payment, acceptance or negotiation is requested under the credit, or 110 per cent of the gross amount of the invoice, whichever is the greater: Article 34. This brings the UCP insurance document requirements in line with those set out in Incoterms 1990.

In terms of the date of the effectiveness of the cover, Article 34 makes it quite clear that banks are not required to analyse the cover terms. If the date of issuance of the insurance document is later than the date of loading on board or taking in charge of the goods in the transport document, banks will reject the tender unless the credit stipulates to the contrary or unless it appears from the insurance document that the cover is effective at the latest from the date of loading on board or taking in charge of the goods.

The applicant must give specific instructions as to the type of cover required: Article 35. Failure to make specific stipulations will enable the bank to accept documents as they are presented without responsibility for any risks covered: Article 35.

Where the credit demands insurance against 'all risks', banks will accept an insurance document which contains any 'all risks' notation or clause, whether or not bearing the heading 'all risks', even if the insurance document indicates that certain risks are excluded, without responsibility for any risk(s) not being covered.

20.6 Non-conforming Tender Made

20.6.1 CONSEQUENCES FOR SELLER

The seller's position under the credit and under the contract of sale, where a tender has been made which is not in conformity with the terms of the credit, is as follows:

(a) The bank can accept the tender and pay out.

(b) The bank can make payment under reserve; see **20.8**.

(c) The bank can lawfully refuse the tender.

(d) Depending on the type of non-conformity the seller/beneficiary, on a refusal to accept the tender, may be able to retender if there is still time (it has already been observed that there is a time restriction on tender of documents under the credit).

(e) Where the bank has lawfully rejected the non-conforming tender and it is no longer possible to make a fresh tender, the seller will have no recourse to the purchaser, e.g. a tender of documents too late under the credit will prevent the seller from presenting them and demanding payment from the buyer under the contract of sale: *Shamisher Jute Mills Ltd* v *Sethia (London) Ltd* [1987] 1 Lloyd's Rep 388.

(f) Where the bank lawfully refuses to accept the tender and it is too late to make a fresh tender, the seller will be liable in damages for non-delivery to the buyer. Where the bank has accepted the tender, the seller may still be liable on the contract of sale, either in damages for non-delivery if the buyer subsequently rejects, or damages for breach of warranty.

20.6.2 DUTY OF THE BANK

Note the following points about the duty of the bank to which documents have been tendered, as required under the credit:

(a) The NB which acts on behalf of the IB and/or CB and the IB and the CB has each to decide and indicate whether to reject or take up the document within a reasonable period, up to a maximum of seven days following the day of the bank's receipt of the documents.

(b) This maximum seven-day period is not cumulative from the time of tender by the beneficiary but applies to each bank in relation to the party tendering to it: Article 13(b).

(c) The bank must within a reasonable time, up to the maximum seven-day period, not only decide whether to take up or refuse the tender but also inform the tenderer of the documents.

(d) Article 14(c) makes it quite clear that the IB must decide on its own whether there has been a tender of documents which appear on their face to comply with the term of the credit. The UCP does not allow the applicant for the credit and its agent, the IB, to come to a joint decision on acceptance or rejection. Article 14(c), however, enables the IB, *once it has decided to reject* a tender, to turn to the applicant for a waiver of the discrepancy (ies). This does not allow an extension of the maximum seven-day period. As to the type of communication indicating acceptance or rejection and what must be stated, Article 14(d) states:

(i) If the issuing bank and/or confirming bank, if any, or a nominated bank acting on their behalf, decides to refuse the documents, it must give notice to that effect by telecommunication, or, if that is not possible, by other expeditious means, without delay but no later than the close of the seventh banking day following the day of receipt of the documents. Such notice shall be given to the bank from which it received the documents, or to the beneficiary, if it received the documents directly from him.

(ii) Such notice must state all discrepancies in respect of which the bank refuses the documents and must also state whether it is holding the documents at the disposal of, or is returning them to the presenter.

As to the penalty for failure in relation to the above, Article 14(e) states:

If the Issuing Bank and/or Confirming Bank, if any, fails to act in accordance with the provisions of this Article and/or fails to hold the documents at the disposal of, or return them to the presenter, the Issuing Bank and/or Confirming Bank, if any, shall be precluded from claiming that the documents are not in compliance with the terms and conditions of the credit.

20.7 Seller's Position where Good Tender Made but Documents Rejected and/or Payment Refused

20.7.1 ACTION FOR THE AMOUNT OF THE CREDIT AGAINST ISSUING BANK/CONFIRMING BANK

The seller/beneficiary can sue the CB on its confirmation, and the IB on its irrevocable undertaking, for the actual amount of the credit plus interest plus any other loss directly resulting from the bank's breach: *Ozalid Group Export* v *African Continental Bank Ltd* [1979] 2 Lloyd's Rep 231.

This remedy must be pursued where the documents are already retained by the bank. In addition, this remedy can be pursued where the beneficiary still has the documents in his/her possession. Whether or not the bank under the credit can insist on steps being taken by the seller/beneficiary to mitigate his/her loss is unclear. Refer to Denning LJ in *Trans-Trust SPRL* v *Danubian Trading Co. Ltd* [1952] 2 QB 297 at p. 305 and also Gutteridge and Megrah, *The Law of Bankers' Commercial Credits,* 7th edn, 1984, Europa Publications.

Where the documents have already been relinquished to the bank, on the bank's acceptance of a bill of exchange, the seller's remedy is an action on the bill of exchange and/or on the promise given in the credit to pay at maturity (Article 9).

20.7.2 ACTION FOR DAMAGES AGAINST ISSUING BANK/CONFIRMING BANK

Where the bank has not retained the documents the seller/beneficiary may decide to accept the IB's/CB's repudiatory breach of contract as bringing the contract to an end. In these circumstances, he/she cannot sue for the amount of the credit, but must mitigate his/her loss by selling the goods elsewhere and suing the bank(s) for the ensuing losses incurred. In essence. damages will be awarded against the bank(s) on the same basis as in an action against the buyer for damages for non-acceptance: *Urquhart Lindsay & Co. Ltd* v *Eastern Bank Ltd* [1922] 1 KB 318.

20.7.3 RECOURSE TO BUYER

The seller can also have recourse to the buyer, if the letter of credit merely operates as a form of conditional payment. Lord Denning in *W. J Alan* v *El Nasr Export & Import* [1972] 2 QB 189 said (at 210):

In my opinion a letter of credit is not to be regarded as absolute payment, unless the seller stipulates, expressly or impliedly, that it should be so. He may do it impliedly if he stipulates for the credit to be issued by a particular banker, in such circumstances that it is to be inferred that the seller looks to that particular bank to the exclusion of the buyer.

If the credit is conditional (as it usually is) the buyer under the contract of sale (a) undertakes to open the correct credit, *and* (b) promises that payment will be made under the letter of credit if the seller fulfils his own contractual obligations.

It must be borne in mind, however, that the action for damages for non-acceptance against the buyer is for breach of the contract of sale. It may be that the c.i.f. or f.o.b. buyer has a defence to the action if the documents rejected have an underlying non-conformity even though not due to the fraud of the seller or his/her agent. If action proceeds against the bank(s) for breach of its/their undertaking in the credit, the defences which it/they can raise are much more limited (see **20.5.2**). There would therefore be a better chance of success and a better chance of obtaining summary judgment in an action pursued against the banks under the credit and/or, where appropriate, on the bill of exchange.

20.8   Payment under Reserve

Banks are aware of their right to reject documents for purely technical irregularities. They are also aware of the importance of letters of credit in the promotion of export transactions. Banks, therefore, do not wish to be obstructive, in the interests of both the applicant for the credit and the beneficiary. Where there is doubt as to the regularity of documents tendered, and/or the irregularity appears to be technical and not substantial, a bank may agree to make payment 'under reserve' to the beneficiary. In *Banque de L'Indochine* v *Rayner* [1983] 1 All ER 1137 the Court of Appeal held that the intention of the parties when the CB made payment under reserve was to oblige the beneficiary to repay the sums paid *on demand*, if the IB had rejected the tendered documents either on its own initiative or on the buyer's instructions. In other words, the obligation to repay was *not* intended by the parties to be dependent on establishing the validity of the reasons for initially making the payment under reserve. Kerr LJ said (at 1144):

> The confirming bank cannot be realistically taken to have agreed to become involved in legal proceedings, if the documents are rejected, by having to sue the beneficiary to recover the money and establishing that the documents did not comply with the credit.

In a counterclaim or subsequent claim for breach of the contract in the credit brought by the beneficiary, to retain or recover the moneys paid out/back, the issue of non-conformity *will* arise. Kerr LJ in the above case expressed the view that there should be implied into the agreement between the paying bank making payment under reserve and the beneficiary a term that the paying bank is only entitled to demand repayment from the seller if the IB rejects the documents for reasons which include at least one of the reasons which caused the paying bank to make payment to the seller under reserve.

20.8.1   IMPORTANCE OF PAYMENT 'UNDER RESERVE' OR UNDER SOME OTHER FORM OF CONTRACT OF INDEMNITY

It is important that the paying bank, intending to make payment against documents which may be rejected by its principal on the grounds of irregularity, should make a 'reserve' payment, or enter into a written contract of indemnity with the beneficiary or the beneficiary's bank. Without this, it would appear that the bank has few rights of recourse to the beneficiary. If there is fraud by the beneficiary or his/her agent the bank may be able to recover in tort for deceit or recover the money paid under a mistake of fact: *Bank Russo-Iran* v *Gordon Woodroffe & Co. Ltd*, *The Times*, 4 October 1972. But in the absence of that, payment made against documents defective *on their face* would appear to prevent recovery by the bank of money paid under a mistake of fact. The bank's conduct in so paying can be regarded as a payment made with knowledge of the facts and thus amounting to a waiver. Unless the bank's principal is prepared to accept the documents and reimburse the paying bank (see **20.10.3**), the bank will be left with its lien over the goods by means of possession of the documents. It will have to realise its loss by dealing with those documents/goods.

Where the bank has paid against documents which contain a latent defect, i.e. one that could not be seen on a reasonable examination of those documents, it is entitled to reimbursement by its principal. It is unclear whether, failing reimbursement by the principal, the bank can recover the money paid, from the beneficiary. It might be possible to argue that in the contract in the credit between the CB and the beneficiary, there exists an implied warranty given by the beneficiary that the documents are genuine and contain no latent defects. Where, therefore, the principal has refused reimbursement (albeit wrongly), the bank may be able to recover from the beneficiary those losses within the contemplation of the parties still remaining after it has dealt with he goods, as damages for breach of warranty. See Goode, *Commercial Law* 1985, Pelican, p. 679.

20.9 Buyer's Position where Bad Tender Made and Documents Rejected and Payment Refused

Where a bank lawfully rejects documents and refuses payment, the following will apply:

(a)   The property in the goods will not pass to the buyer if, as is usual in the c.i.f. and f.o.b. contract, the passing of property is dependent on payment. If property has passed before payment, property in the buyer will revest in the seller on rejection of the documents by the bank.

(b)   Where the seller does not retender conforming documents or is not in a position to do so, the buyer can proceed to sue the seller for damages for non-delivery.

20.10 Buyer's Position where Bank Paid Out Wrongfully

Note that payment out will be wrongful where:

(a)   the documents did not conform on their face; or

(b)   the bank was aware of compelling evidence of a fraud perpetrated by the beneficiary or his/her agent; or

(c)   it is illegal to honour the credit by the law of the place where performance is due; or

(d)   an injunction is in existence prohibiting the bank from paying out.

The consequences of a wrongful payment out are as follows.

20.10.1   BUYER REFUSES TO ADOPT TRANSACTION

Since the IB, through the actions of its agents, is in breach of its mandate with its principal, the buyer, the latter can refuse to adopt the transaction and thus refuse to pay the amount of the credit to the IB. The IB, in its turn and on the same grounds, will refuse to reimburse the paying bank. When the buyer refuses to adopt the transaction, property in the goods, which under the contract of sale passed to the purchaser on payment, appears to be abandoned by the purchaser via the IB to the paying bank.

20.10.2   CLAIM FOR DAMAGES AGAINST ISSUING BANK

Although the buyer has refused to adopt the transaction *vis-à-vis* the IB, he/she may still wish to pursue a claim for damages against the IB, for loss suffered as a result of the wrongful payment out. In that action the IB *could* rely on UCP, Article 18(a), which provides:

> Banks utilising the services of another bank or other banks for the purpose of giving effect to the instructions of the applicant do so for the account and at the risk of such applicant.

The IB could also rely on Article 18(b), which provides:

> Banks assume no liability or responsibility should the instructions they transmit not be carried out, even if they have themselves taken the initiative in the choice of such other bank(s).

The effect of these Articles is that the IB can escape liability even though, had no AB/CB been used, the IB would have been liable. The buyer however, can attack these exclusion provisions on the basis that there has been a fundamental breach to which, as a matter of construction, the clauses do not apply and/or can argue that the clauses are ineffective under the Unfair Contract Terms Act 1977, s. 3.

20.10.3   BUYER ADOPTS TRANSACTION

Alternatively, the buyer can decide to adopt the transaction, take up the documents and reimburse the IB (who in turn will reimburse the AB/CB), reserving his/her right to damages against the IB for the acts of its agent, the AB/CB.

Where there is a defect in the goods as well as the documents, damages awarded against the bank will usually be nominal. The reason for this is that the buyer still has the right to reject the goods because:

(a) The right to reject the goods etc. is not lost even though the defects could have been seen on a reasonable examination of the documents. The acceptance of the documents by the CB or by the AB as agent of the IB under an irrevocable credit is given to the seller as a principal and not as agent of the buyer.

(b) The buyer can make restitution to the seller as he/she took up the documents and thus did not abandon the goods to the banks.

Where the defect is in the documents alone, the buyer cannot treat the bank's acceptance as ineffective in relation to the seller, and claim reimbursement from the seller under the contract of sale. However, the buyer may be able to recover his/her loss of profit on a sub-sale if the documents tendered were rejected by a sub-purchaser *if* this loss was within the contemplation of the IB. See Goode, *Commercial Law*, 1985, Penguin, pp. 668/70.

20.11 Buyer's Position where Conforming Tender Made but Documents Rejected and Payment Refused

If the credit is a form of conditional payment, the buyer, on failure by the bank to pay against a conforming tender of documents, is liable on his/her contract of sale to the seller for the non-payment, usually in an action for damages for non-acceptance. The buyer can (subject to Article 18(a) and (b)), seek an indemnity against the IB for any liability he/she incurs to the seller.

20.12 Use of Injunctions

In many cases, the bank, under the credit, pays against documents conforming on their face with the requirements of the credit, the buyer and the banks at the payment stage being unaware that the goods themselves are defective or that they have been shipped out of time or that there has been fraud by the beneficiary. The buyer is, in these circumstances, obliged to reimburse the bank. If the buyer is made aware of the defective nature of the goods, shipment out of time or fraud by the beneficiary before payment under the credit falls due, can the buyer prevent payment out? Apart from his/her powers of persuasion, the buyer could in some situations prevent payment out (and thus discharge the obligation on him/her to reimburse) by obtaining an interlocutory injunction either against the IB or against the seller preventing a drawing under the credit. Note the following points concerning injunctions.

20.12.1 DOCUMENTS CONFORM ON THEIR FACE

Where the defects in the goods, or the fact of shipment out of time, are not manifest on the face of the documents, no injunction will lie against either the bank or the seller preventing a payment out or drawing on the credit. The credit is isolated from the sale transaction — the parties deal in documents not in goods. In *Hamzeh Malas & Sons* v *British Imex Industries Ltd* [1958] 2 QB 127, Jenkins LJ said (at 129) that an elaborate commercial system had been built up on the footing that a confirmed letter of credit constituted a bargain between the bank and the vendor of the goods, which imposed on the banker an absolute obligation to pay irrespective of any dispute there might be between the parties as to whether or not the goods were up to contract.

If these defects exist on the face of the document an injunction can be obtained, although strictly speaking it will not be necessary as the buyer is not in these circumstances obliged to reimburse the bank. However, despite the superficial conformity of the documents, payment out can be enjoined in the following circumstances.

20.12.2   PAYMENT ILLEGAL

The banks can be enjoined from making payments if to make payment would be illegal at the place for performance of the payment obligation.

20.12.3   BENEFICIARY GUILTY OF FRAUD

An injunction can be obtained where the beneficiary or his/her agent is guilty of fraudulent misrepresentation in relation to the documents. However, the burden placed on the applicant for the injunction is difficult to discharge. This is because it may be difficult to distinguish between fraudulent activity and, e.g., inaccuracies in documents, through shipment of defective goods, incurred with no intention to deceive: see *Korea Industry Co. Ltd* v *Andoll Ltd* [1990] 2 Lloyd's Rep 183 (Sing. CA). The applicant must also show that the bank knows that any demand made for payment will be fraudulent. The courts are very keen to prevent the injunctive procedure being used to interfere with the operation of a credit when in reality the complaint is a mere defective shipment, not a fraudulent activity: *Discount Records Ltd* v *Barclays Bank Ltd* [1975] 1 WLR 315. The court requires the fraud (of which the bank must be aware) to be that of the beneficiary or his/her agent (*United City Merchants* v *Royal Bank of Canada* [1982] 2 All ER 720) and requires evidence of fraud to be put before it of a standard described in *Bolivinter* v *Chase Manhattan Bank* [1984] 1 All ER 351, where the Court of Appeal gave an indication of the factors to be considered by the courts on an *ex parte* application against the bank for the injunction. Donaldson MR said:

> Judges who are asked, often at short notice and *ex parte,* to issue an injunction restraining payment by a bank under an irrevocable letter of credit or performance bond or guarantee, should ask whether there is any challenge to the validity of the letter, bond or guarantee itself. If there is not, or if the challenge is not substantial, prima facie no injunction should be granted, and the bank should be left free to honour its contractual obligations, although restrictions may well be imposed on the freedom of the beneficiary to deal with the money after he has received it. *The wholly exceptional case where an injunction may be granted is where it is proved that the bank knows that any demand for payment already made, or which may thereafter be made, will clearly be fraudulent. But the evidence must be clear, both as to the fact of fraud and as to the bank's knowledge. It would certainly not normally be sufficient that this rests on the uncorroborated statement of the customer,* for irreparable damage can be done to a bank's credit in the relatively brief time which must elapse between the granting of such an injunction, and an application by the bank to have it discharged.

Again, in 1984 in *United Trading Corp.* v *Allied Arab Bank Ltd* [1985] 2 Lloyd's Rep 554 Ackner LJ, in the Court of Appeal, elaborated on what the court required to 'establish fraud' in an application for an interlocutory injunction to prevent a bank honouring a performance bond. (The same principles apply to the obtaining of injunctions to prevent payment out under a performance bond as under a letter of credit: *Edward Owen Engineering Ltd* v *Barclays Bank International Ltd* [1978] 1 All ER 976.) Ackner LJ said:

> We would expect the court to require strong corroborative evidence of the allegation, usually in the form of contemporary documents particularly emanating from the beneficiary. In general, for the evidence of fraud to be clear, we would also expect the beneficiary to have been given an opportunity to answer the allegation and to have failed to provide any adequate answer in circumstances where one could properly be expected. If the court considers that on the material before it the only realistic inference to draw was that of fraud, then the seller would have made out a sufficient case of fraud.

In conclusion, therefore, it will not be sufficient to establish a 'seriously' arguable case that there was good reason to suspect fraud on the part of the beneficiary; it will be necessary to establish a good arguable case that the only realistic inference is one of fraud.

Even if evidence to establish a good arguable case that the only realistic inference is one of fraud has been put before the court, the injunction may still be refused. In *Tukan Timber Ltd* v *Barclays Bank* [1987] 1 Lloyd's Rep 171 Hirst J held that this was one of those rare cases where the strict burden of proof had been satisfied — the evidence of fraud was clear, both as to the fact and as to the bank's knowledge. However, the injunction was refused on the facts because the bank against which the injunction was sought did not intend to pay out under the credit. Moreover, Hirst J stated that even if an intention to pay out had been established, in applying the *American Cyanamid* principle, the bank would suffer uncompensatable damage if the injunction were granted. He said (at 177):

> [O]n the assumption that the bank were to pay on the faith of a further submitted receipt and it turned out at the trial that they should not have done, the plaintiff would have a cast-iron claim against them for damages for breach of contract which the banks are obviously in a position to meet.... I am therefore not satisfied that the plaintiffs would in such circumstances suffer uncompensatable damages. On the other hand, having regard to the great importance generally to the bank of honouring letter of credit obligations, I think that the damage to them would be uncompensatable by the plaintiffs' cross-undertaking, if they were injuncted from honouring the letter of credit, and it was subsequently held that the injunction should not have been granted.

Thus, even though the plaintiff may have cleared the difficult initial hurdle of establishing clear evidence of fraud of which the bank is aware, the injunction may still be refused.

Nevertheless, it behoves the bank to consider very carefully the state of the evidence before it pays out. If the beneficiary is fraudulent *and* at the time of tender the bank has clear evidence to that effect, any payment out will put the bank in breach of contract with its principal. On the other hand, if it were to refuse to pay out, in any subsequent action brought by the beneficiary, fraud by the beneficiary would have to be established by the bank on the balance of probabilities if judgment and damages are not to be awarded against the bank. The bank may decide that its best course is to refuse a payment out, on an undertaking given by the principal or a third party to reimburse the bank for any loss it suffers in consequence.

As to the use of a *Mareva* on the proceeds of a credit paid out, see *The Bhoja Trader* [1981] 2 Lloyd's Rep 256.

Even though the applicant for the credit has clear evidence of fraud and has duly informed his/her agent, the issuing bank, he/she must choose the party against whom he/she will proceed for an injunction. The interlocutory relief is only available if there is an underlying cause of action. There is a contractual nexus between the applicant and the issuing bank/beneficiary. No such contract exists between the applicant for the credit and a confirming bank, thus a cause of action must be based in tort, on establishing a duty of care. Additionally, it may be necessary, in order to pursue the application for interim relief, to show that the cause of action is justiciable within the jurisdiction.

20.13 Bank's Security where Reimbursement is Refused by its Principal

One form of security is in the property in the goods which, on payment, vested in the buyer. When reimbursement is refused by the principal, property appears to be abandoned to the bank.

The bank can realise its loss, or some of it, by selling these goods. It can do this either by dealing with the documents while the goods are still in transit or by taking delivery of the goods from the ship and dealing with the goods themselves.

Where a bill of lading is made out *to order* and indorsed to the bank both these means are available. The bank is in possession of a document of title to its order which it, in turn, can transfer to a third party. In addition, as the holder of the bill of lading, the bank can demand delivery of the goods from the ship.

Where a bill of lading is tendered and accepted naming the buyer as consignee but not to his/her order, neither of these methods are available. The situation is the same where a seaway bill is tendered. The bank will only be able to demand the goods from the ship in its own right if it has been named as consignee.

Even where the bank has had the foresight to insist in the credit that the seaway bill name the bank as the consignee, the lack of negotiability of the documents means that the goods cannot be dealt with on the high seas by means of dealing with the documents.

Where a multimodal transport document has been used, the bank could encounter problems as with the seaway bill. However, it is very common for the multimodal transport document to purport to be negotiable and is thus made out to order. Where the multimodal transport document has been indorsed over to the bank, the latter might be able to demand delivery from the ship or deal with the goods by means of the document if it can successfully argue that the document is a true bill of lading or that a custom in the trade recognises such a document as negotiable.

The tender and acceptance of a delivery order will not enable the bank to claim delivery of the goods from the ship unless the order is directed to the ship and the ship promises to deliver to the bank. This independent promise is called an attornment. This need for an attornment to the party who is to receive possession of the goods from the ship will also make it cumbersome for the bank to sell the goods whilst they remain in transit.

If the bank still suffers loss after a dealing with the goods, it can pursue a claim for breach of contract against its principal if the failure to reimburse was wrongful. Otherwise they could pursue a claim for damages for breach of warranty against the beneficiary, for failing to tender genuine documents or for tendering documents that contained a latent defect.

20.14 Further Reading

Goode, R.M., *Commercial Law,* rev. ed. 1985, Pelican.
Benjamin/Guest, *Sale of Goods,* 4th ed. 1992, Sweet & Maxwell.
Gutteridge/Megrah, *Law of Bankers' Commercial Credits,* 7th ed. 1984. Europa Publications.
Schmitthoff, C., *Export Trade: Law, and Practice of International Trade,* 9th ed. 1990, Sweet and Maxwell.
Jacks, *Documentary Credits,* 1991, Butterworths.

The latest Revision of the UCP, published in 1993 (UCP 500), may be obtained from International Chamber of Commerce, 14/15 Belgrave Square, London SWI 8PS.

20.15 Examples of Transport Documents

Documentary credits are advised by letter, telex or the interbank worldwide SWIFT communications system. Bills of exchange forms can be obtained from printers or stationers or drawn up on company or blank sheets of paper.

Example 1: Unconfirmed Credit: Sight Draft

NATIONAL BANK LTD [2]

DOCUMENTARY CREDITS DEPT

2970 FLEET STREET BRANCH

MILKEMDRY & CO. LTD [3]
WEAVERS WHARF
SHOREDITCH
LONDON E8

10th NOVEMBER 1995 DATE [1]

Dear Sirs

OUR REFERENCE NO. ABC/1/2345
TO BE QUOTED IN ALL CORRESPONDENCE

IRREVOCABLE CREDIT NO. 7898 [4]
OF BANK OF LIBERIA NEW YORK [5]

We are today informed by cable from Bank of Liberia, New York that they have established an Irrevocable Credit in your favour for account of Baby Foods Inc. [7] Down Town New York to the extent [8] US$ 14,365.40 (say US dollars Fourteen thousand, three hundred and sixty five and cents forty only).
available for your drafts [9] on Bank of Liberia [10] at sight [11] to be accompanied by the following documents.

1. Signed invoice in triplicate.

2. Full set of CLEAN ON BOARD MARINE BILLS OF LADING, made out to order, blank endorsed, marked 'freight paid' and 'Notify Quayside Collections Inc. Down Town NY'.

[12]

3. Certificate of Origin issued by a Chamber of Commerce.

[6]

4. Certificate of Insurance in triplicate, covering marine and war risks up to buyer's warehouse, for invoice value of goods plus 10%

covering: [13] 5000 kilo sacks of milk powder.

Evidencing shipment from London to New York c.i.f. between 1st December 1995 and 3rd January 1996. [14]

Partial shipments permitted. [15]

Transhipment not permitted. [16]

The expiry date of this credit is 24th January 1996 [17] which is the latest date for negotiation [18] in London.

All drafts [19] drawn under this credit must be marked 'Drawn under Irrevocable Credit No. 7898 dated 10th November 1995'.

Bank of Liberia, New York undertakes that all drafts drawn under and in conformity with the terms of this credit will be duly honoured provided that they are marked as being so drawn. [20]

We are requested to advise you of the terms of the credit which is irrevocable [21] on the part of our principals **but does not bear our confirmation**. This advice is given for your guidance only and conveys no engagement by us. Any draft negotiated by us under the credit will be subject to recourse to yourselves. [22]

[6] { Subject to Uniform Customs and Practice for Documentary Credits (1993 Revision) International Chamber of Commerce Publication No. 500. [23]

Yours faithfully

Example 2: Draft to Accompany Documents under Credit in Example 1

London 4th January 1996

US$ 14,365.40

AT SIGHT OF THIS FIRST OF EXCHANGE (SECOND AND THIRD OF THE SAME TENOR BEING UNPAID), PAY TO OUR ORDER THE SUM OF US dollars

Fourteen thousand, three hundred and sixty five and cents forty only for value received.

Drawn under Irrevocable Credit No. 7898 dated 10th November 1995.

TO: Bank of Liberia   FOR AND ON BEHALF OF
       New York   Milkemdry & Co. Ltd

....
Director

NOTES TO EXAMPLE 1

(References to articles are references to the Uniform Customs and Practice for Documentary Credits 1993, Revision ICC No. 500.)

[1]   This date gives some idea of when this letter of credit reaches the beneficiary (see note 3). It may be important to establish exactly when the letter of credit reaches the hands of the beneficiary because it is at this stage that the undertaking of the Bank of Liberia becomes contractual and cannot be withdrawn. (see *Hamzeh Malas* v *British Imex Industries* [1958] 2 QB 127).

[2]   This is the advising or correspondent bank. Its letter advises the beneficiary of the opening of the credit (see note 21), but as can be seen from note 22 it does not add its own confirmation. Its function will be to pay out the amount of the credit on receipt by it of a conforming tender, although of course it is within its rights to refuse payment at any time.

[3]   This is the beneficiary of the credit. In order to receive payment, Milkemdry must tender documents including its own invoice(s). Milkemdry will not be able to transfer part of this credit to its own supplier as the credit has not been designated as 'transferable' (Article 48(b)). There will *not* therefore be a second beneficiary under this credit.

If, therefore, Milkemdry wishes to finance a supply contract, it must ask the buyer to amend the instruction to the Bank of Liberia or open a second independent credit in favour of his/her supplier on the 'security' of this first credit (this arrangement is called a 'back-to-back' credit) *or* arrange an assignment of the *proceeds* of the first credit to his supplier (Article 49).

[4]   Under Article 6(b) and (c) of the UCP the credit must clearly indicate whether it is irrevocable or revocable. This is obviously satisfied here, and again at note 21. However, a failure to indicate whether the credit is revocable or irrevocable will cause the credit to be treated as *irrevocable*. Remember where the credit is treated as irrevocable there can be no amendment or cancellation without agreement of all the parties to the credit once this letter of credit reaches the beneficiary. Thus once the letter is received the beneficiary knows even before the goods are shipped that he/she has an assurance of payment from the bank.

[5]   The Bank of Liberia is the issuer of the irrevocable credit. It is called the issuing bank.

[6]   The remaining section of this letter of credit (apart from that section within notes 21 and 22) sets out the terms of the irrevocable letter of credit.

[7]   Here is indicated the customer of the issuing bank, the party that instructed the Bank of Liberia and which will put them in funds before or after the date for payment falls due, and which will pay a commission to the issuing bank. Baby Foods Inc. is the purchaser of the goods from Milkemdry & Co. Ltd.

[8]   This is the amount up to which the beneficiary is entitled to claim payment. The bank will pay against documents including an invoice for a lesser sum as partial shipments are permitted (see note 15). However, sums claimed cannot exceed that set out in the credit.

[9]   This indicates that it will be necessary to tender a bill of exchange ('draft') along with the other documents required to be tendered and set out at note 12, and that the drawer of it must be the beneficiary — Milkemdry & Co. Ltd. See Example 2.

[10]   The bill of exchange must be drawn on the Bank of Liberia. See Example 2.

[11]   The bill must be drawn 'at sight'. This means Milkemdry & Co. Ltd can demand *payment* on presentation of the bill of exchange. See Example 2.

[12]   Here are set out the documents required to be tendered. The credit requires tender of a full set of marine bills of lading. Reference should therefore be made to Article 23. As is usual where payment is to be made by a bank under the credit against the bill of lading, it is required to be to order and blank endorsed. A blank endorsement makes the bill of lading payable to bearer. Thus the bank as the holder of it can deal with the goods by means of the documents if the need arises. When the bank is put in funds by its principal or the documents are released to the customer under a *trust receipt,* the bill of lading can be effectively transferred by mere delivery. Where a bill of lading has been made out to order, with no named consignee, the notify box on the bill of lading has to be filled in. This will either be filled with the name of the purchaser or with that of a forwarding agent who will be acting as agent of the ultimate holder of the bill of lading in arranging for taking delivery of the goods. In our example, Quayside Collections Inc. is the relevant forwarding agent and will usually be informed by the shipping company of the expected arrival of the ship so that it can make arrangements for a prompt collection from the vessel. It is usual for a complete set of original bills of lading to be tendered when payment is made through the banking system (see Article 23(a)(iv)). How many originals will be demanded from the carriers depends on many factors, including the requirements of the purchaser. It is not common to demand the issue of more than four. The bill of lading itself will indicate how many originals have been issued. The invoice tendered must bear a description of the goods which corresponds with the description in the credit (see Article 37(c)). Under Article 43(a) the tender must take place not later than 21 days after the date of shipment. See also Article 42.

[13]   The documents tendered must relate to the specified quantity in the requisite packing units. Since the goods are to be shipped in units there will be no 5 per cent tolerance on the overall amount shipped (Article 39(b)). Note that partial shipments are allowed (see note 15). Thus the bank will pay portions of the credit against documents representing shipments of kilo sacks of milk powder numbering fewer than 5,000. The final tender, however, must not cover a quantity which takes the overall amount above that stated in the credit.

The bank can refuse to pay against a tender of documents in which there is an inconsistency in terms of quantity or description (see Articles 13 and 14). Even though the bill must specify amounts not exceeding that set out in the credit, the banks will still, in the absence of contrary instructions, accept bills of lading in which the statement as to quantity will not operate as a representation by the party issuing the bill of lading, e.g. where the statement as to quantity is qualified by 'shipper's load and count' or 'said by shipper to container' or words of similar effect (Article 31).

[14]   The letter of credit indicates that the documents must state the port of loading and discharge. They must indicate that the goods have been *shipped* as opposed to merely *received for shipment* on a date(s) between 14 December 1995 and 3 January 1996. See Article 23. The transport document should contain this information.

The nature of the sales contract, e.g. c.i.f. or f.o.b. will not be indicated in the bill of lading. It is usually indicated in the invoice.

[15] This letter of credit indicates partial shipments are allowed. Nevertheless, even without the indication, partial shipments/drawings will be allowed. In order to make partial shipments unacceptable, the credit must so stipulate (Article 40). Note therefore in Article 40 circumstances which will not amount to a partial shipment.

[16] Although this credit prohibits transhipment, banks will pay against documents, including a transport document, which incorporate a printed clause giving the right to tranship (Article 23(d)(ii)). This appears to be so even though the carrier undertakes no responsibility for the on-carriage of the goods where a transhipment does take place, since there is no requirement in Article 23 that in such circumstances the entire ocean carriage is covered by one and the same bill of lading.

[17] Apart from having to tender the documents not later than 21 days after the date of shipment (Article 43), Milkemdry & Co. Ltd must tender the documents on or before 24 January 1996 (Article 42(a)).

[18] This negotiation here is a reference to Milkemdry & Co. Ltd the drawer/payee of the bill of exchange negotiating the bill of lading to National Bank Ltd, the advising bank, The negotiation will be by indorsement and delivery of the bill of exchange to National Bank Ltd which becomes the holder of the bill of exchange. The negotiation of bill(s) of exchange and accompanying documents will take place against payment of the sum set out in the bill, or bills, up to the amount allowed under the credit. The National Bank, as holder, will then demand payment of the amount of the bill(s) from its principal, the Bank of Liberia. Note, as National Bank Ltd has not added its own confirmation to the irrevocable letter of credit, it can negotiate the bill of exchange, preserving its rights of recourse against its prior indorser, Milkemdry & Co. Ltd (see Note 22). If, therefore, the Bank of Liberia refuses to reimburse National Bank, the latter can either sue on its agency contract with the principal if the refusal is wrongful or it can claim the amount of the bill back from Milkemdry by virtue of its right of recourse. The beneficiary Milkemdry & Co. Ltd, if the refusal to pay is wrongful, can in its turn successfully sue the Bank of Liberia, *not* on the bill(s) of exchange as the Bank of Liberia will not have 'accepted', but on the undertaking in the irrevocable credit. See Article 10 and note 20. See **Figure 20.2.**

The Bank of Liberia can only justify the refusal to pay on the following grounds:

(a) bad tender
(b) fraud by the beneficiary
(c) illegality at the place of performance of the credit
(d) set off of a debt owed to it by Milkemdry (*Hong Kong & Shanghai Banking Corp.* v *Kloeckner* [1989] 3 All ER 513).

[19] See Example 2.

[20] The Bank of Liberia is under no obligation to pay unless the bill of exchange tendered is so marked.

[21] This makes it absolutely clear that the undertaking of the issuing bank is irrevocable thereby complying with Article 6(b), UCP.

[22] Clear indication here that this letter of credit does not in any way have added to it a confirmation of National Bank and emphasises that the bank's rights of recourse as a holder of the bill of exchange are maintained.

[23] The effect of this is to incorporate the UCP (500 Revision) as express terms of the contract between the Bank of Liberia and Milkemdry. Refer to *Forestal Mimosa Ltd* v *Oriental Credit Ltd* [1986] 2 All ER 400.

Figure 20.2   Negotiation of bill of exchange to bank advising of credit

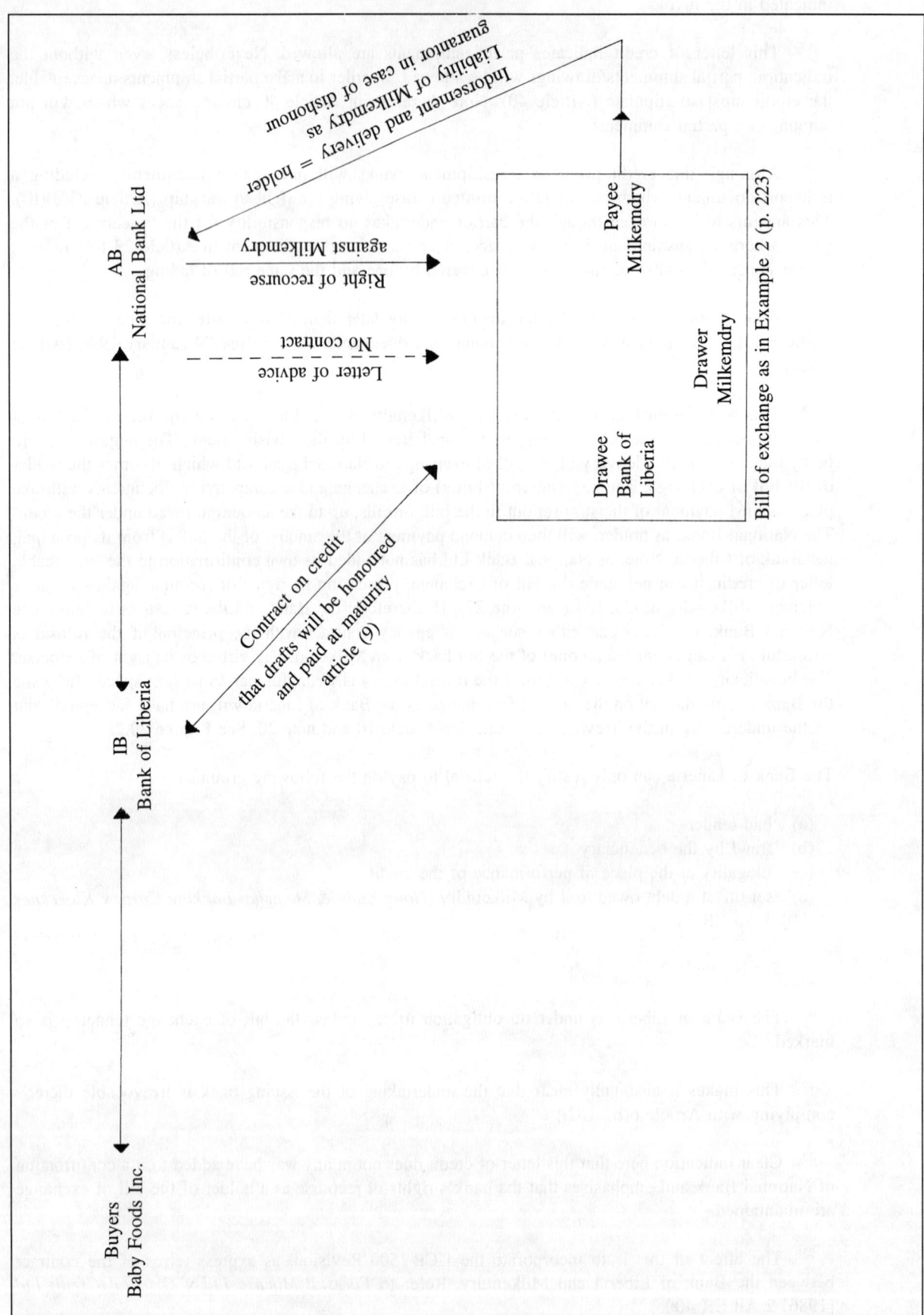

Example 3: Irrevocable Confirmed Acceptance Credit

NATIONAL BANK LTD[2]

DOCUMENTARY CREDITS DEPT

2970 FLEET STREET BRANCH

10th NOVEMBER 1995 DATE[1]

MILKEMDRY & CO. LTD[3]
WEAVERS WHARF
SHOREDITCH
LONDON E8

Dear Sirs

OUR REFERENCE NO. ABC/1/2345
TO BE QUOTED IN ALL CORRESPONDENCE

IRREVOCABLE CREDIT NO. 7898[4]
OF BANK OF LIBERIA NEW YORK[5]
AND WHICH BEARS THE CONFIRMATION OF
NATIONAL BANK LTD[6]

We are today informed by cable from Bank of Liberia that they have established an Irrevocable Credit in your favour for account of Baby Foods Inc.[8] Down Town New York to the extent[9] US$ 14,365.40 (say US dollars Fourteen thousand, three hundred and sixty five and cents forty only) available for your drafts[10] on us[11] at ninety days after sight[12] until 24th January 1996[13] on or before which date your drafts on us will be accepted[14] if accompanied by the undermentioned documents evidencing shipment[16] from London to New York c.i.f. between 1st December 1995 and 3rd January 1996.

[7]

1. Signed invoice in triplicate

[15]

2. Full set of combined transport documents made out to order and blank endorsed marked 'freight collect'.

3. Certificate of Insurance in triplicate, covering marine and war risks up to buyer's warehouse for invoice value of goods plus 10%

    covering:[17] 5,000 kilo sacks of milk powder.

All drafts[18] drawn under this credit must be marked 'Drawn under Irrevocable Credit No 7898 date 10th November 1995

We undertake to honour such drafts on presentation provided they are drawn and presented in conformity with the terms of the credit.[19]

[7] { Subject to the Uniform Customs and Practice for Documentary Credits (1993 Revision) International Chamber of Commerce Publication No. 500.[20]

Yours faithfully

Example 4: Draft to Accompany Documents under Credit in Example 3

London 4th January 1996

US$ 14,365.40

AT 90 DAYS AFTER SIGHT OF THIS FIRST OF EXCHANGE (SECOND AND THIRD OF THE SAME TENOR AND DATE BEING UNPAID), PAY TO OUR ORDER THE SUM OF US dollars

Fourteen thousand, three hundred and sixty five and cents forty only for value received.

Drawn under Irrevocable Credit No. 7898 dated 10th November 1995.

TO: National Bank Ltd   FOR AND ON BEHALF OF
            2970 Fleet Street   Milkemdry & Co. Ltd
            London EC1

                                     ....
                                       Director

NOTES TO EXAMPLE 3

[1]   This date gives an indication of when this letter of credit reached the hands of Milkemdry. On receipt by Milkemdry the undertakings of both the Bank of Liberia and National Bank become binding. See note 1 to Example 1.

[2]   This is the advising *and* confirming bank. This letter of credit not only informs Milkemdry of the opening of an irrevocable credit by Bank of Liberia but as we can see from note 6 and note 19 it has added its own undertaking to honour drafts drawn in conformity with the credit and presented according to the terms of the credit. Article 9 indicates that in these circumstances the CB, in agreeing to accept the bill of exchange, also agrees under the credit to pay against the bill of exchange on its maturity.

[3]   See note 3 to Example 1.

[4]   This avoids any doubt about the irrevocable nature of the credit opened by the Bank of Liberia and thus complies with Article 6(b) UCP.

[5]   See note 5 to Example 1.

[6]   Here is a clear indication that National Bank give an independent promise to the beneficiary. The terms of that promise are set out at notes 19 and 20 (and see Article 9), and becomes binding on receipt y the beneficiary of the letter of credit, see note 1 to Example 1.

[7]   The remaining section of this letter, apart from note 19, sets out the terms of the irrevocable credit.

[8]   See note 8 to Example 1.

[9]   See note 8 to Example 1. In this letter of credit, partial shipments are permitted since there is no specific prohibition (Article 40).

[10]   This indicates that it will be necessary to tender a bill of exchange ('draft') drawn by the beneficiary, and accompanied by the documents set out at note 15.

[11]   The bill(s) of exchange must be drawn on National Bank. See Example 4.

[12] The bill(s) must be drawn at ninety days after sight — see Example 4. This means that on presentment for acceptance of the bill of exchange plus accompanying documents, the documents are retained on 'acceptance' but nevertheless Milkemdry still has to await a considerable amount of time before receiving payment if it retains the bill. An option available to Milkemdry is to negotiate the bill of exchange against payment to a third-party bank. See Figure **20.3**.

Figure 20.3   Negotiation of bill of exchange to bank not involved in documentary credit mechanism

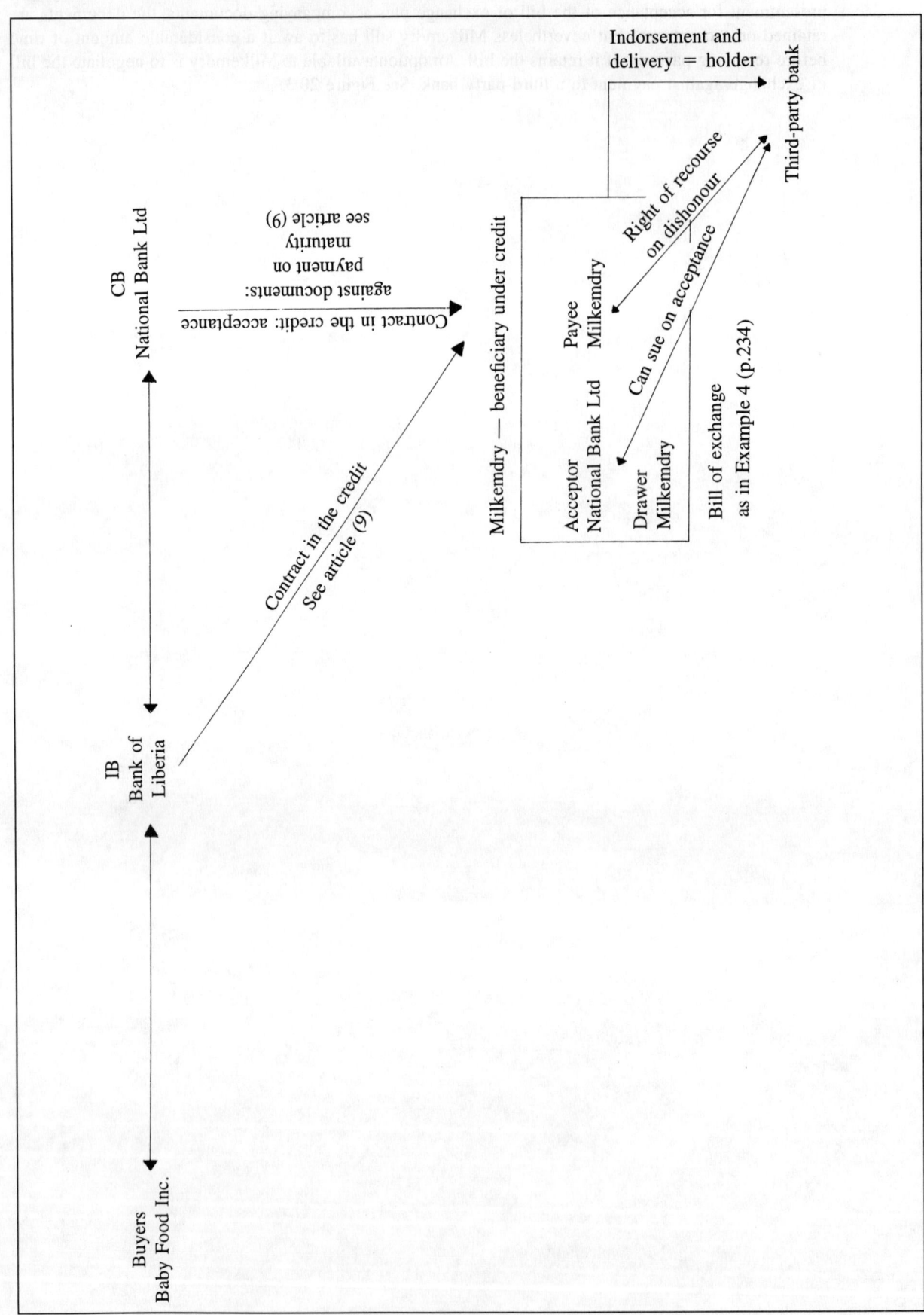

The third-party bank will present the bill of exchange for payment on the due date. On dishonour, the third-party bank can sue National Bank Ltd on its acceptance or exercise a right of recourse against its prior indorser — Milkemdry. The third-party bank cannot sue National Bank Ltd on the *credit*. However, if the bill of exchange is returned to, or retained by, Milkemdry the latter can sue *on the credit* by virtue of the confirmation given by National Bank Ltd *or* on the bill of exchange by virtue of National Bank Ltd's acceptance, as either holder for value (retention of bill) or holder in due course by derivation (return of bill).

[13]   This indicates the expiry date of the credit. See note 17 to Example 1.

[14]   This indicates that the role of the confirming bank is to 'accept' the bill of exchange as opposed to negotiating it.

[15]   Here are set out the documents required to be tendered. It includes the tender of a full set of combined transport documents. As to 'full set', see note 12 to Example 1. For further requirements in relation to the combined transport document refer to Article 26. Notice that the document is required to be made out to order and blank endorsed — whether this suffices to make the document a document of title at common law is unclear.

[16]   Notice here that even though the tender of a combined transport document will suffice, it must be one evidencing the shipment of the goods, i.e. the credit is stipulating for the tender of an on board transport document. See note 14 to Example 1.

[17]   See note 13 to Example 1.

[18]   See Example 4.

[19]   The promise in the confirmation is to *honour* and pay drafts at their maturity, if (i) drawn as on the terms of the credit and (ii) presented as on the terms of the credit. Therefore a failure to accept *or* make payment on the due date if (i) and (ii) are satisfied gives the beneficiary a contractual remedy against National Bank Ltd *on the credit* as well as an action on the bill of exchange if 'accepted'. See note 12.

[20]   The effect of this is to incorporate the UCP (500 Revision) as express terms of the contracts in the credit and in the confirmation. Refer to *Forestal Mimosa Ltd* v *Oriental Credit Ltd* [1986] 2 All ER 400.

Example 5

There is now reproduced with the kind permission of Barclays Bank PLC an example of a documentary credit and an example of each of the documents required to be tendered under it:

(a)   bill of lading
(b)   bill of exchange
(c)   invoice
(d)   certificate of insurance.

Documentary Credit ## BARCLAYS

Barclays Bank PLC
1 Union Court, London EC2P 2HP

Date: 20th July 1995

DOCUMENTARY CREDITS DEPARTMENT

SPECIMEN   IRREVOCABLE CREDIT NO. UTDC 65432

To be quoted in all drafts and correspondence

Beneficiary Spears and Wadley Ltd Adderley Road Hackney, London E8 1XY	Advised through
Accreditor Woldal Ltd New Road Kowloon, Hong Kong	To be completed only if applicable Our cable of Advised through

Dear Sir(s)

In accordance with instructions received from The Downtown Bank & Trust Co.
we hereby issue in your favour a Documentary Credit for £4108
(say) Four thousand one hundred and eight pounds sterling   available by your drafts
drawn on   US

at sight
for the   100% c.i.f. invoice value accompanied by the following documents:

1.   Signed Invoice in triplicate
2.   Full set of clean Combined Transport Bills of Lading made out to order
      and blank endorsed, marked 'Freight Paid' and 'Notify Woldal Ltd., New
      Road, Kowloon, Hong Kong'
3.   Insurance Policy or Certificate in duplicate, covering Marine and War Risks
      up to buyer's warehouse for invoice value of the goods plus 10%.

Covering the following goods:-
    400 Electric Power Drills

To be shipped from   London   to   Hong Kong c.i.f.
not later than   10th August 1995
Partshipment   not permitted   Transhipment   permitted
The credit is available for   presentation to us   until 31st August 1995

Documents to be presented within 21 days of shipment but within credit validity.

Drafts drawn hereunder must be marked "Drawn under Barclays Bank PLC 1 Union Court, London
                branch, Credit number UTDC 65432
We undertake that drafts and documents drawn under and in strict conformity with the terms
of this credit will be honoured upon presentation.

Yours faithfully

R.E. Dennings

Co-signed (Signature No. 9847)   Signed (Signature No.10247)

(a) Bill of lading

BILL OF LADING FOR COMBINED TRANSPORT SHIPMENT OR PORT TO PORT SHIPMENT

Shipper		
Speirs and Wadley Ltd. Adderley Road Hackney London E8 1XY England	**OVERSEAS CONTAINERS LIMITED**	B L No 45969648 Booking Ref 1234567 Shipper's Ref Job 5678

Consignee

To Order   **SPECIMEN**

OCL

Notify Party Address	Place of Receipt Applicable only when this document is used as a Combined Transport B l of Lading
Woldal Ltd. New Road Kowloon Hong Kong	Speirs and Wadley Ltd. Adderley Road Hackney London E8 1XY England

Intended Vessel and Voy No		Place of Delivery Applicable only when this document is used as a Combined Transport B l of Lading
Cardigan Bay	0415	Woldal Ltd. New Road Kowloon Hong Kong

Intended Port of Loading
London

Intended Port of Discharge
Hong Kong

Marks and Nos Container Nos	Number and kind of Packages description of Goods	Gross Weight (kg)	Measurement (cbm)
WL 124 HONG KONG 1/5	5 Wooden Cases containing 400 ELECTRIC POWER DRILLS Model LM 425 2 Speed (900RPM/2400RPM) 425 Watt high-torque motor 2 chucks – 12.5mm and 8mm supplied with each drill	950	2.376

ABOVE PARTICULARS AS DECLARED BY SHIPPER

✱ Total No of Containers/Packages
Packages or pieces   5

Movement
LCL Depot/LCL Depot

Freight and Charges (indicate whether prepaid or collect)

Origin zone transport charge   Prepaid

Origin Terminal Handling/LCL Service Charge   Prepaid

Ocean Freight   Prepaid

Destination Terminal Handling/LCL Service Charge   Prepaid

Destination zone transport charge   Prepaid

ICS
CTB
April 78

Received by the Carrier from the Shipper in apparent good order and condition (unless otherwise noted herein) the total number or quantity of Containers or other packages or units indicated✱ stated by the Shipper to comprise the Goods specified above for Carriage subject to all the terms hereof (INCLUDING THE TERMS ON THE REVERSE HEREOF AND THE TERMS OF THE CARRIER'S APPLICABLE TARIFF) from the Place of Receipt or the Port of Loading whichever is applicable to the Port of Discharge or the Place of Delivery whichever is applicable in accepting this Bill of Lading the Merchant expressly accepts and agrees to all its terms conditions and exceptions whether printed stamped or written or otherwise incorporated notwithstanding the non signing of this Bill of Lading by the Merchant When this document calls for Combined Transport it is a negotiable Combined Transport Document the terms of which are based upon the Uniform Rules for a Combined Transport Document (ICC Publication No 298)

Number of Original Bills of Lading
Two   (02)

Place and Date of Issue
London   01 08 1995

IN WITNESS of the contract herein contained the number of originals stated opposite has been used one of which being accomplished the others to be void

For the Carrier   A.J. S⟨illary⟩

239

(b)   Bill of exchange

SPECIMEN

£4.108

London
11th August 1995

AT SIGHT OF THIS SOLA OF EXCHANGE PAY TO OUR ORDER THE SUM OF

STERLING POUNDS FOUR THOUSAND ONE HUNDRED AND EIGHT ONLY FOR

VALUE RECEIVED

Drawn under Irrevocable Credit of Barclays Bank PLC

1 Union Court, London. Number UTDC 65432 dated 20th July 19...

For and on behalf of
SPEIRS AND WADLEY LTD

Director

To: Barclays Bank PLC
      1 Union Court,
      London EC2P 2HP.

(c) **Invoice**

SPECIMEN

INVOICE FACTURE FACTURA	RECHNUNG FACTUUR		

Seller (Name Address VAT Reg No)		C C C N No 8505
Speirs and Wadley Ltd. Adderley Road Hackney London E8 1XY England	Invoice No and Date (Tax Point) 247 11 Aug 1995	Seller's Reference Job No. 5678
	Buyer's Reference 124	

Consignee	Buyer (if not Consignee)
Woldal Ltd. New Road Kowloon Hong Kong	

	Country of Origin of Goods EEC United Kingdom	Country of Destination Hong Kong
	Terms of Delivery and Payment CIF Kowloon Hong Kong Irrevocable Documentary Credit UTDC 65432	

Vessel/Aircraft etc Cardigan Bay	Port of Loading London
Port of Discharge Hong Kong	

Marks and Numbers Numbers and Kind of Packages Description of Goods	Quantity	∗	Amount (State Currency)
WL 124 HONG KONG 1/5	5 Wooden Cases containing 400 ELECTRIC POWER DRILLS Model LM 425 2 Speed (900RPM/2400RPM) 425 Watt high-torque motor 2 chucks – 12.5mm and 8mm supplied with each drill	400	£10.27	£4108.00

	TOTAL £4108.00 Stg
Freight £210 Insurance £30	Gross Weight (kg) 950 / Cube (m³) 2.376

	Name of Signatory J McDonald Chief Clerk
VAT Reg. No. 241 8235 77	Place and Date of Issue London 11 Aug 1995
It is hereby certified that this invoice shows the actual price of the goods described that no other invoice has been or will be issued and that all particulars are true and correct	Signature J McDonald

380 1

C SITPRO OVERLAYS 1981 V1

241

(d) Certificate of insurance

ORIGINAL   LLOYD'S

Lloyd's Agent at Hong Kong
s authorised to adjust and settle on behalf
of the Underwriters and to purchase on
behalf of the Corporation of Lloyds in
accordance with Lloyd's Standing
Regulations for the Settlement of Claims
Abroad any claim which may arise on this
Certificate

Exporters
Reference

THIS CERTIFICATE
REQUIRES ENDORSEMENT
Job No. 5678

SPECIMEN

Certificate of Insurance No. C 8700/**100051**

This is to Certify that there has been deposited with the Committee of Lloyd's an Open Cover effected by *Barclays Insurance Brokers International Limited* of Lloyd's, acting on behalf of *Speirs and Wadley Limited* with Underwriters at Lloyd's, dated the *First* day of *January* 19 . . ., and that the said Underwriters have undertaken to issue to *Barclays Insurance Brokers International Limited* Policy/Policies of Marine Insurance at Lloyd's to cover, up to *£100,000* in all by any one steamer *or sending by air and or road and or rail and or conveyance Power Drills other Interest held covered.* to be shipped on or before the *Thirty-first* day of *December* 19 . . ., from any port or ports, place or places in *the United Kingdom* to any port or ports, place or places in *the World. other voyages held covered* and that *Speirs and Wadley Limited* are entitled to declare against the said Open Cover the shipments attaching thereto.

for the Committee of Lloyd's

Conveyance	From	
Cardigan Bay	London	
Via/to	**To**	**INSURED VALUE/Currency**
Hong Kong	Kowloon, H. K.	£4520 Stg.

Marks and Number	Interest
WL 124 HONG KONG 1/5	5 Wooden Cases containing 400 ELECTRIC POWER DRILLS Model LM 425 2 Speed (900RPM/2400RPM) 425 Watt high-torque motor 2 chucks – 12.5mm and 8mm supplied with each drill

(3) We hereby declare for Insurance under the said Cover interest as specified above so valued subject to the terms of the Standard Form of Lloyd's Marine Policy providing for the settlement of claims abroad and to the special conditions stated below and on the back hereof

Institute Cargo Clauses (A) (1 1 82) or Institute Cargo Clauses (Air) (excluding sendings by post) (1 1 82) as applicable
Institute War Clauses (Cargo) (1 1 82) or Institute War Clauses (Air Cargo) (excluding sending by Post) (1 1 82) or Institute War Clauses (sendings by Post) (1 1 82) as applicable
Institute Strikes Clauses (Cargo) (1 1 82) or Institute Strikes Clauses (Air Cargo) (1 1 82) as applicable
General Average and Salvage Contribution payable in full irrespective of insured or contributing values

Underwriters agree losses, if any, shall be payable to the order of Speirs and Wadley Limited on surrender of this Certificate.

(6) **In the event of loss or damage which may result in a claim under this Insurance, immediate notice should be given to the Lloyd's Agent at the port or place where the loss or damage is discovered in order that he may examine the goods and issue a survey report.**

(Survey fee is customarily paid by claimant and included in valid claim against Underwriters.)

This Certificate not valid unless the Declaration is signed by
SPEIRS AND WADLEY LIMITED

Dated at London   1 Aug 1994
p p *Speirs and Wadley Limited*

Signed W. H. Mein

Brokers Barclays Insurance Brokers International Limited
India House 81 84 Leadenhall Street London EC3A 3DJ

14478/9

21 The Carriage of Goods by Sea

In performance of the contract of sale, the goods may have to be transported by sea. The vessel may arrive with some or all of the goods deteriorated or damaged; the vessel and the goods may not arrive at all. It is the party who bears the risk of this loss or damage under the contract of sale who may need to recoup his/her loss from the carrier.

We need to consider both the sale contract between the buyer and seller, and the contract of carriage between either the buyer or seller and the carrier. The interplay between the two sets of rights and duties created by the respective contracts does give rise to complex questions as to who may bring an action. Further, as there are various ways in which shipowners, charterers, freight forwarders etc. may arrange between themselves how they will conduct the business of transporting the goods, questions will arise as to against whom an action is to be brought.

We will consider first the question of who may sue in: (a) contract, and (b) tort.

21.1 Right to Sue on Contract of Carriage

The difficulties which arise here stem primarily from the doctrine of privity of contract.

Where the person bearing the loss under the contract of sale is a party to the contract of carriage, the position is straightforward: that person may sue on that contract of carriage. The first thing to ascertain, therefore, is who made the contract of carriage with the carrier, always bearing in mind the possibility of the seller having acted as *agent* for the buyer.

A seller under a contract on c.i.f. terms will have entered into the contract of carriage with the carrier in his/her own right, whether that contract be a charterparty or a contract of carriage evidenced by a bill of lading. If, therefore, goods are lost or damaged while still at the seller's risk, he/she can sue in contract as an original party to the contract of carriage.

Under an f.o.b. contract, identifying the original contracting party is more complex and will ultimately depend on an analysis of the facts. The seller may have found and nominated the ship and booked the shipping space. The bill of lading may have been issued to the seller, naming the seller as shipper. It may be that although the bill of lading has been issued to the seller, nominating the seller as shipper, the buyer has chartered the vessel or booked shipping space upon it. Sometimes the bill of lading will have been issued to the buyer naming him as shipper. All the various circumstances must be looked at to determine whether the buyer contracted as principal or whether the seller contracted as principal or acted for the f.o.b. buyer as undisclosed principal. Consider the circumstances in *The Athanasia Comininos* [1990] 1 Lloyd's Rep 277; *The Captain Gregos (No. 2)* [1990] 2 Lloyd's Rep 395.

However, situations frequently arise where goods are lost or damaged but, by virtue of the contract of sale, the loss is borne by a party other than the one who entered into the contract of carriage. In particular:

(a)   Under a contract of sale on f.o.b. terms the buyer may have entered into the contract of carriage, but the goods are damaged by the carrier, his/her servants or agents before risk under the sale contract has passed to the buyer, e.g. during loading but prior to goods passing the ship's rail. The question here arises as to whether, and if so upon what basis, the seller may benefit under the contract of carriage made with the buyer.

(b)   The seller may, in performance of a contract of sale on f.o.b. or c.i.f. terms, enter into the contract of carriage as a principal, but the loss or damage occurs to the goods at a time when the risk in those goods has already, under the sale contract, passed to the buyer. The question here arises as to whether, and if so upon what basis and in what circumstances, the buyer may benefit under a contract of carriage made with the seller or establish the existence of an independent contract with the carrier.

These situations will be considered in turn.

21.2   Seller may Benefit under Buyer's Contract

The courts have considered various legal routes to enable a seller to pursue a contractual claim in circumstances where the buyer has entered into the carriage contract. The most recent development is the ability of the seller to pursue a contractual remedy by virtue of the operation of COGSA 1992 where the buyer rejects the documents/goods and returns the bill of lading. See s. 2(2)(b).

21.2.1   CONTRACT EVIDENCED BY BILL OF LADING

According to *Pyrene Co. Ltd* v *Scindia Navigation Co. Ltd* [19541 2 All ER 158 the seller can participate in the contract entered into by the buyers, on the basis of agency. Devlin J stated: 'where, as in this case, he [the buyer] has not got the property at the time of the contract of carriage and does not intend to acquire it before the contract begins to operate he must act as agent'. However, the seller does not appear to participate fully in the contract of carriage. Devlin J went on to say in the *Pyrene* case that it was not intended by all three parties that the seller should be a party to the whole contract — it was intended that the seller should take the benefits of the contract which appertained to his/her interest therein, taking them subject to whatever qualification with regard to them the contract imposed.

As an alternative to agency Devlin J suggested the implication of a contract between the carrier and the f.o.b. seller, on the principle in *Brandt* v *Liverpool, Brazil and River Plate SN Co. Ltd* [1924] 1 KB 575. By delivering the goods alongside the ship, the seller impliedly invites the shipowner to load them; the shipowner by lifting them impliedly accepts that invitation. The implied contract so created incorporates the shipowner's usual terms. Devlin J stated: 'The shipowner would not contract for the loading of the goods on terms different from those which he offered for the voyage as a whole.' Nevertheless, Devlin J found difficulties in the adoption of this route to the implication of a contractual relationship between the carrier and the seller for the following reasons:

(a)   It would mean that if the goods were not lifted there would be no contract.

(b)   It might be difficult to infer an intention on the part of the shipowner to make a new contract. In many cases he will suppose that he is acting under a contract already made with the purchaser.

(c)   It might be difficult to infer a similar intention on the part of the seller. He would suppose that loading would be dealt with under the contract of carriage entered into with the f.o.b. purchaser.

21.2.2   CHARTERPARTY

Sometimes, as in *The Dunelmia* [1970] 1 QB 289 the f.o.b. buyer enters into a charterparty contract with the carriers. The bill of lading received by the buyer from the carrier would not appear to have a contractual function at all. The agency principle in *Pyrene* would mean that the buyer acted as agent of the seller when entering into a charterparty contract in respect of 'the benefits of the contract which appertain to his [the seller's] interest therein....'.

But note that although the f.o.b. buyer may charter the ship, the bill of lading may be issued to the seller. In these circumstances a contract evidenced by the bill of lading might exist between the f.o.b. seller and carrier. See *The Athanasia Comninos* [1990] Lloyd's Rep 277.

21.2.3   **CONTRACTUAL RIGHTS ON REJECTION**

Where, before delivery of goods by the carrier, an f.o.b. buyer rejects the tender of documents and therefore also the goods, he will in the appropriate manner (i.e., indorsement and delivery, or delivery) return the bill of lading to his seller. Even though the seller had not entered into a contract of carriage, he/she will, by virtue of becoming a 'holder' of the bill of lading (see COGSA 1992, s. 5(2)), have transferred to and vested in him all rights of suit under the contract of carriage (i.e., contract contained in or evidenced by that bill of lading: see COGSA 1992, s. 5(1)) as if he had been a party to that contract (see COGSA 1992, s. 2(1)).

Where, after delivery of the goods by the carrier, an f.o.b. buyer rejects the goods, he again will, in the appropriate manner, re-transfer the bill of lading to his seller. In these circumstances, even though the bill of lading no longer operates as a document of title at common law, i.e., will not operate as a symbol of the goods because the goods have been delivered, the seller, as 'holder', will have transferred to and vested in him all rights of suit in or evidenced by the bill of lading as the rejection emanates from a contract of sale made before delivery by the carrier: see COGSA 1992, s. 2(2)(b).

The above applies to a 'shipped' or 'received for shipment' bill of lading in transferable form.

In circumstances where a seaway bill is issued to a buyer, COGSA 1992 will vest contractual rights to sue in the seller if, on rejection but before delivery of the goods, the buyer varies his shipping instructions to the carrier identifying the seller as the person to whom delivery of the goods to which the seaway bill relates should be made: see COGSA 1992, s. 2(1)(b). If there is no change of shipping instructions prior to delivery by the carrier, COGSA 1992 will not operate to transfer rights to sue on a contract contained in or evidence by the seaway bill.

21.3   Buyer may Benefit under Seller's Contract

Where a buyer wishes to benefit from a contract of carriage entered into by the seller in his own right, the following arguments may be available to him/her in order to pursue directly or indirectly a contractual remedy.

21.3.1   **CONTRACTUAL REMEDY BY VIRTUE OF THE OPERATION OF THE CARRIAGE OF GOODS BY SEA ACT 1992 (STATUTORY RIGHT OF SUIT)**

This Act applies to the following documents — bill of lading, seaway bill, and ship's delivery order — issued after 15 September 1992. For the position in relation to bills of lading issued before 16 September 1992, refer to the **Commercial Practice Manual 1993/94**).

21.3.1.1   **Bill of lading**
'Bill of lading' means a received for shipment/shipped bill of lading in transferable form: see s. 1(1) and (2)(a) and (b).

A person who receives a bill of lading as defined above needs to show that he has become 'the lawful holder of a bill of lading' (see s. 2(1)(a)) in order to have transferred to and vested in him 'all rights of suit under the contract of carriage as if he had been a party to that contract': s. 2(1).

By 'contract of carriage' is meant that contract contained in or evidenced by the bill of lading: s. 5(1). Thus, if his transferor was a seller with a charterparty contract with the carrier, and for whom the bill of lading has no contractual function, it is not the charterparty contract which is transferred but the contract contained in or evidenced by the bill of lading.

Under COGSA 1992, s. 5(2)(c), a 'holder' of the bill of lading is a person:

(a) 'with possession of the bill who, by virtue of being the person identified in the bill, is the consignee of the goods to which the bill relates';
(b) 'with possession of the bill as a result of the completion, by delivery of the bill, of any indorsement of the bill or, in the case of a bearer bill, of any other transfer of the bill';
(c) 'with possession of the bill as a result of any transaction by virtue of which he would have become a holder falling within paragraphs (a) or (b) above had not the transaction been effected at a time when possession of the bill no longer gave a right (as against the carrier) to possession of the goods to which the bill relates'.

Section 5(2)(c) must be read with s. 2(2). Although by virtue of s. 5(2)(c) the possessor of the bill of lading is a 'holder' even though the bill of lading no longer operates as a document of title at common law, under s. 2(2) rights of suit will be transferred only if he becomes the holder of the bill:

(a)   by virtue of a transaction effected in pursuance of any contractual or other arrangements made before the time when such a right to possession ceased to attach to possession of the bill; or
(b)   as a result of the rejection to that person by another person of goods or documents delivered to the other person in pursuance of any such arrangements.

Thus, as an example of the operation of s. 2(2)(a), if a c.i.f. contract for the sale of widgets between A and B is made in January, delivery overside the ship is made in April, followed by transfer of the bill of lading to B in May, B will become a holder, as the bill was transferred by virtue of the January sale contract made before delivery in April.

The holder of the bill of lading has to be a 'lawful' holder. Section 5(2) states:

... a person shall be regarded for the purposes of this Act as having become the lawful holder of a bill of lading wherever he had become the holder of the bill in good faith.

21.3.1.2   Seaway bill

A seaway bill is defined as referring to a document which is not a bill of lading (i.e., not in transferable form) but which acts as a receipt for the goods and contains or evidences a contract for the carriage of goods by sea and which identifies the person to whom delivery of the goods is to be made by the carrier in accordance with that contract: s. 1(3). Such a definition would include a 'straight-consigned' bill of lading.

By virtue of s. 2(1)(b), the person to whom delivery of the goods to which the seaway bill relates is to be made by the carrier in accordance with the contract of carriage, is the person who has transferred to and vested in him all rights of suits under the contract of carriage.

It is therefore clear that in order to establish a right to sue in contract, the buyer who is not an original party to the contract of carriage does not have to prove his receipt of the seaway bill. Neither is it necessary to tender the seaway bill. However, the buyer must prove he/she is the party to whom the seller has instructed delivery is to be made. The combined effect of s. 1(3)(b), s. 2(1)(b) and s. 5(3) is to preserve the ability of the shipper to alter his shipping instructions and thus change the name of the deliveree at any time before delivery.

The contract of carriage, the rights of which are transferred, is the contract of carriage contained in or evidenced by the seaway bill: s. 5(1).

21.3.1.3   Ship's delivery order

A ship's delivery order is defined in s. 1(4) as referring to a document which is not a bill of lading or a seaway bill but which contains an undertaking which:

(a)   is given under or for the purpose of a contract for the carriage by sea of the goods to which the document relates or of goods which evidence those goods; and

(b)   is an undertaking by the carrier to a person identified in the document to deliver the goods to which the document relates to that person.

By virtue of s. 2(1)(c), contractual rights to sue are transferred to and vested in the person 'to whom delivery of the goods to which the ship's delivery order relates is to be made'. Again, as with the seaway bill, in order to establish contractual rights to sue under the Act where not an original contracting party, there is no need to prove receipt. Neither is it necessary to tender the ship's delivery order. However, it will be necessary to prove that he/she is the party entitled to delivery of the goods. In this regard it must be noted that ship's delivery orders are sometimes issued in which the undertaking is given to a named person 'or order', i.e., at the direction of the named person. The combined effect of s. 1(4)(b), s. 2(1)(c) and s. 5(3) is to enable the named party to nominate a new deliveree.

The contract of carriage which is transferred is that 'under or for the purposes of which the undertaking contained in the order is given': s. 5(1)(b). But note s. 2(3), which states:

The right vested in any person by virtue of the operation of subsection (1) above in relation to a ship's delivery order—

(a)   shall be so vested subject to the terms of the order; and
(b)   where the goods to which the order relates form a part only of the goods to which the contract of carriage relate, shall be confined to rights in respect of the goods to which the order relates.

21.3.1.4   Goods cease to exist/cannot be identified

Whether the document used is a bill of lading, seaway bill or ship's delivery order, transfer of contractual rights is not affected by the fact that goods to which the document relates:

(a)   cease to exist after the issue of the document; or
(b)   cannot be identified (whether because they are mixed with other goods or for any other reason).

See s. 5(4)(a) and (b).

21.3.2   IMPLICATION OF CONTRACT

Although the enactment of COGSA 1992, and thus the greater availability of statutory rights of suit, has reduced the need to rely on implication of a contract, it cannot be ignored altogether. Circumstances will occur where no statutory right of suit arises, e.g., where no shipping document is used, or the document used does not fall within the ambit of the Act. What follows is a brief summary of the present state of the law defining the circumstances required to exist for the implication of a contract between the party obtaining delivery (the deliveree) and the party giving delivery when requested (the deliveror). Note, however, that in relation to the case law, there would now be differences in the types of document presented in requesting delivery.

In *Brandt* v *Liverpool, Brazil and River Plate SN Co. Ltd* [1924] 1 KB 575, Bankes LJ, in reviewing the authorities, stated (at 589):

[I]t has clearly been established that where the holder of a bill of lading presents it and offers to accept delivery, if that offer is accepted by the shipowner, the holder of the bill of lading comes under an obligation to pay the freight and to pay the demurrage if any ... the contract so made by that offer and acceptance covers, so as to include, the terms of the bill of lading.

Similarly, in *Cremer* v *General Carriers SA* [1974] 1 WLR 341 it was held that a contract, on the terms of the original bill of lading, came into existence between the shipowner and the purchaser when the latter tendered a ship's delivery order (see **18.6.1**) incorporating the terms of the bill of lading, paid the freight and received delivery of the goods.

A contract has not been implied between a carrier as deliveror and a party requesting delivery, in circumstances where the party requesting delivery acts as an agent only. See *The Aliakmon* [1983] 1 Lloyd's Rep 203.

A contract has been implied even though no bill of lading has been tendered. The giving of an undertaking on those occasions when the bill of lading was not presented, was treated as sufficient (*The Elli 2* [1985] 1 Lloyd's Rep 107). A contract can be implied if, although no freight is due, demurrage is outstanding (*The Elli 2 (supra)*). In *The Elli 2*, May LJ stated that:

> no such contract should be implied on the facts of any given case unless it is necessary to do so: necessary that is to say, in order to give business reality to a transaction and to create enforceable obligations between parties who are dealing with one another in circumstances in which one would expect that business reality and those enforceable obligations to exist.

Subsequently, in *The Aramis* [1989] 1 Lloyd's Rep 213, the Court of Appeal held that where there was no delivery, there was no basis for implying a contract: that where the delivery or part delivery of a consignment was entirely consistent with the performance of obligations and rights of the parties under their existing contractual arrangement with others, no contract could be implied. There would have to be evidence of performance of an act, which indicated that the bill of lading governed the carrier and receiver's relationship. Stuart-Smith LJ stated (at 229):

> The shipowner has an obligation to make delivery of the goods to the holder of the bill of lading, an obligation undertaken to the shipper; moreover, the holder of the bill of lading has a right to receive the goods, although it is not a right he can directly enforce against the shipowner, because he has no title to the goods nor do any rights of suit pass under the 1855 Act. I would accept that performance by the shipowner of his obligation to the shipper could amount to consideration for a promise by the holder of the bill of lading. But consideration is not the real problem here... What the court has to determine is whether that is evidence of a new contract between the shipowners and the holder of the bill of lading to regulate their dealings on the terms of the bill of lading. Since there is no evidence of any express agreement, it has to be inferred from the conduct of the parties. If their conduct is equally referable to and explicable by their existing rights and obligations, albeit such rights and obligations are not enforceable against each other, there is no material from which the court can draw the inference. It is only if their conduct is unequivocally referable to or explicable by one or more of the rights or obligations contained in the bill of lading that there is factual material from which the court can draw the inference that a contract has been entered into between them.

Thereafter, in *The Captain Gregos (No. 2)* [1990] 2 Lloyd's Rep 395, there was before the court an action for short delivery in which the ship owner was trying to argue the implication of a contract with the receivers of goods, in order to bring in the operation of Article III, r. 6 of the Hague-Visby Rules — a time bar applicable to carriage contracts.

In the circumstances, no freight was paid, nor an undertaking to pay freight given to the shipowner, by the receiver of the goods. No bill of lading was presented, nor an undertaking to present given. Nevertheless the Court of Appeal from the facts of the case felt it necessary to imply a contract (between BP and the shipowner) in order to give business reality to the transaction between them and create the obligations which 'as we think, both parties plainly believed to exist'.

The Court of Appeal distinguished the decision of Court of Appeal in *The Aramis*:

(a) The receivers were the owners of the cargo before discharge began.
(b) The receivers had very clearly and explicitly consented to the carriage of the goods on terms incorporating charterparty conditions normally in use for tankerships, which would include the Hague-Visby Rules.

Most recently in *The Gudermes* [1993] 1 Lloyd's Rep 311, purchasers of a cargo of fuel oil sought to recover from the shipowners the cost of transhipment of the cargo. The cargo in question was required to be kept at a certain temperature in order to prevent congealing. No heating coils were available on *The Gudermes*. In consequence the ultimate receivers rejected the cargo on arrival of the ship at Ravenna, on the basis that it might clog their underwater sealine to the receiving terminal. The plaintiffs thereupon procured and paid for transshipment of the cargo onto the *Sea Oath* off Malta, heated the cargo on board and subsequently delivered at Ravenna.

The plaintiffs contended that as a result of the dealings between the parties in connection with the transhipment, there resulted a *Brandt* v *Liverpool* contract between themselves and the defendants.

It was urged, before Hirst J in the Commercial Court at first instance ([1991] 1 Lloyd's Rep 456), that *The Captain Gregos* had superseded *The Aramis* (supra) and that therefore if there were evidence of cooperation between the shipowner and the indorsee beyond the bare facts in *The Aramis,* a mutual contract would automatically be inferred.

Hirst J stated as follows:

> I am unable to accept this submission ... In my judgment no implied contract can be inferred unless it is necessary to give reality to the transaction, and unless conduct can be identified referable to the contract contended for which is inconsistent with there being no such contract; and it is fatal to the implication of such a contract if the parties would or might have acted exactly as they did in the absence of such a contract, as was clearly laid down in both the earlier cases. In my judgment, *The Captain Gregos* laid down no new principle, but rather applied the well-established doctrine to the particular facts of that case; it does however show that evidence of a sufficient degree of cooperation taken by itself may be enough to meet the established test.

The Court of Appeal accepted what Hirst J stated:

> For our part, we uphold the judge's direction entirely. But there are two points in it that we need to emphasize. First, it is not enough to show that the parties have done something more than, or something different from, what they were already bound to do under obligations owed to others. What they do must be consistent only with there being a new contract implied and inconsistent with there being no such contract ... there was some discussion about offer and acceptance and consideration; but in our judgment these matters are not critical. What we have to do is look at all the facts, and consider the problem in the round.

> Delivery off Malta went further than, and was inconsistent with, the rights and liabilities of the owners and Mitsui under any existing contract with another party. The owner's obligation was to deliver at a port to be nominated, and the nominated port was Ravenna. Mitsui under their purchase contract with the charterers were, we assume, ... entitled to have orders given to the vessel to discharge at Mitsui's nominated port, which again was Ravenna.

> In the event Mitsui and the owners agreed that discharge should take place off Malta. It is certainly arguable as Mr Boyd was prepared to allow, that this agreement had legally binding effect by itself and that neither Mitsui nor the owners could thereafter have demanded discharge somewhere else. But on further consideration we do not find that there must have been a contract, express or implied, from those facts alone. All that happened was that both parties were prepared to cooperate in finding a solution to the problem that had arisen. The owners, with the agreement of the charterers, sent the vessel to Malta; but they did not necessarily conclude a new contract with Mitsui that the vessel would discharge there, even if the operation should turn out to be unduly difficult or dangerous or expensive....

21.3.3   SELLER SUING ON BUYER'S BEHALF

The COGSA 1992 divorces transfer of contractual rights to sue from the transfer of property in the goods. Therefore, where the Act applies, a party can obtain statutory rights to sue without being the owner of the goods. However, there will still be circumstances where COGSA 1992 does not apply and thus a non-owner, with no statutory right of suit but who bears the risk of the loss, would wish the owner as original contracting party to sue on his behalf.

The c.i.f. purchaser (and where relevant the f.o.b. purchaser) could ask the seller to sue, as the principal contracting party, on the buyer's behalf by relying on the principle ennunciated in *The Sanix Ace* [1987] 1 Lloyd's Rep 465, where it was held that the *owner* of goods was entitled to sue and recover damages in respect of loss or damage to those goods. In contract, the right to recover substantial damages can be proved by proving possession or ownership of the goods. As soon as the goods suffer damage, the owner of the goods suffers loss. The fact that the plaintiff has contracts of sale which enable him/her to collect the price from his/her buyer does not disentitle him/her from recovery of full damages. Full damages assessed by reference to the sound arrived value of the goods are not affected by the fact that the owner of the goods has sold them on at a higher price. It is the loss to the proprietary or possessory interest that is compensated, not some other or different economic loss. Thus where (as in *The Sanix Ace)* property has not passed to the purchaser at the time the loss or damage occurs the purchaser bearing the risk can ask the seller to sue on his/her behalf, the seller being able by virtue of retention of ownership to recover substantial damages.

Where COGSA 1992 does not apply, a c.i.f. or f.o.b. purchaser, although becoming owner of the goods before their loss or damage, does not obtain statutory contractual rights of suit. In these circumstances the purchaser can ask the principal contracting party, to sue on his behalf and recover substantial damages on the principle in *Dunlop* v *Lambert* (1839) 6 Cl & Fin 600, as explained in *The Albazero* [1976] 3 All ER 129. The normal position in English law is that, apart from nominal damages, a party to a contract can only recover in an action for damages for breach of contract the actual loss which that party has himself/herself sustained, However, this is subject to an exception in the case of a commercial contract concerning goods where it is in the contemplation of the parties that the proprietary interest in the goods may be transferred from one owner to another after the contract has been entered into and before the breach which causes loss or damage to the goods. In these circumstances, an original party, if this is the intention of them both, is treated in law as having entered into the contract for the benefit of all persons who have or may acquire an interest in the goods before they are lost or damaged and is entitled to recover by way of damage for breach of contract the actual loss sustained by those for whose benefit the contract is entered into.

The House of Lords in *The Albazero* restricted the operation of the principle in *Dunlop* v *Lambert* to those situations where there is no contract between the carrier with whom the shipper contracted and the party who actually suffered the loss. Lord Diplock said:

> The complications, anomalies and injustices that might arise from the co-existence in different parties of rights of suit to recover under separate contracts of carriage which impose different obligations on the parties to them, a loss which a party to one of those contracts alone has sustained, supply compelling reasons why the rule in *Dunlop* v *Lambert* should not be extended to cases where there are two contracts with the carrier covering the same carriage and under one of them there is privity of contract between the person who actually sustains the loss and the carrier by whose breach of that contract it was caused.

The buyer cannot compel the original contracting party to the contract of carriage to sue on his/her behalf. The consignor's right of action against the carrier for breach of contract has never been considered as trust property, nor would courts of equity compel the consignor to exercise his/her right of action for the benefit of the purchaser — 'whatever rights they [the purchasers] have, spring up when the consignor has recovered judgment.' The remedy of the purchaser now is an action for money had and received. Against this sum the seller is not entitled to any set-off in respect of costs incurred by him/her in the action and not recoverable from the carrier on taxation.

Note COGSA 1992, s. 2(4) which makes it clear that in those circumstances where a person with an interest in goods sustains loss or damage but by virtue of the operation of the Act contractual rights of suit are vested in another person, that other person shall be entitled to exercise those rights for the benefit of the person who sustained the loss or damage. For example, a bank under a documentary credit may be named as consignee in a bill of lading. On payment out by the bank to the seller, property in the goods will vest in the buyer. As holder, it will be the bank who has the right to sue (unless it transfers on the bill of lading to the buyer), although it would hold the proceeds for the account of the buyer unless there has been 'abandonment' by the buyer.

21.3.4 ASSIGNMENT AS A TERM OF THE CONTRACT OF SALE

The inability of a person both at common law and under COGSA 1992 to compel the party with right of suit to sue on his/her behalf should cause the buyer to insist in his/her contract that rights to sue be exercised for the buyer's account, or that such rights be assigned. However, notice of the assignment must be given to the carrier. Note that if what is to be assigned is seller's rights of suit under a contract of carriage, it may be a charterparty contract and not that which is contained in or evidenced by a bill of lading or seaway bill.

21.4 Suing in Tort

A party may be able, and indeed may wish, to proceed in tort for negligence in the carriage of the goods. (Note that it may be in the carrier's interest to prove the existence of a contract in order to try and bind the other party to the carrier's conditions of carriage.) However, in order to proceed in the tort of negligence, the party seeking to bring the action must have had the proprietary or possessory interest in the goods at the time the loss or damage occurred (*The Aliakmon* [1986] 2 All ER 145) and must be in a position to prove negligence.

21.5 Party to be Sued on Contract of Carriage or in Tort

Once it has been determined which party can proceed with an action on the contract of carriage or in tort, it must be decided which party is to be sued in the action.

21.5.1 UNIMODAL TRANSPORT

This problem will be dealt with first on the basis that there is just one mode of transport — by sea — with one vessel being used for the whole transport operation.

21.5.1.1 Carriage on a general ship: no charterparty

Where the ship is **not** under charter, the legal carrier and the actual carrier are one and the same — the shipowner. The master or loading broker issues bills of lading or other shipping documents as agent of the shipowner; the master and crew remain under the direction and control of the shipowner. This means that the shipowner can be sued both in contract (including an implied contract) and in tort for loss or damage occurring to the goods whilst in his/her custody. (See **Figure 21.1.**)

Figure 21.1   Shipowner can be sued in contract and tort by shipper and may be sued by the consignee/indorsee in tort, and in contract if COGSA 1992, s. 2 applies or an implied contract exists

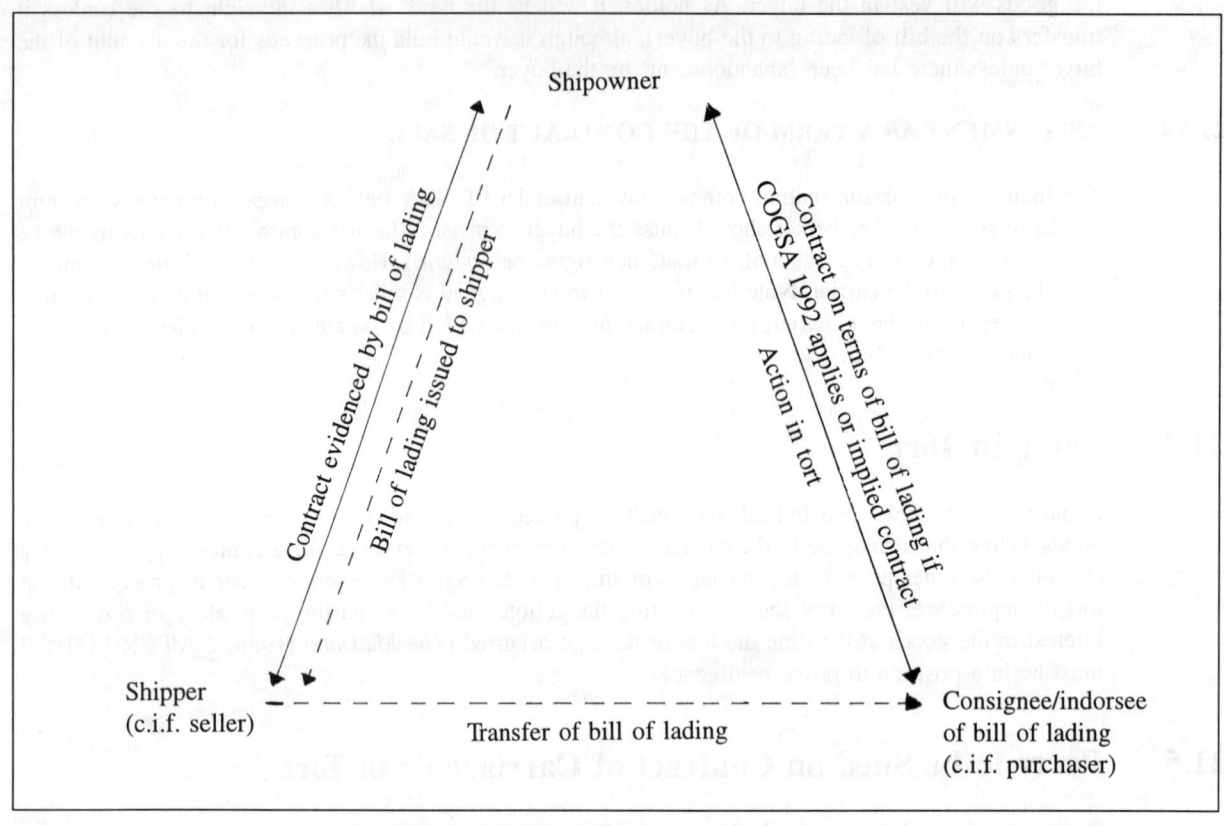

21.5.1.2   Carriage on a ship chartered by demise

Where the ship is chartered by demise the charterer takes over the control and direction of the ship and crew. The party signing the bill of lading will be signing as agent of the charterer, *not* of the shipowner. In consequence the contract of carriage will be with the charterer by demise: *Baumoll Manufacktur von Carl Scheibler* v *Furness* [1893] AC 8. Since the charterer by demise takes over the ship and steps into the shoes of the shipowner, he/she is also the actual carrier of the goods and can be sued on an implied contract and in tort for negligence in the carriage of the goods. The charterer by demise is both the legal and actual carrier. (See **Figure 21.2.**). See also *The Stolt Loyalty* [1995] 1 Lloyd's Rep 598 as to the interpretation of 'owner' and the potential problem of whom to sue when there is a short time bar, e.g., Article III, r. 6 of the Hague-Visby Rules.

Figure 21.2 Charterer by demise can be sued in contract and tort by shipper and may be sued by consignee/indorsee in tort, and in contract if COGSA 1992, s. 2 applies or an implied contract exists

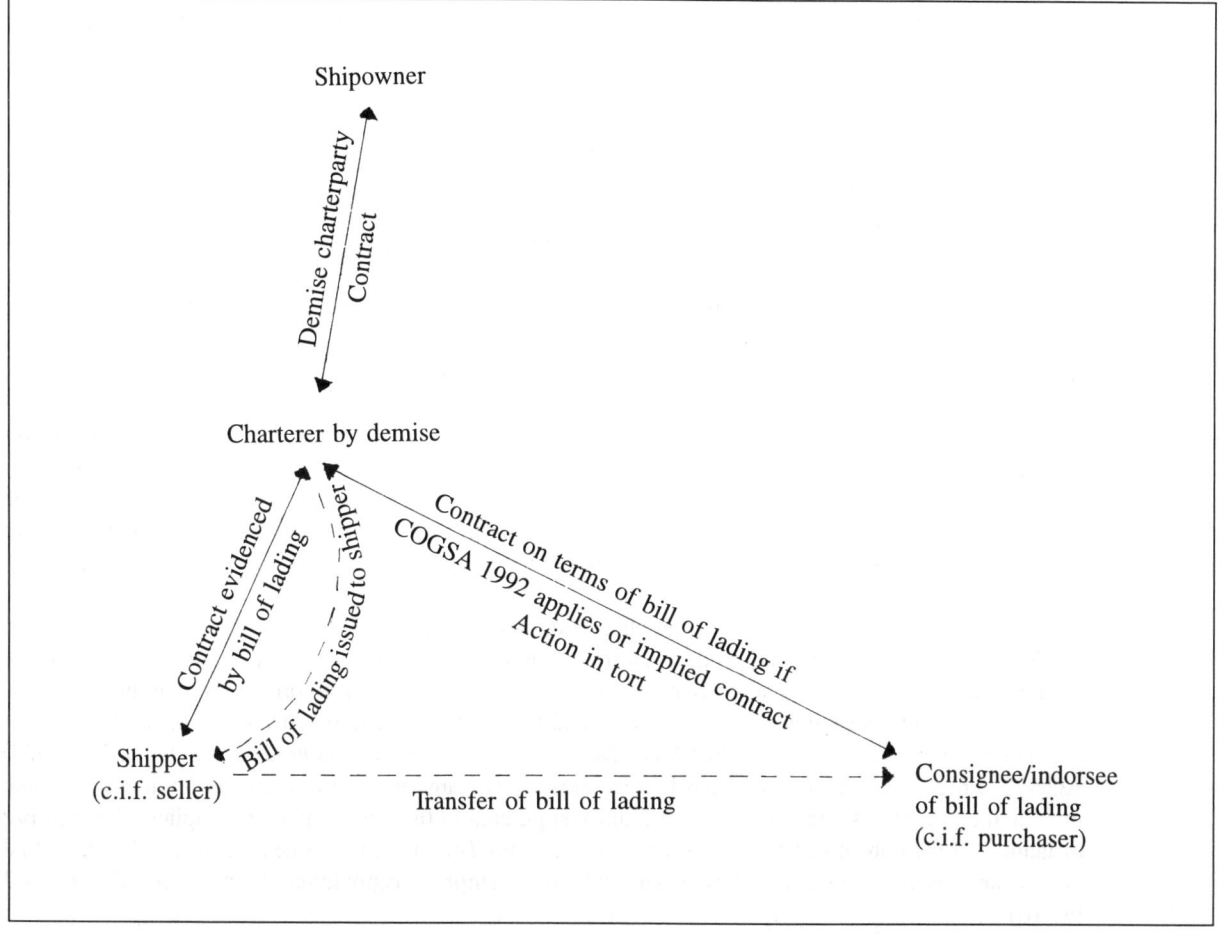

21.5.1.3 Carriage on a time- or voyage-chartered ship

Where the ship is time- or voyage-chartered the situation is more complex. Firstly, it is much more difficult to determine as a matter of construction who is the legal carrier of the goods, but the following can be noted:

(a) Where the master signs the bill of lading he will usually be treated as signing under his usual authority as agent of the shipowner or charterer by demise. See *Sanderman v Scurr* (1866) LR 2 QB 86, but see also *The Venezuela* [1980] 1 Lloyd's Rep 393; *The Rewia* [1991] 2 Lloyd's Rep 325 (CA).

(b) Even though the *charterparty* contains a clause stating that the master shall sign as agent of the charterer, this limitation on the master's usual authority will not affect the shipper or consignee/indorsee unless they have notice of the limitation. Mere knowledge of the existence of a charterparty will not amount to sufficient notice of its contents: *Manchester Trust v Furness* [1895] 2 QB 539.

(c) Where the bill of lading is signed by the charterer, as authorised agent of the master, since the master is treated as acting as agent of the shipowner or charterer by demise, the legal carrier will be the shipowner or charterer by demise: *Tillmanns & Co. v SS Knutsford Ltd* [1908] 1 KB 185; *The Rewia* (*supra*).

(d) Where the bill of lading is signed by the charterer in his/her own name, he/she will be the legal carrier: *The Okehampton* [1913] p. 173 (but see (e) below). However, if *in fact* the charterer had authority to contract on behalf of, e.g., the shipowner, it may be that the holder of the bill of lading can sue the shipowner on the bill of lading contract as an undisclosed principal. (See *Scrutton on Charterparties,* 19th edn, 1984, Sweet and Maxwell, art. 17.)

(e) Demise clauses: bills of lading commonly contain a clause which attempts to prevent the time or voyage charterer from becoming the legal carrier of the goods. These clauses are called 'demise' clauses or 'identity of carrier' clauses. The following is an example:

If the ship is not owned by, or chartered by demise to the company or line by whom the bill of lading is issued (as may be the case notwithstanding anything that appears to the contrary) this bill of lading shall take effect only as a contract with the owner or demise charterer as the case may be, as principal, made through the agency of the said company or line who act as agents only and shall be under no personal liability whatsoever in respect thereof.

See *The Berkshire* [1974] 1 Lloyd's Rep 185; *The Jalamohan* [1988] 1 Lloyd's Rep 443.

See also *The Ives* [1995] 2 Lloyd's Rep 144 where the bill of lading was signed by the master, as agent for the time charterer. There was in the bill of lading a 'demise' clause and a charterer's indemnity clause. The court held that in order to determine who were the true contracting parties it was necessary to examine the whole document and to consider the whole context in which it came into existence. The court held that the master signed the bill of lading as agent for the time charterer who in turn, having authority by virtue of the indemnity clause to sign bills of lading on behalf of the owner, acted as agent for the shipowner. The contractual carrier was the shipowner.

The validity of these clauses does not appear to be in doubt. In *The Jalamohan* Hirst J stated: 'Whatever the position may be in other jurisdictions, I reject the suggestion that under English law there is anything anomalous about demise clauses'. Even if the contract of carriage is governed by the Hague-Visby Rules (see **21.7** ff.), the clause will not be treated as a nullity. The Rules do not govern the *choice* of carrier but are concerned with his/her liabilities etc. See R. M. Goode, *Commercial Law,* 1982, Pelican Books, p. 606.

(f) Where a ship is time- or voyage-chartered, since the charterer does not take over the running of the ship, the legal carrier may well be a different party from the actual carrier, i.e. the party in control of ship and crew. It is the actual carrier who must be sued in an action in tort for the negligent carriage of the goods. But note the actual carrier may be able to rely on the terms of the bill of lading contract between shipper and legal carrier. See *Elder Dempster & Co. Ltd* v *Paterson Zochonis & Co. Ltd* [1924] AC 522, where the reception of goods by the actual carrier amounted to a 'bailment upon terms, which include the exceptions and limitations of liablity stipulated in the known and contemplated form of bill of lading'. If the consignee/indorsee is suing on an *implied* contract, it will be a contract with the actual carrier, and not the carrier (if different) with whom the shipper originally contracted. (See **Figure 21.3 (a)–(d).**)

Figure 21.3(a) Where, on the facts, *shipowner* is the legal carrier

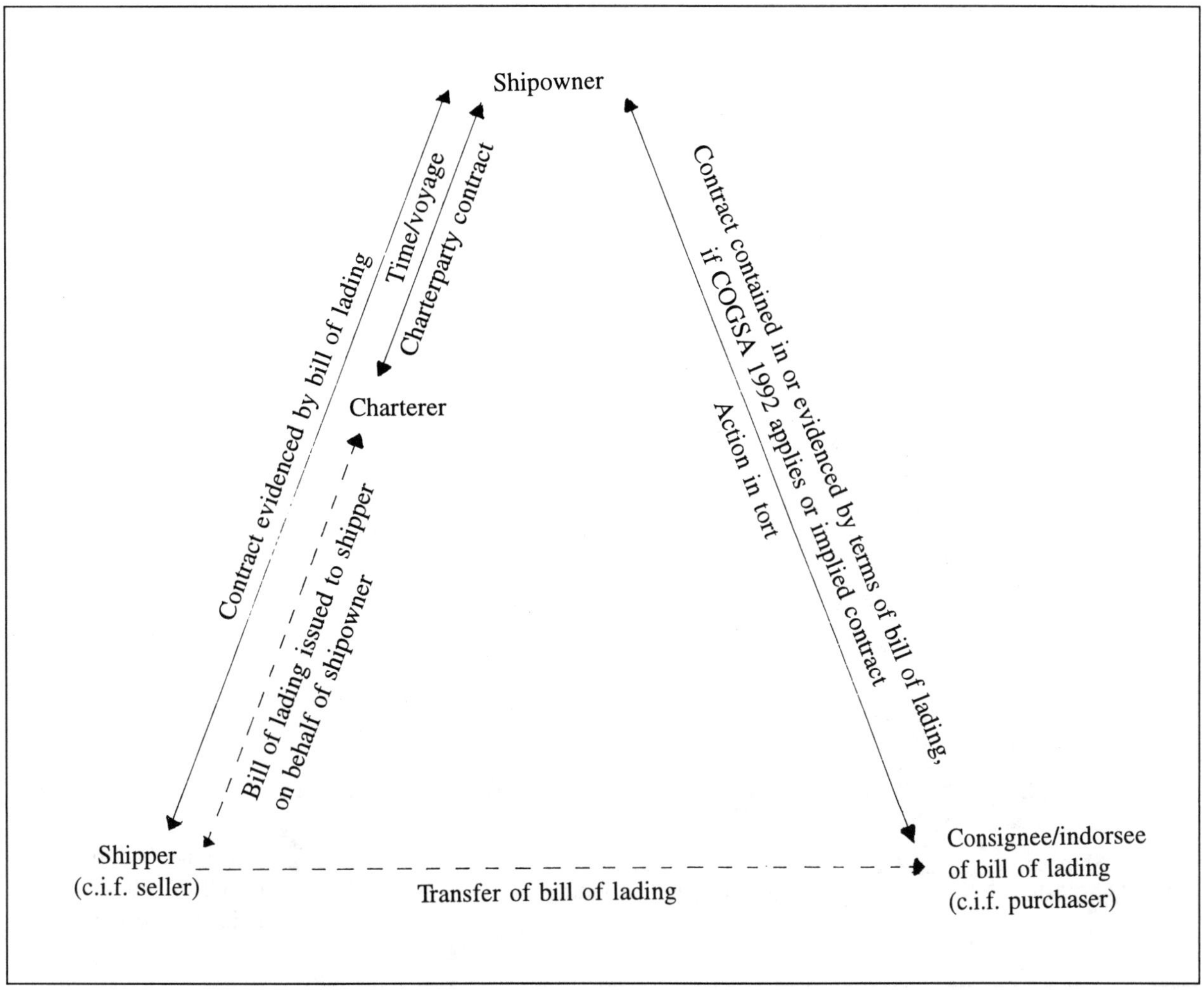

Shipowner

Contract evidenced by bill of lading

Time/voyage
Charterparty contract

Contract contained in or evidenced by terms of bill of lading,
if COGSA 1992 applies or implied contract

Action in tort

Charterer

Bill of lading issued to shipper
on behalf of shipowner

Shipper
(c.i.f. seller)

Transfer of bill of lading

Consignee/indorsee
of bill of lading
(c.i.f. purchaser)

Figure 21.3(b) Where, on the facts, the *time/voyage charterer* is the legal carrier

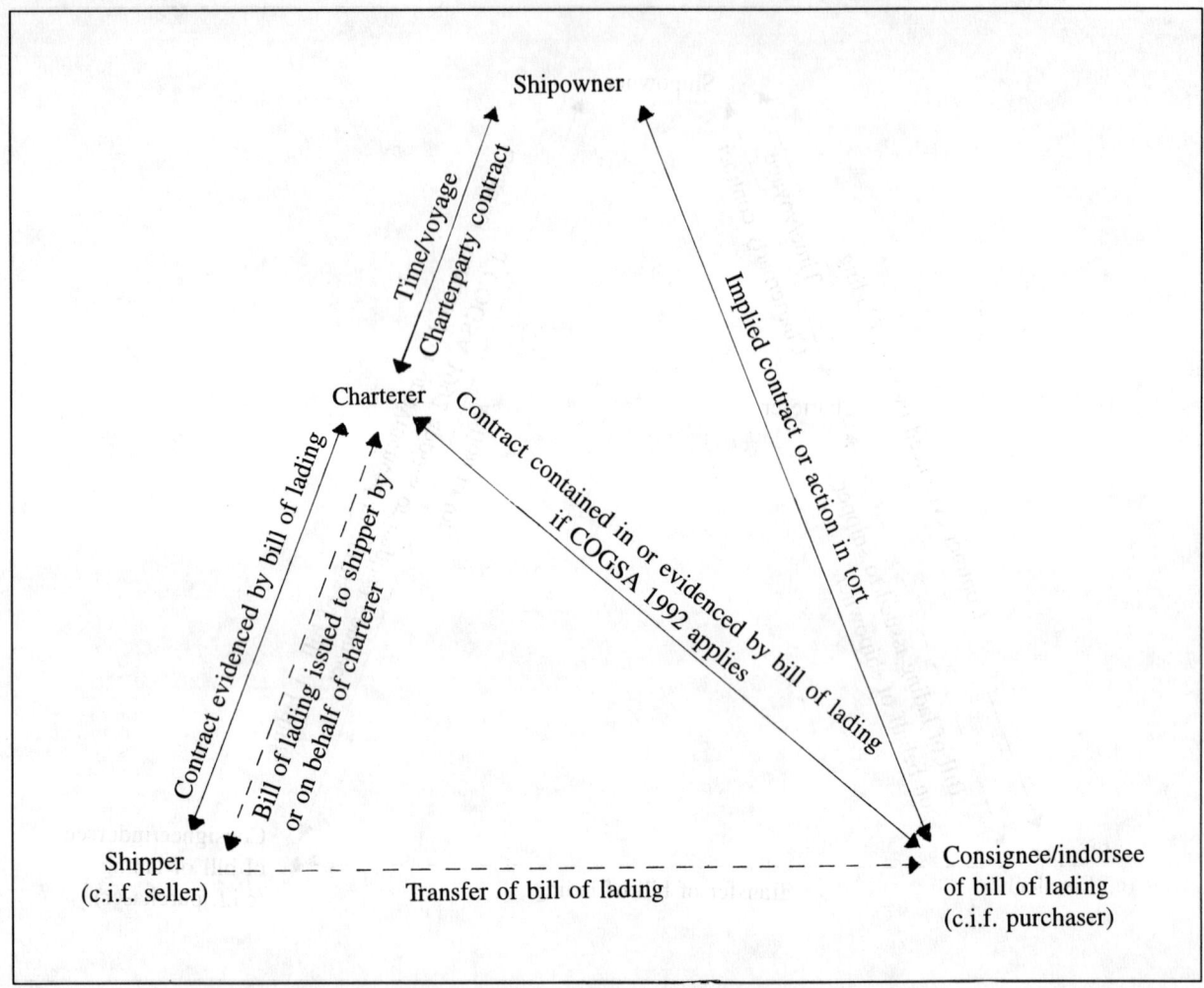

Figure 21.3(c) Where, on the facts, the *demise charterer* is the legal carrier

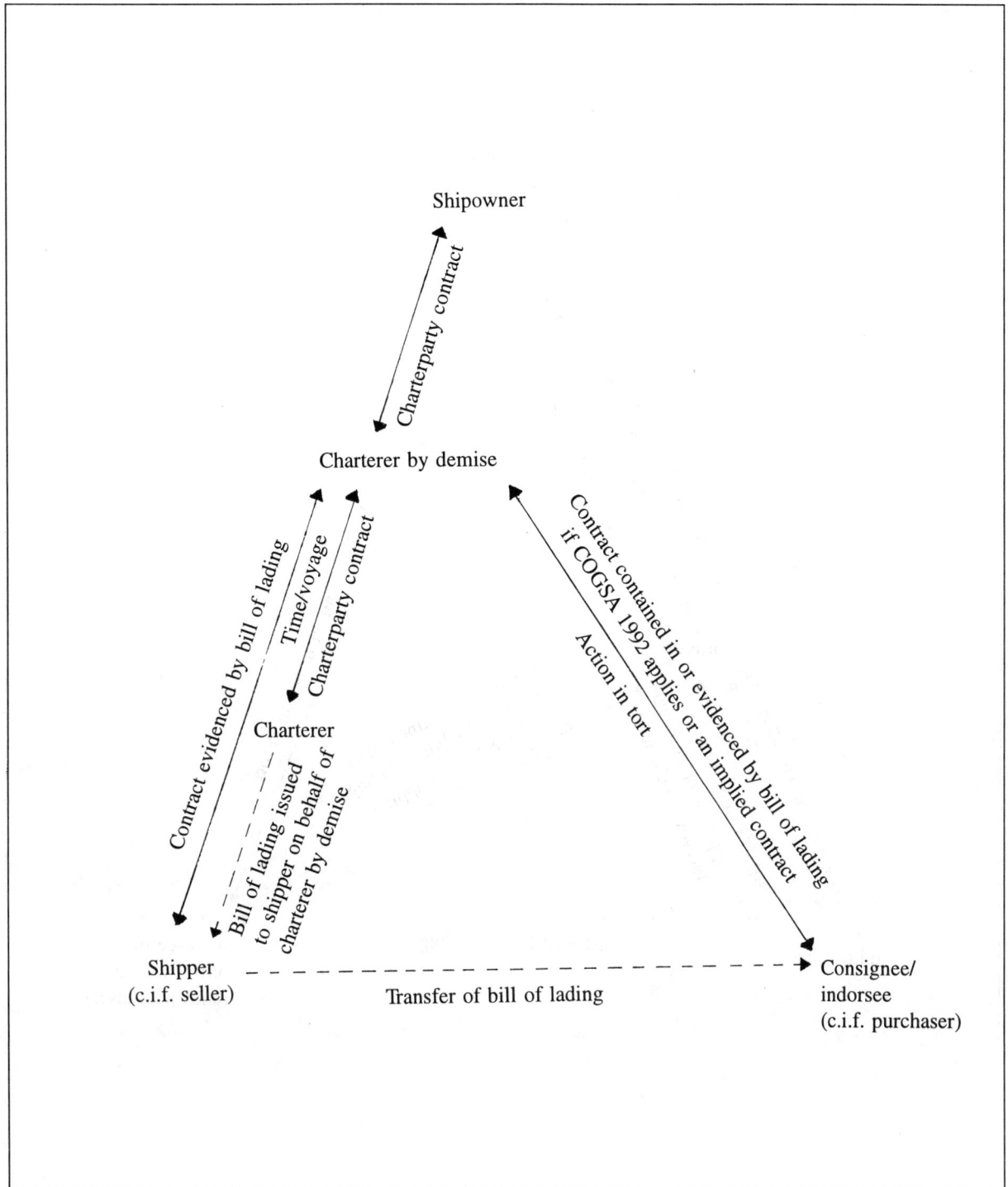

Figure 21.3(d) Where, on the facts, the *time/voyage charterer* is the legal carrier

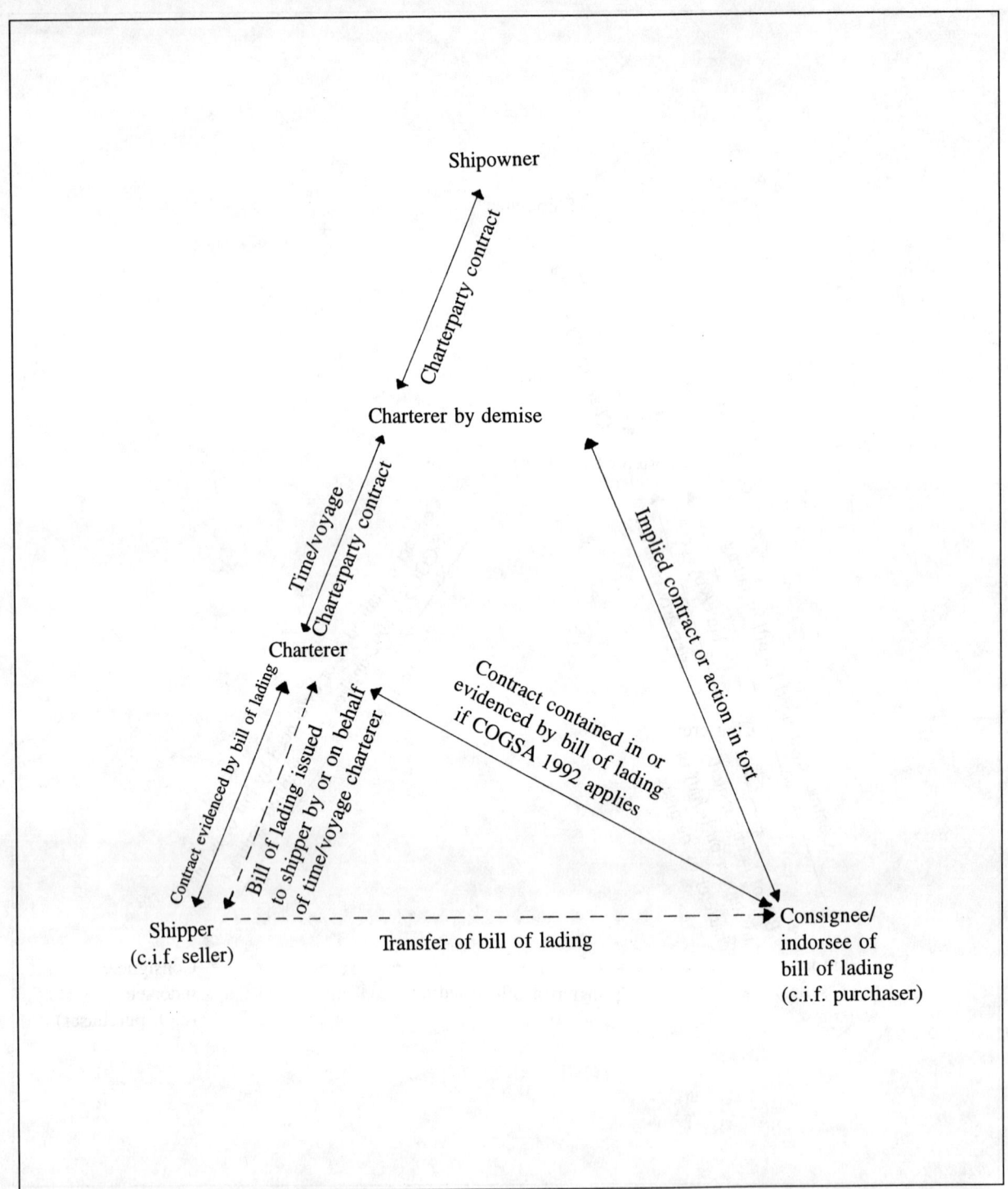

21.5.2   MULTIMODAL TRANSPORT

Where goods are to be transported using various methods of transport, the goods owner/manufacturer will have the task of making arrangements for each stage of the carriage and thus entering into two or more transport contracts. If loss or damage occurs, the goods owner/manufacturer will need to determine at what stage the loss or damage occurred and sue the party responsible for the goods at that stage — a very cumbersome, expensive procedure, and at times an impossible task. Where the goods are to be transported in a container it is highly likely that several modes of transport will be required, and unless the goods owner/manufacturer is a large concern with its own shipping department, it will use the services of a freight forwarder. The freight forwarder will deal with all the administrative matters, find willing transporters and, if necessary, arrange the packaging and handling of the goods. But is the legal position of the goods owner/manufacturer improved?

21.5.2.1   Freight forwarder — as agent

The capacity in which the freight forwarder acts depends on the terms of the individual contract and the facts of the case. It may be that in the circumstances, the freight forwarder acts in its traditional capacity only — as an agent. It does not undertake legal responsibility for the carriage of the goods through all its stages but contracts with the carriers on behalf of its customer. The goods owner/manufacturer will still, in the event of loss or damage, have to determine the stage in the voyage at which the loss/damage took place and sue the appropriate party.

Where the freight forwarder is carrying on a groupage business, e.g. 'stuffing' the goods of several goods owners/manufacturers into one container, it will usually obtain a 'groupage' bill of lading from the sea carrier in its own name. This, for obvious reasons, is not released to the various goods owner/manufacturer. Instead the freight forwarder will issue a 'house' bill of lading to its customers.

The following clause is commonly found in the 'house' bill of lading or 'certificate of shipment', as it is otherwise known:

(a)   The undersigned freight forwarders are authorised to enter into contracts with carriers and others involved in the execution of the transport, subject to the latter's usual terms and conditions.

(b)   The undersigned do not act as carriers but as forwarding agents. In consequence they are only responsible for the careful selection of third parties instructed by them, subject to the conditions of clause (c) hereunder.

(c)   The undersigned are responsible for delivery of the goods to the holders of this document through the intermediary of a delivery agent of their choice. They are not responsible for acts or omissions of carriers involved in the execution of the transport or of other third parties. The undersigned forwarding agents will, on request subrogate their claims against carrier and other parties.

Note in **Figure 21.4** that *if* the goods are sold on during their transit, and are lost or damaged en route, the c.i.f. purchaser cannot sue the carrier on the contract contained in the groupage bill of lading as it is not transferred to him/her. He/she cannot sue the carrier on the 'house' bill of lading as it is not issued by the carrier but by the freight forwarder. COGSA 1992 does not apply to transfer rights to sue. He/she cannot sue the actual carrier on an implied contract as he/she cannot demand the goods from the ship, *only* from the freight forwarder or its agent at the place of destination.

He/she *can* sue in tort the actual carrier with responsibility for those goods at the time the loss or damage took place.

Figure 21.4 Where, on the facts, freight forwarder acts as agent only — shipment of mixed container load

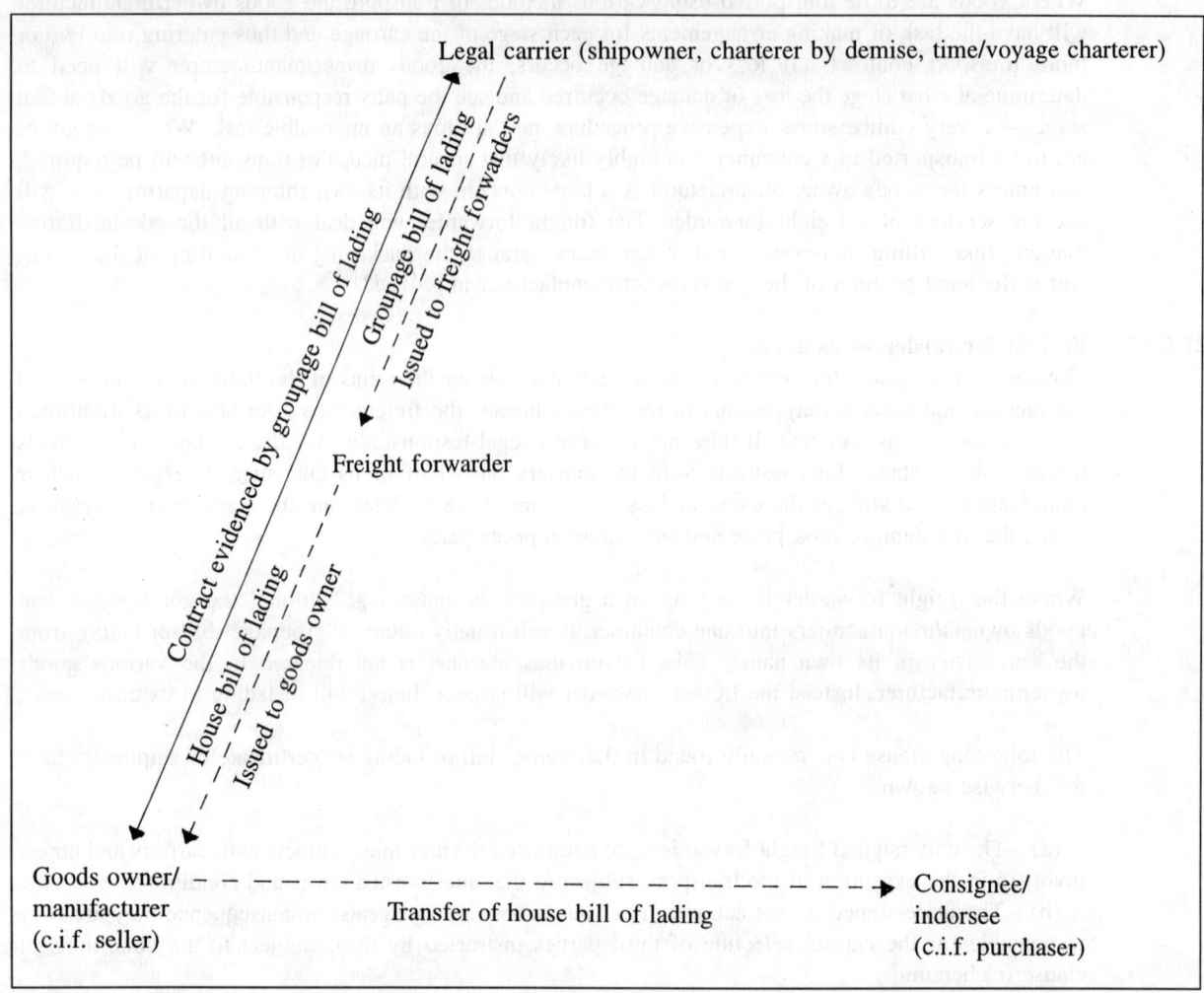

Legal carrier (shipowner, charterer by demise, time/voyage charterer)

Groupage bill of lading
Issued to freight forwarders

Contract evidenced by groupage bill of lading

House bill of lading
Issued to goods owner

Freight forwarder

Goods owner/
manufacturer
(c.i.f. seller)

Transfer of house bill of lading

Consignee/
indorsee
(c.i.f. purchaser)

21.5.2.2 Freight forwarder — as principal

The development of modern transport methods has also seen a parallel development of the responsibilities undertaken by freight forwarders. Today, it is not uncommon for the freight forwarder to agree to act as a principal, i.e. its contract with the goods owner/manufacturer is one of services, not agency. In agreeing to act as principal, it agrees to act as legal carrier of the goods for all stages and modes of transport, whether or not it actually undertakes any part of the carriage process itself. We call such a freight forwarder a multimodal transport operator (MTO).

The MTO issues to its customer a document, called a combined transport document or sometimes, a combined transport bill of lading, which sets out the undertaking of the MTO to act as legal carrier.

The following is an example of such an undertaking.

> The MTO, in accordance with and to the extent of the provisions contained in this MT document, and with liberty to sub-contract, undertakes to perform and/or in his own name to procure performance of the combined transport and delivery of the goods, including all services which are necessary to such transport from the place and time of taking the goods in charge to the place and time of delivery and accepts responsibility for such transport and such delivery.

In the event, therefore, of loss or damage occurring en route, the goods owner/manufacturer can pursue his contractual claim against the MTO. There is no privity of contract between the goods owner/manufacturer and the actual carriers of the goods. Nevertheless it may still be necessary to pinpoint the stage in the transit process at which loss or damage occurred if the MTO's liability is solely determined by the convention applying to that stage in the carriage process during which the loss or damage took place.

21.5.2.3 Sub-bailment

It is important to note the Privy Council decision in *The K. H. Enterprise* [1994] 1 Lloyd's Rep 593, in which the Privy Council held, relying on the authority of *Gilchrist Watt and Saunders Pty Ltd* v *Fork Products Pty Ltd* [1970] 2 Lloyd's Rep 1 and *Morris* v *C. W. Martin & Sons Ltd* [1965] 2 Lloyd's Rep 63, that where goods are sub-bailed by the first carrier to a second carrier, the sub-bailee second carrier becomes the bailee of the goods vis-à-vis the original bailor by voluntarily receiving possession of the original bailor's goods. In addition the sub-bailees are to be viewed as bailees for reward. Lord Goff stated:

> ... if the sub-bailment is for reward the obligation owed by the sub-bailee to the owner must likewise be that of a bailee for reward, notwithstanding that the reward is payable not by the owner but by the bailee.

The Privy Council also held that the second carrier viewed as bailee of the goods vis-à-vis the original bailor, can rely on the terms of the sub-bailment in so far as they were authorised by the original bailor. Lord Goff stated:

> ... if the effect of the sub-bailment is that the sub-bailee voluntarily receives into his custody the goods of the owner and so assumes towards the owner the responsibility of a bailee, then to the extent that the terms of the sub-bailment are consented to by the owner, it can properly be said that the owner has authorised the bailee so to regulate the duties of the sub-bailee in respect of the goods entrusted to him, not only towards the bailee but also towards the owner.

> ... once it is recognised that the sub-bailee by voluntarily taking the owner's goods into his custody, ipso facto becomes the bailee of those goods vis-à-vis the owner, it must follow that the owner's rights against the sub-bailee will only be subject to terms of the sub-bailment if he has consented to them, i.e., if he has authorised the bailee to entrust the goods to the sub-bailee on those terms.

Figure 21.5   Where freight forwarder acts as a principal

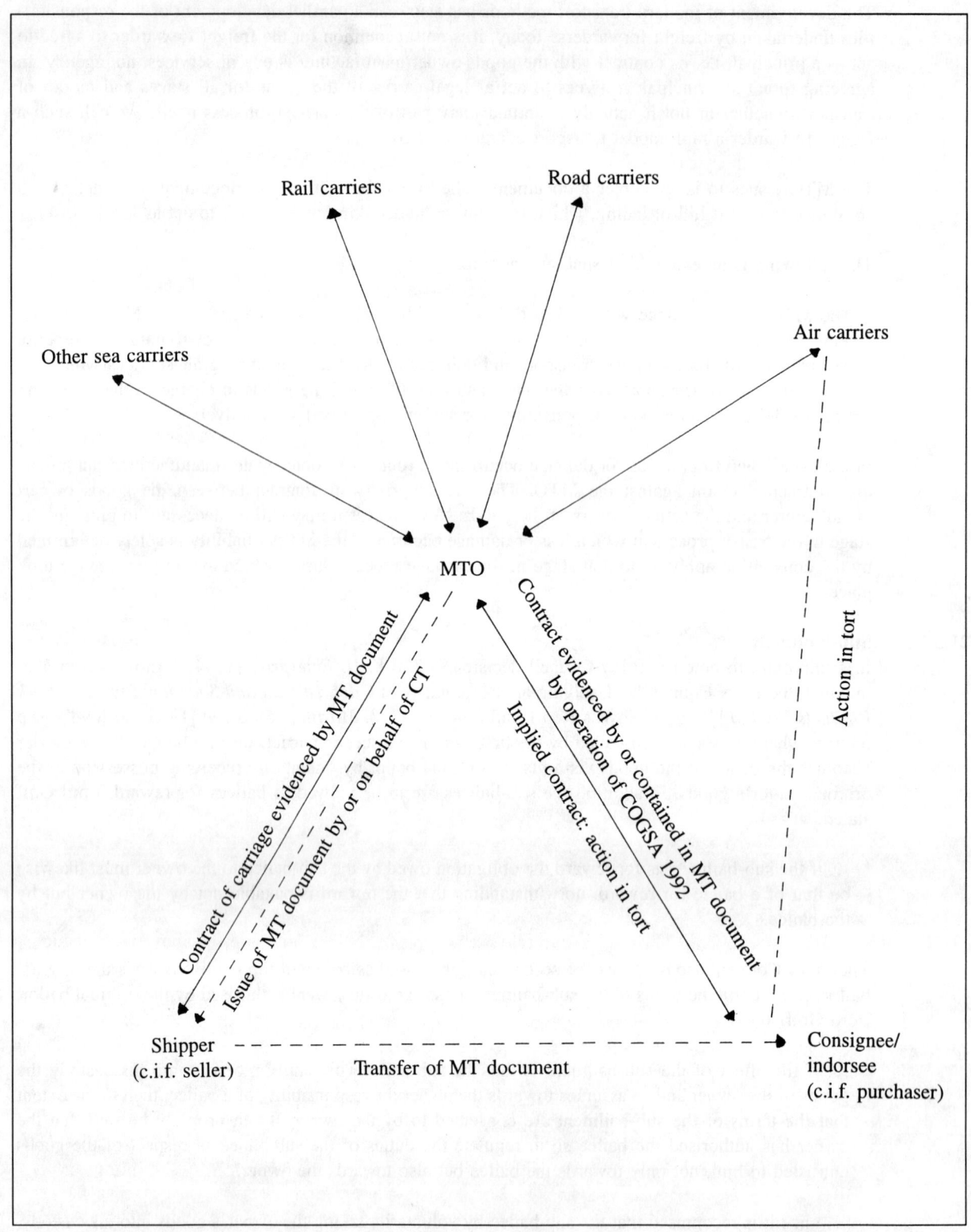

21.5.2.4   **Multimodal transport operator as sea carrier**

In **Figure 21.5,** note that where the MT document is issued to the shipper and is then transferred to the consignee/indorsee, the latter may be able to rely on COGSA 1992, s. 2, to sue the MTO sea carrier on the contract contained in the MT document. There is, in addition, the possibility of an implied contract, and an action in tort where loss or damage occurred at a time when the MTO was the bailee of those goods. An action in tort is available against the other carriers on the same basis.

Compare the MTO who undertakes legal responsibility for all stages of the voyage even though the goods are no longer in his/her custody with that of the sea carrier who issues a 'through' bill of lading in which the carrier issuing the document only agrees to act as agent of the shipper/consignee/indorsee in the forwarding of the goods. The following clause is commonly to be found in 'through' bills of lading.

> The freight received is inclusive of the cost of forwarding to ... which will be arranged through the present carrier acting as agent for the shipper and/or consignees of the goods without any liability whatsoever, the conditions of such forwarding to be covered by the current lawful forms of contract. To avoid the tendering of separate documents at each stage of the voyage, delivery at destination will be given only on due presentation of one of these sets of bills of lading unto ... or to his or their assignee and notice to this effect shall be included in the on-carrier's bill of lading or other freight contracts.

21.6   Terms of the Contract of Carriage

We now need to discuss where one looks to find the terms of the contract, if a contractual action is to be pursued.

21.6.1   CARRIAGE ON A GENERAL SHIP

Where the quantity of goods to be transported is not such as to necessitate the hiring of a ship or part of it for the voyage, the shipper will ship his goods on a 'general' ship. The shipping document issued, at the request of the shipper, will usually be either a bill of lading or a seaway bill. Note that under the Hague-Visby Rules the carrier is required, on demand of the shipper, to issue a bill of lading. Both the bill of lading and seaway bill act as a receipt for the goods. They will both contain, or at least evidence, a contract of carriage. The contract of carriage is not usually made on the issue of the bill of lading/seaway bill but will have been concluded at an earlier moment, e.g., on delivery of the goods into the custody of the shipping line: *Heskell* v *Continental Express* [1950] 1 All ER 1033.

Only the bill of lading, 'shipped' and in transferable form, will, in addition to the above two functions, operate as a document of title at common law.

On transfer of the bill of lading, rights of suit under the contract contained in or evidenced by the bill of lading are transferred to and vested in the 'holder' of the bill of lading: see COGSA 1992, s. 2(1) and s. 5(2). Once the contract has been transferred the 'holder' can sue for breaches of contract occurring before the bill of lading was transferred: *Monarch* v *Karlshamms* [1949] AC 196.

On transfer of the seaway bill rights of suit evidenced by or contained in the seaway bill are transferred to the person to whom delivery is to be made: COGSA 1992, s. 2(1).

It might still be important to consider the existence of an implied contract. It will therefore be necessary to consider what are the terms of this implied contract. Case law indicates that, in general, the terms of the implied contract are those of the document being presented or to be presented: see *Brandt* v *Liverpool Steam Navigation Co.* [1924] 1 KB 575; *The Elli 2* [1985] 1 Lloyd's Rep 107. Equally, where the document tendered refers to the terms of another shipping document those terms may be found to be the terms of the implied contract: see *Cremer* v *General Carriers SA* [1974] 1 WLR 341. However, it would appear that not all the terms will be incorporated into the implied contract.

In *The Athanasia Comninos,* a decision of the Commercial Court in 1979, but reported at [1990] 1 Lloyd's Rep 277, Mustill J in considering the terms to be imported into an implied contract stated (at 281):

[I]t cannot automatically be assumed that such a contract involves the consignee in all the obligations to which the shipper becomes subject, when he ships the goods and becomes party to the bill of lading. To my mind, the reported cases from which this notion of an implied contract is derived, make it clear that the consignee by taking delivery of the goods under the bill of lading, assumes only those rights and liabilities created by the contract of carriage which concern the carriage and delivery of the goods, and the payment therefore. The consignee is placed in this position, not by operation of law, but because the acts of presentation and delivery make it reasonable to assume that the parties intended such rights and liabilities to become mutually binding between them.

Thus in relation to a claim by shipowners against the receivers of the goods for the carriage of a dangerous cargo, Mustill J continued:

I can however, see no ground for extending this implication to embrace a warranty by the consignee as to the fitness of the goods for carriage. In the ordinary case, the person named as consignee stands in no relation to the goods at the moment of shipment. At most, he is the person to whom, if all goes well, they will ultimately be delivered at destination. There is to my mind no reason to assume, from the bare facts of presentation and delivery, that the parties intended the consignee to be made subject to a retrospective liability for acts with which he had nothing to do.

Remember that where the shipper is shipping goods on a 'general' ship but the ship is already under time or voyage charter, there is the additional problem of determining the carrier with whom the shipper contracts (**21.5.1.3**). It might, on the facts, be the case that the voyage charterer is the legal carrier and is thus the other party to a contract evidenced by or contained in a bill of lading. However, when ascertaining the existence of an *implied* contract on the terms of the bill of lading, that contract, if it exists at all, will be between the actual carrier (i.e. the shipowner or charterer by demise) and the holder of the bill of lading. (See **Figure 21.3(b)**.)

21.6.2   CARRIAGE UNDER A CHARTERPARTY

The shipper may feel that the quantity of goods to be transported necessitates the chartering of a ship or part of it. This will either be a voyage charterparty contract or, if the shipper will be shipping similar quantities over a period of time, a time charterparty. It is the charterparty to which the parties will turn to determine the terms of their carriage contract. Nevertheless, the shippers may still ask for the issue of a bill of lading. The bill of lading in these circumstances functions as a document of title and a receipt for the goods; it does *not* usually perform a contractual function. It is the charterparty which continues to govern the rights and liabilities of the shipper and the carrier: *Temperley SS Co.* v *Smyth* [1905] 2 KB 791, where Collins MR stated:

The broad distinction between the position of a charterer who ships and takes a bill of lading, and an ordinary holder of a bill of lading is, I think, that in the former case, there is the underlying contract of the charterparty which remains, until it is cancelled and taking a bill of lading does not cancel it in whole or in part unless it can be inferred from the inconsistency of the terms of the two documents, that it was intended to do so.

See also *The Filiatra Legacy* [1991] 2 Lloyd's Rep 337.

When the bill of lading issued to the charterer is transferred to a holder, the contract of carriage (the rights of which are transferred) is the contract contained in or evidenced by the bill of lading (COGSA 1992, s. 2(1) and s. 5(1)), *not* the charterparty contract. However, that does not mean to say that the charterparty has no relevance to the holder. Very often the bill of lading will purport to incorporate charterparty terms into the 'bill of lading contract': See **21.6.3**.

It is not always the case that the shipper of the goods will arrange carriage of the goods. In **18.4.1** we noted that purchasers contracting on f.o.b. terms can and quite often do arrange the shipment themselves. The importer may arrange shipment on a ship chartered by him/her and yet the shipper may require the issue of a bill of lading to himself/herself. In these circumstances the bill of lading can perform a contractual function in the hands of the shipper — *The Athanasia Comninos* a decision of 1979 but now reported in [1990] 1 Lloyd's Rep 277. The bill of lading when transferred does not usually become the contract between the carrier and the charterer: see *The Dunelmia* [1970] 1 QB 289, where it was held that the charterparty prima facie governed the contract between the carrier and the charterer (an f.o.b. importer), unless altered by the parties expressly or impliedly. Where the charterparty authorised the master to sign the bill of lading 'without prejudice to the charterparty' there could be no such implication. The words meant that the rights of the charterer against the carrier and vice versa were to be preserved. See also *The Athanasia Comninos (supra)*.

Figure 21.6(a) Identification of contracts where exporter charters the ship

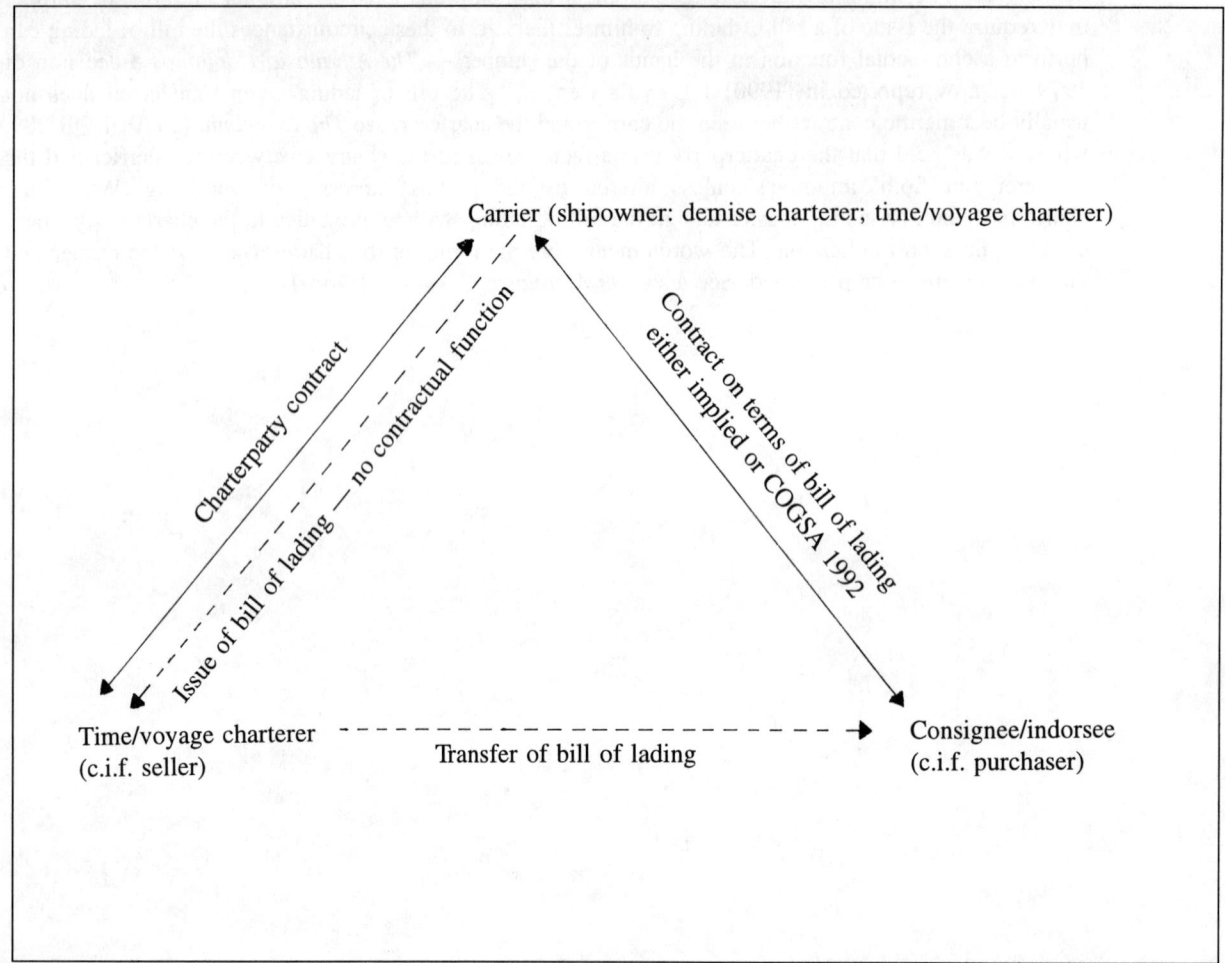

Figure 21.6(b) Identification of contracts where importer charters the ship

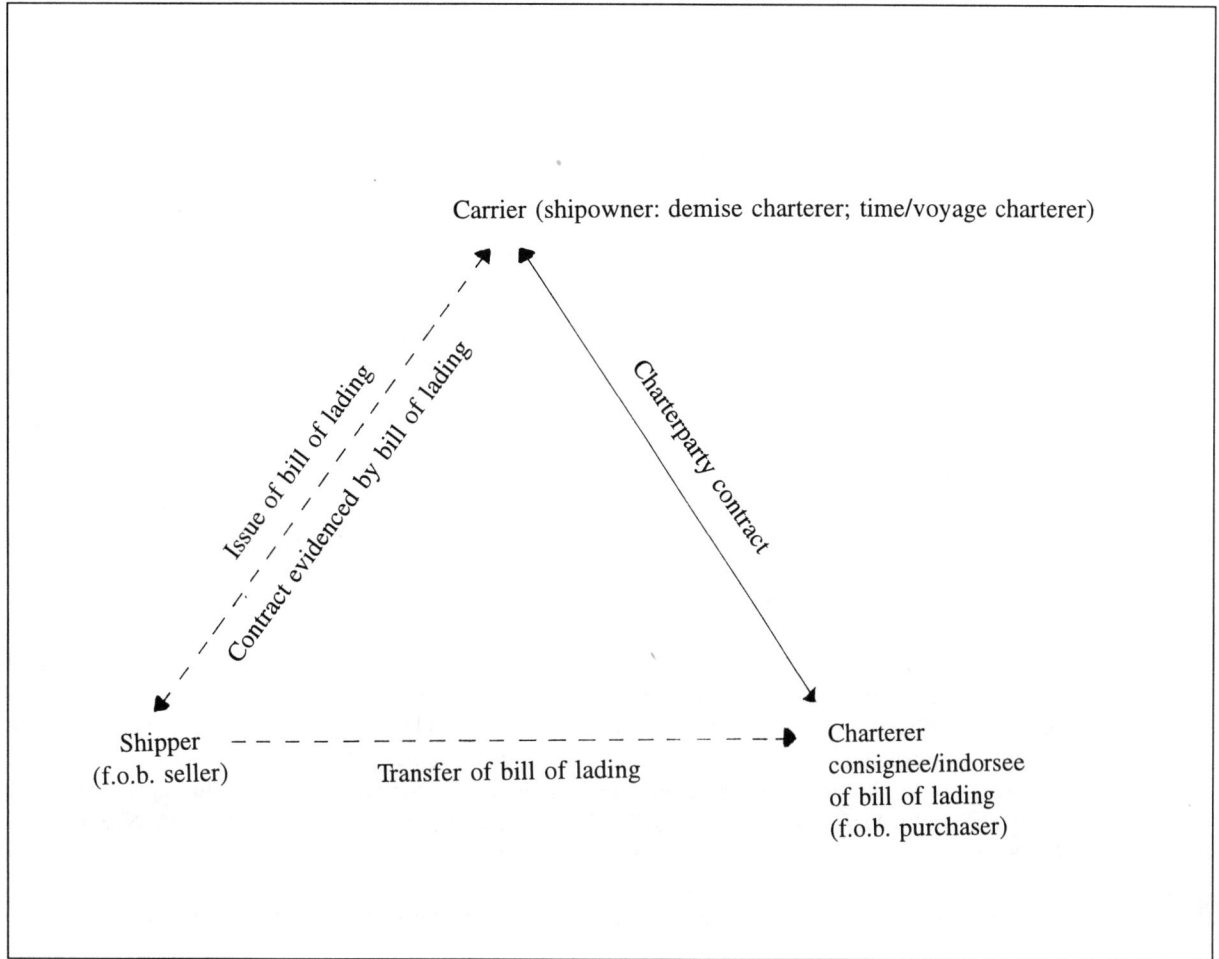

21.6.3 INCORPORATION OF CHARTERPARTY TERMS

Even though the bill of lading has a contractual function either *as* the contract of carriage or as *evidence* of it and even though a holder of it may be a stranger to the charterparty, it is common to introduce terms of the charterparty into the bill of lading contract.

The following are the principles to be considered when deciding whether any, and if so what, terms of the charterparty have been incorporated into the bill of lading.

21.6.3.1 General words of incorporation in the bill of lading

There must be general words of incorporation in the bill of lading. Sir John Donaldson in *Skips A/S Nordheim* v *Syrian Petroleum* [1984] 1 QB 599 said (at 616):

> The starting-point had always to be the provisions of the bill of lading contract producing initial incorporation. What had to be sought was *incorporation,* not *notice* of the existence of terms of another contract which was not incorporated.

21.6.3.2 Construction of incorporating clause

The incorporating clause in the bill of lading must be construed in order to see whether any term prima facie falls within it. Several of these incorporating clauses have received judicial interpretation.

'Freight and all other conditions as *per* charterparty'

This phrase has been interpreted to incorporate into the bill of lading contract all those conditions of the charterparty which are to be performed by the consignee of the goods, e.g. the payment of demurrage: *Gullischen* v *Stewart* (1884) 13 QBD 317. The stipulations covered by the clause are limited to conditions ejusdem generis with the payment of freight: *Thomas* v *Portsea SS Co.* [1912] AC 1. The words will not suffice to incorporate into the bill of lading contract clauses excluding the carrier's liability *(Russell* v *Niemann* (1864) 34 LJCP 10) or conclusive evidence clauses *(Hogarth Shipping Co.* v *Blythe, Green* [1917] 2 KB 534).

'All other terms and conditions and exceptions as *per* charterparty, including negligence clauses'

e.g. *Thomas* v *Portsea SS Co. (supra).*

'All other terms and exceptions contained in the charterparty are herewith incorporated'

e.g. *Van Liewen* v *Hollis* [1920] AC 239; *Hogarth Shipping Co.* v *Blythe, Green (supra).*

'All other terms, conditions, clauses and exceptions contained in the said charterparty, apply to this bill of lading and are deemed to be incorporated therein'

e.g. *Aktieselskabet Ocean* v *Harding* [1928] 2 KB 371.

These wide incorporating clauses allow the carrier under the bill of lading contract to escape liability by relying on a negligence exclusion clause in the charterparty, because it will have been effectively incorporated into the bill of lading contract. The words 'all conditions, clauses, terms' will only, however, incorporate stipulations from the charterparty which are germane to shipment, carriage or discharge of the cargo and payment of freight etc. These terms do not cover a stipulation which falls outside the business of carriage of the goods, e.g. an arbitration clause: *The Annefield* [1971] P 168; *Skips A/S Nordlheim* v *Syrian Petroleum (supra).*

21.6.3.3 Incorporation of arbitration clause

In order to incorporate an arbitration clause *specific* words of incorporation must be used, *which must be contained in the bill of lading itself.* A stipulation in the charterparty that all the bills of lading issued thereunder will incorporate the charterparty's arbitration clause will be of no relevance.

In *Skips A/S Nordheim v Syrian Petroleum (supra)*, the bill of lading stated that 'all conditions and exceptions of [the] charterparty including the negligence clause are deemed to be incorporated in the bill of lading'. The charterparty specifically provided that all bills of lading issued pursuant to the charter should incorporate by reference all terms and conditions of the charter including the terms of the arbitration clause. It was held by the Court of Appeal that the bill of lading could not be construed as incorporating the arbitration clause of the charterparty. Sir John Donaldson MR said (at 615-16):

> The starting-point for the resolution of this dispute must be the contract contained in or evidenced by the bill of lading, for this is the only contract to which the shipowners and the consignees are both parties. What the shipowners agreed with the charterers, whether in the charterparty or otherwise, is wholly irrelevant, save in so far as the whole or part of any such agreement has become part of the bill of lading contract. Such an incorporation cannot be achieved by agreement between the shipowners and the charterers. It can only be achieved by the agreement of the parties to the bill of lading contract and thus the operative words of incorporation must be found in the bill of lading itself.

Compare *The Merak* [1965] P 223, where words purporting to incorporate in the bill of lading 'All terms, conditions, clauses and exceptions contained in the charterparty' were held to be adequate to incorporate into the bill of lading contract the arbitration clause in the charterparty because, although there was no specific incorporation in the bills of lading, the charterparty arbitration clause expressly provided that it should be applied to disputes arising out of the charterparty or any bill of lading issued thereunder. This decision was distinguished and explained by Oliver LJ in *Skips A/S Nordheim v Syrian Petroleum* (at p. 622) on the basis that the words of incorporation were there held to be of such strength and width that they could not, in the absence of some strong indication to the contrary, be cut down or restricted. Thus, all clauses were to be applied, subject only to the test of inconsistency. Refer also to *The Federal Bulker* [1989] 1 Lloyd's Rep 103.

21.6.3.4   Consistency with express terms of bill of lading

When the term has prima facie been incorporated, it must be examined to see whether it is consistent with the express terms of the bill of lading. In *Gardner v Trechmann* (1885) 15 QBD 154 it was held that the words 'other conditions as *per* charterparty' in the bill of lading did not make the indorsee of the bill of lading liable for part of the *charter* freight. Under the bill of lading the goods were deliverable on payment of freight as stated in the *bill of lading*.

In *Kish v Taylor* [1912] AC 604 a charterparty fixed the rate of freight and stated that the shipowner had a lien for dead freight. The bill of lading issued under the charterparty referred to payment of freight at a specified rate and stated 'All other conditions as *per* charterparty'. The charterers failed to load a full and complete cargo. On arrival at the port of destination, the shipowner claimed a lien on the goods for dead freight, as set out in the charterparty. The indorsees of the bill of lading argued that *Gardner v Trechmann* applied. The House of Lords held that dead freight was merely damages for breach of contract by the charterers in failing to load a full cargo. It was not freight as such and therefore the clause in the charterparty claiming a lien for dead freight was not inconsistent with the terms of the bill of lading and could be incorporated.

In *The Merak (supra)*, the plaintiffs argued that even though there might be a prima facie incorporation of the arbitration clause into the bill of lading contract, since the Hague Rules applied to that contract, the arbitration clause must in any event be rejected as inconsistent with Article III, r. 6 of the Hague Rules, which provided for the bringing of 'suit' against the carriers. (The wording is the same under the Hague-Visby Rules.) It was held that since the Hague Rules applied internationally and Article III, r. 6 did not specify any particular mode of procedure for the settlement of disputes, the wording in Article III, r. 6 must be interpreted so as to cover different modes of procedure in different countries. 'Suit' therefore in this context could not be limited to action before the English courts. Arbitration was an accepted method of enforcing rights under a contract. Refer to *The Amazona* [1989] 2 Lloyd's Rep 130.

Where a clause is prima facie incorporated into a bill of lading to which the Hague-Visby Rules apply, but which purports to exclude or reduce the liability of the carrier below that set out in those Rules, the incorporation will be held ineffective as contravening Article III r. 8 of those Rules and thus be inconsistent with the terms of the bill of lading contract. One such instance is where the clause lays down a limitation period shorter than the one year prescribed by the Rules within which suit may be brought against the carrier. Refer to *The Amazona (supra)*.

21.6.3.5 Intention of parties to the bill of lading contract

The intention of the parties to the bill of lading contract will be considered, even if there is no inconsistency with express provision of the bill of lading.

In *Miramar Maritime Corp.* v *Holborn Oil Trading* [1984] 3 WLR 1 the bill of lading purported to incorporate all the terms of the charter (except payment and rates of freight), including a demurrage clause rendering the charterers liable for demurrage. The owners claimed that the demurrage clause thereby incorporated into the bill of lading rendered the consignees of the cargo, as holders of the bill of lading, directly liable for the demurrage incurred. It was held in the House of Lords that on the true construction of the language of the bill of lading it was the intention of the parties to the bill of lading contract that the charterers alone should be liable for demurrage. There was no rule of construction that the clauses in the charterparty which were directly relevant to the shipment, carriage or delivery of the goods and which imposed obligations on the charterer, were presumed to be incorporated into the bill of lading with the substitution of 'charterer' by the phrase 'bill of lading holder'. Lord Diplock said (at 6):

> So if the owners are right in their contention [that the bill of lading holder is liable for demurrage] every consignee to whom a bill of lading covering any part of the cargo is negotiated, is not only accepting personal liability to pay to the owners freight, as stated in the bill of lading, but is also accepting blindfold a potential liability to pay an unknown and wholly unpredictable sum for demurrage which may, unknown to him, already have accrued or may subsequently accrue without any ability on his own part to prevent it, even though that sum may actually exceed the delivered value of the goods to which the bill of lading gives title... I venture to assert that no business man who had not taken leave of his senses would intentionally enter into a contract which exposed him to a potential liability of this kind; and this, in itself, I find to be an overwhelming reason for not indulging in verbal manipulation of the actual contractual words used in the charterparty so as to give to them this effect when they are treated as incorporated in the bill of lading.

21.6.4 CARRIAGE FOR WHICH FREIGHT FORWARDER IS RESPONSIBLE

Where the freight forwarder undertakes responsibility as a carrier during the transport of the goods, it is the combined transport document which he issues which will set out the terms of his contract of carriage.

21.6.5 WHOM TO SUE: PROBLEMS OF EVIDENCE

It is worth pointing out that the evidence available to the goods owner before action is brought as to the stage at which damage or loss took place may not be decisive. Did it occur before the carrier took custody of the goods or not? In addition, even if the evidence as to *when* the damage took place is pretty clear, it may not be so clear as to *why* it happened. Was it due to the shipment, by the seller, of goods not fit to withstand the ordinary incidents of the voyage? If the answer to that question is yes, would it still be possible successfully to sue the carrier on the basis of the operation of estoppel? The limitation period in an action on a contract of sale is six years from the date of the breach. In those contracts of carriage governed by the Hague-Visby Rules suit cannot be brought more than one year after delivery of the goods or the date when delivery should have taken place: Hague-Visby Rules, Article III, r. 6. In the circumstances the purchaser may feel it is in his best interest to commence action against the carrier as well as the seller of the goods. Where, on the evidence before the court, the loss or damage took place before the provisional delivery point in the c.i.f. or f.o.b. contract (e.g. before shipment) and yet whilst the goods were in the custody of the carrier, judgment may be obtained against both seller and carrier. Where the evidence shows the loss or damage to have occurred after the provisional delivery by the seller and to be not due to defects existing before the provisional delivery point, there will be no finding of liability against the seller. Where carriage of goods is multi-modal and no one carrier has undertaken responsibility for the overall transport, it may be necessary, bearing in mind the difficulties of proving when the damage took place during the transit (especially if the goods have been transported by container) and the severely short limitation periods that can apply to an action brought against the carrier(s), to issue writs against some or all of the carriers involved in the carriage of the goods.

21.7   The Hague-Visby Rules

Where loss and damage has occurred to the goods during transport and it is sought to bring an action in contract against the carrier, not only must the contractual document be studied, but also consideration must be given to the question of whether the contract is subject to the Hague-Visby Rules. These Rules were implemented in the United Kingdom by means of the Carriage of Goods by Sea Act (COGSA) 1971. These Rules implement certain amendments to the Hague Rules brought into force in the United Kingdom by means of the Carriage of Goods by Sea Act 1924. The 1971 Act has repealed the 1924 Act and reintroduced the original Hague Rules with the various amendments to them. The Hague-Visby Rules lay down minimum duties and liabilities on the part of the carrier, from which they permit no derogation. When they apply, they thus limit the carrier's freedom to contract.

21.7.1   CIRCUMSTANCES IN WHICH THE HAGUE-VISBY RULES APPLY

The Hague-Visby Rules apply as laid down in Article X thereof and as provided by COGSA 1971, s. 1(3) and (6). The criteria fall under three headings:

(a)   the scope of the voyage;
(b)   the status of the document to which they may apply;
(c)   the nature of the goods.

21.7.1.1   The voyage
The Hague-Visby Rules apply only in the following situations:

(a)   Where the port of shipment is a port in the UK: COGSA 1971, s. 1(3) and Article X.
(b)   Where the ports of shipment and destination are UK ports: COGSA 1971, s. 1(3) (i.e. the rules will apply to UK coastal trade).
(c)   Where the voyage is between ports in two different states, *and*:

(i)   The bill of lading is issued in a contracting state: Article X(a). (Note that the ports of shipment and destination need not be in contracting states, as long as they are in different states and the bill of lading has been issued in a contracting state.) Or,
(ii)   The carriage is from a port in a contracting state: Article X(b). (Note that where the port of shipment is in a contracting state, it is irrelevant that the port of destination is not in a contracting state nor the bill of lading issued in a contracting state.) In (a)–(c) the Rules will have statutory force without any express incorporation of them into the contract.

(d)   Where the voyage is between ports in different states and the contract contained in or evidenced by the bill of lading provides that the Hague-Visby Rules should apply: Article X(c).
(e)   Whether or not the carriage is between ports in different states, where the contract contained in or evidenced by the bill of lading expressly provides that the Hague-Visby Rules shall apply: COGSA 1971, s. 1(6)(a).
(f)   Whether or not the carriage is between ports in different states, where the contract is contained in or evidenced by a non-negotiable receipt marked as such, and expressly provides that the Hague-Visby Rules are to govern the contract, as if the receipt were a bill of lading: COGSA 1971, s. 1(6)(b).

In (d)–(f) the Hague-Visby Rules shall have statutory force, by virtue of their direct incorporation into the contract.

(g)   If the contract of carriage (either evidenced by or contained in the bill of lading) provides that the legislation of any state which gives effect to the Rules is to govern the contract (Article X(c)). In this situation the Hague-Visby Rules will have statutory force. See *The Komninos S* [1991] 1 Lloyd's Rep 370 (CA).

21.7.1.2   Documents

It is not sufficient to identify the type of voyage for the purpose of ascertaining the applicability of the Hague-Visby Rules. It is also necessary to consider the type of document used or contemplated. The Hague-Visby Rules apply 'to contracts of carriage covered by a bill of lading or any similar document of title': Article I(b) and COGSA 1971, s. 1(4). See *Pyrene Co. Ltd* v *Scindia Navigation Co. Ltd* [1954] 2 All ER 158.

The phrase 'similar document of title' probably refers to documents which by custom in the trade are used to transfer possession. In *Kum* v *Wah Tat Bank Ltd* [1971] 1 Lloyd's Rep 439. the mate's receipt was treated by local custom as a document of title on the Singapore-Sarawak routes. It is unclear whether 'through' bills of lading, combined transport documents and waybills fall within the phrase, but as to waybills see s. 1(6)(b).

The rules apply only '... *from the moment at which such bill of lading or similar document of title regulates the relations between a carrier and a holder of the same*'. (See **21.3** and **Figure 21.6(a)** and **(b)** for a consideration of when a bill of lading has contractual force.)

Even though the document used or contemplated does not fall within the category 'bill of lading or similar document of title', the Hague-Visby Rules shall have *statutory* force through a voluntary contractual tie where:

(a)   the contract is contained in or evidenced by a non-negotiable receipt (e.g. a seaway bill) *marked as such*; and

(b)   the contract expressly provides that the Rules are to govern the contract '*as if the receipt were a bill of lading*': COGSA 1971, s. 1(6)(b).

Although the receipt must be marked 'non-negotiable' (*The European Enterprise* [1989] 2 Lloyd's Rep 185), whether the wording emphasised in (b) above must actually be set out in the receipt is the subject of conflicting decisions at first instance. See *The Vechscroon* [1982] 1 Lloyd's Rep 301 where Lloyd J held that general words of incorporation sufficed to give the Rules statutory force; and *The European Enterprise* [1989] 2 Lloyd's Rep 185 where Steyn J held that the phrase as emphasised above must be used, or at least similar wording. In addition, Steyn J held that in order for the Rules to have statutory force, the receipt must expressly provide that the whole body of Rules apply.

Note: not all the Rules are incorporated by statute where s. 1(6)(b) applies. Article III, r. 4 (second sentence) and Article III, r. 7 are inapplicable. See s. 1(6)(b).

Where there is an express incorporation but the document is not marked as non-negotiable, unless the document can be treated as a 'similar document of title' to a bill of lading, the Hague-Visby Rules will have contractual force only, by virtue of an express incorporation.

21.7.1.3   Goods

Even though the voyage falls within Article X or COGSA 1971, s. 1(3) and a bill of lading or 'similar document of title' has or is to be issued, the Hague-Visby Rules will not have statutory force in relation to animals or deck cargo (Article I(c)) unless there has been an express incorporation of the Hague-Visby Rules into the bill of lading or non-negotiable receipt: COGSA 1971, s. 1(7).

For the purposes of the applicability of the Rules, deck cargo is not simply cargo carried on deck, but cargo which is carried on deck *with* a statement in the contract of carriage that the goods are or will be carried on deck. Therefore a clause in the bill of lading giving liberty to carry on deck unaccompanied by any statement in the bill of lading that the goods are or will be carried on deck, will not enable the cargo to be classed as deck cargo under Article l(c): *Svenska Traktor Akt.* v *Maritime Agencies (Southampton) Ltd* [1953] 2 QB 295.

21.7.2   EXCLUSIVE JURISDICTION CLAUSES

Where proceedings against the carrier have been commenced in the English courts, if the carriage of the goods falls within Article X or COGSA 1971, s. 1(3) or (6), the English courts will apply the Hague-Visby Rules.

The carrier may seek to rely on an exclusive jurisdiction clause. However, where the English court is the forum and the carriage falls within Article X or s. 1(3) or (6), the court will not immediately apply the proper law of the contract to determine the validity of the exclusive jurisdiction clause. It will initially apply COGSA 1971 and the Rules it implements. Under Hague-Visby Rules, Article III, r. 8:

> Any clause, covenant, or agreement in a contract of carriage relieving the carrier or the ship from liability for loss or damage, to, or in connection with goods, arising from the negligence, fault or failure in the duties and obligations provided in this article or lessening such liability otherwise than as provided in these Rules, shall be null and void and of no effect...

Thus where it is established that the foreign court chosen as the exclusive forum would apply a domestic substantive law which would result in a reduction of the liability of the carrier *below* that set out in the Rules (either by exclusion or limitation), the English court will treat the choice of forum clause as of no effect: *The Hollandia* [1982] 3 All ER 1141. This does not mean that the English court awards itself jurisdiction to hear the action. On an application to stay the proceedings in the English court, the burden of proof is now on the defendant carrier to show (without the exclusive jurisdiction clause) that there is another more appropriate forum to hear the action: *The Hollandia (supra)*. (But note, where the exclusive jurisdiction clause falls within Article 17 of the Brussels Convention on Jurisdiction, the English court has no discretion. The English court will have no jurisdiction.)

The same principle applies where the parties have chosen as the proper law of the contract a system of law which would lessen the liability of the carrier below that set out in the Rules. The chosen law clause, in so far as it lessens the carrier's liability in connection with the goods will be null and void: Article III, r. 8; *The Hollandia (supra)*.

This does not mean that the parties' chosen proper law is ignored. In relation to those parts of the contract of carriage to which the Hague-Visby Rules do not apply, e.g. claim for freight, the English court can and usually will apply the chosen proper law.

Be aware that action brought in a forum in breach of an exclusive jurisdiction clause may well mean the action is statute-barred under Article III, r. 6. See *The Havhelt* [1993] 1 Lloyd's Rep 523.

21.7.3   STAGE IN VOYAGE DURING WHICH RULES APPLY

Once it has been determined that in all the circumstances, the Rules apply to the contract of carriage, it is necessary to determine at what *stage* the Hague-Visby Rules begin to operate on the contract of carriage. Article I(e) defines 'carriage of goods' as covering the period from the time when the goods are loaded to the time they are discharged from the ship. It is made clearer in Article II and Article III that they apply during loading and discharge. It is to be noted, however, that in *Pyrene* v *Scindia Navigation Co. Ltd* [1954] 2 All ER 158 (a case dealing with the applicability of the Hague Rules but the position in this respect is the same under the Hague-Visby Rules), Devlin J stated obiter that although Article I(e) and Article II referred to the Rules applying from the loading through to the discharging process this did not mean that the Rules, with all the immunities and the limitation of liability, applied to the whole loading and discharging processes. The object of the Rules is not to define the scope of the contract of carriage but the terms on which that service is to be performed — *not* that the carrier shall load and shall do it properly, but that the carrier shall do whatever loading he/she does properly and carefully. See also *G.H. Renton* v *Palmyra Trading* [1957] AC 149. Refer to the Court of Appeal decision on an Ord. 14 application in *The Coral* [1993] 1 Lloyd's Rep 1 for application of the *Pyrene* decision.

The Rules do not apply to restrict the carrier's freedom of contract pre-loading and post-delivery: Article VII.

21.8   Duties of Carrier under the Hague-Visby Rules

21.8.1   SEAWORTHY SHIP: ARTICLE III RULE 1

21.8.1.1   Duties

As at common law, the carrier is under a duty to provide a seaworthy ship. However, unlike the position at common law, the Rules do not place an absolute duty on the carrier: COGSA 1971, s. 3. In its place is a duty, before and at the beginning of the voyage, to exercise due diligence to provide a ship which is seaworthy, properly manned, equipped and supplied, and in every way fit to receive, carry and preserve the goods — in other words, a ship which is both seaworthy and cargoworthy: Article III, r. 1.

The duty under Article III, r. 1 commences 'before and at the beginning of the voyage'. This means the period from at least the beginning of loading until the vessel starts on her journey: *Maxine Footwear* v *Canadian Government Merchant Marine* [1959] AC 589. The duty under Article III, r. 1 does not operate throughout the transit of the goods — it finishes once the vessel begins its contractual voyage: *The Makedonia* [1962] P 190. Thus defects in a ship occurring en route which render the ship unseaworthy but which are not referable to a state of affairs existing at the time the ship began its contractual voyage, will not enable the shipper/consignee/indorsee to argue a breach of Article III, r. 1.

At common law, the doctrine of stages applies, in which the ship has to be seaworthy only for the first stage of the voyage, the duty to provide a seaworthy ship being resurrected at the intermediate fuelling stages of the contractual voyage. Under the Rules, the doctrine of stages no longer applies — the ship must be seaworthy at the time the ship begins performance of its contract of carriage in relation to the goods then shipped: *The Makedonia (supra)*.

There will be *de facto* unseaworthiness where, for example:

(a)   The ship is not reasonably fit at the time of sailing to receive, carry and discharge the cargo delivered to it, to the specified destination: *The Good Friend* [1984] 2 Lloyd's Rep 586: *The Gudermes* [1991] 1 Lloyd's Rep 456.
(b)   The condition of the ship at the time of sailing makes port authority action at a subsequent contractual port inevitable, e.g. fumigation of the ship: *Ciampa* v *British Steam Navigation Co.* [1915] 2 KB 774.
(c)   The cargo is stowed in such a way, at the time of sailing, that the safety of the ship is endangered: *Kopitoff* v *Wilson* (1876) 1 QBD 377.

Bad stowage which merely affects other cargo does not make the ship unseaworthy: *Elder, Dempster* v *Paterson, Zochonis* [1924] AC 522.

Where there is a temporary impediment existing at the time of sailing which causes delay in completion of the voyage, the ship is not unseaworthy: *The Acquacharm* [1982] 1 WLR 119.

In considering whether there is *de facto* unseaworthiness at the commencement of the contractual voyage, it must be noted that the duty is one of provision of a ship which is *reasonably* fit to withstand the ordinary perils of the journey.

The duty placed on the carrier is one of due diligence to provide a seaworthy ship; this duty will not be discharged by the exercise of personal diligence by the carrier. In other words, the carrier does not discharge the burden of proving due diligence by proving that he/she engaged competent experts to perform and/or supervise making the ship seaworthy. In *Riverstone Meat Co. v Lancashire Shipping Co.* [1961] AC 807 it was held in the House of Lords that the obligation placed on the carrier to make the ship seaworthy was one of due diligence by whomsoever it might be done, even when the work was delegated to independent contractors and called for technical or special knowledge or experience and even though the negligence was not apparent to the carrier.

21.8.1.2   Burden of proof

If the cargo owner is alleging a breach of Article III, r. 1, he/she has to show:

    (a)   *de facto* unseaworthiness at the commencement of the contractual voyage; and

    (b)   a causal connection between the unseaworthiness and the loss: *The Europa* [1908] P 84.

Sometimes the facts themselves afford prima facie evidence of unseaworthiness, for example if the ship sinks or permits ingress of water shortly after leaving port and for no apparent reason. See *Madras v P & O* [1924] 18 Lloyd's Rep 93; *Anderson v Morice* (1876) 1 App Cas 713.

It is not necessary to show that the unseaworthiness was the cause of the loss. It will be sufficient if the unseaworthiness was a cause of the loss: *Monarch v Karlshamns* [1949] AC 196; *Smith, Hogg and Co. v Black Sea and Baltic General Insurance Co.* [1940] AC 997.

The burden then shifts to the carrier, who will be liable unless he/she can show due diligence by himself/herself and his/her servants and agents: Article IV, r. 1.

21.8.1.3   Consequences of breach of Article III, rule 1

The carrier, if he/she fails to discharge the burden under Article IV, r. 1, will be liable for the loss, even though there were other *co-operating* causes for which he/she could otherwise rely on an exclusion clause in Article IV, r. 2(a)–(q). Thus we call the obligation to provide a seaworthy ship under Article III, r. 1 an overriding obligation. See *Mediterranean Freight Service Ltd v BP Oil International Ltd, The Times* 27 July 1994.

Where a breach of Article III, r. 1 has occurred, whether the cargo owner can treat the contract as repudiated will depend on the consequences of the breach: *Hong Kong Fir Shipping Co. Ltd v Kawasaki Kisen Kaisha Ltd* [1962] 2 QB 26:

> The express or implied obligation of seaworthiness is neither a condition nor a warranty, but one of that large class of contractual undertakings one breach of which might have the effect ascribed to a breach of condition under the Sale of Goods Act and a different breach of which might have only the same effect as that ascribed to a breach of warranty.

21.8.2   OBLIGATION PROPERLY AND CAREFULLY TO CARRY THE GOODS: ARTICLE III, RULE 2

21.8.2.1   Duties

At common law the carrier is absolutely responsible for delivering the goods received by him/her in the same condition as when they were shipped, unless:

    (a)   the loss or damage resulted from one of the common law exceptions; *and*

    (b)   there has been no negligence on the part of the carrier.

Thus, at common law, the issue of lack of care in relation to the carriage of the goods (the burden resting on the cargo owner) only arises once there is reliance by the carrier on a common law exception.

The exceptions enabling the carrier at common law to escape liability are as follows:

(a)   act of God, e.g. frost, high winds, lightning, fog;
(b)   act of the Queen's enemies;
(c)   inherent vice (i.e. the inherent quality of the goods shipped, defective packing);
(d)   jettison.

Under the Hague-Visby Rules, the obligation on the carrier in relation to the carriage of the goods is no longer absolute. In its place is a duty to 'properly and carefully load, handle, stow, carry, keep, care for and discharge the goods carried': Article III, r. 2. See *The Captain Gregos* [1990] 1 Lloyd's Rep 310.

This obligation arises as soon as that part of the loading operation which the carrier has undertaken commences, and extends throughout the contractual voyage until that part of the discharge operation undertaken by the carrier has been completed. It is in this respect a far wider duty than that under Article III, r. 1.

Article III, r. 2 is expressly subject to Article IV. The Hague-Visby Rules have both increased the number of exclusions from liability on which the carrier can rely and yet prohibited the carrier from introducing yet more exclusion clauses. Before we consider these clauses individually we need to consider the burden of proof.

21.8.2.2   Burden of proof
The burden is initially on the claimant to prove on the balance of probabilities:

(a)   that the goods were received by the carrier in good condition; and
(b)   that they were missing/damaged when delivered at destination.

This raises the inference that the damage or loss occurred whilst the goods were in the custody of the carrier.

In respect of the burden placed on the claimant under (a), for proof that the goods were received by the carrier in good condition the claimant will need to consider initially the probative value of the bill of lading. Normally the shipper will have filled in the bill of lading, setting out the number of packages or the quality or weight of the goods to be carried; he/she may set out the number of packages and the weight. The shipper, after delivering the goods to the carrier, can demand the issue of (i.e. signing of) the bill of lading showing the number of packages *or* pieces *or* quality *or* weight: Article III, r. 3(b).

Where the carrier issues the bill of lading with a statement as to quantity, weight etc., that will amount to prima facie evidence of the receipt by the carrier of goods of that quantity, weight etc.: Article III, r. 4. The carrier must contest the evidence of loss or damage in the prima facie case made out by the claimant. Where, however, the claimant is a transferee in good faith of the bill of lading, the carrier is estopped from adducing evidence to show that he/she never received goods of that quantity, weight etc. Note that the estoppel does not operate in relation to documents other than a bill of lading or similar document of title: see COGSA 1971, s. 1(7).

The carrier's duty is only to issue a bill of lading with one of the above items. In addition the carrier is not bound to issue a bill of lading with any of the above if he/she reasonably suspects that they do not accurately represent the goods received or if he/she has had no reasonable means of checking the goods: Article III, r. 3 proviso. Thus the carrier can qualify a representation in the bill of lading as to quantity, weight etc. with the words 'unknown' or 'shipper load and count' or 'said by shipper to contain', thereby making it possible for him/her to deny the probative value of the bill of lading.

Article III, r. 3 also imposes an obligation on the carrier to issue a bill of lading, on the demand of the shipper, showing the apparent order and condition of the goods on receipt. The probative force of the statement 'shipped in apparent good order and condition' is qualified since it only amounts to evidence or conclusive evidence where the condition or damage complained of could be seen on a reasonable external examination: *Silver* v *Ocean SS Co.* [1930] 1 KB 416. 'Apparent' means that which can be seen on a reasonable external examination. Bearing this in mind, a statement that goods were shipped in apparent good order and condition will amount to prima facie evidence against the carrier when sued by the shipper: Article III, r. 3. However, when the claimant is the transferee of the bill of lading, the carrier will be estopped from adducing evidence as to an overtly defective condition of the goods on shipment: Article III, r. 4. The estoppel does not operate in relation to non-transferable documents: see COGSA 1971, s. 1(7) and **21.12**.

Looking again at the first part of the burden of proof placed on the claimant, this may easily be discharged by putting in evidence the bill of lading. If on the facts the bill of lading does not amount to evidence of the quantity or weight etc, of the goods received or of a particular condition of the goods (e.g. where goods have been sealed in a container at the exporter's premises), evidence must come from another source, e.g. from an independent inspector at the time of receipt or shipment.

Once the claimant has discharged the burden under (a) and (b), the legal burden then shifts to the carrier to show that the cause of the loss or damage falls within one or more of the exceptions: *The Torenia* [1983] 2 Lloyd's Rep 210:

> Where the facts disclose that the loss was caused by the concurrent causative effects of an excepted and a non-excepted peril, the carrier remains liable. He can only escape liability to the extent that he can prove that the loss or damage was caused by the excepted peril alone.

Where the carrier has satisfied the legal burden, that may well be the end of the matter, either because the exception excludes liability for negligence (e.g. Article IV, r. 2(a)(b)) or because in discharging the legal burden, the carrier was obliged to prove the absence of negligence by himself/ herself or his/her servants or agents: Article IV, r. 2(q).

With respect to the other exceptions, however, the position is probably the same as at common law, where negligence has the effect of rendering inoperative another specific exception. Thus the claimant can still defeat the carrier's reliance on specific exceptions under Article IV, r. 2 by showing lack of care on the carrier's etc. part.

21.8.2.3 Exclusions from liability: Article IV, rule 2

The exclusions from liability contained in Article IV, r. 2 include the following:

'Act, neglect or default of the master, mariner, pilot, or the servants of the carrier in the navigation or in the management of the ship': Article IV, r. 2(a).

It will be observed that this exclusion covers only an act, neglect or default in the management or navigation of the ship. See *Gosse Millard* v *Canadian Government Merchant Marine Ltd, The Canadian Highlander* [1929] AC 223, where a distinction was drawn between want of care of cargo and want of care of vessel indirectly affecting the cargo. See also *The Washington* [1976] 2 Lloyd's Rep 453. This exception does *not* cover the actual fault or privity of the *carrier* himself/herself.

'Fire, unless caused by the actual fault or privity of the carrier': Article IV, r. 2(b).

Under this exception, the carrier will not be liable for loss or damage resulting from fire, even though caused by the negligence of his/her servants or agents. The carrier will, however, be liable if the loss was caused by his/her own 'actual fault or privity' *or* if the fire resulted from unseaworthiness of the ship in breach of Article III, r. 1. This will be so whether the unseaworthiness was due to the carrier's actual fault or privity or the negligence of his/her servants or agents. If the unseaworthiness was *a* cause of the loss albeit a cooperating cause, the carrier will be liable for the whole loss (see **21.8.1.3**).

In the following circumstances, the carrier can escape liability even though the fire did result from his/her actual fault or privity and/or unseaworthiness. Under Merchant Shipping Act 1995, s. 186 where the fire occurs (a) on board (b) a British ship, the carrier can escape liability, unless the case falls under sch. 7, Article 4, i.e. unless it is proved that the loss resulted from his/her personal act or omission, committed with the intent to cause such loss, or recklessly and with knowledge that such loss would probably result. Note that COGSA 1971, s. 6(4) has been amended to provide that for the purposes of Hague-Visby Rules, Article VIII, Merchant Shipping Act 1995, s. 186, is a provision relating to limitation of liability. See s. 1A COGSA 1971 inserted by virtue of s. 314 and sch. 13 Merchant Shipping Act 1995.

'Perils, dangers and accidents of the sea or other navigable waters': Article IV, r. 2(c)
This exception covers perils of the sea, rivers, harbours and ports. It does not, however, cover 'that natural and inevitable action of the wind and waves which results in what may be described as wear and tear ...': *The Xantho* (1887) 12 App Cas 503. Furthermore, the accident which has occurred must not be one which can also occur on land, e.g. the exception does not cover loss caused by rats, cockroaches, lightening, fog etc.

The carrier has to show that the loss or damage was caused by the peril of the sea in the sense of damage which is a natural and necessary consequence of perils of the sea: *The Thrunscoe* [1897] P 301. It not infrequently happens, however, that a cooperating cause of the loss by perils of the sea is the unseaworthiness of the ship itself, in which case the carrier will be liable for the whole loss unless he/she can show that he/she fulfilled the duty to exercise diligence to make the ship seaworthy: Article IV, r. 1; Article IV, r. 2(p); *The Torenia* [1983] 2 Lloyd's Rep 210.

'Act or omission of the shipper or owner of the goods, his agent or representative': Article IV, r. 2(i)
The carrier can rely on this exception where, e.g., he/she proves that damage is due to bad stowage which had been undertaken at the direction of the shipper: *Ismail* v *Polish Ocean Lines* [1976] 1 All ER 902. If the carrier wants to argue that the shipper omitted to ship the number of articles as stated in the bill of lading, he/she may be estopped from adducing such evidence.

'Wastage in bulk or weight or any other loss or damage arising from inherent defect, quality or vice of the goods': Article IV, r. 2(m)
This is part of the common law exception of inherent vice. The carrier will be arguing that the wastage etc. arises from the unfitness of the goods to withstand the ordinary incidents of the voyage, bearing in mind the degree of care which the carrier is required by his/her contract to exercise in relation to the goods.

The carrier may be estopped from relying on this exception where the defect in the goods could be seen on a reasonable external examination and there was a statement in the bill of lading that the goods were shipped in apparent good order and condition.

'Insufficiency of packing': Article IV, r. 2(n)
This covers the situation where goods are not sufficiently well packed to withstand the ordinary incidents of the voyage. It has been suggested that this exception will allow the carrier to escape liability for loss caused to goods through the insufficiency of packing of *other* goods: *Goodwin Ferreira* v *Lamport Holt* [1929] All ER 623. Again, depending on the nature of the insufficiency, the carrier may be estopped from relying on this exception where there is a statement in the bill of lading, 'shipped in apparent good order and condition'.

'Insufficiency or inadequacy of marks': Article IV, r. 2(o)
This exception is narrow and will only cover *inadequacy* or *insufficiency* of the marks, and will not cover incorrect marks. Under Article III, r. 3 the carrier can be asked by the shipper to issue, on receipt of the goods, a bill of lading showing the leading marks necessary for the identification of the goods. However, the carrier is not compelled to issue the bill of lading showing these marks if they are not shown clearly on the coverings or the goods themselves if uncovered, or if these marks will not remain legible throughout the voyage, or if he has no means of checking that the markings on the goods are

as described in the bill of lading (e.g. where the goods are in a container), or where he is asked to record on the bill of lading marks which he suspects do not tally with the marks on the goods actually received.

In the hands of the shipper the bill of lading will be prima facie evidence against the carrier that the carrier received the goods as marked. The carrier can contest that evidence by showing that the marks were incorrect or can discharge the legal burden placed on him/her by showing that the inability to deliver the goods as marked in the bill of lading was due to their insufficiency under Article IV, r. 2(o) or some other peril (e.g. Article IV, r. 2(c)), As against the transferee, the carrier will not be estopped from acquiring evidence as to the inadequacy or insufficiency of the marks, but will be estopped from adducing evidence that the marks on the bill of lading were incorrect.

'Any other cause arising without actual fault or privity of the carrier, or without the fault or neglect of the agents or servants of the carrier, but the burden of proof shall be on the person claiming the benefit of this exception to show that neither the actual fault or privity of the carrier nor the fault or neglect of the agents or servants of the carrier contributed to the loss or damage': Article IV, r. 2(q)

This is the general exception on which the carrier will rely if he/she cannot avoid liability by relying on a specific exception. Essentially the carrier is proving performance of the duty under Article III, r. 2. The carrier cannot escape liability for breach of Article III, r. 2 by stating that, e.g. he/she employed a competent crew, but must prove lack of negligence by himself/herself, his/her servants and agents: *International Packers* v *Ocean SS Co.* [1955] 2 Lloyd's Rep 218; *Leesh River Tea Co.* v *British India Steam Navigation Co.* [1967] 2 QB 250.

21.8.3 OBLIGATION NOT TO DEVIATE UNJUSTIFIABLY

21.8.3.1 Justifiable/reasonable deviation

The Hague-Visby Rules preserve this common law obligation not to deviate, but extend the circumstances in which a deviation will be justifiable. Under Article IV, r. 4, a deviation is justified if:

(a) It is made in saving or attempting to save a life at sea (also justifiable at common law).
(b) It is made in saving or attempting to save property at sea (not justifiable at common law).
(c) Any reasonable deviation, e.g. to repair the ship (also justifiable at common law).

As to what is a reasonable deviation Lord Atkins in *Stag Line Ltd* v *Foscolo, Mango and Co. Ltd* [1932] AC 328 said:

The true test seems to be what departure from the contract voyage might a prudent person controlling the voyage at the time make and maintain, having in mind all the relevant circumstances existing at the time including the terms of the contract and the interests of all the parties concerned but without obligation to consider the interest of anyone as conclusive.

A deviation will be reasonable where it is necessary to repair the ship; this is so even though the defect amounted to breach of the obligation to provide a seaworthy ship: *Kish* v *Taylor* [19121 AC 604. Lord Atkinson said: 'It is the presence of the peril and not its cause, which determines the character of the deviation'. See also *The Al Taha* [1990] 2 Lloyd's Rep 117.

21.8.3.2 Determining whether there has been deviation

Before we can consider whether the deviation is justifiable or not, and its effect on the contract, we must determine whether or not there has been a deviation. In order to do this the contractual route must be ascertained. This will be:

(a) a specified route in the bill of lading; or
(b) if no route has been specified, the usual route. If there is no evidence given of the 'usual' route, it will be presumed to be the direct geographical route: *Reardon, Smith* v *Black Sea & Baltic General Insurance Co.* [1939] AC 562.

However, most bills of lading contain a clause which gives the carrier liberty to deviate. That clause is a term of the contract, and forms part of the definition of the contractual voyage. A detour to a port under the clause will *not*, therefore, amount to a deviation. Nevertheless, the courts restrict the ambit of liberty to deviate clauses by following the principle that a liberty to deviate clause will be construed in the light of the intended voyage. Lord Jenkins in *G.H. Renton v Palmyra Trading* [1956] 1 All ER 209 said:

> One must consider the particular contract into which the parties have entered, and if there be some printed condition which would defeat the object and intention of the parties to the contract, it should be limited or disregarded and this applies especially in the case of perishable goods. Where a bill of lading is concluded by means of a printed form comprising general conditions into which the parties write, type or otherwise incorporate the terms agreed upon in respect of the particular transaction in view (for example, the termini of the voyage contracted for) and if the printed condition is found to be inconsistent with or repugnant to the main object and intention of the bill of lading as disclosed by the terms specially agreed, the court will limit or modify the conflicting printed condition to the extent necessary to enable effect to be given to such main object and intention, or in the case of complete repugnancy, reject it.

In *Leduc v Ward* (1888) 20 QBD 475, where a bill of lading reserved a liberty to call at any ports in any order, the court restricted the operation of the liberty clause to such ports 'as would naturally and usually be ports of call on the voyage named'.

21.8.3.3   Consequences of deviation

Article IV, r. 4 states that where a justifiable deviation has taken place, neither the Rules nor the contract of carriage has been breached, and the carrier is not liable for any loss resulting therefrom. This probably means that the carrier is not, by reason of the deviation, deprived of the benefit of an exception, even though he/she would not have encountered the peril had the contractual route been followed.

The consequences of an unjustifiable deviation are not dealt with in the Rules at all. However, at common law an unjustifiable deviation is treated as a fundamental breach. In *Hain v Tate & Lyle* [1936] 2 All ER 597. Lord Atkins stated:

> I venture to think that the true view is that departure from the voyage contracted to be made is a breach by the shipowner of his contract, a breach of such a serious character that, however slight the deviation, the other party to the contract is entitled to treat it as going to the root of the contract and to declare himself as no longer bound by any of the contract terms...

The other party to the contract, therefore, has a choice whether to keep the contract alive or treat it as terminated. Where the contract is treated as terminated, the parties are excused further performance *from the time of the deviation*: *Hain v Tate & Lyle (supra)* — '*the* charterer became entitled to treat the contract as at an end from the date of the repudiation'. See also *STC v Golodetz* [1989] 2 Lloyd's Rep 286-287.

The question therefore arises as to whether the carrier can rely on a clause excluding him/her from liability where loss or damage has occurred to the goods after an unjustifiable deviation by the carrier and the other party to the contract has treated the contract as terminated. Lord Wilberforce in *Photo Productions Ltd v Securicor Transport Ltd* [1980] 1 All ER 556 said:

> When, in the context of a breach of contract one speaks of 'termination' what is meant is no more than that the innocent party, or in some cases, both parties are excused from further performance. Damages in such cases are then claimed under the contract, so what reason in principle can there be for disregarding what the contract itself says about damages, whether it liquidates them, or limits or excludes them?

However, in deviation cases the accepted view has always been to treat the carrier as an insurer and therefore liable for loss or damage to the goods even though unconnected with the deviation, unless the carrier can show that the loss or damage falls within a common law exception and that the loss would have occurred deviation or no deviation: *Stag Line v Foscolo, Mango* [1932] AC 328; *Thorley v Orchis SS Co.* [1907] 1 KB 660; *International Guano v MacAndrew* [1909] 2 KB 360.

Lord Wilberforce in *Photo Productions v Securicor* recognised the special position of the carrier in deviation cases:

> I must add a brief observation on the deviation cases. It may be preferable that they should be considered as a body of authority *sui generis* with special rules derived from historical and for commercial reasons.

It is no longer the case, however, that goods will be treated as uninsured at sea in the event of an unjustifiable deviation and thus there is no longer any reason to treat the deviation cases as falling under special principles. In fact, in *The Antares (Nos 1 and 2)* [1987] 1 Lloyd's Rep 424, Lloyd LJ expressed the view that deviation cases should now be assimilated into the ordinary law of contract.

We need also to consider the effect of termination for unjustifiable deviation on payment of freight, time bars and the limitation of liability.

21.8.3.4 Effect of termination of contract on freight

No contractual freight is claimable, even if the ship has arrived at the port of destination, unless the obligation to pay freight has already fallen due before the deviating event, i.e. the contract stipulates payment of advance freight. Although the carrier will not be able to claim freight payable on delivery he/she may still, however, be able to recover a reasonable sum by way of freight on a *quantum meruit* basis: *per* Wright and Maugham LJJ in *Hain SS Co. v Tate & Lyle* [1936] 2 All ER 597.

21.8.3.5 Effect of termination of contract on time bar

In *The Antares (supra)*, where there was an unauthorised stowage of cargo on deck (a form of deviation), it was argued that, as in route deviations, the special rules applied, with the effect of preventing the carrier from relying on the time bar in Article III, r. 6. (Article III, r. 6 prevents suit being brought more than one year after discharge or after the time when the discharge should have taken place.) The Court of Appeal was not prepared to treat the stowage on deck as falling within the category of special cases referred to by Lord Wilberforce in *Photo Productions v Securicor (supra)*. The substantive doctrine of fundamental breach did not apply to deck cargo and it was a matter of construction whether exclusion clauses applied to this unauthorised stowage on deck. See also *The Chanda* [1989] 2 Lloyd's Rep 494.

Where the Rules have statutory force, it may be that even though the special rules referred to by Lord Wilberforce apply to route deviations, Article III, r. 6 will survive the termination of the contract by virtue of its statutory existence and apply to limit the time within which action should be brought. On interpretation of Article III, r. 6, refer to *The Amazona* [1989] 2 Lloyd's Rep 130; *The Havhelt* [1993] 1 Lloyd's Rep 523.

21.8.3.6 Effect of termination of contract on limitation of liability

In relation to Article IV, r. 5, which limits the liability of the carrier, the editors of *Scrutton on Charterparties* take the view that the carrier may still be able to limit his/her liability under Article IV, r. 5 because of the words 'in any event', if the Rules have statutory effect under COGSA 1971. s. 1(3) as opposed to merely contractual application.

21.8.3.7 Affirmation

In many cases, the fact of deviation will only become known to the other party to the contract at the time the ship arrives. There is here every reason for treating the contract as terminated, e.g. the contractual rates of freight no longer apply.

If the fact of deviation becomes known during the transit, unless the other party indicates that he/she is no longer bound by the contract, he/she may be treated as having waived the right to treat the contract as at an end. See *Hain* v *Tate & Lyle* [1936] 2 All ER 597, where the charterers were held to have waived their right to treat the contract as discharged when, with knowledge of the deviation, they allowed the ship to load at a subsequent port. The transferee of the bill of lading is not bound by the waiver of the indorser/consignor: *Hain* v *Tate & Lyle (supra)*.

If the contract is affirmed it is kept alive for the benefit of both parties. The shipowner can rely on all exceptions for loss or damage occurring before or after deviation but he remains liable for loss or damage resulting from the unjustifiable deviation.

21.9   Calculation of Damages under the Hague-Visby Rules

Article IV, r. 5(b) provides that:

    (a)   where goods are lost, the damages awarded will represent the value the goods would have had at the time and place at which they ought to have been delivered,

    (b)   where goods arrive damaged the claimant will recover the difference between the sound arrived value and the actual arrived value.

The editors of *Scrutton on Charterparties* make the following point:

Article IV, r. 5(b) contains a new provision relating to the computation of damages. The purpose of this provision is not clear. One possible view is that it is intended to provide an additional upper limit to the amount recoverable, thus eliminating claims for consequential loss. Alternatively, the intention may have been to provide a yardstick for the calculation of damages, without necessarily providing that the sum recoverable consists *only* of the damages so calculated. Whichever interpretation is correct, the application of the sub Rule in practice is likely to give rise to difficulty.

The editor of *Carver's Carriage by Sea* (13th edn, 1982, Sweet and Maxwell) takes the same view: '*Scrutton's* comment is accepted. The rule is of no assistance, but a potential source of nuisance to the common law of England'.

21.10   Limitation of Liability under the Hague-Visby Rules

There are two types of limitation of liability to be considered:

    (a)   package limitation, where the limit is calculated according to the number of packages or units lost or damaged; and

    (b)   tonnage limitation, where the limit is calculated by reference to the tonnage of the ship.

21.10.1   PACKAGE LIMITATION

Article IV, r. 5(a), as amended by s. 1(A) of COGSA 1971, sets out the formula for the package limitation as follows:

    (a)   666.67 units of account *per* package or unit; or

    (b)   2 units of account *per* kilogramme of the gross weight of the goods lost or destroyed.

The courts will impose that which produces the higher limit.

'Unit of account' is defined in Article IV, r. 5(d) as amended by s. 1A COGSA 1971, which provides:

The unit of account mentioned in this article is the special drawing right as defined by the International Monetary Fund. The amounts mentioned in sub-para (a) of the paragraph shall be converted into national currency on the basis of the value of that currency on a date to be determined by the law of the court seized of the case.

By virtue of s. 1A COGSA 1971, Article IV, r. 5(d) shall have effect as if the date mentioned were the date of the judgment in question.

By virtue of Article III, r. 8 any clause in a contract of carriage subject to the Hague-Visby Rules which purports to reduce the limits of the carrier's liability will be null and void. On the other hand, Article IV, r. 5(g) specifically provides that a clause increasing the carrier's liability will be valid.

21.10.1.1   Goods carried in containers

Specific provision is made for the calculation of the package limit where the goods are carried in containers. Article IV, r. 5(c) resolves two problems:

(a)   Whether it is the containers or the individual packages inside the containers that are to be considered the packages or units: Article IV, r. 5(c) provides that where:

    (i)   goods are shipped in a container, pallet or similar article of transport, and
    (ii) the individual packages inside the container etc. have been enumerated in the bill of lading,

each package or unit so enumerated will attract its own limit. Thus, if the individual packages or units have not been so enumerated, the container will be the package for the purpose of calculating the limitation sum.

(b)   The 'enumeration' in itself might have given rise to problems. As stated in **21.8.2.2** a carrier is not obliged to issue a bill of lading containing a statement by the shipper as to the quantity or number of packages etc. where the carrier is not in a position to check the veracity of that statement. Where the goods have been shipped in a container the shipper's statement will be qualified, therefore, by the words 'said to contain'. However, although the words 'said to contain' do prevent the bill of lading from operating as evidence of the contents of the container for other purposes, Article IV, r. 5(c) does make such 'enumeration' effective for the purposes of limitation.

21.10.1.2   Hague-Visby provisions — no reliance on package limitation

The carrier can be prevented from relying on the limits of liability where:

(a)   The shipper declares the nature and value of the goods before shipment *and* inserts the nature and value of the goods into the bill of lading: Article IV, r. 5(a). Note that the insertion of the nature and value of the goods does not in itself prevent the carrier from contesting those statements. Under Article IV, r. 5(f) the declaration amounts to prima facie evidence only.

(b)   The *carrier* (or his alter ego) has, through his/her own act or omission, with intent to cause damage, or recklessly and with knowledge that damage would probably result, caused the loss or damage: Article IV, r. 5(e). Refer to *The European Enterprise* [1989] 2 Lloyd's Rep 185.

The limitation of liability rule only applies to loss or damage to or in connection with the goods. The claimant may be able to sue the carrier for loss due to a fraudulent or negligent misrepresentation, e.g. representations made by the carrier in the bill of lading. Not only will Article IV, r. 5 not apply but the measure of damages will be the loss the claimant has suffered as a result of taking up the bill of lading and paying against it, i.e. the difference between the price of the goods and the actual arrived value.

21.10.1.3   Tonnage limitation

The Hague-Visby Rules do not, however, lay down any method for computing the tonnage limitation of a ship. Instead, Article VIII provides that the Rules do not affect the rights and obligations of the carrier under any statute for the time being in force in relation to the limitation of liability. Thus the national provisions for tonnage limitation are preserved. The English statutory provisions are contained in the Merchant Shipping Act 1995.

In *The Benarty* [1984] 3 All ER 961, Dunn LJ stated:

> That provision [Article IV, r. 5] is known as the 'package limitation' and it is crucial to the construction of Article VIII to distinguish between the package limitation on the one hand and the tonnage limitation on the other... The High Contracting parties [to the Hague/ Hague-Visby Rules] were careful to preserve their national provisions for tonnage limitation. They achieved that partly by the provisions of Article VIII and partly by the use of the words 'otherwise than as provided in the Rules' in Article III, r. 8, which brings in Article VIII as an exception to the provision rendering any clause which lessens the liability of a carrier null and void... I would construe the words 'any statute' in Article VIII as meaning what they say, namely any statute, whether English or foreign, dealing with tonnage limitation.

It will be observed that although the limitation figure may not, by a clause in the contract of carriage, be reduced to below that calculated in accordance with Article IV, r. 5(a), national statutory provisions may have the effect of so doing.

21.11   Action in Tort

Article IV, *bis* provides:

> The defences and limits of liability provided for in these Rules shall apply in any action against the carrier in respect of loss or damage to goods covered by a contract of carriage whether the action be founded in contract or in tort.

In *The Captain Gregos* [1990] 1 Lloyd's Rep 310, the Court of Appeal held that the Rule was intended to regulate the rights and duties of the parties to the bill of lading contract, not non-parties. Thus in an action in tort by a cargo owner for negligent carriage of goods, the carrier will not be able to argue the applicability of exclusion clauses under the Rules or the limitation of liability under Article IV, r. 5 *unless* he is able to demonstrate a contractual nexus between the parties.

21.12   Estoppels

The carrier, through the master or other agent, may make statements in the shipping document issued, as to the quantity, weight, packing marks and apparent order and condition of the goods. If goods are lost or arrive damaged, the carrier may want to say that the goods lost were never received/shipped at all, or that they were already in a damaged condition when received/shipped by the carrier. If the cargo owner can successfully argue estoppel then the carrier cannot adduce any evidence showing non-receipt/non-shipment of goods, or receipt/shipment of damaged goods.

At common law, a claimant, in order to establish an estoppel, must show that:

(a)   he/she relied on a representation; and
(b)   he/she acted on the representation to his/her detriment.

However, following the decision in *Grant v Norway* (1851) 10 CB 665, the signatory of the shipping document, e.g., the master or loading broker, cannot bind the carrier by signing e.g., a bill of lading for goods that were never shipped. Thus no common law estoppel can be established against the carrier in relation to misstatements as to quantity.

Nevertheless, under the Hague-Visby Rules, where the document contains misstatements as to quantity and the document is a bill of lading or similar document of title, the statements are conclusive against the carrier.

Where the Hague-Visby Rules do not apply, in relation to shipped/received for shipment transferable bills of lading issued after 15 September 1992, the *Grant* v *Norway* rule is ousted by virtue of COGSA 1992, s. 4, which states:

A bill of lading which—

    (a)   represents goods to have been shipped on board a vessel or to have been received for shipment on board a vessel; and
    (b)   has been signed by the master of the vessel or by a person who was not the master but had the express, implied or apparent authority of the carrier to sign bills of lading

shall, in favour of a person who has become the lawful holder of the bill, be conclusive evidence against the carrier of the shipment of the goods, or, as the case may be, of their receipt for shipment.

A party relying on misstatements in a seaway bill or straight-consigned bill of lading will have to argue the existence of a common law estoppel and will still be subject to the rule in *Grant* v *Norway*. See Article III, r. 4 of the Hague-Visby Rules and COGSA 1971, s. 1(6)(b); COGSA 1992, s. 4.

21.13   Position of Former Holder of Bill of Lading, Seaway Bill/Ship's Delivery Order

The shipper under a bill of lading ceases to have contractual rights once the bill of lading has been transferred in such a way as to make the transferee a new holder of the bill of lading: COGSA 1992, s. 2(5)(a).

The shipper can of course become a 'holder' by virtue of transfer of the bill of lading to him, e.g., on rejection of the goods, in which case contractual rights will be transferred to him by virtue of s. 2(1)(a), s. 2(2)(b), s. 5(2)(c).

Where the shipper initially entered into a charterparty contract, transfer of the bill of lading will not deprive him of rights to sue under the charterparty contract. The contract of carriage identified under COGSA 1992, of which contractual rights will be transferred, is the contract of carriage contained in or evidenced by the bill of lading: COGSA 1992, s. 5(1).

By virtue of COGSA 1992, s. 2(5)(b), on transfer of the bill of lading to a new 'holder', each former 'holder' loses contractual rights to sue on the bill of lading contract.

In relation to seaway bills, it must be remembered that the shipper (unless there is contractual provision to the contrary in the contract of carriage) will preserve his right of disposal of the goods. COGSA 1992, s. 2(1)(b) provides that by virtue of being the person to whom delivery of goods to which the seaway bill relates is to be made, that person has transferred to and vested in him all rights of suit under the contract of carriage. If contractual rights were not also preserved for the shipper, COGSA 1992, s. 2(1) would effectively mean that contractual rights would vest in the original consignee, with no ability on the part of the shipper to change delivery instructions as 'all right of suit will have been transferred'. With this problem in mind COGSA 1992, s. 2(5) indicates that the shipper also retains right of suit — 'the operation of [s. 2(1)] shall be without prejudice to any rights which derive from a person's having been an original party to the contract contained in or evidenced by a seaway bill...'.

COGSA 1992, s. 2(5) also makes it clear that in relation to a ship's delivery order, the contractual rights of the party to the underlying contract of carriage, in pursuance of which the ship's delivery order was issued, are retained even though s. 2(1) indicates that contractual rights in the underlying contract of carriage are transferred to and vested in the party to whom delivery should be made. The carrier can avoid the possibility of two separate contractual actions by taking in the bill of lading before issue of the ship's delivery order.

As with the bill of lading, COGSA 1992, s. 2(5)(b) indicates that intermediate parties are divested of contractual rights once they cease to be a party to whom delivery under the seaway bill or delivery order is to be made.

21.14 Actions Brought by the Carrier

Thus far, only actions against the carrier have been discussed. However, the carrier will be entitled to claim in respect of breaches of contract on the part of the charterer, shipper or receiver. Paragraph **21.15** will deal with the carrier's entitlement to freight. Here we will consider the carrier's right to an indemnity in respect of incorrect statements recorded on the bill of lading and the shipment of dangerous goods.

21.14.1 INACCURACIES ON BILL OF LADING

Where the carrier has been estopped from adducing evidence as to the correct marks on the goods or as to the quantity or weight etc. of the goods at the time of receipt or shipment and thus has to pay damages to the consignee or indorsee of the bill of lading, Article III, r. 5 enables the carrier to claim an indemnity from the shipper against all loss, damage and expenses arising or resulting from the inaccuracies. Article III, r. 5 does not, however, enable the carrier to recover from the shipper loss incurred as a result of the statement 'shipped in apparent good order and condition'.

A carrier concerned about the condition of goods delivered into his/her custody, might be willing to issue a 'clean' bill of lading if the shipper or a third party agrees to indemnify the carrier for loss incurred in consequence. These contracts of indemnity are sometimes unenforceable. In *Brown Jenkinson* v *Percy Dalton* [1957] 2 All ER 844 it was held that even though the carrier does not intend or desire that anyone should be defrauded, by making in the bill of lading a representation of fact that he knows to be false with intent that it should be acted upon, he is committing the tort of deceit and the promise to indemnify is thereby given for an unlawful consideration. Lord Morris did say, however:

> There may perhaps be circumstances in which indemnities can properly be given. Thus if a carrier thinks that he has detected some faulty condition with regard to the goods to be taken on board he may be assured by the shipper that he is entirely mistaken. If he is so persuaded, it may be that he could honestly issue a clean bill of lading whilst taking an indemnity in case it was later shown that there had in fact been some faulty condition. Each case depends on its facts.

21.14.2 DANGEROUS GOODS

The carrier may have suffered loss directly or indirectly from the shipment of dangerous cargo. As to the meaning of 'dangerous' refer to *The Athanasia Comninos* [1990] 1 Lloyd's Rep 277. At common law, the shipper impliedly undertakes that the goods shipped are not dangerous when properly carried. Goods may be dangerous within the common law principle if they are liable to cause detention of the ship: *Mitchell* v *Steel* [1916] 2 KB 610. Ignorance on the part of the shipper of the dangerous nature of the goods appears to be no defence: *Brass* v *Maitland* (1856) 6 E & B 470. The implied undertaking does not arise if the carrier was expressly notified of the dangerous nature of the goods or the carrier knew or ought to have known of their dangerous nature: *Brass* v *Maitland*.

By Article IV, r. 6, where dangerous goods are shipped, the carrier may, whether he/she was knowledgeable of their nature or not, land them and destroy or render them innocuous, without incurring any liability to pay compensation. Where the carrier had knowledge of the nature of the goods he/she can only land, destroy or render innocuous without liability to pay compensation in those circumstances where the goods became a danger to ship and cargo. Further, where the goods are shipped without the carrier's knowledge, the carrier may claim from the shipper 'all damages and expenses directly or indirectly arising out of or resulting from such shipment'.

However, where the carrier's contract with the shipper enables the carrier to recover, even though the carrier was aware of the nature of what he/she was carrying, Article IV, r. 6 will not prevent recovery: *Chandris* v *Isbrandtsen-Moller* [1951] 1 KB 240:

> The article is not intended as a code. It is not meant altogether to supplant the contract of carriage but only to control on certain topics the freedom of contract which the parties would otherwise have. I see no reason why it should not be silent on such topics as the consequence of shipping cargo with the consent of the master, leaving the matter to be regulated by the parties themselves.

It appears that Article IV, r. 6 is confined in its operation to the shipment of goods which are physically dangerous, i.e. it does not cover goods which, owing to legal obstacles to their carriage or discharge, may involve detention of the ship. See also *The Athanasia Comninos* [1990] 1 Lloyd's Rep 277.

The shipowner's rights under Article IV, r. 6 are subject to the performance by him/her of the overriding duty under Article III, r. 1, to make the ship seaworthy: see *Mediterranean Freight Services Ltd* v *BP Oil International Ltd, The Times* 27 July 1994.

21.14.3   WHOM MAY THE CARRIER SUE?

As COGSA 1992 has divorced the transfer of contractual rights from the passing of property, a concurrent transfer of rights and vesting of liabilities would mean that parties who, e.g. are 'holders' of a bill of lading but with no proprietary interest in the goods would be automatically potentially liable to the carrier, e.g. a bank under a documentary credit to which a bill of lading has been indorsed by a seller in order to obtain payment.

The Act circumvents this problem by providing under s. 3(1) that the person who has rights vested in him/her by virtue of s. 2(1) of the Act, will be subject to liabilities only if:

(a)   he/she takes or demands delivery from the carrier of any of the goods to which the document relates; or

(b)   he/she makes a claim under the contract of carriage against the carrier in respect of any of those goods; or

(c)   he/she is a person who, at a time before those rights were vested in him/her, took or demanded delivery from the carrier of any of those goods.

Thus the issuing bank, under a documentary credit, as 'holder' of a bill of lading, will not by virtue of being 'holder' be subject to liabilities. The bank must take/demand delivery or make a claim under the contract of carriage in order to attract disabilities.

Section 3(1) indicates that the party taking/demanding delivery etc. shall become 'subject to the same liabilities under that contract *as if he had been a party to that contract* (emphasis added). It would appear, therefore, that the party taking/demanding delivery etc. will be subject to all liabilities, including those incurred before becoming a 'holder' or 'deliveree'. Thus, against such a party, an action can be pursued by the carrier for advance freight, demurrage incurred at the port of loading, and for loss caused by shipment of a dangerous cargo. The section would also appear to encompass losses incurred by the carrier by virtue of inaccuracies in the bill of lading, recoverable by virtue of Article III, r. 5 of the Hague-Visby Rules and/or by virtue of undertakings given by the shipper in the contract of carriage.

'All liabilities' will cover only liabilities in respect of goods to which a ship's delivery order relates, where the goods form part of a bulk consignment: s. 3(2).

The Act preserves the liabilities of the original party to the contract of carriage: s. 3(3).

21.15 Freight

The remuneration for the carriage of goods is called 'freight'.

21.15.1 AT COMMON LAW

The right of the carrier to claim freight only arises on delivery of the goods at the usual discharging place at the contractual port of destination. If the carrier is prevented from carrying the goods to the port of destination, even if the cause is beyond his control, the carrier cannot claim any part of the freight.

If the carrier has been prevented from completing the voyage by an act or default of the shipper, the carrier is entitled to damages: *Aktieselskabet Olivebank* v *Dansk SIF* [1919] 2 KB 162.

If the ship has arrived at the port of destination, freight must still be paid even if the goods are damaged or deteriorated and even if the damage has been caused by the negligence of the crew. Freight will not be paid, however, on those goods which are so badly damaged or deteriorated as to have lost their identity: see *Asfar* v *Blundell* [1896] 1 QB 123; *The Caspian Sea* [1980] 1 Lloyd's Rep 91. Thus freight can be claimed pro rata on that which arrives and on that which arrives damaged without loss of identity.

21.15.2 CONTRACTS OF CARRIAGE

Such contracts invariably vary the common law rules on freight. Note that the Hague-Visby Rules do not govern this aspect of the contract of carriage.

The parties may agree on 'lump sum' freight, which is a sum stipulated to be paid for the use of the ship or a portion of it. The sum is usually calculated on the basis of the deadweight capacity of the ship. Where freight is payable on a lump sum basis, and the ship arrives at the port of destination but delivers less than the quantity stated in the bill of lading as shipped, the carrier is still entitled to full freight: *Ritchie* v *Atkinson* (1808) 10 East 295; *Merchant Shipping Co.* v *Armitage* (1873) LR 9 QB 99.

If the ship arrives but no bill of lading goods are delivered it is unclear whether the carrier can recover his full freight. One view is that lump sum freight is really in the nature of a rent to be paid for the use and hire of the ship on the agreed voyage and thus freight is payable if the ship completes the voyage with or without cargo. Another view is that lump sum freight is an amount which is paid after 'the entire discharge and right delivery of the cargo'.

The parties may have agreed that freight should be payable but calculated on the intake quantity: *The Metula* [1978] 2 Lloyd's Rep 5. As in the case with lump sum freight, loss of goods en route will not prevent the carrier from claiming the freight sum ascertained on shipment. In *The Metula* some goods were delivered. The court at first instance stated that in order for the freight to be recovered, something more than a minimal amount must be delivered.

Where lump sum freight is payable but the ship delivers short of destination, no freight is payable unless there is an express or implied agreement on the part of the deliveree of the goods to pay freight pro rata on that part of the journey accomplished. To justify an implied agreement, there must be a voluntary acceptance of the goods at the intermediate port, despite an ability and willingness on the part of the carrier to forward the goods to the port of destination.

21.15.3 ADVANCE FREIGHT

This has been called an 'irrevocable payment at the risk of the shipper'. Where the contract calls for advance freight it does not make payment of freight dependent on delivery of the goods. It is a question of construction of the contract whether the parties intended an advance payment to be irrevocable or a mere payment in advance but still dependent on delivery.

Sometimes freight is payable on delivery 'lost or not lost'. This has the same effect as a clause for advance freight proper. The amount to be paid on delivery is calculated on the basis of what is shipped, and that sum must be paid even if the ship fails to arrive.

Where goods are lost before the payment obligation arises, there can be no claim for advance freight. In *Compania Naviera General SA* v *Kerametal* [1982] Com LR 257, the bill of lading demanded 75 per cent of the freight within five days after the master signed the bill of lading. The ship sank before the *five* days were up and the carrier sought to argue that the obligation to pay advance freight arose as soon as the bill of lading was signed, this obligation being coupled with an option to postpone payment for up to five days. Sir John Donaldson MR did not accept this. He held that there was no obligation to make any payment of or on account of freight until the expiry of the five-day period, but before that had occurred the contractual basis of the obligation had been undermined by the loss of the cargo and the vessel. It is therefore of importance to ascertain from the wording of the freight clause exactly when the obligation to pay the advance freight has fallen due.

Advance freight properly so called can be made payable at various points — on shipment, on signing of the bills of lading, at a defined length of time after shipment, on sailing, on final sailing etc. Where freight is payable 'on sailing' the obligation to pay the advance freight arises when the ship fairly starts from her place of loading ready for sea intending there and then to commence the voyage: *Sea Insurance Co.* v *Blogg* [1898] 2 QB 398. Where freight is payable on 'final sailing' the obligation to pay arises when the ship is fairly clear of the port.

It is, further, possible that a freight clause will provide for payment of advance freight at a particular time but that it should be deemed earned at an earlier time. In *Bank of Boston Connecticut* v *European Grain and Shipping* [1989] 1 All ER 545 a charterparty clause stated 'freight shall be prepaid within five days of signing and surrender of final bills of lading; full freight deemed to be earned on signing bill of lading'. The bills of lading were signed on 14 July, surrendered on 26 July but the charterparty was treated as terminated for repudiatory breach on 22 July. The charterers argued that by accepting the shipowner's repudiation of the charterparty, they had lawfully brought the charterparty to an end before the shipowner's right to be paid freight had accrued. The House of Lords held that on proper construction of the freight clause the shipowner's right to freight had accrued on completion of the signing of the bill of lading; it was the mere payment that was postponed until five days after the bills of lading were delivered to the shippers. Therefore, by the time of termination the shipowner's indefeasible right to freight had already fallen due.

Where part of the freight has been paid in advance and the ship arrives at destination with part of the cargo missing, the advance freight is not to be regarded distributively as payment of so much *per* ton, leaving a balance *per* ton of the cargo delivered to be paid on delivery. The advance is to be treated as a payment in advance of the whole amount payable on delivery. Thus if 75 per cent of the freight is paid in advance and 75 per cent of the cargo is delivered, the carrier cannot claim 25 per cent of freight on the cargo delivered. If 75 per cent of the freight is paid and 75 per cent of the cargo is delivered, nothing more is payable: *Allison* v *Bristol Marine Insurance Co.* (1876) 1 App Cas 209.

21.15.4   RULE AGAINST DEDUCTION

Where the carrier can claim freight (under a bill of lading or a voyage charterparty) the rule against deduction applies. This means that the cargo owner cannot set off damages owed to him/her by the carrier: see *The Brede* [1973] 2 Lloyd's Rep 333; *The Aries* [1977] 1 All ER 398; *Bank of Boston Connecticut* v *European Grain and Shipping (supra)*.

An action against the carrier must, therefore, be brought in a separate action or on a counterclaim. It is important to remember that a counterclaim is deemed to commence on the same date as the original action. Whereas a carrier can bring his claim for freight within six years of his cause of action arising, the other party to the contract of carriage, when suing for loss or damage to the goods, will only have one year from discharge under the Hague-Visby Rules: see Article III, r. 6. The counter claiming cargo owner might find his claim statute barred.

21.16 Contracting States to the Hague-Visby Rules

The following are contracting states to the Hague-Visby Rules:

France; Norway; Poland; Germany; Lebanon; The Netherlands (in Europe); Switzerland; Sri Lanka; Sweden; Syria; Singapore; Finland; Tonga; Denmark; Belgium; Egypt; Ecuador; The United Kingdom plus Isle of Man; Bermuda; British Antarctic Territory; British Virgin Islands; Cayman Islands; Falklands Islands; Gibraltar; Hong Kong; Montserrat; The Turks and Caicos Islands; Greece.

21.17 Further Reading

Goode, R.M., *Commercial Law,* rev. ed. 1985, Pelican.
Schmitthoff, C., *Export Trade: The Law and Practice of International Trade,* 9th ed., 1990, Sweet & Maxwell.
Scrutton, T., *On Charterparties,* 19th ed. 1984, Sweet & Maxwell.

21.18 Examples of Transport Documents

Herein enclosed is a selection of transport documents, reproduced with the kind permission of Cunard Ellerman, 12-20 Camomile Street, London EC3 and the Baltic and International Maritime Council (BIMCO) of Copenhagen, Denmark.

The documents have been filled in to give you a better idea of how they operate in practice.

EXAMPLE 1: BILL OF LADING FOR COMBINED TRANSPORT SHIPMENT OR PORT TO PORT SHIPMENT USED FOR PORT TO PORT SHIPMENT

BILL OF LADING FOR COMBINED TRANSPORT SHIPMENT OR
PORT TO PORT SHIPMENT

		B/L No.

SHIPPER

CHEMICAL COMPRESSORS LTD.

CUNARD ELLERMAN

BOOKING REF.

MEDITERRANEAN CONTAINER SERVICES

SHIPPERS REF.

CONSIGNEE

PREVITI SPA (or order)

Ellerman Lines plc
12-20 Camomile Street, London EC3A 7EX
Telephone 071-283 4311   Telex 884771/2
Facsimile 071-283 1767

NOTIFY PARTY AND ADDRESS It is agreed that no responsibility shall attach to the Carrier or his Agents for failure to notify the Consignees of the arrival of the goods (see Clause 20 on the reverse).

LAMANNA TRANSPORTI
1234 VIA VECCHIA
NAPLES

PLACE OF RECEIPT (Applicable only when this document is used as a Combined Transport Bill of Lading)

VESSEL AND VOY. No.
BORGIA 0415

PLACE OF DELIVERY (Applicable only when this document is used as a Combined Transport Bill of Lading)

PORT OF LOADING   LONDON

PORT OF DISCHARGE   NAPLES

MARKS AND Nos. CONTAINER Nos.	NUMBER AND KIND OF PACKAGES, DESCRIPTION OF GOODS	GROSS WEIGHT Kg	MEASUREMENT M³
	4 X 20' CONTAINERS	8,800 kos	
HLCU 2482823	STC 19 PACKAGES TOOLS PARTS	12,963 kos	
HLCU 2306948	STC 33 PALLETS CRUDE KYANITE	18,878 kos	
HLCU 2340855	STC 33 PALLETS CRUDE KYANITE	18,878 kos	
HLCU 2451587	STC 33 PALLETS CRUDE KYANITE	18,878 kos	

SPECIMEN

ABOVE PARTICULARS AS DECLARED BY SHIPPER BUT NOT ACKNOWLEDGED BY THE CARRIER (SEE CLAUSE 11)

✱TOTAL No. OF CONTAINERS/PACKAGES RECEIVED BY THE CARRIER

4 CONTAINERS

MOVEMENT
FCL DEPOT/FCL DEPOT

Received by the Carrier from the Shipper in apparent good order and condition (unless otherwise noted herein) the total number or quantity of Containers or other packages or units indicated in the box opposite entitled "✱ Total No. of Containers/Packages received by the Carrier" for Carriage subject to all the terms and conditions hereof (INCLUDING THE TERMS AND CONDITIONS ON THE REVERSE HEREOF AND THE TERMS AND CONDITIONS OF THE CARRIER'S APPLICABLE TARIFF) from the Place of Receipt or the Port of Loading whichever is applicable, to the Port of Discharge or the Place of Delivery, whichever is applicable. One original Bill of Lading must be surrendered, duly endorsed, in exchange for the Goods. In accepting this Bill of Lading the Merchant expressly accepts and agrees to all its terms and conditions whether printed, stamped or written or otherwise incorporated, notwithstanding the non-signing of this Bill of Lading by the Merchant.

FREIGHT AND CHARGES (Please tick)	Prepaid	Collect
Origin Inland Haulage Charge	☐	☐
Origin Terminal Handling/LCL Service Charge	☐	☐
Ocean Freight	☑	☐
Destination Terminal Handling/LCL Service Charge	☑	☐
Destination Inland Haulage Charge	☐	☐

PLACE AND DATE OF ISSUE
LONDON   01.09.1995

IN WITNESS of the contract herein contained the number of originals stated opposite have been issued, one of which being accomplished, the others to be void.

NUMBER OF ORIGINAL BILLS OF LADING
03/THREE

For the Carrier:
S. RISEDEN SMITH

ICS
CT B/L
April 78

EXAMPLE 2: BILL OF LADING FOR COMBINED TRANSPORT SHIPMENT OR PORT TO PORT SHIPMENT USED FOR COMBINED TRANSPORT

BILL OF LADING FOR COMBINED TRANSPORT SHIPMENT OR PORT TO PORT SHIPMENT

B/L No.

BOOKING REF.

SHIPPERS REF.

SHIPPER

CHEMICAL COMPRESSORS LTD.

CUNARD ELLERMAN

MEDITERRANEAN CONTAINER SERVICES
Ellerman Lines plc
12-20 Camomile Street, London EC3A 7EX
Telephone 071-283 4311   Telex 884771/2
Facsimile 071-283 1767

CONSIGNEE

ORDER

NOTIFY PARTY AND ADDRESS It is agreed that no responsibility shall attach to the Carrier or his Agents for failure to notify the Consignees of the arrival of the goods (see Clause 20 on the reverse).

SHANTUNG CORP
137 LIBERATION AVENUE
SUCHOW CHINA

PLACE OF RECEIPT (Applicable only when this document is used as a Combined Transport Bill of Lading)

MANCHESTER

VESSEL AND VOY. No.

THE FORMOSA II

PORT OF LOADING

LONDON

PLACE OF DELIVERY (Applicable only when this document is used as a Combined Transport Bill of Lading)

DEPOT 10 A
SUCHOW OLD TOWN

PORT OF DISCHARGE

SHANGHAI

MARKS AND Nos. CONTAINER Nos	NUMBER AND KIND OF PACKAGES; DESCRIPTION OF GOODS	GROSS WEIGHT Kg	MEASUREMENT M³
TPHU 423894/1	1 X 40' CONTAINER STC	4,000 kos	
	24 PALLETS MONOFIL WASTE	16,480 kos	

SPECIMEN

ABOVE PARTICULARS AS DECLARED BY SHIPPER BUT NOT ACKNOWLEDGED BY THE CARRIER (SEE CLAUSE 11)

✱TOTAL No. OF CONTAINERS/PACKAGES RECEIVED BY THE CARRIER

1 CONTAINER

MOVEMENT   LCL DEPOT/LCL DEPOT

Received by the Carrier from the Shipper in apparent good order and condition (unless otherwise noted herein) the total number or quantity of Containers or other packages or units indicated in the box opposite entitled "✱ Total No. of Containers/Packages received by the Carrier" for Carriage subject to all the terms and conditions hereof (INCLUDING THE TERMS AND CONDITIONS ON THE REVERSE HEREOF AND THE TERMS AND CONDITIONS OF THE CARRIER'S APPLICABLE TARIFF) from the Place of Receipt or the Port of Loading whichever is applicable, to the Port of Discharge or the Place of Delivery, whichever is applicable. One original Bill of Lading must be surrendered, duly endorsed, in exchange for the Goods. In accepting this Bill of Lading the Merchant expressly accepts and agrees to all its terms and conditions whether printed, stamped or written or otherwise incorporated, notwithstanding the non-signing of this Bill of Lading by the Merchant

FREIGHT AND CHARGES (Please tick)	Prepaid	Collect
Origin Inland Haulage Charge	☑	☐
Origin Terminal Handling/LCL Service Charge	☑	☐
Ocean Freight	☑	☐
Destination Terminal Handling/LCL Service Charge	☑	☐
Destination Inland Haulage Charge	☑	☐

PLACE AND DATE OF ISSUE

LONDON   01.09.1995
IN WITNESS of the contract herein contained the number of originals stated opposite have been issued, one of which being accomplished, the other(s) to be void.

NUMBER OF ORIGINAL BILLS OF LADING

03/THREE

For the Carrier

S. RISEDEN-SMITH

ICS
CT B/L
Apr 75

EXAMPLE 3: COMBINED TRANSPORT DOCUMENT

Code Name: "COMBIDOC"

Consignor

CHEMICAL COMPRESSORS LTD.

CT Doc No

Reference No

Negotiable

COMBINED TRANSPORT DOCUMENT

Issued by The Baltic and International Maritime Conference (BIMCO) and the International Shipowners Association (INSA), subject to International Chamber of Commerce Uniform Rules for a Combined Transport Document (ICC Publication No. 298)

July 1st, 1977

Consigned to order of

ORDER

Notify address

SHANTUNG CORP.
137 LIBERATION AVENUE
SUCHOW CHINA

Place of receipt		
MANCHESTER		

Ocean vessel	Port of loading	Name of sub-contractors for carriage by inland waterways *
THE FORMOSA II	LONDON	

Port of discharge	Place of delivery	Date of sub-contract for carriage by inland waterways *
SHANGHAI	SUCHOW	

Marks and Nos.	Quantity and description of goods	Gross weight, kg, Measurement, m³
TPHU 423894/1	1 X 40' CONTAINER	4,000 kos.
	STC	
	24 PALLETS MONOFIL WASTE	16,480 kos.
	SHIPPERS LOAD AND COUNT	

SPECIMEN

Particulars above declared by Consignor

Freight and charges

PREPAID

RECEIVED the goods in apparent good order and condition and, as far as ascertained by reasonable means of checking, as specified above unless otherwise stated.

The CTO, in accordance with and to the extent of the provisions contained in this CT Document, and with liberty to sub-contract, undertakes to perform and/or in his own name to procure performance of the combined transport and the delivery of the goods, including all services which are necessary to such transport from the place and time of taking the goods in charge to the place and time of delivery and accepts responsibility for such transport and such services.

One of the CT Documents must be surrendered duly endorsed in exchange for the goods or delivery order.

IN WITNESS whereof CT Document(s) has/have been signed in the number indicated below, one of which being accomplished the other(s) to be void.

Freight payable at	Place and date of issue
LONDON	MANCHESTER 01.09.1985
Number of original CT Documents	Signed for the Combined Transport Operator (CTO)
03/THREE	S. RISEHOLME SMITH

As agent(s) to the CTO

Note:
The Merchant's attention is called to the fact that according to Clauses 10 to 12 of this CT Document, the liability of the CTO is, in most cases, limited in respect of loss of or damage to the goods and delay. The liability of the CTO in respect of loss or damage occurring during carriage by inland waterways shall be covered by the provisions of his contract with the sub-contractors mentioned above (*) and dated as likewise indicated (*).

p.t.o.

EXAMPLE 4: NON-NEGOTIABLE WAYBILL

NON-NEGOTIABLE WAYBILL

CUNARD ELLERMAN

Waybill No
Booking Ref.
Shipper's Ref.

Shipper

CHEMICAL COMPRESSORS LTD.

Received in apparent good order and condition except as otherwise noted the total number of Containers or other packages or units enumerated * for Carriage from the Place of Receipt to the Place of Delivery subject to the terms hereof. Delivery will be made to the Consignee named, or his authorised agent, on production of proof of identity at the Place of Delivery. Should the Consignee require delivery elsewhere than at the Place of Delivery as shown below then written instructions must be given by the Consignee to the Carrier or his agent. Should delivery be required to be made to a party other than that named as Consignee, authorisation must be given in writing by the Shipper to the Carrier or his Agent.

Consignee

CHINA STATE IMPORT/EXPORT CORP.

Carrier

Notify Party/Address

SHANTUNG CORP
137 LIBERATION AVENUE
SUCHOW CHINA

Place of Receipt

MANCHESTER

Vessel and Voy. No.

THE FORMOSA II   0435

Port of Loading   LONDON

Port of Discharge   SHANGHAI

Place of Delivery

DEPOT 10 A
SUCHOW OLD TOWN

Marks and Nos; Container Nos;	Number and kind of Packages; description of Goods	Gross Weight (kg)	Measurement (cbm)
TPHU	1 X 40' CONTAINER	4,000 kos	
423894/1	STC		
	24 PALLETS MONOFIL WASTE	16,480 kos	
	SHIPPERS LOAD AND COUNT		

SPECIMEN

ABOVE PARTICULARS AS DECLARED BY SHIPPER

* Total No of Containers Packages
1 CONTAINER

Movement
LCL DEPOT/LCL DEPOT

Freight and Charges (indicate whether to be prepaid or collect)
Origin Inland Haulage Charge
Origin Terminal Handling LCL Service Charge
Ocean Freight
Destination Terminal Handling LCL Service Charge
Destination Inland Haulage Charge

This Waybill is deemed to be a contract of carriage as defined in Article 1 (b) of the Hague Rules and Hague Visby Rules, but it is not a document of title to the Goods. The Contract evidenced by this Waybill is subject to the Carrier's standard Bill of Lading terms and conditions and tariff for the relevant trade, copies of which may be obtained from the offices of the Carrier and those of his authorised Agents Except for live animals, and Goods which are stated herein to be carried on deck, and are so carried, these terms and conditions are warranted, in respect of the sea portion of the Carriage, to apply the Hague Rules or the Hague Visby Rules, whichever would have been applicable if the Carrier had issued a Bill of Lading instead of this Waybill
Unless instructed to the contrary by the Shipper, the Carrier will, subject to the aforesaid terms and conditions, process cargo claims with the Consignee named in this Waybill. Such settlement, if any, shall be a complete discharge of the Carrier's liability to the Shipper. The Shipper accepts the said standard conditions on his own behalf, on behalf of the Consignee and the owner of the Goods and warrants that he has authority to do so.

ICS
CTWB
April 78

Number of Original Waybills
ONE

Place and date of issue
London   01.09.95

Signature for Carrier
S. RUSEDEN-SMITH

294

EXAMPLE 5: NON-NEGOTIABLE WAYBILL

CODE NAME: "GENWAYBILL"

Shipper BERESFORD FOODSTUFFS LTD	NON-NEGOTIABLE GENWB No. GENERAL SEA WAYBILL FOR USE IN SHORT-SEA DRY CARGO TRADE Reference No.

Consignee (not to order)

BRUCKMANNN SERVICES PLC

Notify address

OSTEL HANS N.V.
87 DELWAIDEDOK
ANTWERP

Vessel THE PIETRO	Port of loading LONDON

Port of discharge
ANTWERP

Description of cargo	Marks and Nos.	Number and kind of packages	Gross weight	Measurement
COFFEE BEANS		3 PALLETS/1000 BAGS		
	LFIU 58D7810		4,200 kg.	
	TOLU 583077D		4,200 kg.	
	ICSU 5704387		4,200 kg.	

Particulars declared by the Shipper

SPECIMEN

(of which   on deck at Shipper's risk; the Carrier not
being responsible for loss or damage howsoever arising)

Issued pursuant to Voyage Charter Party indicated hereunder	**SHIPPED** on board the cargo specified above, according to Shipper's declaration in apparent good order and condition – unless otherwise stated herein – weight, measure, marks, numbers, quality, contents and value unknown, for delivery at the port of discharge or so near thereto as the Vessel may safely get, always afloat.
Charter Party (Code name, place and date of issue)	The cargo shipped under this Waybill will be delivered to the Party named as Consignee or its authorised agent, on production of proof of identity without any documentary formalities. The Carrier to exercise due care ensuring that delivery is made to the proper party. However, in case of incorrect delivery, no responsibility will be accepted unless due to fault or neglect on the part of the Carrier. FOR CONDITIONS OF CARRIAGE SEE OVERLEAF.
Freight payable in accordance therewith.	Freight payable at Place and date of issue PREPAID London 01.09.95
	Signature S. ROSEDEN-SMITH

Printed and sold by

21.19   Carriage of Goods by Sea Act 1971 (1971, c. 19)

1. Application of Hague Rules as amended

(1)   In this Act, 'the Rules' means the International Convention for the unification of certain rules of law relating to bills of lading signed at Brussels on 25th August 1924, as amended by the Protocol signed at Brussels on 23rd February 1968 and by the Protocol signed at Brussels on 21st December 1979—[Inserted by section 314 and Schedule 13 Merchant Shipping Act 1995].

(2)   The provisions of the Rules, as set out in the Schedule to this Act, shall have the force of law.

(3)   Without prejudice to subsection (2) above, the said provisions shall have effect (and have the force of law) in relation to and in connection with the carriage of goods by sea in ships where the port of shipment is a port in the United Kingdom, whether or not the carriage is between ports in two different States within the meaning of Article X of the Rules.

(4)   Subject to subsection (6) below, nothing in this section shall be taken as applying anything in the Rules to any contract for the carriage of goods by sea, unless the contract expressly or by implication provides for the issue of a bill of lading or any similar document of title.

(5)   The Secretary of State may from time to time by order made by statutory instrument specify the respective amounts which for the purposes of paragraph 5 of Article IV of the Rules and of Article IV bis of the Rules are to be taken as equivalent to the sums expressed in francs which are mentioned in sub-paragraph (a) of that paragraph.

(6)   Without prejudice to Article (c) of the Rules, the Rules shall have the force of law in relation to—

(a)   any bill of lading if the contract contained in or evidenced by it expressly provides that the Rules shall govern the contract, and

(b)   any receipt which is a non-negotiable document marked as such if the contract contained in or evidenced by it is a contract for the carriage of goods by sea which expressly provides that the Rules are to govern the contract as if the receipt were a bill of lading,

but subject, where paragraph (b) applies, to any necessary modifications and in particular with the omission in Article III of the Rules of the second sentence of paragraph 4 and of paragraph 7.

(7)   If and so far as the contract contained in or evidenced by a bill of lading or receipt within paragraph (a) or (b) of subsection (6) above applies to deck cargo or live animals, the Rules as given the force of law by that subsection shall have effect as if Article I(c) did not exclude deck cargo and live animals.

In this subsection 'deck cargo' means cargo which by the contract of carriage is stated as being carried on deck and is so carried.

1A. Conversion of special drawing rights into sterling [Inserted by section 314 and Schedule 13, Merchant Shipping Act 1995]

(1)   For the purposes of Article IV of the Rules the value on a particular day of one special drawing right shall be treated as equal to such a sum in sterling as the International Monetary Fund have fixed as being the equivalent of one special drawing right—

(a)   for that day; or

(b)   if no sum has been so fixed for that day, for the last day before that day for which a sum has been so fixed.

(2)   A certificate given by or on behalf of the Treasury stating—

(a)   that a particular sum in sterling has been fixed as aforesaid for a particular day; or

(b)   that no sum has been so fixed for a particular day and that a particular sum in sterling has been so fixed for a day which is the last day for which a sum has been so fixed before the particular day,

shall be conclusive evidence of those matters for the purposes of subsection (1) above; and a document purporting to be such a certificate shall in any proceedings be received in evidence and, unless the contrary is proved, be deemed to be such a certificate.

(3)   The Treasury may charge a reasonable fee for any certificate given in pursuance of subsection (2) above, and any fee received by the Treasury by virtue of this subsection shall be paid into the Consolidated Fund.

(4)   For section 6(4) substitute—

(4)   It is hereby declared that for the purposes of Article VIII of the Rules section 186 of the Merchant Shipping Act 1995 (which entirely exempts shipowners and others in certain circumstances for loss of, or damage to, goods) is a provision relating to limitation of liability.

(5)   Article IV of the Rules shall continue to have effect with the following amendments—

(a)   for 'the equivalent of 10,000 francs' substitute '666.67 units of account';

(b)   for '30 francs per kilo' substitute '2 units of account per kilogramme'; and

(c)   for paragraph 5(d) substitute—

(d)   The unit of account mentioned in this Article is the special drawing right as defined by the International Monetary Fund. The amounts mentioned in sub-paragraph (a) of this paragraph shall be converted into national currency on the basis of the value of that currency on a date to be determined by the law of the Court seized of the case.

(6)   Article 4, paragraph 5(d) of the Rules shall continue to have effect as if the date there mentioned were the date of the judgment in question.

(7)   Article X of the Rules shall continue to have effect as if references to a Contracting State included references to a State that is a contracting State in respect of the Rules without the amendments made by the Protocol signed at Brussels on 21st December 1979 as well as to one that is a contracting State in respect of the Rules as so amended, and section 2 shall have effect accordingly.

2.   *Contracting States, etc.*

(1)   If Her Majesty by Order in Council certifies to the following effect, that is to say, that for the purposes of the Rules—

(a)   a State specified in the Order is a contracting State, or is a contracting State in respect of any place or territory so specified; or

(b)   any place or territory specified in the Order forms part of a State so specified (whether a contracting State or not),

the Order shall, except so far as it has been superseded by a subsequent Order, be conclusive evidence of the matters so certified.

(2)   An Order in Council under this section may be varied or revoked by a subsequent Order in Council.

3.   *Absolute warranty of seaworthiness not to be implied in contracts to which Rules apply*

There shall not be implied in any contract for the carriage of goods by sea to which the Rules apply by virtue of this Act any absolute undertaking by the carrier of the goods to provide a seaworthy ship.

4.   *Application of Act to British possessions, etc.*

(1)   Her Majesty may by Order in Council direct that this Act shall extend, subject to such exceptions, adaptations and modifications as may be specified in the Order, to all or any of the following territories, that is—

(a)   any colony (not being a colony for whose external relations a country other than the United Kingdom is responsible),

(b)   any country outside Her Majesty's dominions in which Her Majesty has jurisdiction in right of Her Majesty's Government of the United Kingdom.

(2)   An Order in Council under this section may contain such transitional and other consequential and incidental provisions as appear to Her Majesty to be expedient, including provisions amending or repealing any legislation about the carriage of goods by sea forming part of the law of any of the territories mentioned in paragraphs (a) and (b) above.

(3)   An Order in Council under this section may be varied or revoked by a subsequent Order in Council.

5.   *Extension of application of Rules to carriage from ports in British possessions, etc.*

(1)   Her Majesty may by Order in Council provide that section 1(3) of this Act shall have effect as if the reference therein to the United Kingdom included a reference to all or any of the following territories, that is—

(a)   the Isle of Man;

(b)   any of the Channel Islands specified in the Order;

 (c) any colony specified in the Order (not being a colony for whose external relations country other than the United Kingdom is responsible);

 (d) any associated state (as defined by section 1(3) of the West Indies Act 1967) specified in the Order;

 (e) any country specified in the Order, being a country outside Her Majesty's dominions in which Her Majesty has jurisdiction in right of Her Majesty's Government of the United Kingdom.

 (2) An Order in Council under this section may be varied or revoked by a subsequent Order in Council.

6. *Supplemental*

 (1) This Act may be cited as the Carriage of Goods by Sea Act 1971.

 (2) It is hereby declared that this Act extends to Northern Ireland.

 (3) The following enactments shall be repealed, that is—

 (a) the Carriage of Goods by Sea Act 1924,

 (b) section 12(4)(a) of the Nuclear Installations Act 1965,

and without prejudice to section 38(1) of the Interpretation Act 1889, the reference to the said Act of 1924 in section 1(1)(i)(ii) of the Hovercraft Act 1968 shall include a reference to this Act.

 (4) It is hereby declared that for the purposes of Article VIII of the Rules section 502 of the Merchant Shipping Act 1894 (which, as amended by the Merchant Shipping (Liability of Shipowners and Others) Act 1958, entirely exempts shipowners and others in certain circumstances from liability for loss of, or damage to, goods) is a provision relating to limitation of liability.

 (5) This Act shall come into force on such day as Her Majesty may by Order in Council appoint, and, for the purposes of the transition from the law in force immediately before the day appointed under this subsection to the provisions of this Act, the Order appointing the day may provide that those provisions shall have effect subject to such transitional provisions as may be contained in the Order.

SCHEDULE

The Hague Rules as amended by the Brussels Protocol 1968

Article I

In these Rules the following words are employed, with the meanings set out below:—

 (a) 'Carrier' includes the owner or the charterer who enters into a contract of carriage with a shipper.

 (b) 'Contract of carriage' applies only to contracts of carriage covered by a bill of lading or any similar document of title, in so far as such document relates to the carriage of goods by sea, including any bill of lading or any similar document as aforesaid issued under or pursuant to a charter party from the moment at which such bill of lading or similar document of title regulates the relations between a carrier and a holder of the same.

 (c) 'Goods' includes goods, wares, merchandise, and articles of every kind whatsoever except live animals and cargo which by the contract of carriage is stated as being carried on deck and is so carried.

 (d) 'Ship' means any vessel used for the carriage of goods by sea.

 (e) 'Carriage of goods' covers the period from the time when the goods are loaded on to the time they are discharged from the ship.

Article II

Subject to the provisions of Article VI, under every contract of carriage of goods by sea the carrier, in relation to the loading, handling, stowage, carriage, custody, care and discharge of such goods, shall be subject to the responsibilities and liabilities, and entitled to the rights and immunities hereinafter set forth.

ARTICLE III

1.   The carrier shall be bound before and at the beginning of the voyage to exercise due diligence to —

(a)   Make the ship seaworthy.

(b)   Properly man, equip and supply the ship.

(c)   Make the holds, refrigerating and cool chambers, and all other parts of the ship in which goods are carried, fit and safe for their reception, carriage and preservation.

2.   Subject to the provisions of Article IV, the carrier shall properly and carefully load, handle, stow, carry, keep, care for, and discharge the goods carried.

3.   After receiving the goods into his charge the carrier or the master or agent of the carrier shall, on demand of the shipper, issue to the shipper a bill of lading showing among other things-

(a)   The leading marks necessary for identification of the goods as the same are furnished in writing by the shipper before the loading of such goods starts, provided such marks are stamped or otherwise shown clearly upon the goods if uncovered, or on the cases or coverings in which such goods are contained, in such a manner as should ordinarily remain legible until the end of the voyage.

(b)   Either the number of packages or pieces, or the quantity, or weight, as the case may be, as furnished in writing by the shipper.

(c)   The apparent order and condition of the goods.

Provided that no carrier, master or agent of the carrier shall be bound to state or show in the bill of lading any marks, number, quantity, or weight which he has reasonable ground for suspecting not accurately to represent the goods actually received, or which he has had no reasonable means of checking.

4.   Such a bill of lading shall be prima facie evidence of the receipt by the carrier of the goods as therein described in accordance with paragraph 3(a), (b) and (c). However, proof to the contrary shall not be admissible when the bill of lading has been transferred to a third party acting in good faith.

5.   The shipper shall be deemed to have guaranteed to the carrier the accuracy at the time of shipment of the marks, number, quantity and weight, as furnished by him, and the shipper shall indemnify the carrier against all loss, damages and expenses arising or resulting from inaccuracies in such particulars. The right of the carrier to such indemnity shall in no way limit his responsibility and liability under the contract of carriage to any person other than the shipper.

6.   Unless notice of loss or damage and the general nature of such loss or damage be given in writing to the carrier or his agent at the port of discharge before or at the time of the removal of the goods into the custody of the person entitled to delivery thereof under the contract of carriage, or, if the loss or damage be not apparent, within three days, such removal shall be prima facie evidence of the delivery by the carrier of the goods as described in the bill of lading.

The notice in writing need not be given if the state of the goods has, at the time of their receipt, been the subject of joint survey or inspection.

Subject to paragraph 6bis the carrier and the ship shall in any event be discharged from all liability whatsoever in respect of the goods, unless suit is brought within one year of their delivery or of the date when they should have been delivered. This period may, however, be extended if the parties so agree after the cause of action has arisen.

In the case of any actual or apprehended loss or damage the carrier and the receiver shall give all reasonable facilities to each other for inspecting and tallying the goods.

6bis.   An action for indemnity against a third person may be brought even after the expiration of the year provided for in the preceding paragraph if brought within the time allowed by the law of the Court seized of the case. However, the time allowed shall be not less than three months, commencing from the day when the person bringing such action for indemnity has settled the claim or has been served with process in the action against himself.

7.   After the goods are loaded the bill of lading to be issued by the carrier, master, or agent of the carrier, to the shipper shall, if the shipper so demands, be a 'shipped' bill of lading, provided that if the shipper shall have previously taken up any document of title to such goods, he shall surrender the same as against the issue of the 'shipped' bill of lading, but at the option of the carrier such document of title may be noted at the port of shipment by the carrier, master, or agent with the name or names of the ship or ships upon which the goods have been shipped and the date or dates of shipment, and when so noted, if it shows the particulars mentioned in paragraph 3 of Article III, shall for the purpose of this article be deemed to constitute a 'shipped' bill of lading.

8.   Any clause, covenant, or agreement in a contract of carriage relieving the carrier or the ship from liability for loss or damage to, or in connection with, goods arising from negligence, fault, or failure in the duties and obligations provided in this article or lessening such liability otherwise than as provided in these Rules, shall be null and void and of no effect. A benefit of insurance in favour of the carrier or similar clause shall be deemed to be a clause relieving the carrier from liability.

Article IV

1.   Neither the carrier nor the ship shall be liable for loss or damage arising or resulting from unseaworthiness unless caused by want of due diligence on the part of the carrier to make the ship seaworthy, and to secure that the ship is properly manned, equipped and supplied, and to make the holds, refrigerating and cool chambers and all other parts of the ship in which goods are carried fit and safe for their reception, carriage and preservation in accordance with the provisions of paragraph 1 of Article III. Whenever loss or damage has resulted from unseaworthiness the burden of proving the exercise of due diligence shall be on the carrier or other person claiming exemption under this article.

2.   Neither the carrier nor the ship shall be responsible for loss or damage arising or resulting from—
   (a)   Act, neglect, or default of the master, mariner, pilot, or the servants of the carrier in the navigation or in the management of the ship.
   (b)   Fire, unless caused by the actual fault or privity of the carrier.
   (c)   Perils, dangers and accidents of the sea or other navigable waters.
   (d)   Act of God.
   (e)   Act of War.
   (f)   Act of public enemies.
   (g)   Arrest or restraint of princes, rulers or people, or seizure under legal process.
   (h)   Quarantine restrictions.
   (i)   Act or omission of the shipper or owner of the goods, his agent or representative.
   (j)   Strikes or lockouts or stoppage or restraint of labour from whatever cause, whether partial or general.
   (k)   Riots and civil commotions.
   (l)   Saving or attempting to save life or property at sea.
   (m)   Wastage in bulk or weight or any other loss or damage arising from inherent defect, quality or vice of the goods.
   (n)   Insufficiency of packing.
   (o)   Insufficiency or inadequacy of marks.
   (p)   Latent defects not discoverable by due diligence.
   (q)   Any other cause arising without the actual fault or privity of the carrier, or without the fault or neglect of the agents or servants of the carrier, but the burden of proof shall be on the person claiming the benefit of this exception to show that neither the actual fault or privity of the carrier nor the fault or neglect of the agents or servants of the carrier contributed to the loss or damage.

3.   The shipper shall not be responsible for loss or damage sustained by the carrier or the ship arising or resulting from any cause without the act, fault or neglect of the shipper, his agents or his servants.

4. *Any deviation in saving or attempting to save life or property at sea or any reasonable deviation shall not be deemed to be an infringement or breach of these Rules or of the contract of carriage, and the carrier shall not be liable for any loss or damage resulting therefrom.*

5.(a) *Unless the nature and value of such goods have been declared by the shipper before shipment and inserted in the bill of lading, neither the carrier nor the ship shall in any event be or become liable for any loss or damage to or in connection with the goods in an amount exceeding the equivalent of 10,000 francs per package or unit or 30 francs per kilo of gross weight of the goods lost or damaged, whichever is the higher.*

(b) *The total amount recoverable shall be calculated by reference to the value of such goods at the place and time at which the goods are discharged from the ship in accordance with the contract or should have been so discharged.*

The value of the goods shall be fixed according to the commodity exchange price, or, if there be no such price, according to the current market price, or, if there be no commodity exchange price or current market price, by reference to the normal value of goods of the same kind and quality.

(c) *Where a container, pallet or similar article of transport is used to consolidate goods, the number of packages or units enumerated in the bill of lading as packed in such article of transport shall be deemed the number of packages or units for the purpose of this paragraph as far as these packages or units are concerned. Except as aforesaid such article of transport shall be considered the package or unit.*

(d) *A franc means a unit consisting of 65.5 milligrammes of gold of millesimal fineness 900. The date of conversion of the sum awarded into national currencies shall be governed by the law of the Court seized of the case.*

(e) *Neither the carrier nor the ship shall be entitled to the benefit of the limitation of liability provided for in this paragraph if it is proved that the damage resulted from an act or omission of the carrier done with intent to cause damage, or recklessly and with knowledge that damage would probably result.*

(f) *The declaration mentioned in sub-paragraph (a) of this paragraph, if embodied in the bill of lading, shall be prima facie evidence, but shall not be binding or conclusive on the carrier.*

(g) *By agreement between the carrier, master or agent of the carrier and the shipper other maximum amounts than those mentioned in sub-paragraph (a) of this paragraph may be fixed, provided that no maximum amount so fixed shall be less than the appropriate maximum mentioned in that sub-paragraph.*

(h) *Neither the carrier nor the ship shall be responsible in any event for loss or damage to, or in connection with, goods if the nature or value thereof has been knowingly mis-stated by the shipper in the bill of lading.*

6. *Goods of an inflammable, explosive or dangerous nature to the shipment whereof the carrier, master or agent of the carrier has not consented with knowledge of their nature and character, may at any time before discharge be landed at any place, or destroyed or rendered innocuous by the carrier without compensation and the shipper of such goods shall be liable for all damages and expenses directly or indirectly arising out of or resulting from such shipment. If any such goods shipped with such knowledge and consent shall become a danger to the ship or cargo, they may in like manner be landed at any place, or destroyed or rendered innocuous by the carrier without liability on the part of the carrier except to general average, if any.*

ARTICLE IV BIS

1. *The defences and limits of liability provided for in these Rules shall apply in any action against the carrier in respect of loss or damage to goods covered by a contract of carriage whether the action be founded in contract or in tort.*

2. *If such an action is brought against a servant or agent of the carrier (such servant or agent not being an independent contractor), such servant or agent shall be entitled to avail himself of the defences and limits of liability which the carrier is entitled to invoke under these Rules.*

3.   *The aggregate of the amounts recoverable from the carrier, and such servants and agents, shall in no case exceed the limit provided for in these Rules.*

4.   *Nevertheless, a servant or agent of the carrier shall not be entitled to avail himself of the provisions of this article, if it is proved that the damage resulted from an act or omission of the servant or agent done with intent to cause damage or recklessly and with knowledge that damage would probably result.*

ARTICLE V

A carrier shall be at liberty to surrender in whole or in part all or any of his rights and immunities or to increase any of his responsibilities and obligations under these Rules, provided such surrender or increase shall be embodied in the bill of lading issued to the shipper. The provisions of these Rules shall not be applicable to charter parties, but if bills of lading are issued in the case of a ship under a charter party they shall comply with the terms of these Rules. Nothing in these Rules shall be held to prevent the insertion in a bill of lading of any lawful provision regarding general average.

ARTICLE VI

Notwithstanding the provisions of the preceding articles, a carrier, master or agent of the carrier and a shipper shall in regard to any particular goods be at liberty to enter into any agreement in any terms as to the responsibility and liability of the carrier for such goods, and as to the rights and immunities of the carrier in respect of such goods, or his obligation as to seaworthiness, so far as this stipulation is not contrary to public policy, or the care or diligence of his servants or agents in regard to the loading, handling, stowage, carriage, custody, care and discharge of the goods carried by sea, provided that in this case no bill of lading has been or shall be issued and that the terms agreed shall be embodied in a receipt which shall be a non-negotiable document and shall be marked as such.

Any agreement so entered into shall have full legal effect.

Provided that this article shall not apply to ordinary commercial shipments made in the ordinary course of trade, but only to other shipments where the character or condition of the property to be carried or the circumstances, terms and conditions under which the carriage is to be performed are such as reasonably to justify a special agreement.

ARTICLE VII

Nothing herein contained shall prevent a carrier or a shipper from entering into any agreement, stipulation, condition, reservation or exemption as to the responsibility and liability of the carrier or the ship for the loss or damage to, or in connection with, the custody and care and handling of goods prior to the loading on, and subsequent to the discharge from, the ship on which the goods are carried by sea.

ARTICLE VIII

The provisions of these Rules shall not affect the rights and obligations of the carrier under any statute for the time being in force relating to the limitation of the liability of owners of sea-going vessels.

ARTICLE IX

These Rules shall not affect the provisions of any international Convention or national law governing liability for nuclear damage.

ARTICLE X

The provisions of these Rules shall apply to every bill of lading relating to the carriage of goods between ports in two different States if:

(a)   the bill of lading is issued in a contracting State,

or

(b)   the carriage is from a port in a contracting State,

or

(c)   the contract contained in or evidenced by the bill of lading provides that these Rules or legislation of any State giving effect to them are to govern the contract,

whatever may be the nationality of the ship, the carrier, the shipper, the consignee, or any other interested person.

22   Marine Insurance — Cargo

22.1   Contract of Marine Insurance

A contract of marine insurance is, in English law, one whereby the insurer undertakes to indemnify the assured against marine losses: Marine Insurance Act 1906, s. 1. (In this section of the Manual all references to statutory sections will be to the Marine Insurance Act 1906 unless otherwise stated.) In s. 1, 'marine losses' are defined as 'losses incident to a marine adventure'. 'Marine adventure' is, in turn, defined in s. 3(2) as occurring where:

(a)   any ship, goods or other moveables (the insurable property) is exposed to 'maritime perils'; or

(b)   the exposure of insurable property to 'maritime perils' endangers the earning or acquisition of any freight, profit, or other pecuniary benefit, or the security for any advances, loan or disbursements; or

(c)   the owner, or other person interested or responsible for, insurable property may become liable to a third party by reason of exposure to 'maritime perils'.

Section 3(2) then proceeds to define 'maritime perils' as 'perils consequent on or incidental to the navigation of the sea, that is to say, perils of the seas, fire, war perils, pirates, rovers, thieves, captures, seizures, restraints, detainments of princes and peoples, jettisons, barratry, and any other perils, either of the like kind or which may be designated by the policy'.

In *Continental Illinois* v *Bathurst* [1985] Lloyd's Rep 625, Mustill J stated:

It is preferable to concentrate on the first part of the definition of 'maritime perils' in s. 3. This identifies the perils as those which are 'consequent on or incidental to the navigation of the sea'. It is only the exposure to perils of this nature which gives the adventure the character of a marine adventure within s. 3(2).

Although the insurable property must thus be exposed to the perils of sea navigation for the contract to qualify as one of *marine* insurance, the contract may nevertheless by its express terms or by a usage in the trade be extended so as to protect the assured against losses on inland waters or against losses on any land risk which may be incidental to the sea voyage: s. 2(1). It is the usual practice these days on cargo insurance for cover to attach 'warehouse to warehouse', that is to say, at the commencement of land transit from the warehouse to the ship at the loading port, to continue during the sea voyage, and to cease on completion of the land transit from the ship at the port of discharge to the warehouse at destination. A clause which provides for this type of extended cover is known as a 'transit clause'.

22.1.1   THE TRANSIT CLAUSE

It is of fundamental importance that the duration of the cover provided by a contract of marine insurance should be clearly defined. If an assured is to recover it must be shown that the loss occurred whilst cover was operational. Some contracts define the duration of cover in terms of time; others provide cover during a voyage, in which case it is particularly important to agree specifically when the voyage will be treated as commencing and terminating.

The Institute Cargo Clauses provide voyage cover and Clause 8 defines its duration. This clause is called a 'transit' clause and provides, *inter alia,* that:

(a)   the insurance attaches from the time the goods leave the warehouse or place of storage for the commencement of the transit;
(b)   it continues during the ordinary course of transit;
(c)   it terminates:

(i)   when the goods arrive at the consignee's warehouse at the destination named in the policy; or

(ii)   when the goods arrive at some other final warehouse or place of storage whether at the destination named in the policy or not, which the assured elects to use either

(1)   for storage other than in the ordinary course of transit; or
(2)   for allocation or distribution

(iii)   in any event, on the expiry of 60 days after completion of discharge at the final port of the voyage, if the goods have not by that time reached the relevant warehouse or place of storage.

The following points should be noted. Insurance cover attaches only when the goods leave the warehouse in *order to commence the insured voyage.* Thus cover will not commence if, for example, the goods have been sent to the packers. Although cover continues during 'the ordinary course of transit', by Clause 8.3 the cover shall nevertheless remain in force during delay beyond the control of the assured, any deviation, forced discharge, reshipment or transhipment, and any variation of the adventure arising from the exercise of a liberty granted to the shipowner or charterer under the contract of carriage. (This provision does *not* render the insurer *liable* for any loss, damage or expenses caused by delay.)

Clause 8 will not apply where the carrier has terminated the voyage at a port short of destination in circumstances beyond the control of the assured. In this situation, under Clause 9, cover will cease unless prompt notice is given to the insurer and a request for continuation of cover made. Once this has occurred, cover will continue but the assured is obliged to pay an additional premium. Cover extended under Clause 9 will cease:

(a)   when the goods are delivered to a buyer at the intermediate port, subject to an overall 60-day limit, after the 'arrival' of the goods insured at the intermediate port; or
(b)   if the assured decides to send the goods on to the original port of destination or to another port during the 60 days, when the goods arrive at the appropriate warehouse set out in Clause 8, but subject to the overall limit of 60 days after completion of discharge.

22.1.2   INSURABLE INTEREST

In order to be able to recover on his/her insurance the assured must have an 'insurable interest' at the time of the loss (s. 6(1)), a requirement specifically set out also in Clause 11.1 of the Institute Cargo Clauses. The assured need not be 'interested' when the insurance is effected.

The assured will have an insurable interest where:

(a)   some physical object capable of being destroyed is exposed to *maritime perils*; and
(b)   the assured stands in some relationship recognised by law or equity to that object, as a result of which he/she may benefit from its safety or due arrival or suffer prejudice from its loss, damage or detention, or may incur liability in respect thereof: s. 5(2).

An obvious example of an 'insurable interest' is absolute ownership of the insurable property. In addition, a buyer has an insurable interest in goods which are at his/her risk: *Inglis* v *Stock* (1885) 10 App Cas 263. Equally, where the seller exercises the right of stoppage in transit and recovers possession of the goods, he/she has an insurable interest. Difficulties do arise in showing the existence of an insurable interest at the appropriate time. Where the seller has parted with possession and property before payment, and the goods are lost or damaged before the seller exercises a right of stoppage on the buyer's insolvency, it is unclear whether the seller had an insurable interest at the time of the loss. A similar problem arises where property and possession have passed, but prior to rejection of the goods by the buyer they are lost or damaged. Again, it is uncertain whether the seller has an existing insurable interest at the time of the loss or damage.

Section 7(1) provides that contingent and defeasible interests are insurable interests. A seller is best advised to insure on a 'sellers interest' basis so as to be protected in circumstances such as those set out above.

There may be circumstances in which the assured had an interest in the goods recognised as an insurable interest at the time the loss or damage occurred and yet there was no insurance cover at that time — for example, goods purchased FOB are lost or damaged before the purchaser has placed the insurance cover but *after* he/she has assumed the risk. Where the purchaser has insured on 'lost or not lost' terms or contracted on Institute Cargo Clause terms, which include the 'insurable interest' Clause 11.2, the policy, when it attaches, will attach retrospectively to cover the time of commencement (if it is a time policy) or first point on the voyage (if it is a voyage policy). If loss occurs during the time or stage in the voyage now covered by the policy, *and* the loss falls within the terms of the policy, *and* the assured was unaware of the loss at the time the contract of insurance was concluded, he/she will recover.

An assured may sue on the contract of insurance in one of two categories. The assured may be one originally interested in the policy as a disclosed or undisclosed principle: *Browning v London Provincial Insurance* (1872) 2 LR 5 AL 273. In this situation the principal must show that he/she had the insurable interest and was covered at the time of the loss or must be able to rely on a 'lost or not lost' clause. Alternatively the assured may be one who obtains a derivative interest on an assignment of the policy to him/her. The assignee need not show that he/she had an insurable interest at the time of the loss, but must show that the assignor had an insurable interest at that time: *J. Aron v Miall* (1928) 34 Com Cas 18.

22.1.3   ASSIGNMENT

If an assured assigns his/her interest in the subject-matter insured, he/she does not thereby assign his/her rights under the contract of insurance: s. 15. However, the policy is assignable unless it contains terms expressly prohibiting assignment: s. 50. A valid assignment under the Marine Insurance Act, s. 51 will take place if:

   (a)   when the assured parts with his/her interest in the subject-matter insured, he/she assigns the policy at that time; or

   (b)   when at the time the assured parts with his/her interest in the subject-matter, there is in existence an express or implied agreement (e.g. in the contract of sale) to assign the policy: *North of England Oil Cake Co. v Archangel Maritime Insurance* (1875) LR 10 QB 249.

Under s. 50(3) the policy can be assigned by endorsement or other customary manner. Where, under s. 51, there has been an ineffective assignment, there can still be an assignment of the right to sue the insurers under the Law of Property Act 1925, s. 136: *Williams v Atlantic Assurance* [1933] 1 KB 81. Nevertheless, in these circumstances, the assignment will have to be in writing (mere endorsement of the marine insurance policy will probably not suffice) and there must be written notice to the debtor, i.e. the insurer.

Under s. 50(2) the assignee is entitled to sue in his/her own name, but the insurer is entitled to set up any defences arising out of the contract which he/she would have had against the assignor, e.g. the insurer can set up against the innocent assignee non-disclosure of a material fact by the assignor: *William Pickersgill & Sons Ltd v London & Provincial Maritime & General Insurance Co.* [1912] 3 KB 614. See also *Colonia Versicherung AG v Amoco Oil Co.* [1995] 1 Lloyd's Rep 570.

Not only must the assured show the capacity in which he/she is claiming under the insurance policy and, where appropriate, his/her assignor's insurable interest existing at the time of the loss, but must also prove a loss by a peril insured against.

22.2   Institute Cargo Clauses

Almost all cargo insurance is now undertaken by means of the use of the new policy forms with the attachment of the Institute Cargo Clauses A, B or C depending on the assured's requirements. The A Clauses are the equivalent of the former 'all risks' policy and will most commonly be used for the carriage of fragile, perishable cargo. The B Clauses provide the most usual form of cover, whilst the C Clauses provide very limited cover indeed.

22.2.1   CONSTRUCTION OF INSTITUTE CARGO CLAUSES

Since the A Clauses cover *all risks of loss or damage to the subject-matter insured except as provided in the exclusion clauses*, the assured discharges the burden placed on him/her when he/she proves that the loss was proximately caused by some event which is an accident. The assured is not bound to go further and prove the exact nature of the accident or casualty which occasioned the loss. In *British & Foreign Marine Insurance* v *Gaunt* [1921] 2 AC 41 Lord Sumner did, however, lay emphasis on the distinction between 'All risks' and (i) inherent vice and (ii) wear and tear. He said (at 57, 58):

> There are, of course, limits to 'all risks' ... [and] the expression does not cover inherent vice or mere wear and tear or British capture. It covers a risk not a certainty; it is something which happens to the subject-matter from without, not the natural behaviour of that subject-matter, being what it is, in the circumstances under which it is carried ... I think, however, that the quasi-universality of the description does affect the onus of proof in one way ... when [the claimant] avers loss by some risk coming within 'all risks' ... he need only give evidence reasonably showing that the loss was due to a casualty, not a certainty or to inherent vice or to wear and tear.

The above statement by Lord Sumner was referred to in *Golodetz et Co.* v *Czarnikow-Rionda* [1979] 2 AERT 726 by Donaldson J, who stated:

> This seems to me to establish that, if an assured claims under an all risks policy on the basis that a loss has occurred due to some accident or casualty without proof of its exact nature, he will necessarily be relying on a change in the condition of the goods rather than on direct evidence of what occurred and that in such circumstances he must prove that this change was not due to the natural behaviour of the subject-matter. If he does not do this, he will be unable to prove the essentially accidental nature of the broad cover provided.

By contrast, where the goods are insured on the B or C Clauses. the burden of proving a loss within the risks covered clauses (Clause 1) remains throughout on the assured. He/she must show with particularity that the goods were damaged during transit by a risk insured against: *Rhesa Shipping Co.* v *Edmunds* [1985] 2 All ER 712; *Reinhart Co.* v *Joshua Hoyle & Sons Ltd* [1961] 1 Lloyd's Rep 346; *Golodetz et Co.* v *Czarnikow-Rionda (supra)*. This last case deals with an all risks policy but the judgment is equally relevant to the burden of proof under B and C Clauses. Donaldson J said:

> However, a claim under an 'all risks' policy can be pursued in a different way ... All risks has the same effect as if all insurable risks were separately enumerated. The assured can, therefore, claim on the basis that he was insured, *inter alia,* against loss or damage by fire. The question then becomes that of whether insurance against fire is unlimited but subject to exceptions for inherent vice, or is limited to fire which does not arise from the inherent nature of the goods insured ... In my judgment, an insurance against 'fire' is an unqualified promise which is subject to the exceptions set out in s. 55(2)(c), Marine Insurance Act 1906, ... This conclusion is in line with the view expressed in *Phillips on the Law of Insurance* that proof of fire suffices to prove a casualty for which the underwriters are liable unless they can show that it occurred as a result of inherent vice.

22.2.2   CONSTRUCTION OF PARTICULAR CLAUSES

There are other points to be noted on the construction of the Institute Cargo Clauses.

22.2.2.1   Risks covered — generally
Clause 1 in A, B and C Clauses covers 'loss or damage to the subject-matter insured'. This expression covers physical loss or damage to the goods but not financial loss not emanating from physical loss or damage, even though the financial loss was caused by a peril insured against (but note the specific cover for expenses under Clause 16).

Clause 1.1 in B and C Clauses enables the assured with regard to those risks/perils therein set out to establish liability on the part of the insurer merely by proving that the loss was 'reasonably attributable' to these perils. All risks and perils set out in Clause 1 of the B and C Clauses are covered by the A Clauses.

22.2.2.2   Entry of water — windstorm damage
B Clause 1.2.3 replaces the traditional formula, 'perils of the sea', found in the old standard SG Policy with the expression 'entry of sea lake or river water into vessel craft hold conveyance container lift van or place of storage'. In order to recover the assured must prove that the loss was *proximately caused* by the occurrence of one or more such circumstances (see Clause 1.2).

Since by Clause 8.1 cover only commences when the goods leave the warehouse or place of storage at the place named therein *for the commencement of the transit*, B Clause 1.2.3, although providing considerable cover for loss or damage caused by sea water or river water, can only apply when the water enters a place where the goods are stowed or stored *during transit*.

The peril will apply even though it cannot be said that the water entered through heavy weather conditions.

However, B Clause 1.2.3 does not cover loss or damage caused by the shifting of the cargo in the hold due to a storm, Neither the B Clauses nor the C Clauses cover mere windstorm damage. Such loss is covered under the A Clauses, but in the B and C Clauses only in the additional event of stranding, grounding, sinking or capsizing (B and C Clause 1.1.2) or collision (B and C Clause 1.1.4). Further, neither B Clauses nor the C Clauses cover rainwater damage but this loss would be covered under the A Clauses.

Since B Clause 1.2.3 does not exist under the C Clauses, loss or damage by the entry of sea water is only recoverable under the C Clauses if the loss is:

(a)   attributable to stranding, grounding, sinking or capsizing (C Clause 1.1.2); or
(b)   attributable to discharge of cargo at a port of distress (C Clause 1.1.5); or
(c)   caused by jettison (C Clause 1.2.2).

22.2.2.3   Stranding, grounding, sinking or capsizing
B and C Clauses 1.1.2 cover the risk of 'vessel or craft being stranded, grounded, sunk or capsized'. In this respect it should be noted that loss or damage need only be reasonably attributable to the risk in Clause 1.1.2. Stranding is taking ground by reason of an accident; grounding is taking ground in the usual course of navigation. Sea water damage and also damage to cargo in the holds reasonably attributable to the above events is covered.

22.2.2.4   General average sacrifice
The risk of 'general average sacrifice' is covered by Clause 1 of the A Clauses and by Clause 1.2.1 of the B and C Clauses. By the Marine Insurance Act 1906, s. 66, there is a general average act where 'any extraordinary sacrifice ... is voluntarily and reasonably made ... in time of peril for the purpose of preserving the property imperilled in the common adventure'. A common example of general average sacrifice is jettison of cargo — if cargo is jettisoned in heavy seas in order to preserve the ship and the

remainder of the cargo, the owner of the jettisoned cargo may recover his/her loss on the insurance. The insurers may then, by subrogation (see below), recover against the owners of the interests saved, who may then, in turn, if insured, recover their contributions from their own insurers. The contributions are calculated pro rata to the value of the property saved by the sacrifice.

22.2.2.5　Jettison
The risk of jettison is covered by Clause 1 of the A Clauses and by Clause 1.2.2 of the B and C Clauses. In most cases jettison would constitute a general average sacrifice covered by A Clauses and Clause 1.2.1 (B and C) (see **22.2.2.4** above), but Clause 1.2.2 will cover, for example, loss where a port authority has ordered the jettison of hazardous cargo.

22.2.2.6　Washing overboard
The A Clauses cover and, by Clause 1.2.2, the B Clauses also cover the risk of loss or damage caused by 'washing overboard'. This risk is not covered in the C Clauses. If the assured seeks to rely on this risk he must show that the goods were *washed* overboard as opposed to being *lost* overboard unless the assured can rely on what is known as a sling loss (see **22.2.2.7** below).

22.2.2.7　Loss whilst loading or unloading
The A Clauses and B Clause 1.3 covers 'total loss of any package lost overboard or dropped whilst loading on to or unloading from vessel or craft'. This risk is not covered in the C Clauses. It should be noted that Clause 1.3 will only allow recovery for total loss. The total loss must have occurred during loading or discharge. It probably extends to those acts during transhipment or transfer to lighters or barges.

22.2.2.8　Collision
Damage by collision is covered under the A Clauses, and is covered by B and C Clause 1.1.4, which provides cover for loss or damage reasonably attributable to 'collision or contact of vessel, craft or conveyance with any external object other than water'. Here it should be noted that under Clause 1.1.4 the loss or damage must have been due to contact with an object *external* to the vessel. Damage due to contact of cargoes during storms is not recoverable thereunder.

22.2.2.9　Fire and explosion
Fire and explosion are covered in any event in the A Clauses. They are covered in the B and C Clauses by Clause 1.1.1. Since this clause requires the assured to show only that the loss is *reasonably attributable* to the fire, heating damage would be covered, as would water damage where water had been used to put out the fire. For the same reason, the clause would allow recovery for loss or damage to goods caused by crushing due to the force of an explosion.

The clause is not confined to fire on a ship, As the transit clause is attached, Clause 1.1.1 will extend to fire and/or explosion at any stage once transit has begun.

22.2.2.10　Overturning or derailment of a land conveyance
This is covered by A Clauses and Clause 1.1.3 of the B and C Clauses.

The addition of the transit clause in B and C Clauses would have less impact if the risks did not include the most common land risk. In addition, the loss or damage need only be *reasonably attributable* to the above.

22.2.2.11　Earthquake, volcanic eruption, lightning
This is covered by A Clauses and B Clause 1.1.6, the effect of which is to extend cover under the B Clauses (not the C Clauses) for loss or damage reasonably attributable to these events, whether during sea **or** land transit.

22.2.2.12　Discharge of cargo at port of distress
The A Clauses and Clause 1.1.5 of the B and C Clauses allows recovery for loss or damage reasonably attributable to discharge of *insured* cargo at a port short of destination.

22.3 Causation

Unlike the A Clauses, where all accidents once transit has commenced are covered unless specifically excluded, the assured with cover under the B or C Clauses has to bring his/her loss within a particular part of Clause 1. In the A Clauses and those risks within Clause 1.2 of the B and C Clauses, the assured has to show the loss was **proximately** caused by an accident (A Clauses) or by a particular peril in Clause 1.2 (B and C Clauses).

22.3.1 MEANING OF 'PROXIMATE'

Where a loss is due to a combination of causes, the question of which is the *proximate* cause is not answered by mere order in time: *Leyland Shipping Co.* v *Norwich Union Insurance Society* [1918] AC 350. The cause which is truly proximate is that which is proximate in terms of efficiency. The choice of the real or efficient cause from out of the whole complex of facts must be made by applying common-sense standards: *Reischer* v *Borwick* [1894] 2 QB 548.

As long as the loss is proximately caused by or, where B and C Clause 1.1 applies, is reasonably attributable to the peril insured against, *negligence* of the master or crew will not enable the insurers to escape liability: s. 55(2)(a).

22.3.2 COMBINATION OF CAUSES

The situation might be such that the loss is found to be caused by two or more causes co-operating together to produce the loss or damage. A distinction must be made between the following situations:

(a)   Where one co-operating cause is within the terms of the policy and the other is *not covered by the terms of the policy at all*. In such a situation, the assured is entitled to recover: see *The Miss Jay Jay,* [1987] 1 Lloyd's Rep 32, where Slade LJ said (at 40): 'The loss is treated as proximately caused by the cause insured against, not withstanding the presence of a concurrent cause not covered by the policy.'

(b)   Where one co-operating cause is within the terms of the policy and the other is *excluded*, the assured is not entitled to recover: see *Wayne Tank & Pump Co.* v *Employers' Liability Assurance Corporation* [1974] QB 57, in which Roskill LJ stated *per curiam* (at 75):

I think that the law in this respect is the same both for marine and non-marine, namely, that if the loss is caused by two causes effectively operating at the same time and one is wholly expressly excluded from the policy, *the policy does not pay.*

22.4 Excluded Risks

Once the assured has proved a loss within the terms of the policy, the burden shifts to the insurers, who can escape liability if they can establish that the loss is specifically excluded: see Donaldson J in *Golodetz et Co.* v *Czarnikow-Rionda* (**22.2.1**).

22.4.1 WILFUL MISCONDUCT OF ASSURED

Clause 4.1, A, B and C Clauses, excludes liability for loss, damage or *expense* attributable to the wilful misconduct of the assured. For example, if the charterer or cargo owner connives with the crew to scuttle the ship, even though loss is proximately caused by the entry of sea water, Clause 4.1 enables the insurer to escape liability for the loss of the *charterer's* cargo as the loss is attributable to the wilful misconduct of the assured.

22.4.2 LEAKAGE, LOSS IN WEIGHT OR VOLUME, WEAR AND TEAR

By Clause 4.2, A, B and C Clauses, there is no cover for ordinary leakage, ordinary loss in weight or volume, or ordinary wear and tear of the subject-matter insured. The exception excludes liability for, e.g., evaporation which occurs in the natural course of events during transit. Thus evaporation caused by stifling conditions in the hold, due to the closure of the hatch covers during heavy weather, would not be caught by the exception. In spite of this, however, such a loss would only be covered in the A Clauses; it is not covered within Clause 1 of the B or C Clauses.

22.4.3   INSUFFICIENCY OR UNSUITABILITY OF PACKING OR PREPARATION

Clause 4.3, A, B and C Clauses, prevents liability attaching for loss, damage or expense *caused* by insufficiency or unsuitability of packing or preparation of the subject-matter insured: *Berk* v *Style* [1955] 3 All ER 625.

'Packing' to which the exclusion applies will include stowage in a container or liftvan if:

    (a)   the stowage was undertaken by the assured or his/her servant (note that this exception is not applicable where stowage is undertaken by an agent); or

    (b)   the stowage was carried out prior to the attachment of the risk.

22.4.4   INHERENT VICE

Clause 4.4, A, B and C Clauses, excludes liability for loss, damage or expense *caused* by the inherent vice or nature of the subject-matter insured (as to meaning of inherent vice see *Noten* v *Harding* [1989] 2 Lloyd's Rep 522). Where there is spontaneous combustion of grain which causes damage to other cargo, there is no liability for grain lost through its own internal processes, but the damage and loss to other cargo affected by heat or fire are recoverable under the A Clauses and under B or C Clauses where loss is reasonably attributable to fire or explosion (Clause 1.1.1). See, e.g., *Sassoon* v *Yorkshire Insurance Co.* (1923) 16 Ll LR 129.

22.4.5   DELAY

Clause 4.5, A, B and C Clauses, excludes liability for loss, damage or expenses proximately caused by delay, even though the delay is caused by a risk insured against.

The following points should be noted:

    (a)   General average expenses and salvage charges even though proximately incurred by delay are recoverable.

    (b)   Under s. 48, in a voyage policy the adventure insured must be prosecuted with reasonable despatch and the insurer will be discharged from liability as from the time when the delay becomes unreasonable unless there is a lawful excuse. However, Clause 8.3 (A, B and C Clauses) keeps the contract alive during *delay beyond the control of the assured.* (This does not mean the insurer is liable. The effect of Clause 8.3 is to preserve the potential liability of the insurer for a loss falling within the terms of the policy, and which is not excluded.)

22.4.6   INSOLVENCY OR FINANCIAL DEFAULT OF OWNERS, MANAGERS, CHARTERERS OR OPERATORS OF VESSEL

Clause 4.6, A, B and C Clauses, excludes loss, damage or expense *arising* from the insolvency or financial default of the owners, managers, charterers or operators of the vessel. For example, if due to financial difficulties, the carrier discharges at a port short of destination, the insurer is not liable for any forwarding expenses incurred by the assured. Nor can the assured recover under Clause 12, the forwarding charges clause, as it is confined to recovery of expenses where transit has been terminated short of destination *by a peril insured against.*

22.4.7   DELIBERATE DAMAGE OR DESTRUCTION BY WRONGFUL ACT

By Clause 4.7, there is no insurance under the B and C Clauses for loss of or damage to the subject-matter insured if this is due to a deliberate and wrongful act of any person or persons.

The standard SG policy covered loss by barratry, which was defined as any wilful wrongdoing by the master or crew to the prejudice of the shipowner or charterer. The B and C Clauses indicate the desire of the insurer not to be bound by this type of loss. This risk can be covered if the assured contracts on the A Clauses, which automatically cover the loss as long as the deliberate act is not that of the *assured*, or if the assured asks for the addition of the 'malicious damage clause', which automatically deletes Clause 4.7 B and C Clauses.

The malicious damage clause reads as follows:

> In consideration of our additional premium it is hereby agreed that Clause 4.7 ... is deemed to be deleted and further that this insurance covers loss or damage to the subject-matter insured caused by malicious acts, vandalism or sabotage, subject always to the other exclusions contained in this insurance.

There is no cover in the B and C Clauses for theft. Since this is a greater possibility when goods are in transit overland, Clause 4.7 can be deleted and the Institute Theft and Pilferage clause added.

22.4.8 NUCLEAR AND ATOMIC WEAPONS

By Clause 4.7 of the A Clauses and by Clause 4.8 of the B and C Clauses there is no liability for loss, damage or expense *arising* from the use of any weapon of war employing atomic or nuclear fission or other like reaction or radioactive force or matter.

It should be noted that this clause excludes liability for loss, damage or expenses from the use of a nuclear weapon in a non-war situation. The addition of war risk insurance will still not allow recovery for the above loss.

22.4.9 UNSEAWORTHINESS OR UNFITNESS OF VESSEL

This is dealt with in Clause 5.1, A, B and C Clauses. Many merchants, when shipping goods, will have no control over the manning and equipping of the ship. Neither will they normally be aware of any inadequacies in these respects. In a voyage policy, there is, under s. 39, an implied warranty that the ship is seaworthy, i.e. reasonably fit to carry the goods or other moveables to the destination contemplated by the policy and reasonably fit in all respects to encounter the ordinary perils of the insured adventure. If the warranty is not exactly complied with, the insurer will be discharged from *all* liability (*not just that relating to unseaworthiness*) *as from the date of the breach*, i.e. the commencement of the sea voyage, but without prejudice to any liability incurred by him before that date: s. 33(3), unless there is an express term in the contract to the contrary, or the insurer waives the breach under s. 34(3): *The Good Luck* [1991] 3 All ER 1, HL.

A breach of this warranty, therefore, could leave the assured cargo owner uninsured, even though there has been no fault on his/her part. Section 33(3) is, however, subject to the express provisions of the policy and, moreover, s. 34(3) enables the insurer to waive the breach of warranty. Indeed, Clause 5.2 in each set of Institute Cargo Clauses states that the insurer waives the breach of warranty but only if the assured or his/her servants were not privy to such unseaworthiness. It is not clear when there must be no knowledge of unseaworthiness by the assured or his/ her servants in order for the waiver clause to operate, but presumably the provision requires an absence of knowledge at the time the warranty operates, i.e. at the commencement of the sea transit. It will be observed that the waiver clause continues to operate even though an agent of the assured has knowledge, e.g. the container transport operator or other type of freight forwarder used by the assured,

Clause 5.2 is *not* a clause excluding liability. Far from it — it is a clause preserving the *potential* liability of the insurer. If the assured can prove a loss within Clause 1 and the insurer cannot rely on an exclusion of liability, the latter will be liable. This brings us to the specific exclusion from liability under Clause 5.1. The operation of Clause 5.2 may have preserved the potential liability of the insurer for *all* losses falling within Clause 1, but he/she can escape liability for the particular loss *arising from:*

(a)   the unseaworthiness of vessel or craft; and/or

(b)   the unfitness of vessel, craft, conveyance container, or liftvan for the safe carriage of the subject-matter insured,

but only if the assured or *his/her servant* were aware of the unseaworthiness or unfitness *at the time the insured cargo was loaded.*

Note that knowledge on the part of a CTO or other freight forwarder of unseaworthiness or unfitness at the time the assured's cargo is loaded, will *not* enable the insurer to escape liability.

22.4.10   WAR

There is an automatic exclusion of war risk cover by Clause 6 of the A, B and C Clauses.

The following points should be noted:

(a)   Piracy is included in the war risk exclusion, 'capture, seizure, arrest, restraint or detachment', in Clause 6.2 of the B and C Clauses. However, 'piracy' is specifically excepted from Clause 6.2 of the A Clauses. Since the A Clauses give 'all risk' cover, piracy is therefore a risk insured against.

(b)   Clause 6.1 shows that the insurer is not liable for loss, damage or expense caused by warlike acts.

(c)   In Clause 6.2 'capture, seizure, arrest' etc. refers to political and executive acts and does not exclude loss caused by judicial process, a risk therefore covered under the A Clauses.

(d)   Clause 6.3 excludes the liability of the insurer for losses due to risks created by hostilities, even though those hostilities have ceased.

(e)   If the assured deletes Clause 6, he will still not get war risk cover under the B and C Clauses unless he asks for it. There is no automatic attachment of war risk cover. The cover in the war clauses is limited to loss or damage to the subject-matter insured. There is no cover for expenses or financial loss suffered as a result of war risks.

22.4.11   STRIKES

Clause 7 deals with strikes exclusion in the A, B and C Clauses.

Even though loss may not be proximately caused by action specified in Clause 7.1, i.e. not caused by strikers, lock-outs etc., the loss will probably be caught by Clause 7.2, which excludes loss *resulting* from strikes, lock-outs etc., even though loss was proximately caused by a peril insured against.

Clause 7.3 excludes loss caused by political activists or terrorists.

Clause 7 excludes liability for expense. If therefore the carrier discharges the goods insured at a port short of destination because the contractual port is strike-bound, the expenses incurred by the assured are not recoverable.

Even with the addition of the Institute Strikes Clauses, which give strike cover, there is no cover for loss, damage or expense arising from the absence, shortage or withholding of labour of any description whatsoever which results from any strike, lock-out, labour disturbance, riot or civil commotion, i.e. cover is only available in respect of loss or damage to goods caused *directly* by strikes etc.

22.5   Types of Loss

The Marine Insurance Act 1906 draws a distinction between total and partial losses. To avoid any doubt, it lays down that any loss other than a total loss is a partial loss: s. 56(1). The Institute Cargo Clauses provide cover for losses which are total or partial. The only instance thereunder where the insurers confine liability to a total loss is B Clause 1.3, where the 'sling loss' must amount to a total loss in order for the assured to be able to recover.

The 1906 Act further subdivides total loss into actual total loss and constructive total loss: s. 56(2). Actual total loss arises when there is a total loss in point of fact. A constructive total loss arises where, although the loss is not a total loss in fact, the commercial realities of the situation are such that the law will recognise it as a total loss. Unless a contrary intention appears from the policy, insurance against total loss includes constructive as well as actual total loss: s. 56(3).

One important distinction between actual and constructive loss is, as will be explained further below, that in the former situation no notice of abandonment need be given: s. 57(2). Indeed, by virtue of the definition of actual total loss, there would be no benefit to the insurer by giving notice. In the case of constructive total loss, such notice is necessary, otherwise the loss will be treated as partial: s. 62(1).

22.5.1 ACTUAL TOTAL LOSS (ATL)

Section 57(1) sets out two categories of ATL:

(a) where the subject-matter insured is wholly destroyed by a peril or perils insured against, or so damaged so to cease to be a thing of the kind insured; or
(b) where the assured is irretrievably deprived of the subject-matter insured by a peril or perils insured against.

As to (b) above, it may be noted that the editors of *Arnould's Law of Marine Insurance and Average* (16th edn, 1981, Sweet and Maxwell) define 'irretrievable deprivation' as occurring:

> where by perils insured against the assured is permanently and irretrievably deprived not only of all present possession and control over the insured goods, but of all hope or possibility of ever ultimately recovering possession of, or further prosecuting the adventure upon, the insured goods.

See, for example, *Roux* v *Salvador* (1836) 3 Bing NC 266 (Ex Ch).

22.5.2 CONSTRUCTIVE TOTAL LOSS (CTL)

Constructive total loss is a concept peculiar to marine insurance. Section 60 defines CTL, and there are two situations in which it arises.

22.5.2.1 Abandonment because actual total loss appears unavoidable
Where the subject-matter insured is reasonably abandoned (i.e. given up for lost) on account of its ATL appearing to be unavoidable, there will be a CTL. Thus under s. 60(2)(i)(a) there will be a CTL where:

(a) the assured is deprived of possession of the goods
(b) by a peril insured against; and
(c) it is unlikely that the assured can recover the insured goods.

The following points should be noted:

(a) There is no need for the goods to be damaged.
(b) Deprivation of possession will include that caused by strandings, groundings or becoming icebound (see *Hall* v *Hayman* [1912] 2 KB 5) but the deprivation of possession by capture, seizure etc. will usually be excluded under the policy, e.g. under Clause 6 of the Institute Cargo Clauses.
(c) 'Unlikely' has been defined as 'unlikely to recover within reasonable time': *Polurrian SS Co. Ltd* v *Young* [1917] 1 KB 922. The prospect of indefinite delay militates against the time being reasonable; *Irvin* v *Hine* [1950] 1 KB 555; *Rodocanachi* v *Elliott* (1873) LR 8 CP 649.

22.5.2.2 Abandonment where the cost of preserving goods would exceed their value when saved
CTL also occurs where the subject-matter insured is reasonably abandoned because it could not be preserved from ATL without an expenditure which would exceed its value when the expenditure had been incurred. Most instances of CTL fall within this category.

Two particular instances relating to cargo insurance are set out in the Act:

(a) The first instance is that set out in s. 60(2)(i)(b) where:

    (i)   the assured is deprived of possession of the goods

    (ii)   by a peril insured against; and

    (iii) the cost of recovering the goods would exceed their value when recovered.

The case of *Rickards* v *Forestal* [1942] AC 50 is an example of such a CTL. In that case, goods belonging to a British assured were being carried on a German ship. On the outbreak of war, the master of the ship decided to obey the instructions of the German Government and return to Germany. It was held that when the master acted upon that determination he possessed the insured goods as servant and agent of the German Government, instead of as bailee of the assured. Thus the assured had been deprived of possession of the goods by an executive act of the German Government — a restraint of princes (which was a peril insured against). Thereafter, in obedience to the instructions of the German Government, the Master put into a Spanish port. He offered to discharge the goods there but only on payment of full freight, discharging expenses and an additional payment of 25 per cent of the value of the goods. It was held that there had been a constructive total loss. Lord Wright said (at 96):

> It would be necessary, if the adventure were to be completed, to obtain space on a vessel bound to [port of destination] or if that were not possible, to England ... for a further transhipment to [port of destination]. There would be heavy agency fees, expenses of transhipment or transhipments, further freight and other expenses in addition to the exorbitant payments demanded at [the Spanish port].

Note that:

    (i)   This type of CTL is not dependent on damage occurring to the goods.

    (ii)   The value with which the cost of recovery is compared is the *value of those goods on arrival* and *not* the valuation stated in the policy: s. 27(4).

(b) The second instance is that set out in s. 60(2)(iii), where:

    (i)   goods are damaged, and

    (ii)   the cost of repairing the damage and forwarding the goods to their destination would exceed their value on arrival.

Points to note are:

    (i)   There is no need for deprivation of possession to have occurred.

    (ii)   The costs of repairing and forwarding which are to be taken into account include those of unshipping the cargo, warehousing, salvage charges, transhipment, etc.

    (iii) As in the situation in (a), the value with which the costs of repairing and forwarding are compared is the *value* (e.g, market value) of the goods on arrival and not the valuation fixed in the policy: s. 22(4).

22.6   Election under Constructive Total Loss

Where there is a CTL, the assured is put to an election: s. 61. He/she can elect to treat the loss as a partial loss or may abandon the subject-matter insured to the insurer and treat the loss as if it were an ATL. The following points may have a bearing on which election is made:

(a) The benefit of treating the loss as a partial loss is that a claim can be made for up to 100 per cent of the insured value, plus retention of whatever remains of the property.

(b)   There is a risk in treating the loss as partial only. Under s. 77(2), if under the same policy a partial loss which has not been repaired or made good is followed by an independent total loss, the assured can only recover in respect of the total loss — if it was caused by a peril insured against.

22.6.1   REQUIREMENTS WHERE ASSURED ELECTS TO TREAT THE LOSS AS CTL

22.6.1.1   Notice of abandonment

Where the assured elects to abandon the subject-matter insured to the insurer and seeks to recover as for a total loss, he/she must give notice of abandonment (s. 62(1)), save that notice of abandonment is not necessary in the following situations:

(a)   Where at the time the assured receives the information of the loss, there would be no possibility of benefit to the insurer if notice were given to him/her: s. 62(7). (It is difficult to know what type of situation this exception is intended to cover. Probably such a loss is already an ATL for which no notice is required anyway.)

(b)   Where its service has been waived by the insurers (as in *Rickards* v *Forestal, supra*). Note that under Clause 17 (A, B and C Clauses) no act of the insurers in recovering, saving or preserving the property insured shall amount to a waiver of notice of abandonment.

22.6.1.2   Time of notice

The notice must be given *in time*. Failure to do so means that the loss will be treated as partial only: s. 62(1).

Since the effect of a valid abandonment is to allow the insurer, if he/she wishes, to take over the assured's interest in the goods (s. 63(1)), it is important that the assured should give notice of abandonment as soon as possible, so that the insurer can use his/her best endeavour to save or preserve etc. the property insured.

Section 62(3) states that notice of abandonment must be given within a *reasonable* time after receipt of reliable information about the loss, i.e. after receipt of reliable information about a state of affairs which justifies giving a notice of abandonment. If the information is 'doubtful', the assured is entitled to a reasonable time to make enquiry. But the assured cannot delay for any other reason.

If the notice is given on facts which do not amount to a constructive total loss, it is ineffective. In *Bainbridge* v *Neilson* (1808) 1 Camp 237 Lord Ellenborough stated:

> The effect of an offer of abandonment is that, if it appears to have been properly made upon supposed facts which turn out to be true, the assured has put himself in a condition to insist on his abandonment. But it is not enough that it was properly made on assumed facts, if it turned out that none such existed,

If, therefore, the notice is given *too early* — it is ineffective.

Again, if at the time the notice is given the facts amounting to a CTL have ceased to exist, the notice is invalid even though the facts upon which the notice was founded were truly reported and were in themselves such as to justify the assured in giving notice of abandonment.

The assured may be best advised in certain situations to serve a series of notices, hoping that one such notice will be given at a time when the circumstances so warrant.

22.6.1.3   Form of notice

The notice, when given, does not have to be in any particular form. It can be in writing or by word of mouth; but in either case, whatever its form, it must be unequivocal, clearly stating the intention of the assured to abandon his/her interest in the goods unconditionally to the insurer: s. 62(2).

Once the notice has been given the insurer will either accept or reject it.

22.6.1.4 Acceptance of notice

If, which rarely happens in practice, the insurer chooses to accept the notice of abandonment, the following consequences arise:

(a) The abandonment will be irrevocable. The assured cannot thereafter change his mind: s. 62(6).

(b) The insurer conclusively admits the sufficiency of the notice and his/her liability for a total loss: s.62(6).

There is no established form of acceptance. It may be expressed or implied from conduct. Mere silence, however, does not indicate acceptance: s. 62(5). Equally, under Clause 17 (A, B and C Clauses), operations in the nature of salvage after receipt of a notice of abandonment will not amount to an acceptance.

22.6.1.5 No acceptance of notice

This is the more usual situation and necessitates the assured in issuing a writ claiming a CTL. However, there may be an additional hurdle for the assured to overcome. The court will consider whether the circumstances amounting to a CTL and for which a valid notice of abandonment may have been issued, continued to exist down to the time at which the writ was issued.

In *Rickards* v *Forestal (supra)* Lord Wright stated:

The doctrine has been clearly established in English law, that the date which is to be taken in ascertaining whether or not there has been a CTL and whether or not a notice of abandonment given by the assured was justified, is at *the time of the issue of the writ* in an action by the assured against the underwriter and this doctrine has not been altered by the Marine Insurance Act.

If, therefore, before the issue of the writ, the assured has the means of getting possession under such circumstances as ought to have induced a prudent man to take possession of them, then his/her right to claim for a total loss is defeated and he/she can claim for a partial loss only.

The situation as at the date of issue of the writ is not considered, however, where the insurers (as they commonly do) agree that the writ shall be deemed to have been issued as on the date on which notice of abandonment was given.

22.6.1.6 Withdrawal of notice

Before the claim is paid, the assured may withdraw his notice and sue for a partial loss only: *Pesquerias Secaderos* v *Beer* (1949) 79 Ll LR 417.

22.6.2 CLAIM FOR PARTIAL LOSS ONLY

The following points should be borne in mind where the claim is, or can only be, pursued for a partial loss:

(a) Where, under the same policy, a partial loss which has not been repaired, or made good, is followed by a total loss, the assured can only recover in respect of the total loss: s. 77(2). 'The less is swallowed up by the greater and both form but one loss' *Knight* v *Faith* (1850) 15 QBD 649. Consequently, if a total loss subsequently occurs, though not by a peril insured against, the assured has no claim of any kind on the policy: *Wilson Shipping Co. Ltd* v *British and Foreign Marine Insurance* [1921] 1 AC 188.

(b) Where a total loss occurs after the policy has expired, the assured can still claim for a partial loss by the peril insured against, as s. 77(2) will not apply.

(c) Even though the total loss occurs after the policy has expired, the assured may be able to recover *under the policy* as for a *total loss* if it can be said to be the result of a sequence of events following in the ordinary course of events from the original loss, by a peril insured against: *Fooks* v *Smith* (1924) 30 Com Cas 97.

(d)   A partial loss is not subsumed by another partial loss. The insurer is liable for successive losses, even though the total amount of such losses exceeds the sum insured: s. 77(1).

(e)   It has not been determined whether partial losses can be added together so as to produce a CTL. The editors of *Arnould on the Law of Marine Insurance and Average* (16th edn, 1981, Sweet and Maxwell) take the view that if the losses are distinct, they should not be added together.

22.7   Consequences of a Valid Abandonment

There will be a valid abandonment when there has been an ATL or a partial loss which is treated by the insurers (on acceptance of notice of abandonment) or by the courts as a CTL. Where there has been a valid abandonment:

(a)   The assured will have abandoned his/her interest in the subject-matter insured: *Barraclough* v *Brown* [1897] AC 615.

(b)   Once the insurer has paid out for an ATL or CTL he/she is entitled to take over the interest of the assured in whatever remains of the subject-matter insured (known as salvage rights): ss. 63(1) and 79(1).

(c)   Once the insurer has taken over the interest of the assured he/she obtains '[t]he right to prosecute all claims which belonged to the assured and rendering him liable to all just demands that might have been made against the assured': *London Assurance Co.* v *Williams* (1892) 9 TLR 96.

22.7.1   INSURER'S OPTION TO ACCEPT ASSURED'S INTEREST

Note that the insurer is not bound to take over the interest of the assured. In the *Barraclough* case *(supra)* the insurers were not sued. *Arnould's Law of Marine Insurance and Average* (16th edn, 1981, Sweet and Maxwell) states that abandonment *per se* does not necessarily vest the property in anyone. It will divest the assured of his/her interest in the goods and give the insurer the option of either accepting the interest or not. Therefore in a case like *Barraclough* the property becomes *res nullius*. If this is correct, it follows that no one can be made liable *qua* owner, though there might be a claim in respect of prior ownership, if such prior owner had by his/her negligence put his/her property in such a position as to cause damage to others (see *Arnould*, op. cit., § 1290).

22.7.2   INSURER'S RIGHTS

The rights of the insurer, once he/she elects to take over the goods, operate retrospectively from the moment of the casualty that gave the right to abandon: *Stewart* v *Greenock Marine Insurance* (1848) 2 HL Cas 179.

The interest in the goods and all proprietary rights incidental thereto taken over, are known as salvage rights. If what the insurer eventually recovers proves to be more than the amount paid to the assured, the insurer is entitled to keep the excess.

By contrast, where the insurer pays out for a partial loss, he/she acquires no rights over the goods or what remains of them: s. 79(2).

22.8   Subrogation

Subrogation is the right of the insurer, on payment of a loss, to stand in the shoes of the assured and avail himself/herself of the latter's rights and remedies, e.g. the right to sue the carrier for loss or damage to the goods. The right of subrogation operates whenever the insurer pays out, be it for a total or a partial loss: s. 79(1) and (2).

Lord Blackburn in *Simpson* v *Thomson* (1877) 3 App Cas 229 at p. 292, compared salvage rights (available on abandonment) with rights of subrogation as follows:

[W]here the owners of an insured ship have claimed or been paid as for a total loss, the property in what remains of the ship, and all rights incident to the property, are transferred to the underwriter as from the time of the disaster in respect of which the total loss is claimed for and paid. The right to receive payment of freight accruing due, but not earned, at the time of the disaster, is one of those rights so incident to the property in the ship, and it therefore passes to the underwriters because the ship has become their property ... This is, at times, very hard upon the insured owner of the ship; he can, however, avoid it by claiming only for a partial loss, keeping the property in himself, and so keeping the right to earn the accruing freight. In such a case he recovers an indemnity for the amount of the loss actually sustained ...

But the right of the assured to recover damages from a third person is not one of those rights which are incident to the property in the ship; it does pass to the underwriters in case of payment for a total loss, but on a different principle. And on this same principle it does pass to the underwriters who have satisfied a claim for a partial loss, though no property in the ship passes.

The following points should be noted:

(a)   The right of subrogation arises only on payment of the loss: s. 79(1) and (2).

(b)   The assured is bound to lend his/her name to proceedings which the insurer decides to instigate against third parties who may be liable for the loss.

(c)   Under Clause 16.2 (A, B and C Clauses) it is the duty of the assured to make any necessary claims against the carrier and the bailees, so as to preserve the insurers' rights of subrogation, e.g. the assured must issue the writ in time so as to preserve the possibility of an action against the carrier. This obligation on the assured does not amount to a warranty, but enables the insurers to cross-claim for damages, which in certain circumstances may be sufficient to extinguish the assured's claim under the policy.

(d)   In exercising rights of subrogation, the insurers are limited to retention of the sums paid out by them to the assured: *Yorkshire Insurance Co.* v *Nisbet Shipping Co.* [1961] 2 WLR 1043.

(e)   In *Castellain* v *Preston* (1883) 11 QBD 380 at p. 386, Brett LJ stated:

The contract of insurance contained in a marine or fire policy is a contract of indemnity, and of indemnity only, and ... this contract means that the assured, in case of a loss against which the policy has been made, shall be fully indemnified, but shall never be more than fully indemnified. This is the fundamental principle of insurance and if ever a proposition is brought forward which is at variance with it, that is to say, which either will prevent the assured from obtaining a full indemnity, or which will give to the assured more than a full indemnity, that proposition must certainly be wrong.

As Cotton LJ at p. 395 stated:

If there is a money or any other benefit received which ought to be taken into account in diminishing the loss or in ascertaining what the real loss is against which the contract of indemnity is given, the indemnifier ought to be allowed to take advantage of it in order to calculate what the real loss is, even although the benefit is not a contract or right of suit which arises and has its birth from the accident insured against....

The difficulty is in determining in what circumstances the benefit can be taken into account by the insurer in determining the sums it is/was required to pay out. The cases of *Burnard* v *Rodocanachi* (1882) 7 App Con 333, *Castellain* v *Preston* (*supra*), *Merrett* v *Capitol Indemnity Corporation* [1991] 1 Lloyd's Rep 169 and *Colonia Versicherung AG* v *Amoco Oil Co.* [1995] 1 Lloyd's Rep 570 establish that an ex-gratia payment to the assured cannot be taken into account by the insurers where on the facts the donor intended only to benefit the assured and not the insurers.

In *Castellain* v *Preston (supra)*, Cotton LJ stated:

... why is a gift not to be taken into account? ... The answer is that when a gift is made afterwards in order to diminish the loss, it is bestowed in such terms as to show an intention to benefit the assured, and to give the insurer the benefit if that would be to divert the gift from its intended object to a different person ...

In *Merrett* v *Capitol Indemnity Corporation (supra)*, Steyn J in giving judgment stated:

The payment by the brokers was a gift, albeit a gift made for commercial rather than purely disinterested purposes. The contracts of re-insurance are contracts of indemnity. The question is, therefore, whether the payment diminishes the loss. Not every gift to an assured diminishes the loss. It is a question of fact in each case whether a gift has or has not been paid in diminution of the loss, and if it is established the payment is intended solely for the benefit of the assured, it has not been paid in diminution of the loss. In that event, it must be disregarded in assessing the assured's recoverable losses.

In *Colonia Versicherung AG* v *Amoco Oil Co. (supra)*, Potter J stated:

... all the judgments in *Castellain* v *Preston* plainly contemplated that certain types of gift would fall to be taken into account if properly to be regarded as paid in diminution of the loss.

The payment can still qualify as a gift intending to benefit only the assured even though the 'gift' is based on commercial considerations, e.g., to retain goodwill as in *Merrett* v *Capitol Indemnity Corporation (supra)*.

However, if in fact the intention of the payment was to compromise disputed claims, the payment ceases to be voluntary and would be regarded as payment made in diminution of the loss. See *Colonia Versicherung AG* v *Amoco Oil Co. (supra)* where this intention was ascertained from the terms of an assignment agreement assigning the rights under the insurance policy, of the ultimate receiver of the cargo, to the original shipper.

As to the question whether it is necessary for there to exist a directly enforceable claim against the giver of the benefit in order for the payment to cease to be 'voluntary', Potter J in the *Colonia* case *supra* stated:

As to the submission that, for an insurer to be entitled to have a sum brought into account in diminution of the loss, that sum must be the product of a right existing in the assured *at the time of the loss*. I do not accept it as correct. The remarks of Cotton LJ in *Castellain* v *Preston* ... were tentative only and were focused upon the position of a sum *ex hypothesi* bestowed by way of gift. If those remarks were intended to have wider application (and it is plain they find no support in the other judgments in that case, or in the judgment of Steyn J in *Merrett* v *Capitol Indemnity Corporation*) they cannot in my view be applicable to the position where payment has been made pursuant to a subsequent agreement specifically directed at compensating the assured for the very losses insured against.

(f) Where payment in diminution of the loss is received by the assured *before* payment out under the insurance policy, the underwriters' subrogatory remedy is the recovery of such a sum up to the amount of the insured loss which represents the difference between sums recovered by the assured from both insurers and wrongdoers and the amount of the insured loss, *as money paid under a mistake of fact. Refer to Lord Browne-Wilkinson in Napier v Hunt (supra), interpreting Stearns v Village Mainreef Goldmining Co. (supra)*:

So far as trusteeship was concerned, there was no fund capable of being the subject-matter of a trust since the moneys were recovered by the assured from the third party ... before the plaintiff insurers settled the insurance claim. It was a case of overpayment by the insurers under a mistake, not subsequent recovery by the assured from a third party of a fund for which the insured was accountable to the insurer.

However, where payment in diminution of the loss is received by the assured from a wrongoer *after* payment out under the insurance policy, the sums recovered are subject to an equitable lien or charge. Lord Browne-Wilkinson said (at 409):

> ... an insurer who has paid over the insurance moneys does have a proprietary interest in moneys subsequently recovered by an assured from a third party wrongdoer. Although many of the authorities refer to that right as arising under a trust, in my judgment, the imposition of a trust is neither necessary nor desirable; to impose fiduciary liabilities on the assured is commercially undesirable and unnecessary to protect the insurers' interests. In my judgment the correct analysis is as follows. The contract of insurance contains an implied term that the assured will pay to the insurer out of the moneys recovered in reduction of the loss the amount to which the insurer is entitled by way of subrogation. That contractual obligation is specifically enforceable in equity against the defined fund (i.e., the damages) in just the same way as are other contracts to assign or charge specific property e.g., equitable assignments and equitable charges. Since equity regards as done that which ought to be done under a contract, this specifically enforceable right gives rise to an immediate proprietary interest in the moneys recovered from the third party. In my judgment, this proprietary interest is adequately satisfied in the circumstances of subrogation under an insurance contract by granting the insurers a lien over the moneys recovered by the assured from the third party. This lien will be enforceable against the fund so long as it is traceable and has not been acquired by a bona fide purchaser for value without notice. In addition to the equitable lien the insurer will have a personal right of action at law to recover the amount received by the assured as money had and received to the use of the insurer.

22.9 Measure of Indemnity

When the assured is able to show that he/she is entitled to recover in respect of a loss covered by the policy, the question will then arise as to the measure of the indemnity. The expression 'measure of indemnity' is explained in s. 67(1) thus:

> *The sum which the assured can recover in respect of a loss on a policy by which he is insured, in the case of an unvalued policy to the full extent of the insurable value, or, in the case of a valued policy to the full extent of the value fixed by the policy, is called the measure of indemnity.*

This indicates, and the following sections further explain, that the amount recovered by the assured will depend on whether the policy is a 'valued' or 'unvalued' policy.

22.9.1 VALUED POLICY

A valued policy is a policy which specifies the agreed value of the subject-matter insured:. s. 27(2). A policy becomes a valued policy if and when the assured completes the valuation clause. In cases where the consignment/shipment is to be covered under a 'floating policy' or 'open cover', the assured (through his/her broker) must, unless the policy provides otherwise, declare the consignment and its value before notice of its loss or its arrival, in order for that consignment to be covered under a valued policy: s. 29(4).

The valuation in a valued policy is conclusive of the insurable value as regards the total or partial loss.

22.9.1.1 Calculation of value

The assured will have worked out the value of the goods by including the prime costs of those goods, freight, premium, commission and probable profit. In the c.i.f. and in those f.o.b. contracts where the seller is obliged to arrange insurance cover, in the absence of a term in the contract of sale or of usage in the trade, the seller is not bound to provide insurance cover on freight payable on delivery or the buyer's probable profit. However, it is usual for the buyer in the contract of sale to demand that the c.i.f. or f.o.b. seller include in the computation, freight charges payable at destination plus a percentage on that computation representing anticipated profits. Insurers cannot demand that the valuation be reopened if e.g. a cargo loss occurs and thus the freight to be paid on delivery of the cargo never in fact becomes payable: *Loders & Nucoline v Bank of New Zealand* (1929) 33 L1 LR 70.

22.9.1.2   Amount payable

Where there is a total loss of the subject-matter insured, the measure of indemnity is, unless the policy otherwise provides, the sum fixed by the policy: s. 68(1).

Where part of the goods is totally lost, the measure of the indemnity is, unless the policy otherwise provides, such proportion of the sum fixed by the policy as the insurable value of the part lost bears to the insurable value of the whole, ascertained as in the case of an unvalued policy: s. 71(1).

Where the whole or any part of the goods or merchandise is delivered damaged at destination, the measure of indemnity is, unless the policy otherwise provides, such proportion of the sum fixed by the policy, as the difference between the gross sound and damaged values at the place of arrival bears to the gross sound value: s. 71(3). Section 71(4) defines 'gross value'.

Thus where the goods have been overvalued, the assured is able to recover more than the true loss. Where they have been undervalued he/she will recover less than his/her actual loss. In summary, the measure of indemnity under a valued policy is worked out on the valuation and not on the loss to the assured.

However, an overvaluation can cause problems to the assured, in that:

(a)   It may be evidence of fraud, which, if proved, will enable the insurers to avoid the policy.

(b)   If not evidence of fraud, it may still entitle the insurers to avail themselves of the doctrine of non-disclosure — if the overvaluation was a material fact — and thus avoid the contract of insurance: *Ionides v Pender* (1874) LR 9 QB 531.

22.9.2   UNVALUED POLICY

This is defined in s. 28:

> *An unvalued policy is a policy which does not specify the value of the subject-matter insured, but, subject to the limit of the sum insured, leaves the insurable value to be subsequently ascertained ...*

Where goods are insured under a 'floating' policy or under 'open cover' and the declaration of shipment/consignment and its value is made after notice of its loss or arrival, that valuation may not be used for the purposes of working out the measure of indemnity and the goods will, accordingly, be treated as insured under an unvalued policy: s. 29(4).

Where goods are insured or treated as insured, under an unvalued policy, the measure of indemnity is worked out on the 'insurable value' unless the policy otherwise provides. The term 'insurable value' in insurance on goods or merchandise is defined in s. 16(3) as, 'the prime cost of the property insured, plus the expenses of and incidental to shipping and the charges of insurance upon the whole'.

The prime cost for the purposes of s. 16 is the market value at the time the risk attaches and not the original invoice value: see *Williams v Atlantic Assurance* [1933] 1 KB 81 *per* Greer LJ, where he said:

> I think the words 'prime cost' in [s. 16] mean the prime cost to the assured at or about the time of shipment, or at any rate at some time when the prime cost can be reasonably deemed to represent their value to their owner at the date of shipment. To hold that the prime cost at a period of boom long past must by statute be taken to be the value at the time when values had diminished by 50 per

cent would have the effect of enabling the assured to recover [under his right of indemnity for loss during the voyage] a sum which would represent a loss incurred long before the voyage started.

If there is no market value for the goods, the courts will treat the commercial value of the goods as the prime cost: *Berger and Light Diffusers Pty Ltd* v *Pollock* [1973] 2 Lloyd's Rep 442.

The following points on insurable value should be noted:

(a)   The insurable value is subject to the limit of the sum insured: s. 28. If the insurable value is found to be more than the sum insured, the assured is treated as his/her own insurer for the excess. If the sum insured exceeds the insurable value, a rateable return of premium is claimable in respect of the amount of overinsurance: s. 84(3)(e).

(b)   The insurable value is assessed as from commencement of the risk and therefore takes no account of increase in market values or the assured's anticipated profits. For this reason, most floating policies and open covers include a 'basis of valuation' clause to supplant the insurable value as defined in s. 16(3), whereunder the insurable value may, e.g., be based on the invoice value and charges plus 15 per cent.

Where there is a total loss under an unvalued policy the measure of indemnity is, unless the policy otherwise provides, the insurable value of the goods: s. 68(2).

Where there has been a total loss of part, the measure of indemnity is, unless the policy otherwise provides, the insurable value of the part lost: s. 71(2).

22.10   Recoverable Expenses of Assured

22.10.1   EXPENSES TO AVERT OR MINIMISE A LOSS

Section 78(4) provides that it is the duty of the assured and his/her agents, in all cases, to take such measures as may be reasonable for the purpose of averting or minimising a loss. That duty is laid down also in Clause 16.1 of the Institute Cargo Clauses (A, B and C). In addition Clause 16.2 enables the assured to recover any expenses incurred in preserving all rights against carriers, bailees or other third parties. These expenses will be recoverable by the assured provided that:

(a)   the subject-matter insured was in danger by a peril insured against (see opening words of Clause 16); and
(b)   the expenses were properly and reasonably incurred.

Once the charges fall within the clause, the insurers will be liable, even though the measures taken failed to avert a loss,

The engagement of the insurers under Clause 16 is supplementary to the contract of insurance. Thus the insurers will be liable for the expenses even though they are also liable to pay out for the total loss. Although, as already noted, a partial loss blends with a subsequent total loss (s. 77(2)), any measures taken to avoid or minimise the partial loss will still be recoverable under Clause 16: s. 77(2).

On the expression 'properly and reasonably incurred', see *Integrated Container Services Inc.* v *British Traders Insurance* [1984] 1 Lloyd's Rep 154. In that case, the assured had taken measures to regain possession of his containers after the lessees of the containers became bankrupt. The policy was against all risks of loss or damage. Insurers argued that the expenses incurred by the assured had not been incurred for the purpose of averting or minimising losses for which the insurers were liable. The Court of Appeal held that:

Since, on the bankruptcy, the containers were open to risk of theft, misuse etc., because the lessees could no longer exercise their duty of care as bailees, the assured was entitled to recover payments made in respect of custom and storage charges in order to obtain possession of the containers, transhipment costs and travelling expenses of those engaged in the operation plus legal fees connected with the transaction.

22.10.2   GENERAL AVERAGE CHARGES

There is a general average act where any extraordinary sacrifice or expenditure is voluntarily and reasonably made or incurred in time of peril for the purpose of preserving the property imperilled in the common adventure: s. 66(2). Once a general average loss has occurred, the assured loser is entitled to a rateable contribution from the other parties interested in the adventure: s. 66(3). The assured liable to make a general average contribution can claim them under Clause 2 (A, B and C Clauses) unless they were incurred to avoid, or in connection with the avoidance of, any cause excluded in Clauses 4 to 7 (A, B and C Clauses).

22.10.3   SALVAGE CHARGES

Salvage is the rescue, by a volunteer (i.e. a stranger to the maritime adventure — a salvor) of a vessel, her cargo or freight from a position or condition of danger and the placing of her/it in a position or state of safety. Charges thus incurred by acting under the maritime law independently of contract are salvage charges proper. They are recoverable under s. 65(1) if they were incurred in preventing a loss by perils insured against. However, Clause 2 (A, B and C Clauses) is wider, in that thereunder recovery is possible in respect of salvage charges even when those charges were not incurred in the avoidance of a peril insured against — so long as they were not incurred in connection with the avoidance of loss from a cause excluded under Clauses 4 to 7.

Salvage charges thus defined are to be distinguished from expenses in the nature of salvage rendered by the assured or his/her agents or any person employed for hire by them. Such charges are recoverable under Clause 16. Note, however, that in contrast to the salvage charges proper under Clause 2 (A, B and C Clauses), they must have been incurred to avert or minimise a loss by a peril insured against.

22.11   Avoidance of Contract for Non-disclosure or Misrepresentation

Even though the assured has proved a loss within the terms of the policy, the insurers may be able to avoid the contract and thus escape all liability on the basis of non-disclosure or misrepresentation of a material fact.

Section 17 lays down that a contract of marine insurance is a contract based upon the utmost good faith, and, if the utmost good faith is not observed by either party, the contract may be avoided by the other party. Insurance is thus *uberrimae fidei*.

In *Banque Financière* v *Westgate Insurance Co.* [1989] 2 All ER 952 the Court of Appeal held that:

> In adapting the well-established principles relating to the duty of disclosure falling on the insured to the obverse case of the insurer himself due account must be taken of the rather different reasons for which the insured and the insurer require the protection of full disclosure. In our judgment, the duty falling on the insurer must at least extend to disclosing all facts known to him which are material either to the nature of the risk sought to be covered or the recoverability of a claim under the policy which a prudent insurer would take into account in deciding whether or not to place the risk for which he seeks cover with that insurer.

This view was endorsed on appeal to the House of Lords — see [1990] 2 All ER 947.

Breach of this duty by the insurers gives the assured the right to rescind the contract of insurance and recover the premium. Breach of the obligation does not give rise to a claim for contractual damages. Refer to Lord Templeman [1990] 2 All ER 959. However, if there is negligence or fraud there will be a cause of action in tort.

The Marine Insurance Act 1906 does not particularise this duty of good faith in relation to the insurers, but does so in part in relation to the assured in ss. 18 to 20.

22.12 Duty of Assured to Disclose

22.12.1 PRE-CONTRACT DISCLOSURE

Under s. 18(1) the assured must disclose every circumstance:

(a) which is material; and
(b) which is known to the assured, or is deemed to be known to the assured,

before the contract is concluded.

Under s. 19, where an agent effects the insurance for the assured, he/she must disclose:

(a) every material circumstance which the assured is bound to disclose (see above) unless the assured received the knowledge too late to communicate it to the agent; and
(b) every material circumstance which is known to himself/herself, or which he/she is deemed to know. The agent is deemed to know every material circumstance which in the ordinary course of business ought to be known by, or to have been communicated to, him/her.

In *Simner* v *New India Assurance Co. Ltd, The Times*, 21 July 1994, the court held that the assured's duty of disclosure was limited to circumstances which were known to the assured, or which the assured is presumed to know in the ordinary course of his/her business. A potential assured is not required to make enquiries or investigate facts outside his/her knowledge for the purpose of complying with his/her duty of disclosure.

Two questions which arise at this stage are:

(a) When is the contract concluded?
(b) When is a circumstance 'material'?

22.12.1.1 When the contract is concluded

Under s. 21, a contract of marine insurance is deemed to be concluded when the 'slip' setting out the assured's proposals is initialled. The initialling of the slip by each company (called 'writing a line'), amounts to an acceptance by the company of an indicated proportion of the risk. There is an immediate, binding contract between the company or underwriting syndicate and the assured: *General Reinsurance Corp.* v *Forsakringsakfiebolaget* [1983] 3 WLR 318; decision applied in *Touche Ross & Co.* v *Baker* [1991] 2 Lloyd's Rep 230. After the initialling of the slip, there is, in relation to the company or syndicate that has signed, no further duty on the assured to volunteer information coming to light after the conclusion of the policy if it *affects the risks already accepted*: *The Litsion Pride* [1985] 1 Lloyd's Rep 437 at p. 511.

22.12.1.2 Materiality

Under s. 18(2), every circumstance is material which would influence the judgment of a prudent insurer in fixing the premium, or determining whether he will take the risk. The House of Lords in *Pan Atlantic Insurance Co. Ltd* v *Pine Top Insurance* [1994] Lloyd's Rep 427 had to consider whether, in order for materiality to be established, it had to be shown that full and accurate disclosure would have led the prudent underwriter to a different decision in relation to accepting or rating the risk, or whether a lesser standard of impact on his mind was sufficient. The appellants, Pan Atlantic, had argued that s. 18(2) and s. 20(2) of the 1906 Act required the disclosure only of such fresh circumstances as would, if disclosed to the hypothetical prudent insurer, have caused him to decline the risk or charge an increased premium. The House of Lords, Lord Lloyd dissenting, rejected this argument. The legislation had not required there to be a 'decisive' or 'conclusive' influence. the phrase 'influence the judgment' was not the same as change of mind. The wording of s. 18(2) and s. 20(2) merely required there to be an effect on the thought processes of the insurer in weighing up the risk. See also *St Paul Fire and Marine Insurance Ltd* v *McConnell* [1995] 2 Lloyd's Rep 116.

22.12.2   WHAT THE ASSURED IS DEEMED TO KNOW

Under s. 18(2) the assured is deemed to know every circumstance which in the ordinary course of business ought to be known by him/her. This will include:

(a)   knowledge of an agent which will be imputed to the principal; and

(b)   information which has reached the assured's office but which has not actually come to the attention of the assured or his/her servants.

22.12.2.1   Knowledge of agent imputed to principal

The question of knowledge of an agent which will be imputed to the principal was discussed by Lord Halsbury LC in *Blackburn* v *Vigors* (1887) 12 App Cas 531 (at 537):

> Some agents so far represent the principal that in all respects their acts and intentions and their knowledge may truly be said to be the acts, intentions and knowledge of the principal.

He did, however, go on to say:

> Other agents may have so limited and narrow an authority, both in fact and in the common understanding of the form of employment, that it would be quite inaccurate to say that such an agent's knowledge or intentions are the knowledge or intentions of his principal.

In other words, not in every case will the knowledge of an agent be imputed to a principal, but only in the case of those agents upon whom the principal relies for information. For example, if a cargo owner wants to take out insurance on goods, he/she is imputed with the knowledge of his/her trading agent as to the condition of those goods. This is because the trading agent has a duty to keep his/her employer informed on all matters affecting the property which is to be insured. The principal is here imputed with the agent's knowledge, irrespective of whether such agent has withheld the information.

In *Berger and Light Diffusers Pty Ltd* v *Pollock* [1973] 2 Lloyd's Rep 442 the fact that a bill of lading in respect of some steel injection moulds was 'claused' (it stated that the moulds were 'unprotected' and 'insufficiently packed') was deemed to be known to the assured, for it was known by their shipping agents.

In *Blackburn* v *Vigors (supra)* the plaintiffs instructed a broker to re-insure an overdue ship. Whilst acting for the plaintiffs, the broker received information material to the risk, but did not communicate this to the plaintiffs. Ultimately the policy was not effected by this first broker. Later the plaintiffs, through other brokers, effected a policy of reinsurance with the defendants. There was no question of the plaintiffs and second broker acting in bad faith. The question was whether the knowledge of the first broker should be imputed to the principal and thus allow the defendants to avoid the policy. In other words, did the first broker fall into the first category of agent as expressed in Lord Halsbury's judgment?

The House of Lords held that the first broker was not one of those agents whose duty it was to give information to the principal. Lord Watson said:

> The cases relating to captains and ship agents did not have any analogy to the cases of agents employed to effect a policy ... they were two different classes of agent. One class was employed for the purpose of communicating to [the principal] the very facts which the law required the principal to divulge to the insurer, the other was employed not to procure or furnish information concerning the ship, but to effect an insurance.

22.12.2.2   Received but unassimilated information

What the assured is deemed to know will also include information which has, in fact, reached his/her office but which has not actually come to the attention of the assured or his/her servants. In *London General Insurance Co.* v *General Marine Underwriters Association Ltd* [1921] 1 KB 104, a few hours before the plaintiff effected a reinsurance with the defendants on a ship, a casualty slip had been posted on the board at Lloyds and had also been sent round to the various insurers, which included the plaintiff and the defendants. Through pressure of work no one noted the casualty slip and the ship was reinsured that afternoon. It was held that the information contained in the slip was a circumstance which, in the ordinary course of business ought to have been known by the plaintiff. The defendants succeeded on their defence of non-disclosure.

22.12.3   WHAT NEED NOT BE DISCLOSED

Under s. 18(3) the following need not be disclosed:

(a)   Any circumstance which diminishes the risk.

(b)   Any circumstance which is known or presumed to be known to the insurers, e.g. an underwriter is presumed to know that war is imminent, or that war is taking place in a particular area of the world. In *London General Insurance Co.* v *General Marine Underwriters Association (supra)* the plaintiff tried to argue that they need not have disclosed the loss of the ship as it was a circumstance which ought to have been known by the defendants. It was held that since the defendants, at the time when they received the casualty slip, had not been asked to cover the ship, the contents of the casualty slip were of no interest to them. Therefore they were not presumed to know the information.

(c)   Any circumstance, as to which information is waived by the insurer. If a fact is disclosed which should put a careful business person on enquiry, and no such enquires are made, then he/she is deemed to have waived disclosure of information which would have been produced by those enquiries.

(d)   Any circumstance which it is superfluous to disclose by reason of any express or implied warranty. For example, under s. 39(1), in a voyage policy there is an implied warranty that at the commencement of the voyage the ship shall be seaworthy for the purpose of the particular adventure insured.

22.12.4   POST-CONTRACT DISCLOSURE

There is still a duty in relation to a post-contract obligation to disclose a fact which is material, *per* Hirst J in *The Litsion Pride* [1985] 1 Lloyd's Rep 437 at p. 512. For example, in order to seek the protection of a held covered clause, the assured must not withhold factors which are material, i.e. which enable the underwriter to fix the rate of additional premium. See *Overseas Commodities* v *Style (supra); Liberian Insurance Agency Inc.* v *Mosse* [1977] 2 Lloyd's Rep 560; *The Litsion Pride (supra)*.

There is in addition a duty in relation to claims not *fraudulently* to misrepresent or fraudulently to fail to disclose material facts. See *The Litsion Pride,* where Hirst J said (at 512):

> However, in contrast to the precontract situation, the precise ambit of the duty in the claims context has not been developed by the authorities; indeed no case has been cited to me where it has been considered outside the fraud context in relation to claims. It must be right, I think, by comparison with the *Style* and *Liberian* cases to go so far as to hold that the duty in the claims sphere extends to culpable misrepresentation or non-disclosure. Further than that there is no need to go on the facts of the present case, nor would it be right to do so in view of this remarkable dearth of authority, which no doubt stems from the fact that in the vast majority of cases this matter is dealt with in the express conditions of the policy.

22.13   Effect of Non-disclosure

22.13.1   INSURERS' ENTITLEMENT TO ELECT

The House of Lords in *Pan Atlantic Insurance Co. Ltd* v *Pine Top Insurance* [1994] 2 Lloyd's Rep 427 has held that in order to avoid the insurance contract the material non-disclosure or misrepresentation must have induced the making of the contract. There was to be implied into the Marine Insurance Act, a requirement that neither material misrepresentation nor non-disclosure would entitle the underwriter to avoid the policy unless it had induced the making of the contract on terms which he would not have accepted if all the material facts had been made known to him. See also *St Paul Fire and Marine Insurance Ltd* v *McConnell* [1995] 2 Lloyd's Rep 116.

The insurers are not obliged to avoid, although affirmation of a contract with knowledge of pre-contract non-disclosure may amount to an election not to rely on the default at all. Hirst J in *The Litsion Pride* said:

> Section 17 provides that the policy *may* be avoided not that it *must* be avoided. In the pre-contract situation, no doubt the assured's default necessarily strikes at the very basis of the contract itself so that when ... the underwriter affirms the contract, it necessarily follows that he is electing not to rely on default but the same considerations do not apply in the case of post-contract default ... In the case of post-contract breach it is open to the underwriters simply to defend the claim without avoiding the policy.

22.13.2 WHEN MUST ELECTION BE MADE

Donaldson J in *Liberian Insurance Agency* v *Moss* [1977] 2 Lloyd's Rep 560 said (at 565):

> The right [to avoid] exists from the time when the contract is made and continues until the insurer with full knowledge of the non-disclosure or misrepresentation, affirms or is deemed to have affirmed the contract... Full knowledge of the facts is essential before there can be any question of affirmation — being put on inquiry is insufficient ... and even when the underwriter has full knowledge of the facts, he is entitled to a reasonable time in which to decide whether to affirm the contract. In a situation in which the underwriter has taken no action to affirm or repudiate the contract and a reasonable time for making up his mind has elapsed, he will be deemed to have affirmed the contract if either so much time has elapsed that the necessary inference is one of affirmation or the assured has been prejudiced by the delay in making an election or the rights of third parties have intervened.

In *CTI Insurance* v *Oceanus Mutual Underwriters Association* [1984] 1 Lloyd's Rep 476 Kerr LJ said:

> Affirmation in the present context means that the underwriter elects to affirm the policy after he has acquired full knowledge of the material facts which would entitle him to avoid it. Having the means of knowledge or having been put on inquiry is not enough...

If no loss has occurred and the insurer is only informed when the goods reach their destination, the effect is that the insurer will usually affirm — to avoid the contract necessitates the return of the premium in the absence of fraud.

22.14 Duty of Assured where Representations are Made

Section 20 is necessary to cover the situation where the assured or his/her agent makes a representation designed to influence the insurer in fixing the premium or in undertaking the risk. Under s. 20 if any *material* representation is made by the assured or his/her agent to the insurer before the contract is concluded then it must be *true*. Whether a representation is 'true' or not must be examined in the light of the type of representation made.

22.14.1 TWO TYPES OF REPRESENTATION

The Act deals with two types of representation: s. 20(3).

22.14.1.1 Representation as to a matter of fact
This means 'a representation that something exists *at the moment*': *Jorden* v *Money* (1854) 5 HL Cas 185. Such a representation is 'true' if it is substantially correct, i.e. 'if the difference between what is

represented and what is actually correct would not be considered material by a prudent insurer': s. 20(4). For instance, in *Pawson* v *Watson* (1778) 2 Comp 785 the assured represented that the ship carried 12 guns and 20 men. In fact she carried 9 guns, 6 swivels, 16 men and 9 boys. This was held to be substantially correct.

22.14.1.2 Representation as to a matter of expectation or belief

A statement such as 'assured expects the ship to sail in 10 days' would come into this category. Such a representation is one of fact but that fact relates not to the subject-matter of the expectation, but to the condition of mind of the person making the statement.

Even though the representation is in terms of a direct and positive assertion, e.g. 'The ship was to sail in 10 days', it will still be regarded as a mere expression of expectation or belief, if this is evident from the position of the parties and all the circumstances of the case. See *Bowden* v *Vaughan* (1809) 10 East 415, where a broker employed to effect a policy on goods represented that 'the ship was to sail in a few days'. The ship did not sail for a month. It was held that this statement, although material to the risk, must be regarded merely as an expression of expectation since the owner of the goods had no control over the time of the ship's sailing. Such a representation is 'true' if it is made in good faith: s. 20(5). In this case the court held that as the representation appeared to have been made bona fide, the policy could not be avoided.

Where a representation is untrue, the insurer may avoid the contract: s. 20(1).

22.15 Breach of Warranty

The insurer might also be able to argue breach of an express or implied warranty which would discharge the insurers from liability as from the date of the breach, unless the breach was waived by the insurers, or an express term in the contract prevented discharge from liability. Until very recently, the exact effect of a breach of warranty on the insurers' liability and the effect on the contract of insurance itself, on a breach of warranty, was unclear. The matter came before the House of Lords in *The Good Luck* [1991] 3 All ER 1. Lord Goff stated:

> [I]f a promissory warranty is not complied with, the insurer is discharged from liability as from the date of the breach of warranty, for the simple reason that fulfilment of the warranty is a condition precedent to the liability or further liability of the insurer. This moreover reflects the fact that the rationale of warranties in insurance law is that the insurer only accepts the risk provided that the warranty is fulfilled ... [I]t follows that the immediate effect of a breach of promissory warranty is to discharge the insurer from liability as from the date of the breach ... Here, where we are concerned with a promissory warranty, i.e., a promissory condition precedent, contained in an existing contract of insurance, non-fulfilment of the condition does not prevent the contract from coming into existence. What it does (as s. 33(3) makes plain) is to discharge the insurer from liability as from the date of the breach. Certainly, it does not have the effect of avoiding the contract *ab initio*. Nor, strictly speaking, does it have the effect of bringing the contract to an end. It is possible that there may be obligations of the assured under the contract which will survive the discharge of the insurer from liability as, for example a continuing liability to pay a premium. Even if in the result no further obligations rest on either parties, it is not correct to speak of the contract being avoided; and it is, strictly speaking, more accurate to keep the carefully chosen words in s. 33(3) of the Act, rather than to speak of the contract being brought to an end, though that may be the practical effect. When, as s. 34(4) contemplates, the insurer waives a breach of a promissory warranty, the effect is that, to the extent of the waiver, the insurer cannot rely upon the breach having discharged him from liability. This is a very different thing from saying that discharge of the insurer from liability is dependent upon a decision by the insurer,

22.15.1 EXPRESS WARRANTIES

No special form of words is necessary to indicate an express warranty; all that is needed is a particular wording which indicates the intention of the parties that a particular fact is warranted: s. 35(1).

Warranties can be divided into two main categories, express and implied.

The following are the more usual examples of express warranties:

(a)   Sailing warranties: this is where there is a promise by the assured that the ship will sail, e.g. on or before 1 May 1990. This is important as far as the insurers are concerned, as they want to be certain that they will be insuring summer risks as opposed to winter risks.

(b)   Warranties as to the number of crew.

(c)   Convoy warranties.

(d)   Warranties as to the goods. See, e.g., *Overseas Commodities* v *Style* [1958] 1 Lloyd's Rep 546, where there was an all risks policy on tins of canned pork warranted all tins marked by manufacturers with a code for verification of the date of manufacture. Many of the tins were not marked in the stipulated manner. On arrival some of the tins were found to be punctured. The assured claimed under the policy. It was held that the underwriter was not liable because of the breach of warranty.

22.15.2   IMPLIED WARRANTIES

In every policy there is an implied warranty of legality (s. 41), and in a voyage policy an implied warranty of seaworthiness (s. 39(1)).

In a voyage policy on a ship or on goods there is an implied warranty that the ship shall be reasonably fit in all respects to encounter the ordinary perils of the seas of the insured adventure, and reasonably fit to carry the goods when she commences the voyage: ss. 39(1) and (4) and 40(2). If the ship is *de facto* unseaworthy at the start of the voyage, then the insured can treat himself/herself as discharged from that time, even though the loss did not occur because of the unseaworthiness and even though the breach of warranty had been remedied before the loss. Nor does it make any difference that the assured was ignorant of the unseaworthiness of the ship.

A consequence of the application of s. 39(1) and s. 33 is that an innocent cargo owner who has had no say in the equipping and manning of the ship, and who in all probability will not be aware of any inadequacies in these respects, will find himself/herself uninsured at sea. Clause 5.2 of the Institute Cargo Clauses remedies this by waiving the breach of the implied warranty as long as the assured or his/her *servant* was not privy to the unseaworthiness at the time the ship started on its voyage.

By contrast, in a time policy there is no such implied warranty of seaworthiness: s. 39(5). However, if *with the privity* of the assured the ship is sent to sea in an unseaworthy state, the insurer is not liable for any loss *attributable* to the unseaworthiness.

22.16   Warranties and Representations Contrasted

A representation, although it may be in writing, is not inserted on the face of the policy or incorporated by reference: *Yorkshire Insurance Co.* v *Campbell* [1917] AC 218. An express warranty, on the other hand, must be included in or written on the policy (normally by insertion in the margin or at the foot of the policy), or incorporated by reference: s. 35(2).

With regard to representations, under s. 20(1) and (2) the insurers are only able to treat themselves as discharged from liability if the misrepresentation was material to the risk. Once it has been determined that the provision *is* a warranty, however, then the question of materiality does not arise. If the warranty has not been exactly complied with, then, although a loss occurs which is unconnected with the breach of warranty, the insurers will be discharged from liability *as from the date of the breach*: s. 33(3).

It should be noted that it is no excuse that before the loss occurred, the breach of warranty was remedied (s. 34(2)), but the following do constitute valid excuses:

(a) Because of a change of circumstances the warranty ceases to be applicable to the circumstances of the contract: s. 34(1). If, for instance, insurers insist on a warranty that the ship sail in convoy because of a war, and before the ship sails, war ceases, then s. 34(1) will apply and the assured will be excused from the consequences of non-compliance.

(b) Compliance with the warranty has become unlawful: s. 34(1).

(c) The insurer has waived compliance: s. 34(3). (See also Clause 5.2 of the Institute Cargo Clauses A, B and C.)

22.17   Further Reading

Arnould, J., *Marine Insurance*, 16th ed. 1981, Sweet & Maxwell.

Schmitthoff, C., *Export Trade: The Law and Practice of International Trade*, 9th ed. 1990, Sweet & Maxwell.

22.18   Examples of Institute Cargo Clauses

These Clauses are reproduced with kind permission of Witherby & Co. Ltd, the publishers, and the Institute of London Underwriters, the source of the Clauses.

INSTITUTE CARGO CLAUSES (A)

RISKS COVERED

1   This insurance covers all risks of loss or of damage to the subject-matter insured except as provided in Clauses 4, 5, 6 and 7 below.   Risks Clause

2   This insurance covers general average and salvage charges, adjusted or determined according to the contract of affreightment and/or the governing law and practice, incurred to avoid or in connection with the avoidance of loss from any cause except those excluded in Clauses 4, 5, 6 and 7 or elsewhere in this insurance.   General Average Clause

3   This insurance is extended to indemnify the Assured against such proportion of liability under the contract of affreightment 'Both to Blame Collision' Clause as in respect of a loss recoverable hereunder. In the event of any claim by shipowners under the said Clause the Assured agree to notify the Underwriters who shall have the right, at their own cost and expense, to defend the Assured against such claim.   Both to Blame Collision Clause

EXCLUSIONS

4   In no case shall this insurance cover   General Exclusions Clause

  4.1 loss damage or expense attributable to wilful misconduct of the Assured

  4.2 ordinary leakage, ordinary loss in weight or volume, or ordinary wear and tear of the subject-matter insured

  4.3 loss damage or expense caused by insufficiency or unsuitability of packing or preparation of the subject-matter insured (for the purpose of this Clause 4.3 'packing' shall be deemed to include stowage in a container or liftvan but only when such stowage is carried out prior to attachment of this insurance or by the Assured or their servants)

  4.4 loss damage or expense caused by inherent vice or nature of the subject-matter insured

  4.5 loss damage or expense proximately caused by delay, even though the delay be caused by a risk insured against (except expenses payable under Clause 2 above)

  4.6 loss damage or expense arising from insolvency or financial default of the owners managers charterers or operators of the vessel

4.7 loss damage or expense arising from the use of any weapon of war employing atomic or nuclear fission and/or fusion or other like reaction or radioactive force or matter.

5 5.1 In no case shall this insurance cover loss damage or expense arising from

unseaworthiness of vessel or craft,

unfitness of vessel craft conveyance container or liftvan for the safe carriage of the subject-matter insured,

where the Assured or their servants are privy to such unseaworthiness or unfitness, at the time the subject-matter insured is loaded therein.

5.2 The Underwriters waive any breach of the implied warranties of seaworthiness of the ship and fitness of the ship to carry the subject-matter insured to destination, unless the Assured or their servants are privy to such unseaworthiness or unfitness.

Unseaworthiness and Unfitness Exclusion Clause

6 In no case shall this insurance cover loss damage or expense caused by

6.1 war civil war revolution rebellion insurrection, or civil strife arising therefrom, or any hostile act by or against a belligerent power

6.2 capture seizure arrest restraint or detainment (piracy excepted), and the consequences thereof or any attempt thereat

6.3 derelict mines torpedoes bombs or other derelict weapons of war.

War Exclusion Clause

7 In no case shall this insurance cover loss damage or expense

7.1 caused by strikers, locked-out workmen, or persons taking part in labour disturbances, riots or civil commotions

7.2 resulting from strikes, lock-outs, labour disturbances, riots or civil commotions

7.3 caused by any terrorist or any person acting from a political motive.

Strikes Exclusion Clause

DURATION

8 8.1 This insurance attaches from the time the goods leave the warehouse or place of storage at the place named herein for the commencement of the transit, continues during the ordinary course of transit and terminates either

Transit Clause

8.1.1 on delivery to the Consignees' or other final warehouse or place of storage at the destination named herein,

8.1.2 on delivery to any other warehouse or place of storage, whether prior to or at the destination named herein, which the Assured elect to use either

8.1.2.1 for storage other than in the ordinary course of transit or

8.1.2.2 for allocation or distribution,

or

8.1.3 on the expiry of 60 days after completion of discharge overside of the goods hereby insured from the oversea vessel at the final port of discharge,

whichever shall first occur.

8.2 If, after discharge overside from the oversea vessel at the final port of discharge, but prior to termination of this insurance, the goods are to be forwarded to a destination other than that to which they are insured hereunder, this insurance, whilst remaining subject to termination as provided for above, shall not extend beyond the commencement of transit to such other destination.

8.3 This insurance shall remain in force (subject to termination as provided for above and to the provisions of Clause 9 below) during delay beyond the control of the Assured, any deviation, forced discharge, reshipment or transhipment and during any variation of the adventure arising from the exercise of a liberty granted to shipowners or charterers under the contract of affreightment.

9   If owing to circumstances beyond the control of the Assured either the contract of carriage is terminated at a port or place other than the destination named therein or the transit is otherwise terminated before delivery of the goods as provided for in Clause 8 above, then this insurance shall also terminate *unless prompt notice is given to the Underwriters and continuation of cover is requested when the insurance shall remain in force, subject to an additional premium if required by the Underwriters,* either

    9.1   until the goods are sold and delivered at such port or place, or, unless otherwise specially agreed, until the expiry of 60 days after arrival of the goods hereby insured at such port or place, whichever shall first occur, or

    9.2   if the goods are forwarded within the said period of 60 days (or any agreed extension thereof) to the destination named herein or to any other destination, until terminated in accordance with the provisions of Clause 8 above.

Termination of Contract of Carriage Clause

10   Where, after attachment of this insurance, the destination is changed by the Assured, *held covered at a premium and on conditions to be arranged subject to prompt notice being given to the Underwriters.*

Change of Voyage Clause

CLAIMS

11   11.1   In order to recover under this insurance the Assured must have an insurable interest in the subject-matter insured at the time of the loss.

    11.2   Subject to 11.1 above, the Assured shall be entitled to recover for insured loss occurring during the period covered by this insurance, notwithstanding that the loss occurred before the contract of insurance was concluded, unless the Assured were aware of the loss and the Underwriters were not.

Insurable Interest Clause

12   Where, as a result of the operation of a risk covered by this insurance, the insured transit is terminated at a port or place other than that to which the subject-matter is covered under this insurance, the Underwriters will reimburse the Assured for any extra charges properly and reasonably incurred in unloading storing and forwarding the subject-matter to the destination to which it is insured hereunder.

This Clause 12, which does not apply to general average or salvage charges, shall be subject to the exclusions contained in Clauses 4, 5, 6 and 7 above, and shall not include charges arising from the fault negligence insolvency or financial default of the Assured or their servants.

Forwarding Charges Clause

13   No claim for Constructive Total Loss shall be recoverable hereunder unless the subject-matter insured is reasonably abandoned either on account of its actual total loss appearing to be unavoidable or because the cost of recovering, reconditioning and forwarding the subject-matter to the destination to which it is insured would exceed its value on arrival.

Constructive Total Loss Clause

14   14.1   If any Increased Value insurance is effected by the Assured on the cargo insured herein the agreed value of the cargo shall be deemed to be increased to the total amount insured under this insurance and all Increased Value insurances covering the loss, and liability under this insurance shall be in such proportion as the sum insured herein bears to such total amount insured.

In the event of claim the Assured shall provide the Underwriters with evidence of the amounts insured under all other insurances.

    14.2   **Where this insurance is on Increased Value the following clause shall apply:** The agreed value of the cargo shall be deemed to be equal to the total amount insured under the primary insurance and all Increased Value insurances covering the loss and effected on the cargo by the Assured, and liability under this insurance shall be in such proportion as the sum insured herein bears to such total amount insured.

In the event of claim the Assured shall provide the Underwriters with evidence of the amounts insured under all other insurances.

Increased Value Clause

BENEFIT OF INSURANCE

15   This insurance shall not inure to the benefit of the carrier or other bailee.   Not to Inure
Clause

MINIMISING LOSSES

16   It is the duty of the Assured and their servants and agents in respect of loss recoverable hereunder   Duty of
Assured
Clause

       16.1   to take such measures as may be reasonable for the purpose of averting or minimising such loss,

             and

       16.2   to ensure that all rights against carriers, bailees or other third parties are properly preserved and exercised

and the Underwriters will, in addition to any loss recoverable hereunder, reimburse the Assured for any charges properly and reasonably incurred in pursuance of these duties.

17   Measures taken by the Assured or the Underwriters with the object of saving, protecting or recovering the subject-matter insured shall not be considered as a waiver or acceptance of abandonment or otherwise prejudice the rights of either party.   Waiver
Clause

AVOIDANCE OF DELAY

18   It is a condition of this insurance that the Assured shall act with reasonable despatch in all circumstances within their control.   Reasonable
Despatch
Clause

LAW AND PRACTICE

19   This insurance is subject to English law and practice.   English Law
and Practice
Clause

NOTE:—It is necessary for the Assured when they become aware of an event which is 'held covered' under this insurance to give prompt notice to the Underwriters and the right to such cover is dependent upon compliance with this obligation.

INSTITUTE CARGO CLAUSES (B)

RISKS COVERED

1   This insurance covers, except as provided in Clauses 4, 5, 6 and 7 below,   Risks Clause

       1.1   loss of or damage to the subject-matter insured reasonably attributable to

       1.1.1   fire or explosion

       1.1.2   vessel or craft being stranded grounded sunk or capsized

       1.1.3   overturning or derailment of land conveyance

       1.1.4   collision or contact of vessel craft or conveyance with any external object other than water

       1.1.5   discharge of cargo at a port of distress

       1.1.6   earthquake volcanic eruption or lightning,

       1.2   loss of or damage to the subject-matter insured caused by

       1.2.1   general average sacrifice

       1.2.2   jettison or washing overboard

       1.2.3   entry of sea lake or river water into vessel craft hold conveyance container liftvan or place of storage,

       1.3   total loss of any package lost overboard or dropped whilst loading on to, or unloading from, vessel or craft.

2   This insurance covers general average and salvage charges, adjusted or determined according to the contract of affreightment and/or the governing law and practice, incurred to avoid or in connection with the avoidance of loss from any cause except those excluded in Clauses 4, 5, 6 and 7 or elsewhere in this insurance. *General Average Clause*

3   This insurance is extended to indemnify the Assured against such proportion of liability under the contract of affreightment 'Both to Blame Collision' Clause as in respect of a loss recoverable hereunder. In the event of any claim by shipowners under the said Clause the Assured agree to notify the Underwriters who shall have the right, at their own cost and expense, to defend the Assured against such claim. *Both to Blaim Collision Clause*

EXCLUSIONS

4   In no case shall this insurance cover
    4.1 loss damage or expense attributable to wilful misconduct of the Assured *General Exclusions Clause*
    4.2 ordinary leakage, ordinary loss in weight or volume, or ordinary wear and tear of the subject-matter insured
    4.3 loss damage or expense caused by insufficiency or unsuitability of packing or preparation of the subject-matter insured (for the purpose of this Clause 4.3 'packing' shall be deemed to include stowage in a container or liftvan but only when such stowage is carried out prior to attachment of this insurance or by the Assured or their servants)
    4.4 loss damage or expense caused by inherent vice or nature of the subject-matter insured
    4.5 loss damage or expense proximately caused by delay, even though the delay be caused by a risk insured against (except expenses payable under Clause 2 above)
    4.6 loss damage or expense arising from insolvency or financial default of the owners managers charterers or operators of the vessel
    4.7 deliberate damage to or deliberate destruction of the subject-matter insured or any part thereof by the wrongful act of any person or persons
    4.8 loss damage or expense arising from the use of any weapon of war employing atomic or nuclear fission and/or fusion or other like reaction or radioactive force or matter.

5   5.1 In no case shall this insurance cover loss damage or expense arising from *Unseaworthiness and Unfitness Exclusion Clause*
            unseaworthiness of vessel or craft,
            unfitness of vessel craft conveyance container or liftvan for the safe carriage of the subject-matter insured,
         where the Assured or their servants are privy to such unseaworthiness or unfitness, at the time the subject-matter insured is loaded therein.
    5.2 The Underwriters waive any breach of the implied warranties of seaworthiness of the ship and fitness of the ship to carry the subject-matter insured to destination, unless the Assured or their servants are privy to such unseaworthiness or unfitness.

6   In no case shall this insurance cover loss damage or expense caused by
    6.1 war civil war revolution rebellion insurrection, or civil strife arising therefrom, or any hostile act by or against a belligerent power *War Exclusion Clause*
    6.2 capture seizure arrest restraint or detainment, and the consequences thereof or any attempt thereat
    6.3 derelict mines torpedoes bombs or other derelict weapons of war.

7   In no case shall this insurance cover loss damage or expense
    7.1 caused by strikers, locked-out workmen, or persons taking part in labour disturbances, riots or civil commotions *Strikes Exclusion Clause*
    7.2 resulting from strikes, lock-outs, labour disturbances, riots or civil commotions

7.3   caused by any terrorist or any person acting from a political motive.

DURATION

8   8.1   This insurance attaches from the time the goods leave the warehouse or place of storage at the place named herein for the commencement of the transit, continues during the ordinary course of transit and terminates either

Transit Clause

       8.1.1   on delivery to the Consignees' or other final warehouse or place of storage at the destination named herein,

       8.1.2   on delivery to any other warehouse or place of storage, whether prior to or at the destination named herein, which the Assured elect to use either

       8.1.2.1   for storage other than in the ordinary course of transit or

       8.1.2.2   for allocation or distribution,

         or

       8.1.3   on the expiry of 60 days after completion of discharge overside of the goods hereby insured from the oversea vessel at the final port of discharge,

        whichever shall first occur.

    8.2   If, after discharge overside from the oversea vessel at the final port of discharge, but prior to termination of this insurance, the goods are to be forwarded to a destination other than that to which they are insured hereunder, this insurance, whilst remaining subject to termination as provided for above, shall not extend beyond the commencement of transit to such other destination.

    8.3   This insurance shall remain in force (subject to termination as provided for above and to the provisions of Clause 9 below) during delay beyond the control of the Assured, any deviation, forced discharge, reshipment or transhipment and during any variation of the adventure arising from the exercise of a liberty granted to shipowners or charterers under the contract of affreightment.

9   If owing to circumstances beyond the control of the Assured either the contract of carriage is terminated at a port or place other than the destination named therein or the transit is otherwise terminated before delivery of the goods as provided for in Clause 8 above, then this insurance shall also terminate *unless prompt notice is given to the Underwriters and continuation of cover is requested when the insurance shall remain in force, subject to an additional premium if required by the Underwriters,* either

Termination of Contract of Carriage Clause

    9.1   until the goods are sold and delivered at such port or place, or, unless otherwise specially agreed, until the expiry of 60 days after arrival of the goods hereby insured at such port or place, whichever shall first occur,

      or

    9.2   if the goods are forwarded within the said period of 60 days (or any agreed extension thereof) to the destination named herein or to any other destination, until terminated in accordance with the provisions of Clause 8 above.

10   Where, after attachment of this insurance, the destination is changed by the Assured, *held covered at a premium and on conditions to be arranged subject to prompt notice being given to the Underwriters.*

Change of Voyage Clause

CLAIMS

11   11.1   In order to recover under this insurance the Assured must have an insurable interest in the subject-matter insured at the time of the loss.

Insurable Interest Clause

    11.2   Subject to 11.1 above, the Assured shall be entitled to recover for insured loss occurring during the period covered by this insurance, notwithstanding that the loss occurred before the contract of insurance was concluded, unless the Assured were aware of the loss and the Underwriters were not.

12 Where, as a result of the operation of a risk covered by this insurance, the insured transit is terminated at a port or place other than that to which the subject-matter is covered under this insurance, the Underwriters will reimburse the Assured for any extra charges properly and reasonably incurred in unloading storing and forwarding the subject-matter to the destination to which it is insured hereunder.

This Clause 12, which does not apply to general average or salvage charges, shall be subject to the exclusions contained in Clauses 4, 5, 6 and 7 above, and shall not include charges arising from the fault negligence insolvency or financial default of the Assured or their servants.

Forwarding Charges Clause

13 No claim for Constructive Total Loss shall be recoverable hereunder unless the subject-matter insured is reasonably abandoned either on account of its actual total loss appearing to be unavoidable or because the cost of recovering, reconditioning and forwarding the subject-matter to the destination to which it is insured would exceed its value on arrival.

Constructive Total Loss Clause

14 14.1 If any Increased Value insurance is effected by the Assured on the cargo insured herein the agreed value of the cargo shall be deemed to be increased to the total amount insured under this insurance and all Increased Value insurances covering the loss, and liability under this insurance shall be in such proportion as the sum insured herein bears to such total amount insured.

In the event of claim the Assured shall provide the Underwriters with evidence of the amounts insured under all other insurances.

Increased Value Clause

14.2 **Where this insurance is on Increased Value the following clause shall apply:** The agreed value of the cargo shall be deemed to be equal to the total amount insured under the primary insurance and all Increased Value insurances covering the loss and effected on the cargo by the Assured, and liability under this insurance shall be in such proportion as the sum insured herein bears to such total amount insured.

In the event of claim the Assured shall provide the Underwriters with evidence of the amounts insured under all other insurances.

BENEFIT OF INSURANCE
15 This insurance shall not inure to the benefit of the carrier or other bailee.

Not to Inure Clause

MINIMISING LOSSES
16 It is the duty of the Assured and their servants and agents in respect of loss recoverable hereunder

16.1 to take such measures as may be reasonable for the purpose of averting or minimising such loss,
and

Duty of Assured Clause

16.2 to ensure that all rights against carriers, bailees or other third parties are properly preserved and exercised

and the Underwriters will, in addition to any loss recoverable hereunder, reimburse the Assured for any charges properly and reasonably incurred in pursuance of these duties.

17 Measures taken by the Assured or the Underwriters with the object of saving, protecting or recovering the subject-matter insured shall not be considered as a waiver or acceptance of abandonment or otherwise prejudice the rights of either party.

Waiver Clause

AVOIDANCE OF DELAY
18 It is a condition of this insurance that the Assured shall act with reasonable despatch in all circumstances within their control.

Reasonable Despatch Clause

LAW AND PRACTICE

19   This insurance is subject to English law and practice.

English Law
and Practice
Clause

NOTE:—It is necessary for the Assured when they become aware of an event which is 'held covered' under this insurance to give prompt notice to the Underwriters and the right to such cover is dependent upon compliance with this obligation.

INSTITUTE CARGO CLAUSES (C)

RISKS COVERED

1   This insurance covers, except as provided in Clauses 4, 5, 6 and 7 below,

Risks Clause

1.1   loss of or damage to the subject-matter insured reasonably attributable to

1.1.1   fire or explosion

1.1.2   vessel or craft being stranded grounded sunk or capsized

1.1.3   overturning or derailment of land conveyance

1.1.4   collision or contact of vessel craft or conveyance with any external object other than water

1.1.5   discharge of cargo at a port of distress,

1.2   loss of or damage to the subject-matter insured caused by

1.2.1   general average sacrifice

1.2.2   jettison.

2   This insurance covers general average and salvage charges, adjusted or determined according to the contract of affreightment and/or the governing law and practice, incurred to avoid or in connection with the avoidance of loss from any cause except those excluded in Clauses 4, 5, 6 and 7 or elsewhere in this insurance.

General
Average
Clause

3   This insurance is extended to indemnify the Assured against such proportion of liability under the contract of affreightment 'Both to Blame Collision' Clause as in respect of a loss recoverable hereunder. In the event of any claim by shipowners under the said Clause the Assured agree to notify the Underwriters who shall have the right, at their own cost and expense, to defend the Assured against such claim.

Both to
Blame
Collision
Clause

EXCLUSIONS

4   In no case shall this insurance cover

4.1   loss damage or expense attributable to wilful misconduct of the Assured

General
Exclusions
Clause

4.2   ordinary leakage, ordinary loss in weight or volume, or ordinary wear and tear of the subject-matter insured

4.3   loss damage or expense caused by insufficiency or unsuitability of packing or preparation of the subject-matter insured (for the purpose of this Clause 4.3 'packing' shall be deemed to include stowage in a container or liftvan but only when such stowage is carried out prior to attachment of this insurance or by the Assured or their servants)

4.4   loss damage or expense caused by inherent vice or nature of the subject-matter insured

4.5   loss damage or expense proximately caused by delay, even though the delay be caused by a risk insured against (except expenses payable under Clause 2 above)

4.6   loss damage or expense arising from insolvency or financial default of the owners managers charterers or operators of the vessel

4.7 deliberate damage to or deliberate destruction of the subject-matter insured or any part thereof by the wrongful act of any person or persons

4.8 loss damage or expense arising from the use of any weapon of war employing atomic or nuclear fission and/or fusion or other like reaction or radioactive force or matter.

5   5.1 In no case shall this insurance cover loss damage or expense arising from

Unseaworthiness and Unfitness Exclusion Clause

        unseaworthiness of vessel or craft,

        unfitness of vessel craft conveyance container or liftvan for the safe carriage of the subject-matter insured,

where the Assured or their servants are privy to such unseaworthiness or unfitness, at the time the subject-matter insured is loaded therein.

5.2 The Underwriters waive any breach of the implied warranties of seaworthiness of the ship and fitness of the ship to carry the subject-matter insured to destination, unless the Assured or their servants are privy to such unseaworthiness or unfitness.

6   In no case shall this insurance cover loss damage or expense caused by

6.1 war civil war revolution rebellion insurrection, or civil strife arising therefrom, or any hostile act by or against a belligerent power

War Exclusion Clause

6.2 capture seizure arrest restraint or detainment, and the consequences thereof or any attempt thereat

6.3 derelict mines torpedoes bombs or other derelict weapons of war.

7   In no case shall this insurance cover loss damage or expense

7.1 caused by strikers, locked-out workmen, or persons taking part in labour disturbances, riots or civil commotions

Strikes Exclusion Clause

7.2 resulting from strikes, lock-outs, labour disturbances, riots or civil commotions

7.3 caused by any terrorist or any person acting from a political motive.

DURATION

8   8.1 This insurance attaches from the time the goods leave the warehouse or place of storage at the place named herein for the commencement of the transit, continues during the ordinary course of transit and terminates either

Transit Clause

8.1.1 on delivery to the Consignees' or other final warehouse or place of storage at the destination named herein,

8.1.2 on delivery to any other warehouse or place of storage, whether prior to or at the destination named herein, which the Assured elect to use either

8.1.2.1 for storage other than in the ordinary course of transit or

8.1.2.2 for allocation or distribution,

or

8.1.3 on the expiry of 60 days after completion of discharge overside of the goods hereby insured from the oversea vessel at the final port of discharge,

whichever shall first occur.

8.2 If, after discharge overside from the oversea vessel at the final port of discharge, but prior to termination of this insurance, the goods are to be forwarded to a destination other than that to which they are insured hereunder, this insurance, whilst remaining subject to termination as provided for above, shall not extend beyond the commencement of transit to such other destination.

8.3 This insurance shall remain in force (subject to termination as provided for above and to the provisions of Clause 9 below) during delay beyond the control of the Assured, any deviation, forced discharge, reshipment or transhipment and during any variation of the adventure arising from the exercise of a liberty granted to shipowners or charterers under the contract of affreightment.

9 If owing to circumstances beyond the control of the Assured either the contract of carriage is terminated at a port or place other than the destination named therein or the transit is otherwise terminated before delivery of the goods as provided for in Clause 8 above, then this insurance shall also terminate *unless prompt notice is given to the Underwriters and continuation of cover is requested when the insurance shall remain in force, subject to an additional premium if required by the Underwriters,* either

9.1 until the goods are sold and delivered at such port or place, or, unless otherwise specially agreed, until the expiry of 60 days after arrival of the goods hereby insured at such port or place, whichever shall first occur, or

9.2 if the goods are forwarded within the said period of 60 days (or any agreed extension thereof) to the destination named herein or to any other destination, until terminated in accordance with the provisions of Clause 8 above.

[margin: Termination of Contract of Carriage Clause]

10 Where, after attachment of this insurance, the destination is changed by the Assured, *held covered at a premium and on conditions to be arranged subject to prompt notice being given to the Underwriters.*

[margin: Change of Voyage Clause]

CLAIMS

11 11.1 In order to recover under this insurance the Assured must have an insurable interest in the subject-matter insured at the time of the loss.

11.2 Subject to 11.1 above, the Assured shall be entitled to recover for insured loss occurring during the period covered by this insurance, notwithstanding that the loss occurred before the contract of insurance was concluded, unless the Assured were aware of the loss and the Underwriters were not.

[margin: Insurable Interest Clause]

12 Where, as a result of the operation of a risk covered by this insurance, the insured transit is terminated at a port or place other than that to which the subject-matter is covered under this insurance, the Underwriters will reimburse the Assured for any extra charges properly and reasonably incurred in unloading storing and forwarding the subject-matter to the destination to which it is insured hereunder.

This Clause 12, which does not apply to general average or salvage charges, shall be subject to the exclusions contained in Clauses 4, 5, 6 and 7 above, and shall not include charges arising from the fault negligence insolvency or financial default of the Assured or their servants.

[margin: Forwarding Charges Clause]

13 No claim for Constructive Total Loss shall be recoverable hereunder unless the subject-matter insured is reasonably abandoned either on account of its actual total loss appearing to be unavoidable or because the cost of recovering, reconditioning and forwarding the subject-matter to the destination to which it is insured would exceed its value on arrival.

[margin: Constructive Total Loss Clause]

14 14.1 If any Increased Value insurance is effected by the Assured on the cargo insured herein the agreed value of the cargo shall be deemed to be increased to the total amount insured under this insurance and all Increased Value insurances covering the loss, and liability under this insurance shall be in such proportion as the sum insured herein bears to such total amount insured.

In the event of claim the Assured shall provide the Underwriters with evidence of the amounts insured under all other insurances.

14.2 **Where this insurance is on Increased Value the following clause shall apply:** The agreed value of the cargo shall be deemed to be equal to the total amount insured under the primary insurance and all Increased Value insurances covering the loss and effected on the cargo by the Assured, and liability under this insurance shall be in such proportion as the sum insured herein bears to such total amount insured.

In the event of claim the Assured shall provide the Underwriters with evidence of the amounts insured under all other insurances.

[margin: Increased Value Clause]

BENEFIT OF INSURANCE

15   This insurance shall not inure to the benefit of the carrier or other bailee.   Not to
                                                                                       Inure Clause

MINIMISING LOSSES

16   It is the duty of the Assured and their servants and agents in respect of loss   Duty of
      recoverable hereunder   Assured
                                                                                       Clause
      16.1   to take such measures as may be reasonable for the purpose of averting
              or minimising such loss,
              and
      16.2   to ensure that all rights against carriers, bailees or other third parties are
              properly preserved and exercised
      and the Underwriters will, in addition to any loss recoverable hereunder, reimburse
      the Assured for any charges properly and reasonably incurred in pursuance of these
      duties.

17   Measures taken by the Assured or the Underwriters with the object of   Waiver
      saving, protecting or recovering the subject-matter insured shall not be   Clause
      considered as a waiver or acceptance of abandonment or otherwise prejudice the
      rights of either party.

AVOIDANCE OF DELAY

18   It is a condition of this insurance that the Assured shall act with reasonable   Reasonable
      despatch in all circumstances within their control.   Despatch
                                                                                       Clause

LAW AND PRACTICE

19   This insurance is subject to English law and practice.   English Law
                                                                and Practice
                                                                Clause

---

*NOTE:—It is necessary for the Assured when they, become aware of an event
which is 'held covered' under this insurance to give prompt notice to the
Underwriters and the right to such cover is dependent upon compliance with this
obligation.*

INSTITUTE STRIKES CLAUSES (CARGO)

RISKS COVERED

1   This insurance covers, except as provided in Clauses 3 and 4 below, loss of   Risks Clause
      or damage to the subject-matter insured caused by
      1.1   strikers, locked-out workmen, or persons taking part in labour disturbances,
             riots or civil commotions
      1.2   any terrorist or any person acting from a political motive.

2   This insurance covers general average and salvage charges, adjusted or   General
      determined according to the contract of affreightment and/or the governing   Average
      law and practice, incurred to avoid or in connection with the avoidance of   Clause
      loss from a risk covered under these clauses.

EXCLUSIONS

3   In no case shall this insurance cover
      3.1   loss damage or expense attributable to wilful misconduct of the Assured
      3.2   ordinary leakage, ordinary loss in weight or volume, or ordinary wear   General
             and tear of the subject-matter insured   Exclusions
                                                                                     Clause
      3.3   loss damage or expense caused by insufficiency or unsuitability of packing
             or preparation of the subject-matter insured (for the purpose of this Clause
             3.3 'packing' shall be deemed to include stowage in a container or liftvan but

only when such stowage is carried out prior to attachment of this insurance or by the Assured or their servants)

3.4 loss damage or expense caused by inherent vice or nature of the subject-matter insured

3.5 loss damage or expense proximately caused by delay, even though the delay be caused by a risk insured against (except expenses payable under Clause 2 above)

3.6 loss damage or expense arising from insolvency or financial default of the owners managers charterers or operators of the vessel

3.7 loss damage or expense arising from the absence shortage or withholding of labour of any description whatsoever resulting from any strike, lockout, labour disturbance, riot or civil commotion

3.8 any claim based upon loss of or frustration of the voyage or adventure

3.9 loss damage or expense arising from the use of any weapon of war employing atomic or nuclear fission and/or fusion or other like reaction or radioactive force or matter

3.10 loss damage or expense caused by war civil war revolution rebellion insurrection, or civil strife arising therefrom, or any hostile act by or against a belligerent power.

4   4.1 In no case shall this insurance cover loss damage or expense arising from

> unseaworthiness of vessel or craft,
>
> unfitness of vessel craft conveyance container or liftvan for the safe carriage of the subject-matter insured,

where the Assured or their servants are privy to such unseaworthiness or unfitness, at the time the subject-matter insured is loaded therein.

4.2 The Underwriters waive any breach of the implied warranties of seaworthiness of the ship and fitness of the ship to carry the subject-matter insured to destination, unless the Assured or their servants are privy to such unseaworthiness or unfitness.

Unseaworthiness and Unfitness Exclusion Clause

DURATION

5   5.1 This insurance attaches from the time the goods leave the warehouse or place of storage at the place named herein for the commencement of the transit, continues during the ordinary course of transit and terminates either

Transit Clause

5.1.1   on delivery to the Consignees' or other final warehouse or place of storage at the destination named herein,

5.1.2   on delivery to any other warehouse or place of storage, whether prior to or at the destination named herein, which the Assured elect to use either

5.1.2.1   for storage other than in the ordinary course of transit or

5.1.2.2   for allocation or distribution,

or

5.1.3   on the expiry of 60 days after completion of discharge overside of the goods hereby insured from the oversea vessel at the final port of discharge,

whichever shall first occur.

5.2 If, after discharge overside from the oversea vessel at the final port of discharge, but prior to termination of this insurance, the goods are to be forwarded to a destination other than that to which they are insured hereunder, this insurance, whilst remaining subject to termination as provided for above, shall not extend beyond the commencement of transit to such other destination.

5.3   This insurance shall remain in force (subject to termination as provided for above and to the provisions of Clause 6 below) during delay beyond the control of the Assured, any deviation, forced discharge, reshipment or transhipment and during any variation of the adventure arising from the exercise of a liberty granted to shipowners or charterers under the contract of affreightment.

6   If owing to circumstances beyond the control of the Assured either the contract of carriage is terminated at a port or place other than the destination named therein or the transit is otherwise terminated before delivery of the goods as provided for in Clause 5 above, then this insurance shall also terminate *unless prompt notice is given to the Underwriters and continuation of cover is requested when the insurance shall remain in force, subject to an additional premium if required by the Underwriters,* either

Termination of Contract of Carriage Clause

6.1   until the goods are sold and delivered at such port or place, or, unless otherwise specially agreed, until the expiry of 60 days after arrival of the goods hereby insured at such port or place, whichever shall first occur,

or

6.2   if the goods are forwarded within the said period of 60 days (or any agreed extension thereof) to the destination named herein or to any other destination, until terminated in accordance with the provisions of Clause 5 above.

7   Where, after attachment of this insurance, the destination is changed by the Assured, *held covered at a premium and on conditions to be arranged subject to prompt notice being given to the Underwriters.*

Change of Voyage Clause

CLAIMS

8   8.1   In order to recover under this insurance the Assured must have an insurable interest in the subject-matter insured at the time of the loss.

Insurable Interest Clause

     8.2   Subject to 8.1 above, the Assured shall be entitled to recover for insured loss occurring during the period covered by this insurance, notwithstanding that the loss occurred before the contract of insurance was concluded, unless the Assured were aware of the loss and the Underwriters were not.

9   9.1   If any Increased Value insurance is effected by the Assured on the cargo insured herein the agreed value of the cargo shall be deemed to be increased to the total amount insured under this insurance and all Increased Value insurances covering the loss, and liability under this insurance shall be in such proportion as the sum insured herein bears to such total amount insured.

Increased Value Clause

     In the event of claim the Assured shall provide the Underwriters with evidence of the amounts insured under all other insurances.

     9.2   **Where this insurance is on Increased Value the following clause shall apply:** The agreed value of the cargo shall be deemed to be equal to the total amount insured under the primary insurance and all Increased Value insurances covering the loss and effected on the cargo by the Assured, and liability under this insurance shall be in such proportion as the sum insured herein bears to such total amount insured.

     In the event of claim the Assured shall provide the Underwriters with evidence of the amounts insured under all other insurances.

BENEFIT OF INSURANCE

10   This insurance shall not inure to the benefit of the carrier or other bailee.

Not to Insure Clause

MINIMISING LOSSES

11   It is the duty of the Assured and their servants and agents in respect of loss recoverable hereunder

Duty of Assured

11.1 to take such measures as may be reasonable for the purpose of averting or minimising such loss, and

11.2 to ensure that all rights against carriers, bailees or other third parties are properly preserved and exercised

and the Underwriters will, in addition to any loss recoverable hereunder, reimburse the Assured for any charges properly and reasonably incurred in pursuance of these duties.

12 Measures taken by the Assured or the Underwriters with the object of saving, protecting or recovering the subject-matter insured shall not be considered as a waiver or acceptance of abandonment or otherwise prejudice the rights of either party.

Clause

Waiver Clause

AVOIDANCE OF DELAY

13 It is a condition of this insurance that the Assured shall act with reasonable despatch in all circumstances within their control.

Reasonable Despatch Clause

LAW AND PRACTICE

14 This insurance is subject to English law and practice.

English Law and Practice Clause

NOTE:-It is necessary for the Assured when they become aware of an event which is 'held covered' under this insurance to give prompt notice to the Underwriters and the right to such cover is dependent upon compliance with this obligation.

INSTITUTE WAR CLAUSES (CARGO)

RISKS COVERED

1 This insurance covers, except as provided in Clauses 3 and 4 below, loss of or damage to the subject-matter insured caused by

1.1 war civil war revolution rebellion insurrection, or civil strife arising therefrom, or any hostile act by or against a belligerent power

1.2 capture seizure arrest restraint or detainment, arising from risks covered under 1.1 above, and the consequences thereof or any attempt thereat

1.3 derelict mines torpedoes bombs or other derelict weapons of war.

Risks Clause

2 This insurance covers general average and salvage charges, adjusted or determined according to the contract of affreightment and/or the governing law and practice, incurred to avoid or in connection with the avoidance of loss from a risk covered under these clauses.

General Average Clause

EXCLUSIONS

3 In no case shall this insurance cover

3.1 loss damage or expense attributable to wilful misconduct of the Assured

3.2 ordinary leakage, ordinary loss in weight or volume, or ordinary wear and tear of the subject-matter insured

3.3 loss damage or expense caused by insufficiency or unsuitability of packing or preparation of the subject-matter insured (for the purpose of this Clause 3.3 'packing' shall be deemed to include stowage in a container or liftvan but only when such stowage is carried out prior to attachment of this insurance or by the Assured or their servants)

3.4 loss damage or expense caused by inherent vice or nature of the subject-matter insured

General Exclusions Clause

3.5 loss damage or expense proximately caused by delay, even though the delay be caused by a risk insured against (except expenses payable under Clause 2 above)

3.6 loss damage or expense arising from insolvency or financial default of the owners managers charterers or operators of the vessel

3.7 any claim based upon loss of or frustration of the voyage or adventure

3.8 loss damage or expense arising from any hostile use of any weapon of war employing atomic or nuclear fission and/or fusion or other like reaction or radioactive force or matter.

4   4.1 In no case shall this insurance cover loss damage or expense arising from

   Unseaworthiness and Unfitness Exclusion Clause

> unseaworthiness of vessel or craft,
>
> unfitness of vessel craft conveyance container or liftvan for the safe carriage of the subject-matter insured,

where the Assured or their servants are privy to such unseaworthiness or unfitness, at the time the subject-matter insured is loaded therein.

4.2 The Underwriters waive any breach of the implied warranties of seaworthiness of the ship and fitness of the ship to carry the subject-matter insured to destination, unless the Assured or their servants are privy to such unseaworthiness or unfitness.

DURATION

5   5.1 This insurance

5.1.1   attaches only as the subject-matter insured and as to any part as that part is loaded on an oversea vessel

   Transit Clause

and

5.1.2   terminates, subject to 5.2 and 5.3 below, either as the subject-matter insured and as to any part as that part is discharged from an oversea vessel at the final port or place of discharge,

or

on expiry of 15 days counting from midnight of the day of arrival of the vessel at the final port or place of discharge,

whichever shall first occur; nevertheless,

subject to prompt notice to the Underwriters and to an additional premium, such insurance

5.1.3   reattaches when, without having discharged the subject-matter insured at the final port or place of discharge, the vessel sails therefrom,

and

5.1.4   terminates, subject to 5.2 and 5.3 below, either as the subject-matter insured and as to any part as that part is thereafter discharged from the vessel at the final (or substituted) port or place of discharge,

or

on expiry of 15 days counting from midnight of the day of re-arrival of the vessel at the final port or place of discharge or arrival of the vessel at a substituted port or place of discharge,

whichever shall first occur.

5.2 If during the insured voyage the oversea vessel arrives at an intermediate port or place to discharge the subject-matter insured for on-carriage by oversea vessel or by aircraft, or the goods are discharged from the vessel at a port or place of refuge, then, subject to 5.3 below and to an additional premium if required, this insurance continues until the expiry of 15 days counting from midnight of the day of arrival of the vessel at such port or place, but thereafter reattaches as the subject-matter insured and as to any part as that part is loaded on an on-carrying oversea vessel or aircraft. During the period of 15 days the insurance remains in force after discharge only whilst the subject-matter insured and as to any part as that part is at such port or place.

If the goods are on-carried within the said period of 15 days or if the insurance reattaches as provided in this Clause 5.2.

5.2.1   where the on-carriage is by oversea vessel this insurance continues subject to the terms of these clauses,
or

5.2.2   where the on-carriage is by aircraft, the current Institute War Clauses (Air Cargo) (excluding sendings by Post) shall be deemed to form part of this insurance and shall apply to the on-carriage by air.

5.3   If the voyage in the contract of carriage is terminated at a port or place other than the destination agreed therein, such port or place shall be deemed the final port of discharge and such insurance terminates in accordance with 5.1.2. If the subject-matter insured is subsequently reshipped to the original or any other destination, then *provided notice is given to the Underwriters before the commencement of such further transit and subject to an additional premium,* such insurance reattaches

5.3.1   in the case of the subject-matter insured having been discharged, as the subject-matter insured and as to any part as that part is loaded on the on-carrying vessel for the voyage;

5.3.2   in the case of the subject-matter not having been discharged, when the vessel sails from such deemed final port of discharge;
thereafter such insurance terminates in accordance with 5.1.4.

5.4   The insurance against the risks of mines and derelict torpedoes, floating or submerged, is extended whilst the subject-matter insured or any part thereof is on craft whilst in transit to or from the oversea vessel, but in no case beyond the expiry of 60 days after discharge from the oversea vessel unless otherwise specially agreed by the Underwriters.

5.5   *Subject to prompt notice to Underwriters, and to an additional premium if required,* this insurance shall remain in force within the provisions of these Clauses during any deviation, or any variation of the adventure arising from the exercise of a liberty granted to shipowners or charterers under the contract of affreightment.

(For the purpose of Clause 5

'arrival' shall be deemed to mean that the vessel is anchored, moored or otherwise secured at a berth or place within the Harbour Authority area. If such a berth or place is not available, arrival is deemed to have occurred when the vessel first anchors, moors or otherwise secures either at or off the intended port or place of discharge

'oversea vessel' shall be deemed to mean a vessel carrying the subject-matter from one port or place to another where such voyage involves a sea passage by that vessel)

6   Where, after attachment of this insurance, the destination is changed by the Assured, *held covered at a premium and on conditions to be arranged subject to prompt notice being given to the Underwriters.*

Change of Voyage Clause

7   **Anything contained in this contract which is inconsistent with Clauses 3.7, 3.8 or 5 shall, to the extent of such inconsistency, be null and void.**

CLAIMS

8   8.1   In order to recover under this insurance the Assured must have an insurable interest in the subject-matter insured at the time of the loss.

Insurable Interest Clause

8.2   Subject to 8.1 above, the Assured shall be entitled to recover for insured loss occurring during the period covered by this insurance, notwithstanding that the loss occurred before the contract of insurance was concluded, unless the Assured were aware of the loss and the Underwriters were not.

9   9.1   If any Increased Value insurance is effected by the Assured on the cargo insured herein the agreed value of the cargo shall be deemed to be increased to the total amount insured under this insurance and all Increased Value insurances covering the loss, and liability under this insurance shall be in such proportion as the sum insured herein bears to such total amount insured. *Increased Value Clause*

In the event of claim the Assured shall provide the Underwriters with evidence of the amounts insured under all other insurances.

9.2   **Where this insurance is on Increased Value the following clause shall apply:** The agreed value of the cargo shall be deemed to be equal to the total amount insured under the primary insurance and all Increased Value insurances covering the loss and effected on the cargo by the Assured, and liability under this insurance shall be in such proportion as the sum insured herein bears to such total amount insured.

In the event of claim the Assured shall provide the Underwriters with evidence of the amounts insured under all other insurances.

BENEFIT OF INSURANCE

10   This insurance shall not inure to the benefit of the carrier or other bailee. *Not to Inure Clause*

MINIMISING LOSSES

11   It is the duty of the Assured and their servants and agents in respect of loss recoverable hereunder *Duty of Assured Clause*

11.1   to take such measures as may be reasonable for the purpose of averting or minimising such loss,
and

11.2   to ensure that all rights against carriers, bailees or other third parties are properly preserved and exercised

and the Underwriters will, in addition to any loss recoverable hereunder, reimburse the Assured for any charges properly and reasonably incurred in pursuance of these duties.

12   Measures taken by the Assured or the Underwriters with the object of saving, protecting or recovering the subject-matter insured shall not be considered as a waiver or acceptance of abandonment or otherwise prejudice the rights of either party. *Waiver Clause*

AVOIDANCE OF DELAY

13   It is a condition of this insurance that the Assured shall act with reasonable despatch in all circumstances within their control. *Reasonable Despatch Clause*

LAW AND PRACTICE

14   This insurance is subject to English law and practice. *English Law and Practice Clause*

NOTE:—It is necessary for the Assured when they become aware of an event which 'held covered' under this insurance to give prompt notice to the Underwriters and the right to such cover is dependent upon compliance with this obligation.

---

23   Jurisdiction of the English Courts

23.1   Introduction

The jurisdiction of the English courts has traditionally been founded on the service of a writ on a defendant who is present or which has presence, within England and Wales, or where the claim exhibits such connections with England and Wales as are defined by RSC ord. 11, r. 1, and the court exercises its discretion in favour of permitting service on a defendant outside the jurisdiction.

However, in 1971 the UK acceded to the Treaty of Rome and became a member of the EEC. By Article 220 of the Treaty, the Member States agreed to enter into negotiations with a view to securing for the benefit of their nationals the simplification of formalities governing the reciprocal recognition and enforcement of judgments of courts and tribunals and of arbitration awards. The negotiations which took place resulted in the Brussels Convention on Jurisdiction and Enforcement of Judgments in Civil and Commercial Matters 1968, which was enacted by the Civil Jurisdiction and Judgments Act 1982 (CJJA 1982), s. 2. The Brussels Convention is contained in sch. 1 to that Act. As the full title of the Brussels Convention shows, its application is limited to civil and commercial matters, and a number of other types of claim are specifically excluded by Article 1 thereof. The San Sebastian Convention which was concluded with Spain and Portugal creates minor amendments to the Brussels Convention. This Convention has been implemented within the UK by the Civil Jurisdiction and Judgments Act 1982 (Amendment) Order 1990 (SI 1990 No. 2591) and brought into force on 1 December 1991.

The Lugano Convention which is very closely modelled on the Brussels Convention on Jurisdiction and the Enforcement of Judgments has extended the same jurisdictional and enforcement rules to those EFTA Member States which ratify it. By virtue of the Civil Jurisdiction and Judgments Act 1991 the Lugano Convention came into force in the United Kingdom on 1 May 1992.

Throughout **Chapter 23** any statutory references will be to the Civil Jurisdiction and Judgments Act 1982 unless otherwise stated. The Convention of 1968 as amended, will be referred to as the Brussels Convention.

Once an action falls within the definition of a 'civil or commercial matter', and is not excluded from the ambit of the Brussels Convention by Article I, significant restrictions will be imposed by the Brussels Convention on the exercise of the traditional rules on jurisdiction exercised by the courts of Contracting States to that Convention irrespective of the domicile of the defendant. As far as the English courts are concerned, this means that RSC ord. 11, and the rule allowing service of a writ on a defendant within the jurisdiction no matter how fleeting his/her visit, cannot apply in the following circumstances:

    (a)   Where proceedings fall within Article 16 and thus for practical considerations are deemed to be within the exclusive jurisdiction of a particular contracting state: Article 16.

    (b)   Where there is an agreement on jurisdiction fulfilling the conditions set out in Article 17. Only the courts of the Contracting State chosen can exercise jurisdiction.

(c)   Where proceedings involving the same cause of action and between the same parties are brought in the courts of different Contracting States. Here jurisdiction shall be declined in favour of the court first seised once jurisdiction of the court first seised is established by the court first seised.

(d)   Where related actions are brought in the courts of different Contracting States, any court other than that first seised may stay its proceedings and on the application of one of the parties may decline jurisdiction if the law of that court permits the consolidation of related actions and the court first seised has jurisdiction over both actions: Article 22.

(e)   Where actions come within the exclusive jurisdiction of courts of several Contracting States, any court other than the court first seised shall decline jurisdiction in favour of that court: Article 23.

To give an example of what has already been stated, an American citizen who has commenced proceedings in France against a fellow American, will be prevented by virtue of Article 21 from pursuing subsequent proceedings involving the same cause of action against the same party within the jurisdiction of the English courts. He would not, however, be prevented from proceeding with an action involving the same cause of action as in proceedings pending in France, in, for example, the courts of the State of Virginia, USA.

Note: Articles 16, 17 and 21–23 impose their own jurisdictional rules.

In addition to the special jurisdictional rules imposed under the aforementioned articles, the Brussels Convention introduces into a civil/commercial action a new criterion for jurisdiction, namely, that of *domicile* in a Contracting State which supersedes traditional jurisdictional rules. There are certain well-defined exceptions, but the basic rule, as set out in Article 2, is that a defendant *domiciled in a Contracting State must be sued in the courts of that State*. The 'domicile' rule is inapplicable if (i) the circumstances fall within Articles 16–18, 21-23, in which case regard is had to the particular exception to determine jurisdiction, or (ii) a plaintiff is able to rely on Articles 5-15 and chooses to sue a defendant domiciled in one Contracting State in another. Remember that where the exceptions (i) or (ii) above apply, traditional rules of jurisdiction do not reassert themselves. Jurisdiction is determined by the exception. For example, a contractual action must be pursued against a French defendant in the French courts as opposed to the courts of any other Contracting State (e.g. an English court), unless, for example, the plaintiff could argue that performance of the obligation at issue has to take place within the jurisdiction of the English courts, thus giving the English courts jurisdiction under Article 5(1). *Note the Convention does not prevent actions being pursued in the courts of a non-Convention territory, e.g. Japan.*

Where the Brussels Convention applies to grant jurisdiction to the English court, the court's wide discretion under the doctrine of *forum non conveniens* is no longer applicable where the contest on jurisdiction is between courts *in Contracting States*. Where the contest arises between the courts of a Contracting and non-Contracting State, the *forum non conveniens* principle is still applicable (*Re Harrods (Buenos Aires) Ltd* [1991] 4 All ER 334, CA).

23.1.1   DOMICILE

The CJJA 1982 ss. 41–42 provide a new definition of domicile to be used by the English courts to determine jurisdiction. Where the defendant is an individual, an English court seised of the matter must apply the definition of domicile in s. 41 to determine whether the defendant is domiciled in the UK or in a non-Contracting State.

If not domiciled within the UK, the English court may have to consider whether the defendant is domiciled in another Contracting State. It must do this by applying the law of that State: Article 52.

Where the defendant is a company or association, the English court will use the definition of domicile under s. 42 to determine whether the defendant is domiciled in any Contracting or non-Contracting State: Article 53. See *The Rewia* [1991] 1 Lloyd's Rep 69; [1991] 2 Lloyd's Rep 325.

Where it has been determined that the proposed defendant is domiciled in the UK the jurisdiction of the English courts will be governed by the Brussels Convention and by the Modified Convention which allocates jurisdiction to a part of the UK, unless the jurisdictional contest is with the courts of a non-Contracting State.

As to the effect of the Brussels Convention on English jurisdiction *in rem* refer to **23.3**.

Do remember that although the jurisdictional rules of the Brussels Convention now form part of the jurisdiction of the English courts, they do not apply to every potential action.

23.2 Rules on Jurisdiction in an Action *in Personam* where Proposed Defendant is not Domiciled in a Contracting State

23.2.1 DEFENDANT WITHIN JURISDICTION

Subject to the circumstances falling within Articles 16-23 (and remember for Articles 16–23 to apply, the action must relate to a civil or commercial matter and not be excluded under Article 1), the English court is competent to hear any case invoked by anyone in the world, as long as the defendant was within the jurisdiction, albeit fleetingly, at the time of service of process. There is no need for the plaintiff or defendant to be domiciled here, or for the matter in dispute to have any connection with the jurisdiction. However, whether the English court chooses to *retain* jurisdiction is another matter. An application can be made under the inherent jurisdiction of the courts, by the defendant to stay the English proceedings on the basis that there is another more appropriate forum that can determine the dispute. The less connection the matter and parties have with the English jurisdiction the easier will be the defendant's task of succeeding in his/her application for a stay. See **23.2.4**.

23.2.2 DEFENDANT OUTSIDE, BUT SUBMITS TO, JURISDICTION

Even though the defendant remains outside the jurisdiction, an English court will have jurisdiction to determine the action, *subject to the operation of Article 16 of the Brussels Convention*, where the defendant submits to the jurisdiction by:

(a) accepting service of process, e.g. by instructing his/her solicitors to accept service: RSC ord. 10, r. 1(4); or
(b) acknowledging service *gratis* and not merely to contest the jurisdiction of the court: RSC ord. 10, r. 1(5); or
(c) agreeing to service on an appointed party within the jurisdiction: RSC ord. 10, r. 3(1); or
(d) bringing an action here, which will enable a counterclaim to be brought against him/her.

23.2.3 DEFENDANT OUTSIDE, AND DOES NOT SUBMIT TO, JURISDICTION

Where the defendant remains outside the jurisdiction and does not submit to the jurisdiction, the English court will still be able to determine the matter in dispute, *subject to the operation of Articles 16-17 and 21-23* of the Brussels Convention, if the provisions of RSC ord. 11 are satisfied. The requirements of RSC ord. 11 are as follows:

(a) The case must fall into one of the categories in RSC ord. 11, r. 1(1)(a)–(q).
(b) The case must be a proper one for service out of the jurisdiction. That is to say, the case must fall within the spirit as well as the letter of the order: *Johnson* v *Taylor Bros & Co.* [1920] AC 144.
(c) The plaintiff must show that he/she has a good cause of action.
(d) The plaintiff must show that the English court is clearly the appropriate forum: The *Spiliada* [1987] AC 460.
(e) The plaintiff must make an *ex parte* application, supported by an affidavit, stating:

    (i)   the paragraphs of RSC ord. 11, r. 1(1) relied upon as giving the court jurisdiction, plus a summary of the facts relied on as bringing the case within the identified paragraph(s);

    (ii)   clearly in what place or country the defendant is or probably may be found;

    (iii)   the belief of the deponent that there is a good cause of action;

    (iv)   the deponent's grounds of belief and source of information;

    (v)   the considerations relied upon as showing that the case is a proper one in which to subject a party outside the jursidiction to proceedings within it;

    (vi)   any features which may reasonably be thought to weigh against the making of the order sought;

and exhibiting copies of documents to which reference has been made in the affidavit.

In most cases the making of the application is a three-stage process. First, the plaintiff has to show that his claim(s) falls within a particular head(s) of ord. 11. This is the 'jurisdictional element' stage. The standard of proof placed on the plaintiff is that of showing a 'good arguable case'. This will be rather more difficult to establish at an *inter partes* hearing as opposed to at the *ex parte* application stage: see *Vitkovice Horni* v *Korner* [1951] AC 869; *Attock Cement Co. Ltd* v *Romanian Bank* [1989] 1 WLR 1147; *E. F. Hutton & Co. (London) Ltd* v *Mofarrij* [1989] 1 WLR 488; *Seaconsar Far East Ltd* v *Bank Markazi* [1993] 3 WLR 756.

The plaintiff must then proceed to the 'merits' element and must establish a 'prima facie' case or 'serious question to be tried'. In *Seaconsar Far East Ltd* v *Bank Markazi (supra)*, Goff LJ stated:

> If in support of the [plaintiff's] *ex parte* application, an affidavit is sworn in proper form deposing to facts which, if proved, provide a sufficient foundation for the alleged cause of action, that should generally be enough for present purposes. This is no doubt what a number of judges have referred to when they have used the expression 'prima facie' case ... The problem arises from the fact that the court will consider, on an application to set aside leave so given, affidavit evidence on the part of the defendant and will take such evidence into account when deciding whether or not to exercise its discretion in favour of the plaintiff. But the court cannot resolve disputed questions of fact on affidavit evidence ... if at the end of the day there remains a substantial question of fact or law or both arising on the facts disclosed by the affidavits which the plaintiff bona fide desires to try, the court should as a rule allow service of the writ ... The standard of proof in respect of the cause of action can broadly be stated to be whether, on the affidavit evidence before the court, there is a serious question to be tried.

In some instances, the merits element will be subsumed within the jurisdictional element, and then the second stage will be omitted, e.g., when the plaintiff is relying on ord. 11, r. 1(1)(e).

Lastly, the court will consider the issue of *forum conveniens*. The plaintiff is required to show that England is clearly the appropriate forum to try the action.

23.2.4   *FORUM NON CONVENIENS*

Where the writ has been served as of right on the defendant using traditional rules, an application for a stay of proceedings can be made by the defendant, either on the basis that circumstances fall within Articles 16–17, 21–23 or that the domicile rule applies (as to which see below), or on the basis of *forum non conveniens*. The *forum non conveniens* principles to be considered were enunciated by Lord Goff in *The Spiliada* [1987] AC 460.

23.2.4.1   Some other available, more appropriate, forum

The stay will only be granted on the grounds of *forum non conveniens* where the court is satisfied that there is some other available forum, having competent jurisdiction, in which the case may be tried more suitably in the interests of all the parties and the ends of justice.

The legal burden is initially on the defendant to persuade the court that there is another available forum which is clearly more appropriate. By this is meant a forum which could be called a 'natural' forum — one with which the action has the most real and substantial connection. It is connecting factors in this sense that the court will first consider, e.g. the law governing the relevant transaction, the places where the parties reside and carry on business.

It will not be sufficient to grant a stay that the defendant can show that the English court is not the appropriate forum. If the defendant cannot show that another forum is clearly *more* appropriate, the stay will be refused.

23.2.4.2 Special circumstances requiring suit to proceed in less appropriate forum

Where the defendant discharges his/her burden and proves that another forum is clearly more appropriate, the burden now shifts to the plaintiff to show that there are special circumstances in which justice requires that the trial should nevertheless take place within the English jurisdiction (a less appropriate forum). The underlying principle is that the court has to consider where the case may be tried 'suitably in the interests of all the parties and for the ends of justice'.

The court will consider all relevant circumstances, including circumstances which go beyond those taken into account when considering connecting factors with another jurisdiction. These circumstances include:

(a)   The plaintiff may not obtain justice abroad, e.g. the judiciary is not independent.
(b)   The plaintiff will be deprived of some advantage that he/she has or will obtain by trial in England, e.g.:

(i)   a personal advantage, e.g. the plaintiff is an English resident;
(ii)   juridical advantages, e.g. an action in England would result in: summary judgment; higher damages in the English courts; an award of interest; cheaper, quicker trial; security obtained for the amount of the claim; a more generous limitation period within the jurisdiction.

The advantage must be real, legitimate, and it must currently exist on a comparison of the English and the other, more appropriate, forum.

The mere fact that the plaintiff has a legitimate personal or juridical advantage in the English proceedings is not decisive. Justice must require that the stay should not be granted. Where, for example, the plaintiff has obtained security, Lord Goff stated in *The Spiliada (supra)* (at 483): '[I]t would not, I think, normally be wrong to allow a plaintiff to keep the benefit of security obtained by commencing proceedings here, while at the same time granting a stay of proceedings in this country to enable the action to proceed in the appropriate forum'. (See CJJA 1982, s. 26.)

Similarly, the fact that the action in the more appropriate jurisdiction is statute barred will not cause the application for a stay to be refused.

Lord Goff said:

Suppose that the plaintiff allowed the limitation period to elapse in the appropriate jurisdiction and came here simply because he wanted to take advantage of a more generous time-bar applicable in this country; or suppose that it was obvious that the plaintiff should have commenced proceedings in the appropriate jurisdiction and yet he did not trouble to issue a protective writ there. In cases such as these I cannot see that the court should hesitate to stay the proceedings in this country, even though the effect would be that the plaintiff's claim would inevitably be defeated by a plea of the time-bar in the appropriate jurisdiction. Indeed, a strong theoretical argument can be advanced for the proposition that if there is another, clearly more appropriate forum for the trial of the action, a stay should generally be granted even though the plaintiff's action would be time-barred there.

23.2.5   *LIS PENDENS*

The existence of foreign proceedings is a relevant factor in the equation when the court has to consider whether the foreign or English forum is clearly more appropriate, particularly in view of the inherent undesirability of concurrent sets of proceedings. The weight to be attached will depend on all the circumstances, including the state of advance of the foreign proceedings. Nevertheless, the existence of foreign proceedings is not a decisive factor in the equation: *Meadows v ICI* [1989] 1 LCR 181; *The Abidin Daver* [1984] 1 All ER 470.

However, under the Brussels Convention. if an action to which the Convention applies is pending in another *Contracting State*, the English court must consider of its own motion, whether it was first seised of the matter. If not it must stay its proceedings until such time as the jurisdiction of the court first seised is established. When the jurisdiction of the court first seised is established, any other court shall decline jurisdiction in favour of the court first seised. There is no discretion: Article 21. The traditional discretion in relation to the doctrine of *lis alibi pendens* is no longer applicable: *Arkright v Bryanston* [1990] 2 Lloyd's Rep 70. Note that the provisions of Article 21 are applicable even though the defendant is not domiciled in a Contracting State (see *Overseas Union Insurance v New Hampshire Insurance* [1992] 1 Lloyd's Rep 204).

23.2.6   EXCLUSIVE JURISDICTION

Note that if the matter falls within the exclusive jurisdiction of the English courts by virtue of Article 16 of the Brussels Convention, the *forum non conveniens/conveniens* principle is inapplicable: unless the court claiming jurisdiction is in a non-Contracting State (*Re Harrods (Buenos Aires) Ltd* [1991] 4 All ER 334). As between courts of Contracting States, Article 16 requires that the English court must take jurisdiction, irrespective of the domicile of the defendant. Where the English court has jurisdiction by virtue of Article 16, no leave is required to issue a writ out of the jurisdiction where there are no pending proceedings in a Contracting State: RSC ord. 11, r. 2.

Again if the matter falls also within the exclusive jurisdiction of the courts of (an)other Contracting State(s), English proceedings must be stayed unless the English court is first seised (Article 23).

23.2.7   FOREIGN JURISDICTION CLAUSES

In an application for leave to serve the writ out of the jurisdiction under ord. 11, leave will be refused where there is in existence a foreign jurisdiction clause, unless it can be attacked on the basis that the contract containing the clauses, or the clause itself, is null and void: *Mackenda v Feldia AG* [1967] 2 QB 590.

In circumstances where the writ has been served as of right on the defendant, application to stay the proceedings will be successful unless the plaintiff:

(a)   successfully attacks the validity of the contract containing the clause, or the clause itself (e.g. on the basis of its being null and void under the Hague-Visby Rules, art. III, r. 8), in which case normal *forum non conveniens* principles apply and the burden lies initially on the defendant to show that other factors (apart from the jurisdiction clause) point to a more appropriate forum; or

(b)   shows that justice demands the stay be refused.

However, if in an action to which the Brussels Convention applies the requirements of Article 17 are met, giving exclusive jurisdiction to the chosen courts of a Contracting State, the English court *must* refuse to exercise jurisdiction. This would appear to be the case even though the chosen Contracting State would not apply the Hague-Visby Rules. The question as to which is the more appropriate forum will not arise. Note that exclusive jurisdiction can be granted to the courts of a Contracting State where *one* of the parties, be it defendant or plaintiff, is domiciled in a Contracting State.

Where neither party to an action to which the Brussels Convention applies is domiciled in a Contracting State, but the courts of a Contracting State other than the United Kingdom have been chosen to exercise jurisdiction, the English courts cannot exercise jurisdiction unless and until the chosen court has declined jurisdiction: Article 17.

23.2.8   ENJOINING FOREIGN PROCEEDINGS

The English court will normally only restrain the plaintiff from proceeding in a foreign court in favour of proceedings in the English courts where the applicant for the injunction shows that the English court would provide the natural forum for the trial of the action, and it would be vexatious or oppressive to allow the foreign proceedings to continue, i.e. the injustice to the defendant if the plaintiff is allowed to pursue the foreign proceedings would outweigh the injustice to the plaintiff if he/she were enjoined from doing so *(Societé Nationale Industrielle Aerospatiale* v *Lee Kui Jak* [1987] 3 WLR 59).

Note that where there are concurrent proceedings, to which the Brussels Convention apply, taking place in the courts of different Contracting States, Articles 21 or 22 will apply. Under Article 21, where the concurrent proceedings involve the same cause of action and the same parties, whichever court is not first seised of the matter must initially stay, and ultimately decline jurisdiction when the jurisdiction of the court first seised is established. Recently the Court of Appeal, in *Continental Bank NA* v *Aeakos Compaña Naviera* [1994] 1 Lloyd's Rep 505, granted an injunction prohibiting the continuation of Greek proceedings, on the basis that an Article 17 jurisdiction agreement required the Greek court to decline to exercise jurisdiction. The injunction was granted despite the fact that the Greek court appeared to be 'first seised' of the action.

23.3   Action *in rem*

This means in substance an action against a thing — an asset of the person who could be sued in an action *in personam*. In an action *in rem*, no personal liability can attach to the person who would be potentially liable *in personam* unless he/she chooses to take part in the proceedings. Any judgment in an action which remains solely *in rem* can only be enforced against the *res, not* against any other personal assets of the person who would be liable *in personam*. See *The Sylt* [1991] 1 Lloyd's Rep 240; *The Nordglimt* [1988] QB 183; *The Sardinia Sulcis* [1991] 1 Lloyd's Rep 201; *The Maciej Rataj* [1992] 2 Lloyd's Rep 552.

The fact that, in the Admiralty writ, there is a reference to a defendant — the party potentially liable *in personam*, e.g., 'The owners of the ship SS Castor ... Defendants' — and an identification of that defendant, albeit by description, does not make the action one against that described defendant. It is still by its nature, at its inception, an action against the *res*. However, take note that *for the purposes of the application of Article 2 of the Brussels Convention*, the Court of Appeal has held in *The Deichland* [1989] 2 All ER 1066, that the party potentially liable *in personam* and described as the defendant in the writ is 'being sued' and must be sued in courts of his/her domicile, if domiciled in a Contracting State, even though the action has remained solely *in rem*, unless the provisions of another jurisdiction Convention can be relied upon (see below).

The commencement of an action *in rem* may very much affect the person who would be liable *in personam* and who is described as the 'defendant' in the writ. The ways in which this can occur are as follows:

(a)   In order to *defend* the *in rem* proceedings, the 'defendant' must either:

(i)   acknowledge *service* of the writ, in so doing the action continues *in rem* and *in personam* (*The Nordglimt (supra)*; *The Kherson* [1992] 2 Lloyd's Rep 261; *The Maciej Rataj* [1992] 2 Lloyd's Rep 552); or
(ii)   acknowledge the *issue* of the writ on the basis that he or she 'desires to take part in the proceedings' (see ord. 75, r. 3(b)). Again, the action has now become one *in personam* as well as *in rem* (*The Prinsengracht* [1993] 1 Lloyd's Rep 41).

Thus the commencement of an action *in rem* can force the 'defendant' to submit to the jurisdiction, even though the absence of the 'defendant' within the jurisdiction, and the inapplicability of RSC ord. 11 or the applicability of the Brussels Convention on Jurisdiction would otherwise prevent action being pursued within this jurisdiction. On submission to the jurisdiction in order to defend, the action proceeds also *in personam*. In consequence the plaintiff is not confined to satisfying his judgment against the *res* but can execute judgment against the other personal assets of the defendant. The benefits of being able initially to pursue an action *in rem* are evident.

(b) In order to *prevent/seek the release from arrest* of the *res,* the 'defendant' will be required to take steps which may be viewed as a submission to the jurisdiction. In consequence there may be added to the value of the *res*, his or her personal liability. The following points should be noted about this:

(i) Where the ship is no longer under the control of the 'defendant', he or she will not usually be concerned about the arrest or potential arrest of the vessel. But see *The Deichland* (*supra*).

(ii) If the ship does remain under the control of the 'defendant', the latter can prevent/seek release from arrest either—

(1) by putting up bail. In *The Prinsengracht* (*supra*) Sheen J stated that 'bail cannot be given without submitting to the jurisdiction. However, the Court of Appeal in *The Anna H* [1995] 1 Lloyd's Rep 11, suggests that whether there has been a submission to the jurisdiction by putting up bail will depend on the construction of the bail bond. Hobhouse LJ stated:

> Similarly, since it is accepted that it is possible to put up bail conditionally reserving the right to challenge the jurisdiction of the court (*The City of Mecca* (1879) 5 PD 28) there are problems about treating the provision of bail, without more, as precluding the ship owner from thereafter exercising his right to challenge the jurisdiction of the court.

(2) by entering a caveat against arrest. The procedure is set out under ord. 75, r. 6. However, in order to enter the caveat, the defendant or his/her solicitor must undertake to acknowledge issue or service of the writ in any action that may begin against the property described in the request, and within three days of receipt of notice of the action, give bail.

In *The Anna H* (*supra*), the Court of Appeal stated that the mere *undertaking* to acknowledge issue/service of the writ or put up bail could not in itself amount to a submission to the jurisdiction of the court. Indeed an acknowledgement of *service* thereafter could not in itself, amount to submission. Hobhouse LJ stated:

> ... an acknowledgement of service does not without more preclude a subsequent challenge to the jurisdiction of the court. Since the time at which the challenge has to be made is postponed until after service of a statement of claim and the fact that, following an unsuccessful challenge, a fresh acknowledgement is necessary (012R8) there are problems about treating a mere acknowledgement of service, or an undertaking to acknowledge issue or service, as being a waiver of the right to challenge the jurisdiction of the Court.... That some right of challenge must subsist is self-evident. The claim in the writ may be one which upon examination does not fall within the admiralty jurisdiction of the court under the 1981 Act. The entry of a caveat against arrest cannot preclude the caveator from raising that objection.

(3) by giving contractual security. In comparison with (1), however, since contractual security is given to the plaintiff, not the court, there can be no question of inherent submission to the jurisdiction. See *The Deichland* (*supra*). This has important consequences. First, a judgment in this action within this jurisdiction is confined in its execution to the value of the contractual security, and, secondly, where no arrest has been effected, the domicile of the 'defendant' i.e., the party potentially liable *in personam* in relation to the action persued *in rem*, within a contracting state to the Brussels Convention on Jurisdiction will prima facie prevent an action *in rem* being proceeded with in this jurisdiction at all. See *The Deichland* (*supra*). The plaintiff in taking contractual security in these circumstances must get the agreement of the defendant to submit to the jurisdiction of the English court and thus obtain an agreement on jurisdiction falling within Article 17.

The commencement of an action in rem may also affect a person who is under no personal liability to the plaintiff at all and who is not, therefore, the defendant to the claim on the writ. An Admiralty action *in rem* can be pursued against a vessel which is no longer, at the time of the arrest, under the control of the person liable *in personam.* In order to prevent the seizure of his income-earning asset the new owner of the vessel can offer to put up contractual security. The contractual security will cover the amount of the plaintiff's claim plus interest and costs, not exceeding the value of the *res.* Note that the new owner's personal liability does not extend beyond the contractual security. There will be no personal liability in relation to the *claim* the subject of the *in rem* action. However, it is worth noting that in those circumstances where the defendant named on the writ — the party potentially liable *in personam* — is domiciled in a contracting state to the Brussels Convention on Jurisdiction, following the decision in *The Deichland (supra),* the plaintiff may still feel it necessary to arrest the ship (no longer under the control of the defendant) in order to be able to maintain the *in rem* action within the jurisdiction.

In rem jurisdiction can only be exercised by the Admiralty Court. The jurisdiction of the Admiralty Court is statutory and is governed by ss. 20–24 of the Supreme Court Act 1981 and s. 27 of the County Courts Act 1984.

There is a restriction on the subject matter of an action which is within the Admiralty Jurisdiction. The claim must fall within s. 20(1)–(6) of the Supreme Court Act 1981, s. 27(1) of the County Courts Act 1984. In relation to problems arising in the carriage of goods by sea, an action *in rem* can proceed where:

    (a)   the claim is for damage done by a ship: SCA 1981, s. 20(2)(e); CCA 1984, s. 27(1)(b);

    (b)   the claim is for loss of or damage to goods carried in a ship: SCA 1981, s. 20(2)(g); CCA 1984, s. 27(1)(d);

    (c)   the claim *arises* out of an agreement *relating* to the carriage of goods in a ship, or to the use or hire of a ship: SCA 1981, s. 20(2)(h); CCA 1984, s. 27(1)(e). See in relation to this provision *Gatoil v Arkwright* [1985] 2 WLR 74; *The Antonis Lemos* [1985] 2 WLR 468. Note also *The Lloyd Pacifico* [1995] 1 Lloyd's Rep 54 in which the court held that to pursue a claim within s. 20(2)(h), the claim must relate to the carriage of goods on an identified ship.

The County Court jurisdiction has a financial restriction, in that the court has no jurisdiction to hear and determine any of the aforementioned claims for an amount exceeding £5,000.

Once the subject matter of the claim falls within SCA 1981, s. 20(1)–(6); CCA 1984, s. 27(1), jurisdiction is territorially unlimited in the sense that it does not matter where the claim arose and irrespective of the domicile or place of business of the owner of the ship (SCA 1981, s. 20(7); CCA 1984, s. 27(4)).

However, note the restriction in relation to both the High Court and the County Court of the Crown Proceedings Act 1947, the State Immunity Act 1978 and, most importantly, the Civil Jurisdiction and Judgments Act 1982 (CJJA).

Under CJJA 1982, the Brussels Convention can apply to superimpose its rules on jurisdiction over traditional jurisdiction *in rem* (*The Deichland* [1989] 2 All ER 1066) where the matter in dispute falls within Article 1. The domicile rule *prima facie* applies, i.e. action must proceed in courts of the contracting state where the defendant is domiciled (*The Deichland, supra*). In addition, the action *in rem* in a contracting state is subject to the rules on jurisdiction contained in Articles 17, 18, 21-23. (Article 16 in theory is applicable but is not likely to apply to an action *in rem.*)

Nevertheless, despite the above, the Brussels Convention indicates, at Article 57, that it shall not affect any convention to which the contracting states are or will be parties and which, in relation to particular matters, govern jurisdiction. Since, under English traditional rules on *in rem* jurisdiction, *arrest* of sea-going ships derives from the Brussels Convention Relating to the Arrest of Seagoing Ships 1952 (the Arrest Convention), once a ship has been *arrested* in an action *in rem,* the rules on jurisdiction contained in the Brussels Convention will not apply *in so far as they are catered for under the Arrest Convention* (*The Nordglimt* [1988] 2 All ER 531). Hobhouse J in *The Nordglimt* stated:

It is clear from the text of the 1968 Convention and the Accession Convention and the Commentaries of Mr Jenard and Prof. Schlosser that the relationship of Conventions such as the 1952 Convention to the 1968 Convention is that of the special to the general. Where special provision is made in the special convention it shall govern; where no special provision is made, the general provision of the 1968 Convention shall apply.

See also *The Anna H* (*supra*).

Now the European Court in *The Maciej Rataj* [1995] 1 Lloyd's Rep 302 has stated:

On a proper construction, Article 57 of the Convention, as amended by the Accession Convention, means that, where a Contracting State is also a contracting party to another convention on a specific matter containing rules on jurisdiction, that specialised convention precludes the application of the provisions of the Brussels Convention only in cases governed by the specialised convention and not in those to which it does not apply.

Note that the English *in rem* jurisdiction over aircraft cargo and freight is not derived from the Arrest Convention. Note also the Collision Convention of 1952 which imposes its own jurisdictional rules (see *The PO* [1990] 1 Lloyd's Rep 419).

There is also, in relation to the Admiralty action *in rem,* a restriction on the *res. The res* must be a ship, or cargo, aircraft or freight when subject to a maritime lien.

It may happen that, since the cause of action arose, the *res* has been dealt with by its owner, e.g. the ship may have been sold, or time chartered, to a third party. Can action proceed against the *res* in these circumstances, and indeed is the complainant confined to pursuing an *in rem* action only against the particular *res* involved in the incident?

Note the following:

(a) where the claim creates a 'maritime lien' then the action *in rem* can proceed against the *res* affected by the lien even though the *res* was sold *before action is brought*. For our purposes a claim falling within SCA 1981, s. 20(2)(e); CCA 1984, s. 27(1)(b), creates a maritime lien on the ship. Essentially the *res* is charged with the lien so that the maritime lien can be enforced by an action *in rem* against the property in whoever's hand it may be. The lien attaches from the time the facts happen which gave rise to the maritime lien and continues binding until discharged.

(b) In relation to claims falling within SCA 1981, s. 20(2)(g); CCA 1984, s. 27(1)(d) and SCA 1981, s. 20(2)(h); CCA 1984, s. 27(1)(e), the following conditions must be satisfied in order to commence an action *in rem* against the ship involved in the incident — the 'relevant' ship:

(i) the claim must have arisen in connection with a ship;

and when the cause of action arose

(ii) the person who would be liable on the claim in an action *in personam* — the *relevant person* — must have been the owner or charterer, or in possession or control of the ship;

(*Note*: (i) 'owner' means registered owner. See *The Evpo Agnic* [1988] 1 WLR 1090.
(ii) 'charterer' includes time charterer. See *The Span Terza* [1982] 1 Lloyd's Rep 225.)

and at the time when *action is brought*

(iii) the relevant person is the beneficial owner of all the shares in the relevant ship or the charterer of it by demise.

(*Note*: (i) 'time when action is brought' means when the writ is issued. See *The Carmenia II* [1963] 2 Lloyd's Rep 152.

(ii)   'beneficial owner' means equitable owner. See *I Congresso del Partido* [1978] QB 500.)

In addition, with regard to claims under s. 20(2)(g) and (h), and a maritime lien claim under s. 20(2)(e), provided conditions (i) and (ii) above are satisfied, an action *in rem* can proceed against any other ship of which, at the time when action is brought, the person who would have been liable *in personam* (the relevant person) was the beneficial owner as respects all the shares in it.

Note the meaning of 'beneficial owner' — see *I Congresso del Partido, supra*. See also *The Aventicum* [1978] 1 Lloyd's Rep 184, 'where damages are claimed by cargo owners and there is a dispute as to the beneficial ownership of the ship, the court in all cases can and in some cases should look behind the registered ownership to determine the true beneficial ownership'. See also *The Evpo Agnic* [1988] 1 WLR 1090.

What happens if the ship, not subject to a maritime lien, but which, according to SCA 1981, s. 21(4), CCA 1984, s. 28, could be served with a writ *in rem*, is sold between issue of the writ and service?

Once the writ *in rem* has been issued, the plaintiff's right of action cannot be defeated by a subsequent change of ownership. See *The Monica S* [1976] 2 Lloyd's Rep 113. It will be the new owners of the ship, not the defendant named in the writ, who will seek to prevent or seek release from arrest, of the vessel, by putting up security.

Note the following *procedural requirements*:

(a)   An Admiralty action *in rem* must be commenced by writ in the prescribed form: RSC ord. 75, r. 3(1).

(b)   The writ indicates that the action is an action *in rem* against the ship, e.g. '*Castor*', or other *res* as may be, describing the property against which the action is brought.

(c)   The plaintiffs are usually described without naming them, e.g. 'owners of cargo lately laden on board the ship *Castor*'.

(d)   The defendants are titled (i) 'the owners of the ship *Castor*', or (ii) 'the demise charterers of the ship *Castor*', or (iii) 'the owner or demise charterers of the ship *Castor*'. The writ may name only one ship, in which case, if there are sister ships, separate writs can be issued for each ship. It is possible for the writ to list all the ships, i.e. the 'relevant one' and/or sister ships. In any event, only one ship can be served with the writ.

(e)   Where the ship named on the writ has been sold before service, the writ will be amended under RSC ord. 20, r. 1 to read, e.g. 'Admiralty Action *in rem* against *Polydeuces* formerly *Castor*' and the defendants will be named as 'the owners of the ship *Castor* now named *Polydeuces*'. The defendant must be the party who was the owner, or charterer, or in possession or control of the ship involved in the incident when the course of action arose *and* was the owner or demise charterer of the 'relevant ship' and/or owner of a sister ship, at the same time the writ was issued. Where the claim creates a maritime lien, the defendant will be the owner or demise charterer of the relevant ship at the time the cause of action arose. The action remains solely an action *in rem* unless and until there is an acknowledgement of service by the defendant with no subsequent application to the court disputing jurisdiction. The new owners can make an application under RSC ord. 75, r. 17 for leave to intervene in the action (see *The Mawan* [1988] 2 Lloyd's Rep 459) and they can give security to prevent the arrest of or obtain release from arrest of the ship. But note that the rights of the intervener are limited to the protection of his interest in the *res*. He can, however, raise defences that the defendant could raise: *The Lord Strathcona* [1925] P 143; *The Byzantium* (1922) 16 Asp 19.

(f)   In the case of claims falling within s. 20(2)(e)–(r) of the SCA 1981, s. 27 of CCA 1984, although the plaintiff can issue more than one writ *in rem*, in respect of the claim, or name more than one ship in one writ *in rem*, the writ *in rem* can be served on one named ship only. Where one writ has identified several named ships, immediately after service on one ship, the writ should be amended by striking out the reference to all other ships: *The Freccia del Nord* [1989] 1 Lloyd's Rep 388.

(g)   The writ is valid for service for 12 months and service cannot be effected outside the jurisdiction. No application can be made for service out, or for substituted service.

(h)   Arrest can be applied for at any time after issue of the writ: ord. 75, r. 5(1). The party asking for arrest must file an affidavit with the particulars as required in ord. 75, r. 5(9). As long as the requirements of ord. 75, r. 5 are complied with, the court has no discretion to refuse a warrant of arrest. It is not a discretionary remedy: see *The Varna* [1993] 2 Lloyd's Rep 253. For the procedure for arresting the ship, refer to *The Johnny Two* [1992] 2 Lloyd's Rep 257. Only one ship can be arrested — that which is served. Where a ship has been arrested without prior service, the writ must be served on the ship arrested.

The Court of Appeal in *The Maciej Rataj* [1992] 2 Lloyd's Rep 552 has held that after an acknowledgement of service has been given in an action *in rem*, the action continues as a hybrid. The action becomes *in personam* but it does not lose its previous character of being an action *in rem*. The European Court of Justice in *The Maciej Rataj* [1995] 1 Lloyd's Rep 302 has decided that for the purpose of Article 21, a 'hybrid' action *in rem* before the court of one Contracting State can involve the same parties as a mere '*personam*' action before the courts of another Contracting State:

> In Article 21 of the Convention, the terms 'same cause of action' and 'between the same parties' have an independent meaning.... They must therefore be interpreted independently of the specific feature of the law in force in each Contracting State. It follows that the distinction drawn by the law of a Contracting State between an action *in personam* and an action *in rem* is not material for the interpretation of Article 21. Consequently, the answer is that a subsequent action does not cease to have the same cause of action and the same object and to be between the same parties as a previous action where the latter, brought by the owner of a ship before a Court of a Contracting State, is an action *in personam* for a declaration that that owner is not liable for alleged damage to cargo transported by his ship, whereas the subsequent action has been brought by the owner of the cargo before a court of another Contracting State by way of an action *in rem* concerning an arrested ship, and has subsequently continued both *in rem* and *in personam* or solely *in personam*, according to the distinctions drawn by the national law of that other Contracting State.

If an action *in rem* is stayed, either by virtue of the Brussels Convention on Jurisdiction or under traditional jurisdictional rules, s. 26 of the CJJA can operate to maintain any security obtained. Section 26(1) of the CJJA states that, where in England and Wales, or Northern Ireland, a court stops or dismisses Admiralty proceedings on the ground that the dispute in question should be submitted to the determination of the courts of another part of the United Kingdom or of an overseas country, the court may, if in those proceedings property has been arrested or bail or other security has been given to prevent or obtain release from arrest, order one of two things. First, that the property arrested be retained as security for the satisfaction of any award or judgment which:

(a)   is given in respect of the dispute in the arbitration or legal proceedings of which those proceedings are stayed or dismissed; and

(b)   is enforceable in England and Wales or, as the case may be, Northern Ireland.

Or, secondly, order that the stay or dismissal of those proceedings be conditional on the provision of equivalent security for the satisfaction of any such award or judgment (a conditional order is not possible if Article 21 applies).

See, in relation to s. 26(2), *The Havhelt* [1993] 1 Lloyd's Rep 523.

23.4   Application of Brussels Convention in Actions *in personam* and *in rem*

23.4.1   ACTIONS IN WHICH BRUSSELS CONVENTION APPLIES

In determining the question of whether the Convention applies, it must be borne in mind that although the Convention applies to 'civil or commercial matters' whatever the nature of the court or tribunal, the Convention does not apply where:

(a)   the matter involves no foreign element: Preamble to the Convention;

(b)   the matter deals with revenue, custom and administrative issues: Article 1;

(c)   the matter deals with the status or legal capacity of natural persons, rights in property arising out of a matrimonial relationship, wills and succession: Article 1(1);

(d)   the matter deals with bankruptcy, proceedings relating to the winding up of insolvent companies or other legal persons, judicial arrangements, compositions and analogous proceedings: Article 1(2);

(e)   the matter relates to social security: Article 1(3).

(f)   arbitration proceedings are involved: as to meaning of 'arbitration', refer to *The Atlantic Emperor* [1992] 1 Lloyd's Rep 342 (EC).

The European Court set out the relevant test as follows:

> In order to determine whether a dispute falls within the scope of the Convention, reference must be made solely to the subject matter of the dispute. If, by virtue of its subject matter such as the appointment of an arbitrator, a dispute falls outside the scope of the Convention the existence of a preliminary issue which the Court must resolve in order to determine the dispute cannot, whatever the issue may be, justify application of the convention.

See further, in relation to the need to identify the eventual subject matter of the dispute: *The Heidberg* [1994] 2 Lloyd's Rep 287; *The Xing Su Hai* [1995] 2 Lloyd's Rep 15.

As to the meaning of 'civil and commercial matters', see *LTU* v *Eurocontrol* [1976] 3 ECR 1541, [1977] 1 CMLR 88.

23.4.2   APPLICABILITY OF THE BRUSSELS CONVENTION: DOMICILE IN A CONTRACTING STATE

Even though the dispute is international in character and falls within the scope of the Convention, it is, in general, necessary to demonstrate that the defendant is domiciled in a Contracting State in order for the Convention to govern jurisdiction. For exceptions to this principle see **23.1.**

23.4.2.1   Domicile of an individual

The Convention, although it fails to define 'domicile', indicates under Article 52 which State's definition of domicile is to be used:

(a)   The Court of a Contracting State seised of the matter shall apply its internal law, i.e. a United Kingdom court seised of the matter shall apply the definition of domicile in CJJA 1982, s. 41(2). For the consequences of domicile, see **23.4.2.3.**

(b)   If a party is not domiciled in the State whose courts are seised of the matter, the court, in order to determine whether that party is domiciled in another Contracting State, shall apply the law of that State, i.e. a United Kingdom court would have to determine whether the defendant was domiciled in another Contracting State by applying the law of that State: Article 52.

23.4.2.2   Domicile of a company or association

Article 53 indicates that the Court of a Contracting State seised of the matter will apply its own concept of 'seat' in order to determine whether the company or association is domiciled in a Contracting or non-Contracting State, i.e. a United Kingdom Court seised of the matter will apply its definition of 'seat' under the provisions of CJJA 1982, s. 42.

23.4.2.3   Consequences of defendant's domicile in a Contracting State

The plaintiff must sue the defendant in the courts of the Contracting State where the defendant is domiciled. The defendant's nationality is ignored: Article 2. For example, in a matter to which the Convention applies, a defendant domiciled in the United Kingdom, must, generally speaking, be sued in the courts of the United Kingdom. The Modified Convention will now apply to allocate jurisdiction to a part of the United Kingdom.

23.4.3   PLAINTIFF'S CHOICE OF JURISDICTION

The primary basis of jurisdiction set out above is supplemented by the following provisions which give the plaintiff the choice of suing the defendant in another Contracting State:

    (a)   special jurisdiction: Articles 5–6A (see **23.5**);
    (b)   jurisdiction in matters relating to insurance: Articles 7–12A (see **23.6**);
    (c)   jurisdiction over consumer contracts: Articles 13–15 (see **23.7**).

The primary basis of jurisdiction is qualified, and the above supplementary provisions restricted, by:

    (a)   exclusive jurisdiction: Article 16 (see **23.8**);
    (b)   agreements on jurisdiction: Article 17 (see **23.9**);
    (c)   submission to the jurisdiction actions: Article 18 (see **23.10**);
    (d)   *Lis pendens* and related actions: Articles 21, 22, 23 (see **23.12** and **23.13**).

23.5   Special Jurisdiction: Articles 5–6A

This special jurisdiction is viewed as a series of exceptions and will be restrictively interpreted: *Somafer v Saar-Ferngas* [1978] 3 ECR 2183, [1979] 1 CMLR 490; *Jakob Handte GmbH v Traitements Mecanochimiques des Surfaces and Another, The Times,* 19 August 1992. It enables the courts of a Contracting State other than that where the defendant is domiciled to exercise jurisdiction at the choice of the plaintiff. The plaintiff's choice is limited, however, by the operation of Articles 16, 17, 21–23.

23.5.1   CONTRACT

If the matter 'relates to a contract', the plaintiff can choose to proceed in the courts of the 'place' of 'performance' of 'the obligation' in question: Article 5(1).

Note the following points about Article 5(1):

    (a) 'Matters relating to a contract'. This phrase has been interpreted in *Jakob Handte GmbH v Traitements Mechanochimiques des Surface* 1993 ILPR 5. The European Court of Justice held that the concept of 'matters relating to a contract' had to be interpreted independently and not according to a relevant national law. The concept 'would not be understood as referring to a situation in which there was no undertaking which had been freely entered into by one party with regard to another': see also *Atlas Shipping Agency (UK) Ltd v Suisse Atlantique Société Darmament Maritime* [1995] Lloyd's Rep 188. In *Trade Indemnity plc v Forsakringsaktiebolaget Njord* [1995] 1 All ER 796, the Court held in Queen's Bench Division that a claim to avoid a contract including a claim in restitution fell within the words 'matters relating to a contract'.
    (b)   Which is the relevant obligation in question? In *Shevanai v Kreischer* [1987] 3 CMLR 782, the European Court held, following *De Bloos v Bouyer* [1976] 3 ELR 1497, that the contractual obligation is that which forms the actual basis of the legal proceedings and not the obligation which characterises the contract, upon which the plaintiff's action may not be based. The court also held that where there are various obligations in issue it is the principal obligation which will determine jurisdiction. See also in this regard *Medway Packaging v Meurer* [1990] 2 Lloyd's Rep 112; *Unicon Transport Group plc v Continental Lines* [1992] 1 All ER 161 (HL). In the *Trade Indemnity plc* case *(supra)* the Court was asked to consider whether the obligation to make full and frank disclosure prior to entry into an insurance contract was an 'obligation' falling within the ambit of Article 5(1). The Court held that 'matters relating to a contract' might extend beyond contracts *stricto sensu* to consensual relationships partaking of the same nature as a contract, and thus the same, more liberal interpretation should extend to the meaning of 'obligation'. Nevertheless, the Court held that since the obligation of full and frank disclosure arose by virtue of equitable principles and not as a matter of contract, even in the more liberal sense, it was not an obligation falling within the wording of Article 5(1).

(c)   Where the parties have not specified the place of performance, this will be determined by the forum applying its rules of private international law: *Tessili* v *Dunlop* [1976] ECR 1473.

(d)   If the parties choose the place of performance for the purposes of Article 5(1), the agreed choice is not subject to Article 17: *Zelger* v *Salinitri* [1980] 1 ECR 89.

(e)   Where a defendant challenges the plaintiff's right to rely on the special jurisdictional rule, as to the standard of proof required of the plaintiff refer to *Tesam Distribution Ltd* v *Schuh Mode Team GmbH Law Society Gazette* 89/38, 20 December 1989.

23.5.2   MAINTENANCE

Although the Convention does not apply to matters such as divorce or separation (see Article 1(1)), in matters relating to maintenance, the plaintiff can, by virtue of Article 5(2), choose to sue in the courts:

(a)   where the plaintiff is domiciled; or

(b)   where the plaintiff is habitually resident (habitual residence will be defined according to national law); or

(c)   where by its own law, the court has jurisdiction to entertain proceedings concerning the status of a person (as long as that jurisdiction is not based on nationality) and the maintenance matter is ancillary to those proceedings.

23.5.3   TORT, DELICT OR QUASI-DELICT

If the matter relates to tort, delict, or quasi delict, the plaintiff can choose to sue the defendant in the courts at the place where the harmful event occurred: Article 5(3).

Note the following about the above provision:

(a)   The European Court in *Kalfelis* v *Schroder* [1988] ECR 5565, held that the words 'relates to a tort' must be treated as an independent concept not defined in accordance with national law, covering all actions which seek to establish the liability of a defendant and which are not 'related to a contract' within the meaning of Article 5(1). A court which does have jurisdiction over an action in so far as it is based on tort, does not have jurisdiction over that action in so far as it is not so based.

(b)   'Where the harmful event occurred' covers both the place where damage occurred and the place of the event giving rise to it, where the two are not identical: see *Biers BV* v *Mines de Potasse d'Alsace* [1978] QB 708.

(c)   Where the defendant challenges the right of the plaintiff to rely on the special jurisdictional rule as to the standard of proof required of the plaintiff, refer to *Tesam Distribution Ltd* v *Schuh Mode Team GmbH* [1990] 1 LPR 149; *Molnlycke* v *Proctor & Gamble Ltd* [1992] 1 WLR 1112.

23.5.4   DAMAGES OR RESTITUTION

The plaintiff can choose to claim damages or restitution against a defendant, in the courts seised of criminal proceedings against that defendant, if the court has jurisdiction under its own law to entertain the civil proceedings: Article 5(4) (English criminal courts have jurisdiction under Powers of Criminal Courts Act 1973, s. 35 as amended by Criminal Justice Act 1988, s. 104; Theft Act 1968, s. 23). However, see Article 11, Annexed Protocol.

23.5.5   BRANCH OR AGENCY

The plaintiff can choose to sue the defendant in the courts where a branch, agency or other establishment of the defendant is situated, as long as the dispute arises out of the operations of the branch or agency: Article 5(5).

Article 5(5) is only intended to apply to disputes between a third party and the parent body: see *De Bloos* v *Bouyer* [1976] ECR 1497, [1977] 1 CMLR 60.

For the meaning of 'branch', 'agency' or 'other establishment', see *De Bloos* v *Bouyer (supra); Somafer* v *Saar Ferngas* [1978] ECR 2183; *Blanckaert and Williams* v *Trost* [1981] ECR 819, [1982] 2 CMLR 1.

23.5.6   TRUSTS

When the defendant is being sued in his/her capacity as settlor, trustee or beneficiary, the plaintiff can choose to sue him/her in the courts of the Contracting State where the trust is domiciled: Article 5(6).

This only applies, however, where the trust is created by statute, or is written or evidenced in writing. The special jurisdiction will not therefore extend to constructive or resulting trusts. Trusts arising under wills or intestacies fall outside the scope of the Brussels Convention: Article 1.

The special jurisdiction only applies to disputes concerning the relationships of the parties to the trust, and does not apply to disputes between third parties and, e.g., trustees. (See the Schlosser Report, para. 120.)

Under Article 53, the court of the Contracting State seised of the matter shall apply its own rules of private international law to determine where a trust is domiciled. A UK court will apply CJJA 1982, s. 45 to determine if the trust is domiciled in the United Kingdom.

23.5.7   SALVAGE

A plaintiff can choose to pursue his/her claims for remuneration for salvage of a cargo or freight in the courts which:

(a)   ordered the cargo or freight to be arrested to secure the payment of remuneration; or
(b)   which could have ordered the arrest but for bail or other security being given: Article 5(7).

This special jurisdiction only applies where it is claimed that the defendant has an interest in the cargo or had an interest in the cargo at the time of the salvage. This special jurisdiction does not extend to remuneration claims for salvage of a *ship*. Where the Arrest Convention of 1952 applies, and the ship is arrested, the Brussels Convention will not apply: Article 57; *The Deichland* [1989] 2 All ER 1066.

23.5.8   CO-DEFENDANTS

A plaintiff can choose to sue the defendant in the courts where a co-defendant is domiciled: Article 6(1) (see *Aiglon* v *Gua Slian* [1993] 1 Lloyd's Rep 164). According to the Jenard Report, p. 26, (see **23.16**) there must be a connection between the claims made against the defendants. Refer to *Kalfelis* v *Bankhaus Schröder Munchmeyer Hengst & Co. 189/87* [1988] ECR 5565 and the Court of Appeal in *The Rewia* [1991] 2 Lloyd's Rep 325. In the *Kalfelis* case the Court ruled:

> the rule laid down in Article 6(1) therefore applies where the actions brought against the various defendants are related when the proceedings are instituted, that is to say where it is expedient to hear and determine them together in order to avoid the risk of irreconcilable judgments resulting from separate proceedings. It is for the national court to verify in each individual case whether that condition is satisfied.

Note Dillon LJ in *Molnlycke AB* v *Proctor & Gamble* [1992] 4 All ER 47: 'Where Article 6 is concerned, the test to be applied for joinder must be, what I would call briefly, the Order 11 test — the test that would have been applied had permission for service had to be obtained under Order 11.' See *The Rewia* [1991] 2 Lloyd's Rep 325.

23.5.9   THIRD PARTIES

The party bringing third-party proceedings can choose to sue the third party in the court having jurisdiction in the original proceedings unless the original proceedings were instituted with the aim of removing him/her from the jurisdiction of the court which would be competent in his/her case: Article 6(2). Where the third-party proceedings do not involve a warranty or guarantee, Article 6(2) requires the existence of a nexus between the main claim and the third-party proceedings: see *Kinnear* v *Falcon Films* [1994] 3 All ER 42.

23.5.10 COUNTERCLAIMS

Where a defendant is sued in the courts of a Contracting State he/she can counterclaim in the courts where the original action was brought even though the defendant to the counterclaim is domiciled in another Contracting State, as long as the counterclaim arises out of the same contract or facts on which the original claim was based: Article 6(3).

23.5.11 RIGHTS *IN REM* IN IMMOVEABLE PROPERTY

By virtue of the Civil Jurisdiction and Judgments Act 1982 (Amendment) Order 1990, a new Article 6(4) has been added. This allows the plaintiff to sue the defendant in the courts of the Contracting State where immoveable property is situated if the matter relates to a contract and the action can be combined with an action against the same defendant in matters relating to rights *in rem* in immoveable property.

23.5.12 LIMITATION OF LIABILITY

Any court which would have jurisdiction over a claim against the shipowner can make a declaration on limitation of liability: Article 6A.

23.6 Jurisdiction in Matters Relating to Insurance: Articles 7–12 (Section 3)

23.6.1 ACTIONS BY INSURED

Jurisdiction under this section only applies where the defendant is domiciled in a Contracting State: Article 7. These provisions give the plaintiff a wide choice of forum against a defendant insurer. The plaintiff can choose to sue the insurer in the courts of the Contracting State where the insurer is domiciled: Article 8(1). Where the insurer is *not* domiciled in a Contracting State but has a branch agency or other establishment in a Contracting State, the insurer is deemed to be domiciled in the Contracting State of the branch, agency or other establishment, if the dispute arises out of the operation of that branch, agency or other establishment: Article 8, and see CJJA 1982, s. 44.

However, the plaintiff can choose to sue the insurer:

(a) in the courts of another Contracting State where the policy holder is domiciled: Article 8(2);
(b) in the courts of a Contracting State where the leading insurer is being sued, where the relevant insurer is a co-insurer: Article 8(3);
(c) in the courts of a Contracting State where a branch, agency or other establishment is situated, as regards disputes arising out of the operations of the branch, agency or other establishment: Articles 7 and 5(5);
(d) in respect of liability insurance, in the courts of the place where the harmful event occurred: Article 9;
(e) in respect of liability insurance, in the courts where the injured party has commenced proceedings against the insured, if the law of those courts permits the joinder: Article 10;
(f) in respect of the insurance of immoveable property, and also moveable property where both are covered by the same insurance policy and both are affected by the event, in the courts of the place where the harmful event occurred: Article 9;
(g) in the courts of a Contracting State if the defendant insurer has submitted to the jurisdiction of the court. See Jenard Report, p. 30 (see **23.16**), and see Article 28.

LAW OF INTERNATIONAL TRADE

23.6.2   ACTIONS BY INSURER

The insurer can only bring proceedings in the courts of the Contracting State where the defendant is domiciled: Article 11 (see *New Hampshire Insurance Co.* v *Strabag Bau AG* [1990] 2 Lloyd's Rep 61). However, when direct action has been properly brought by the injured party against the insurer, the same court shall have jurisdiction against the policy holder or the insured where the law governing direct action permits the joinder: Articles 10–11.

Equally, the insurer can bring a counterclaim in the courts where, by virtue of section 3, the original claim is pending: Article 11. The insurer may be able to proceed in the court of a Contracting State where the defendant has submitted to the jurisdiction: see Jenard Report, p. 30 (see **23.16**) and see Article 18. Where section 3 applies, it will not be possible for a plaintiff to rely on the other special bases of jurisdiction (apart from Article 5(5)): Article 7.

23.6.3   OUSTING THE JURISDICTION

The parties can oust the operation of s. 3 by an agreement on jurisdiction complying with the provisions of Article 12 (and see Article 17, third paragraph). Refer to *S. & W. Berisford* v *New Hampshire* [1990] 1 Lloyd's Rep 454. It is not clear whether an agreement on jurisdiction under Article 12 must also comply with the formalities under Article 17.

The provisions of section 3 are also subject to the exclusive jurisdiction provision in Article 16.

23.7   Jurisdiction over Consumer Contracts: Articles 13–15 (Section 4)

Section 4 only applies where the defendant is domiciled in a Contracting State: Article 13. These provisions enable the court of a Contracting State other than that in which the defendant is domiciled to exercise jurisdiction against a defendant at the choice of the plaintiff. The plaintiff is given a wide choice if he/she is the consumer. In relation to this, where a defendant is being sued by a consumer and is not domiciled in a Contracting State, that party will be deemed to be domiciled in the Contracting State of a branch, agency or other establishment, in disputes arising out of the operations of that branch, agency or establishment: Article 13, and see CJJA 1982, s. 44.

23.7.1   REQUIREMENTS FOR APPLICATION OF SECTION 4

The section only covers a contract concluded by a consumer. A consumer is a person who concludes a contract for a purpose outside his/her trade or profession: Article 13. The section only applies if the contract, the subject of the proceedings, falls within one of the following categories:

(a)   a contract for sale of goods on instalment credit terms: see *Bertrand* v *Ott* [1978] ECR 1431, [1978] 3 CMLR 499;
(b)   a contract for a loan, repayable by instalments, made to finance the sale of goods;
(c)   a contract for any other form of credit made to finance the sale of goods;
(d)   any other contract for the supply of goods or for the supply of services where:

(i)   in the State of the consumer's domicile, the conclusion of the contract was preceded by a specific invitation addressed to the consumer, or by advertisement; and
(ii)   the consumer took the steps necessary for the conclusion of the contract in the State of his/her domicile: Article 13.

23.7.2   CONSEQUENCES OF OPERATION OF SECTION 4

If the above requirements for the operation of section 4 are met, the consequences are as follows:

(a)   The consumer can sue the other party to the contract in the courts of the Contracting State in which that party is domiciled, or in the courts of the Contracting State in which the consumer is domiciled.

(b)   As regards a dispute arising out of the operations of a branch, agency or other establishment, the consumer can sue the other party in the court of the place in which the branch, agency or other establishment is situated: Articles 13 and 5(5).

(c)   Proceedings can only be brought against the consumer in the courts of the Contracting State in which the consumer is domiciled (the 'deemed domicile' provisions do not apply): Article 14. However, the other party can counterclaim against the consumer in the courts in which, in accordance with s. 4, the original claim is pursued: Article 14.

(d)   The operation of section 4 can probably be avoided where a defendant has submitted to the jurisdiction of a Contracting State: Article 18.

(e)   With the exception of Article 5(5), parties pursuing claims which fall within section 4 cannot rely on the other special bases of jurisdiction under the Convention.

(f)   The operation of section 4 can be avoided by an agreement as to jurisdiction by the parties which complies with the provisions of Article 15 (and see Article 17, third paragraph). It is unclear whether the terms of Article 15 must also comply with the formal requirements of Article 17: see Schlosser Report, para. 161 (see **23.16**).

The provisions of section 4 are also subject to the exclusive jurisdiction provision in Article 16.

23.8   Exclusive Jurisdiction: Article 16

In certain matters the Brussels Convention gives exclusive jurisdiction to the courts of a particular Contracting State: Article 16. The courts of other Contracting States not given exclusive jurisdiction must declare of their own motion that they have no jurisdiction: Article 19. Article 16 takes precedence over Articles 17, 18, 21 and 22.

Allocation of jurisdiction under Article 16 is not dependent on domicile. This provision thus further restricts the application of the traditional rules as to jurisdiction in the courts of Contracting States.

23.8.1   APPLICATION OF ARTICLE 16

The application of Article 16 cannot be evaded by submission to the jurisdiction under Article 18 or by means of a jurisdiction clause under Article 17. Article 16 applies where the matter is principally concerned (Jenard Report, p. 34, see **23.16**) with the following.

23.8.1.1   Rights *in rem* of immoveable property
Article 16 states that the courts of the Contracting State where the property is situated shall have exclusive jurisdiction: Article 16(1). Where the property is situated in more than one Contracting State, Article 23 will apply. Any court other than the first seised of the matter must decline jurisdiction.

23.8.1.2   Tenancies of immoveable property
Article 16(1), as amended by Civil Jurisdiction and Judgments Act 1982 (Amendment) Order 1990, states that the courts of the Contracting State in which the property is situated shall have exclusive jurisdiction except where the tenancy is concluded for temporary private use for a maximum of six consecutive months, in which case the courts of the Contracting State in which the defendant is domiciled shall have jurisdiction provided that the landlord and the tenant are natural persons and are domiciled in the same Contracting State.

23.8.1.3   Constitution, dissolution and decisions of company or association
Article 16 applies where the matter concerns the validity of the constitution, nullity or dissolution of a company, or association, or the decisions of the organs of a company or association. This provision does not apply to proceedings relating to the winding up of insolvent companies etc. (see Article 1(2) and the Schlosser Report, paras 57–58, see **23.16**).

Article 16(2) states that the courts of the Contracting States in which a company or association has its seat shall have exclusive jurisdiction. A UK court seised of the matter will apply the special definition of 'seat' in CJJA 1982, s. 43(2) to ascertain whether it has exclusive jurisdiction under Article 16(2).

If the company or association has no seat within the UK under s. 43(2), the UK court will apply s. 43(6) to determine whether there is a seat within another Contracting State for the purpose of Article 16. Where the company or association has more than one seat (see Article 53), a court other than that first seised of the matter must decline jurisdiction: Article 23.

23.8.1.4 Validity of entries in public registers

Article 16(3) states that the courts of the Contracting State where the public register is kept will have exclusive jurisdiction.

23.8.1.5 Patents, trademarks, designs and other similar rights

Article 16 applies where the matter concerns the registration or validity of patents, trademarks, designs, or other similar rights required to be deposited or registered. Article 16(4) states that the courts of the Contracting State where the deposit or registration has been applied for, or has taken place, or where by international convention the deposit or registration is deemed to have taken place, shall have exclusive jurisdiction.

23.8.1.6 Enforcement of judgments

Article 16(5) states that the courts of the Contracting State where the judgment has been or is to be enforced shall have exclusive jurisdiction. See *AS-Autoteile Service GmbH* v *Malhe* [1986] 3 CMLR 321, (1986) 11 ECR 98.

23.9 Agreements on Jurisdiction: Article 17

23.9.1 CONDITIONS REQUIRED FOR OPERATION OF ARTICLE 17 (AS AMENDED BY CIVIL JURISDICTION AND JUDGMENTS ACT 1982 (AMENDMENT) ORDER 1990)

The courts of a Contracting State must exercise jurisdiction with no discretion to refuse if the following conditions are satisfied:

(a) the courts of the Contracting State have been granted jurisdiction by *agreement* of the parties; and

(b) at least one of the parties is domiciled in the Contracting State; and

(c) the parties have agreed that the court or courts of a Contracting State are to have jurisdiction to settle any dispute which has arisen or which may arise in connection with a particular legal relationship; and

(d) the agreement must be either:

(i) in writing; or

(ii) evidenced in writing; or

(iii) in a form which accords with the practice the parties have established; or

(iv) in international trade or commerce, in a form which accords with a usage of which the parties are or ought to be aware and which in such trade or commerce is widely known to, and regularly observed by, parties to contracts of the type involved in the particular trade or commerce concerned.

Note the following points about the Article 17 provision:

(a) There must have been *agreement* of the *parties* to grant jurisdiction to the courts of a Contracting State: *Dresser UK Ltd* v *Falcongate Freight Management* [1992] QB 502 (bailor/bailee relationship); *Partenreederei Ms Tilly Russ* v *Haven* [1985] QB 931 (assignment); *IP Metal* v *Ruote (No. 2)* [1994] 2 Lloyd's Rep 560; *Denby* v *Hellenic Mediterranean Lines* [1994] 1 Lloyd's Rep 320.

(b) If the above conditions are satisfied, the chosen court of a Contracting State has no discretion to decline to exercise jurisdiction in relation to courts of other Contracting States. It is, however, able to exercise its *forum non conveniens* principle where the contest is with the courts of a non-Contracting State: *Re Harrods (Buenos Aires) Ltd* [1991] 4 All ER 334.

(c) If the above conditions are satisfied, the jurisdiction agreement is of conclusive effect. In consequence, an Article 17 jurisdiction agreement takes precedence over the provisions of Articles 21 and 22: *Kloeckner* v *Gatoil Overseas Inc.* [1990] 1 Lloyd's Rep 177; *Continental Bank NA* v *Aeakos Compañia Naviera* [1994] 1 Lloyd's Rep 505; *Mark Denby* v *The Hellenic Mediterranean Lines* [1994] 1 Lloyd's Rep 320.

(d) An Article 17 agreement on jurisdiction cannot oust the operation of Article 16: Article 17.

(e) An Article 17 agreement on jurisdiction can be ousted by submission to the jurisdiction: Article 18; *Elefanten Schuh GmbH* v *Jacqmain* [1981] ECR 1671.

(f) If the agreement was entered into for the benefit of one party only, the party retains the right to bring proceedings in any other court which has jurisdiction by virtue of the Convention: Article 17; *Anterist* v *Credit Lyonnais* [1987] 1 CMLR 33.

(g) If condition (a) above is missing, i.e., parties have conferred jurisdiction on courts of a non-Contracting State, a subsequent contest with the courts of a Contracting State, e.g., courts of the defendant's domicile in a Contracting State, will enable the court of the Contracting State to consider *forum non conveniens* principles: *Re Harrods (Buenos Aires) Ltd (supra)*.

(h) Where condition (b) is missing, i.e., neither party is domiciled in a Contracting State, the courts of a Contracting State not chosen by the parties cannot exercise jurisdiction unless and until the chosen Contracting State court decides not to exercise jurisdiction: Article 17. Since the defendant is not domiciled in a Contracting State, the court will apply its traditional rules on jurisdiction subject to Articles 16 and 21–23.

23.10 Submission to the Jurisdiction: Article 18

Submission to the jurisdiction of a court of a Contracting State will be effective to grant that court jurisdiction unless:

(a) the submission was to contest jurisdiction only (see *Elefanten Schuh* v *Jacqmain* (supra)): *CHW* v *GJH* [1982] ECR 11 89, [1983] 2 CMLR 125; or

(b) submission would evade the exclusive jurisdiction of the court of another Contracting State under Article 16 (see Article 19).

The rules of procedure of the court of the Contracting State seised of the matter will be applied to determine whether or not the defendant has submitted to the jurisdiction. (See Jenard Report, p. 38, **23.6** and *The Xing Su Hai* [1995] 2 Lloyd's Rep 15.)

23.11 Exclusive Jurisdiction with One Court Only: Article 19

Where a court of a Contracting State is seised of a claim which is principally concerned with a matter over which the courts of another Contracting State have exclusive jurisdiction by virtue of Article 16, it shall declare of its own motion that it has no jurisdiction,

23.12 *Lis Pendens:* Article 21

Where proceedings involving the same 'cause of action' and between the 'same parties' are brought in the courts of different Contracting States, any court other than the court first seised of the matter shall stay its proceedings until such time as the jurisdiction of the court first seised is established. Once established any court not first seised shall decline jurisdiction in favour of the court first seised: Article 21.

The following points should be noted about this provision:

(a)   A Court before which proceedings are pending, will not have to consider the date on which it became 'seised' of the proceedings until it has determined that the sets of proceedings are before the courts of different Contracting States and involves the 'same cause of action' and are between 'the same parties'.

The European Court in *Gubisch Maschinefabrik* v *Palumbo* [1989] EC 420 has held that the term *lis pendens* has an independent meaning:

> Article 21, together with Article 22 on related actions, is contained in section 8 of Title II of the Convention; that section is intended, in the interests of the proper administration of justice within the Community, to prevent parallel proceedings before the courts of different Contracting States and to avoid conflicts between decisions which might result therefrom. Those rules are therefore designed to preclude, in so far as is possible and from the outset, the possibility of a situation arising such as that referred to in Article 27(3), that is to say, the non-recognition of a judgment on account of its irreconcilability with a judgment given in a dispute between the same parties in the State in which recognition is sought... Having regard to the aforesaid objectives of the Convention and to the fact that Article 21, instead of referring to the term *lis pendens* as used in the different national legal system of the Contracting States, lays down a number of substantive conventions as components of a definition, it must be concluded that the term used in Article 21 in order to determine whether a situation of *lis pendens* arises must be regarded as independent.

Under Article 21, a *lis pendens* situation will arise where firstly the sets of proceedings involve the 'same cause of action'. The European Court in the *Gubisch* case has stated that in addition the actions must have the 'same subject matter'. In that case the parties were engaged in two legal proceedings in different Contracting States which were based on the same 'cause of action', i.e., the same contractual relationship. However one set of proceedings asked the court for discharge or rescission of the contract, the other proceedings asked for performance of the contract. The European Court held that both actions involved the same subject matter as the question whether the contract was binding lay at the heart of the two actions.

Subsequently, in *The Maciej Rataj* [1995] 1 Lloyd's Rep 302, the European Court in indorsing its earlier decision in *Gubisch* stated:

> For the purposes of Article 21 of the Convention, the 'cause of action' comprises the facts and the rule of law relied on as the basis of the action.

> Consequently, an action for a declaration of non-liability, such as that brought in the main proceedings in the case by the shipowners, and another action, such as that brought subsequently by the cargo owners on the basis of shipping contracts which are separate but in identical terms, concerning the same cargo transported in bulk and damaged in the same circumstances, have the same cause of action.

> The 'object of the action' for the purposes of Article 21 means the end the action has in view.

> The question accordingly arises whether two actions have the same object when the first seeks a declaration that the plaintiff is not liable for damages as claimed by the defendants, while the second commenced subsequently by those defendants seek on the contrary to have the plaintiff in the first action held liable for causing loss and ordered to pay damages.

> As to liability, the second action has the same object as the first, since the issue of liability is central to both actions. The fact that the plaintiff's pleadings are couched in negative terms in the first action whereas in the second action they are couched in positive terms by the defendant, who has become plaintiff, does not make the object of the dispute different.

> As to damage, the pleas in the second action are the natural consequence of those relating to the finding of liability and thus do not alter the principal object of the action. Furthermore, the fact that a party seeks a declaration that he is not liable for loss implies that he disputes any obligation to pay.

In those circumstances ... on a proper construction of Article 21 of the Convention, an action seeking to have the defendants held liable for causing loss and ordered to pay damages has the same cause of action and the same object as earlier proceedings brought by that defendant seeking a declaration that he is not liable for loss.

The European Court in *The Maciej Rataj (supra)* gave the following decision in relation to the meaning of the 'same parties':

(i)   a 'hybrid' action *in rem* and *in personam* and an action purely *in personam* can involve the 'same parties';

(ii)   where two actions involve the same cause of action and some but not all of the parties to the second action are the same as the parties to the action commenced earlier in another Contracting State, the second Court ... is required to decline jurisdiction only to the extent to which the parties to the proceedings before it are also parties to the action previously commenced; it does not prevent the proceedings from continuing between the other parties.

In addition,

(iii)   Parties will be the 'same parties' for the purposes of Article 21, even though they are plaintiff in one action and defendant in the other. See *Gubisch Maschinefabrik v Palumbo (supra)*.

(b)   the court having determined that it must consider when it was 'seised' of the proceedings, must of its own motion apply its own internal law to determine when it became 'seised' of the matter and must apply the internal law of the other Contracting State to determine when the court of that Contracting State became 'seised': see *Zelger v Salinitri (No. 2)* [1985] 3 CMLR 366. However, when considering the internal law of the other Contracting State, if there is a dispute as to the date on which the court of another Contracting State became 'seised' of proceedings and there is insufficient evidence to determine this issue, it is for the court of that other Contracting State to determine that date: see *Polly Peck International v Citibank, The Times,* 20 October 1993.

(c)   The European Court in *Zelger v Salinitri (supra)* has held that the court first seised 'is the one before which the requirements for proceedings to become definitively pending are first fulfilled, such requirments to be determined in accordance with the national law of each of the courts concerned'.

(d)   In order to determine when, under English law, for the purposes of Articles 21 and 22 (below) an English court is 'seised', a distinction must be drawn between actions *in personam* and *in rem*.

In actions *in personam*, the Court of Appeal in *Dresser UK v Falcongate* [1992] 2 WLR 319 rejected the notion that proceedings were 'definitively pending' on issue of a writ for service within the jurisdiction, but held the proceedings to be 'definitively pending' on service of the writ. However, Bingham LJ stated *obiter* that proceedings would also have become 'definitively pending' where provisional relief had been granted against the potential defendant prior to service of the writ. More recently, the Court of Appeal in *The Sargasso* [1994] 3 All ER 180 was asked to follow the *obiter dictum* of Bingham LJ in *Dresser v Falcongate* and rule that the granting of leave to issue and serve a writ out of the jurisdiction coupled with the issue of the writ would amount to the definitive pending of proceedings. The Court of Appeal in *The Sargasso* rejected the notion of any exception to the 'date of service' rule in *Dresser v Falcongate*.

The requirement on the part of a national court to find a date of 'definitive pendency' which reflects and respects the general concept of a 'decisive, conclusive, final or definitive litigational relationship between the courts and litigants' has been re-emphasised in *Grupo Torras SA v Al-Sabah* [1995] 1 Lloyd's Rep 374. The court in this very complex multi-partite litigation went on to hold that whether there were proceedings in different Contracting States involving the same cause of action and between the same parties on related proceedings has to be decided as at the date when the Court gave judgment on that issue. In addition, to determine which court was first seized of proceedings, there was to be applied, a simple test of chronological priority, ignoring any amendments of the cause of action or parties which might otherwise be treated under national law as having retrospective effect.

Mance J stated in relation to chronological priority:

'The defendants' submission was that it is open to any national court to apply any national rule of pendency which it chooses, including a rule creating retrospective pendency. Thus, in the defendants' submission, if the Quail proceedings in their original form were (at best) only related proceedings in relation to the present English proceedings, their amendment on May 18th 1993 meant that they became proceeding within Article 21 which were under Spanish law to be regarded as having been pending from June 9th 1992. Alternatively, if they remained no more than related actions, they were under Spanish law related actions which fell to be treated as pending *in their amended form* since June 9th 1992. Such submissions do not marry with a 'simple test of chronological priority'. It is difficult to think that the Convention contemplates retrospective satisfaction of the criteria of Article 21 requiring 'the same cause of action' and 'the same parties'. Indeed, if the submissions were right, it would mean that it was open to the Quail co-plaintiffs to join in the Quail proceedings retrospectively by amendment at any time up until the day of any judgment given in any English action involving them and by so doing to put themselves in a position to assert under Article 21 or 22 that the Spanish Court was first seised.

The court in the *Grupo Torras* case, in accepting the date of service as the date of definitive pendency had then to consider the position where there were multiple defendants served at different times. The court held that in these circumstances the date of definitive pendency is the date of first service on any of the defendants.

Mance J stated:

But the reality is that, once one defendant has been served, the proceedings have entered a new phase. The plaintiff thereafter no longer disposes, either in practical terms or in law, of complete freedom of action. It is most unlikely that he will wish to serve one defendant in one jurisdiction and bring separate proceedings against another in a second ... service on the first defendant served, whether domestic or foreign, does in a clear sense mark a Rubicon.

In actions *in rem*, proceedings are 'definitively pending' from the moment of service of the writ or arrest of the ship, whichever is the earlier. When the ship is already under arrest, proceedings will be 'definitively pending' from the moment the writ is issued: see *The Freccia del Nord* [1989] 1 Lloyd's Rep 388.

(e)   Any court not 'first seised' shall decline to exercise jurisdiction in favour of the court 'first seised' or, where there is a dispute as to the jurisdiction of the court 'first seised', the court shall stay its proceedings until jurisdiction of the court 'first seised' is established. Once established, the court not 'first seised' must decline to exercise jurisdiction: Article 21. When the court 'declines' to exercise jurisdiction under Article 21, those proceedings are not considered a nullity. If the court had no jurisdiction in the first place, no *lis pendens* problem would arise: see Hobhouse J in *The Nordglimt* [1988] 2 All ER 531.

(f)   Where an Article 17 argument is raised in the court not first seised, that court is not obliged to leave the question of jurisdiction to the court first seised but can consider the Article 17 issue itself: *Kloeckner & Co. v Gatoil Overseas Inc.* [1990] 1 Lloyd's Rep 177; *Mark Denby v Hellenic Mediterranean Lines* [1994] 1 Lloyd's Rep 320.

The conclusive effect of an agreement on jurisdiction under Article 17 is such that it takes precedence over the provisions of Article 21 (and Article 22): see *Continental Bank v Aeakos Compañia Naviera* [1994] 1 Lloyd's Rep 505.

(g)   The Brussels Convention itself provides for actions to be pending in more than one jurisdiction, e.g. supplementary jurisdiction under Article 5 (see **23.5**). However, Article 21 also extends to actions pending in different Contracting States using traditional rules, e.g. where the defendant is not domiciled in a Contracting State (Jenard Report, pp. 20–21, see **23.16**).

(h)   Article 21 applies to concurrent actions in different Contracting States. If concurrent proceedings are pending in a non-Contracting State, Article 21 will not apply. In consequence, the court of a

Contracting State hearing a matter by virtue of the exercise of jurisdiction under the convention will not be able to decline jurisdiction on the basis that it was not first seised of the matter. It will, however, be able to consider the exercise of its jurisdiction on *forum conveniens/non-conveniens principles* (*Re Harrods (Buenos Aires) Ltd* [1991] 4 All ER 334).

23.13 Related Actions: Article 22

The third paragraph of Article 22 provides that actions are deemed to be related where they are so closely connected that it is expedient to hear and determine term together to avoid the risk of irreconcilable judgments resulting from separate proceedings.

The European Court in *The Maciej Rataj* (*supra*) has held that in order to achieve the proper administration of justice, Article 22 must be interpreted to cover all cases where there is a risk of conflicting decisions, even if the judgments can be separately enforced and their legal consequences are not mutually exclusive. On the basis of the question placed before it the European Court concluded:

> It is sufficient, in order to establish the necessary relationships between, on the one hand, an action brought in a Contracting State by one group of cargo owners against a shipowner seeking damages for harm caused to part of the cargo carried in bulk under separate but identical contracts, and, on the other, an action in damages brought in another Contracting State against the same shipowners by the owners of another part of the cargo shipped under the same conditions and under contracts which are separate from but identical to those between the first group and the ship owner, that separate trial and judgment would involve the risk of conflicting decisions, without necessarily involving the risk of giving rise to mutually exclusive legal consequences.

23.14 Exclusive Jurisdiction with more than One Court: Article 23

Where actions come within the exclusive jurisdiction of courts in Contracting States, any court other than the court first seised shall decline jurisdiction in favour of that court: Article 23.

23.15 Access to Interim Relief within the Jurisdiction

Whether or not a party is domiciled in a Contracting State, the Brussels Convention can apply to prevent an English court from exercising its traditional rules on jurisdiction. The effect of this would be that in denying access to a complainant to pursue his/her substantive claim in the English courts, the complainant might have been denied the opportunity to 'freeze' assets within the jurisdiction by means of a *Mareva* injunction. Refer to *The Siskina* [1978] 1 Lloyd's Rep 1, which stated that English courts can only grant a *Mareva* if the underlying action is justiciable within the jurisdiction.

This decision is now reversed where the conditions in s. 25 of the CJJA 1982 are satisfied (s. 25 was specifically enacted to enable the court to exercise powers contained in Article 24 of the Brussels Convention):

Interim relief in England and Wales and Northern Ireland in the absence of substantive proceedings

25.—(1) The High Court in England and Wales or Northern Ireland shall have power to grant interim relief where—
(a) proceedings have been or are to be commenced in a Contracting State other than the United Kingdom or in a part of the United Kingdom other than that in which the High Court in question exercises jurisdiction; and
(b) they are or will be proceedings whose subject-matter is within the scope of the 1968 Convention as determined by Article 1 (whether or not the Convention has effect in relation to the proceedings).

    (2)   On an application for any interim relief under subsection (1) the court may refuse to grant that relief if, in the opinion of the court, the fact that the court has no jurisdiction apart from this section in relation to the subject-matter of the proceedings in question makes it inexpedient for the court to grant it.

    (3)   Her Majesty may by Order in Council extend the power to grant interim relief conferred by subsection (1) so as to make it exercisable in relation to proceedings of any of the following descriptions, namely—

    (a)   proceedings commenced or to be commenced otherwise than in a Contracting State;

    (b)   proceedings whose subject-matter is not within the scope of the 1968 Convention as determined by Article 1;

    (c)   arbitration proceedings.

    (4)   An Order in Council under subsection (3)—

    (a)   may confer power to grant only specified descriptions of interim relief;

    (b)   may make different provision for different classes of proceedings, for proceedings pending in different countries or courts outside the United Kingdom or in different parts of the United Kingdom and for other different circumstances; and

    (c)   may impose conditions or restrictions on the exercise of any power confered by the Order.

    (5)   An Order in Council under subsection (3) which confers power to grant interim relief in relation to arbitration proceedings may provide for the repeal of any provision of section 12(6) of the Arbitration Act 1950 or section 21(1) of the Arbitration Act (Northern Ireland) 1937 to the extent that it is superseded by the provisions of the Order.

    (6)   Any Order in Council under subsection (3) shall be subject to annulment in pursuance of a resolution of either House of Parliament.

    (7)   In this section 'interim relief, in relation to the High Court in England and Wales or Northern Ireland, means interim relief of any kind which that court has power to grant in proceedings relating to matters within its jurisdiction, other than—

    (a)   a warrant for the arrest of property; or

    (b)   provision for obtaining evidence.

In order for s. 25 to operate, the following two conditions must be satisfied.

    (a)   proceedings must have been or must be about to be commenced in the courts of a Contracting State other than the UK; and

    (b)   the subject matter of the proceedings must fall within the scope of the Convention as set out in Article 1.

Note that it is *not* necessary for the applicability of s. 25 that the jurisdictional rules of the Brussels Convention should apply to the proceedings. See *X* v *Y and Y Establishment* [1989] 2 Lloyd's Rep 561.

23.16   Interpretation of the Brussels Convention

Any question as to the meaning or effect of any provision of the Conventions shall (if there is no referral to the European Court) be determined in the United Kingdom courts in accordance with the principles laid down by, and any relevant decision of, the European Court: CJJA 1982, s. 3(1).

Judicial notice must be taken of any decision of, or expression of opinion of, the European Court in relation to the meaning and effect of the provisions of the Conventions: CJJA 1982, s. 3(2).

Equally, a court of the United Kingdom may consider the following reports when addressing itself to the meaning or effect of the provisions of the Conventions (CJJA 1982, s. 3(3)):

    (a)   Report on the Convention on Jurisdiction and the Enforcement of Judgments in Civil and Commercial Matters signed at Brussels, 27 September 1968, by Mr P. Jenard (Official Journal of the European Communities 1979 C 59/1).

(b)   Report on the Convention signed at Luxembourg, 9 October 1978, on the Association of the Kingdom of Denmark, Ireland and the United Kingdom of Great Britain and Northern Ireland to the Convention on Jurisdiction and the Enforcement of Judgments in Civil and Commercial Matters and to the Protocol on its interpretation by the Court of Justice by Professor Dr Peter Schlosser (Official Journal of the European Communities 1979 C 59/71).

Where the Modified Convention applies, a United Kingdom court shall take note of any relevant principles laid down by, and decisions of, the European Court, with regard given and appropriate weight attached to both the Jenard and Schlosser Reports: CJJA 1982, s. 16(3). As to when the Modified Convention applies, see **23.4.1.**

23.17   Further Reading

Cheshire and North, *Private International Law,* 12th ed., 1992, Butterworths.
Collier, J.G., *Conflict of Laws,* 1988, Cambridge University Press.

24 Arbitration

24.1 Classification of Arbitration Agreements

A dispute will not be referred to the method of dispute resolution known as arbitration unless the parties **agree** to arbitrate. This can only occur by means of:

(a) An arbitration clause included in the underlying contract between the parties or concluded separately prior to the existence of the dispute. In this situation the parties are agreeing to refer *future* disputes to arbitration.

(b) A separate agreement to refer *existing* disputes to arbitration.

An existing dispute arbitration agreement commonly arises through the conduct of the parties. For example, if no objection is taken to an arbitrator's lack of jurisdiction to deal with the claim an implied agreement to arbitrate will be construed — an *ad hoc* submission and both parties will be bound by an award on the merits of the claim: *The Amazona* [1989] 2 Lloyd's Rep 130. Be aware, though, that if such an implied agreement is not reduced into written form, the Arbitration Acts will not apply. Their applicability depends on the existence of a 'written agreement to submit present or future differences to arbitration, whether an arbitrator is named therein or not' (AA 1950, s. 32).

In consequence, although the oral arbitration agreement is still valid at common law, it will not be subject to the supportive and supervisory power of the court.

Under English law, the relationships between the parties and the arbitrator, and between the separate parties, are viewed in terms of private law. However, although the agreement dominates, it may well be subject to legislation which governs the ability of the courts to enforce, support, supervise and intervene in the arbitral process. This legislation is to be found in the Arbitration Acts 1950, 1975 and 1979.

24.1.1 PROPER LAW OF THE ARBITRATION

The arbitration agreement, although it is viewed as distinct from the substantive agreement into which it may have been incorporated (*Bremer Vulkan Schiffbau* v *South Indian Shipping Corp.* [1981] 1 Lloyd's Rep 253), usually take as its proper law, the proper law of the substantive agreement. See *Union of India* v *McDonnell Douglas* [1993] 2 Lloyd's Rep 48.

Under English principles of the conflict of laws, it is the proper law of the arbitration agreement which governs substantive issues, e.g. the validity of the arbitration agreement, the question whether a dispute lies within the scope of the arbitration agreement. Where the proper law of the arbitration is not expressed, the arbitrator must, if English law governs the manner in which the arbitration is to be conducted, i.e. English law is the curial law, determine whether the proper law can be implied or whether a system of law can be identified with which the arbitration agreement has its closest and most real connection. The factors to be considered in both these lines of enquiry are in practice the same and include determination of the 'seat' of the arbitration (this carries great weight); the nationalities of the parties; place(s) where contract was made and to be performed; language of the arbitration, and the contract.

It is nevertheless true that the parties can agree that their agreement to arbitrate disputes be governed by one law but that the procedures to be adopted in any arbitration under that agreement be governed by another law. See *Union of India* v *McDonnell Douglas* (*supra*).

24.1.2 CURIAL LAW

It is true to say that the curial law, i.e., the law governing the conduct of the arbitration expressly chosen by the parties, is usually the law of the 'seat' of the arbitration. In *Union of India* v *McDonnell Douglas* (*supra*), Saville J stated:

> If the parties do not make an express choice of procedural law to govern their arbitration then the Court will consider whether they have made an implicit choice. In this circumstance the fact that the parties have agreed to a place for the arbitration is a very strong pointer that implicitly they must have chosen the laws of that place to govern the procedures of the arbitration. The reason for this is essentially common sense. By choosing a country in which to arbitrate the parties have, *ex hypothesi*, created a close connection between the arbitration and that country and it is reasonable to assume from their choice that they attached some importance to the relevant laws of that country i.e. those laws which would be relevant to an arbitration conducted in that country. Indeed English law at least has turned its face against the notion that it is possible to have arbitral procedures that are wholly unconnected with any national system of law at all. . . .

> It is clear from the authorities that English law does admit of at least the theoretical possibility that the parties are free to choose to hold their arbitration in one country but subject to the procedural laws of another ... It seems to me that the jurisdiction of the English Court under the Arbitration Act over an arbitration in this country cannot be excluded by an agreement between the parties to apply the laws of another country, or indeed by any other means unless such is sanctioned by those Acts themselves.

Thus there will have to be an analysis of the arbitration agreement to determine its 'seat'. Where there is no express choice of 'seat' the choice can be implied from, for example, the chosen set of arbitral rules associated with a particular country, e.g. LCIA Rules associated with England; proper law of the arbitration agreement; nationality of the parties; parties as state agencies — desire for arbitration to take place on neutral territory.

24.2 Jurisdiction of the Arbitrator

An arbitrator cannot make a legally enforceable award in relation to matters for which he/she has no jurisdiction.

The jurisdiction of the arbitrator emanates from the arbitration agreement and subsumed within that, the terms of the arbitrator's appointment.

24.2.1 CHALLENGING THE JURISDICTION OF THE ARBITRATOR ON THE BASIS OF A DEFECTIVE CONTRACT

The jurisdiction of the arbitrator can be challenged on the basis that a defect in the underlying contract destroys the arbitration agreement and with it, the arbitrator's authority.

Note the following points about this:

(a) Where the arbitration agreement has a separate existence from the underlying contract, a sufficiently widely drawn arbitration agreement will enable the arbitrator to make a binding award as to the initial validity or legality of the underlying contract. See *Harbour Assurance Co. (UK) Ltd* v *Kansa General International Insurance Co. Ltd* [1992] 1 Lloyd's Rep 81; [1993] 1 Lloyd's Rep 455.

The arbitration agreement will have separate existence where (i) an *ad hoc* arbitration is concluded after the contract is made or after a dispute has arisen, or (ii) a written contract and written arbitration agreement are executed at the same time in separate documents. (See *Harbour Assurance Co. (UK) Ltd* v *Kansa General International Insurance Co. Ltd (supra).)*

(b)   Where the arbitration agreement is embedded in the contract, English law has developed the principle of 'separability' under which in certain circumstances the arbitration agreement is viewed as separate from the underlying contract. In this way, the arbitration agreement is not affected by the termination of the underlying contract for repudiatory breach (*Heyman* v *Darwins* [1942] AC 356), frustration of the contract *(Kruse* v *Questier & Co. Ltd* [1953] 1 Lloyd's Rep 310), supervening illegality *(Prodexport State Company for Foreign Trade* v *E.D. & F. Man Ltd* [1972] 2 Lloyd's Rep 375), avoidance for non-disclosure, misrepresentation, fraud, duress (*Mackender Hill and White* v *Feldia AG* [1966] 2 Lloyd's Rep 449; *Harbour Assurance Co. (UK) Ltd* v *Kansa General International Insurance Co. Ltd* (*supra*)).

The effect of the principle of separability in the above circumstances is that the arbitration agreement remains as the foundation of the arbitrator's authority and a sufficiently widely drawn agreement enables the arbitrator to make a binding ruling on termination, frustration, etc. of the underlying contract and make a second binding award dealing with monetary claims and cross-claims.

In *Harbour Assurance Co. (UK) Ltd* v *Kansa General International Insurance Co. Ltd (supra)* the court had to consider whether the principle of separability extended to the initial invalidity or illegality of the underlying agreement, i.e. voidness *ab initio*. Steyn J, in relation to invalidity, stated at p. 92:

> Provided that the arbitration clause itself is not directly impeached (e.g. by a *non est factum* plea), the arbitration agreement is as a matter of principled legal theory capable of surviving the invalidity of the contract … My conclusion is therefore that the separability principle, as applicable also to cases of the initial invalidity of the contract, is sound in legal theory.

However, at p. 95, Steyn J felt constrained by precedent to prevent the principle of separability from applying to contracts affected by initial illegality: 'In any event, while the distinction between initial invalidity and illegality is not one which in my view should nowadays prevail, I am constrained by high authority to hold that it does prevail'. In the Court of Appeal, reported at [1993] 1 Lloyd's Rep 455, the Court endorsed the decision of Steyn J in relation to initial invalidity but went on to hold that the courts were not obliged by authority to prevent arbitrators from determining the issue of initial illegality. The self-contained arbitration contract collateral to the containing contract had to be construed according to its terms and with regard to the relevant factual situation to determine whether the clause covered the issue of initial invalidity or illegality. The arbitrator will not be able to make a binding ruling where the attack is on the initial validity or legality of the *arbitration* contract. Ralph Gibson LJ stated in relation to this:

> Mr Justice Steyn said that the question of fraud or initial illegality was *capable* of being referred to arbitration. He did not qualify the clearly stated principle that if the validity of the arbitration clause itself is attacked the issue cannot be decided by the arbitrator. His reference to direct impeachment was as I understood his judgment, to distinguish an attack upon the clause otherwise than by the logical proposition that the clause falls within the containing contract. When it is said that the contract was induced by fraud it may well be clear, that if it was, the making of the independent arbitration clause was also induced by fraud. There is, further, the power of the Court under s. 24(2) of the 1950 Act, considered by Mr Justice Steyn at p. 89 of his judgment.

> Next, as to illegality, the question whether the particular form of illegality will, if proved, render void both the contract and the arbitration clause must depend upon the nature of the illegality and, as Lord Justice Hoffmann pointed out in the course of argument, when it is said to consist of acts prohibited by statute, upon the construction of the relevant provisions of the statute.

(c)   Where the challenge to the jurisdiction of the arbitrator is that the arbitration agreement itself is void for vagueness, mistake, duress, etc., Steyn J said, at p. 86, 'all such disputes fall outside the scope of the arbitration agreement, no matter how widely drawn, and are obviously outside the arbitrator's jurisdiction'.

24.2.2   CHALLENGING THE JURISDICTION OF THE ARBITRATOR WHERE THERE IS NO ATTACK ON THE VALIDITY OF THE ARBITRATION AGREEMENT

Assuming a valid arbitration agreement exists, challenge can be made to the jurisdiction of the arbitrator on the following bases:

(a)   The arbitrator does not have the qualifications prescribed by the contract/has disqualifications prescribed by the contract.

(b)   The arbitrator has not been properly appointed.

(c)   There is no 'dispute'/'claim' in existence at the time of the arbitration; or the dispute falls outside the scope of the arbitration agreement.

Note in relation to basis (c):

(i)   It may be necessary to determine whether there is a 'dispute' or 'difference' to which the arbitration agreement requires submission to arbitration. In *Ellerine Brothers (Pty) Ltd* v *Klinger* [1982] 1 WLR 1375, Templeman LJ stated: 'There is a dispute until the defendant admits that the sum is due and payable'. Endorsing that statement, Saville J in *Hayter* v *Nelson and Home Insurance Co.* [1990] 2 Lloyd's Rep 265 stated:

In my judgment in this context neither the word 'dispute' nor the word 'difference' is confined to cases where it cannot then and there be determined whether one party or the other is in the right. Two men — have an argument over who won the University Boat Race in a particular year. In ordinary language they have a dispute over whether it was Oxford or Cambridge. The fact that it can be easily and immediately demonstrated beyond any doubt that the one is right and the other is wrong does not and cannot mean that that dispute did not in fact exist. Because one man can be said to be indisputably right and the other indisputably wrong does not, in my view, entail that there was therefore never any dispute between them.

(ii)   As to the 'scope' of the arbitration agreement, whether it be drafted widely or very specifically, 'each arbitration clause must be construed in the context of the contract as a whole, and the meaning of a particular formula may be broader or narrower depending on the nature of the transaction, the circumstances in which the arbitration clause came into existence, and the other provisions of the contract' (Mustill and Boyd, 2nd edn, 1989, p. 119). Bearing in mind the above, reference is made to the following decisions.

In *Ethiopian Oilseeds & Pulses Export Corporation* v *Rio del Mar Foods Inc.* [1990] 1 Lloyd's Rep 86, an arbitration clause in which 'any *dispute arising out of* or *under* this contract shall be settled by arbitration' was construed as covering a plea for rectification. The words 'arising out of' were to be given a wide interpretation covering disputes *other* than one as to the very existence of the contract itself so as to give effect to the parties' presumed intention not to have two sets of proceedings.

The phrase 'arising out of a contract' has enabled the following types of claim to fall within the ambit of the arbitration clause: any form of ancillary relief claim (*Mantovani* v *Carapelli SpA* [1980] 1 Lloyd's Rep 37); claims in tort where it was commercially realistic to treat the contract as central to the whole dispute in tort (*The Playa Larga* [1983] 2 Lloyd's Rep 171).

Note the discussion on the possible difference in scope of 'arising out of a contract' and 'arising under a contract' in *Ethiopian Oilseeds & Pulses Export Corporation* v *Rio del Mar Foods Inc. (supra)* and the decision of the Court of Appeal in *Fillite Runcorn* v *Aqua-Left (a firm)* (1989) 45 Build LR 27.

In *Harbour Assurance* v *Kansa (supra),* the Court of Appeal ruled that the arbitration agreement which stated that '... all disputes and differences arising out of this agreement shall be submitted to the decision of two arbitrators covered the issue of illegality of the containing contract. Ralph Gibson LJ said:

> the parties were indeed presupposing, that 'The agreement' had some relevant existence. For this purpose, I think 'this agreement' means the act of the parties recorded in the document which contain the mutual promises which they have made. The meaning and effect of those promises with reference to their subsequent acts would be determined according to law and if necessary, under the proviso for arbitration.

In *The Ermoupolis* [1990] 1 Lloyd's Rep 160, an arbitration clause in a bill of lading was expressed to apply to 'any dispute arising in any way whatsoever out of this bill of lading'. The court had to consider whether cargo interests' claim in conversion fell within the ambit of the clause. Steyn J said, at p. 164:

> The owners say that the claim in conversion is independent of the bill of lading contract and not in any way dependent upon it or founded upon its terms. Consequently, it is argued, the claim in conversion falls outside the scope of the arbitration clause. Cargo interests emphasise however, that the bill of lading operates also as an acknowledgment of the receipt of the cargo, and that there is a very real and close connection between the contractual claim in respect of short delivery and the claim in conversion in respect of that very same delivery. Clearly, the matters to be proved, and therefore the potential issues greatly overlap. That such closely related claims should be subject to different forms of dispute resolution, arbitration and litigation, possibly in different jurisdictions, would, in my view, hold no attraction for the reasonable businessman versed in the business of shipping ...

Steyn J, on the construction of the clause and relying on decisions including *The Playa Larga (supra),* held that the claim in conversion fell within the ambit of the clause. See also *The Angelic Grace* [1995] Lloyd's Rep 87.

(iii)   It may be necessary not only to consider the scope of the arbitration agreement but also the scope of the submission to the arbitrator in order to determine his/her jurisdiction.

In *The Ermoupolis (supra),* although the arbitration agreement was drafted very widely indeed, the arbitrators were appointed in respect of 'claims *arising under* the bill of lading'. Steyn J would not accept that in the circumstances the submission was narrower than the agreement. He said, at p. 165: 'Here I am dealing not with the construction of an arbitration agreement evincing a consensual mode of dispute resolution but with acts of appointment of arbitrators after a short delivery dispute has arisen'. In *Antaios Compania SA* v *Salen Rederierna AB* [1984] 2 Lloyd's Rep 235, at p.238, Lord Diplock said:

> if detailed semantic or syntactical analysis of words in a commercial contract is going to lead to a conclusion that flouts business common sense, it must be made to yield to business common sense. That approach seems to me to be *a fortiori* applicable to the arguments based on the words in the telexes of appointment. In my view the common-sense view is that the words 'claims under the bill of lading' were, in the context, simply a shorthand reference for the shortage claim without any definition or delineation of the precise causes of action at that stage.

However, in *The World Era* [1992] 1 Lloyd's Rep 45, an arbitration clause provided *inter alia* that 'any and all differences and disputes of whatsoever nature arising out of this charter shall be put to arbitration in the City of [London] pursuant to the laws relating to arbitration there in force'. The terms of appointment of arbitration only referred to a claim by charterers against disponent owners of a vessel. The court held that the terms of the appointment did not enable the claimant/charterers to pursue in arbitration under the terms of that appointment, claims for losses suffered by undisclosed principals. It was a new cause of action, not included in the original reference which was confined to claims for losses by the charterer/claimants in their own right. Hobhouse J. said, at p. 52:

To recover in the right of another is to assert a cause of action of that other person. Such a cause of action had at no time been referred to directly or indirectly prior to the delivery of the draft amended pleading in 1990. On the face of it, it is a new cause of action not included in the original reference which only included claims based upon a cause of action of Petrolsea and losses which Petrolsea was entitled to recover in its own right.

(iv)   An award 'in excess of jurisdiction' means there is an absence of jurisdiction in relation to a particular dispute or part of a dispute. Whether or not an award is in excess of jurisdiction requires careful consideration of the scope of the submission.

(v)   The arbitrator only has jurisdiction over disputes in existence at the time of his/her appointment: *London and North Western and Great-Western Joint Rly Companies* v *Billington* [1899] AC 79 — unless the terms of his/her appointment enable him/her to consider future disputes or there is an *ad hoc* submission in relation to a dispute arising after his/her initial appointment.

The arbitrator has jurisdiction to grant an amendment to a claim which will enable inclusion of a claim which existed at the time of his/her appointment, and which fell within the scope of the arbitration agreement and his/her appointment. (See *The Ermoupolis (supra).*)

(d)   The claimant/defendant is not a party to the agreement. Even though a party to the arbitration is not an original party to the arbitration agreement, he/she is able to or indeed may be required to participate in the arbitration/make a valid appointment of an arbitrator, if he/she has succeeded to the rights of the original party legitimately. Succession to the rights of original parties can arise by, for example, operation of law; e.g. assignment.

In *The 'Jordon Nicolov'* [1990] 2 Lloyd's Rep 11, Hobhouse J., at p. 15, stated:

The scope of any assignment must, of course, ultimately be determined by the terms of that assignment. But where the assignment is the assignment of the cause of action, it will, in the absence of some agreement to the contrary, include as stated in s. 136 all the remedies in respect of that cause of action. The relevant remedy is the right to arbitrate and obtain an arbitration award in respect of the cause of action. The assignee is bound by the arbitration clause in the sense that he cannot assert the assigned right without also accepting the obligation to arbitrate. Accordingly it is clear both from the statute and from a consideration of the position of the assignee that the assignee has the benefit of the arbitration clause as well as of the other provision of the contract.

Indeed, if an assignment has taken place after the assignor has appointed an arbitrator, the arbitrator has jurisdiction to make an award in favour of the assignee. Hobhouse J. at p.19, said:

I consider that there is no authority which precludes me from holding that the assignee is entitled to enforce the assignor's rights in the pending arbitration or which shows that the arbitrators do not have jurisdiction and the duty, if the assignee is otherwise entitled to succeed in the merits, to make an award in favour of the assignee.

However, Hobhouse J. made it clear that for the assignment to take full legal effect, notice of the assignment must be given not only to the other party to the dispute but the assignee must intervene in the arbitration by giving notice to the arbitrator or arbitrators. In *Baytur SA* v *Finagro Holding SA* [1991] 4 All ER 129, the Court of Appeal held that (Lloyd LJ): 'an assignee does not automatically become a party to a pending arbitration on the assignment taking effect in equity. Something more is required. He/she must *at least* give notice to the other side, and submit to the jurisdiction of the arbitrator.

In the *Baytur* case the assignor company had dissolved before either step had taken place. The Court of Appeal held that the immediate consequence was that the arbitration lapsed and any award made thereunder was a nullity since an arbitration required two or more parties and there could not be a valid award when one of the parties had ceased to exist.

24.3 Powers of the Arbitrator

Assuming the arbitrator has jurisdiction to make a valid award, we will consider very briefly the powers that he/she can exercise during the course of the reference.

(a) The parties in the contract are able to express the powers of the arbitrator subject only to the following limitations:

(i) parties cannot give the arbitrator powers, the exercise of which will be against public policy;
(ii) the expressed power cannot affect someone *not* a party to the reference;
(iii) the court reserves to itself those powers which affect the liberty of the subject, i.e. the arbitrator cannot possess the *coercive* powers of the court if there is a failure to comply with orders made by the arbitrator.

(b) The Arbitration Act 1950, s. 12, implies the following arbitral powers into the written arbitration contract, unless a contrary intention is expressed:

(i) the parties to the arbitration can be required to submit to examination by the arbitrator, subject to legal objection — AA 1950, s. 12(1);
(ii) the parties to the reference and witnesses can be examined on oath or affirmation — AA 1950, s. 12(1) and (2);
(iii) the arbitrator shall have the power to administer the oath or affirmation of the parties or witnesses;
(iv) the arbitrator has the power to order the disclosure and inspection of documents, subject to legal objection — AA 1950, s. 12(1);
(v) the concluding words of s.12(1) enable the arbitrator to order the doing of all other things which during the proceedings on the reference are required, e.g. order exchange of pleadings.

The powers implied under s. 12(1), (2), (3) and (4) do not enable the arbitrator to make orders which are not directly concerned with the decision-making process, nor do they give the arbitrator the full powers of the judge, i.e. the ability to deploy personal remedies for contempt of court or for non-compliance with an order.

The Arbitration Act 1950, s. 13A, which came into force on 1 January 1992, enables the aribtrator to make an award dismissing any claim in a dispute referred to him if there has been inordinate and inexcusable delay. See *L'office cherifien* v *Yamashita Ltd* [1993] 3 All ER 686. However, it would be an error of law for an arbitrator to dismiss a claim within the limitation period unless there were special circumstances. See *Lazenby* v *McNicholas Construction* [1995] 2 Lloyd's Rep 30.

24.4 Jurisdiction of the Court

The existence of an arbitration agreement does not negate the jurisdiction of the English court. Usually when an arbitration is in process, the English court will only be concerned to exercise procedural powers in relation to the reference. However, in certain circumstances, the English court will consider the merits of a claim.

24.4.1 INTERLOCUTORY PROCEDURAL POWERS OF COURT IN AID OF THE ARBITRATION

In relation to the conduct of arbitration proceedings, derived from a written arbitration agreement, the intcrlocutory procedural powers of the court are set out in the Arbitration Act 1950, s. 12(6). Section 12(6) sets out a number of procedural orders available from the High Court 'for the purpose of and in relation to a reference'. In such circumstances, the High Court has the same power of making the orders as it has 'for the purpose of and in relation to an action or matter in the High Court'.

24.4.1.1 Application

Where an action is already pending in the High Court, the applicant will usually use an ordinary interlocutory summons — ord. 73, r. 3(3).

Where there is no pending action, application is made on originating summons in Form no. 10 in Appendix A, set out in White Book, Volume 2 — see ord. 73, r. 3(3).

Where the party to be served is abroad, service out of the jurisdiction of the originating summons is permissible with the leave of the court provided that the arbitration to which the summons relates is (a) governed by English law, or (b) has been, or (c) is being, or (d) is to be held within the jurisdiction — see ord. 73, r. 7(1). In *The Atlantic Emperor* [1992] 1 Lloyd's Rep 342, the European Court of Justice held that the Brussels Convention does *not* affect *any* matters connected with arbitration. Therefore, even though the party to be served is domiciled in an EEC country, leave will still be required. It will not be sufficient to try and serve the originating summons with a Brussels Convention endorsement.

The application for leave under ord. 73, r.7(1) is supported by an affidavit which must set out the grounds upon which the application is made and show in what place or country the person to be served may be found. The burden is upon the applicant to show that the case is a proper one for service out of the jurisdiction.

Difficulty might arise in showing the case is a proper one for service out of the jurisdiction where the arbitration is 'seated' abroad. In *Channel Tunnel Group and France Manche SA v Balfour Beatty Construction* [1992] 2 All ER 609, Staughton J, although required to make a decision on the extent of its jurisdiction under s. 12(6) (h), stated at p. 623:

> ... I do not believe that an English court has jurisdiction to exercise all the power in the Arbitration Act 1950 in the case of an arbitration held abroad, even if the parties have agreed to English curial law ... and in the converse case, where parties arbitrate here but agree on the procedural law of a foreign country, it seems to me that at least some of the powers conferred by the English Act could still be exercised.

In relation to those arbitrations seated abroad, but where there is an express choice of English curial law, Staughton J quoted from Mustill and Boyd, 2nd edn 1989, at p. 91:

> the English Court would be highly unlikely to assume jurisdiction to intervene in the reference or to set aside or remit the award. Any attempt to exercise powers to appoint arbitrators or to give ancillary relief, such as orders for the inspection of property would in fact present formidable difficulties of enforcement. Moreover, the prospect of two courts exercising supervisory powers over the same reference at the same time would appear to be unacceptable.

24.4.1.2 Interlocutory orders

Under the Arbitration Act 1950, s. 12(6)(h), the High Court has the power to award an interim injunction or appoint a receiver in aid of an arbitration. Under s. 12(6)(f), the court has the power to provide a claimant in an arbitration with security for the payment of any award which he/she may obtain. Under s. 12(6)(g), the court has the power to order the detention, preservation or inspection of any property or thing which is the subject of the reference or as to which any question may arise. The court can authorise for any of the above purposes, any person to enter upon or into any land or building in the possession of any party to the reference, or authorise any samples to be taken or any observation to be made or experiment to be tried which may be necessary or expedient for the purpose of obtaining full information or evidence.

It will be possible for the claimant to apply *ex parte* for an injunction. If he/she does so, whether or not he/she has commenced arbitration proceedings. the plaintiff must, in the draft minute of the order, undertake to issue an originating summons claiming the injunctive relief granted in the *ex parte* order.

When a *Mareva* injunction is granted *ex parte,* it is usually granted up to a specified period after the final award is made (usually 21 days). In the circumstances, the return date on the originating summons is left blank. If the plaintiff subsequently wishes to apply for an extension of the injunction (e.g. in aid of execution of the arbitration award) he/she should issue a summons in the action commenced by originating summons.

If the plaintiff, at the time he/she applies for his/her injunction, has not yet commenced arbitration proceedings, he/she should give an undertaking to 'commence arbitration proceedings against the intended defendant forthwith'.

The House of Lords has held that none of the powers conferred on the Court by the AA 1950, which includes s. 12(6), is available to the court in respect of an arbitration conducted abroad under a law which is not the law of England. See *Channel Tunnel Group* v *Balfour Beatty Ltd* [1993] 1 All ER 664.

Note that the CJJA 1982, s. 25(1) does not as yet enable interim relief to be granted in England in aid of arbitration proceedings 'seated' abroad.

However, the House of Lords in the *Channel Tunnel* case (*supra*) did accept that the court had power to grant an interlocutory injunction under s. 37 of the SCA 1981 in support of a cause of action which the parties had agreed should be the subject of a foreign arbitration. This was so even though the proceedings in England had been stayed so that the agreed method of adjudication could take place, since the cause of action remained potentially justiciable before the English court despite the stay.

Some arbitration agreements contain what are known as *'Scott* v *Avery'* clauses. These clauses postpone accrual to the plaintiff of a cause of action to be pursued in the High Court until after an arbitral award has been obtained. These clauses do not preclude the High Court from granting relief *under s. 12(6)* in relation to a claim advanced in arbitration.

The High Court also has the power to order security for arbitration costs (s. 12(6)(a)); the giving of evidence by affidavit (s. 12(6)(c)); the examination on oath of any witness before an officer of the High Court or any other person, and the issue of a commission or request for the examination of a witness out of the jurisdiction (s. 12(6)(d)); the preservation, interim custody or sale of any goods which are the subject matter of the reference (s. 12(6)(e)).

The power to order discovery of documents and interrogatories under s. 12(6)(b) has been repealed by virtue of the Courts and Legal Services Act.

Note that the powers of the arbitrator and the High Court may be co-extensive. To determine this you will need to look at the arbitration agreement and AA 1950, s. 12(1). But remember tough coercive powers are available to the court but not to the arbitrator. Refer to *The Argenpuma* [1984] 2 Lloyd's Rep 563; *The Golden Trader* [1974] 1 Lloyd's Rep 378; *Richco International Ltd* v *International Industrial Food Co. SAL* [1989] 2 Lloyd's Rep 106.

24.4.2   ARREST OF A SHIP

The provisions of the Arbitration Act 1950, s. 12(6) do not enable the court to arrest a ship in aid of an arbitration: *The Rena K* [1979] 1 All ER 397; *The Tuyuti* [1984] 2 Lloyd's Rep 51. Therefore, in order to obtain the arrest of a ship (and hopefully replace it with other security), it will be necessary to start a substantive action *in rem* within the jurisdiction. The existence of an arbitration agreement, unless of the *Scott* v *Avery* type, does not deprive the English court of its jurisdiction *in rem: The Vasso* [1984] 1 Lloyd's Rep 235. Once an action *in rem* is commenced and a ship arrested, the ability to maintain the arrest (or retain any security put up to obtain the release of the vessel) where the action is *in rem* is to be stayed, depends on the operation of the Civil Jurisdiction and Judgments Act 1982, s. 26.

Under s. 26 of the Civil Jurisdiction and Judgments Act 1982, it is no longer necessary for the court to be satisfied that a stay of *in rem* proceedings may well not be final, in order to exercise its discretion and refuse to release the security. By virtue of s. 26, the vessel will be released only on the provision of sufficient security to cover the amount of the claim, plus interest and costs, on the basis of the plaintiff's reasonably arguable best cause of action. See *The Bazias 3* [1993] 1 Lloyd's Rep 101.

As to stay of proceedings, see **24.4.6.**

24.4.3   JURISDICTION OF THE COURT AFTER THE GRANT OF THE AWARD

There follows four ways in which the courts can help a party dissatisfied with the arbitration and/or the award.

(a)   Under AA 1950, s. 23(2) there is statutory jurisdiction to *set aside* an award made pursuant to a written arbitration agreement (i) where the arbitrator has misconducted him/herself or the proceedings (see, e.g. *Sociedad Iberica De Molturacion SA* v *Nidera Handels Compagnia BV* [1990] 2 Lloyd's Rep 240), and (ii) where the award has been improperly procured.

(b)   Under AA 1950, s. 22(1) there is a statutory jurisdiction to *remit* the matters initially referred to arbitration by virtue of a written arbitration agreement, or any of them, for the reconsideration of the arbitrator.

The jurisdiction of the Court under s. 22(1) is wholly unlimited: *King* v *Thomas McKenna Ltd* [1991] 1 All ER 653, where it was held in the Court of Appeal that:

> The jurisdiction of the Court under s. 22 of the 1950 Act to remit an award to an arbitrator was wholly unlimited and not confined to the four traditional grounds of remission, i.e. where the award was defective *on its face,* where there had been misconduct on the part of the arbitrator, where there had been an admitted mistake and the arbitrator had asked that the matter be remitted and where additional evidence had been discovered after the making of the award, but extended to any case where, notwithstanding that the arbitrator had acted with complete propriety, some aspect of the dispute which had been the subject of the reference had not, due to mishap or misunderstanding, been considered and adjudicated upon as fully as or in a manner which the parties were entitled to expect and it would be inequitable to allow any award to take effect without some further consideration by the arbitrator. However, in exercising its discretion the Court had to bear in mind that the jurisdiction to remit was designed to remedy deviations from the route which the reference should have taken towards its destination of an award, and not to remedy a situation in which, despite having followed an unimpeachable route, the arbitrator had made errors of fact or law and as a result had reached an award which was not that which the Court would have reached.

Note: the High Court does not have jurisdiction to set aside or remit an award on an arbitration agreement on the ground of error of fact or law on the face of the award: AA 1979, s. 1(1).

(c)   Jurisdiction at common law to declare the award a nullity.

(d)   Under AA 1979, s. 1(2), limited jurisdiction to hear an appeal on a question of law arising out of an award made under a written arbitration agreement. For a consideration of the principles to be considered in deciding whether leave to appeal should be granted, refer to AA 1979, ss. 1 and 3 (exclusion agreements) and *The Nema* [1982] AC 724. As an example of application of *The Nema* principle, refer to *Ipswich Borough Council* v *Fisons* [1990] 2 WLR 108 (CA).

24.4.4   EXCLUSION AGREEMENTS

The 1979 Arbitration Act gives the parties to the arbitration agreement the right by means of a written exclusion agreement to exclude the right of recourse to the courts on questions of law under ss. 1(2) and 2 in the following circumstances:

(a)   Where the arbitration agreement falls within the definition of a 'domestic' arbitration agreement at the time the agreement is made: AA 1979, s. 3(7). The exclusion agreement is only valid if entered into after the commencement of the arbitration (AA 1979, s. 3(6)) in respect of which the award is made or, as the case may be, in which the question of law arises.

(b)   Where the arbitration agreement is non-domestic, an exclusion agreement is, with the following exceptions, valid whether made before or after the commencement of the relevant arbitration. Where the non-domestic arbitration agreement relates to disputes concerning a maritime, insurance or commodity transaction the exclusion agreement is only valid in relation to the award or preliminary question if made after the commencement of the relevant arbitration. or if the award or question of law to be referred relates to a contract which is expressed to be governed by a law other than the law of England or Wales: AA 1979, s. 4.

The arbitral rules of the following institutions which the parties to an international arbitration agreement agree shall govern their arbitration, include an agreement to exclude the supervisory powers of the court under AA 1979, s. 1(2) and 2: Rules of London Court of International Arbitration 1985 ED (LDIA Rules); International Chamber of Commerce Rules of Conciliation and Arbitration 1988 ED (ICC Rules).

The right given by the 1979 Act to the parties to a non-domestic arbitration agreement to exclude recourse to the courts for review of an arbitral award or for a decision on a preliminary point of law, affords recognition to the dislike of parties to commercial contracts to arbitrate within jurisdictions where review by the courts is possible. The appeal procedures when used will serve to delay enforcement of the award. For the same reason, AA 1979, s. 1(6A) and (7), s. 2(2A) and (3) impose restrictions on the right of appeal from the High Court to the Court of Appeal.

24.4.5   PROCEDURE

For procedure for applications under AA 1979, ss. 23(2), 22(1) and 1(2), refer to RSC ord. 73 and the example brief in Appendix 2 and comments thereto.

Where the attack on the award is that it is made without jurisdiction, the application can be made by originating notice of motion, or by writ, or originating summons: ord. 73, r. 1(3). Where the attack on the award is that it does not satisfy the requirements of a valid award, e.g. under the arbitration agreement, application for declaration must be begun by writ or originating summons.

Unlike applications to remit/set aside and application for leave to appeal which have severely circumscribed time periods during which the relevant application must be made, action for declaration that an award is a nullity on the grounds of absence of jurisdiction can be brought within six years from the date of the award.

24.4.6   STAY OF PROCEEDINGS

The existence of an arbitration agreement does not deprive the English court of jurisdiction to hear a claim. However, the English court can choose not to exercise that jurisdiction and stay the court proceedings. To determine the extent, if any, of the discretion, a distinction is drawn between *domestic* and *non-domestic* written arbitration agreements. In relation to the latter, if certain conditions are fulfilled, the court has no discretion but *must* stay the proceedings.

Under the Arbitration Act 1975, s. 1(4) a *domestic* arbitration agreement is one which does *not* provide expressly or by implication, for arbitration is a state, other than the United Kingdom and to which neither:

(a)   an individual who is a national of, or habitually resident in, any state other than the United Kingdom, nor

(b)   a body corporate which is incorporated in, or whose central management and control is exercised in, any state other than the United Kingdom,

is a party *at the time the proceedings are commenced.*

Under AA 1975, s. 1 where at the time legal proceedings are commenced there is in existence:

    (a)   a written arbitration agreement
    (b)   which is *not* a domestic arbitration agreement, and
    (c)   the legal proceedings relate to a matter agreed to be referred, and
    (d)   both the plaintiff to the legal proceedings and the applicant for the stay are parties to the arbitration agreement, or are claiming through or under such parties, and
    (e)   the application for a stay is made after acknowledgment of service but before delivery of pleadings *or the taking of any other steps in the proceedings by the applicant*

the court *must* stay the proceedings, unless the party opposing the stay can satisfy the court that

    (i)   the arbitration agreement is null and void, or
    (ii)   the arbitration agreement is inoperative or incapable of being performed, or
    (iii)   there is in fact no *dispute* between the parties with regard to the matter agreed to be referred.

Note:

1.   If the party opposing the stay cannot satisfy the court in respect of one of the matters (i)–(iii)above, the order to stay is mandatory. The court has no power to impose terms as a condition of an order for a stay: *The Rena K* [1978] 1 Lloyd's Rep 545.

2.   In (c) above, there may well be a 'dispute' which falls within the ambit of the arbitration clause, and yet the opponent of the application for the stay may satisfy the court that there is in fact no dispute between the parties with regard to the matter agreed to be referred. Refer to *Hayter* v *Nelson and Home Insurance Co.* [1990] 2 Lloyd's Rep 265 in which Saville J read the words 'there is not in fact any dispute' as meaning 'there is not in fact anything disputable'. Saville J quoting with approval Parker LJ in the Court of Appeal in *Home and Overseas Insurance Co. Ltd* v *Mentor Insurance Co. (UK) Ltd* [1989] 1 Lloyd's Rep 473:

> It seems to me to be clear from the passage quoted from Lord Justice Parker's judgment, that when considering an application for summary judgment, a factor to be taken into account is the existence of an arbitration agreement between the parties; so that only in the simplest and clearest cases, i.e. where it is readily and immediately demonstrable that the respondent has no good grounds at all for disputing the claim, should that party be deprived of his contractual right to arbitrate. In the context of the 1975 Act, this means that only in such cases can the court be satisfied that there is not in fact any dispute between the parties with regard to the matter agreed to be referred.

See also the Court of Appeal in *Channel Tunnel Group and France Manche SA* v *Balfour Beatty Construction Ltd* [1992] 2 All ER 609.

3.   A defendant to an action can only maintain his application for a stay of proceedings under Arbitration Acts by acknowledging he/she and the plaintiff are parties to an arbitration agreement. Yet if the defendants wished to challenge the existence of the contract they would lose their right to a stay. In these circumstances, the defendants should prima facie be granted a stay of proceedings under Supreme Court Act 1981, s. 49 and an adjournment of any application made for a stay under Arbitration Acts, pending the outcome of separate proceedings commenced by the defendant to determine the contractual issue. Refer to *The Amazona* [1989] 2 Lloyd's Rep 130.

Where the arbitration agreement is 'domestic' at the time legal proceedings are commenced, reference must be made to AA 1950, s. 4(1) which sets out the powers of the court to stay the legal proceedings. Under s. 4(1), the applicant for the stay must prove:

    (a)   the existence of a written agreement to submit present or future disputes to arbitration;

(b)   the agreement falls within the ambit of s. 4(1);

(c)   the legal proccedings are brought in respect of a matter(s) agreed to be referred to arbitration;

(d)   both the plaintiff to the legal proceedings and the applicant for the stay are parties to the arbitration agreement or are claiming through or under such a person;

(e)   the application to a stay is being made after acknowledgment of service and before delivery of pleadings or the taking of any other steps in the proceedings by the applicant;

(f)   the applicant is ready and willing to do all things necessary for the proper conduct of the arbitration.

If the above requirements are satisfied, the applicant has a prima facie right to a stay, which will usually be granted unless the party opposing the application persuades the court that there are good reasons why a stay should not be granted.

The following points can be noted about AA 1950, s. 4(1):

(a)   The courts take the view in relation to applications under s. 4(1) that, in general, agreements to arbitrate should be enforced. A comparatively heavy burden is placed on the respondent to the application.

(b)   The court has a discretion as to the terms upon which the stay will be granted, e.g. stay can be granted on condition the applicant gives security for costs, or the court may order a stay of some only of the issues in the proceedings.

(c)   The plaintiff to the action is entitled to summary judgment with no stay of proceedings where there is no defence to the claim. Parker LJ, in *Home and Overseas Insurance Co. Ltd* v *Mentor Insurance Co. (UK) Ltd* [19891] Lloyd's Rep 473, said:

> The purpose of O.14 is to enable a plaintiff to obtain a quick judgment where there is plainly no defence to the claim. If the defendant's only suggested defence is a point of law and the court can see at once that the point is misconceived, the plaintiff is entitled to judgment. If at first sight the point appears to be arguable but with a relatively short argument can be shown to be plainly unsustainable the plaintiff is also entitled to judgment ... In cases where there is an arbitration clause it is in my judgment the more necessary that full scale argument should not be permitted. The parties have agreed on their chosen tribunal and a defendant is entitled prima facie to have the dispute decided by that tribunal in the first instance, to be free from the intervention of the courts, until it has been so decided and thereafter, if it is in his favour, to hold it unless the plaintiff obtain leave to appeal and successfully appeals ... In very clear cases a plaintiff is no doubt entitled to his summary judgment notwithstanding the clause ... if the point of law relied upon by the defendant raises a serious question to be tried which calls for detailed argument and mature consideration the point is not suitable to be dealt with in O.14 proceedings.

Refer also to *Hayter* v *Nelson and Home Insurance Co.* [1990] 2 Lloyd's Rep 265.

(d)   For the procedure where the defendant to the action wishes to challenge the existence of arbitration agreement, see *The Amazona* [1989] 2 Lloyd's Rep 130.

Where in breach of the arbitration agreement, court action has been commenced in foreign courts, there can be no stay of the foreign proceedings by the English courts. However the defendant to the foreign proceedings can apply to the English courts for an injunction against the plaintiff to the foreign proceedings. The injunction is unlikely to be granted unless the plaintiff to the foreign proceedings is, or has assets within, the jurisdiction and is thus amenable to the coercive powers of the courts.

Where the arbitration agreement is *not* in writing, neither AA 1950, s. 4(1) nor AA 1975, s. 1 can be relied upon. Nevertheless, a party to the legal proceedings can rely on the inherent jurisdiction of the court to stay proceedings which it considers to be frivolous, vexatious, oppressive or an abuse of the process of the court. (Procedure on application for a stay under AA 1975, s.1 or AA 1950, s. 4 — refer to RSC ord. 12, r. 8.)

24.5   Enforcing the Award

If the award is not honoured, the aggrieved party can proceed to sue the offending party for breach of the promise implied in the arbitration agreement to honour a valid award. This is called 'action on the award'. Service of the writ overseas would depend on the application of normal jurisdictional rules. See RSC ord. 11, r. 1(1)(m).

In certain circumstances the aggrieved party can rely on AA 1950, s. 26 which enables him/her to apply for *an order* giving leave to enforce an award in the same manner as a judgment or to apply for *a judgment* in terms of the award.

Where a party seeks to enforce a 'convention' award either by 'action on the award' or by virtue of AA 1950, s. 26 (a 'convention' award) only certain defences are permissible to the enforcement of the award. These are set out at AA 1975, s. 5(1). A 'convention award' is defined as 'an award made in pursuance of an arbitration agreement in the territory of a state, other than the United Kingdom, which is a party to the New York Convention', AA 1975, s. 7.

Where a party seeks to enforce a 'foreign award' either by 'action on the award' or by virtue of AA 1950, s. 26 certain conditions are required to be satisfied. These are set out at AA 1950, s. 37. The definition of a 'foreign award' is set out at AA 1950, s. 35. Under ord. 73, r. 10, an application for leave under AA 1950, s. 26 to enforce an award on an arbitration agreement can be made *ex parte*. If the court directs that a summons be issued, the summons shall be an originating summons in form no. 10 in Appendix A. Service out of the jurisdiction of an originating summons for leave to enforce the award is permissible with leave of the court whether or not the arbitration is governed by English law, ord. 73, r. 7(1)(A).

24.6   Advantages of Arbitration

There are no jurisdictional problems. Arbitration also avoids the problems of sovereign immunity and overcomes the sensitivities some states might experience in being subject to the decisions of the courts of other states. These last two problems are likely to occur when the other contracting party is a state agency.

Arbitration enables the parties to choose a 'neutral seat' because an arbitration agreement can be 'sited' anywhere. Yet, at the same time, a party willing to move on 'siting' can insist on a particular proper law to apply to the arbitration agreement, and perhaps even insist on a curial law different from that of the 'seat'. The parties, of course, can also choose the building in which the arbitration will take place. Not an insignificant factor when a rather 'down-at-heel' commercial court is the only other alternative.

It may be difficult to enforce a judgment abroad, as there may be no reciprocal enforcement arrangements in operation. For example, it is at the moment very difficult to enforce a judgment in some East European countries. The New York convention on the recognition and enforcement of foreign arbitral awards, given effect in this country under the Arbitration Act 1975, sets out the procedure for enforcing a foreign award here. Since, in addition, some 70 to 80 countries so far have also ratified the convention, an English award will prove comparatively easy to enforce. The adoption of this convention by so many countries is really the key to the success of international arbitration.

Another advantage of arbitration is that arbitrators can be chosen who have expertise in the particular field concerned. Again this is most important in relation to those countries (e.g. East European countries) where the courts so far, from the nature of the political system, have had little or no experience of commercial arbitration.

In arbitration there need be no publicity, and there is also a choice of procedures — language etc. There is such flexibility in terms of procedure that essentially the parties can gear the arbitration the way they want it.

24.7 Disadvantages of Arbitration

Far from being able to say these days that arbitration speeds up the decision-making process, in many instances, parties to the reference, especially by using the intervening powers of the court, can slow things down.

Another disadvantage is that by the nature of arbitration, it does not deal with third-party problems, e.g. where respondent to the reference wants to join a third party, such as his/her supplier. There needs to be, in these circumstances, an agreement to 'string arbitration'.

24.8 Further Reading

Mustill/Boyd, *Commercial Arbitration,* 2nd ed. 1989, Butterworths.
Atkins Court Forms, 2nd ed., service to date, Butterworths.

24.9 Arbitration Act Provisions

24.9.1 ARBITRATION ACT 1950: GENERAL PROVISIONS

24.9.1.1 Section 4

(1) If any party to an arbitration agreement, or any person claiming through or under him, commences any legal proceedings in any court against any other party to the agreement, or any person claiming through or under him, in respect of any matter agreed to be referred, any party to those legal proceedings may at any time after appearance, and before delivering any pleadings or taking any other steps in the proceedings, apply to that court to stay the proceedings, and that court or a judge thereof, if satisfied that there is no sufficient reason why the matter should not be referred in accordance with the agreement, and that the applicant was, at the time when the proceedings were commenced, and still remains, ready and willing to do all things necessary to the proper conduct of the arbitration, may make an order staying the proceedings.

24.9.1.2 Section 7

Where an arbitration agreement provides that the reference shall be to two arbitrators, one to be appointed by each party then, unless a contrary intention is expressed therein—

(a) if either of the appointed arbitrators refuses to act, or is incapable of acting, or dies, the party who appointed him may appoint a new arbitrator in his place,

(b) if, on such a reference, one party fails to appoint an arbitrator, either originally, or by way of substitution as aforesaid, for seven clear days after the other party having appointed his arbitrator, has served the party making default with notice to make the appointment, the party who has appointed an arbitrator may appoint that arbitrator to act as sole arbitrator in the reference and his award shall be binding on both parties as if he had been appointed by consent:

Provided that the High Court or a judge thereof may set aside any appointment made in pursuance of this section.

24.9.1.3 Section 8 (as amended by Arbitration Act 1979, s. 6(1))

(1) Unless a contrary intention is expressed therein, every arbitration agreement shall, where the reference is to two arbitrators, be deemed to include a provision that the two arbitrators may appoint an umpire at any time after they are themselves appointed, and shall do so forthwith if they cannot agree.

(2) Unless a contrary intention is expressed therein, every arbitration agreement shall, where such a provision is applicable to the reference, be deemed to include a provision that if the arbitrators have delivered to any party to the arbitration agreement, or to the umpire, a notice in writing stating that they cannot agree, the umpire may forthwith enter on the reference in lieu of the arbitrators.

(3) At any time after the appointment of an umpire, however appointed, the High Court may, on the application of any party to the reference and notwithstanding anything to the contrary in the arbitration agreement, order that the umpire shall enter upon the reference in lieu of the arbitrators and as if he were a sole arbitrator.

24.9.1.4   Section 10 (as amended by Arbitration Act 1979, s. 6(3) and Administration of Justice Act 1985, s. 58)

(1)   In any of the following cases—

(a)   where an arbitration agreement provides that the reference shall be to a single arbitrator, and all the parties do not, after differences have arisen, concur in the appointment of an arbitrator;

(b)   if an appointed arbitrator refuses to act, or is incapable of acting, or dies, and the arbitration agreement does not show that it was intended that the vacancy should not be supplied and the parties do not supply the vacany;

(c)   where the parties or two arbitrators are required or are at liberty to appoint an umpire or third arbitrator and do not appoint him;

(d)   where an appointed umpire or third arbitrator refuses to act, or is incapable of acting, or dies, and the arbitration agreement does not show that it was intended that the vacancy should not be supplied, and the parties or arbitrators do not supply the vacancy;

any party may serve the other parties or the arbitrators, as the case be, with a written notice to appoint or, as the case may be, concur in appointing, an arbitrator, umpire or third arbitrator, and if the appointment is not made within seven clear days after the service of the notice, the High Court or a judge thereof may, on application by the party who gave the notice, appoint an arbitrator, umpire or third arbitrator who shall have the like powers to act in the reference and make an award as if he had been appointed by consent of all parties.

(2)   In any case where—

(a)   an arbitration agreement provides for the appointment of an arbitrator or umpire by a person who is neither one of the parties nor an existing arbitrator (whether the provision applies directly or in default of agreement by the parties or otherwise), and

(b)   that person refuses to make the appointment or does not make it within the time specified in the agreement or, if no time is so specified, within a reasonable time

any party to the agreement may serve the person in question with a written notice to appoint an arbitrator or umpire and, if the appointment is not made within seven clear days after the service of the notice, the High Court or a judge thereof may, on the application of the party who gave the notice, appoint an arbitrator or umpire who shall have the like powers to act in the reference and make an award as if he had been appointed in accordance with the terms of the agreement.

(3)   In any case where—

(a)   an arbitration agreement provides that the reference shall be to three arbitrators, one to be appointed by each party and the third to be appointed by the two appointed by the parties or in some other manner specified in the agreement; and

(b)   one of the parties 'the party in default' refuses to appoint an arbitrator or does not do so within the time specified in the agreement or, if no time is specified, within a reasonable time, the other party to the agreement, having appointed his arbitrator, may serve the party in default with a written notice to appoint an arbitrator and, if the appointment is not made within seven clear days after the service of the notice, the High Court or a judge thereof may, on the application of the party who gave the notice, appoint an arbitrator on behalf of the party in default who shall have the like powers to act in the reference and make an award (and, if the case so requires, the like duty in relation to the appointment of a third arbitrator) as if he had been appointed in accordance with the terms of the agreement.

(4)   Except in a case where the arbitration agreement shows that it was intended that the vacancy should not be supplied, paragraph (b) of each of subsections (2) and (3) shall be construed as extending to any such refusal or failure by a person as is there mentioned arising in connection with the replacement of an arbitrator who was appointed by that person (or, in default of being so appointed, was appointed under that subsection) but who refuses to act, or is incapable of acting or has died.

24.9.1.5   Section 12(6)

The High Court shall have, for the purpose of and in relation to a reference, the same power of making orders in respect of—

(a)   security for costs;

(b)   discovery of documents and interrogatories [repealed by the Courts and Legal Services Act 1990];

(c)   the giving of evidence by affidavit;

(d)   examination on oath of any witness before an officer of the High Court or any other person, and the issue of a commission or request for the examination of a witness out of the jurisdiction.

(e)   the preservation, interim custody or sale of any goods which are the subject matter of the reference;

(f)   securing the amount in dispute in the reference;

(g)   the detention, preservation or inspection of any property or thing which is the subject of the reference or as to which any question may arise therein, and authorising for any of the purposes aforesaid any persons to enter upon or into any land or building in the possession of any party to the reference, or authorising any samples to be taken or any observation to be made or experiment to be tried which may be necessary or expedient for the purpose of obtaining full information or evidence; and

(h)   interim injunctions or the appointment of a receiver;

as it has for the purpose of and in relation to an action or matter in the High Court;

Provided that nothing in this subsection shall be taken to prejudice any power which may be vested in an arbitrator or umpire of making orders with respect to any of the matters aforesaid.

24.9.1.6   Section 18

(1)   Unless a contrary intention is expressed therein, every arbitration agreement shall be deemed to include a provision that the costs of the reference and award shall be in the discretion of the arbitrator or umpire, who may direct to and by whom and in what manner those costs or any part thereof shall be paid, and may tax or settle the amount of costs to be so paid or any part thereof, and may award costs to be paid as between solicitors and client.

(2)   Any costs directed by an award to be paid shall, unless the award otherwise directs, be taxable in the High Court.

(3)   Any provision in an arbitration agreement to the effect that the parties or any party thereto shall in any event pay their or his own costs of the reference or award or any part thereof shall be void, and this Part of this Act shall, in the case of an arbitration agreement containing any such provision, have effect as if that provision were not contained therein:

Provided that nothing in this subsection shall invalidate such a provision when it is a part of an agreement to submit to arbitration a dispute which has arisen before the making of that agreement.

(4)   If no provision is made by an award with respect to the costs of the reference, any party to the reference may, within fourteen days of the publication of the award or such further time as the High Court or a judge thereof may direct, apply to the arbitrator for an order directing by and to whom those costs shall be paid, and thereupon the arbitrator shall, after hearing any party who may desire to be heard, amend his award by adding thereto such directions as he may think proper with respect to the payment of the costs of the reference.

(5)   Section sixty-nine of the Solicitors Act 1932 (which empowers a court before which any proceeding is being heard or is pending to charge property recovered or preserved in the proceeding with the payment of solicitors' costs) shall apply, as if an arbitration were a proceeding in the High Court, and the High Court may make declarations and orders accordingly.

24.9.1.7   Section 19

(1)   If in any case an arbitrator or umpire refuses to deliver his award except on payment of the fees demanded by him, the High Court may, on an application for the purpose, order that the arbitrator or umpire shall deliver the award to the applicant on payment into court by the applicant of the fees demanded, and further that the fees demanded shall be taxed by the taxing officer and that out of the money paid into court there shall be paid out to the arbitrator or umpire by way of fees such sum as may be found reasonable on taxation and that the balance of the money, if any, shall be paid out to the applicant.

(2) An application for the purposes of this section may be made by any party to the reference unless the fees demanded have been fixed by a written agreement between him and the arbitrator or umpire.

(3) A taxation of fees under this section may be reviewed in the same manner as a taxation of costs.

(4) The arbitrator or umpire shall be entitled to appear and be heard on any taxation or review of taxation under this section.

24.9.1.8   Section 22

(1) In all cases of reference to arbitration the High Court or a judge thereof may from time to time remit the matters referred, or any of them, to the reconsideration of the arbitrator or umpire.

(2) Where an award is remitted, the arbitrator or umpire shall, unless the order otherwise directs, make his award within three months after the date of the order.

24.9.1.9   Section 23

(1) Where an arbitrator or umpire has misconducted himself or the proceedings, the High Court may remove him.

(2) Where an arbitrator or umpire has misconducted himself or the proceedings, or an arbitration or award has been improperly procured, the High Court may set the award aside.

(3) Where an application is made to set aside an award, the High Court may order that any money made payable by the award shall be brought into court or otherwise secured pending the determination of the application.

24.9.1.10   Section 24

(1) Where an agreement between any parties provides that disputes which may arise in the future between them shall be referred to an arbitrator named or designated in the agreement, and after a dispute has arisen any party applies, on the ground that the arbitrator so named or designated is not or may not be impartial, for leave to revoke the authority of the arbitrator or for an injunction to restrain any other party or the arbitrator from proceeding with the arbitration, it shall not be a ground for refusing the application that the said party at the time when he made the agreement knew, or ought to have known, that the arbitrator, by reason of his relation towards any other party to the agreement or of his connection with the subject referred, might not be capable of impartiality.

(2) Where an agreement between any parties provides that disputes which may arise in the future between them shall be preferred to arbitration, and a dispute which so arises involves the question whether any such party has been guilty of fraud, the High Court shall, so far as may be necessary, to enable that question to be determined by the High Court, have power to order that the agreement shall cease to have effect and power to give leave to revoke the authority of any arbitrator or umpire appointed by or by virtue of the agreement.

(3) In any case where by virtue of this section the High Court has power to order that an arbitration agreement shall cease to have effect or to give leave to revoke the authority of an arbitrator or umpire, the High Court may refuse to stay any action brought in breach of the agreement.

24.9.1.11   Section 25

(1) Where an arbitrator (not being a sole arbitrator), or two or more arbitrators (not being all the arbitrators) or an umpire who has not entered on the reference is or are removed by the High Court or the Court of Appeal, the High Court may on the application of any party to the arbitration agreement, appoint a person or persons to act as arbitrator or arbitrators or umpire in place of the person or persons so removed.

(2) Where the authority of an arbitrator or arbitrators or umpire is revoked by leave of the High Court or the Court of Appeal, or a sole arbitrator or all the arbitrators or an umpire who has entered on the reference is or are removed by the High Court or the Court of Appeal, the High Court may, on the application of any party to the arbitration agreement, either—

(a) appoint a person to act as sole arbitrator in place of the person or persons removed; or

(b) order that the arbitration agreement shall cease to have effect with respect to the dispute referred.

(3) A person appointed under this section by the High Court or the Court of Appeal, as an arbitrator or umpire, shall have the like power to act in the reference and to make an award as if he had been appointed in accordance with the terms of the arbitration agreement.

(4) Where it is provided (whether by means of a provision in the arbitration agreement or otherwise) that an award under an arbitration agreement shall be a condition precedent to the bringing of an action with respect to any matter to which the agreement applies, the High Court or the Court of Appeal, if it orders (whether under this section or under any other enactment) that the agreement shall cease to have effect as regards any particular dispute, may further order that the provision making an award a condition precedent to the bringing of an action shall also cease to have effect as regards that dispute.

24.9.1.12 Section 27

Where the terms of an agreement to refer future disputes to arbitration provide that any claims to which the agreement applies shall be barred unless notice to appoint an arbitrator is given or an arbitrator is appointed or some other step to commence arbitration proceedings is taken within a time fixed by the agreement, and a dispute arises to which the agreement applies, the High Court, if it is of opinion that in the circumstances of the case undue hardship would otherwise be caused, and notwithstanding that the time so fixed has expired, may, on such terms, if any, as the justice of the case may require, but without prejudice to the provisions of any enactment limiting the time for the commencement of arbitration proceedings, extend the time for such period as it thinks proper.

24.9.2 ARBITRATION ACT 1975

24.9.2.1 Section 1

(1) If any party to an arbitration agreement to which this section applies, or any person claiming through or under him, commences any legal proceedings in any court against any other party to the agreement, or any person claiming through or under him, in respect of any matter agreed to be referred, any party to the proceedings may at any time after appearance, and before delivering any pleadings or taking any other steps in the proceedings, apply to the court to stay the proceedings; and the court, unless satisfied that the arbitration agreement is null and void, inoperative or incapable of being performed or that there is not in fact any dispute between the parties with regard to the matter agreed to be referred, shall make an order staying the proceedings.

(2) This section applies to any arbitration agreement which is not a domestic arbitration agreement; and neither section 4(1) of the Arbitration Act 1950 nor section 4 of the Arbitration Act (Northern Ireland) 1937 shall apply to an arbitration agreement to which this section applies.

(3) In the application of this section to Scotland, for the references to staying proceedings there shall be substituted references to sisting proceedings.

(4) In this section 'domestic arbitration agreement' means an arbitration agreement which does not provide, expressly or by implication, for arbitration in a State other than the United Kingdom and to which neither—

(a) an individual who is a national of, or habitually resident in, any State other than the United Kingdom; nor

(b) a body corporate which is incorporated in, or whose central management and control is exercised in, any State other than the United Kingdom;
is a party at the time the proceedings are commenced.

24.9.3 ARBITRATION ACT 1979

24.9.3.1 Section 1

(1) In the Arbitration Act 1950 (in this Act referred to as 'the principal Act') section 21 (statement of case for a decision of the High Court) shall cease to have effect and, without prejudice to the right of appeal conferred by subsection (2) below, the High Court shall not have jurisdiction to set aside or remit an award on an arbitration agreement on the ground of errors of fact or law on the face of the award.

(2) Subject to subsection (3) below, an appeal shall lie to the High Court on any question of law arising out of an award made on an arbitration agreement; and on the determination of such an appeal the High Court may by order—

    (a)   confirm, vary or set aside the award; or

    (b)   remit the award to the reconsideration of the arbitrator or umpire together with the court's opinion on the question of law which was the subject of the appeal;

and where the award is remitted under paragraph (b) above the arbitrator or umpire shall, unless the order otherwise directs, make his award within three months after the date of the order.

    (3)   An appeal under this section may be brought by any of the parties to the reference—

    (a)   with the consent of all the other parties to the reference; or

    (b)   subject to section 3 below, with the leave of the court.

    (4)   The High Court shall not grant leave under subsection (3)(b) above unless it considers that, having regard to all the circumstances, the determination of the question of law concerned could substantially affect the rights of one or more of the parties to the arbitration agreement; and the court may make any leave which it gives conditional upon the applicant complying with such conditions as it considers appropriate.

    (5)   Subject to subsection (6) below, if an award is made and, on an application made by any of the parties to the reference—

    (a)   with the consent of all the other parties to the reference, or

    (b)   subject to section 3 below, with the leave of the court,

it appears to the High Court that the award does not or does not sufficiently set out the reasons for the award, the court may order the arbitrator or umpire concerned to state the reasons for his award in sufficient detail to enable the court, should an appeal be brought under this section, to consider any question of law arising out of the award.

    (6)   In any case where an award is made without any reason being given, the High Court shall not make an order under subsection (5) above unless it is satisfied—

    (a)   that before the award was made one of the parties to the reference gave notice to the arbitrator or umpire concerned that a reasoned award would be required; or

    (b)   that there is some special reason why such a notice was not given.

24.9.3.2   Section 2

    (1)   Subject to subsection (2) and section 3 below, on an application to the High Court made by any of the parties to a reference—

    (a)   with the consent of an arbitrator who has entered on the reference or, if an umpire has entered on the reference, with his consent, or

    (b)   with the consent of all the other parties,

the High Court shall have jurisdiction to determine any question of law arising in the course of the reference.

    (2)   The High Court shall not entertain an application under subsection (1)(a) above with respect to any question of law, unless it is satisfied that—

    (a)   the determination of the application might produce substantial savings in costs to the parties; and

    (b)   the question of law is one in respect of which leave to appeal would be likely to be given under section 1(3)(b) above.

24.9.3.3   Section 5

    (1)   If any party to a reference under an arbitration agreement fails within the time specified in the order or, if no time is so specified, within a reasonable time to comply with an order made by the arbitrator or umpire in the course of the reference, then, on the application of the arbitrator or umpire or of any party to the reference, the High Court may make an order extending the powers of the arbitrator or umpire as mentioned in subsection (2) below.

    (2)   If an order is made by the High Court under this section, the arbitrator or umpire shall have power, to the extent and subject to any conditions specified in that order, to continue with the reference in default of appearance or of any other act by one of the parties in like manner as a judge of the High Court might continue with proceedings in that court where a party fails to comply with an order of that court or a requirement of rules of court.

    (3)   Section 4(5) of the Administration of Justice Act 1970 (jurisdiction of the High Court to be exercisable by the Court of Appeal in relation to judge-arbitrators and judge-umpires) shall not apply in relation to the power of the High Court to make an order under this section, but in the case of a

reference to a judge-arbitrator or judge-umpire that power shall be exercisable as in the case of any other reference to arbitration and also by the judge-arbitrator or judge-umpire himself.

(4)   Anything done by a judge-arbitrator or judge-umpire in the exercise of the power conferred by subsection (3) above shall be done by him in his capacity as judge of the High Court and have effect as if done by that court.

(5)   The preceding provisions of this section have effect notwithstanding anything in any agreement but do not derogate from any powers conferred on an arbitrator or umpire, whether by an arbitration agreement or otherwise.

(6)   In this section 'judge-arbitrator' and 'judge-umpire' have the same meaning as in Schedule 3 to the Administration of Justice Act 1970.

Appendix—Instructions to Counsel with Model Drafts

LEEDSUNITED SHIPPING CO./

LEEDSUNITED SHIPPING LTD

v.

COMPANIA NAVIERA STRACHAN SA

MV 'BATTY'

INSTRUCTIONS TO COUNSEL

Abbott, Carver & Co.,
Temple
London EC4 123A

LEEDSUNITED SHIPPING CO./LEEDSUNITED SHIPPING LTD

vs.

COMPANIA NAVIERA STRACHAN SA

MV 'BATTY'

___

INSTRUCTIONS TO COUNSEL

___

Counsel is instructed on behalf of the Respondent charterers in the arbitration, Compania Naviera Strachan SA. Counsel has herewith the award together with the Reasons for the Award. Counsel will see that the award went against the client. The client is disgruntled and wants to appeal or to take any other steps to challenge the award as may be available.

The client has explained that it has only now 'set the wheels in motion' to dispute the award as its City of London office was, at the beginning of April, severely damaged in a terrorist attack. Alternative premises had to be found and during the process of relocation, the papers relating to this matter were for a time mislaid,

The client is particularly concerned with two aspects of the award. First, it seems that the arbitrator disregarded the rule that deviation abrogates the charterparty contract, and awarded freight notwithstanding that there was a deviation (paragraphs 14 and 15 of the Reasons for the Award). This is a rather important point of law which must arise often and one in which, it seems to instructing solicitors, the arbitrator erred in law.

Second, the arbitrator seems to have failed to decide which of the Claimants was entitled to sue on the charterparty. She said that she 'had no reason not to accept the assertion of the owners that Leedsunited Shipping Company Ltd were the true Claimants' (paragraph 17 of the Reasons), notwithstanding that there was no evidence at all on the point at the hearing. Yet, illogically, she went on to make an award in favour of 'the Owners' without distinction.

The client is determined that the award be challenged. Accordingly Counsel is instructed to settle such originating notice(s) of motion and/or summons(es) for leave as may be necessary, together with suitable affidavit(s) in support.

IN THE MATTER OF THE ARBITRATION ACTS 1950-1979

AND

IN THE MATTER OF AN ARBITRATION

BETWEEN

(1) LEEDSUNITED SHIPPING COMPANY LTD

or

(2) LEEDSUNITED SHIPPING LTD

Claimants
(Time Chartered Owners)

and

COMPANIA NAVIERA STRACHAN SA

Respondents
(Charterers)

MV 'BATTY'

Charterparty dated 6th February 1993

_____

INTERIM FINAL ARBITRATION AWARD

_____

WHEREAS:

1.   By a voyage charterparty on a Gencon form dated Madrid 6th February 1993 the first or second Claimants (hereinafter referred to as 'the Owners') chartered the M.V. Batty to the Respondents (hereinafter referred to as 'the Charterers') for the carriage of a part cargo of copper from Dar Es Salaam to two ports at Charterers' option out of Izmir, Saloniki and Istanbul.

2.   The said charterparty provided, inter alia, that should any disputes arise between the Owners and the Charterers they should be referred to arbitration in London in accordance with 'British law'.

3.   Disputes arose between the parties as detailed hereafter. The parties appointed me, JOHANNA OLDENDORFF of CHARTER HOUSE, St MARY AXE, London El as the sole arbitrator.

4.   The Owners claimed US$33,595.73 in respect of the balance of freight provided for in the charterparty, together with interest and costs. They argued that that sum was indisputably owing to them and that it could appropriately be awarded to them in an interim award. The Charterers denied liability for the claim. Alternatively, they argued that any interim award should be made on terms that secured them with regard to any counter-claims that they had against the Owners under the charterparty.

5.   The application for the interim award was heard on 1st March 1995 at Lloyd's of London, Lime St, London EC3. The parties were represented by solicitors and counsel. The Charterers requested me to make a reasoned award and my reasons are hereby attached to and form part of this my award.

6.   NOW I, the said JOHANNA OLDENDORFF having taken upon myself the burden of this reference, having considered the written evidence submitted to me and listened to the arguments of counsel for the parties, having concluded that this is a proper case for the exercise of my discretion to make an interim award and, furthermore, that the interim award should not have any conditions as to the provision of security attached to it, DO HEREBY MAKE, ISSUE AND PUBLISH this my INTERIM FINAL AWARD as follows:

(A)   I FIND that the Owners' claim succeeds in the amount of US$30,446.15 and no more.

(B)   I THEREFORE AWARD AND ADJUDGE that the Charterers shall forthwith pay to the Owners US$30,446.15 (Thirty Thousand, Four Hundred and Forty-Six Dollars and Fifteen Cents) together with interest thereon at the rate of 8% per annum from 13th March 1993 to the date of this my INTERIM FINAL AWARD.

(C)   I FURTHER AWARD AND ADJUDGE that the Charterers shall bear their own and the Owners' costs of the reference insofar as they relate to this interim final award (the latter to be taxed if not agreed) together with the costs of this my interim final award which I hereby tax and settle in the sum of £750.00 PROVIDED that if, in the first instance, the Owners shall have paid any part of the said costs of this my award they shall be entitled to an immediate refund from the Charterers of the sum so paid.

(D)   I DECLARE that this award is FINAL as to the matters hereby determined and I reserve to myself the right to make a further award or awards as may be appropriate in respect of other outstanding differences between the parties in this reference.

GIVEN under my hand in London this 30th day of MARCH 1995

....

Sole Arbitrator   Witness

MV 'BATTY'

Charterparty dated 6th February 1993

REASONS FOR AND FORMING PART OF THE

INTERIM FINAL ARBITRATION AWARD

1. This arbitration concerned an application for an interim award for a balance of freight allegedly payable under a voyage charterparty. The Charterers denied liability for the claim on the grounds that the vessel had deviated from the route that she should have followed. They argued that the deviation constituted a repudiatory breach of the charterparty. They argued that although the Owners would doubtless be entitled to quantum meruit freight which could be awarded in a final award, they were not entitled to freight which could properly be awarded to them in an interim award. Alternatively, they argued that if the Owners would normally be entitled to an interim award for freight, the existence of their counter-claims meant that either an interim award should not be made or, alternatively, it should be made on terms that effectively gave them the same security for their counter-claims as their retention of the freight.

2. The MV 'BATTY' is a 1973 built tweendecker with a deadweight of 18,000 tons. She was fixed on Gencon form charterparty to carry a part cargo of 28,000 metric tonnes of blister copper (up to 3% more or less at Charterers' option) from Dar Es Salaam to two ports at Charterers' option out of Izmir, Saloniki and Istanbul.

    The freight rate was US$45 per metric tonne 'LINER IN/FREE OUT'.

    Additional clause 17 provided:

    > Full freight less 2.5% address commission is payable within 10 (ten) banking days after signing and release of bills of lading to: ROYAL BANK OF SCOTLAND ...
    > Full freight is deemed earned on shipment and discountless and non-returnable vessel and/or cargo lost or not lost. . . .

3. 2,799.644 metric tonnes of blister copper were loaded at Dar Es Salaam. The relevant bills of lading were dated 28th February 1993 and were released immediately after issue. According to the charterparty terms, freight in the gross amount of US$125,983.98 was earned and became payable on or by 13th March 1993.

4. After loading the copper cargo at Dar Es Salaam, the vessel sailed south via Durban and the Cape of Good Hope. The Charterers' case was that the vessel should have sailed to the Mediterranean via the Suez Canal and the route actually followed by the vessel was a deviation from that envisaged by the parties when agreeing the charterparty.

5. On 14th May 1993 an agreement was concluded between the Owners and the sub-charterers pursuant to which the sub-charterers, Chapman Co. Ltd paid direct to the Owners freight at the rate of US$33 per metric tonne in the total amount of US$92,388.25. Without prejudice to a possible claim for the whole of the charterparty freight, in this application for an interim award, the Owners claimed the difference between the charterparty freight and the money received from Chapman. In calculating their possible claim, they in fact failed to take account of the 2.5% address commission which was to be deducted from the freight. The net charterparty freight was US$122,834.40 and consequently the maximum that could be recovered under the application for an interim award was for the balance of US$30,446.15.

6. As previously mentioned, the Owners' claim for the balance of freight was advanced without prejudice to their possible right to claim all of the charterparty freight from the Charterers. In addition, in the application for an interim award the Owners did not pursue a claim for demurrage, which was left over

for a future date. Furthermore, solely for the purposes of the interim award application, the Owners were prepared to advance their case on the basis that the route followed by the vessel did constitute a deviation from the route envisaged by the charterparty contract. However, they reserved the right at a future date to argue that the route followed was in fact a permissible, customary route and/or the Owners were protected from the possible consequences of the deviation as a result of the protection afforded them by printed clause 20, the deviation clause which read:

> The vessel has liberty to call at any port or ports in any order, for any purpose, to sail without pilots, to tow and/or assist vessels in all situations, and also to deviate for the purpose of saving life and/or property.

7.   The Owners argued that, even though the payment obligation was postponed, the freight became due as soon as the cargo was shipped. They relied upon the House of Lords decision in *The Dominique* [1989] 1 Lloyd's Rep 431, in which the court had to consider a very similar clause, although there the freight was deemed earned on signing bills of lading whereas here it was on shipment.

8.   The Owners accepted (solely for the purposes of the application) that the deviation represented a repudiatory breach of the charterparty and indeed an indication before loading of their intention to sail via the Cape of Good Hope represented an anticipatory repudiatory breach. However, they argued that the Charterers had either affirmed the contract by accepting the cargo or, alternatively, had failed to accept the repudiatory breach within a reasonable time so that the contract remained binding. The Charterers argued that the deviation simply abrogated the contract and the freight provisions of it did not survive the abrogation.

9.   On 16th February 1993 the Owners advised their chartering brokers that the vessel would proceed to South Africa. In a telex passed on to the Owners by their brokers on 18th February, the Charterers protested and insisted that the vessel sail west-bound otherwise 'regret unable to authorise shipment'. On the same day the Owners responded, alleging that a guarantee of direct sailing from the port of loading to the port of discharge had neither been requested nor granted. The telex pointed out that loading had in fact already started. On 19th February the Charterers responded, insisting that the vessel should 'perform a normal rotation' from Dar Es Salaam to Turkey. The telex concluded:

> If vessel already started loading we are ready to respect terms of C/P provided, repeat, provided Owners performing northbound trip on a normal rotation otherwise holding them fully responsible all consequences arising out of cargo damage, capital and interest costs of copper on board, eventual problems of receivers factories at destination due lack of cargo in proper time.

10.   The Owners argued that the Charterers discovered the intention to sail south by 13th February and their permitting the cargo to be loaded with the benefit of that knowledge represented an affirmation of the contract because loading started only on 17th February. The Charterers, however, argued that it was difficult for them to obtain an accurate picture of what was happening at the loading port and therefore they were unable to make an informed decision about the future of the charterparty until after the vessel had sailed. Furthermore, they argued that the actual loading operations were in the hands of the shippers.

11.   Both during and after the hearing I was referred to a large number of telexes from which both parties sought to derive support. The crucial telex, however, seemed to me to be the telex of 19th February quoted above. It is clear from that telex that the Charterers did not know whether or not loading had actually started. Certainly earlier telexes showed that there had been considerable uncertainty about the vessel's berthing prospects and how much cargo was actually available. That telex seemed to me to support the Charterers' argument that they did not know precisely what was happening at the loading port and, above all, they did not make a positive decision to load the vessel in the knowledge that she was definitely going to sail via the Cape of Good Hope. Furthermore, their readiness to 'respect terms of C/P' was conditional on the vessel sailing northwards, failing which they reserved their right to hold the Owners responsible for all consequences. Clearly such a qualified and resigned acceptance of the voyage going ahead once cargo had started being loaded could scarcely represent an affirmation of the

contract. On the other hand, I was also satisfied that it could not represent an acceptance by the Charterers of the anticipatory repudiatory breach which was constituted by the advice to the Charterers of the Owners' intention to sail southwards.

12. I was therefore satisfied that prior to the vessel sailing from Dar Es Salaam there had therefore been neither an affirmation of the contract by the Charterers nor an acceptance by them of an anticipatory repudiatory breach by the Owners.

13. Nor did the Charterers accept the Owners' repudiatory breach of the charterparty until considerably after completion of discharge at Istanbul, which occurred on 5th June 1993. In a telex of 9th April 1993 the Charterers' solicitors made it clear that their clients had not yet decided whether or not to accept the deviation as a repudiation of the contract. They stated:

> It is settled law that if our clients decide to accept the deviation as a repudiation of the contract, your clients have no entitlement to the C/P freight. Our clients will not be in a position to make a decision on this until we hear from you with the information requested ..... above .....

On 15th July 1993 the Charterers' solicitors referred to their clients' entitlement to receive information about the vessel's whereabouts 'before deciding whether to accept the deviation as a repudiation or to affirm the charterparty and reserve the right to claim damages.... Your clients failed to provide the requisite details and our clients were never placed in a position in which they could choose between repudiation and affirmation. Accordingly they are still entitled to treat your clients' conduct as a repudiation of the charterparty.'

It was only in submissions dated 3rd September 1994. served in response to the application for an interim award, that the Charterers' solicitors stated that their clients considered that the deviation amounted to repudiation of the charterparty, which precluded the recovery of charterparty as opposed to quantum meruit freight.

14. I was satisfied that apparently not before service of the submissions in response to the application for an interim award and certainly not prior to the completion of discharge and delivery of the cargo did the Charterers accept the Owners' repudiatory breach of the charterparty. The very latest reasonable moment for acceptance of a repudiatory breach was, it seemed to me, delivery of the cargo. It is, of course trite law that a repudiatory breach that is not accepted does not affect the continuing rights and obligations of both parties under the contract. Here there was no timely acceptance. Consequently, in order to defeat the Owners' prima facie right to freight on the grounds of deviation, the Charterers had to show that the deviation automatically abrogated the contractual right to freight even if there was no acceptance by them of the repudiatory breach. The Owners relied on a passage from page 262 of the current edition of Scrutton on charterparties. There it is stated:

> In the event of a deviation not treated as a repudiation of the contract of carriage it seems clear that the contractual right of freight remains unimpaired.

The Charterers, however, pointed to note 76 on that page in which it is suggested that, in the case of the loss covered by an exception in the bill of lading occurring before the deviation, the ship owner would not be entitled to rely on the exception. Why, the Charterers asked, should a freight clause survive if an exemption clause would not?

15. I was referred to the House of Lords decision in *Tate & Lyle* v *Hain Steamship Co. Ltd* [1936] 2 All ER 597. Both parties accepted that the comments in that case on this point were obiter dicta because there the freight was payable at destination. The Charterers pointed to the judgment of Lord Wright who concluded that a deviation abrogated a contract completely, including the right to claim contractual freight. However, Lords Atkin and Maugham (the only other Law Lords who gave reasoned judgments) merely treated a deviation as a breach of condition, which had to be accepted before the obligation to pay contractual freight was no longer binding. I was also referred to the Australian decision of *Thiess Bros.* v *Australian Steamships* [1955] 1 Lloyd's Rep 459 in which it was held that where freight was

payable on shipment, it could be recovered notwithstanding a subsequent unjustifiable deviation. It seemed to me that the majority of the reasoned judgments in the *Tate & Lyle* case and the *Thiess Bros.* case supported the conclusion stated by the learned editors of Scrutton, their conclusion also being one to which one should attach independent weight. I therefore concluded that the right to freight had not been abrogated as a result of the deviation which in this case had not been accepted as a repudiatory breach of the contract prior to the discharge and delivery of the cargo.

16. As a result of the extended voyage, the Charterers were exposed to claims from their sub-charterers, Chapman. Indeed, they had been obliged to post security of US$75,000 in respect of such claims. Although *The Dominique* [1989] 1 Lloyd's Rep 431 confirmed that such a claim could not be set-off against a liability for freight, the Charterers asked that I exercise the discretion recognised as being vested in arbitrators in *The Angelic Grace* [1980] 1 Lloyd's Rep 288 to make a conditional award so as to secure the Charterers in the event of their being ordered to pay the withheld freight to the Owners. They asked that an order as to payment should be made conditional on the Owners providing security for a claim by Chapman. However, it did not seem to me that such an order would be appropriate. In making an interim award for freight, an arbitration tribunal is essentially declaring that there was no justification at all for the freight having been withheld in the first instance. Although understandably a charterer may be unhappy about losing his security, it would be neither desirable nor fair that a charterer who fails to fulfil his undoubted obligation to pay freight without deduction should manage to achieve a better position by an award against him being made conditional on the provision of security than a charterer who pays in full in the first instance. To grant security under these circumstances would be to undermine the well-established and repeatedly affirmed right to payment of freight in full, however anomalous that right might be. For the same reason, the fact that the Charterers had secured the Owners for their claim for the balance of freight could not affect the entitlement of the Owners to an award for the payment of the withheld freight.

17. There was a dispute about the correct identity of the Claimant Owners. In the charterparty (which had apparently been drawn up by the Charterers' brokers but not signed by either party), the Owners were identified as Leedsunited Shipping Ltd of London as Time Chartered Owners. The claimants, however, argued that the Time Chartered Owners should be correctly identified as Leedsunited Shipping Company Ltd, an associated Gibraltar company. Indeed, they had instituted High Court proceedings seeking a declaration to that effect and also rectification of the charterparty contract to reflect it. I had been appointed both on behalf of Leedsunited Shipping Company Ltd and Leedsunited Shipping Ltd. In the points of claim the claim was advanced on behalf of Leedsunited Shipping Company Ltd or, failing that, Leedsunited Shipping Ltd. The Owners asked that, in the event of their being successful, money should be awarded to Leedsunited Shipping Company Ltd, Leedsunited Shipping Ltd merely being named as a claimant but no finding in their favour being made. I could see no objection to that course of action. Although the Charterers correctly argued that an award could only be made in favour of a party entitled to commence the proceedings, they did not advance a positive case that the contractual intention of the parties was *not* that Leedsunited Shipping Company Ltd should act as the Time Chartered Owners. I was not referred to any pre-fixture negotiations that could shed light on the intention of the parties. In the absence of a positive case as to what had been the intention of the parties, I had no reason not to accept the assertion of the Claimant Owners that Leedsunited Shipping Company Ltd were the true Claimants. There was no possibility of the Charterers being faced with double jeopardy, because satisfaction of an award in favour of Leedsunited Shipping Co. Ltd as the Claimants who had carried the cargo would preclude a further claim by an associated company purporting to be the correct claimant and basing its claim on the same performance of the same contract.

18. Clearly it was appropriate to award interest from the date when the freight should have been paid. Since the Claimant Owners had been successful, they were obviously entitled to the costs relating to the interim award application. Obviously the award in no way affects the rights of either party to bring any further claims or counter-claims arising under the charterparty contract.

MV 'BATTY' — NOTES ON THE ANSWERS TO THE BRIEF

1.   The correct legal analysis of the Plaintiff Charterers' complaint against the way this award was made is somewhat difficult. There are three possible ways in which the Plaintiffs' complaints may be put:

(a)   First, that the award was made without jurisdiction because it was and is not clear which claimant was party to the arbitration agreement. The Charterers' arguments are that (1) in the absence of any evidence on the point the court is not (and the arbitrator was not) able to conclude which claimant was owner, and therefore neither claimant can prove that it was party to an arbitration agreement (on whom is the burden of proof?); or (2) the likelihood in the absence of evidence is that Leedsunited Shipping Ltd were the owners, being named in the charterparty, but both claimants appear to have asked for an award in favour of Leedsunited Shipping Co. Ltd (paragraph 17). Therefore the person who was (probably) party to the contract was not asking for an award, and the party asking for an award was probably not party to the contract.

(b)   If the above points do not go to jurisdiction, they provide a defence to the Charterers. The argument is that the claim must fail because there is no evidence of which claimant is entitled to the freight and, as the burden of proof is on the claimant, each has failed to prove its claim. The arbitrator therefore erred in law. This argument is supported by the different but similar case of *The Jordan Nicolov* (Hobhouse J).

(c)   The Charterers raised this point as a defence (paragraph 17) but the arbitration declined to determine it, thereby derelicting her duty to decide defences raised and committing technical misconduct.

2.   There is also a fairly straightforward (and well-known) point of law whether the effect of a deviation is to abrogate automatically and retrospectively the right to contractual freight earned on shipment.

3.   In theory the following documents are required:

(a)   Notice of motion for declaration of lack of jurisdiction. This application can be made without leave, and by notice of motion (ord. 73, r. 2(3)), and is convenient because the application can be combined with applications (c) and (f) (see below) which must be made by notice of motion.

(b)   Affidavit in support of (a) (which will, however, do little other than recite the facts that appear in the reasons to the award).

(c)   Notice of motion for the award to be set aside or remitted for error of law under s. 1 of the 1979 Act. This cannot be made without leave (s. 1(3) of the 1979 Act). It must be made by notice of motion (ord. 73, r. 2(2)). As a matter of practice no affidavit is permitted: the point of law must be one that appears from the award itself.

(d)   The application for leave to appeal for error of law under s. 1 of the 1979 Act may (and should for convenience) be made by summons in the action (once the notice of motion is issued): ord. 73, r. 2(3).

(e)   Affidavit in support of (d) giving evidence of the importance of the point of law (realistically, only the deviation point is an important point; the point about the wrong party seems to be entirely one-off).

(f)   Notice of motions for remission for misconduct under s. 22 of the 1950 Act. This application can be made without leave. It must be made by notice of motion (ord. 73, r. 2(1)).

(g)   Affidavit in support of (f) (which will do little, however, than put in evidence the facts recitedin the reasons).

(h)   The Plaintiff also needs an extension of the time limits under ord. 73, r. 5: time summons in the action.

(i)   Affidavit in support of (h).

(j)   Leedsunited Shipping Co. Ltd is a Gibraltar company (paragraph 17). In theory leave to serve the originating notice of motion is required. The application is *ex parte* by affidavit under ord. 73, r. 7(1)(b). In practice, leave is almost always dispensed with because in the case of an English arbitration a party who has obtained an award will have London solicitors. However, the point, although obscure and not significant, would be worth mentioning.

4.   Documents (a) (c) and (f) can and probably should, for convenience, notwithstanding that (c) requires leave, be combined into the same originating notice of motion (but there is nothing wrong with issuing separate notices of motion). Documents (d) and (h) can be made by the same summons (but there is nothing wrong with separate summonses). Affidavits (b), (e), (g), (i) and (j) could be combined into one affidavit, although this would be a bit cumbersome. A sensible approach would be to combine (b) and (g) into one affidavit, swear (e) on its own, and combine (i) and, if necessary, (j).

5.   There is no draft affidavit (i) in support of the time summons (h), and no affidavit in support of the application for leave to serve the originating notice of motion out of the jurisdiction (j). Students may, if they wish, draft these two documents either separately or as suggested in paragraph 4 above.

IN THE HIGH COURT OF JUSTICE   1995 Folio....
Queen's Bench Division
Commercial Court

In the matter of the Arbitration Acts 1950-1979

And in the matter of an Arbitration

BETWEEN

<table>
<tr><td>Compania Naviera Strachan SA</td><td>Plaintiffs (respondents)</td></tr>
<tr><td>and</td><td></td></tr>
<tr><td>(1) Leedsunited Shipping Company Ltd
(2) Leedsunited Shipping Ltd</td><td>Defendants (claimants)</td></tr>
</table>

NOTICE OF ORIGINATING MOTION

TAKE NOTICE that the High Court of Justice, Queen's Bench Division, Commercial Court, Royal Courts of Justice, Strand, London, will be moved on   day the   day of 1995 at   o'clock in the   noon or so soon thereafter as counsel may be heard on behalf of the above named Plaintiffs (who were respondents in the arbitration and charterers of the vessel 'Batty') in respect of the Interim Final Arbitration Award dated 30 March 1995 ('the award') of the arbitrator herein, Ms Johanna Oldendorff, for orders that:

(1) It is declared that the award is not binding on the Plaintiffs on the grounds that it was made without jurisdiction; alternatively

(2) The award be set aside and or remitted for errors of law under s. 1 of the Arbitration Act 1979, for reconsideration by the arbitrator; alternatively

(3) The award be remitted to the arbitrator under s. 22 of the Arbitration Act 1950 for reconsideration by the arbitrator.

(4) The costs of this application and of the arbitration be paid by the Defendants to the Plaintiffs.

AND FURTHER TAKE NOTICE that the grounds of the applications are as follows:

Declaration

1.   The charterparty as drawn up but not signed, which incorporated the arbitration clause, named the Second Defendants (the London company) as time chartered owners (paragraph 17 of the reasons). The Defendants both purported to commence arbitration and both asserted that the true owners under the charterparty were the First Defendants (the Gibraltar company). The Defendants as claimants both asked for an award in favour of the First Defendants. The Defendants adduced no evidence on the issue as to which of the Defendants was the true owner and party to the charterparty.

2.   The burden of proof is on the correct Defendants, who assert that they were party to a contract with an arbitration clause and who claim under that contract, to prove that they were party to the contract.

The First Defendants asserted this but did not prove it. The Second Defendants did not assert it. Therefore the arbitrator could, and the court can, only conclude that neither of the Defendants can prove they were party to the contract. It follows that neither of the Defendants can establish that the arbitrator had jurisdiction and the court should hold that the arbitrator did not have jurisdiction. See, by analogy, *The Jordan Nicolov* [1990] 2 Lloyd's Rep 11.

3.　Alternatively, insofar as there was any evidence, it was that the brokers drew up the (unsigned) charterparty naming the Second Defendants as disponent owners. This makes it more likely than not, in the absence of other evidence, that the Second Defendants were party to the contract, and the First Defendants were not. Both Defendants, however, asked for an award in favour of the First Defendants. There was no jurisdiction to make an award in favour of the First Defendants because on the evidence they were not party to the contract; and no jurisdiction to make an award in favour of the Second Defendants because no such award was asked for.

4.　In any event the arbitrator did not have jurisdiction, as she purported to do, to make an award in favour of 'owners' without deciding which Defendant was the owner.

5.　Therefore the award was made without jurisdiction and is not binding on the Plaintiffs.

Errors of law

6.　The Plaintiffs disputed the correct identity of the claimants in the arbitration (paragraph 17 of the reasons).

7.　The burden of proof was on the Defendant claimants in the arbitration to prove their entitlement to freight. For this purpose one or other of the Defendant claimants had to prove that they were party to the charterparty.

8.　The Defendants adduced no evidence on this point, confining themselves to assertion (paragraph 17 of the reasons). Therefore as a matter of law neither of the Defendant claimants discharged the burden of proof of showing that it was entitled to freight.

9.　The arbitrator therefore should have found that each of the Defendants' claims failed: see *The Jordan Nicolov* [1990] 2 Lloyd's Rep 11.

10.　The arbitrator erred in law in deciding that in the absence of evidence she could accept the assertion of the claimants that the First Defendants were the true claimants (paragraph 17 of the award).

11.　Further or alternatively, the application before the arbitrator proceeded on the basis that the owners deviated from the contractual route and the arbitrator made no finding that the charterers elected to waive the deviation (see paragraphs 8 to 10 of the reasons).

12.　As a matter of law, unless the charterer elects to waive the deviation, the deviation abrogates the contract of carriage retrospectively, including any exceptions applying to events, and any obligations as to freight accruing, prior to the deviation: Scrutton on charterparties, pp. 261–2 (see footnotes 73 to 74 and 76 especially); *Thorley* v *Orchis* [1907] 1 KB 660; *Internationale Guano* v *McAndrew* [1909] 2 KB 360; *Hain* v *Tate and Lyle* (1936) 41 Com Cas 350 per Lord Wright.

13.　Therefore, upon deviation, the Defendants ceased to be entitled to and the Plaintiffs ceased to be liable for any contractual freight.

14.　The arbitrator erred in law in that she held the right to contractual freight survived the deviation.

Remission for misconduct

15. The Plaintiffs disputed the identity of the correct claimant (paragraph 17 of the reasons). The Plaintiffs thereby asserted the defence that each of the claimants was not the party entitled to the freight.

16. The arbitrator failed and refused to decide these defences which were raised by the Plaintiffs. The arbitrator thereby misconducted herself and or the proceedings. Alternatively, the issues between the parties were not determined and there occurred a procedural mishap.

IN THE HIGH COURT OF JUSTICE   1995 Folio....
Queen's Bench Division
Commercial Court

In the matter of the Arbitration Acts 1950-1979
And in the matter of an Arbitration

BETWEEN

                          Compania Naviera Strachan SA   Plaintiffs (respondents)

                                    and

                    (1) Leedsunited Shipping Company Ltd
                    (2) Leedsunited Shipping Ltd   Defendants (claimants)

                          ―――――――――――――――

                                 SUMMONS

                          ―――――――――――――――

LET all parties attend the Commercial Judge in chambers, Royal Courts of Justice, Strand, London
WC2A 2LL, on   day the   day of   1995 on the hearing of applications by the
Plaintiffs in respect of the arbitration award of the arbitrator, Ms Johanna Oldendorff, for

   (1) an order that the time limited by ord. 73, r. 5 for the service of the Notice of Motion herein,
the affidavit evidence in support and this summons insofar as it seeks leave to appeal, be extended to
7 days after any order herein;

   (2) leave to appeal under s. 1 of the Arbitration Act 1979 on the points of law, set out in the Notice
of Motion herein, and

   (3) costs to be in cause.

[etc.]

[name] 1st
Plaintiffs
Sworn on (date)

1995 Folio....

IN THE HIGH COURT OF JUSTICE
Queen's Bench Division
Commercial Court

In the matter of the Arbitration Acts 1950-1979
And in the matter of an Arbitration

BETWEEN

<table>
<tr><td>Compania Naviera Strachan SA</td><td>Plaintiffs (respondents)</td></tr>
<tr><td>and</td><td></td></tr>
<tr><td>(1) Leedsunited Shipping Company Ltd
(2) Leedsunited Shipping Ltd</td><td>Defendants (claimants)</td></tr>
</table>

[draft] AFFIDAVIT

I [NAME] of [identify position] MAKE OATH and SAY as follows:

1. I am [please fill in details]. I make this affidavit from information contained in the documents and the matters to which I depose are true to the best of my knowledge and belief. I make this affidavit in support of the Plaintiffs' applications for a declaration that the award dated 30 March 1995 was made without jurisdiction, alternatively that the award should be remitted for misconduct or mishap.

2. There is now produced to me marked '   1' a true copy of the award and the reasons given by the arbitrator. The Defendants were claimants in the arbitration and their claim was for freight as owners under the charterparty against the Plaintiffs as charterers.

3. It will be seen from paragraph 17 of the reasons that the charterparty was drawn up (albeit unsigned) naming the Second Defendants as disponent owners, but that both Defendants purported to arbitrate as claimants, asserted (without evidence) that the true claimant were the First Defendants, and asked for an award in the name of the First Defendants. It is to be observed that the Plaintiffs had a counterclaim against the true disponent owner, which would not as a matter of law rank as a set off against freight. The assertion by the Defendants was therefore convenient for them, because the counterclaim is likely to be more difficult to enforce against the First Defendants (a Gibraltar company) than against the Second Defendants (a London company).

4. The arbitrator 'had no reason not to accept the assertion' that the First Defendants were the true claimants, and she made an award in favour of the 'owners', but distinguishing between the First and Second Defendants. From paragraph 17 of the reasons it is apparent that the arbitrator did not act on the basis of any evidence (there being none) as to the identity of the correct claimant, and did not try to decide the identity of the correct claimant.

5. In these circumstances the Plaintiffs contend that the award was made without jurisdiction, or the arbitrator committed misconduct, or there was a procedural mishap, on the grounds set out in the Notice of Motion. The Plaintiffs also contend that the arbitrator erred in law. The Plaintiffs ask for appropriate relief as set out in the Notice of Motion.

Plaintiffs
Sworn on [date]
1995 Folio....

IN THE HIGH COURT OF JUSTICE
Queen's Bench Division
Commercial Court

In the matter of the Arbitration Acts 1950-1979
And in the matter of an Arbitration

BETWEEN

Compania Naviera Strachan SA

Plaintiffs (respondents)

and

(1)   Leedsunited Shipping Company Ltd
(2)   Leedsunited Shipping Ltd

Defendants (claimants)

AFFIDAVIT

I [NAME] of [identify position] MAKE OATH and SAY as follows:

1.   I am [please fill in details]. I make this affidavit from information contained in the documents and the matters to which I depose are true to the best of my knowledge and belief. I make this affidavit in support of the Plaintiffs' applications for leave to appeal against the interim final arbitration award dated 30 March 1995 on the grounds of error of law set out in the notice of motion.

2.   There is now produced to me marked '   2' a true copy of the award and the reasons given by the arbitrator. The Defendants were claimants in the arbitration and their claim was for freight as owners under the charterparty against the Plaintiffs as charterers.

3.   One of the points of law on which the Plaintiffs wish to appeal is whether the effect of a deviation, where the charterer has not elected to waive the deviation, is retrospectively to abrogate the contract of carriage so that the carrier can, after a deviation, no longer recover freight earned even before the deviation. This is a point on which different views have been expressed in the cases and which is discussed in the textbooks. The arbitrator herself in paragraph 15 of her reasons refers to an apparent difference of view in the House of Lords in *Hain* v *Tate & Lyle* between Lord Wright on the one hand, and Lords Atkin and Porter on the other.

4.   The point is of considerable importance to the shipping trade and is not, in my belief, a one-off point.